ENCYCLOPEDIA OF
CHINESE FILM

ENCYCLOPEDIA OF CHINESE FILM

Yingjin Zhang and **Zhiwei Xiao**

With additional contributions from
**Ru-shou Robert Chen, Shuqin Cui, Paul Fonoroff,
Ken Hall, Julian Stringer, Jean J. Su,
Paola Voci, Tony Williams, Yueh-yu Yeh**

Edited by
Yingjin Zhang

London & New York

First published 1998
by Routledge
11 New Fetter Lane, London EC4P 4EE
29 West 35th Street, New York, NY 10001

© Routledge 1998

Typeset in Baskerville and Optima by The Florence Group, Stoodleigh, Devon
Printed and bound in Great Britain by Redwood Books, Trowbridge, Wiltshire

British Library Cataloguing in Publication Data
A catalogue record for this book is available from the British Library

Library of Congress Cataloging-in-Publication Data
Zhang, Yingjin.
    Encyclopedia of Chinese Film/Yingjin Zhang and Zhiwei Xiao;
    with additional contributions from Ru-shou Robert Chen . . . [et al.];
    edited by Yingjin Zhang.
        p.   cm..
    Includes bibliographical references and indexes.
    (alk. paper)
    1. Motion pictures—China—Encyclopedias.   2. Motion pictures—
Taiwan—Encyclopedias.   I. Xiao, Zhiwei.   II. Title.
PN1993.5.C4Z53   1998
791.43′0951′03—dc21   98–18267
                    CIP

ISBN 0-415-15168-6

For Mimi, Alex and David

Contents

Part I: Historical essays

Part II: Main entries 73

Plates

Notes on contributors

Ru-shou Robert Chen (RC) received his Ph.D. in Critical Studies from the School of Cinema-TV, the University of Southern California in the USA and is Associate Professor of Cinema Studies at National Taiwan College of Arts. He is the author of two Chinese books, *Historical and Cultural Experience in New Taiwan Cinema* (1993b) and *Screen Empire* (1995), and a contributor to *Film Appreciation* and other magazines in Taiwan.

Shuqin Cui (SC) received her Ph.D. in Cultural Studies from the University of Michigan and is Assistant Professor of Chinese at Southern Methodist University in the USA. Her essay is included in *Transnational Chinese Cinemas*, ed. by S. Lu (1997a).

Paul Fonoroff (PF) received his MFA from the School of Cinema–TV, the University of Southern California in the USA and is the film critic for *South China Morning Post* in Hong Kong and host of 'Movie World', a weekly Mandarin-language cinema programme broadcast in China. He is the author of *Silver Light: A Pictorial History of Hong Kong Cinema, 1920–1970* (1997) and has contributed to *Renditions* and other publications in Hong Kong.

Ken Hall (KH) received his Ph.D. in Spanish-American Literature from the University of Arizona and is Associate Professor of Spanish at the University of North Dakota in the USA. He is the author

of *Guillermo Cabrera Infante and the Cinema* (1989, Newark, Delaware: Juan de la Cuesta Hispanic Monographs) and *John Woo: Painting the True Colors of the Hero* (1999, Jefferson, N.C.: McFarland & Co., forthcoming). He has translated two of Infante's works: *A Twentieth Century Job* (1991, London and New York: Faber & Faber) and *Mea Cuba* (1994, London: Faber & Faber; New York: Farrar, Straus & Giroux). He is a contributor to *Encyclopedia of World Literature in the 20th Century*, *Literature/Film Quarterly*, *University of Dayton Review*, *Hispanofila*, and *Classical and Modern Literature*.

Julian Stringer (JS) studied film at the University of North London, UK and currently researches Hong Kong and Japanese cinema as a doctoral student of Comparative Literature at Indiana University in the USA. He has contributed articles to *Asian Cinema*, *Cineaction*, *Film Quarterly*, *Millennium Film Journal*, *Monthly Film Bulletin*, *Screen* and two critical anthologies.

Jean J. Su (JJS) is a graduate student of Library and Information Science at Indiana University in the USA. During the 1980s she was an editor of Western literature with Haixia Literature and Art Press in China and contributed to *Chinese and Foreign Film* and other magazines.

Paola Voci (PV) studied Chinese cinema at Beijing Film Academy and currently researches Chinese and Japanese cinema as a doctoral student of East Asian Languages and Cultures at Indiana University in the USA. She has contributed to *Journal of Modern Literature in Chinese*.

Tony Williams (TW) received his Ph.D. in Theology from Manchester University, UK and is Associate Professor of English and Area Head of Film Studies at Southern Illinois University in the USA. He is the author of *Jack London: The Movies* (1992, Los Angeles: David Rejl), *Hearths of Darkness: The Family in the American Horror Film* (1996, New Jersey: Fairleigh Dickinson University Press) and *Larry Cohen: Radical Allegories of an American Filmmaker* (1997, Jefferson, N.C.: McFarland & Co). He is also co-editor (with Jean-Jacques Malo) of *Vietnam War Films* (1994, also from McFarland) and (with Rocco Fumento) of *Jack London's The Sea Wolf* (1998, Carbondale: Southern Illinois University Press). He has contributed articles to *Cinema Journal*, *Cineaction*, *Movie*, *Viet Nam Generation* and *Wide Angle*.

Zhiwei Xiao (ZX) received his Ph.D. in Modern East Asia from the University of California at San Diego and is Assistant Professor of History at California State University at San Marcos in the USA. He has contributed articles to *American Historical Review* and *China Review International* as well as to *Transnational Chinese Cinema* (1997) and *Romance, Sexuality, Identity* (1999).

Yueh-yu Yeh (YY) received her Ph.D. in Critical Studies from the School of Cinema–TV, the University of Southern California in the USA and is teaching film at Hong Kong Baptist University. She is the co-author of 'Narrating National Sadness: Cinematic Mapping and Hypertextual Dispersion' (a multimedia monograph) and a contributor to *Film Appreciation* in Taiwan.

Yingjin Zhang (YZ) received his Ph.D. in Comparative Literature from Stanford University and is Associate Professor of Chinese, Comparative Literature, and Film Studies at Indiana University in the USA. He is the author of *The City in Modern Chinese Literature and Film: Configurations of Space, Time, and Gender* (1996) and the editor of *China in a Polycentric World: Essays in Chinese Comparative Literature* (1998) and *Romance, Sexuality, Identity* (1999), all from Stanford University Press. He has contributed articles to three critical anthologies in English and over a dozen journals in the USA, China, Hong Kong and Taiwan.

Note to the reader

This reference work is designed to provide, first of all, a comprehensive coverage of Chinese film in its historical, cultural, geopolitical, generic, thematic and textual aspects; and, secondly, a critical guide to assist the reader to navigate through these multiple aspects and to locate the exact information needed.

In addition to the main body of entries on film people, film synopses, genres and subjects presented in alphabetical order, this encyclopedia contains the following special features:

1   Six historical essays on Chinese, Hong Kong and Taiwan cinemas as well as their inter-actions with and their relations to the West. Conveniently placed before the main entries, these essays offer surveys of the developments of Chinese film in different geopolitical locations and the Western presence in China throughout the twentieth century.

2   The **Classified contents list** in the front matter includes subject listings of topics, genres, themes, and a chronological list of film entries. From generic, historical and thematic angles, these essay entries treat topics not usually covered by film reviews and critical studies.

3   Important items are cross-referenced throughout the work to direct the reader to related subjects discussed in other entries and historical essays. Such cross-references are marked by bold face for surnames or terms (**Zhang Yimou**, John **Woo**, **martial arts film**) and by **See also**: at the end of some entries.

4   To facilitate the reader's research, **Further reading** included at the end of many entries furnishes a briefly annotated guide to secondary sources, most of them in English.

5   The **Bibliography** near the end of the work lists hundreds of secondary sources, with asterisks marking essential items. A list of **Select Internet web sites** points to the contin-uous addition of information on line that is relevant to Chinese film around the world.

6   The **Index of titles** provides an alphabetical list of all films and television dramas (including the Western ones) mentioned in the work, and the accompanying Pinyin romanizations help the Chinese specialist to identify the original Chinese titles.

7   The **Index of names** (with years of birth and death if available) and **Index of studios** both contain Pinyin romanizations and are designed to facilitate the reader's search for names that are mentioned in other entries.

8   A **Glossary** of Pinyin romanizations, Chinese characters and English (or other) equiva-lents further assists the China specialist to move between Chinese titles or names and their English translations.

For clarity, the Pinyin form is used throughout the work, except for proper names and bibli-ographic data. With regard to people from Hong Kong and Taiwan, efforts are made to include the standard or the most commonly used romanizations of their names in existing publications. Regional diversity is similarly reflected in the names of film characters. Dates following film titles are usually those of the production years, but inconsistencies occur from time to time because there is no single authoritative text to refer to when questions arise. In any case, the reader can safely assume that approximately six months exist between the production and the release dates.

Acknowledgements

From Yingjin Zhang:

I should like to thank Fiona Cairns of Routledge and five anonymous reviewers of the original proposal for their critical input that shaped the initial design of this project in 1995. I am particularly grateful for several institutional grants I received in 1995–7: from Indiana University, an Outstanding Junior Faculty Award, three Summer Faculty Fellowships, a Research Leave Supplement, a Short-term Faculty Exchange in China, other research and travel funds, and a course reduction; from the University of Michigan, a Postdoctoral Research Fellowship and a travel grant; from the University of Chicago, Stanford University and the Harvard-Yenching Library, four library travel grants. My thanks also go to all contributors for their cooperation and creative input; to Tony Williams and especially Julian Stringer for reading and revising earlier drafts; to my other colleagues and friends across the Pacific, notably Dudley Andrew, Cheng Jihua, Leo Ou-fan Lee, Eugene Eoyang, Paul Pickowicz, Wang Renyin and Zhang Longxi; to the China Research Center for Film Arts, Beijing, for providing illustrations. I am grateful to Routledge for the care that has been taken in copy-editing the manuscript. Last but not least, I owe my achievements to Su, Mimi and Alex, without whose love and understanding the completion of this project would not have carried as much significance to my career.

From Zhiwei Xiao:

I should like to acknowledge that the present project was conceptualized by Yingjin Zhang in 1995. Besides being a co-author, Yingjin also did all the organizational work and final editing. I am particularly grateful for Yingjin's abundant patience with and continuous confidence in me, which made our collaboration on this book a pleasant experience. In writing the history portion of this work, I am indebted to Hu Jubin at the China Film Archive in Beijing and Yin Hong from Beijing Normal University. Finally, I want to thank my wife Lydia for her never failing support, which allows me to concentrate on my research and writing, and even to feel good after feeling guilty for not taking my fair share of family responsibilities.

From all the contributors:

Thanks to Peggy Hsiung-Ping Chiao, Joan Hawkins, Xiaozhao Huang, Shiho Maeshima and Andrew Straw, as well as to the Central Motion Picture Company in Taipei, the National Film Archive of the ROC and the Taiwan Film Centre.

Abbreviations

aka	*also known as*
b.	*born*
BFA	Beijing Film Academy
CCP	Chinese Communist Party
CMPC	Central Motion Picture Company (Taiwan)
d.	*died*
dir.	*directed by*
FF	Film Festival
GHA	Golden Horse Awards (Taiwan)
GIO	Government Information Office (Taiwan)
GRA	Golden Rooster Awards (China)
HFA	Hundred Flowers Awards (China)
HKFA	Hong Kong Film Awards
HKIFF	Hong Kong International Film Festival
KMT	Kuomintang (the Nationalist party in China and Taiwan)
MBFT	Ministry of Broadcasting, Film and Television (China)
MP&GI	Motion Picture & General Investment (Hong Kong)
MTV	Music Television
PRC	The People's Republic of China (mainland China)
sc.	*screen writer*
ROC	The Republic of China (Taiwan)
ZDX	Zhongguo dianyingjia xiehui (Chinese Film Association, Beijing)
ZDYYZ	Zhongguo dianying yishu yanjiu zhongxin (China Research Center for Film Art, Beijing)

Classified contents

Teng Wenji (*b.* 1944)
Ti Lung (Di Long, *b.* 1946)
Tian Fang (1911–74)
Tian Han (1898–1968)
Tian Hua (Liu Tianhua, *b.* 1928)
Tian Zhuangzhuang (*b.* 1952)
Ting Shan-hsi (Ding Shanxi, *b.* 1936)
Tsai Ming-liang (Cai Mingliang, *b.* 1958)
Tseng Chuang-hsiang (Zeng Zhuangxiang,
    b. 1947)
Tsui Hark (Xu Ke, *b.* 1952)
Wan Jen (Wan Ren, *b.* 1950)
Wan Laiming (*b.* 1899)
Wang Danfeng (Wang Yufeng, *b.* 1925)
Wang Ping (Wang Guangzhen, *b.* 1916)
Wang Renmei (Wang Shuxi, 1914–87)
Wang Tung (Wang Tong, *b.* 1942)
Wang Xiaoshuai
Wang Xin'gang (*b.* 1932)
Wang Yin (1900–88)
Wang Yu (*b.* 1944)
Wong, Anthony (Huang Qiusheng, *b.* 1961)
Wong, Che Kirk (Huang Zhiqiang, *b.*
    1949)
Wong Jing (Wang Jing, *b.* 1956)
Wong, Joey (Wang Zuxian, *b.* 1967)
Wong Kar-Wai (Wang Jiawei, *b.* 1958)
Wong, Raymond (Huang Baiming, *b.* 1948)
Woo, John (Wu Yusen, *b.* 1946)
Wu Di
Wu Nien-chen (Wu Nianzhen, *b.* 1952)
Wu Tianming (*b.* 1939)
Wu Wenguang (*b.* 1956)
Wu Yigong (*b.* 1938)
Wu Yin (Yang Ying, *b.* 1909)
Wu Yonggang (1907–82)
Wu Ziniu (*b.* 1953)
Xia Gang (*b.* 1953)
Xia Meng (*b.* 1932)
Xia Yan (Shen Duanxian, Shen Naixi,
    1900–95)
Xian Xinghai (1905–45)
Xie Fei (*b.* 1942)
Xie Jin (*b.* 1923)
Xie Tian (Xie Hongkun, Xie Jun, *b.* 1914)
Xie Tieli (*b.* 1925)
Xu Xinfu (1897–1965)
Yam, Simon (Ren Dahua, *b.* 1955)

Yan Chuntang (?–1949)
Yang, Edward (Yang Dechang, *b.* 1947)
Yang Hansheng (Ouyang Benyi, Ouyang
    Jixiu, *b.* 1902)
Yang Xiaozhong (Yang Baotai, Mi
    Tisheng, 1899–1969)
Yeoh, Michelle (Michelle Khan, Yang
    Ziqiong, *b.* 1962)
Yim Ho (Yan Hao, *b.* 1952)
Ying Yunwei (Ying Yuchen, Ying
    Yangzhen, 1904–67)
Yu Lan (Yu Peiwen, *b.* 1921)
Yu Ling (Ren Xigui, Yu Cheng, You Jing,
    b. 1907)
Yuan Muzhi (Yuan Jialai, 1909–78)
Zhang Jianya (*b.* 1951)
Zhang Junxiang (Yuan Jun, *b.* 1910)
Zhang Junzhao (*b.* 1952)
Zhang Nuanxin (1940–95)
Zhang Ruifang (*b.* 1918)
Zhang Shankun (1905–57)
Zhang Shichuan (1889–1953)
Zhang Yimou (*b.* 1950)
Zhang Yu (*b.* 1957)
Zhang Yuan (*b.* 1963)
Zhang Zeming (*b.* 1951)
Zhao Dan (Zhao Fengxiang, 1915–80)
Zheng Junli (Zheng Zhong, Qian Li,
    1911–69)
Zheng Zhengqiu (Zheng Fangze, Zheng Bo
    Chang, Zheng Yao Feng, 1888–1935)
Zhou Jianyun (1893–1967)
Zhou Xiaowen (1954)
Zhou Xuan (Su Pu, 1918–57)
Zhu Shilin (1899–1967)

VI Synopses: a chronological list

1905 *Conquering Jun Mountain*, aka *Dingjun
    Mountain*
1913 *The Difficult Couple*
    Zhuangzi Tests His Wife
1921 *Sea Oath*
    Yan Ruisheng
1922 *Cheng the Fruit Seller*, aka *Laborer's Love*
1923 *Orphan Rescues Grandfather*
1927 *Revived Rose*
    Romance of the Western Chamber, aka
    Way Down West

Part I
Historical essays

Chinese cinema

Zhiwei Xiao

1 Introduction

The first film was shown in China in 1896. Since that time, this new medium has gradually sunk its roots in the country to become one of the most important forms of popular entertainment. Unlike artists working with other media and genres introduced into China from the West – such as oil painting, symphonic music and spoken drama – Chinese filmmakers had no indigenous traditions to draw on in their efforts to assimilate this foreign novelty. Yet over the century they have completely mastered the art of filmmaking and their works have earned international recognition. To date, more than six hundred Chinese titles have won film **awards** at various international film festivals, including Cannes, Berlin, Locarno, Nantes, New York, Toronto and Venice.

Many distinctive features developed by Chinese film over the last hundred years are the result and testimony of the particular kinds of interaction linking culture and politics in twentieth-century China. As a form of mass entertainment, Chinese film has been affected by historical forces in an unique way. To understand fully Chinese cinema's recurring motifs and images, predominant narrative modes and thematic orientations requires a thorough knowledge of both the industry's internal development and the historical changes taking place in society at large. In fact, one of Chinese film's most striking attributes is the way it has responded and reacted to political events. Hence, any narrative history of Chinese film must be informed by an understanding of the general history of the country.

The conventional narrative of Chinese film history is usually divided into eight distinct periods: (1) early experiments, (2) the 1920s, (3) the Nanjing decade, (4) wartime, (5) post-war revival, (6) the first seventeen years of the PRC, (7) the Cultural Revolution and (8) the New Era. Each of these periods corresponds to a specific phase of socio-political development in modern Chinese history.

Further reading
S. Li (1991), containing essays on periodization and other methodological issues; ZDX (1995: 1–32), a discussion of film historiography.

2   Early film activities, 1896–1921

The first period begins with the introduction of film into China in 1896 and ends with the release of the first Chinese-made long feature, **Yan Ruisheng** (*dir*. Ren Pengnian, 1921). During this period, China saw her final days of imperial rule under the Manchu Dynasty, which was overthrown by the revolutionaries in 1911. But the founding of the new republican government did not immediately bring wealth and power, two goals sought by the revolutionaries. On the contrary, the political disintegration that had already become evident in the late nineteenth century only escalated during the early Republican period. Following the death of Yuan Shikai, the first president of the Republic of China, the era of warlordism began. Meanwhile, Western and Japanese imperialists increased their political and economical exploitation of China. China's defeat in the 1895 Sino-Japanese war and the Allied intervention following the Boxer Uprising of 1900 marked the high tide of imperialism in China. It was in this context of increasing foreign penetration and intensifying internal conflict that film was first imported.

On 11 August 1896 in Shanghai, a Spaniard named Galen Bocca exhibited the first motion picture to a Chinese audience at an entertainment centre called Xu Garden (Xuyuang) where variety shows and acrobatic performances were given daily. A year later, an American came to China and screened movies at a number of teahouses in the city. These screenings lasted for more than ten days and created a sensation. At this time, as in most parts of the world, movies were considered a novelty and were viewed as popular entertainment. Early films mostly took as their subject matter exotic places and peoples, thus reinforcing the view of film as exotica. Films shown in China during this period include *The Tsar's Visit to Paris*, *The Serpent Dance in Florida*, *The City of Madrid*, *The Spanish Dance*, *The Exhausted Mule* and *The Boxer*.

These titles illustrate both the nature and the appeal of early movie shows. One Chinese described what he saw: 'I recently saw some American electric shadowplays (*yingxi*) that contained wonderful scenes and were full of surprises. One scene showed two cute dancing blondes, who were then replaced by another scene of two Western wrestling men. One other scene showed a bathing woman. In yet another scene, a man tried to sleep but was annoyed by insects. He got up, caught a few insects and put them in his mouth, which made the audience laugh. In one other scene, a magician covered a woman with a blanket. When he unfolded the blanket the woman was gone. Minutes later the woman reappeared from behind the blanket.' This early eyewitness account suggests that the first movies to be screened in China had not yet developed mature narrative techniques and were mostly one-reelers. But works reminiscent of the two most important filmmakers of the day, the Lumière brothers and Méliès, were presented to Chinese audiences. The short film about a man trying to sleep arguably reminds one of the Lumières' own brand of cinematic realism, while the story of the magician seems to borrow heavily from Méliès' famous techniques. These two diametrically opposed orientations in filmmaking were to have tremendous impact on later developments, and they were to be echoed in China as well as throughout the rest of the world.

That foreigners played such a prominent role in the early development of film in China should come as no surprise. China was not alone among non-Western nations in this regard. As an industrial enterprise, film first had to establish itself in the exhibition and distribution sectors in China, because there was hardly any native film production. As a result, the majority of early titles shown in China were Western imports, and all the first-run theatres were located in foreign concessions and owned by foreign interests.

Chinese film production began in 1905. A photographer named Ren Fengtai (1850–1932), who owned a photographic studio in Beijing, built the city's first movie theatre at the turn of the century as a sideline business venture. By that time, moviegoing had become so fashionable that the supply of foreign films could not keep pace with demand. So Ren decided to make his own films. In spring 1905, with the help of his assistants, Ren filmed a segment of **Conquering Jun Mountain**, featuring Tan Xinpei (1847–1917), then the 'King of Beijing Opera', and he continued to film some more stage performances by Tan and other renowned Beijing opera singers later that year. The fact that the earliest films attempted to integrate the new Western medium with traditional Chinese theatre says much about the terms on which film was adopted by pioneering Chinese filmmakers. In 1909, Ren's studio was mysteriously destroyed by fire, and his brief adventure in film came to an end.

Besides Ren's **filmed stage performances**, a number of other experimental short features were also made during the 1910s, although without exception all these early productions involved foreigners who either worked as technicians or provided finance for pioneering Chinese filmmakers. Among the many foreign filmmakers who came to China, the American Benjamin Brodsky was the first to set up a studio, Asia (Yaxia) Film Company. Apart from a **documentary** entitled *China*, Brodsky also produced a couple of shorts before entrusting his business to another American named Yashell. Yashell, who was interested in making films about Chinese life with Chinese casts, hired **Zhang Shichuan** to manage the new business. Within four years Asia Film Company had produced about eighteen films, including the first Chinese short feature, The **Difficult Couple** (1913).

Although Asia Film Company was the first to start, the Commercial Press's Motion Picture Department actually became the industry leader. As a publishing house, the Commercial Press's involvement in filmmaking was initially only minor. In 1917, an American filmmaker arrived in China to launch a big movie venture. However, in two years he had spent all his money and not produced anything particularly significant, with the result that he had to sell his film equipment for a return ticket to the USA. The Commercial Press seized the opportunity to acquire all of his equipment for only three thousand yuan (Chinese dollars). In 1920, the Board of Trustees of the Commercial Press officially approved the formation of the Motion Picture Department, and within a year the department had expanded its production base by purchasing more equipment from the USA. Besides producing films, the Motion Picture Department of the Commercial Press developed film stock for other studios.

In addition to Asia Film Company and the Motion Picture Department, two other smaller studios were also involved in filmmaking. Based in Hong Kong, Huamei (Sino-American) Films, managed by **Li Minwei**, produced **Zhuangzi Tests His Wife** (1913), while the Shanghai-based Huanxian (Fantasy) Film Company was headed by Zhang Shichuan and Guan Haifeng. Each of these companies produced only one film before going bankrupt. In total, only five studios, including Ren Fengtai's sideline venture, made films in the 1910s.

Since no equivalent for the term film was available in traditional Chinese vocabulary, expressions such as 'electrical shadowplay' (*dianguang yingxi*) or simply 'electric shadow' (*dianying*) were soon deployed. These terms are suggestive of how Chinese people understood what film was taken to be. While the 'electric' component of this expression emphasized the technical aspects of this new medium, 'shadowplay' was simply an appropriation of an existing Chinese word referring to a traditional form of popular entertainment called *piying xi* (leather shadowplay). The techniques and operating principles of the Chinese shadowplay are quite similar to that of the motion picture. In this form of Chinese folk art, human and animal figures are carved out of leather (mostly donkey skin, which is why in many parts of China this art is also called *lü piying* – donkey skin shadowplay) and projected on to a screen. While the puppeteers and light sources are kept to one side of the screen, the audience watches the movements and shadowy images from the other side. An example of this practice can be found in **To Live** (*dir.* **Zhang Yimou**, 1994), where the protagonist was originally a shadowplay artist. Understandably, when the Chinese first saw motion pictures, they likened them to their traditional shadowplay, and because of this similarity, some Chinese are still claiming to this day that the origins of motion pictures should be traced to the traditional shadowplay in China.

While 'electric shadowplay' was the earliest Chinese expression for movies, other terms such as 'Western shadowplay' were also used. In fact, during the 1910s and early 1920s, 'shadowplay' was the most frequently used word for movies. It was not until the early 1920s that the Chinese began to use the current word, 'electric shadow' (*dianying*), to refer to the motion pictures. This progression in terminology is indicative of the progression in Chinese understanding of film as an imported medium. Obviously, the Chinese were increasingly aware of the medium's technical dimensions and so began to realize the incongruity of likening movies to traditional Chinese shadowplays.

Outside of questions of naming, the early Chinese response to movies was nothing short of enthusiastic. While some commented on how the representation of the world in movies provides the supreme demonstration of the illusive nature of reality, others were more impressed by film realism. People were amused, amazed and ultimately entertained by this new technology and the various possibilities it presented. As more films were imported into China, film watching also became more popular. In 1904, when Empress Dowager Cixi celebrated her seventieth birthday in the imperial palace, the British embassy in Beijing presented her with a film projector and several reels of film. Unfortunately, though, the generator exploded during the screening at the party, and Cixi, taking this as a bad omen, ordered the prohibition of any future film exhibition in the Forbidden City.

Cixi's ruling may have prevented her officials from seeing any more films within the confines of the imperial palace, but film attracted an ever larger audience outside the palace walls. In 1901, the first theatre houses exclusively devoted to movies appeared in Hong Kong and Taiwan. The first theatre in Beijing appeared in 1907, while around the same time movie theatres were being built in Shanghai by Western and Japanese businessmen. By 1926, the number of movie theatres in China had mushroomed to 106, with a total seating capacity of 68,000, figures that do not take into account other entertainment sites, such as YMCAs, where films were shown regularly. Despite many failures, the development of film in these three decades prepared Chinese filmmakers for the bigger strides they were to make in the next phase.

See also: theatre and film

Further reading
Zhong *et al.* (1997), a historical study of early film exhibition and film audiences.

3   The movie craze of the 1920s

During the 1920s, Chinese industry and national economy enjoyed a brief respite from foreign competition due to the destructive effects of World War I in Europe. The Western powers, preoccupied with post-war reconstruction, relaxed their grip on China. The war had also significantly cut supplies from Europe and so created a shortage of available films for exhibition. While this situation allowed Hollywood to step in and fill the vacuum, it also gave Chinese filmmakers a share of the market. Furthermore, as the popularity of movies increased, so did the demand for full-length feature films. Theatre owners could no longer satisfy audiences with programmes consisting of only short films. To cater to this market demand in 1921, Chinese filmmakers produced three long features: ***Yan Ruisheng***, ***Sea Oath*** (*dir.* Guan Haifeng, 1921) and *The Vampire* (*dir.* **Dan Duyu**, 1921).

Yan Ruisheng was based on a sensational Shanghai murder case of 1920. The case involved a young man named Yan Ruisheng who killed a prostitute for money. The victim, Wang Lianying, was not an ordinary hooker, but a concubine of great renown in the pleasure quarters of Shanghai, where she bore the title 'Queen of the Flowers'. The case received huge publicity. The Shanghai Cinema Studies Society decided to make a film about it and asked Yan's good friend Chen Shouzhi to play Yan. Chen not only looked like Yan, he had the same mannerisms. In the hope of achieving a sense of authenticity, the studio also found a former prostitute to play the victim.

Sea Oath concerns a **romance** between a modern girl named Fuzhu and her artist lover. After they have declared their love for each other, Fuzhu then decides to leave the artist when she is tempted by a wealthy suitor. However, Fuzhu's conscience awakens at her wedding and she goes back to the artist. The latter, angry, refuses to see her. The girl then goes to the seashore with the intention of committing suicide, but the artist arrives just in time to rescue her. The two are reconciled and live happily ever after. At a time when arranged marriage was still the dominant practice, the 'free love' between Fuzhu and the artist in this film represents a challenge to tradition. Interestingly, the narrative of *Sea Oath* looks rather Western, thus rendering the film both refreshing and outlandish. The film was a commercial success. Its female lead, Yin Mingzhu, who was a well known figure in Shanghai society, soon became one of the earliest Chinese film stars.

The third long feature was *The Vampire*. Its director, Guan Haifeng, based the film on a French detective story so as to cash in on the detective and **thriller** genres that were in vogue at that time, especially among younger audiences. *The Vampire* centres on the kidnapping of Doctor Bao and his rescue by the girl who loves him. The evil characters are mainly beautiful young women who live in a secret cave, a fact that, together with the use of special effects, contributed to the film's success at the box-office.

An important backdrop to the growth of the Chinese film industry in the 1920s was the relative freedom enjoyed by filmmakers operating in places such as Shanghai. The political fragmentation of China by the warlords had, ironically, created an environment in which intellectual pluralism and cultural diversity could flourish, and film's rapid growth at this time was directly linked to this *laissez-faire* condition. The absence of any effective government spared the Chinese film industry direct state interference, a luxury that it would never again enjoy for the remainder of the century.

During this decade, moviegoing became a fashionable pastime for city dwellers, and film stars began to join ranks with social celebrities. Many adventurous capitalists were eager to invest in the film business. In response to the movie craze, the number of theatres rose dramatically throughout the country, and new film studios mushroomed in Shanghai and other major cities. Many businessmen who had earlier refused to take film seriously now began to get involved in production and exhibition. By the mid-1920s, a total of 176 studios had been established in the country, 146 of them in Shanghai alone.

The mushrooming of film studios may have been indicative of a new enthusiasm for film, but it would be wrong to see the 1920s as the golden age of Chinese cinema. In fact, very few studios survived for more than a year, and even fewer actually produced any films. Most of these studios were started by opportunist capitalists looking to make some quick money. With only a few thousand yuan in their pockets, they borrowed equipment, shot pictures in rented studios and cast family members with no prior acting experience. The manner in which these studios were operated was bound to produce films of poor quality. And yet, by increasing the market supply of films, they substantially reduced a film's per copy price. What had sold for 7,000–8,000 yuan per copy in the early 1920s could sell for only 1,000–2,000 yuan by the middle of the decade. As a result, a large number of mediocre and junk films flooded the movie theatres.

This situation worried the established film studios. They accused the smaller studios of damaging the healthy growth of the film industry by alienating Chinese audiences from domestically produced films and so driving them to better-produced foreign titles. In 1928, setting out to squeeze out their small rivals, six major movie establishments in Shanghai – Mingxing, Minxin, Da Zhonghua-Baihe, Shanghai Film Company, China Theatre and Youlian – joined forces to form a corporation named 'Liuhe' (the United Six). In their manifesto, Liuhe stressed the need to advance the Chinese film industry by improving production quality. The real issue, however, was the elimination of the rival studios. Liuhe's strategy of 'fighting poison with poison' (*yidu gongdu*) meant not only that the new corporation was going to compete with the smaller studios by duplicating what the latter planned to produce, but that it was going to do it with more capital, better equipment, bigger stars and a faster rate of production. By all accounts, the strategy worked, because by the late 1920s fewer than a dozen film studios were still in business.

While engaging in direct combat with small studios, the major studios also appealed to the government to establish official control over the industry in the hope of further weakening their rivals. They won public sympathy by resorting to nationalistic rhetoric, arguing that in order to fight off foreign dominance of China's film market, it was necessary to stamp out the irresponsible smaller studios. By the late 1920s, the Kuomintang (KMT) government had begun its censorship operation, with films dealing with martial arts, **legends and myths** among the first targets. Since most of the smaller studios were completely dependent on profits generated by these genres, the government's action directly threatened their existence. Although the major studios were also involved in making these types of movies, their production base was more diversified, and so they could better adapt to new government policies. After this self-structuring from within and government intervention from without, the Chinese film industry moved toward a period of further consolidation in the 1930s.

See also: censorship and film; detective film; genre films; love and marriage; martial arts film

Further reading
S. Hong (1995), on commercial films of the 1920s; C. Tan (1995), a survey of early cinema.

4   Early film people

In the early days, Chinese filmmakers mainly came from the *xinxi* (i.e., new Western-style spoken drama) tradition. Theatre was traditionally one of the most popular performing arts in China. At the turn of the century, there was an enormous audience for Beijing opera and various regional operas. At this time, some returned Chinese students introduced Western-style plays to Chinese audiences. This new form of theatre, called *xinxi* or *wenmingxi* (civilized play), was particularly popular with young people because it dealt with contemporary issues and events.

In formal terms, the Western-style theatre took a more naturalistic approach to stage design and acting, differing markedly from the highly stylized and 'expressive' aesthetic traditions of Chinese theatre. For this reason, it was easier for the 'new theatre' to make the transition from theatre to film. For instance, **Zheng Zhengqiu**, the 'founding father' of Chinese cinema, began his career as a professional Beijing opera critic, and wrote, directed and acted in a number of 'new plays' before starting to make films. Another important film producer of the 1920s–30s, **Shao Zuiweng**, who founded Tianyi Film Company in 1925 and subsequently directed many films, also had previous experience as a theatre manager. When he made the transition to filmmaking, he brought the entire staff of his theatre with him.

Film actors and actresses were even more closely linked to the 'new theatre' movement, but unlike the 'brain power' of the film industry – screen writers, studio managers and directors – who mainly came from well-to-do families, film actors and actresses were usually recruited from the lower social strata. This situation arose because in traditional society acting was considered a lowly occupation, one which respectable families would not let their sons and daughters enter. Popular perceptions of actresses equated them with dancing girls and prostitutes. Not surprisingly, then, the social ritual of electing a reigning 'Queen of Movie Stars' was conducted in exactly the same fashion as the election of the 'Queen of the Flowers' in late Qing. However, movie stars themselves felt superior to their fellow entertainers. On one occasion, a group of film actors took offence at an advertising poster that listed their names beneath those of *mingpiao* (famous opera performers) and *minghua* (famous flowers, that is, prostitutes).

The lack of respect given movie stars was a major obstacle to the development of Chinese cinema. It deterred many talented people from entering a world looked upon as corrupt. The relatively low salaries paid to film actors and actresses also reflected this social status. During the 1920s, for instance, film actresses were usually paid between one and four yuan a day, hardly a handsome income. As movies became more established in the late 1920s and early 1930s, the major studios developed a casting system. A small group of 'stars' were paid fees for every film in which they appeared, in addition to their base salaries. The basic cast were just paid a regular monthly salary. For instance, **Hu Die** (Butterfly Wu), one of the leading female stars of the 1920s–30s, earned a monthly salary of 2,000 yuan, at that time the highest salary for a Chinese movie star, while Ai Xia (? – 1935), a member of the basic cast of Mingxing Film Company, made slightly over 100 a month. The leading male star at Lianhua, **Jin Yan**, sometimes referred to as 'the king of cinema', earned only 320 yuan a month, while a 1930s dancing girl could make as much as 1,100. Although movie stars enjoyed greater social prestige than dancing girls, the lack of financial incentives made many stars abandon the film world and join dance clubs instead. The consequent shortage of talented actors created a situation whereby, as some contemporary observers complained, anyone who appeared in a movie was treated as a star, regardless of their actual abilities.

Like movie stars elsewhere, Chinese actors had tremendous mass appeal. They set fashion trends and were invited to conduct opening ceremonies and promote domestic products. They were also the subject of gossip. Although stars were not necessarily guilty of the sins they were accused of, their private lives were put under constant public scrutiny. Because of their social influence, efforts were made to mould them into living models for society. Such efforts ranged from open criticism and ridicule of some stars' 'libertine' life-styles to the publicly offered advice of good intent; that is, from the offering of best film actor/actress awards to the studio's direct interference in the private lives of its stars. The suicides of Ai Xia and **Ruan Lingyu** well illustrate the social pressures faced by, in particular, female stars. On the whole, though, few actors or actresses were as politically committed as the screen writers and film critics.

During the 1920s, fiction writers from the Mandarin Duck and Butterfly school figured prominently in the world of film. Many films produced in the 1920s were either scripted by them or adapted from their works. This literary genre was enormously popular with urban readers, and many in the film industry shared the sentiments of its writers. In comparison with the radical May Fourth intellectuals, these writers were much more ambivalent about Western culture. Written in traditional narrative styles, their works featured protagonists torn between the forces of the old and the new.

It might be argued that before the 1930s very few people were committed to politics. When it came to writing film scripts, even a figure such as **Hong Shen**, otherwise an outspoken social critic and iconoclast of the New Culture movement, wrote in a more subdued manner. In many ways Hong's scripts resembled those of the Mandarin Duck and Butterfly writers. But that is not to say that early Chinese filmmakers were not concerned with socio-political issues. On the contrary, one of the most accomplished film directors of the period, Ren Pengnian, portrayed patriotic heroes elevating the interests of the nation above those of personal love in two films, *Secret Told at Last* (1922) and *Umbrella of Patriotism* (1923). Zheng Zhengqiu stated that his *Orphan Rescues Grandfather* (1923) dramatized the importance of education. Similarly, *Abandoned Woman* (*dir.* Li Zeyuan, **Hou Yao**, 1924) addressed the complex issue of women's liberation. In many ways, socially conscious filmmakers of later generations inherited their sense of responsibility from this founding generation.

Further reading
X. He (1982), on Zhang Shichuan and Mingxing; C. Tan (1992a,b), two studies of Zheng Zhengqiu.

5   The Nanjing decade, 1927–37

The founding of the KMT Nanjing government in 1927 signalled the beginning of the end for the lawless situation that had marked the second phase of development in Chinese film history. The new regime's efforts at political centralization and ideological control ushered in a new era of state intervention in cultural and intellectual life. In the early 1930s, as the Nationalists gradually consolidated their control, they began to exert more authority over the entertainment industry. The establishment of the National Film Censorship Committee in 1931 was just one example of the government's efforts at constructing a new national culture. State censorship was designed to enlist the services of the modern media in the project of national reconstruction and so dictate what could or could not be produced. This political intervention was to have a tremendous impact on film's development during the 1930s, and its legacy can still be seen in mainland China and Taiwan today.

In addition to state involvement, two other factors also shaped the film industry during the 1930s. Firstly, the increasing Japanese aggression against China created a sense of national crisis. Secondly, a group of dedicated underground Communist writers and film critics managed to infiltrate the film industry. The combination of these political and historical forces was to change the course of Chinese film history.

The developments at three studios best reflect these trends. One of the oldest and most important studios in China, Mingxing Film Company, was founded in 1922 by **Zhang Shichuan**, **Zhou Jianyun**, **Zheng Zhengqiu**, Ren Jinping and Zheng Zhegu, all of whom recognized film's potential for financial profit and social reform. Indeed, the twin drives to make money and provide a positive moral influence on society dominated the company's history. While Zhang Shichuan is representative of the more pragmatic, profit-oriented approach, Zheng Zhengqiu was more idealistic about film's social responsibility. Zhang wanted to make entertaining films free of moral didacticism. Zheng, on the other hand, strongly believed in providing audiences with moral guidance.

The company's first productions apparently followed Zhang's line of thinking. After its début, a newsreel about a French general's visit to Shanghai, Mingxing churned out three comedies and one drama on subjects ranging from Charlie Chaplin's visit to Shanghai to a real-life case of patricide. However, these films failed to generate the expected profits and placed the company in financial trouble. Only after the commercial success of **Orphan Rescues Grandfather** in 1923 was the company able to regain financial strength. The success of this morally explicit film seemed to prove that Zheng was right to insist on film's social responsibility. Besides, commercial success and moral didacticism were not mutually exclusive. Mingxing later produced a series of movies in a similar pattern, all of which presented the struggle between good (e.g., motherly love, philanthropy, education) and evil (e.g., old social customs, warlords, the tyranny of the traditional **family**). Good always triumphed in the end.

In some ways, it was this emphasis on moral didacticism that opened the door for the leftist filmmakers of the early 1930s. As one of the general managers of the company, Zheng may not have shared leftist ideology, but he certainly shared a belief in film's social and moral responsibilities. Such shared belief lay behind the company's decision to hire a group of well-known leftists for its script department. It is no coincidence that Mingxing was actively engaged in producing leftist films in the early 1930s.

Lianhua Film Company was founded in 1930 by **Luo Mingyou**, who had started a theatre business while still a student at Beijing University. Luo's strong sense of mission would eventually lead him to a Christian priesthood, but in the early years it revealed itself in the way he managed business and selected films. Under his management, Zhenguang Theatre in Beijing earned a reputation for showing quality films in the early 1920s. His low price admission fees allowed more people to enjoy movies. Ironically, Luo's seemingly nonchalant attitude toward profit actually brought in more revenue. By the late 1920s, Luo managed more than twenty movie theatres and controlled the entire distribution network in Northern China.

In 1929, Luo went to Shanghai and persuaded two studios, Minxin and Great China-Lily (Da Zhonghua-Baihe), to jointly set up a new company. Minxin was founded by **Li Minwei** in Hong Kong on 14 May 1923 and moved to Shanghai in 1926. Great China-Lily, as the name suggests, was the result of a merger between Great China and Lily in 1926. The new company employed a group of highly educated people noted for their progressive 'Westernized' views. The alliance of Luo's distribution network in Northern China and the production capabilities of these two Shanghai studios led to the establishment of Lianhua Film Company. On Lianhua's board of trustees were: He Dong, a millionaire from Hong Kong; Xiong Xiling, the former prime minister of Duan Qirui's Beijing government; Feng Gengguang, general manager of the Bank of China; Yu Fengzhi, wife of the Northeastern warlord Zhang Xueliang; Luo Wengan, foreign minister of the Nanjing government and Luo Mingyou's uncle; and Luo Xuefu, Luo's father and chair of the Hong Kong Chamber of Commerce. With so many powerful figures, Lianhua Film Company enjoyed close ties with the Nanjing government.

In its manifesto, Lianhua declared its mission to elevate art, promote culture, enlighten the masses, and rescue China's film industry from degeneration and deterioration. Such pronouncements were very much in accord with cultural policies of the Nanjing government. As a highly respected studio, Lianhua staffed its management, writing, directing and acting departments with well-educated people. Many employees had Western education and a 'progressive' outlook. Lianhua produced twelve films in its first two years. The first two releases, *Memories of the Old Capital* and **Wild Flower** (both *dir*. **Sun Yu**, 1930), greatly impressed audiences and brought a new look to domestic production. Many titles deal with pressing contemporary issues. Too melodramatic to qualify as realism, they nevertheless engaged social conditions of the 1930s.

Lianhua's films rejected the highly theatrical and exaggerated acting styles of the new theatre in favour of an emphasis on the cinema's visual potential. Their sophisticated use of montage, camera angle, lighting and visual effects sets them apart. Many contemporary observers believed that the emergence of Lianhua ended the prevalence of such genres as martial arts and **ghosts and immortals**. In this regard, Lianhua initiated a new trend for social films. Between 1930 and 1937, the studio produced ninety-four titles, including the well known *Humanity* (*dir*. **Bu Wancang**, 1932), **Big Road** (*dir*. Sun Yu, 1934), **New Woman**, **Song of the Fishermen** (both *dir*. **Cai Chusheng**, all 1934), **Goddess** (1934) and *Little Angel* (1935, both *dir*. **Wu Yonggang**). In contrast to Mingxing, whose audience came mostly from the leisure class, Lianhua established a loyal following among the better educated, especially young students.

Financially independent, Lianhua voluntarily cooperated with the KMT government, mainly because of Luo's close ties to Nanjing. When the KMT authorities prepared to set up their own film studio in the mid-1930s, Luo was appointed advisor to the planning committee, and he was among the delegation of Chinese industrialists later sent by the government on a tour of Europe and the USA. In return, Lianhua produced *Iron Bird* (*dir*. Yuan Congmei, 1934) in support of

Plate 1   *Memories of the Old Capital* (1930)

the government's call for public support. By late 1935, Lianhua had released *Little Angel* and *The Spirit of the Nation* (*dir.* Luo Mingyou, 1935), both of which aimed to advance the New Life Movement sponsored by the government. In this regard, Lianhua contrasted drastically with Mingxing, which on more than one occasion refused to take orders from the government.

Tianyi was founded in 1925 by the Shao (Shaw) brothers, with the oldest, **Shao Zuiweng**, in charge. During the 1920s, Tianyi opposed the imitation of Western models and took the lead in making 'genuinely' Chinese films. To ensure such authentic 'Chineseness', a number of Tianyi productions were based on popular legends and myths or adapted from classical literature. Far removed from contemporary social concerns, these movies catered largely to the tastes of the lower classes. Tianyi productions of the 1920s were usually scorned by progressive-minded critics who charged that they perpetuated superstitious beliefs, lacked historical accuracy in their costume dramas and were of lowly artistic standard. Nevertheless, out of the 140 studios operating in Shanghai during the 1920s, Tianyi was one of only a dozen to survive into the 1930s. It even managed to become one of the three major movie establishments in the country. From 1930 to 1937, it produced a total of sixty-two films, second only to Mingxing and Lianhua.

After the Japanese invaded Manchuria in September 1931, a strong nationalistic sentiment swept China. Suddenly, entertainment and fantasy films seemed irrelevant and frivolous. Films addressing nationalistic concerns found an enthusiastic audience. Tianyi, which had long been notorious for churning out commercial flicks, was pressured into adjusting its policies. Beginning in 1932, the studio made several films dealing with the national crisis caused by Japanese aggression. For instance, *Two Orphan Girls from the Northeast* (*dir.* **Li Pingqian**, 1932) concerns two girls forced to flee their invaded homeland in Northeastern China. Stranded in Shanghai, they meet a young doctor and both fall in love with him. But when the Japanese attack Shanghai in 1932, the two sisters put aside their personal feelings, join a medical team and nurse the wounded soldiers. Touched by the two girls' patriotic spirit, the doctor also offers his services. *Struggle* (*dir.* Qiu Qixiang, 1933), another Tianyi production, calls for rapprochement between warring Chinese in the name of the fight against the common Japanese enemy. The story centres on a young peasant whose wife has been raped and killed by an evil landlord. The peasant joins the Chinese resistance and, getting the chance to avenge himself on the evil landlord, decides to save his bullets for the Japanese instead.

These films reflected the change of mood among Chinese filmmakers as well as among the general audience. Indeed, audiences now seemed to demand films that addressed their concerns. In this context the making of socially responsible films was not necessarily incompatible with the earning of profit. It is no exaggeration to say that the large number of serious films produced in the early 1930s was the result of the studios' attempt to respond to changed tastes. It was against this backdrop that leftist cinema made its first appearance.

See also: comedy; costume drama; documentary; family; ghosts and immortals; leftist film; martial arts film; melodrama

Further reading
Li and Hu (1996), a history of silent cinema; M. Severson (1996), a report of Chinese silent films screened in Italy; ZDYYZ (1996), a large collection of historical material on silent cinema.

6   Leftist film

The term leftist film refers to a group of titles produced in the 1930s highly critical of the KMT government. They usually depict society's dark side, express indignation over social injustice and advocate radical social reform. It is a mistake, however, to assume that all leftist films were made by leftist filmmakers. In fact, their producers came from diverse cultural and political backgrounds. Some, such as **Bu Wancang**, **Zhang Shichuan** and **Zheng Zhengqiu**, were veteran film directors of the 1920s. They took the view that film ought to promote social progress and improve people's living conditions. Because of their conviction, their films consistently dramatize the misfortunes of the working class, the sufferings of the weak and powerless, and the moral corruption of the rich and powerful. But their critiques of social injustice were rooted in a humanistic concern for the downtrodden, whereas people like **Tian Han**, **Xia Yan** and **Yang Hansheng** were committed underground Communists with specific political agendas and interests. Their primary objective was to discredit the KMT government by highlighting its widespread failures. The portrayal of poverty, injustice, class conflict, and the moral decay of the rich and powerful in leftist films thus served a subversive purpose. Finally, there were people like **Cai Chusheng**, Sun Yu and **Wu Yonggang** who, while not Communists themselves, were persuaded by leftist ideals and formed alliances with leftist filmmakers. Films by this last group of people contributed significantly to the development of the leftist cinema movement.

Although the beginnings of the leftist cultural movement in China can be traced to the 1928 debate on revolutionary literature, leftist cinema was not set in motion until the 1931 formation of the League of Leftist Performing Artists. This organization included a number of Communist intellectuals who were to play important roles in the leftist cinema movement. As the brainchild of the Chinese Communist Party (CCP), the League served in the front line of the party's ideological war against the Nationalists. Among other things, the League's manifesto stressed the need to develop proletarian cinema. In the following year, Xia Yan, Zheng Boqi and Qian Xingcun (**Ah Ying**) were invited by Mingxing's management to join its script department. Meanwhile, Tian Han was offered a position as screen writer by Lianhua and appointed Director of the Script Division by Yihua Film Company. Thus, the creative nucleus of China's three major studios was under the influence of the CCP. In 1932, Xia Yan organized the 'Communist cinema group', whose members included Qian Xingcun, Wang Chenwu, Shi Linghe, and **Situ Huimin**. The group was accepted by the League as a subdivision and subject to the direct leadership of the CCP's Cultural Committee. The combination of able leadership, individual talent and ingenuity, and favourable circumstances resulted in the production of a large number of leftist films that exerted an influence throughout the industry.

The true identity of Communist workers was kept secret. After the purge of 1927, in which thousands of Communists were arrested and killed by the Nationalists, no one in the film industry wanted to be openly associated with the CCP, although many harboured sympathy for leftist platforms. Some studio producers and managers, such as Lianhua's Luo Mingyou and Mingxing's Zheng Zhengqiu, and, to some extent, even a number of Nationalist officials, shared the view that film must play a positive role in China's social progress by doing more than just offering entertainment. Such sentiments provided a fertile and relatively protected ground for Communist activity in the film industry. Indeed, leftist films were mainly characterized by their focus on social problems, which chimed well with the industry's general shift toward more socially conscientious positions. To some extent, the serious nature – rather than the critical edge – of leftist films was congruous with cultural policies of the KMT government, as both lashed out at what was considered frivolous subject matter. Since the early 1930s, the regime had encouraged films concerned with national issues, and in this respect some leftist titles were more in keeping with state policies than the escapist fantasies of entertainment movies. When it came to selecting films to represent China at international film festivals, the Nationalist censors picked titles later identified as leftist.

The reasons for the Nationalist censors' tolerance of leftist film are extremely complex. Certainly, ambiguity over what actually constituted a leftist film generated a good deal of confusion for both the censors and studio managers. In addition, factional power struggles within the KMT government reduced the effectiveness of control over the film industry. Finally, some Nationalist officials, including many film censors, were in sympathy with the views expressed by leftist cinema. After all, the Nanjing government was not a monolithic entity, and from time to time more liberal-minded opinions managed to hold sway. These factors allowed for the production and exhibition of films antagonistic to the regime. For example, *Twenty-Four Hours in Shanghai* (*dir.* **Shen Xiling**, 1933) portrays the hardships endured by ordinary city dwellers in their daily lives. *Wild Torrents* (*dir.* **Cheng Bugao**, 1933) tells the story of flood victims' confrontation with an evil landlord. *The Uprising* (*dir.* **Xu Xinfu**, 1933) sympathizes with the salt workers who rebelled against the capitalists. Other films, such as *Dawn Over the Metropolis* (*dir.* Cai Chusheng, 1933), *Plunder of Peach and Plum* (*dir.* **Yuan Muzhi**, 1934), *Big Road*, *Goddess*, *New Woman* and *Street Angel* (*dir.* Shen Xiling, 1937), share similar ideological orientations.

In addition to producing a large number of influential films, the leftists also controlled the public forum of film **criticism**. In their capacity as editors of, or contributors to, several major newspaper columns, leftist critics dominated the public discourse on cinema. Their views on film had tremendous influence over directors and studio managers. By making a concerted effort to engage and discredit their political opponents, leftist film critics greatly shaped public opinion.

But the political thrust of leftist film, particularly its evocation of class struggle, irritated many right-wing Nationalists who found the film industry's turn to the left disturbing and worried that such radical ideology might fan already widespread social discontent. Because the Film Censorship Committee, the only government agency authorized to deal with such matters, took a rather lenient attitude towards film censorship, right-wing Nationalists found it difficult to stop the production and exhibition of politically antagonistic films by official means. So they took matters into their own hands. In the early morning of 12 November 1933, a group armed with sticks and bricks stormed Yihua and trashed its equipment. In addition to leaving pamphlets full of slogans such as 'Eradicate the Communists', they also posted a public letter and signed themselves as members of the 'Anti-Communist Squad of the Film Industry in Shanghai'. The next day many film studios in Shanghai received letters warning them of the menace of Communism. The studios were instructed to stop hiring leftists. These letters and pamphlets identified filmmakers like Tian Han and Xia Yan, and listed the titles of films considered suspect.

Right-wing Nationalists also blamed the government film censors for allowing these films to pass through their office, and they accused the censors of being blind to Communist propaganda. Their scare tactics were effective. Within a few weeks, many of the known leftist filmmakers were in hiding. Although Lianhua and Mingxing continued to produce a few more leftist titles, Yihua reverted to the production of just entertainment films. Yet the movement's influence remained strong. The legacy of leftist film was not only revived in the late 1940s; it also continues to inspire filmmakers of the 1980s–90s.

See also: censorship and film

Further reading
C. Berry (1989b), a brief discussion of leftist film; Bo Chen (1993), a large collection of historical material on the leftist cinema movement; N. Ma (1989), a critical analysis of leftist film.

7   Soft film

The violent right-wing Nationalist response to the leftist film group reveals the fierceness and intensity of the fight to control film production. Yet not everyone took such a partisan position. Some considered it sad that film had become so politicized and began to stress the medium's other values. They rejected the didacticism so prevalent in many leftist films by calling film 'ice-cream for the eyes' – sensuous, pleasing and devoid of politics. They complained that leftist films were dominated by ideology and lacked artistic refinement. They believed that a film's representation of life should remain 'soft' – a quality that resembled film stock itself. The type of film thus promoted has been termed soft cinema.

The champions of soft cinema included artists, poets, film critics and screen writers, most notably Liu Na'ou (1900–40), Mu Shiying, Huang Jiamo and Huang Tianshi. They began to publish essays in early 1933 calling for a new approach to filmmaking. In their view, the primary function of film was to entertain the audience, to please their senses and make them feel good, rather than to lecture them and force ideas down their throats. As one essay put it, movies should be 'ice-cream for the eyes and a couch for the soul'. Advocates of soft cinema accused leftist films of over-emphasizing content and neglecting form. For them, leftist film did nothing but expose social ills and peddle propaganda for the CCP.

Understandably, the leftists responded with torrents of counter accusations. Critics argued that as there was nothing soft about poverty, injustice and class conflict, films must confront hard social realities. But the leftists' triumph over soft cinema in film **publications** did not stop the industry's drift away from serious films. By the mid-1930s, the majority of film directors and screen writers had softened their critical stance and begun to stress the values of entertainment. Following the commercial success of ***Girl in Disguise*** (*dir*. Fang Peilin, 1936), a film scripted by Huang Jiamo, a significant number of films were made using the same formula: engaging story, sensational event, fantastic visual effects and apolitical world view.

The rise of soft cinema in the mid-1930s had its roots in political history. Ever since 1905, filmmakers had oscillated between two approaches, one focusing on film's entertainment value, the other on its social function. This division may not be absolute, but it has always existed. The two box-office hits of the 1920s, ***Yan Ruisheng*** and ***Orphan Rescues Grandfather***, represent two early examples of this split. The commercial concern held sway until the early 1930s. Films of ghosts and immortals, legends and myths, as well as tales of martial arts heroes and heroines, were industry staples during the 1920s. By the early 1930, however, a series of changes turned the industry toward the production of more socially conscious films. This development contributed to the rise of leftist cinema. Soft cinema, a reaction to the excesses of leftist filmmaking, advocated a revival of the legacy of entertainment films of the 1920s. But at the same time, its emphasis on the importance of artistic refinement and good craftsmanship reflected a sincere concern to improve the quality of Chinese film.

Further reading
Bo Chen (1993: 142–74), contains original pro and con articles on soft cinema.

8   Sound film

The world's first sound film, *The Jazz Singer* (*dir*. Alan Crosland, 1927), was publicly screened in the USA on 6 August 1927. Four months later, Shanghai had its own encounter with this new invention. On 16 December 1927, the city's Hundred Stars Theatre showed a number of American sound documentaries and exhibited relevant equipment after the performance, so that the audience could learn the operating principles of the new technology. By 1929, Olympic Theatre, the only movie theatre in Shanghai equipped with sound facility, was showing the first feature-length American sound film, *The Wings* (*dir.* William Wellman, 1927). Sound's popularity encouraged other prestigious movie theatres to install the new equipment as well. Because of the huge costs involved, the majority of movie houses in Shanghai could only afford to show silent films. However, since Hollywood had now turned to the production of sound films, the supply of silents could only be met by Chinese studios. Movie houses were thus put under pressure to make the transition.

In general, Chinese filmmakers felt ambivalent about the coming of talkies. On the one hand, they realized that sound represented the future of filmmaking and were keenly aware of the necessity of adopting the new technology. On the other hand, the transition from silent to sound required extra capital: both studios and theatres needed to be renovated, and such funds were not immediately available to Chinese filmmakers always plagued by investment shortages. Interestingly, with Hollywood switching to talkies, Chinese filmmakers saw an opportunity to expand a domestic market previously dominated by American products. They concluded that the language barrier, a minor factor during the silent era, would soon amount to a major obstacle for foreign films. In addition, the majority of Chinese-owned movie houses were technically incapable of showing sound films: they had no choice but to show silents. Here was a golden opportunity for growth and development. According to this point of view, there was no urgency or incentive for the Chinese film industry to make the transition from silent to sound, and as a result, Chinese studios continued to churn out silent movies well into the mid-1930s. Some of the most important films of this period, such as **Big Road**, **New Woman** and **Goddess**, were made without sound.

Yet the Chinese apprehension about sound could only slow down, not prevent, the period of transition. In early 1931, both Mingxing and Youlian finally released sound films. Mingxing premièred **Sing-Song Girl Red Peony** (*dir.* Zhang Shichuan), starring **Hu Die**, on 15 March at New Light Theatre, while Youlian screened *Yu the Beauty* (*dir.* Chen Kengran, 1931) at Olympia Theatre on 24 May. In both cases, dialogue and song were not synchronized on the soundtrack, but recorded first on a phonograph and then broadcast during screenings. Only dialogue and singing were recorded, and no background sounds were included. Despite such limitations, the two films were a huge box-office success. Audiences enthusiastically swarmed the theatres, forcing other studios to reconsider their position.

On 1 July 1931, Huaguang Film Company publicly screened *Reconciliation* (*dir.* Xia Chifeng, 1931), the first Chinese film to feature a real soundtrack. Three months later, Tianyi released its own first sound film, *A Singer's Story* (*dir.* **Li Pingqian**, 1931). These films were produced using foreign experts. In the case of *Reconciliation*, post-production was completed in a sound studio in Japan, while the participation of foreign technicians in the making of *A Singer's Story* proved crucial to its success. With the release of these films, the Chinese film industry finally entered the sound era. Although silent films continued to be produced, they were gradually phased out by the late 1930s.

Further reading

W. Guan (1976), a memoir of early Chinese cinema and its connection with the West; Hong Kong Arts Centre (1984), a collection on the films of the 1920s–30s, with synopses; L. Lee (1999), on the urban milieu of Shanghai in the 1930s; P. Pickowicz (1991), a historical survey of the 1930s, with emphasis on urban corruption.

9   Wartime film, 1937–45

The fourth period of Chinese film history begins with the outbreak of the second Sino-Japanese war in 1937. During the next eight years, the war of resistance was to overshadow every aspect of Chinese life, including the production of film in both occupied and unoccupied areas. In the wartime capital, Chongqing, Central Film Studio (Zhongdian) and China Motion Picture Studio (Zhongzhi), both run by the KMT government, employed a large number of patriotic filmmakers who continued to work with anti-Japanese themes. In the occupied areas, Manchurian Motion Pictures (Manying) in Changchun served as a propaganda machine for the Japanese, whereas film studios in Shanghai turned to the production of entertainment films. Some historians view many Shanghai genre films as constituting a passive resistance to Japanese attempts at indoctrination through Japanese propaganda films. Wherever they were produced, though, films tended to reflect the uniqueness of wartime conditions.

The outbreak of war in 1937 brought film production to a halt. Japanese bombardments of Shanghai caused severe damage to many studios. Mingxing's facilities were completely destroyed, Lianhua was soon dissolved, and Tianyi was relocated to Hong Kong. As the situation stabilized, film production resumed in two separate areas: the unoccupied and the occupied.

In the unoccupied areas, film production was concentrated around Central Film Studio, which operated briefly in Wuhan and then in Chongqing. Other filmmakers scattered around places like Hong Kong and Taiyuan also played their part. Before Hong Kong fell to the Japanese in 1941, its filmmakers produced a number of patriotic titles. Except for ***Orphan Island Paradise*** (*dir.* **Cai Chusheng**, 1939) and a few others, most Hong Kong productions belonged to Cantonese movies, which had formerly been banned by the KMT government. When the Japanese took over Hong Kong, Chongqing became the centre of film production in the unoccupied areas. China Motion Picture Studio and Central Film Studio both released a number of highly acclaimed wartime films, including ***Protect Our Land*** (*dir.* **Shi Dongshan**, 1938), *Children of China* (*dir.* **Shen Xiling**, 1939), ***Storm on the Border*** (*dir.* **Ying Yunwei**, 1940) and *Japanese Spy* (*dir.* Yuan Meiyun, 1943). Needless to say, as a part of the government's propaganda machine, the dominant themes of these films were **nationalism** and Chinese resistance.

In the occupied areas, film production was centred around two places. While Shanghai resumed its leadership in filmmaking as soon as the situation stabilized, Changchun, a city in Northeastern China, hosted Manchurian Motion Pictures, brainchild of the collaboration between the Japanese and their puppet regime, Manchukuo.

Until the outbreak of the Pacific War, Chinese filmmakers in Shanghai were in a peculiar position. Because of the existence of the foreign concessions, they were protected by British–French neutrality and so relatively free from direct Japanese harassment, and a group of patriotic intellectuals were able to continue influencing public opinion through their control of journals and newspapers. Taking advantage of the situation, some patriotic filmmakers managed to produce films, such as ***Mulan Joins the Army*** (*dir.* **Bu Wancang**, 1939), in which strong nationalistic sentiments were wrapped in a historical framework. However, the majority of films produced in Shanghai during this 'isolated island' (*gudao*) period were far removed from contemporary political life.

As early as 1939, the Japanese had sponsored the formation of China Film Company (Zhongying), which controlled the distribution of Shanghai produced movies in Manchuria and other occupied areas. Many Shanghai industry heads were concerned about profits and therefore reluctant to make films likely to offend the Japanese. Instead, they turned to politically safer subject matter. Detective, horror, **romance** and other entertainment genres dominated the market during this period. After Pearl Harbour, the Japanese military moved into the International Settlements as well as the French Concession. Numerous newspapers and magazines were closed for their alleged anti-Japanese bent. Meanwhile, the Japanese proceeded to tighten their control over the Chinese film industry by launching China United Film Production Corporation (Zhonglian) in early 1942. This organization subjected all the film-producing facilities in Shanghai to Japanese control, even though the acting managers were all Chinese, including wartime mogul **Zhang Shankun**. Under these conditions, the resistance and defiance demonstrated by some Chinese filmmakers in the early years of the occupation all but disappeared. The best they could do was to assume a stance of 'passive resistance' by making commercial flicks in an attempt to deflect the Japanese usage of film as a vehicle for ideological indoctrination.

Besides Shanghai, Manchurian Motion Pictures also produced a large number of films during the war. Founded in August 1937 in Changchun under the financial as well as political sponsorship of the Japanese and their puppet regime, Manchukuo, Manchurian Motion Pictures produced more than six hundred films between 1937 and 1945. Not surprisingly, most of these films, including three hundred newsreels, served as propaganda for Japanese military expansion in Asia. In February 1938, Manchurian Motion Pictures set up a branch studio in Beijing (then called Beiping). Unlike China United Film Production Corporation, which always maintained the facade of Chinese management, Manchurian Motion Pictures was under direct and total control of the Japanese. In fact, many of its key staff members were Japanese. After Japan surrendered in 1945, Manchurian Motion Pictures was taken over by the KMT government, but not before the Communists grabbed a substantial portion of its film production facilities. These formed the basis of Northeast (Dongbei) Film Studio, the predecessor of what is today's Changchun Film Studio.

See also: Cantonese cinema; propaganda and film

Further reading
S. Stephenson (1999), a critical study of the actress Li Xianglan and the Shanghai film audience.

10 The post-war revival, 1945–49

The fifth period of Chinese film history stretches from the end of the war to the founding of the People's Republic of China (PRC) in October 1949. During these four years, the Communists and the Nationalists engaged in a ferocious civil war which ended in the Nationalist defeat and retreat to Taiwan. The military conflict between the two parties was paralleled by the equally intense battle for influence over public opinion through control of modern media like film. Both sides tried to use film for political ends. While the Nationalists took steps to nationalize the film industry and so increase government supervision over production, Communist and leftist filmmakers deliberately set out to produce subversive films that undermined the legitimacy of the KMT regime. These polemical weapons played an important role in bringing about the demise of the KMT regime.

One important development during the war was the trend towards consolidation of the industry. While the Japanese-controlled China United Film Production Corporation brought all Shanghai studios under one management system, and Manchurian Motion Pictures monopolized film production and **distribution** in Northern China, in Chongqing, the KMT government's wartime capital, Central Film Studio and China Motion Picture Studio incorporated all independent filmmaking in the unoccupied areas. In both cases, governments were actively involved in the process of centralization under a unified national authority. This trend continued after the war as the KMT government confiscated both China United Film Production Corporation and Manchurian Motion Pictures as enemy properties. Meanwhile, the Central Film Services, a government agency formed in 1943 to oversee film distribution, took control of a large number of theatres and monopolized the distribution system. With most production facilities under its control, Central Film Studio quickly expanded its operation, setting up two branches in Shanghai and one in Beijing. The industry came the closest it had ever come to being nationalized.

The films produced by Central Film Studio can be divided into three groups. The first group includes such titles as *Loyal Family* (*dir*. **Wu Yonggang**, 1946), *Code Name Heaven No. 1* and *From Night to Dawn* (both *dir*. Tu Guangqi, both 1947). These films are strongly pro-government. *Loyal Family* shows how an ordinary Chinese family maintains its loyalty to the KMT government during the war. *Code Name Heaven No. 1* glorifies the Nationalist underground agents. *From Night to Dawn* gives the government an extremely positive role in the reconstruction of rural China. The second group consists of films that were meant to entertain rather than indoctrinate audiences. These films usually focus on romantic triangles, crime and punishment, or music and song. The romantic songs in *The Singer* (*dir*. Fang Peilin, 1946) and the melancholy mood of *Turning Back* (*dir*. **Yang Xiaozhong**, 1948), for instance, were markedly removed from contemporary politics. The third group of films were produced by leftist filmmakers employed at Central Film Studio. These films preserved the leftist legacy of the 1930s by presenting critical views of society. While ***Dream in Paradise*** (*dir*. **Tang Xiaodan**, 1947) depicts injustices in post-war China, ***Diary of a Homecoming*** (*dir*. Yuan Jun, 1947) satirizes the corrupt Nationalist officials who take over private property in Shanghai.

While some leftist filmmakers continued to work within the confines of government-controlled studios, others set up their own. In 1946, **Yang Hansheng**, **Cai Chusheng** and **Shi Dongshan** formed Lianhua Film Society and recruited a number of their former Lianhua colleagues. Within a year they had completed ***Eight Thousand Li of Cloud and Moon*** (*dir*. Shi Dongshan, 1947) and the first part of ***Spring River Flows East*** (*dir*. Cai Chusheng, **Zheng Junli**, 1947). The success of these two films led to Lianhua Film Society's merger with Kunlun Film Company in 1947. The reorganized Kunlun attracted a large number of leftist filmmakers and became the centre of 'progressive' filmmaking. In addition to completing the second part of *Spring River Flows East*, a masterpiece of leftist filmmaking, Kunlun also produced other highly acclaimed films, notably ***Myriad of Lights*** (*dir*. **Shen Fu**, 1948), ***Female Fighters*** (*dir*. **Chen Liting**), *An **Orphan on the Streets*** (*dir*. Zhao Ming) and ***Crows and Sparrows*** (*dir*. Zheng Junli, all 1949).

However, not all private studios were antagonistic to the government. Some sought a neutral position by keeping their distance from both the government and the leftists. One such studio was Wenhua, previously known for its high level of artistry. The impressive list of Wenhua releases includes ***Phony Phoenixes***, ***Night Inn*** (both *dir*. **Huang Zuolin**), ***Long Live the Mistress!*** (*dir*. **Sang Hu**, all 1947), ***Spring in a Small Town*** (*dir*. **Fei Mu**, 1948) and ***Sorrows and Joys of a Middle-Aged Man*** (*dir*. Sang Hu, 1949). *Spring in a Small Town*, in particular, has been regarded as one of the best films of the pre-1949 period. Wenhua's films represent the humanistic tradition of Chinese filmmaking at its best. However, the majority of films produced by other private studios tended to give the audience what it wanted by offering sex scandals, sensational news, cheap thrillers and romantic encounters. Titles such as *Thorny Rose* (*dir*. Yang Xiaozhong), *Pink Bomb* (both 1947) and *Beauty's Blood* (1948, both *dir*. **Xu Xinfu**) are indicative of their general thematic orientation.

Although the country's political instability limited the industry's potential to grow, the four years from 1946 to 1949 witnessed a spectacular revival of filmmaking. Chinese films now surpassed those of previous decades in both quantity and quality. When the CCP came to power in 1949, the new regime inherited a vital industry with a rich legacy and a framework for nationalization already laid out by the Nationalists.

Further reading

Y. Bao (1985), a survey of pre-1949 film; R. Bergeron (1977), a history of Chinese film up to 1949; J. Cheng *et al.* (1963), a two-volume film history from the Communist perspective; Y. Du (1988), a two-volume film history from the Nationalist perspective; J. Ellis (1982), a report on early Chinese cinema screened in Italy; L. Gongsun (1977), an anecdotal history of early Chinese film; P. Wilson (1987), a study of Northeast Film Studio.

11   Film in the PRC: the first seventeen years, 1949–66

The Communist victory of 1949 brought profound changes to Chinese society and film. Before 1949, political authorities could only influence film production. In some cases, film studios could even refuse to act on requests by the government. After 1949, however, the state enjoyed complete control of every aspect of filmmaking, often in the most tyrannical manner. The development of film in the People's Republic of China (PRC) was, therefore, drawn ever closer into the orbit of party politics.

During the first seventeen years of the PRC, the CCP implemented a series of policies that drastically changed the country. The party abandoned any pretence of being a democratic coalition and openly defended its 'proletarian dictatorship'. The numerous political campaigns not only acted to suppress dissident voices, but also purged the party of those who dared question or oppose Mao Zedong, the supreme CCP leader. Economically, the state nationalized the country's finance, industry, transportation and other key areas and transformed China into a socialist planned economy modelled after the Soviet Union. These dramatic social and economic changes were accompanied by an intense effort to launch an ideological battle for control of people's minds. Film was transformed from primarily a mass entertainment into a machine of political indoctrination. With just a few exceptions, films produced between 1949 and 1966 reflect the party's political and ideological agenda more than the tastes of the film **audience**.

The CCP has always considered film an important propaganda weapon. Its involvement with the medium began as early as 1932, when Xia Yan formed an underground Communist cell in Shanghai with the specific goal of penetrating the film industry. During the war of resistance, many Communist intellectuals worked in the propaganda department of the coalition government under Chiang Kai-shek's leadership. When Japan surrendered in 1945, the CCP took over part of Manchurian Motion Pictures and used it as a basis for the building of its own film studio. In Shanghai, underground CCP members not only infiltrated the Nationalist-controlled Central Film Studio, together with other private studios, but also set up their own company. Consequently, when the CCP finally took control of the country in 1949, it immediately moved to nationalize the film industry. Even before the founding of the PRC in October, the party's central committee had set up the Central Film Bureau in April 1949. This agency was in charge of all matters related to film production, exhibition and **distribution**. In essence, it was the highest authority in charge of the entire film industry.

By November 1949, the CCP had not only established a firm control over the film industry nationwide, it also owned and operated three major film studios producing eighty per cent of the country's total output. As early as October 1946, the CCP had turned part of Manchurian Motion Pictures into Northeast Film Studio, with staff members drawn mostly from the group who made newsreels in Yan'an, the Communist headquarters during the war. Although Northeast produced a large number of newsreels, it did not release its first feature film, ***Bridge*** (*dir.* Wang Bin), until April 1949.

The beginnings of Beijing Film Studio can be traced to January 1949, when the Communist army entered the city and seized the branch belonging to Central Film Studio. In April, the military turned it over to the newly formed civilian government, which then organized what was initially called Beiping Film Studio. A former actor and veteran CCP member, **Tian Fang** was appointed as first general manager of the studio, and the studio changed its name to Beijing along with the city in October 1949.

Shanghai Film Studio was officially founded on 16 November 1949. The newest among the three studios, it was the best equipped and had the largest production capability. The material basis of Shanghai Film Studio comprised confiscated film-producing equipment formerly owned by the Nationalists. Shanghai Film Studio also attracted the largest number of veteran filmmakers. In comparison with their colleagues in Northeast and Beijing, they tended to have much more experience of feature film production.

In accordance with a CCP political platform that envisioned several stages in the country's social, political and economic transformation, the PRC government's initial policy with regard to private studios was to encourage their growth. Of the seven studios not associated with the government, four received loans totalling twenty-one million yuan. The government also provided film stock and equipment. Considering the economic blockade imposed on China by hostile international forces led by the USA, not to mention China's military involvement in Korea, the government seemed quite generous in allocating its resources to private studios.

But the policy began to change once a number of studios produced titles considered to deviate from the party line. From the party's point of view, these problematic films, which amounted to a betrayal of the government's trust, demonstrated the necessity for tighter ideological control. For many filmmakers, the nationwide campaigns against *The* **Life of Wu Xun** (*dir.* **Sun Yu**, 1950), *Commander Guan* (*dir.* **Shi Hui**, 1951) and *Husband and Wife* (*dir.* **Zheng Junli**, 1951) signalled a difficult time ahead, as official criticism adversely affected their distribution and box-office returns. In 1952, all private studios 'willingly' merged with the state-controlled Shanghai Film Studio, and private studios were nonexistent for the next three decades.

In the meantime, the state set out to establish more studios of its own. After first launching the military-affiliated August First (Bayi) Film Studio in August 1952, officials approved the establishment of five more provincial studios by the late 1950s: Xi'an Film Studio in Shanxi, Pearl River Film Studio in Guangdong, Emei Film Studio in Sichuan, Tianshan Film Studio in Xinjiang and Inner Mongolian Film Studio in Inner Mongolia. These studios, along with Changchun (formerly Northeast), Beijing (Formerly Beiping), Shanghai and August First, produced the bulk of films between the 1950s and the 1980s.

One of the reasons the PRC government reorganized the film industry was that the party wanted to use film effectively, as a vehicle for the teaching of new values and new ideas. Due to their sense of mission, the officials in charge probably did not consider their work political indoctrination. They were simply trying to bring 'good' films to the people. What was considered good or bad, however, was dictated by the specific political needs of the moment.

Soon after the CCP came into power, it began to purge Western films, especially Hollywood productions. Even before the outbreak of the Korean war, the PRC had taken steps to reduce the influence of Western cinema. In addition to limiting the number of days Western films could be shown in theatres, the government sponsored negative publicity campaigns. With China preparing to enter the Korean conflict, the party orchestrated anti-American parades throughout the country, and the watching of American films became socially stigmatized. It did not take long for the general denunciation of the USA to turn into the specific denunciation of Hollywood. To substantiate official charges, numerous personal accounts of the harm done to Chinese people by American films were published. This campaign was obviously effective, because by October 1950 American films had all but disappeared from China.

After driving American films out of the market, the government filled the resulting vacuum with Soviet Union and Eastern European imports. Dubbing these films became an important part of the studios' daily schedule. Between 1949 and 1952, a total of 180 Soviet films were dubbed. To further encourage the attendance of Soviet films, the state lowered ticket prices for urban dwellers. However, imported Soviet films did not immediately catch on, in part because of audience unfamiliarity with Russian culture and history. Chinese exposure to Soviet film in the pre-1949 period had been limited to a few private screenings sponsored by the Soviet Embassy and attended mostly by leftist intellectuals. To help Chinese audiences understand Soviet films, the news media published essays and reviews with background information and synopses. Meanwhile, Chinese filmmakers were sent to the Soviet Union for advanced training, and Soviet filmmakers were invited to teach in China's newly established Beijing Film School, later the famous Beijing Film Academy (BFA). With the help of official sponsorship, Soviet films soon replaced American films' former position in the marketplace.

For the CCP, the banning of American films and the introduction of Soviet films were only the initial steps in the plan to produce domestic titles that could further the cause of socialism. Early productions from the state-controlled studios illustrate some characteristics of this new cinema. In **Bridge**, workers' revolutionary enthusiasm is portrayed as the driving force behind the completion of a difficult construction project, whereas the chief engineer's expertise is represented more as obstacle than asset. In **Daughters of China** (*dir.* **Ling Zifeng**, Zai Qiang, 1949), a sense of nationalism and heroism prevails throughout. The **White-Haired Girl** (*dir.* Wang Bin, **Shui Hua**, 1950) depicts the oppression of Chinese peasants under the old regime and their liberation by the **Communist revolution**. And *Shangrao Concentration Camp* (*dir.* Sha Meng, Zhang Ke, 1951) glorifies the sacrifice and devotion of Communists imprisoned by the Nationalists.

In 1950, the government developed a quota system to subject studios to an annual production plan. For instance, the Film Bureau forecast a total of eighteen films for 1951, of which at least three should deal with the CCP's war against the Japanese and the Nationalists, four to five with **socialist construction**, two with land reform and **rural life**, two with world peace, one with science, one with issues of ethnic minority, one with cultural matters, and one with children. This system of allocating specific subject matter continues to serve as a basic working model for the state because it can carry the party's political priorities at any given time.

This quota system theoretically applied only to state-controlled studios, which meant that private studios were exempt. But by approving and disapproving film scripts, the Film Bureau retained a great deal of power over what private studios could produce in the early 1950s. In fact, the party's distrust of private studios grew after the national campaign against *The Life of Wu Xun*. This **biography** was written and directed by the veteran director Sun Yu, who had earlier played a major role in the leftist cinema movement. Although production began in 1948, the film was not completed until 1950. The story was based on the life of the historical figure Wu Xun, an illiterate peasant determined to change the destiny of the poor by giving them an education. In contrast to his friend who joined the peasant rebels, Wu sought change within the existing system.

When the film was released, it initially received extremely favourable reviews. Several major newspapers in Beijing and Shanghai published articles praising it as a breakthrough in historical drama and an illustration of the peasants' awakening to the power of culture. But when Mao Zedong saw it, he found serious deviations from revolutionary ideology and orchestrated a nationwide condemnation. Beginning on 16 May 1951, *People's Daily*, the official party organ, published a series of articles criticizing both the historical figure Wu Xun and the film of his life. On 20 May, Mao himself wrote an editorial questioning Wu's class background and essentially 'conformist' stance. In addition, Mao alleged that the reviewers who praised the film lacked understanding of Marxist doctrines. Following Mao's lead, a national campaign to denounce *The Life of Wu Xun* was launched. Between May and late July 1951, an overwhelming number of articles were published in major newspapers and journals. In June, Mao's wife, Jiang Qing, led an investigative team to Wu Xun's home town with the aim of collecting evidence in support of Mao's denunciation. A 45,000-word report, published in *People's Daily* between 23 and 28 July 1951, claimed, amongst other things, that the real Wu opposed peasant revolution, that his attempts at building schools came to nothing and even helped 'repair' the feudal establishment, that he had ties with the local underworld and extracted money from people, and that his school was never exclusively for children from poor families.

With Mao's editorial and Jiang's investigative interventions, the fate of *The Life of Wu Xun* was sealed. Not only was the film banned, but all involved in making, distributing and promoting it were subject to tremendous political pressure. Many had to offer 'self criticism' or recant their views in public. Most important of all, the ban and the campaign served as a warning to intellectuals throughout the country. They should familiarize themselves with Marxist teachings and pay attention to the party's view of history. Any deviation from the official line would carry serious consequences.

The campaign against *The Life of Wu Xun* had a chilling effect on the entire film industry. The rate of production dropped drastically in the early 1950s. Given the financial risks involved, private studios found it particularly difficult to operate under a system of strict censorship and began to merge with state-owned studios. Filmmakers became more concerned with not making political mistakes than being artistically creative or even productive. In 1956, following the de-Stalinization in the Soviet Union, Mao encouraged candid criticism of his regime during the Hundred Flowers period (1956–7). His chosen slogan was taken from an ancient expression: 'Let a hundred flowers bloom, let a hundred schools of thought contend.' Now the term refers to a period of pluralism in intellectual life. Scholars, writers and filmmakers responded to Mao's call with an often bitter denunciation of many aspects of life under the CCP's rule, with the latter in particular voicing their resentment toward heavy-handed interference from studio management, the Film Bureau and the Ministry of Propaganda. While some complained about censorship, others ridiculed the uneducated party officials who meddled in the complicated process of film production. A number of films from this period also veered away from the party line. For instance, the first **comedy** produced in the PRC, *Before the New Director Arrives* (dir. Lü Ban, 1956), ridicules officials who try to curry favour with their superiors. Another film, *Loyal Partners* (dir. Xu Changlin, 1957), casts intellectuals as the heroes, a major departure from mainstream **representations of intellectuals** over previous years.

This atmosphere of political openness was short-lived. Alarmed by the discontent revealed during the Hundred Flowers period, particularly from the intellectual community, Mao launched the Anti-Rightist Campaign in June 1957 to suppress dissident voices. As a result, many in the film industry were labelled Rightists. Both *Before the New Director Arrives* and *Loyal Partners* were recalled from circulation, and several people involved in their production were publicly condemned. Shanghai Film Studio was particularly hard hit. Several veteran filmmakers, including **Shi Hui**, **Wu Yin** and **Wu Yonggang**, were labeled Rightists. After the campaign, filmmakers became even more nervous. They were now to toe the party line more carefully than ever before.

See also: children's film; dubbed foreign film; ethnic minorities, film of; historical film; science and education film

Further reading
D. Hsiung (1960), a preview of PRC films of the 1960s.

12 Socialist realism

Besides imposing specific subject matter on filmmakers, the state also dictated specific aesthetic principles and creative procedures. In 1950, **Yuan Muzhi**, the first Director of the Film Bureau, suggested that 'revolutionary realism' be followed as a general rule. In other words, while depicting post-1949 social conditions, filmmakers must take up a revolutionary or progressive position. They must identify with the party's interests. Yuan specifically warned filmmakers not to identify with the petty bourgeoisie and not to cater to the tastes of politically backward urban dwellers. Critical realism of the 1930s had been concerned with representing reality the way it appeared, which meant that authenticity and accuracy were primary objectives. Revolutionary realism, however, demanded that post-1949 reality be understood from a politically correct perspective, obtainable only through devout loyalty to the party line. According to this logic, truth was not to be found on the surface; the party alone could grasp the real, deeper truths. Therefore, only by following the party could an artist get closer to the Truth.

As the Soviet influence increased, socialist realism was introduced as a new slogan. Socialist realism refers to a set of aesthetic values imposed on writers and artists by Stalin, who believed that socialist reality demanded a new approach to creative activity. Central to this Socialist version of realism was the requirement that writers and artists identify with the party's point of view. If a conflict between an artist's view and the party's view arose, the individual perspective must be abandoned in favour of the party's. In this sense, socialist realism was in essence not very different from the concept promoted earlier by the CCP itself. However, the party decreed that, although China still had a long way to go before it would transform itself into a socialist nation, enough socialist elements were already in place. Filmmakers must look for those elements and not concentrate on temporary problem areas. The message was clear: sing the party's praises and do not criticize life in China under the CCP.

During the Hundred Flowers period, the view of socialist realism as the only correct creative method was challenged. Critics of socialist realism proposed a new approach combining revolutionary realism with revolutionary romanticism. Although this new synthesis was further removed from the realist principles still found in both revolutionary realism and socialist realism, the radical social changes initiated during the Great Leap Forward in the late 1950s helped revolutionary romanticism gain a following. From the point of view of its advocates, China was changing too rapidly to validate any realist representations of social life. Given the speed of progress, any verbatim adherence in the arts was doomed to become outdated. Therefore, in order to represent such a fast-changing society in a truly accurate and realistic fashion, one must be guided by a futuristic vision of revolutionary ideals.

Dictated by these guidelines for revolutionary romanticism, filmmakers were frequently pressured into presenting an ideal picture of reality by means of distortion, exaggeration or complete falsification. For instance, historical evidence shows that, during the land reform movement of the 1950s, the majority of peasants resented collectivization. Yet films dealing with this subject had to show how enthusiastic peasants were to join and work for People's Communes. The reason for this discrepancy between history and representation is simple: the party – or rather, Mao himself – believed that collectivization represented the future of agriculture in China. According to the party line, the peasants' reluctance to participate was nothing less than backward thinking, correctable given time, so that films should focus on what reality ought to look like, not how it actually appeared. Typical examples of this 'romantic' approach include *Steel Man and Iron Horse* (*dir.* Lu Ren) and *Love the Factory as One's Home* (*dir.* Zhao Ming, both 1958). Such films were not only conceptually simplistic and naive; they were also technically craggy. Once produced to meet the studio quotas, they were often forgotten by audiences and filmmakers.

The failure of the Great Leap Forward to transform the country radically in 1958, together with the subsequent economic and natural disasters which claimed millions of lives in rural China, forced the CCP to re-evaluate its policies. Under political pressure within the party, Mao went into semi-retirement in the early 1960s. A group of moderate leaders then took responsibility for economic reconstruction, including the reduction of the massive operation of People's Communes across the country. In the cultural and intellectual realms, the new leadership also reversed many of its earlier policies by taking a new, more moderate approach to cultural activities. New censorship regulations decreed that, when determining whether the problem in a controversial film is political or artistic in nature, it should be treated as an artistic problem, for the time being at least.

By the early 1960s, after a decade of integrating art and politics, Chinese filmmakers had successfully learned to combine the two in a more sophisticated way and so come closer to developing an aesthetic of socialist realism. Their success is evident in films such as *Legend of the Banner* (*dir.* Ling Zifeng, 1960), **Revolutionary Family** (*dir.* Shui Hua), **Red Detachment of Women** (*dir.* **Xie Jin**, both 1961), **Naval Battle of 1894** (*dir.* Lin Nong, 1962) and **Early Spring in February** (*dir.* **Xie Tieli**, 1963). These films fulfilled the party's ideological expectations with their thematic emphasis on class struggle, the Communist revolution, nationalism and socialist construction. At the same time, they are also marked by a high level of artistic achievement and appealed to the popular audience.

As interest in China's traditional culture began to surge in the early 1960s, filmmakers turned to the production of **filmed stage performances**. Based on traditional operas, films like *Women Warriors of the Yang Family* (1960), *Boar Forest* (1962, both *dir.* **Cui Wei**, Chen Huaiai) and *Dream of the Red Chamber* (*dir.* Cen Fan, 1962) were well received by both party officials and audiences. But serious efforts were also made to depict life in post-1949 China. Three light comedies stand out as representative: *Big Li, Young Li and Old Li* (*dir.* Xie Jin), **Li Shuangshuang** (*dir.* Lu Ren, both 1962) and *Satisfied or Not* (*dir.* Yan Gong, 1963).

The release of these films in the early 1960s, together with the laughter they brought forth, suggests a more relaxed political climate than that of the late 1950s. But this 'cultural thaw', as some people have called it, soon came to a halt. A new political storm was gathering momentum on the horizon, and when it came, it swept the nation like nothing ever seen before.

Further reading
J. Lösel (1980), a history of PRC film from 1949 to 1965; L. Lee (1991), on the literary tradition of social realism; Rayns and Meek (1980), a dossier of background information.

13   The Cultural Revolution, 1966–76

Although the Cultural Revolution officially began in 1966, its overture started with a speech delivered by Mao in December 1963, in which he stated that problems were abundant in the fields of literature and arts and that cultural officials who had deviated from the party line were now on the verge of yielding to the revisionist camp. Under the political pressure, the CCP's Department of Propaganda and the Ministry of Culture launched a rectification campaign, with the film industry singled out as primary focus. Within a few months, ten films, including *City Without Night* (*dir.* **Tang Xiaodan**, 1957), *The Lin Family Shop* (*dir.* **Shui Hua**, 1959), *Southern Wind Blowing North* (*dir.* **Shen Fu**, 1963) and *Early Spring in February*, were identified as targets for public criticism.

Once the Cultural Revolution was set in motion, Mao's wife, Jiang Qing, expanded the blacklist to a total of fifty-four films. She accused these of advocating erroneous ideas and selected some twenty titles for nationwide re-release so as to provide the people with negative examples. In the process of this political 'witch hunt', not only were the films made in the first seventeen years of the PRC completely trashed, but the legacy of leftist cinema from the pre-1949 period also came under attack. Moderate cultural officials were removed from their posts; many filmmakers were sent to re-education camps; some were even imprisoned on false charges. Film studios across the country were placed in the hands of a small party faction in charge of the new movement. According to these ultra-leftist ideologues, the total destruction of the old establishment was a necessary step in the construction of a new world order.

A prime target of attack, feature film production was suspended for several years. As for new construction projects, a decision was made in June 1968 that the eight model revolutionary operas (*yangban xi*) supervised by Jiang Qing should be adapted for the screen. After going through numerous revisions, *Taking Tiger Mountain by Stratagem* was released in 1970. Within the next two years, the remaining seven operas were also produced. Obviously, those films were made for political reasons. The theoretical elaboration of the 'success' of the original plays, as well as the film adaptations, was meant to propose a new set of guidelines for revolutionary filmmaking, namely the 'principles of three prominences' (*san tuchu*) that give exclusive attention to a film's central hero. In this sense, the film adaptation of model plays became the model for filmmaking. Based on these highly formulaic opera movies, a small number of feature films – including some remakes of earlier war films – were produced in the mid-1970s. They actively promote ultra-leftist ideology by serving the interests of radical factions within the party.

During the ten years of the Cultural Revolution, China witnessed the most radical and bloody political turmoil of its recent history. Government offices and schools were closed; students and workers formed factions and started fighting each other, first with sticks and stones and then with knives and guns; and a portion of the urban population was forced to settle in the remote countryside or border regions. The chaos lasted until Mao's death in 1976. As far as film was concerned, the state became more involved in production than at any other time in the century, and political criteria were always of the utmost importance. For many veteran filmmakers, the Cultural Revolution was a chapter in Chinese film history that contained practically nothing good.

See also: filmed stage performances; war film

Further reading
C. Berry (1982), a study of narrative models during the Cultural Revolution; P. Clark (1984), on the film industry in the 1970s; J. Leyda (1972), a film history from the beginnings to the 1960s.

14   The new era and beyond, 1976–96

When Deng Xiaoping took control and implemented a series of economic reforms in the late 1970s, China entered a new era. The country slowly changed from a centrally planned economy to a market-oriented economy. Foreign investments were encouraged, and new technologies eagerly sought. The new interest in advanced Western 'know how' soon spilled over to the realms of culture and ideology as well. More and more students were sent abroad to study in foreign universities, and an increasing number of foreign books, music and movies began to circulate. By no means democratic by Western standards, the CCP government under Deng's leadership became more liberal than it had ever been. It was against this backdrop that Chinese film made its quantum leap.

In the aftermath of the Cultural Revolution, the events of the recent past continued to over-shadow film production. Many films produced in the late 1970s were hardly distinguishable from the propaganda films of the Cultural Revolution period. The revolutionary aesthetic formulated over previous decades was still rigidly observed in films like *The October Storm* (*dir.* Zhang Yi, 1977) and *Traces of Tears* (*dir.* Li Wenhua, 1979). The primary purpose of these films was to pay lip service to the current leadership by denouncing the 'Gang of Four' (i.e., Jiang Qing and her clique). After all, official propaganda at this time decreed that the Gang of Four was to blame for all the evils of the past decade.

As far as film is concerned, one of the most significant changes of the new era was that film-makers began to explore the trauma caused by political radicalism from diverse perspectives. For instance, in its examination of the psychological impact of political repression, ***Bitter Laughter*** (*dir.* Yang Yanjin, Deng Yimin, 1979) was concerned not so much with political correctness as with the integrity of ordinary people facing political pressure. *The **Legend of Tianyun Mountain*** (*dir.* **Xie Jin**, 1980) traced the origins of political repression to the Anti-Rightist Campaign of the late 1950s. In so doing, the film criticized the party's cultural policies and placed the Cultural Revolution in a broader historical perspective. These two films exemplify the technical advances being made in this transition phase: they rely heavily on devices like flashbacks and voice-overs seldom favoured by socialist realism.

By the early 1980s, the cinematic focus on the 'wounds' or 'scars' (*shanghen*) of the Cultural Revolution was gradually being replaced by an interest in a variety of new subjects and issues. The formulaic categorization of characters prevalent in the earlier decades had largely been abandoned. Intellectuals, scientists, urban youth, overseas Chinese, and the aristocrats of the Qing dynasty all made their appearance on the screen, some for the first time in the PRC period. The depoliticization of the film industry in the early 1980s also allowed for a more realistic approach to contemporary life. In ***At the Middle Age*** (*dir.* Wang Qimin, **Sun Yu**, 1982), poor living conditions and a distrust of intellectuals are presented as serious problems. In *The Corner Forsaken by Love* (*dir.* Zhang Qi, 1981), poverty and ignorance are portrayed as causing such evil practices as arranged marriages, traditions attacked by the first generation of filmmakers back in the 1920s.

As economic reform gained momentum in the mid-1980s, people's lives were profoundly affected by the resulting drastic changes. The filmmakers directed their attention to the new problems now confronting China. In *Alarm Bell* (*dir.* Ma Erlu, Wen Yan, 1981), the protagonist is a determined reformer who overcomes numerous obstacles to turn his debt-ridden factory into a profit-earning enterprise. Similar stories and characters can be found in other contemporary films focused on the subject of reform.

The frustrations and problems experienced by many people in the reform era led to a cultural reflection movement. After all, resistance to social progress does not emanate from political authorities alone. The country's leading intellectuals began to search for the roots of social practices not compatible with the modern world. They came to regard traditional Chinese values and beliefs as the biggest obstacle to China's drive towards modernization. Many middle-aged directors, also known as the **Fourth Generation**, came to participate in this critical re-examination of traditional culture. Noted titles here include ***Sacrificed Youth*** (dir. **Zhang Nuanxin**), ***Good Woman*** (*dir.* **Huang Jianzhong**, both 1985), *A **Girl from Hunan*** (*dir.* **Xie Fei**, 1986) and ***Old Well*** (*dir.* **Wu Tianming**, 1987).

Nevertheless, the most original contribution to this process of cultural reflection came from a group of young directors labeled the **Fifth Generation**. The group's landmark film, ***Yellow Earth*** (*dir.* **Chen Kaige**, 1984), attracted international attention for its visually striking images of the barren landscape in Northwestern China and the entrenched traditions that have burdened peasants' lives there for thousands of years. In the film's powerful final scene, the crowd of illiterate and superstitious peasants comes to resemble the torrents of the Yellow River – the familiar symbol of Chinese civilization itself. The boy named Hanhan is groping his way against this human tide, trying to reach the Communist soldier standing against the backdrop of a bright sky. In an earlier scene, Hanhan's sister had drowned in the water while attempting to cross the Yellow River. The audience is therefore left to wonder whether the boy will be crushed by the human tide at the end. Such a critical view of traditional Chinese culture remains a dominant theme throughout the films of the late 1980s and early 1990s. ***Raise the Red Lantern*** (*dir.* Zhang Yimou, 1991), for instance, presents the oppressive, backward and inhumane aspects of traditional Chinese life.

However, these serious concerns for history, culture and reality were soon swept aside by a rising tide of moral cynicism, political apathy and existential anxiety in the late 1980s. One of the most outspoken cynics of this time is a young Beijing novelist named Wang Shuo. In a number of films either scripted by him or adapted from his popular fictional works, such as ***Transmigration*** (*dir.* **Huang Jianxin**, 1988) and *Half Flame, Half Brine* (*dir.* **Xia Gang**, 1989), traditional notions of morality, decency and integrity are relentlessly ridiculed. What had been regarded as sacred and saintly is represented as hypocritical or even farcical. The opening scene of *The **Trouble Shooters*** (*dir.* Mi Jiashan, 1988), where a policeman directs traffic, illustrates Wang Shuo's vision of chaos surrounding symbols of authority. Although the policeman's hand gestures and his bodily movements are choreographed gracefully, he is completely ignored. The following shots of skyscrapers, cars and pedestrians in the street, children in the playground, and a manic pop singer performing on stage, are intercut into a collage of confusing sights and sounds that suggest both the dynamism and disarray of contemporary Chinese life. As far as Chinese filmmaking is concerned, the influence of Wang Shuo's vision is that, at least for a while, films dealing with serious subjects appeared silly, naive or even phony. Wang's influence on representations of **urban life** has been particularly strong, as demonstrated by ***In the Heat of the Sun*** (*dir.* **Jiang Wen**, 1994) and other urban films of the mid-1990s.

However, the widespread cynicism of the late 1980s has not prevented other filmmakers from exploring different avenues. Since the early 1990s, three major trends in Chinese film-making have emerged: (1) 'commercial film' (*shangye pian*) or 'entertainment film' (*yule pian*); (2) 'mainstream film' (*zhu xuanlü dianying*) or propaganda film; and (3) **art film**. On the one hand, under financial pressure resulting from the restructuring of the old system of production and distribution, major studios have competed with one another to produce a large number of commercial films. These titles follow the formula of successful **genre films** from Hong Kong, Taiwan and, to a lesser extent, Hollywood, by relying increasingly on sex, violence and abnormal characterizations for box-office appeal. On the other hand, the government has regained some control over the film studios by sponsoring a series of blockbuster war films, as well as biographies of its top leaders and model workers. Like the productions of the 1950s–60s, these 'mainstream' propaganda films glorify the Communist revolution, legitimize the party's rule and promote its policies.

Finally, in spite of the dominance of entertainment and propaganda films in the 1990s, a small number of filmmakers have continued to make art films. Titles by this last group demonstrate diverse ideological orientations, aesthetic tastes and stylistic concerns. Many Fourth Generation directors, particularly those on the faculty of BFA, have maintained their stature by consistently making quality films. The glory of the Fifth Generation, however, has gradually faded because most of their films, financed by foreign capital, are now aimed at the international film festival circuit and have thereby become increasingly irrelevant to concerns of the mass Chinese audience.

A new development in the 1990s is the emergence of the so-called **Sixth Generation** directors, who arrived at a time when the industry had suffered huge financial losses and could no longer afford to take risks with inexperienced youngsters as it had done earlier with the Fifth Generation. As a consequence, a handful of Sixth Generation titles fared even worse than their predecessors in terms of domestic mass appeal. In fact, many Sixth Generation directors have started as independent filmmakers producing films outside the studio system before being brought back into the state-owned circuit, if they so choose. In spite of their difficult financial and political situation, however, the emergence of a Sixth Generation has brought a new dynamism to the Chinese film industry. Their films provide evidence of real talent. There is no doubt that they will follow the footsteps of their predecessors by playing a major role in the future development of Chinese film.

See also: cultural reflections

Further reading

R. Bergeron (1984), a history of PRC film up to 1983; H. Chen (1989), an official history of PRC film in two volumes; P. Clark (1987a), a book-length study of PRC film; Eder and Rossell (1993), a catalogue on the period with interviews; M. Feng *et al.* (1992), a film history from the beginnings to the 1980s; X. Hu (1986), a history of Changchun Film Studio; L. Liu (1992), a dissertation on socialist realism of the 1980s; P. Pickowicz (1989), a study of popular film and political thought in post-Mao China; Rayns (1992, 1993, 1996), three reports on the 1990s; Semsel *et al.* (1993), a collection of Chinese film reviews; M. Shao (1988), on films of the reform era; X. Wu (1992), a dissertation on the film industry since 1977; ZDX (1985), an official collection of surveys of various studios and genres in PRC film; Chengshan Zhang (1989), an excellent study of film genres and directors of various generations; X. Zhang (1997), a theoretical work on the 1980s; Zhong and Shu (1995), a textbook history compiled for BFA; X. Zhou (1985), a historical study of screen writing as a literary genre over the century.

Hong Kong cinema

Paul Fonoroff

1   In the beginning: The silent era, 1896–1932

The history of cinema in Hong Kong is nearly as old as the history of cinema itself, though the first three decades produced little in the way of actual filmmaking in the colony. In 1896, a camera crew of the Lumière Brothers reportedly visited Hong Kong. The earliest surviving films lensed in the territory are brief documentary snippets shot by the Edison Company in 1898. Dramatic filmmaking made its début in 1909, when the Shanghai-based Asia Film Company came south to the colony to make the silent short *Stealing the Roast Duck*. The producer and cinematographer was an American, Benjamin Brodsky (some sources spell his name 'Brasky'), who had founded Asia the same year. The **comedy** centred around three characters: 'Fatty', 'Skinny Thief', and 'Cop'. The latter two roles were played by men who would have a lasting impact on the early years of Hong Kong cinema. Liang Shaopo (Leung Siu-po), who played the thief and also directed *Stealing the Roast Duck*, would a decade later co-found the city's first major studio and direct some of the earliest feature films. **Li Beihai** (Lai Pakhoi), who played the policeman, directed the colony's first silent feature-length movie in 1925 and the first talking picture in 1933. Brodsky terminated his Shanghai film venture in 1913, returning to the USA via Hong Kong. While there, he met with former colleague Lai Pak-hoi and his brother **Li Minwei** (Lai Man-wai), and decided to invest in their new movie company, Huamei (Wah Mei, which literally means 'China–America'). Huamei's first (and only) production was ***Zhuangzi Tests His Wife*** (1913), which goes down in the history books as the first wholly Hong Kong-produced dramatic short film. The story revolves around the philosopher Zhuangzi who stages his own death in order to test his wife's virtue. The film was directed by Li Minwei, reputedly the 'Father of Hong Kong cinema'. He also essayed the role of Zhuangzi's

Plate 2   *Zhuangzi Tests His Wife* (1913)

wife, with elder brother Li Beihai playing the philosopher and Yan Shanshan (Yim San-san, 1896–1952, Minwei's wife) a servant girl. The film enters the history books on another count, with Yan the first actress to appear on the Chinese screen.

The film stock used in Hong Kong was imported from Germany, a situation which came to a halt with the outbreak of World War I. The colony's nascent movie business also came to a halt, beginning a slow revival eight years later when Li Minwei and brothers Li Beihai and Li Haishan (Lai Hoi-san) founded Minxin (China Sun), Hong Kong's first fully-fledged film studio. In addition to producing the colony's first newsreels, Minxin also filmed Hong Kong's first feature-length dramatic film, *Rouge* (1925).

This Hong Kong 'first' was shot not in Hong Kong but in Guangzhou (Canton), for a multitude of reasons. Minxin's Hong Kong studio was located on Ngan Mok (Silver Screen) Road, a new street whose lack of a water supply made it impossible for the studio to operate a film processing laboratory. The obstacles continued when the Hong Kong government dragged its feet on issuing Minxin a permit to build an actual shooting stage, forcing the filmmakers to journey north to Guangzhou. The movie was finally completed in 1925 and proved a box-office hit. *Rouge* was very definitely a family affair, written and directed by Li Beihai, starring Li Minwei and another wife of Minwei's, Lin Chuchu (Lam Cho-cho, 1904–79). Chuchu is Hong Kong's first true movie star, with a career spanning both silent and talking pictures, from 1925 until her retirement in 1953.

Before Minxin could follow up its *Rouge* success with another film, the Great Strike of 1925–6 had broken out. This was a huge anti-imperialist protest that turned the colony into an economic ghost town for sixteen months. It is estimated that nearly 40 per cent of the population of

600,000 took part in the strike, causing a temporary closure of most businesses, including movie theatres. Li moved Minxin to Shanghai, and Hong Kong's 'Silver Screen' Road was never again home to a film studio.

Approximately ten movies were produced in Hong Kong during 1924–5, by nearly as many small film companies. The Great Strike spelled the end of them all. Most closed their doors for good while a few relocated to Guangzhou, which for a brief period was a rival to Hong Kong as the Hollywood of South China. Between 1925 and 1930, no movies were produced in Hong Kong while about a dozen were shot in Guangzhou, more than the colony's entire output up to that time. But once it became feasible to resume shooting in Hong Kong, Guangzhou's film industry quickly disappeared. A heavy tax on film stock was one factor. Others included inconsistent governmental policies regarding both censorship and Cantonese dialect cinema in an era when Mandarin was being promoted as the national language (*guoyu*). Guangzhou would never again pose a serious threat to the supremacy of Hong Kong as a film-making centre. In 1956, the Chinese government established Guangzhou's Pearl River (Zhujiang) Studio, which over the next three decades produced some 150 features, less than the average annual Hong Kong output during that period.

With the cessation of the Great Strike, cinema houses gradually resumed operation. The colony's first movie magazine, *Silver Light* (Yinguang), began publication in 1926 but only lasted a few issues. In 1930, production was revived with the founding of the Hong Kong Film Company by Li Beihai. Hong Kong's movie business entered the 'major leagues' with the 1930 merger of Minxin with a handful of Shanghai and Tianjin film companies to form the Lianhua Film Company (United Photoplay Service), one of China's most influential studios before World War II. Most of the capital funding Lianhua was from Hong Kong, hence the main head-quarters were formally located in the colony. However, Hong Kong's filmmaking facilities at this time could not compete with Shanghai, which had already earned the nickname 'Hollywood of the East'. Thus, the bulk of Lianhua's movie-making activities took place in the northern metropolis. A Hong Kong branch studio headed by Li Beihai was set up in 1931. Though only a handful of movies were completed before it was closed down in 1934, Lianhua's Shanghai operation continued to flourish until its demise upon the outbreak of the Sino-Japanese War in 1937. Hong Kong's Lianhua history may have been brief, but it had a strong impact on the future of Cantonese cinema, providing training for a number of directors and actors who would be major figures for the following three decades.

2   Cantonese talkies

Less than thirty dramatic shorts and features were produced in Hong Kong during the silent era, from *Stealing the Roast Duck* in 1909 to *Post-Marital Problems* (*dir.* Shek Yau-yu, 1934). Hong Kong silent films were barely a footnote in the context of Chinese (i.e., Shanghai) cinema. This is a situation that would change dramatically with the birth of Cantonese talking pictures in 1933. It was an innovation that began not in Cantonese-speaking Hong Kong or Guangzhou, but in Shanghai. The first Cantonese talkie, *The Platinum Dragon* (*dir.* **Tang Xiaodan**, 1933), was produced by Xue Juexian (Sit Kok-sin, 1904–56) at Shanghai's Tianyi Studio, one of China's largest film companies. Sit, who served as *The Platinum Dragon*'s director, scriptwriter, and star, adapted his own Cantonese opera, which itself was an adaptation of the 1926 Hollywood film *The Duchess and the Waiter*, starring Aldolphe Menjou and Florence Vidor. The movie was a box-office success in Hong Kong, Guangzhou, Singapore, Malaya, and other Southeast Asian cities with large Cantonese-speaking populations. The owners of Tianyi Studio, a·group of brothers surnamed Shaw, immediately recognized the potential of Cantonese pictures, and in 1934 established a branch studio in Hong Kong. In 1937, they closed down Tianyi's Shanghai operation and renamed the Hong Kong studio Nanyang (South Seas). Other studios would follow, making the Shaws the most prolific producers in post-World War II Hong Kong cinema.

Whereas silent films enjoyed far less mass appeal than Cantonese opera, talking pictures not only competed with but eventually overtook the opera stage. The vast majority of stars from the 1930s–50s had their initial training in Cantonese opera, and this art form had a profound influence on cinematic style and content throughout the first three decades of Hong Kong's talking pictures. Recruiting opera superstars like Sit Kok-sin, Ma Shizeng (Ma Sze-tsang), Tan Lanqing (Tam Lan-hing), Xin Ma Shizeng (Sun-Ma Sze-tsang), Guan Dexing (Kwan Tak-Hing, *b*. 1906) and others gave Hong Kong movies a jump-start at the box office and an appeal beyond the borders of tiny Hong Kong.

Following *The Platinum Dragon*, the second Cantonese talking picture, *Singing Lovers* (1934), was produced not in Hong Kong but in the USA by Grandview (Daguan) Film Company. The studio was founded in San Francisco in 1933, by Chinese-American Zhao Shushen (Chiu Shu-sen, *b*. 1904), and re-established in Hong Kong in 1935. Grandview was one of the only studios to survive World War II, not ceasing operations until 1958. *Singing Lovers* was directed by Moon **Kwan**, who helped establish both Grandview and Lianhua's Hong Kong branch, and was one of the most influential directors during the early years of Hong Kong movies.

After the demise of Lianhua's Hong Kong branch, former studio boss **Li Beihai** founded the colony's first talking picture studio, Zhonghua (China), and directed Hong Kong's first partial-talkie, *Conscience* (1933), and the first all-talkie, *The Fool's Wedding Night* (1934). By 1935, Hong Kong was firmly established as one of the major filmmaking centres of Asia.

See also: adaptations of drama and literature

3   The first golden age of Cantonese movies

While the Mandarin-dialect film industry in Shanghai was racked by an economic depression and the outbreak of the Sino-Japanese War in 1937, Hong Kong's Cantonese cinema flourished from the mid-1930s until the early 1940s, with steady growth until the Japanese invasion on 8 December 1941. During this period, over 500 features were produced, covering a variety of genres and creating a number of superstar performers and directors. Chief among the actors was Wu Chufan (Ng Cho-fan, 1911–93), the 'Movie Emperor of the South China'. He made his début in 1932 and, before retiring in 1966, not only starred in approximately 250 films but was also instrumental in his behind-the-screen roles as studio boss, producer and screenwriter.

Directors who came to the fore during this period were Li Tie (Lee Tit, *b*. 1913), Wu Hui (Ng Wui, *b*. 1912), and Chen Pi (Chan Pei); superstars included Huang Manli (Wong Man-lei, *b*. 1913), **Pak Yin**, Zhang Ying (Cheung Ying, 1918–86), Zhang Huoyou (Cheung Wood-yau, *b*. 1909), and the list goes on. Each artist would make hundreds of films in careers extending beyond World War II till the decline of the traditional Cantonese film in the 1960s.

Being a British colony, Hong Kong was buffeted from the first four years of the war. The Japanese invasion of Shanghai on 13 August 1937, in which all of the city save the foreign concession areas was occupied, caused the temporary closure of the entire Shanghai Mandarin dialect film industry. Three of the largest studios in Shanghai – Lianhua, Mingxing (Star), and Tianyi – closed their doors forever, with the last making a permanent move to Hong Kong. Some of Shanghai's leading lights scurried to the British-controlled enclave. For the first time, Mandarin dialect films were produced in Hong Kong, though Cantonese pictures remained in the overwhelming majority.

There had always been a close connection between the film industries of Shanghai and Hong Kong, dating back to the days of *Stealing the Roast Duck*. However, throughout the silent and early talkie eras, Cantonese movies were considered very much the 'poor cousin' of their northern counterparts, technically crude and lower-budgeted than the glossy Mandarin movies of Shanghai. The relationship was somewhat analogous to that between Hollywood and Britain during the same era. With the outbreak of war, the situation was reversed. Rather than the multitude of British filmmakers journeying to Hollywood, it was 'Hollywood' Shanghai movie people making the move to 'little' Hong Kong. For the first time, Mandarin movies were shot in the colony. Though just a handful, it was a harbinger of things to come when, after World War II, Hong Kong would overtake Shanghai to become the world's leader in Mandarin film production.

Among the Shanghai movie moguls to move temporarily south was **Zhang Shankun**. He was head of Xinhua (Hsin Hwa, literally meaning 'New China'), the largest Chinese studio between the outbreak of the Sino-Japanese War in 1937 and the outbreak of the Pacific War in December 1941. Zhang Shankun used Shanghai stars and a Shanghai director (**Bu Wancang**) to make the colony's first Mandarin movie, *Sable Cicada* (1938), and a handful of others before closing down his Hong Kong operation. After the War, Zhang would settle permanently in the colony and re-establish Hsin Hwa after co-founding such influential Mandarin studios as Yonghua (Yung Hwa) and Great Wall (Changcheng).

A group of leftist Shanghai filmmakers also came south and made some socially conscious Mandarin films, like ***Orphan Island Paradise*** (1939), *The Boundless Future* (1941, both *dir.* **Cai Chusheng**) and *White Clouds of Home* (*dir.* **Situ Huimin**, 1940). Directors Cai Chusheng and Situ Huimin, and screenwriter **Xia Yan**, would later play prominent roles in the PRC movie world before their denouncement during the **Cultural Revolution**.

Themes of **nationalism** figured more and more in Hong Kong motion pictures. Though fettered by colonial censorship laws that forbade the identification of the enemy as specifically Japanese – after all, Britain and Japan were at peace until the end of 1941 – Hong Kong film-makers had considerably more freedom than their Shanghai counterparts to inject overt patriotic sentiments into their movies. *Life Line* (*dir.* Moon **Kwan**, 1935) led the way, followed by dozens of Cantonese patriotic dramas and the leftist Mandarin movies mentioned above. Mandarin and Cantonese filmmakers from all sides of the political spectrum helped found the Southern China National Defence Film Movement, and were also instrumental in instituting a Clean-Up movement to rid Hong Kong cinema of its feudalistic and superstitious content. The Clean-Up campaign met with little success and was relaunched a decade later, in the aftermath of World War II.

Naturally, audiences can take only so much 'realism'. Like Hollywood fare, the vast majority of Cantonese movies were escapist in nature. These included the Busby Berkeley-style **musical** *Eighth Heaven* (*dir.* Sit Kok-sin) and *Stage Glamour* (both 1938), the latter made in both Mandarin and Cantonese versions by transplanted Shanghai director **Tang Xiaodan**. Another movie made in both Cantonese and Mandarin versions was the heart-rending **melodrama** *Rouge Tears* (1938, Mandarin version *dir.* **Wu Yonggang**; Cantonese version *dir.* Chen Pi), a co-production between Shanghai's Xinhua and Hong Kong's Nanyue (Nam Yuet) studios. Both versions starred Shanghai movie queen **Hu Die** (Butterfly Wu) who, though raised in the Mandarin-speaking north, was from a Cantonese family. Her linguistic skills would serve her well after settling permanently in Hong Kong following World War II.

The flow of talent between Shanghai and Hong Kong was very much a mutual affair. Much like David Selznick hiring Britisher Vivien Leigh for *Gone With the Wind* (*dir.* Victor Fleming, 1939), Xinhua brought Cantonese film's top *ingénue*, Nancy Chan (Chen Yunshang, *b.* 1919) to Shanghai in 1939 to star in the most anticipated Mandarin production of the year, **Mulan Joins the Army** (*dir.* Bu Wancang). Like Leigh, Chan was a resounding success, and reigned as the new queen of the Shanghai screen until retiring upon her marriage in 1943. She returned to the colony after World War II and made a brief comeback in the early 1950s in order to help former mentor Zhang Shankun re-establish Xinhua on Hong Kong soil.

It seemed as though nothing could stop the prosperity of the Hong Kong movie business, a success reflected in the colony's growing number of cinema houses. In 1938, there were twenty-eight theatres in Kowloon and Hong Kong: thirteen on the island and fifteen on the peninsula. With the population of the colony about 1.2 million, it meant that Hong Kong possessed more theatres per person than Shanghai, which had sixty theatres for a population of 3 million. At the time, there were less than 300 theatres in the whole of China, compared to approximately 20,000 in the USA.

See also: censorship and film; genre films

4   The Japanese occupation, 1941–5

No one could have foreseen that the flourishing film business would come to a dead halt on 8 December 1941. On the first days of the Japanese invasion of Hong Kong, the airport was bombed and, along with it, Grandview Studio located nearby. By Christmas 1941, the entire colony was occupied, and Hong Kong cinema came to a stop until early 1946. The only dramatic feature shot in Hong Kong for nearly four years was *The Day of England's Collapse* (1943), produced by a Japanese film company, which told of the invasion from the invader's point of view.

Cantonese film production did not cease entirely. Grandview's Hong Kong facilities may have been destroyed, but they still had their San Francisco headquarters. Though not as technically advanced, with only 16mm camera equipment, twenty-one black-and-white and four colour features were shot between 1941 and 1946. Among them was *All That Glitters* (*dir.* Chiu Shu-sen, 1942, released in Hong Kong in 1947), which is generally credited as the first all-colour Cantonese film.

The devastation by the Japanese was so complete that it was over one year after Hong Kong's liberation in August 1945 that the first film of the post-war era, and the first feature film produced in over four years, *Flames of Passion* (*dir.* Mok Hong-see), was released. Significantly, this was a Mandarin dialect film, and a signal of things to come. With civil war raging in China between the Communists under Mao Zedong and the Nationalists under Chiang Kai-shek, many Shanghai filmmakers set up temporary or permanent residency in Hong Kong. Some were political refugees, left wingers who felt their freedom was too restricted in Shanghai or who even faced the risk of imprisonment. Others motives were more economic. Inflation was rampant in China. For instance, between November 1948 and the Communist take-over of Shanghai in May 1949, the cost of Shanghai's leading film magazine escalated from 20 cents local currency to $600,000. Hong Kong's Mandarin film industry was the chief beneficiary of this talent exodus, and by 1950 the colony had surpassed Shanghai as the centre for Mandarin filmmaking.

5   The rise of Mandarin movies

Between 1946 and 1952, the two-way traffic of movie personnel between Shanghai and Hong Kong reached a new peak. After 1949, numerous 'right-wing' filmmakers emigrated from the newly-formed PRC to the colony, a flood which was reduced to a trickle after an 'artistic rectification campaign' in 1951 and the nationalization of the last privately-operated film studios in 1952. On the other side of the political spectrum, many left-wing filmmakers returned to the motherland after 1949, the last batch being a group deported by the Hong Kong government for political activities in the early 1950s. Tragically, many of these patriotic artists would be persecuted and have their careers ruined during the Anti-Rightist Campaign of 1957 and the Cultural Revolution.

Hong Kong's first major Mandarin studio was Great China (Da Zhonghua), which rented the pre-World War II Nanyang Studio facilities. Great China recruited essentially its entire roster of stars and directors from Shanghai, and produced thirty-four Mandarin films (and eight Cantonese features) during 1946–9. In terms of script and style, the films were indistinguishable from their Shanghai counterparts, often with stories taking place in Shanghai rather than Hong Kong. The Shaw family decided to get into the Mandarin film business themselves in 1949, re-occupying the Nanyang Studio which they renamed Shaw and Sons (Shaoshi fuzi). In 1957, the studio was reorganized, with the filmmaking operation going under the name of Shaw Brothers (Shaoshi xiongdi), headed by Run Run (Shao Yifu) and Runme Shaw (Shao Renmei, 1901–85), which became the largest filmmaking operation in Hong Kong history.

Other significant Mandarin studios from the early post-war period were Yonghua and Great Wall, both co-founded by former Shanghai movie mogul **Zhang Shankun**. After Zhang's departure from Great Wall in 1950, it became the leading left-wing studio in the colony, later joined by 'sister' left-wing studios Fenghuang (Phoenix) and the Cantonese Xinlian (Sun Luen). Zhang meanwhile re-established his Shanghai Xinhua Studio in Hong Kong, which in the late 1950s enjoyed great success with a series of light musicals starring 'Little Wildcat' Zhong Qing (*b.* 1932), her vocals dubbed by singing superstar Yao Li.

Shaw's chief rival in the late 1950s and 1960s was Cathay (Guotai), whose filmmaking operation went under the banner of MP & GI (Dianmao), or Motion Picture & General Investment. Originally a major distributor of Hong Kong movies in Southeast Asia, Cathay went into the movie-making business in 1955 when it took over the management of Yonghua. Cathay boss Lu Yuntao (Loke Wan Tho) is considered a giant among movie moguls, a man whose love for movies was reflected in the high production values and literate scripts of MP & GI. An early example of the polished studio product was a family **comedy**, *Our Sister Hedy* (*dir.* Tao Qin, 1957), one of the most delightful films of its era.

The competition between Shaw's and MP & GI was intense. Directors like Tao Qin (1915–69) and stars like Linda **Lin Dai** (who from her début in 1953 till her suicide in 1964 was continually in the front ranks of Mandarin stardom) were lured from one studio to the other. This culminated in the early 1960s with a series of 'double' productions, like *The Magic Lamp* (1965, Shaw's version *dir.* Yue Feng; MP & GI version by numerous directors) and *Fate in Tears and Laughter* (MP & GI version *dir.* Wang Tianlin; Shaw's version by their entire roster of directors), in which one studio announced the project and the other employed its full roster of stars and behind-the-screen personnel in order to rush a rival version out before its competitor.

MP & GI lost its competitive edge with studio boss Loke's death in a plane crash in 1964. Without his guidance, the Cathay product lost its special sparkle, and by 1972 the organization closed down its filmmaking operation. The studio site was taken over by Golden Harvest which, with the help of Bruce **Lee** and Jackie **Chan**, became the new industry leader.

Shaw's supremacy in the Mandarin movie field was further solidified by political events across the border. The left-wing Great Wall and Fenghuang studios, longtime bastions for quality films with a social message, were strongly affected by the Cultural Revolution raging in China from 1966 to 1976. While the Great Wall–Fenghuang films in the late 1950s and early 1960s were 'progressive' rather than overtly 'propagandistic' in nature, the films' content became increasingly 'leftist' and out of touch with mainstream audience tastes. Furthermore, the Hong Kong riots of 1967 made anything labelled 'Communist' unattractive to a large segment of the local population. Matters were not helped by the retirement of Great Wall's reigning movie queen, **Xia Meng**, in 1967; the arrest of other stars for Communist political activities; and the 'defection' of Fenghuang leading man Gao Yuan (*b.* 1933) to Shaw's. The left-wing studios continued to make movies, but were never able to regain their position as giants in the Hong Kong film industry. Great Wall, Fenghuang, and Sun Luen merged in 1982 to form Sil-Metropole (Yindu) Organization, home of some of the more innovative and critically acclaimed films of social problems in the 1980s–90s, like *Ah Ying* (*dir.* Allen **Fong**, 1983), *Gangs* (1988) and *Queen of Temple Street* (1990), both *dir.* Lawrence Ah Mon (Liu Guochang).

See also: Shaw, Run Run; social problems, film of

Further reading
HKIFF (1983), on post-war Mandarin and Cantonese films; HKIFF (1993), on Mandarin films and popular songs of the 1940s–60s.

6   The second golden age of Cantonese cinema

In the multi-dialect Hong Kong film industry, Mandarin movies on the average had higher budgets, greater technical polish, and longer shooting schedules than their Cantonese, Amoy (or Fukienese) and Swatow (Chaozhou) counterparts. But it was Cantonese cinema that enjoyed the greatest audience popularity from the inception of talking pictures in the 1930s until the late 1960s, reaching a peak in the two decades following World War II. As many as 200 Cantonese films were produced each year during this period, a good number of them belonging to the genre of Cantonese opera.

Unlike other genres or sub-genres such as detective films, backstage musicals, and James Bond knock-offs, Cantonese opera movies (i.e., **filmed stage performances**) were uniquely un-Hollywood in their ultra-theatricality, traditional Chinese music, and non-naturalistic performing styles. Over 500 opera movies were produced in the 1950s, reaching a peak of over eighty released in 1958. Another 200 were made in the early 1960s, but by the mid-1960s the trend had played itself out. By the decade's end, the genre was extinct. John **Woo** attempted a Cantonese opera revival with *Princess Chang Ping* (1975). It enjoyed a certain box-office success, ranking fourth for the year. But with this one exception, the Cantonese opera movie effectively died by 1965.

But the importance of the opera movie, especially from 1955 to 1965, cannot be underestimated. Theatre owners and film producers eagerly embraced the genre. Opera movies were fairly inexpensive and fast to make, with an average shooting schedule of under two weeks. These stage-bound classical productions required virtually no location shooting, and the sets could be recycled from film to film. And the loyalty of the legions of opera fans could not be overlooked. The biggest opera stars of the era enjoyed huge popularity on both stage and screen, and their movies had a 'guaranteed' box office that the Cantonese cinema's non-opera stars often lacked.

The number one screen team in Cantonese opera consisted of Ren Jianhui (Yam Kim-fai) and Bai Xuexian (Pak Suet-sin). During 1951–61 they co-starred in fifty-nine movies, with a final 'farewell' film in 1968. Yam usually assumed the male lead, not only in movies set in a bygone age, but also in contemporary non-operatic roles. Such 'gender-bending' is a convention from the opera stage, and was readily accepted by contemporary audiences. Part of Yam's huge audience following consisted of matrons who considered 'her' the ideal screen lover, hence Yam's nickname of 'opera fans' sweetheart'.

In Mandarin cinema, a northern Chinese folk opera style called 'huangmei diao' (literally, 'yellow plum melodies') became all the rage. Beginning with *Diau Charn of the Three Kingdoms*, (*dir.* **Li Han-hsiang**, 1958), and continuing until the mid-1960s, these costume 'yellow plum' operas became the major trend in Mandarin pictures, their popularity eventually eclipsed by the rise of 'new style' martial arts and kungfu pictures later in the decade. It is interesting to note that at a time when Hong Kong was undergoing rapid modernization and Westernization, both Cantonese and Mandarin cinema audiences flocked to films of a decidedly traditional mode.

Of course, opera was but one genre that flourished in Cantonese cinema during the 1950s–60s. Swordplay films, the forerunner of Bruce **Lee** kungfu movies, were extremely popular. Chief among these was the Wong Fei-hung (Huang Feihong) series of motion pictures. A Cantonese martial arts performer and upholder of righteousness, Wong (1847–1924) and his exploits had become legendary through martial arts novels and newspaper serials. In 1949, his story finally came to the screen in *The True Story of Wong Fei-hung* (*dir.* Wu Pang), starring Kwan Tak-Hing. Over the next two decades, Wu Pang (Hu Peng, *b.* 1910) would direct a total of fifty-eight 'Wong Fei-hung' movies starring Kwan, making this the most prolific series in the history of Cantonese cinema, reaching a peak in 1956 with twenty-four Wong movies! The series was revived in the 1980s–90s by producer-director **Tsui Hark**'s *Once Upon a Time in China, I–VI*, with Jet **Li** and Wing Chow (Zhao Wenzhuo) variously assuming the lead. Another notable Wong Fei-hung was Jackie **Chan**, in one of his earliest successes *Drunken Master* (*dir.* Yuen Woo-ping, 1978) and *Drunken Master II* (*dir.* Lau Kar-leung, 1994).

Post-war Cantonese cinema may have been prolific, but the majority of costume and contemporary dramas, comedies, operas and others were cheap productions, some dubbed 'seven-day wonders' because they were shot in a week. A growing number of artists were devoted to making Cantonese cinema much more than the opera and martial arts films which were the backbone of the industry. This was the spirit behind the Southern China Film Industry Workers Union, founded in 1949. Many of the union's members went on to found Union Film Enterprises (Zhonglian), a studio whose production methods and finished product represent a peak to what is generally acknowledged as the golden age of Cantonese cinema. Founded in 1952 and disbanded in 1967, Union produced forty-four films, many now acknowledged as classics of Cantonese cinema. Particularly noteworthy are Union's realistic dramas like *In the Face of Demolition* (*dir.* Li Tie, 1953), with an all-star cast including twelve-year-old Bruce Lee, which reflected the post-war housing crisis in the colony; and adaptations of literature, like *Family* (*dir.* Wu Hui, 1953) based on Ba Jin's critically acclaimed novel. Equally significant are the ideas embodied by the studio, which was run as a collective. Though Union's roster of stars included the biggest names in the business, actors received equal pay regardless of the size of their roles or their standing in the popularity polls.

The Southern China Film Industry Workers Union was politically leftist, with close ties to mainland China. On the other side of the political spectrum was the Hong Kong & Kowloon Cinema & Theatrical Enterprise Free General Association, a 'Free China' Taiwan-affiliated organization established in 1955. The 'left' and 'right' rarely associated socially, and never on screen. This also extended to movie distribution. While a few Great Wall and Fenghuang movies were released in China – a territory from which Shaw's and Cathay were excluded – left-wing productions could never be screened in the even more profitable markets of Taiwan and most Southeast Asian locales, as well as the American Chinatown theatre circuits.

While Cantonese and Mandarin dialect movies were the most popular in Hong Kong, there were two other important dialect industries. About 400 Amoy dialect and 200 Swatow movies were produced in the 1950s and early 1960s. Few of these films were released in Hong Kong, their chief markets being the Amoy and Swatow-speaking communities in Taiwan, the Philippines, and Southeast Asia.

See also: adaptations of drama and literature; detective film; genre films; kungfu film; martial arts film; swordplay film

Further reading
HKIFF (1978, 1982a, 1986a, 1996a), on Cantonese cinema of the 1950s–60s.

7   The decline of Cantonese cinema

Cantonese movie production remained prolific throughout the early 1960s, with nearly one thousand Cantonese features made in 1960–4. By the mid-1960s, it was a different story. Though Hong Kong society had changed markedly from the early post-war years, Cantonese movies had changed little since the 1930s. Audiences began to taper off. Cantonese film production dropped from 211 films in 1961 to seventy-one in 1969, thirty-five in 1970, and only one in 1971. The 1967 founding of TVB, the colony's first non-subscription, non-cable television station, was another factor in the temporary demise of Cantonese pictures, though television would later prove to be a major factor in the revival of Cantonese-language cinema.

The final days of the 'traditional' Cantonese film were dominated by two youth idols, Chen Baozhu (Connie Chan, *b*. 1949) and Josephine **Siao**, and child star Feng Baobao (Bobo Fung, *b*. 1953, the 'Hong Kong Shirley Temple'). They were the most popular of a group of teen idols collectively known as the 'Seven Princesses' (*qi gongzhu*), who alone and in various combinations appeared in a series of 'youth' films in the late 1960s. Chan and Siao were the most prolific of the group. Together or separately, for example, they starred in 58 of the 105 Cantonese movies released in 1967. These movies covered a wide variety of genres, from traditional opera films to Hollywood-tinged Cantonese musicals. By the early 1970s, both had retired to pursue their higher education. Siao soon returned to the screen, and two decades later achieved new heights as the most critically acclaimed and highest-salaried female star in the movies, winning Best Actress honours in Hong Kong, Taiwan, and Berlin FF for **Summer Snow** (*dir.* Ann **Hui**, 1994).

Further reading
I.C. Jarvie (1979), on the significance of the demise of Cantonese movies.

8   The 1970s: The rise of kungfu, comedy and kungfu comedy

With the departure of these youth idols from the screen, the absence of new stars, and intense audience dissatisfaction with Cantonese cinema, Cantonese cinema simply ceased to exist. Between February 1971 and September 1973, there was not one new Cantonese film released in Hong Kong, a situation that would have been beyond the realm of speculation just a few years earlier. Ironically, Hong Kong cinema was about to burst on the world scene in an unprecedented manner.

On the critical front, King **Hu**'s martial arts masterpiece *A **Touch of Zen*** (1970) became the first Hong Kong movie to receive critical acclaim at a non-Asian film festival, winning an award at the 1975 Cannes FF. Even more significant was the worldwide box-office success of a succession of kungfu movies starring Bruce **Lee**. *The Big Boss* (*dir*. Lo Wei) was number one at the Hong Kong box office in 1971; ***Return of the Dragon*** (*dir*. Bruce Lee) and *Fist of Fury* (*dir*. Lo Wei) number one and two respectively in 1972; and ***Enter the Dragon*** (*dir*. Robert Clouse) number two in 1973. The movies enjoyed considerable popularity in Europe and North America as well as Asia. Lee became Hong Kong's first bona fide international superstar, and the most famous Chinese on earth with the possible exception of Chairman Mao. For better or worse, Bruce Lee and cheaply made kungfu pictures became virtually synonymous with 'Hong Kong cinema'.

The rise of Bruce Lee also put the Golden Harvest (Jiahe) Film Company on the map. Founded in 1970, Golden Harvest took over the Cathay studio site in 1971. Thanks to its association with Lee and, later, Jackie **Chan**, Golden Harvest eventually surpassed Shaw's as the colony's largest filmmaking enterprise.

Beginning with the mid-1970s, the distinctions between 'Mandarin' and 'Cantonese' cinema disappeared. While the percentage of Mandarin releases shrank from 100 per cent in 1972 to 20 per cent in 1979, there were no longer separate Mandarin and Cantonese film entities in the pre-1971 manner. Rather, there was one 'Hong Kong' cinema. Post-dubbing of dialogue had replaced synchronized-sound recording, with the dubbed Cantonese version released in Hong Kong and Malaysia, and the dubbed Mandarin version distributed in Taiwan and Singapore.

In addition to kungfu, a major box-office force on the home front came about with the rise of new style Cantonese comedies, beginning with *The House of Seventy-Two Tenants* (*dir*. Chu Yuan, 1973). The only Cantonese-dialect release of the year, and the first since 1971, the movie was heavily influenced by television in technique and on-camera personalities. The film outgrossed even Bruce Lee's *Enter the Dragon*, and proved that television, far from being the nemesis of Hong Kong cinema, had replaced the opera stage as the major training ground for cinematic talent. Throughout the following decades, virtually every major star and a majority of directors had their start on the small screen, particularly in TVB soap operas and other dramatic series.

Two actors who enjoyed popularity on television before making their screen débuts were the famous brothers Michael **Hui** (Xu Guanwen) and Sam Hui (Xu Guanjie, *b*. 1948). After making auspicious film débuts separately, they teamed for the first time on the big screen in *Games Gamblers Play* (*dir*. Michael Hui), which became the top-grossing film of 1974. The Hui Brothers' wacky sense of humour and satirical take on Hong Kong society struck a responsive chord with local audiences, and their subsequent films ranked number one at the box office: *The Last Message* (1975), *The Private Eyes* (1976), *The Contract* (1978) and *Security Unlimited* (1981, all *dir*. Michael Hui). *The Private Eyes*, moreover, was the biggest box-office hit of the entire 1970s decade.

Comedy and kungfu combined in the action films starring Jackie Chan, the biggest star to emerge in the late 1970s. *Drunken Master* was number two at the box office in 1978, with *Fearless Hyena* (*dir*. Jackie Chan, Luo Kong) making it to number one in 1979. Throughout the 1980s–90s, Chan remained a major force in Hong Kong movies, with a significant following in Japan. After many attempts, in the 1990s he became the first 'kungfu' star since Bruce Lee to enjoy success in North America.

The 1970s is considered by many critics to be something of a wasteland. The rise of kungfu action was marked by a corresponding decline in well-crafted screenplays. Technical standards ebbed, with the zoom lens and 'wide screen' leading to a lack of attention to screen composition. The abandonment of synchronized-sound dialogue further gave the movies a tinny, unnatural quality. In the late 1970s, the crass commercialism was put into perspective by the founding in

1977 of the Hong Kong International Film Festival. Their annual retrospectives of Hong Kong cinema focused attention on the commercial local film industry as one with a cultural and artistic side that was not to be neglected. However, it would be nearly twenty years before the Hong Kong government finally approved funding for the Hong Kong Film Archives, giving 'official' recognition to the important place Cantonese and Mandarin movies have had in local culture.

In 1978, a group of young filmmakers, many of them graduates from overseas film schools who served their apprenticeship in Hong Kong television, began making movies that attempted to break away from the popular kungfu and comedy that was now the norm. **Yim Ho**'s *The Extras* (1978), **Tsui Hark**'s *The Butterfly Murders* (1979), Ann **Hui**'s *The Secret* (1979), and Allen **Fong**'s *Father and Son* (1981) and others were hailed at the time as the dawn of a New Wave in Hong Kong cinema. But the 'wave' turned out to be a mere ripple, with many of the young filmmakers absorbed by the commercial movie establishment they had ostensibly sought to transform.

See also: action film

Further reading
W. Eberhard (1972), an introduction with synopses; S. Fore (1994), on Golden Harvest and globalization of Hong Kong cinema; HKIFF (1980, 1981), on martial arts film; HKIFF (1984), on 1970s films; HKIFF (1985), on Hong Kong comedies.

9   The 1980s: Cops, comedy, comic cops, and a new prosperity

The decade's movies were populated with cops and gangsters, both in serious and comic treatments. The early 1980s was dominated by a new studio, Cinema City (Xinyi cheng). Founded in 1980 by Carl **Mak**, Dean Shek (Shi Tian, *b.* 1950), and Raymond **Wong** (Huang Baiming), the film company applied 'assembly line' script techniques to a series of big budget comedies that proved extremely popular with the Hong Kong public. Chief among these were the *Aces Go Places*, a collection of James Bond-style farces whose ticket sales reached number one in 1982, 1983, and 1984, with further sequels ranking third in 1985 and sixth in 1989. Golden Harvest also scored box-office hits with Jackie **Chan**'s *Police Story* (*dir.* Jackie Chan, 1985) and its numerous sequels. *Lucky Stars* action comedy series (1983–5), starring Chan and Sammo **Hung**, were also audience-pleasers, reaffirming the supremacy of 'kungfu comedy' as a major force in Hong Kong cinema.

Cinema City displayed a serious side when, in conjunction with Tsui Hark's Film Workshop (Dianying gongzuo shi), it produced *A **Better Tomorrow*** (*dir.* John **Woo**), the number one box-office hit of 1986 and a landmark in Hong Kong cinema. Not only did it revive and redefine the career of John Woo, who would later become the first Hong Kong director to break into mainstream Hollywood, *A Better Tomorrow*'s style was a major influence on Hong Kong filmmaking for years to come. The movie also established **Chow Yun-Fat** as Hong Kong's number one superstar, a position he would hold for the remainder of the decade until he, like his mentor Woo, decamped to Hollywood.

A Better Tomorrow ushered in a cycle of 'triad' films, exploring and glorifying the Hong Kong underworld. Dozens of similarly-themed blood fests were churned out until audiences and producers went on to the next trend, screwball farces. A refreshing antidote to the triad clones was *Gangs*, the directorial début of Lawrence Ah Mon, a decidedly unglamorous look at youth gangs that enjoyed considerable critical success in 1988.

Another popular trend was ghost stories, both contemporary comedies like *Encounters of the Spooky Kind* (*dir.* Sammo **Hung**, 1980) and supernatural costume dramas like *A **Chinese Ghost***

Story (*dir.* **Ching Sin Tung**, 1987). A minor trend was a series of vampire comedies, begin-ning with ***Mr Vampire*** (*dir.* Lau Kwoon-wai, 1985).

With the decline of Shaw's as a primary filmmaking centre, another major player came to the fore in the mid-1980s. D&B Films (Debao), founded in 1985, excelled at middle-class come-dies, like the multi-sequelled *It's a Mad Mad World* and *Heart to Hearts* series. Like Golden Harvest, with its Gala circuit, and Cinema City, with its Golden Princess circuit, D&B had its own theatre chain, the D&B circuit, consisting mostly of theatres leased from Shaw's. With three major cinema chains devoted to first-run Hong Kong films, the local product dominated cinema screens far more than Hollywood imports. By the early 1990s, there was a total of five chains, an excess of screens which ultimately proved detrimental to the local industry. By then, both D&B and Cinema City had been replaced by new players, with Golden Harvest remaining a commanding force in the industry.

The Mainland Chinese market, closed to Hong Kong filmmakers for decades, gradually began to reopen during the 1980s with a series of co-productions between Hong Kong and Chinese film companies. *Shaolin Temple* (*dir.* Zhang Xinyan, 1982) was a huge hit and estab-lished Jet **Li** as an international kungfu star and serious rival to Jackie Chan. Veteran director Li Han-hsiang returned to China to make such epic historical films as *The **Burning of the Imperial Palace*** and ***Reign Behind a Curtain***, both of which made it into the top ten box-office hits of 1983. Bluebird (Qingniao), the film company founded by former Great Wall star Xia Meng, enjoyed considerable box-office and critical success with ***Boat People*** (*dir.* Ann **Hui**, 1982), one of the first contemporary-themed Hong Kong films to be shot on location in China in forty years. In 1984, Bluebird had one more award winner with Yim Ho's ***Homecoming***, another contemporary-themed drama.

However, China became chiefly a venue for Hong Kong filmmakers to shoot costume martial arts epics, like Jackie Chan's *Drunken Master, II* (1994) and two instalments of Tsui Hark's *Once Upon a Time in China* series. The trend reached a peak in the early 1990s, when the Chinese censors put a brake on most co-productions, reducing the flood to a trickle by the mid-1990s.

On the Hong Kong front, censorship became a prickly issue. Since the 1950s, the Television and Entertainment Licensing Authority (TELA) and its previous incarnations had been censoring movies for their political content. In the 1980s, the film world discovered that TELA actually had no legal authority to do so. A clause was added to the censorship code making it illegal for movies to stir up bad relationships with 'neighbouring territories', a veiled reference to China. Thus, a scene depicting Chinese troops shooting down protesting students could be legally excised from a Hong Kong production, while similar scenes would be approved if they took place in 'foreign' countries. In *A Better Tomorrow, III* (*dir.* Tsui Hark, 1989), for instance, it was Vietnamese Communist troops who shot down protesting students, though the parallels to the Tiananmen Square massacre were obvious.

In the wake of 4 June 1989, Hong Kong movies briefly became politicized in a manner that had previously not existed. Hong Kong peoples' concerns about 1997 were expressed in numerous movies, like *Farewell, China* (*dir.* Clara **Law**, 1990), with its dour picture of displaced Chinese emigrants in the USA. Numerous gangster films and comedies made sarcastic comments about the Chinese Communists. Political satire reached a high point with *Her Fatal Ways* (*dir.* Alfred Cheung, 1990), in which a Ninotchka-type Chinese cadre comes to the colony and experiences at first hand the clash of cultures inherent in 'one country two systems'. Though the satire was mild, theatres with close mainland ties refused to screen the movie, and despite the concerns of the Hong Kong public towards both 'June Fourth' and '1997', there never emerged one movie that maturely reflected these sentiments. The clause about offending neigh-bouring territories was eventually scrapped from a new censorship ordinance in the 1990s, but in the run-up to 1997 Hong Kong filmmakers became even more reluctant to make any political statements potentially offensive to the new masters.

On the other hand, the rating system instituted in 1988 served to open up Hong Kong's screens for more adult content in both local and imported movies. The ratings consisted of three categories, with Category 3 (restricted to viewers over 18) reserved for the kind of violence and sex that would previously have been snipped out of local releases. 'CAT 3' quickly became synonymous with 'soft-core porn', and indeed led to a spate of cheaply made sex films as well as raw-edged slices of life like *Queen of Temple Street* and 'artistic' erotic movies, like the classically-themed *Sex and Zen* (*dir.* Michael Mak, 1991).

The 1980s saw the Hong Kong film industry beginning to receive more serious attention at home. Hong Kong's own version of the Oscars, the Hong Kong Film Awards (HKFA), was inaugurated in 1981. The Hong Kong, Kowloon and New Territories Motion Picture Industry Association was founded in 1987, and the Hong Kong Directors Guild established in 1988. Other guilds were formed in the following five years, including those for cinematographers, performing artists, stunt men, scriptwriters and so on. Hong Kong cinema received official sanction as an art form worthy of study and preservation with the belated setting up of the Hong Kong Film Archives in the 1990s. It was long overdue, as all but four of the 500 feature films made before World War II, and perhaps one third of the 5,000 motion pictures filmed in the first four decades after the war, were already lost for ever.

See also: Category 3 film; censorship and film; gangster film; ghosts and immortals, film of; historical film

Further reading
H. Chiao (1987), a major collection of articles on Hong Kong cinema of the 1980s; D. Chute (1988), a report on Hong Kong filmmaking; HKIFF (1982b, 1986b), on 1980s films; C. Li (1985), on 1980s films; S. Teo (1994), on Hong Kong New Wave cinema.

10   The 1990s: Growing recognition abroad and dwindling audience at home

The 1990s began with Hong Kong cinema at the peak of its prosperity. Production was booming, reaching 165 features in 1993, the highest annual total in quarter of a century. Local audiences flocked to local films. In 1992, the top twelve box-office movies were Hong Kong productions, the highest ranking foreign import, *Basic Instinct* (*dir.* Paul Verhoeven, 1992), coming in at thirteen. Hong Kong movies had a healthy export market to Taiwan, Korea, Singapore, and Malaysia.

The industry was a veritable beehive of activity, with a roster of stars in such demand that they simultaneously shot as many as five films. Top among the stars was Stephen **Chow** (Zhou Xingchi), whose special brand of nonsense farce, called *moleitau* in Cantonese, was all the rage. With **Chow Yun-Fat**'s temporary retirement from the screen, the younger Chow was anointed the new king of the Cantonese screen. Among his dozen or so credits in 1992 were the top four grossing movies of the year. Stephen Chow was virtually a genre unto himself, first with a series of contemporary farces, like the gambling comedy *All For the Winner* (*dir.* Yuen Fui, Jeff Lau), the top-grossing picture of 1990, and *Fight Back to School* (*dir.* Gordon Chan), the number one hit of 1991. When the trend changed to costume pictures, so did Chow's comedies. There was the historic farce *Justice, My Foot!* (*dir.* Johnny To), the top hit of 1992, and *Flirting Scholar* (*dir.* Lee Lik-chee), the number one local hit of 1993, the latter trailing *Jurassic Park* (*dir.* Steven Spielberg, 1993) to come in number two over all.

The most prolific filmmaker was **Wong Jing**. He produced, directed, and/or wrote over one hundred films during the decade, covering all genres and exemplifying the commercialism of Hong Kong cinema. Win's (Yongsheng) Films, founded in 1985 by Jimmy Heung (Xiang Huasheng), became one of the most powerful movie companies following the success of such gambling-themed movies as ***God of Gamblers*** (*dir*. Wong Jing), the number-one picture of 1989 starring Chow Yun-Fat. This started a mini-trend in gambling movies, including the Win's-produced *God of Gamblers II* (*dir*. Wong Jing), starring Stephen Chow. It was the number two hit of 1990, right on the heels of Stephen Chow's *All for the Winner* (whose Chinese title is literally translated as 'Saint of Gamblers').

During the early 1990s, it seemed as if every Hong Kong movie could turn a profit, if not at home then abroad. The number of theatre chains screening Cantonese films expanded to five, which meant that as many as five new pictures might be released in any week. This created an unhealthy situation. Since there were only a half dozen or so stars whose names could pre-sell a film, they were under constant pressure from 'triad' gangster elements to make movies that were frequently substandard in quality. Overworked stars not only could not prepare properly for multiple roles at once; they also wreaked havoc on production schedules. Movies were rushed into production without completed scripts. Violence became an underlying theme not only on screen in action films, but off-screen, where competition between rival companies sometimes became rough. In 1992, leading members of the film industry took to the streets in protest about triad violence in the movie business.

These issues – triad violence, overworked stars, excessive production – became moot just a couple of years later as Hong Kong cinema descended into its deepest depression since World War II. Restrictions regarding Hollywood exports in such overseas markets as Korea and Taiwan were liberalized, leading to a decrease in imports from Hong Kong. At home, escalation of ticket prices – from a top ticket price of HK $6 in 1974 to $20 in 1984, $30 in 1989, and $60 in 1996 – coupled with the burgeoning market for laser, video, and VCD, led to a sharp downturn in cinema attendance. Pirated VCDs would hit the market within weeks, or even days, of a film's theatrical release. A more lethal blow was the public's lack of enthusiasm for the local product.

After the craze for costume swordplay films waned in the early 1990s, producers could not find another trend to capture the audience's imagination. This led to more variety in subject matter than in previous years, with a handful of exceptional productions. Gordon Chan took the police story to new heights with *Final Option* (1994), Derek Yee (Er Dongsheng) brought depth to a traditional love story in ***C'est la vie, mon chéri*** (1993), and Pete Chan (Chen Kexin, *b.* 1962) had a critical hit with the **romance** *Comrades: Almost a Love Story* (1996). There was the usual quota of action movies, a popular mini-trend emerging in the mid-1990s with the glorification of young triads in the *Young and Dangerous* (*dir*. Andrew Lau, 1996) series. On the art film circuit, movies by **Wong Kar-Wai** enjoyed a certain cachet, with critical verdicts ranging from high art to pretentious pseudo-art.

Other than Jackie Chan and Stephen Chow, there were virtually no stars who guaranteed packed houses. Production decreased, as did the number of cinema screens devoted to Hong Kong films. Ironically, it was during this period that Hollywood began to become aware of Hong Kong cinema. John Woo, Tsui Hark, Ringo **Lam**, and other directors moved to Los Angeles, as did stars like Chow Yun-Fat and Michelle **Yeoh**. With the 1997 hand-over, Hong Kong cinema was in a doldrums from which few predicted recovery. The possible opening of the huge China market was viewed as a potential financial saviour, though even an audience of one billion across the border would do little to restore the enthusiasm Hong Kong audiences once felt for the local product. The miracle of Hong Kong cinema as one of the most prolific in the world, a trend-setter across East Asia, and a serious rival to Hollywood both at home and abroad, had not so much come to an end but entered a new phase.

Further reading

A. Abbas (1997: 16–47), on the cinematic articulation of the *déjà disparu* in the 1980s–90s; H. Cai (1995), a historical survey of eighty years of filmmaking; Hammond and Wilkins (1996), a handbook on Hong Kong cinema; C. Li (1993a), a collection of reviews; Y. Li (1994), on cinema and social changes; J. Stringer (1996/7), on the concept of camp in Hong Kong cinema; E. Yau (1994a), on Hong Kong's images of mainland China.

Taiwan cinema

Ru-Shou Robert Chen

1 Early formation, 1901–45

From its very beginnings, Taiwan cinema has been a potpourri of diverse cultural, linguistic and other elements. Due to the historically unique circumstances of Taiwan, the history of Taiwan cinema is about films made in Taiwan, whether they have been financed and directed by Japanese, Chinese or Taiwanese. Moreover, a Taiwan film may use one or more of several different languages and dialects – Japanese, Taiwanese or Mandarin, depending on different social and historical circumstances.

The world's first public showing of cinema took place in the Grand Café of Paris in 1895, the same year the Qing Dynasty signed with Japan the Treaty of Shimonoseki, under which Taiwan was ceded to Japan and which initiated the fifty-year Japanese occupation (1895–1945). Cinema came to Taiwan in 1901, two years before it arrived in mainland China. In the same year, the Japanese produced the first film made in Taiwan, a **documentary** on Japan's rule over Taiwan.

In the early history of Taiwan cinema, the Japanese were the dominant force behind all three stages of film operations – production, **distribution** and exhibition. Even though Taiwan did not make its own films until 1921, films from all over the world were shown there, among them *Judex* (*dir*. Louis Feuillade, 1916), Chaplin's shorts and Buster Keaton's *Sherlock Jr.* (1924). Japan, however, provided the majority of the films then shown to Taiwanese audiences. China was another main source of movies, and the first Chinese import was *The Revival of an Old Well* (*dir*. **Dan Duyu**, 1923) from Shanghai, the centre of China's film industry. No matter where the films came from, all were required to carry Japanese subtitles, or be dubbed in Japanese in the case of sound films.

Taiwan began to produce feature films in 1921, when the Japanese governor decided to use the medium to spread Japanese culture among the Taiwanese. A 'circuit movie group' was set up under the Culture Bureau. The first film the group made, *Eyes of the Buddha* (*dir*. Tanaka King, 1922), was about a Chinese official who tried to force a Taiwanese girl to marry him until a young Japanese came to the rescue. In one dramatic sequence, the eyes of a Buddha flashed and frightened away the official. The first Taiwanese film actor who appeared in this movie was subsequently fired from his real job as a bank teller because acting was looked down upon as a lowly and disreputable activity.

In 1925 the Taiwan Motion Picture Study Society was established, the first such organization aspiring to produce motion pictures by and for the Taiwanese. Its first film, *Whose Fault Is This?* (*dir.* Liu Xiyang, 1925), another hero-saves-beauty movie, did not meet public expectations and was a failure. But *Bloodstain* (*dir.* Zhang Yunhe, 1929), made by the same people, turned out to be an enormous success. The first film to use Taiwanese aborigines as actors, it tells the story of a girl and her lover who go into the mountains to search for and take revenge upon her father's killer. It is also evident from the division of labour that Japanese still controlled the major technical aspects. Director, cameramen and lighting technicians were Japanese; Taiwanese had to be content with being actors or doing make-up and other minor jobs, while aborigines were merely extras or small-part performers. On the whole, the production set-up reflected the uneven power relationship between the colonizer and the colonized.

Another group, the Taiwan Motion Picture Production Office, made two popular movies: *Wu Feng the Righteous Man* (*dir.* Ando Talo, Jiba Hiroki, 1932), which tells of a Qing Dynasty official Wu Feng who sacrifices his life to stop aborigines from killing people, and *Map of the Seven-Star Cave* (*dir.* Jiba Hiroki, 1933), a story about the fight over a treasure map. Both were made as Taiwanese–Japanese co-productions, which was the only way of providing some security for the Taiwan film business. Capital came from Taiwan sources; casts could include both Taiwanese and Japanese, although again the main production personnel such as editors, photographers, and the director were Japanese.

The state of film production in this early period encountered four problems: (1) Since movie-making was not regarded in Taiwan as a permanent business, no long-term organization or regular investment existed, and after a film was done everyone involved in it had to find other jobs. (2) Lacking formal technical training, Taiwanese filmmakers had to rely on the Japanese to fill positions requiring specialized skills. (3) Like elsewhere in the world, Taiwan had few good screenplays at the time. (4) A very harsh film censorship (harsher even than in Japan proper) awaited every finished film.

Once motion pictures had appeared as a new cultural medium, the Taiwanese learned to incorporate it into its indigenous cultural production. Two special features marked early film showings. One was the *rengasi* (*rensageki* in Japanese, meaning 'chained drama') whereby films were used to complement stage plays. When the play's narrative came to a point where an exterior setting was needed or the stage facilities were insufficient to present such scenes (e.g., the main character jumping into a river or people taking a ferry), backdrops would be removed and a film on that subject would be projected on a screen at the back of the stage. After this was done, the stage play continued with its story. Thus, live performance was 'chained' to film as the two modes alternated.

The other feature was the *benzi* (*benshi* or *katsuben* in Japanese), a person who stood or sat to the left of the movie screen. In other countries, such a person was called a 'talker' or 'explainer' for silent films. In Japan and Taiwan, however, the *benzi* was not only a narrator and voice actor but also a commentator-reader and audience representative. Part of his function was to interpret a film, to react to the film as a viewer and to convey reactions to the audience. Working under licence in Taiwan, the *benzi* often obtained a higher billing than the star of a movie. He (always a male) had to follow a pre-censored script to explain the film, but he could comment on the story using his own manner of expression, and the police would sometimes censure the *benzi* for foul or politically dangerous language. The *benzi* – most of them intellectuals who later became leaders in many other fields – became quite important in Taiwan's socio-political context, in that they could express the people's dissatisfaction. Their comments on the movies gave the audiences a better understanding of their plight as colonialized Taiwanese.

Before the second Sino-Japanese war began in 1937, Shanghai was one of the major sources of film imports, and Shanghai film companies had branches or agencies in Taiwan. Although the war did not, at first, stop the imports of Shanghai films, the Japanese government became much more restrictive in its censorship and regulation. Japanese customs authorities in Taiwan designed a highly complicated procedure for inspecting such imports. Films were reviewed right at the harbour; those with anti-Japanese contents would be confiscated on the spot. If a film passed customs, a heavy import duty still had to be paid, after which a censorship board reviewed it again before permission was granted for public showing. Images of China's national flag, Dr. Sun Yat-Sen (1866–1925) and Generalissimo Chiang Kai-shek (1887–1975) were deleted.

The flow of films from Shanghai was entirely cut off when the war escalated to its highest point. Nevertheless, from 1923 (when the first Chinese film was shown in Taiwan) to 1945 (when the Japanese occupation ended) more than 300 Chinese films were seen by the Taiwanese. Although the importation of Chinese movies was forbidden during the war, films made in Manchuria (a vast region in Northeastern China occupied by Japanese armed forces before and during World War II) could be seen in Taiwan's theatres. Japan apparently hoped that these Manchurian movies would help to reconcile the Taiwanese to Japanese rule and wean them away from their historical, social and cultural ties with China.

As mentioned earlier, Taiwanese–Japanese co-production was once the only way films could be made in Taiwan. Influences from Japanese culture were omnipresent. *Love Tide* (*dir.* Tani, 1926), a film about a young Japanese who travels to Taiwan and falls in love with a Taiwanese girl, even copied the stylized performance of Japan's No plays. The Japanese director and photographer dominated the production and made the film into a box-office disaster since the Taiwanese simply could not accept this genre of acting. Such films further alienated the Taiwanese audience because of cultural disparities.

A distribution and exhibition system appeared in Taiwan as early as in 1915. Japanese-run circuit film companies were set up to handle the circulation and screening of films in different cities, and soon movies shown in Tokyo could be seen in Taipei within a month. In the 1930s, Hollywood companies like Paramount and Universal either set up offices in Taiwan or put the Taiwanese market under the management of their Tokyo branches.

In the early days films were frequently shown outdoors, since there were not enough theatres (only forty-nine in 1941) to screen the limited number of prints of a film circulated around the island. After 1942, theatres were classified into three different categories. Those in class A (the biggest one in Taipei had 1,632 seats) were first-run theatres showing mainly Japanese films and charging higher ticket prices. Class B theatres were either second-run houses or those showing Taiwanese and Chinese movies. Most of them lacked air conditioning. Class C theatres were open-air establishments sometimes used for stage plays.

Until the end of World War II, 70 per cent of the audience were Japanese. This figure can be taken as an indication that the Japanese were richer than the Taiwanese and that movie-going was for the privileged. But the Taiwanese also had other forms of entertainment, and many still preferred indigenous art performances such as puppet plays and local operas.

See also: censorship and film; dubbed foreign film

2   Destruction and restoration, 1945–59

The four years following the end of World War II, 1945–9, were among the most devastating in the history of Taiwan cinema. Politically, the Communists and the Nationalists were fighting a civil war on the mainland. The Shanghai film industry, a long-time film supply centre for Taiwan, stopped production and was forced to evacuate to Hong Kong and Taiwan. Mainland Chinese took over film industries established by the Japanese and continued to exploit Taiwanese workers. Due to inflation, the price of a movie ticket rose to an exorbitant 3,000 Old Taiwan (OT) dollars in 1948, compared with less than two OT dollars in 1945. And in less than a year, it had further sky-rocketed to 5,000 OT dollars. (The price of rice at that time was 2,000 OT dollars a kilogram. Movie-going thus became an unimaginable luxury.)

Not a single feature film was produced during this period except for a few documentaries on the scenery of Taiwan. One reason was the unavailability of film stock from Shanghai; another was the lack of film technicians. Taiwan's film industry had relied heavily on the Japanese technicians who were sent back to Japan, along with 480,000 other Japanese, after World War II. The vacuum was soon filled by film personnel from Shanghai, but these people spent their time fighting over control of the film equipment and theatres originally owned by the Japanese, and the infrastructure of Taiwan's film industry was affected. It was subsequently reorganized and divided among three companies: the Central Motion Picture Company (CMPC, formerly the Agriculture Education Motion Picture Company, owned by the ruling party KMT), which made anti-Communist feature films; the China Motion Picture Studio (owned by the Ministry of National Defence), which specialized in military education documentaries; and the Taiwan Motion Picture Studio (owned by the Taiwan Provincial Government), which produced social education newsreels.

The provisional government ruled at first that no Japanese films were to be shown. But this ruling was later abolished for two reasons: there were not enough movies to fill the gap left by the Japanese films; and, secondly, Chinese theatre owners could not make a profit under such restrictions. Hence, until the mid-1960s, movie theatres screened Chinese, Japanese, Taiwanese, and Hollywood films as usual.

In 1950, after a four-year hiatus, CMPC started making feature films. In line with the government's propaganda policy, films were made to reveal the inhumanity of the Communists, with self-explanatory titles such as *Awakening from Nightmare* (*dir.* Zhong You, 1950), *Black List* (*dir.* Chen Rui, 1951), and *Advice to the Communist Spy* (*dir.* Zhong You, 1952), the last openly exhorting Communist agents and sympathizers to surrender themselves to the authorities. On the other hand, the KMT government tried to heal the wounds caused by clashes between mainlanders and Taiwanese with films such as *Never to Part* (*dir.* **Xu Xinfu**, 1951) and *Beautiful Island* (*dir.* Chen Wenquan, 1952), which presented idyllic pictures of life in Taiwan. Films were also used as a vehicle to promote government policy. *Spring on Earth* (*dir.* **Bu Wancang**, Fang Wuling, 1952) was about the agricultural reform and its benefit to Taiwanese farmers, while another film, *Spring Comes to the Rice Field* (*dir.* Zhong You, 1952), showed the improvements in the farmers' lives after the reform.

After World War II, Hollywood films took over the biggest slice of the world market, and of Taiwan's as well. In 1954, for example, 238 American films were shown, as against only 104 Chinese films, including those in Mandarin, Cantonese, and Fukienese. New film gimmicks created by Hollywood to compete with television were also introduced. Three-D movies came to Taiwan in 1953; CinemaScope, in 1954; VistaVision, in 1954; and Stereophonic sound, in 1954. At the end of this period Hollywood controlled 70 per cent of the market share.

The year 1955 was an important one for Taiwan's film industry. CMPC initiated a series of film projects using American financial aid. It also leased unused studios to other film companies. Hong Kong filmmakers who sided with the KMT regime came to Taiwan to make their films. The KMT government welcomed them by granting them subsidies. From then on, films made in Hong Kong for Taiwanese consumption were also counted as domestic production in government statistics. Nineteen fifty-five was also the year that Taiwanese-dialect films started to dominate the local market. Twenty-one films were made in 1956; thirty-eight in 1957. The highest point was reached in 1958, when eighty-two Taiwanese-dialect films were made, including a hand-puppet film and five films made in Hong Kong by Taiwanese film crews. (Production of Taiwanese-dialect films rose to another peak in 1966, and then again in 1971.)

The popularity of these Taiwanese-dialect films in the 1950s is understandable. Most of the films were adaptations of stories from Taiwanese **legends and myths**, stories that the audiences knew by heart. Some were popular because well-known folk songs were used; others were adapted from real-life crime stories. An important contribution by these Taiwanese-dialect films is that they provided filmmakers from Shanghai, most them unemployed after evacuating to Taiwan, with opportunities to practice their skills. In 1957, the first Taiwanese-dialect film festival was held in Taipei. Film **awards** for Best Director, Best Actor and others were selected by fourteen judges, although the award for Best Film was left vacant. Audiences cast their votes to choose the most popular actor and actress. But the Taiwanese-dialect films were out of production in the late 1970s for two reasons: (1) the government declared Mandarin the official language, and (2) the government never bothered to subsidize nor designed measures to promote the ill-structured Taiwanese-dialect film industry. It was not until the rise of the New Taiwan Cinema movement (see below) that the audience could hear Taiwanese again in theatres.

Taxation was the biggest problem in this period. One estimate was that, when all kinds of tax items were added up, the government took 70 per cent of the gross income from every film shown. According to another source, movie theatres could only retain 1.57 New Taiwan (NT) dollars from every A class ticket (10.00 NT dollars) sold. Two dollars went to a 'donation for national construction'; another 1.25 dollars to 'national defence'. The audiences also paid one dollar to help relocate military dependants, and 40 cents for relief to the 'suffering mainland Chinese compatriots', in addition to an entertainment tax and numerous other taxes. Exhibitors claimed at the time that Taiwan had the most expensive movie tickets in the world, although without taxes they would also have been the cheapest.

The number of movie theatres increased rapidly – from forty-nine in 1941 to 347 in 1953. Audience figures could reach 600,000 daily. Many theatres installed air conditioning, while the open-air theatres gradually dropped out of business.

In order to consolidate its control and to stop Communist ideology from filtering into Taiwan, the government began a movement in 1954 to expunge 'three evils': leftist materials (red), pornographic literature (yellow), and sensational inside stories (black). As part of this movement, a film censorship law was proclaimed in 1955, under which it was decreed that films should be created for the purpose of anti-Communism and refrain from questioning the legitimacy of the KMT government, attacking government leaders, harming Taiwan–US relations, or revealing the dark side of Taiwan society. Violation of this law could expose filmmakers to such sanctions as licence revocation, imposition of fines, film confiscation, or a jail term.

See also: adaptations of drama and literature; documentary education film; propaganda and film

Further reading

L. Ye (1995), on post-war Taiwan cinema.

3   Revitalization and decay, 1960s–70s

The 1960s is recognized as the golden era in the history of Taiwan cinema. Taiwan ranked third among Asian countries in total number of feature films produced in 1966, next only to Japan and India. Taiwanese-dialect cinema experienced another renaissance with the production of 144 films in 1966; 116 in 1967; and 115 in 1968. Mandarin films also rose in quantity as well as in quality. The year 1968 was the first in which Mandarin films produced in Taiwan exceeded the 100 mark (116). A total of 398 were produced between 1968 and 1970, equivalent to 11 per month. Films made in Taiwan began to dominate the overseas Chinese market in Hong Kong, Southeast Asia and elsewhere. Meanwhile Taiwan's own movie theatres increased from 374 in 1953 to 734 in 1967. Box-office earnings of Chinese (Mandarin) films rivalled those of Hollywood movies in Taiwan, and many theatre chains in Taipei switched from showing only foreign films to screening Chinese films. It is estimated that every citizen of Taiwan (population: 12 million) on average watched ten movies in 1967, as against only four in 1951 (population: 4 million).

After the government-sponsored CMPC restructured itself in 1963, the new manager, Kung Hung, advanced 'wholesome realism' (*jiankang xieshi zhuyi*) as the guideline for filmmaking. The object of wholesome realism, according to him, was to 'reveal the bright side of social reality' and 'to promote good qualities of humanity such as sympathy, care, forgiveness, consideration and altruism'. Wholesome realism was supposed to lead the audience 'to do the right thing'.

The subject matter of wholesome realism revolved around the lives of working class people, and at the same time highlighted Taiwan's economic development. Unlike Italian neorealism which was largely devoted to exposing social problems, films of wholesome realism dignified characters in the films who earned a living through their labour. *Head of Street, End of Lane* (*dir.* **Lee Hsing**, 1963) portrayed commoners who had been evacuated from mainland China to Taiwan and who dreamed of going back to their home towns after saving enough money. ***Oyster Girl*** (*dir.* Li Jia, Lee Hsing, 1964), the first wide-screen colour feature film made in Taiwan, described the simple life of a family engaged in breeding oysters. Another film, *Beautiful Duckling* (*dir.* Lee Hsing, 1964), which won the accolade of Best Film in the Taipei Golden Horse Awards (GHA), showed how the government helped a family of duck raisers through economic hardships by lending them money to modernize their equipment.

At the same time as those films of wholesome realism were produced, other **genre films** such as kungfu or swordplay, **costume drama** and **melodrama** were popular and thus became major forces competing in theatres. One major competition was films based on popular folk ballads originally from Huangmei, a region in Southeast China. Huangmei opera movies were revived by the Hong Kong film industry. *The Love Eterne* (*dir.* **Li Han-hsiang**, 1963), a tragic ancient love story similar to that of Romeo and Juliet, was the most successful film in this genre. It was shown during sixty-two consecutive days at the three largest theatres in Taipei to audiences totalling 721,929, most of whom saw the film more than once. Three reasons account for the overnight success of this film. First, its 'free love, or death' theme was in accord with people's reaction to the old custom of arranged marriage. Second, the downbeat, sentimental mood of the Huangmei melody genre catered to the feelings of a repressed general public. Third, the film's **nostalgia** provided some comfort to mainland Chinese stranded in Taiwan, and thus had a cathartic effect on a large audience. Nevertheless, its escapist and pessimistic tone was seen as detracting from the KMT government's war preparations to 'reconquer the mainland'. The concept of wholesome realism was therefore brought forward in an effort to influence people's attitudes and focus their attention on present-day concerns in Taiwan.

The films of wholesome realism also stood in direct opposition to romantic melodrama films made in Taiwan, mostly adaptations from the works of woman writer **Chiung Yao**. Her novels depicted either teacher–student love or love triangles (or polygons) among young people. Such films created an emotional world of their own, in which heroines were without exception beautiful, passionate and very independent, while the heroes were handsome, romantic and melancholy. Invariably, one of them would be from a rich family where she (or he) had a tyrant father whose opposition made their ideal marriage almost impossible. The venues of this world were limited to three locations: living room, dancing hall, and coffee shop. Hence the films were commonly called 'three-location movies' (*santing dianying*). These unrealistic, dream-like films were very popular among young people – mainly high school students and factory workers. The best-known director in this genre was Liu Jiachang (*b.* 1941), who set a record by finishing a film in three days without the benefit of a script. His films typically used his own songs to bridge the narrative, showed lovers running on a beach – time and again in slow motion – and invariably featured a rebellious male or female protagonist.

Another genre, the **martial arts film**, was also popular in the 1960s. Many such films figured among the top ten box-office hits between 1966 and 1969 and were among the first films that attracted Western attention to the film industry in Hong Kong and Taiwan. This genre was in constant flux in terms of its mode of representation. For instance, all kinds of weapons (e.g., swords, knives, sticks and clubs) were employed at first. Then films appeared in which only fists and legs were used, such as those featuring Bruce **Lee**, whose films were Hong Kong productions. Another type of **kungfu film** mixed **comedy** with violent fighting sequences and focused on the way the hero practised his kungfu (shown in slow motion). Some characteristics, however, were common to all the kungfu films: anachronism, stereotyped characters and identical narrative structure, generally blended with pseudo-patriotism and an irrational xenophobic attitude. Foreigners, especially the Japanese, were often portrayed as bad guys and ultimately beaten by the good Chinese guys. The genre cannot be overlooked, however, since 500 or more kungfu films were made in the 1970s, representing 42 per cent of Taiwan's total production. The effect of these martial arts films was to transport the audience to another time and space, where justice could be done and evil avenged. They provided a kind of escape from the oppressive political climate in real life. The authorities were, however, quite tolerant toward these films because the dichotomy (good vs. evil and right vs. wrong) underlying the stories did not conflict with the official ideology.

Government-backed film studios, on the other hand, were busy making high-budget war films, which were popular because of their spectacular battle scenes, some containing slow motion shots of dead bodies flying through the air. Since this genre fitted in with the government's policy of propagating patriotism, two such films received Best Film awards at Taipei GHA ceremonies.

Taiwan cinema of the 1960s–70s developed around a number of veteran directors who, for better or for worse, set the tone for these major genres. They treated their films seriously and further motivated other people, technicians and actors, to perfect their skills. The first of them is Lee Hsing. Starting his career in the Taiwanese-dialect film industry, Lee had already been famous for his films of wholesome realism back in the 1960s. After directing several melodramas, which all failed at the box office, he picked up ideas from nativist literature (*xiangtu wenxue*) to make films using the realist style but taking a more critical attitude toward problems resulting from industrialization. Examples are his *A Boat in the Ocean* (1978), *Story of a Small Town* and *Good Morning, Taipei* (both 1979), all portraying rural life on the eve of Taiwan's economic transition. The films brought him fame again and won him a record-breaking three consecutive awards of Best Film in Taiwan.

Three other major directors besides Lee Hsing determined the trend and convention of major genres – and their popularity – in Taiwan cinema. King **Hu** was the first internationally known director in Taiwan cinema. His *A **Touch of Zen*** (1970) won the Grand Prix of the Commission Supérieure Technique at the 1975 Cannes Film Festival (FF). Acclaimed for its fast-paced cutting, constant change of lens, and conventions borrowed from Peking opera, *A Touch of Zen* begins with a simple theme of revenge, then develops into a highly sophisticated narrative involving, as the English title suggests, the ideas of Zen Buddhism and other metaphysical concepts. The film can hardly be classified with the period's martial arts genre, as it deviates so extensively from the norms that one would have to redefine the genre itself according to director King Hu's own terms. His later works followed the same pattern and employed similar plots, and established him in the category of an *auteur*. His international success opened another page in the history of Taiwan cinema.

Another director, **Pai Ching-jui**, who learned his filming skills in Italy in the 1960s, made twenty-one films between 1971 and 1979, an average of more than two films a year. Most of his works in this period were adaptations of Chiung Yao's novels. In 1977 he made news by bringing a team to Europe and shooting three films at the same time, using the same actor as the protagonist but pairing him off with three different actresses.

The films of the last important director, Song Cunshou (*b*. 1930), were controversial by virtue of their seemingly deviationist topics: *Story of Mother* (1972) presents a licentious mother and her unforgiving son; *Outside the Window* (1972) depicts the love between a high school student and her teacher; and *The Diary of Didi* (1978) narrates a girl's coming of age through pregnancy. But these subjects all revolved around his real concern: humanism, namely, how to reconcile one's inner passion with a rigid and intolerant outside world.

The 1970s was an important era for Taiwan in terms of its political, economic, and cultural transformation. The death of Chiang Kai-shek in 1975 further accelerated this process of change. Yet, at the same time, a series of political setbacks – expulsion from the United Nations in 1971, the signing of the Shanghai Communiqué between the USA and the PRC in 1972, and Taiwan's termination of diplomatic relations with Japan in 1972 and with the US in 1979 – created mixed feelings among Taiwan's people.

In an effort to stave off another possible defeat, the KMT government used officially-backed films to rekindle patriotism among the Taiwanese and to promote the ideology of anti-Communism. Films like *The Man Who Carries the National Flag* (*dir.* Liu Jiachang), *The Story of Daniel* (*dir.* Liu Weibing) and *Snowflake* (*dir.* Liu Jiachang, all 1973) were anti-Communist propaganda films. Another type of film took military events of the Sino-Japanese war (1937–45) as subject matter to remind audiences of the Nationalists' successes against the Japanese invaders. There were also a few military propaganda films such as *The Spirit of the Huangpu Military Academy* (*dir.* Liu Jiachang, 1978), which were aimed at encouraging young people to join the army.

Meanwhile, Taiwan's rapid economic growth brought many benefits to the film industry as a whole. Starting in 1973, a customs tax on imported film stock was cut by half, as was also the case for exported products. Films were categorized as trade goods rather than cultural items, and film companies could obtain rebates from the government when processing films abroad. The government also encouraged overseas Chinese filmmakers to come to Taiwan and use local talents.

The economic transformation in the 1970s opened the way for the existence of independent or privately-owned film companies, forty of which went into regular production. The government encouraged independent film production by subsidizing the film companies, assigning import quotas for foreign films, presenting GHA each year and according customs tax discounts for the purchase of foreign film stock and equipment. These measures stimulated the investment of more and more capital in the film industry.

In 1975 the Foundation for the Development of the Motion Picture Industry in the Republic of China was established under the auspices of the Government Information Office (GIO). Its function was to build up a better filmmaking environment, train film technicians, expand overseas markets, and preserve materials on Taiwan cinema. Film Library was subsequently established in 1978. In 1992 it was upgraded and became the China Film Archive in Taipei. After three years' preparation, the Film Archive was voted in as a full member of the International Federation of Film Archives in 1995.

As the economy prospered, more films were produced. A total of 2,150 films went into production in the 1970s. Sudden affluence also led to the emergence of a middle class who could afford to buy more movie tickets. Total attendance in the mid-1970s continued to increase in spite of the inroads of television. Ominously, however, the average number of movies watched annually by each Taiwanese had not increased; it remained at 10, as in the late 1960s, and the overall rise in film attendance was primarily a consequence of a rapid growth in the island's population, then up to 15 million.

See also: filmed stage performances; independent film; love and marriage; swordplay film; war film

Further reading
H. Chiao (1993a), on Li Han-hsiang and his Guolian Studio; R. Huang (1994), a book on propaganda films in Taiwan; W. Eberhard (1972), an introduction with synopses.

4   New Taiwan Cinema, 1980s

Taiwan cinema had one of its most schizophrenic periods in the 1980s. On the one hand, its endemic problems gradually worsened. On the other, it gained international prestige from the short-lived New Taiwan Cinema movement (1982–6), and especially from **Hou Hsiao-hsien**'s *A City of Sadness* (1989).

Politically, more and more countries in the 1980s recognized the PRC as the one and only legitimate Chinese government, thus relegating the KMT government in Taiwan to a diplomatic limbo. For the film industry, such political isolation meant the loss of overseas markets in Southeast Asia and elsewhere. Economically, Taiwan had gone through industrialization in the late 1970s. But, instead of helping the declining film industry, Taiwan's economic success only hastened its demise.

Revenues from martial arts and melodrama films, the box-office mainstays of Taiwan's film industry in the 1970s, were deteriorating when the 1980s began. Economic success had the effect of changing the tastes of the audiences, who no longer wanted to be taken into a world of fantasy where lovers spent all their time talking about their feelings without doing anything else, or where a swordsman would sacrifice everything simply to kill an adversary. The allure of immediate and unrestrained material gratification attracted the audiences to other genres: films exploiting sex and violence, glorifying gambling and fraud, or showing scenes of Taiwan's underworld. Movie screens became filled with nude bodies, gun battles, gambling scenes and the gangster Big Boss. These works were ironically labelled 'social realism' films by their producers, who showed little regard for their deleterious influence on society as a whole. Yet sensational new topics could only capture the audiences for a short time. Movie audiences soon turned their backs on such films, as they had on the martial art films and romantic melodramas before. College and university students prided themselves on not going to such domestic productions. The film industry came to an impasse when almost all Taiwan film companies began to lose money.

At this time, the influx of Hong Kong films had begun to loom large on the horizon. Escapist, imitative and superficial were some of the adjectives once used to describe Hong Kong cinema. But the late 1970s had seen the rise of New Wave cinema in Hong Kong, and about sixty new directors, most of them trained abroad, made their débuts during 1975–9. Their refreshingly realistic and socially conscious works held up a mirror to aspects of Hong Kong society that had been long ignored by Hong Kong cinema. They exposed the myth of urban prosperity, the dissatisfaction of youth, the uncertainty about Hong Kong's future and identity, and the myriad problems and societal changes of the Crown Colony. Even though these films were eventually absorbed into the mainstream commercially-oriented production system, they had by then successfully revolutionized Hong Kong cinema. Films from Hong Kong now resembled Hollywood films: well-packaged, meticulous in all details of content and form. Taiwanese audiences welcomed these films, which not only entertained but also touched upon certain social, cultural and political issues encountered in Taiwan also. Their impact on Taiwan's film industry was immediately felt when, starting in 1981, they carried away major categories at the annual GHA. Alarmed by the fact that Hong Kong cinema was dominating not only the awards but the box office as well, many film people desperately wanted a change in the system.

The government was not unaware of the crisis. The new GIO director at that time, James Soong, took many initiatives to help rebuild the financially beleaguered industry. Starting from 1983, he reorganized the annual GHA to honour artistic innovation rather than 'policy approved' content, and to have the films judged by professionals instead of government representatives. He created the GHA International FF to bring in award-winning foreign films that might raise local standards. In a bid to stimulate the concern of intellectuals for Taiwan cinema, he initiated the Campus Film Festival in 1984, which brought filmmakers to university campuses where they could communicate directly with the students. He encouraged sending films out to compete in international film festivals, updated the infrastructure of film law to meet current needs, and raised the medium to the level of a cultural enterprise. He proclaimed three goals for the film industry: that Taiwan cinema should be 'professional, artistic, and international'.

Both the challenge from Hong Kong and the GIO's positive encouragement contributed to the birth of the New Taiwan Cinema movement in the early 1980s. An additional factor that made the movement possible was the return to Taiwan of a group of film students at a time when the CMPC had been specifically instructed by the government to offer opportunities to new filmmakers. Some of the returnees immediately tried their hand at filmmaking, others joined newspapers and became film critics, and together they created a new film culture. The so-called 'new film critics' soon became extremely influential among audiences due to their serious attitude toward cinema. Their efforts gave rise to a generation of serious film viewers and helped promote films made by young directors.

In sum, Taiwan's dying film industry earnestly tried to revitalize itself in the early 1980s, and it did achieve some successes. New Taiwan Cinema not only was the first conscious attempt to build a serious film culture in Taiwan, but also set a high standard for creative integrity and produced a significant body of works. Numerous films were sent abroad and won international awards, most notable among them *In Our Time* (*dir.* Tao Dechen, Edward **Yang**, **Ko Yicheng**, **Chang Yi**, 1982), *Growing Up* (*dir.* **Chen Kun-hou**), *Sandwich Man* (*dir.* Hou Hsiao-hsien, **Tseng Chuang-hsiang**, **Wan Jen**), *That Day on the Beach* (*dir.* Edward Yang, all 1983), *Jade Love* (*dir.* Chang Yi, 1984), *Taipei Story* (1985) and *Terrorizer* (1986, both *dir.* Edward Yang). All were products of those young directors emerging from the New Taiwan Cinema movement.

The movement began in 1982 with the release of *In Our Time*, a portmanteau film by four new directors. This film belonged to one type of New Taiwan Cinema which attempted to

Plate 3   *Taipei Story* (1985)

represent Taiwan and its history from a macro level. The film described Taiwan's social and economic development by relating four different stories, which, connected together, recounted Taiwan's modernization process from the 1960s to the 1980s, from the age of radio to that of TV, and from the countryside to the city. The importance of this film, according to Edward Yang, one of the four directors and a major figure of the movement, lay in the fact that 'it was perhaps the first attempt in cinema to recover the Taiwan past, one of the first films in which we began to ask ourselves questions . . . questions about our origins, our politics, our relation to mainland China, and so on'.

Another type of New Taiwan Cinema was more personal, often taking the form of the film-maker's own autobiography, childhood memories or personal experiences. While these films also dealt with the history of Taiwan, they tended to rest on a micro level. Representative of this type are Hou Hsiao-hsien's early works: *A **Time to Live, a Time to Die*** (1985) was based on Hou's childhood memory, *A **Summer at Grandpa's*** (1984) on that of the writer **Chu Tien-wen**, and ***Dust in the Wind*** (1986) on that of the screen writer **Wu Nien-chen**.

In spite of their different emphases, the collective memory of the past becomes the thematic preoccupation of New Taiwan Cinema. *A Time to Live, a Time to Die*, for example, portrays the tragedies of mainland Chinese exiled to Taiwan after 1949, and the subsequent formation of a distinctive Taiwanese consciousness among the younger generation.

Besides dealing with the past, some dominant themes of New Taiwan Cinema are problems resulting from modernization, such as gradual deterioration of the patriarchy, crisis in the urban nuclear family and juvenile delinquency. *Taipei Story*, for example, reflects on problems of interpersonal relationship caused by the economic transformation. *Terrorizer*, on the other hand, represents a nightmarish image of modern urban environment.

As for stylistic innovations, those new directors make an effort to develop a new cinematic language that stands apart from the dominant mode of the classical Hollywood narrative. The way they tell a story in their films, if there is indeed a story, tends to be elliptical. Unlike Hollywood, narrative flow in those films is never clearly defined. Sometimes it is multi-directional: more than two story lines are perceived simultaneously, as in *Terrorizer*. Most of the time those films do not have what we usually associate with a 'regular' film – a beginning, a middle, and a climactic ending. They are more like pieces of one's lived experience cut loose and sent drifting along in one's memory. Hou's early works used this type of narrative strategy.

In order to achieve the 'lifelike' atmosphere, the new directors restrain camera movement, simply letting the camera stand still so that the story will unfold itself. Because most of the films are shot on location, they rely heavily on natural sources rather than artificial lighting. A mixture of drama with documentary footage is commonly found from those films, thus rendering a more vivid and creative viewing experience.

The new directors are keenly aware of composition in space and depth. A long-take, deep-focus shot becomes the trademark of their films. They even utilize off-screen space, suggesting to the audience that there is a bigger space outside the frames that define and confine the screen. Equally important is the dialectical juxtaposition of sound and image. *Terrorizer* is a good example. We can find at least two scenes in the film where voice and image do not match. Voice-over from the sound track is telling one thing, while the image on the screen is showing another. In another scene a series of images is used to 'tell' a story, but the whole scene is intentionally kept silent. Voice-over, usually female, is another trademark in New Taiwan Cinema. It is sometimes employed as a frame device, appearing at the beginning and the end of the film. In other places it is used to connect missing points in the narrative or to signal the lapse of time, as in **Kuei-mei, A Woman** (*dir.* Chang Yi, 1985).

New Taiwan Cinema prefers ordinary, insignificant people to heroic or historical figures. In *Sandwich Man*, for instance, protagonists in three different episodes are a 'sandwich man', two salesmen and a working-class family. For those roles, new filmmakers favour the use of non-professional people as their actors. They are instructed 'to play themselves' in front of the camera. We can find many improvisation pieces from those films. Another important feature is the **representations of women**. One group of films from New Taiwan Cinema capture women's repression and suffering in addition to reflecting the struggles and dilemmas of their search for new identities.

The use of languages in New Taiwan Cinema reflected a growing awareness of indigenous Taiwanese culture and its colonial experiences. As a reaction against the KMT government's policy of monolingualism (speaking only Mandarin in films), *Sandwich Man* initiated a flow of films using Taiwanese and Hakka, two major dialects in Taiwan, and Japanese, the ex-colonizer's language. By adopting Taiwanese as the means of communication, as well as the symbol of cultural identity, New Taiwan Cinema transformed the then dying Taiwanese-dialect cinema into a new artistic form.

Also striking is the strong solidarity among the new filmmakers. They cooperated instead of competing with each other – on screen as well as off screen. Some seven to eight major directors, for example, appeared together in *That Day on the Beach*, and Hou Hsiao-hsien acted as the protagonist in *Taipei Story*. On the other hand, it is Hou who financed – by mortgaging his own house – Edward Yang's *Terrorizer*.

New Taiwan Cinema also transformed the viewing habits of the audience. They can no longer sit passively for the film to begin and finish, but have to engage themselves in the narrative. While watching a film, they must actively select, reflect, and sometimes reach their own conclusions. Edward Yang's open-ended style always invites his audiences to determine the fate of certain characters, such as the 'missing' husband in *That Day on the Beach*. His *Terrorizer* provides more than one ending for audiences to determine an appropriate outcome for the chilling story. Challenges such as these, however, would inevitably become a burden to people who are accustomed to the Hollywood formula of identification, and might explain why many outstanding works of New Taiwan Cinema have been denounced by conservative critics as being cold, alienating and obscure.

The New Taiwan Cinema movement peaked around 1985, but as a whole it soon ground to a halt. Taiwan productions were outperformed and outsold in a market strongly controlled by films from Hong Kong, although it remains to be explained exactly why Taiwan, with a population three times greater than Hong Kong's, fell so far behind the latter in filmmaking. One factor was perhaps the dearth of topics for the new directors. The day finally came when audiences simply felt tired of watching the director's childhood stories, for there was no longer any need to remind people of Taiwan's past. Taiwan's investors, too, were put off by the uneven box-office records of the new directors. Most of their films lost money, although their mediocre financial performance had to do with Taiwan's limited market, which simply could not support so many directors at the same time. Paradoxically, the wealth of the Taiwanese posed one of the biggest threats to the film industry: instead of movies, people began to enjoy other recreational diversion such as TV, VCR, laser disc players, KTV, MTV, and various outdoor activities.

For whatever causes, New Taiwan Cinema as a cohesive concept was dead by 1987. Just when some film critics were about to moan the death of Taiwan cinema, Hou Hsiao-hsien's *A City of Sadness* brought home a Golden Lion at the 1989 Venice FF, an unprecedented honour in the history of Taiwan cinema. *A City of Sadness* continued all good qualities that made New Taiwan Cinema internationally known: reflection of a colonial past, long takes and static long-shots, off-screen voice-over, and the life of common people set against a background of political upheaval and financial deprivation.

In addition to these innovative styles, *A City of Sadness* was praised for its exposure of political taboos of Taiwan's past. After the lifting of martial law in 1987 and the implementation of various reform policies that followed the death of President Chiang Ching-kuo (Jiang Jingguo, 1910–88), *A City of Sadness* was the first film to confront the Incident of 28 February 1947, a massacre of Taiwanese activists by the Nationalist troops. The film is basically a **family** saga, since the family is the mirror and symbol of society in Chinese culture. It spans the years from 1945, which marked the end of the Japanese colonial period, to 1949, the year of the Communist takeover of mainland China and the establishment of Chiang Kai-shek's government-in-exile in Taiwan. Four sons of the Lin family met their fate tragically: the eldest is murdered; the second, mentally impaired after being classified as a traitor; the third, lost in the war after being drafted by the Japanese; the youngest, arrested for his involvement in the 28 February Incident.

Interestingly enough, Hou chose the youngest son, a deaf-mute, as the protagonist to witness the massacre. This daring decision reflects the historical irony that details of the Incident are not fully revealed by the government even today. It also foregrounds the dilemma of the Taiwanese at that time, being colonial subjects between Japan and China. Reactions from the audience varied. Some praised Hou's courage to address such an important historical event and believed he was doing the right thing. Some, on the other hand, thought that Hou was not sufficiently portraying the atrocity. As for Hou himself, *A City of Sadness* is an endeavour 'to understand who I am at a time when my country has embarked on the same quest [to redefine Taiwan's cultural identity]'.

Further reading

H. Chiao (1988), a major collection of articles on New Taiwan Cinema; R. Chen (1993a, b), two books on New Taiwan Cinema; Y. Li (1986a, b), two source books; S. Hoare (1993), on film adaptations of nativist literature; T. Sato (1992), a discussion of the New Wave.

5   Recent developments, 1990s

As *A City of Sadness* wrapped up a decade of vital, exciting change in Taiwan cinema, it also marked an optimistic beginning for the 1990s. The government set aside more funding than ever before to strengthen Taiwan's film industry. Starting from 1992, film was finally singled out for special protection as a 'cultural enterprise' and qualified for increased government support. A two-day national conference on film was held in 1992. More than 250 participants, including government officials, filmmakers and scholars, gathered to discuss problems related to the development of the film industry. The year 1993 was designated as the 'National Film Year'. Its idea was to give the industry another opportunity to deepen its roots and at the same time to expand its overseas markets.

All these efforts did lift the spirit of the film industry as a whole, resulting in the production of numerous quality films. Veteran directors and first-timers competed for awards at international film festivals around the world. Hou strengthened his status as an *auteur* with a number of new award-winning films, gaining a Georges Delerue award at Flanders FF for *The **Puppet Master*** (1993) and Best Film award at Asian FF for ***Good Men, Good Women*** (1995) and ***Goodbye, South, Goodbye*** (1996). In a semi-autobiographic style, *The Puppet Master* recounted the story of the real-life puppet master Li Tien-lu (*b.* 1909) during the Japanese occupation era. *Good Men, Good Women* continued the political thrust of *A City of Sadness* by tracing back to the Nationalist White Terror of the 1950s. And *Goodbye, South, Goodbye* brought us to the modern underworld of Taiwan. Hou seemed much more familiar with characters in the last film because they demonstrate that Taiwan is being devoured by greed, lust and violence.

Another veteran director, **Wang Tung** (*b.* 1942), released *The **Hills of No Return*** (1992) and thus completed his 'Taiwan Trilogy' – the other two being ***Strawman*** (1987) and ***Banana Paradise*** (1989). In 1993, *The Hills of No Return* won Best Film award at Taipei GHA and at Shanghai FF, as well as Special Jury prize at Singapore FF. Edward Yang's *A **Brighter Summer Day*** (1991), a story of juvenile delinquency in Taiwan of the 1950s, received Special Jury prize at Tokyo FF and Best Film award at Asian FF, both in 1991. Yang himself was awarded Best Director prize at the 1991 Nantes FF and at the 1992 Singapore FF. Yang's ***Mah-jong*** (1996), a satirical account of human relationships in modern Taipei, received Special Jury prize at Berlin FF and was compared to Woody Allen's *Manhattan* (1979) by some film critics.

More encouraging signs were found among new directors, sometimes called the 'second wave' of Taiwan New Cinema. **Tsai Ming-liang** worked for TV before moving into filmmaking. His first two films, ***Rebel of the Neon God*** (1992) and ***Vive l'amour*** (1994) probed the loneliness of young Taipei urbanites. *Rebel of the Neon God* was an intertwined story of four Taipei youths. No other terms could describe their state of mind better than boredom, alienation and self-annihilation. The film took Best Film award at the 1993 Turin FF and Special Jury prize at the Singapore FF, and made Tsai a cinematic spokesman for Generation X. Tsai's *Vive l'amour*, the winner of the second Golden Lion for Taiwan at the 1994 Venice FF, became an instant classic. It used only three main characters, who altogether spoke less than 100 lines of dialogue, and it contained no musical score throughout the film. At the end of the film, Tsai had the actress weeping for seven minutes in a long shot. Tsai's third feature, and the most depressing of the three, was *The River* (1997), which foretold the breakdown of the traditional patriarchal system in Taiwan. Three members in a family – the homosexual father, the mother and the son – did not appear together in the same frame until very late in the film. Near the end of the film, the son cruised a gay bath-house and was shocked to find his father giving him oral sex. The first film in Taiwan to depict such a taboo topic, it brought home a Silver Bear from the 1997 Berlin FF.

Another high-profile new director is Ang **Lee**, who had stayed at home writing screenplays for six years before being given a chance to direct his first film, *Pushing Hands* (1991). The film won Special Jury prize at Taipei GHA and Best Film award at Asian FF. Lee's next works, *The **Wedding Banquet*** (1992) and ***Eat Drink Man Woman*** (1994), proved even bigger successes. After *The Wedding Banquet* won a Golden Bear at the 1993 Berlin FF, both films successfully entered the art cinema market in Europe and North America. Lee's three films centred around Chinese family values. Thematic conflicts in these films (e.g., individual vs. family, modern vs. tradition, love vs. duty, East vs. West) appealed directly to modern audiences. Lee certainly knew how to mix Chinese culture with an international flavour that could be enjoyed at both a refined and a popular level. These films led Lee along the road to a Hollywood big-budget, international production, *Sense and Sensibility* (1995), an adaptation of Jane Austen's famous novel. This Western family drama was nominated for an Oscar as the Best Foreign Film.

Unlike Tsai Ming-liang and Ang Lee, Wu Nien-chen is more interested in **rural life**. A playwright turned director, Wu soberly and mildly reminisced about his miner father in his directorial début, *A Borrowed Life* (1994). The film succeeded in portraying a typical Japanese-educated father, familiar to Taiwanese audiences young and old. After winning Best Film award at Turin FF, Wu proceeded with his next project, *Buddha Bless America* (1996). A comic political satire, the film dramatized the ways in which a US military exercise had interrupted the life of innocent Taiwanese villagers and challenged a widely believed myth in the 1950s–60s: 'Everything is good and big in America'. Instead of looking at Taiwan's past with sadness and nostalgia (as in *A City of Sadness*), *Buddha Bless America* opened up a new possibility: critical reflection with laughter.

Tropical Fish (*dir.* Chen Yuxun, 1995) also brought forth rare laughter from the Taiwanese audience. Made by a former TV director, the film had two dumb gangsters coming directly from *Home Alone* (*dir.* Chris Columbus, 1990) who foiled an attempt to kidnap a rich child. The underlying message of *Tropical Fish* was intended for students who have suffered under the strict entrance examination system. Another film from a first-timer, *Ah Chung* (*dir.* Zhang Zuoji, 1997), tells of a youth who sacrificed himself for the sake of family, religious belief and peer pressure. The film won Special Jury prizes at Asian FF and Pusan FF in South Korea, and earned Best Director award at Thessaloniki FF in Greece.

Unfortunately, winning international awards has not stopped the slump in domestic ticket sales. Box-office failures give film investors a legitimate reason to transfer money to Hong Kong and mainland China, producing what they call the 'cinema of three Chinas'. The only hopes left for many young directors are first to apply for government funding, and then to find a theatre willing to show their films. As mentioned earlier, theatres in Taiwan have long been dominated by Hollywood and Hong Kong movies. In the 1990s, Taiwan produces an average of less than twenty films a year. Compared with its golden age in the 1960s–70s, the Taiwan film industry is indeed in a state of serious crisis. It remains to be seen when and how Taiwan cinema will recover from this precarious situation and continue in the next century.

See also: adaptations of drama and literature

Further reading

F. Chen (1988), a book of history; F. Chen (1994), a generational line-up of Taiwan directors; J. Cheng (1995), on the film industry in the 1990s; H. Chiao (1996a), three interviews on the Second Wave directors; T. Lee (1995), a study of Taiwan cinema of the 1990s; S. Lü (1961), the earliest book on Taiwan film history; S. Shen (1995), a report on changes in Taiwan film investment; F. Wang (1995), on the 'barren soil' of the film industry; W. Wang (1995), a collection of film reviews.

Transnational cinema: mainland China, Hong Kong and Taiwan

Yingjin Zhang

Transnational Chinese cinema is a critical term formulated in the early 1990s to account for the transnational capital flow in the making of many new Chinese films and to capture the changing nature of cultural, regional and geopolitical differences in Chinese filmmaking. One thing is evident from the three historical accounts of Chinese cinemas in the mainland, Hong Kong and Taiwan in the preceding pages: there is a long tradition of communication and cooperation between China and Hong Kong, between Hong Kong and Taiwan, and between Taiwan and the mainland.

In the 1920s–30s, close ties and friendly cooperation between Hong Kong and Shanghai film studios, especially Minxin, Lianhua, Mingxing and Tianyi, helped filmmakers in both places to bring their feature productions to the first golden age in Chinese film history. The flow of Hong Kong capital to Shanghai in the 1920s and the flow of Shanghai money and talents to Hong Kong during the war benefited the two cities. In terms of **genre films**, the long-standing Shanghai influences were visible in Hong Kong productions of not only the **martial arts film** but also a type of **historical film** that features **costume drama**. The second flow of Shanghai film people to Hong Kong in the late 1940s and the early 1950s brought in the **melodrama** that addresses a wide variety of **family** and social problems. **Zhu Shilin**'s film realism of the 1950s–60s, as embodied in *New Widow* (1956) and *Between Tears and Smiles* (1964), represents an uninterrupted continuation of the Shanghai realist tradition of the 1940s, in films like ***Eight Thousand Li of Cloud and Moon*** (*dir*. **Shi Dongshan**) and ***Spring River Flows East*** (*dir*. **Cai Chusheng**, **Zheng Junli**, both 1947). In Taiwan, when government studios resumed feature productions in the 1950s–60s, they relied on veteran directors, like Yuan Congmei (*b*. 1916) and Zhang Ying (*b*. 1919) who made their début in Chongqing in the 1940s, and thus ensured a continuity in the KMT propaganda tradition. The humanist concerns in non-partisan Shanghai studios like Wenhua, which produced ***Spring in a Small Town*** (*dir*. **Fei Mu**, 1948) and ***Sorrows and Joys of a Middle-Aged Man*** (*dir*. Sang Hu, 1949), were carried on in film romances in Taiwan, especially those based on **Chiung Yao**'s novels. Interestingly, after sweeping across the Taiwan and Hong Kong markets in the 1960s–70s, Chiung Yao films (and several TV series) were produced in the mainland in the 1980s, and some of them, like *Wanjun* and *The Silent Wife* (both 1987), are actually remakes of the same Taiwan titles (1964 and 1965, respectively).

On the other side, the influences of Hong Kong films in Taiwan are so strong that Hong Kong titles (classified as 'domestic' in Taiwan) have dominated the Taiwan market for decades. The names of two famous Hong Kong directors, King **Hu** and **Li Han-hsiang**, are associated with two dominant genres in Taiwan, the kungfu or **swordplay film** and costume drama, respectively. Because both directors made films in Taiwan as well, some Taiwan scholars would rather classify them as Taiwan directors. The 'traffic' of film people, however, is not just a one-way journey from Hong Kong to Taiwan. In fact, some Taiwan directors moved to Hong Kong and became famous there. One example is **Chang Che**, whose kungfu films produced in Hong Kong contributed to the genre's revival in the 1960s–70s. Besides, many superstars in Hong Kong were originally Taiwan actresses, such as Sylvia **Chang**, **Lin Ching Hsia** and Joey **Wong**.

After a long period of suspension, Hong Kong resumed its investment in the mainland in the 1980s. As they did in Taiwan, Hong Kong filmmakers brought in martial arts and historical films, and Li Han-hsiang took the lead with his costume dramas *The **Burning of the Imperial Palace*** and ***Reign Behind a Curtain*** (both 1983). Co-productions between Hong Kong and the mainland have increased dramatically since then, and Taiwan investors have been eager to channel their money through Hong Kong. By the early 1990s, the cooperation among those three areas has become so intertwined that sometimes it is hard to find distinctive regional styles. For instance, ***My American Grandson*** (1991), which had a Hong Kong woman director (Ann **Hui**), a Taiwan screenwriter (**Wu Nien-chen**), and mainland actors, resembles a Taiwan film; ***Five Girls and a Rope*** (1991; see *The **Wedding Maidens***), which had a Taiwan director (Yeh Hong-wei, *b.* 1963), mostly Taiwan actresses, but a mainland screenwriter (Ye Weilin), looks rather like a mainland **Fifth Generation** work. Indeed, co-productions have made the classification of a film's 'nationality' extremely difficult. For example, ***Farewell My Concubine*** (1993) may be classified as a mainland film according to the original 'nationality' of its director, **Chen Kaige**, who nevertheless resides in the USA. It may also be a Taiwan film according to the 'nationality' of its producer, **Hsu Feng**, an actress who made her name in King Hu's kungfu films. Or it may well be a Hong Kong film according to the 'nationality' of its registered production company, Tomson Film, through which the Taiwan investment was channelled to the mainland.

As is evident in the case of *Farewell My Concubine*, or earlier in ***Raise the Red Lantern*** (*dir.* **Zhang Yimou**, 1991), which was financed by Qiu Fusheng (*b.* 1947), who owns Era (Niandai) International based in Taiwan, film co-productions in the 1990s have led to a kind of cultural 'unification' prior to a 'political unification' – to quote Peggy Chiao, a leading film scholar in Taiwan – among the three Chinese areas. Films by mainland directors are routinely screened at annual Hong Kong FFs and Taipei GHAs. At the 1994 Taipei Golden Horse FF, for instance, these four films by mainland directors are listed as Hong Kong (and hence 'domestic') productions: *The **Story of Qiuju*** (*dir.* Zhang Yimou, 1992), ***Sparkling Fox*** (*dir.* **Wu Ziniu**, 1993), ***Back to Back, Face to Face*** (*dir.* **Huang Jianxin**), ***Red Firecracker, Green Firecracker*** (*dir.* **He Ping**, both 1994). These titles were programmed along with two Taiwan films and five other Hong Kong films by real Hong Kong directors. In the 1990s, at least one mainland actor (Xia Yu) and one actress (Joan **Chen**, who is now a Chinese-American) have won top prizes at Taipei GHAs, and Taiwan films have also been awarded prizes at mainland film festivals, such as those held in Shanghai and Zhuhai. Hong Kong superstars are big names on the mainland, too, and enjoy a regular fan magazine coverage. Several noted Hong Kong directors made co-productions in the mainland, such as **Yim Ho** with *The **Day the Sun Turned Cold*** (1994) and Ann Hui with *An **Interrupted Love*** (1997).

Somewhat surprisingly, a prominent figure who contributed to the increasing cooperation among filmmakers in the three Chinese areas is Christopher Doyle (*b.* 1952), or Du Kefeng as he is called in Chinese. Born in Australia, Doyle has established himself as one of the most sought after cinematographers in East Asia during the 1990s. He was behind the success of many critically acclaimed or award-winning art films. In Taiwan, he worked for Edward **Yang** on *That Day on the Beach* (1983) as well as for Stan **Lai** on *Peach Blossom Land* (1993) and *The Red Lotus Society* (1994); in Hong Kong, he worked for **Wong Kar-Wai** on *Days of Being Wild* (1991), *Chungking Express*, *Ashes of Time* (both 1994) and *Fallen Angels* (1995), as well as for Stanley **Kwan** on *Red Rose, White Rose* (1994); in mainland China, he was a co-producer of *Beijing Bastards* (*dir*. **Zhang Yuan**, 1993), an independent feature, and served as cameraman for **Chen Kaige**'s *Temptress Moon* (1995).

Considering the long list of Chinese films that won prestigious **awards** at Cannes, Berlin, Venice and other international FF, Chinese cinema has become truly international in its impact. A number of new mainland directors, such as **Ning Ying**, **Wang Xiaoshuai** and Zhang Yuan, were able to shoot films because they received awards or grants from international film festivals. As a result, their films are more likely to be exhibited in Hong Kong, Taiwan and the West than in mainland China. Meanwhile, a new development in the mid-1990s is the emigration of Hong Kong talents to the West. Noted directors John **Woo**, Ringo **Lam** and **Tsui Hark** moved to the USA and directed Hollywood action films. Action superstars **Chow Yun-Fat**, Jet **Li** and Michelle **Yeoh** soon followed suit. Clara **Law** and Eddie Fong (*b.* 1954) moved to Melbourne. The former directed *Floating Life* in 1996, Australia's first foreign-language feature. Examples like these demonstrate that the transnational aspects of filmmaking in mainland China, Hong Kong and Taiwan need to be fully assessed in conjunction with the intra-cultural and inter-regional factors that combine to make contemporary Chinese cinema a fascinating subject to study.

See also: action film; art film; independent film; kungfu film; propaganda and film; romance; social problems, films of

Further reading
H. Chiao (1991a, b), two studies of Hong Kong and Taiwan films; H. Chiao (1993c), an informative piece on cooperations among the three areas; HKIFF (1994, 1995), on the relationships between Hong Kong and Shanghai or China in general; S. Lu (1997a), a collection of essays on the transnational aspects of Chinese filmmaking; E. Yau (1993), on 'international fantasy' and new Chinese cinema.

Chinese film in the West

Yingjin Zhang

Since the mid-1980s, Chinese film has made a strong impact in the West (i.e., Europe, North America and Australia). Chinese films from the mainland, Hong Kong and Taiwan have won film **awards** at international film festivals such as Berlin, Cannes, Locarno, Montreal, Nantes, Persaro, Rotterdam, Tokyo, Toronto, Turin, and Venice. Mainland and Taiwan art films, Hong Kong gangster, martial arts and **comedy** films were regularly screened in art-theatre houses in the West. Some were successfully marketed by the commercial theatre chains and earned huge profits, such as ***Farewell My Concubine*** (*dir*. **Chen Kaige**, 1993) and ***Eat Drink Man Woman*** (*dir*. Ang **Lee**, 1994).

There is a long tradition of film-cultural exchange between China and the West. The Hollywood presence in Shanghai was a significant factor in the Chinese film market during the 1920s–40s. Although Hollywood has never dominated Hong Kong the way it did in old Shanghai, it began to hit the Taiwan market once the government lifted its import quota for foreign film there. Newly released Hollywood films can be seen in Taiwan and Hong Kong with Chinese subtitles. In the mid-1990s, the mainland government began to import 'ten major foreign films' each year, most of them Hollywood titles, such as *The Fugitive* (*dir*. Andrew Davis, 1993), *Forrest Gump* (*dir*. Robert Zemeckis, 1994), *Die Hard with a Vengeance* (*dir*. John McTiernan, 1995) and *Broken Arrow* (*dir*. John **Woo**, 1996). These dubbed foreign films (in Chinese soundtrack) enjoy a popularity rarely obtained by the majority of domestic features. Nevertheless, the fact that the director of *Broken Arrow* is originally from Hong Kong points to an East–West film exchange from the opposite direction.

As evident in the three historical accounts of Chinese film in the mainland, Hong Kong and Taiwan in the preceding pages, many early Chinese filmmakers had the Western world in mind when they started business. ***Zhuangzi Tests His Wife*** (*dir*. **Li Beihai**, 1913), the first Hong Kong short feature, is reputedly also the first Chinese film ever to be exported to the West. Other silent titles, such as ***Cheng the Fruit Seller*** (*dir*. **Zhang Shichuan**, 1922) and ***Song of China*** (*dir*. **Fei Mu**, **Luo Mingyou**, 1935), carried both Chinese and English subtitles, presumably for export purposes (a videotape version of the latter is now available at Facets Multimedia, Inc. in Chicago, the USA). ***Romance of the Western Chamber*** (*dir*. **Hou Yao**, 1927), the film adaptation of a classic Chinese drama, was given a promotional English title, *Way Down West*, to invoke the famous *Way Down East* (*dir*. D.W. Griffith, 1920) in Shanghai audiences familiar with Western films. Translated in French as *La Rose de Pu-Chui*, *Romance of the Western Chamber* was screened in Paris from 20 April to 3 June 1928 – concurrently with *Ben-Hur* (*dir*. Fred Niblo, 1926) and *Joyless Streets* (*dir*. G.W. Pabst, 1922), the latter a German film.

The export of Chinese films to be screened in Chinese communities in Southeast Asian countries is a practice as old as the Chinese film industries, especially in Hong Kong. But the export of Chinese films to the English-speaking audiences in the West did not constitute a significant trend until the 1970s, when King **Hu** and **Chang Che** revived the **martial arts film** in Hong Kong and Taiwan. Soon, Bruce **Lee**, who grew up in the USA and became a kungfu superstar in Hong Kong, enjoyed a worldwide reputation for his impressive performance in such titles as *Fist of Fury* (*dir.* Lo Wei, 1972) and ***Enter the Dragon*** (*dir.* Robert Clouse, 1973). After Lee's untimely death in 1973, his screen image as a kungfu master was taken over by another Hong Kong star, Jackie **Chan**. Chan made himself a more likeable screen idol by softening Lee's seriousness in fighting and blending comic elements into the genre. Chan's success in the West is best exemplified in his ***Rumble in the Bronx*** (*dir.* Stanley Tong, 1994).

Chan has helped to bring Western attention to another genre, the gangster film, which has long been the staple of the Hong Kong film industry. The most notable directors of this genre include John **Woo**, Ringo **Lam** and **Tsui Hark**. Hong Kong superstars like Jackie Chan, **Chow Yun-Fat** and Michelle **Yeoh** have fascinated the world with their thrilling performances. They have become cult figures in the West, and their photos regularly appear in Western fan magazines. So successful is the Hong Kong gangster film that the three major directors named above moved to the USA and started shooting Hollywood action films, such as *Hard Target* (*dir.* John Woo, 1993) and *Maximum Risk* (*dir.* Ringo Lam, 1996). These directors were soon joined by action Hong Kong superstars Chow Yun-Fat and Michelle Yeoh.

The traffic of film people to the West also occurred in Taiwan and mainland China. Ang **Lee**, who grew up in Taiwan and was trained in the USA, made his directorial début in

Plate 4   *Rumble in the Bronx* (1994)

Taiwan and won international acclaim with *The **Wedding Banquet*** (1992) and *Eat Drink Man Woman* (1994). He returned to the USA and directed *Sense and Sensibility* (1995), which won a Golden Bear at the 1996 Berlin FF. Joan **Chen**, a mainland actress who won Best Actress award at the 1980 HFA, went to the USA and starred in *The Last Emperor* (*dir.* Bernardo Bertolucci, 1987), the TV series *Twin Peaks* (*dir.* David Lynch *et al.*, 1990), and other titles. She returned to Asia to play lead roles in *The **Temptation of a Monk*** (*dir.* Clara **Law**, 1993) and *Red Rose, White Rose* (*dir.* Stanley **Kwan**, 1994). Chen's co-star in *The Last Emperor*, John Lone (Zun Long, *b.* 1952), has also appeared in many films produced in Hong Kong and in the West, such as *Year of the Dragon* (*dir.* Michael Cimino, 1985), *Shanghai 1920* (*dir.* Leong Po-chih, 1991) and *M. Butterfly* (*dir.* David Cronenberg, 1993). Another actress from *The Last Emperor*, Vivian Wu (*b.* 1969), who was born in Shanghai, went on to star in *The Joy Luck Club* (*dir.* Wayne Wang, 1993) and *The Pillow Book* (*dir.* Peter Greenaway, 1997). In addition, Jet **Li**, a mainland martial arts champion who became a superstar in Hong Kong, has also reportedly worked on Hollywood films such as *Black Mask* (1997).

Parallel to the Western 'discovery' of contemporary Chinese film talents, another kind of discovery took place in the early 1980s, this time early Chinese films. The China Film Archive in Beijing cooperated with its European counterparts and organized several film retrospectives, showcasing Chinese films of the 1920s–40s in Western Europe and North America. Some of the retrospectives have resulted in the publication of festival catalogues with detailed listings of film synopses and biographic entries. In the 1980s–90s, Chinese films produced in the mainland, Hong Kong and Taiwan are regularly invited to participate in international film festivals, and many of them have won top prizes.

Apart from showcasing their films in the West, Chinese filmmakers also make co-productions with other countries. *The Kite* (*dir.* Wang Jiayi, Roger Pico, 1958), is a children's **fantasy film** co-produced with France. ***Red Cherry*** (*dir.* Ye Daying, 1995), a co-production with Russia with Chinese and English subtitles, scored a domestic box-office record in the mainland. Other than co-productions with the West, Chinese directors occasionally made films outside the Chinese-speaking communities. As early as the 1930s, *Singing Lovers* (*dir.* Moon **Kwan**, 1934) was produced by Grandview (Daguan) Film based in San Francisco. Obviously an exceptional case, *Singing Lovers* foreshadows an alternative mode of film production for Chinese filmmakers, especially those who left their homelands in the 1980s–90s. For instance, Dai Sijie, a little known Chinese director in France, shot ***China, My Sorrow*** (1989), a politically sensitive feature about the **Cultural Revolution**. Chen Kaige, eminent member of China's **Fifth Generation**, raised funds in the West to produce his avant-garde film, ***Life on a String*** (1991). Clara Law, who had emigrated with her screenwriter-director husband Eddie Fong (*b.* 1954) from Hong Kong to Melbourne in the early 1990s, made *Floating Life* (1996), Australia's first foreign-language feature. In numerous other less known cases, Chinese emigrés (e.g., Mabel Cheung (*b.* 1950) and **Peng Xiaolian**) have made documentaries and short features in the West.

By the mid-1990s, it is clear that Chinese film, in addition to attaining a solid international reputation, has also gone transnational in filmmaking, film **distribution** and exhibition. Such a new international and transnational aspect of Chinese film is perfectly embodied in the figure of **Zhang Yimou**, a mainland director who has won a Golden Bear and a Golden Lion, as well as two Oscar nominations for Best Foreign Film. His films are regularly financed by investors from Taiwan, Hong Kong and Japan. In 1996, he was invited by an Italian producer to direct a film based on Puccini's *Turandot*.

See also: adaptations of drama and literature; art film; avant-garde, experimental or exploratory film; children's film; documentary; dubbed foreign film; gangster film; kungfu film

Further reading

R. Armes (1987), on third world film and the West; R. Bergeron (1996/97), experience with Chinese film in Europe; M. Dolcini (1978), a collection of essays on Chinese cinema; Eder and Rossell (1993), *Ombre elettriche* (1982), *Ombres électriques* (1982), Quiquemell and Passek (1985), Rayns and Meek (1980), all European festival programmes or collections on Chinese films.

Foreign films in China

Zhiwei Xiao

Film was introduced into China by Westerners in the late nineteenth century. Since then, China's film market had been dominated by foreign films until 1950 when the PRC adopted a policy that opposed Western cultural influence. Although domestic film production began as early as 1905, the chronic shortage of capital, technical personnel and political instability prevented the domestic film industry from being competitive in the market. Hence, imported foreign films flooded China's big cities.

In the 1900s–20s, three types of Western films came to China in tandem. First, it was the detective films and thrillers that attracted Chinese audiences during the 1910s. Then, with the end of World War I, war films and films about the military prowess of the Western countries became the box-office attractions in the 1920s. Finally, the human drama of love and **romance** gained unrivalled popularity among the Chinese audience from the mid-1920s. Stars such as Charlie Chaplin, Harold Lloyd, Douglas Fairbanks and Lilian Gish were familiar household names to many urban Chinese.

Under the old unequal treaty system, China did not have control over its customs and could not impose any restrictions on the quantity of the imported foreign films. As a result, films of foreign origin dominated China's film market until the late 1940s. While Hollywood productions had the largest market share, French, English and German films also had a significant following. Sometimes they competed with each other. Americans frequently complained that the British authorities in the International Settlement jealously protected their films by subjecting American productions to the most stringent censorship. In reality, there was a certain intrinsic quality about Hollywood films that had more mass appeal than European films in general. Not surprisingly, it was also the Americans who took the lead in the effort to build 'Hollywood of the East' in Shanghai. Although the plan was aborted, partly at least because of the resistance from the nationalistic Chinese filmmakers, the scheme was indicative of Hollywood's interest and enthusiasm in tapping the China market. For most of the first half of the twentieth century, Hollywood maintained an unrivalled position in China. Major film studios such as Paramount, Universal and Columbia all had branch offices in China. During the Pacific War, Western (including American) films disappeared from China. Despite a drastic increase in number, Japanese films never totally dominated China's film market as Hollywood had done. When the war was over in 1945, Western films regained control of China's film market.

Although the KMT government tried to protect the domestic film industry by implementing a series of policies aimed at curbing the influence of foreign films, these policies had little impact because China did not have control over its customs until after the outbreak of Pacific War.

Plate 5   Hollywood films in Shanghai

After the war, the KMT government was engaged in a civil war with the Communists and heavily dependent on US military support. Hence it was in no position to stop American films from flooding China's market again.

After the founding of the PRC government, the Communists immediately published *Temporary Regulations Regarding the Importation of Foreign Films* in July 1950, which proposed restrictions on imported foreign films. By October 1950 the Korean War had broken out and the CCP government imposed a total ban on American films. At the same time, a large number of films from the former Soviet Union and Eastern European countries were introduced to a Chinese audience. But because the domestic film industry also increased its output from the mid-1950s, the proportion of Soviet films in the overall film market fell far below the level achieved by Hollywood in the pre-1949 period. By the early 1960s, as Sino-Soviet relations began to deteriorate, Soviet and other Eastern European films were gradually disappearing from China.

The fact is that the Communist regime never stopped importing foreign films. During the 1960s and the early 1970s, a small number of films from 'fraternal' socialist countries, such as North Korea, Romania, Albania and Vietnam, were shown in China. However, although Western and Soviet films were banned to the public, high-ranking officials, film scholars and a few filmmakers trusted by the government continued to enjoy the privilege of viewing those films in private screenings.

After the **Cultural Revolution**, Western films were reintroduced to the Chinese audience. Initially preference was given to those films that were critical of the capitalist system. For instance, they might portray the dark side of Western society or deal with political corruption in Western governments. Gradually the list expanded to include films on neutral subjects, such as romance and World War II. As economic reform picked up its pace, the restriction on foreign films began to relax. In 1984 the Chinese government co-sponsored with the US Embassy in China an American Film Week. Five American films, *Star Wars* (*dir.* George Lucas), *The Turning Point* (*dir.* Herbert Ross, both 1977), *On Golden Pond* (*dir.* Mark Rydell, 1981), *Kramer vs. Kramer* (*dir.* Robert Benton, 1979) and *Coal Miner's Daughter* (*dir.* Michael Apted, 1980), were selected for this occasion and went on a five-city tour in China. Somewhat to the surprise of American scholars, among these five films, *Kramer vs. Kramer*, not *Star Wars*, was best liked by Chinese audiences.

Despite its new open door policy, the Chinese government continued to impose a quota system and limited the number of foreign films for public screening. The purpose was to protect the domestic film industry. A major shift in policy took place in 1994 when the Ministry of Broadcasting, Film and Television (MBFT) decided to import ten major foreign titles each year. It was a substantial change because, until then, foreign films shown in China had been limited to a few 'oldies' and contemporary B movies. Now, films such as *The Fugitive* (*dir.* Andrew Davis, 1993), *Forrest Gump* (*dir.* Robert Zemeckis) and *True Lies* (*dir.* James Cameron, both 1994), were shown in China shortly after they premièred in the USA. Their enormous popularity among the Chinese audience stimulated a new interest in movie going, although at the same time they also put tremendous pressure on domestic film production. As China strives to enter the World Trade Organization in the late 1990s, the future of foreign films in China looks bright indeed.

See also: censorship and film; detective film; Hong Kong cinema (in Historical Essays); love and marriage; Taiwan cinema (in Historical Essays); thriller; war film

Further reading
M. Cambon (1995), a study of American films in Shanghai prior to 1949.

Part II
Main entries

action film

A type of film that revels excessively in scenes of action such as car chases, gun fights and other kinds of physical stunts, violence and bloodshed. For over fifty years in Chinese film history, the action film has never been a popular genre, partly because of an entrenched Chinese preference for theatricality and narrative plot, and partly because of a persistent emphasis on the moral function of entertainment throughout most of the twentieth century. If one really insists on a typically Chinese type of action in the early period, then martial arts or **kungfu film** may perhaps qualify as a sibling of the action film in the West. However, even that qualification begs the question, for in a majority of Chinese martial arts films up to the 1970s, the triumph of moral integrity is usually given priority over the mere spectacle of kungfu fights.

In the minds of Western viewers, Chinese action films may be closely associated with, or even largely equivalent to, gangster films from Hong Kong. This association is correct as far as one has in mind the dominant influence the Hong Kong genre has exerted on the markets of both Taiwan and mainland China since the 1980s. To understand the Chinese action film, therefore, one has to know much more about Hong Kong gangster films.

Indeed, that Hong Kong has invested so heavily in the production of gangster films should come as no surprise. After all, crime films are popular in all capitalist societies. The genre provides filmmakers with a useful means of exploring themes of class mobility and male bonding, the maintenance of social boundaries and the limits of state power. The specifically Chinese variant of the gangster figure – the Triad, or Tong – has been the subject of countless Hong Kong productions since the mid-1980s.

At the same time, Hong Kong has probably been plagued by more gangster activity inside the movie industry than has any other film-producing region. The Triads' show business connections stretch notoriously far, run notoriously deep. Numerous acts of mob violence against stars, managers, producers, and directors have provided tabloid newspapers with a steady stream of lurid headlines. But the industry has at times fought back. In January 1992, for example, a mass demonstration against Triad involvement in the Hong Kong film industry drew appearances by such superstars as Jackie **Chan**, Joey **Wong**, **Chow Yun-Fat** and Amy Yip.

Most Hong Kong gangster films are routine generic products. However, a few have distinguished themselves through conceptual or stylistic innovation. One of the more intelligent contributions remains Johnny **Mak**'s *Long Arm of the Law* (1984), and one of the more successful, John **Woo**'s *A Better Tomorrow* (1986). While the former dealt head-on with troubling political issues, the latter promoted the gangster to tragic romantic figure by transposing chivalric values into the late capitalist world. Along with subsequent John Woo classics such as *The Killer* (1989) and *Hard Boiled* (1993), any list of other notable Hong Kong gangster films must include *As Tears Go By* (*dir.* **Wong Kar-Wai**, 1988), *City on Fire* (1987), *Full Contact* (1992, both *dir.* Ringo **Lam**), *A Moment of Romance* (*dir.* Benny Chan, 1990), and *Tiger on the Beat* (*dir.* Liu Chia Liang, 1988).

As a sub-strand of the gangster film, the true-life crime drama has also proved popular. Sometimes called 'Big Time' films, titles like *To Be Number One* (*dir.* Poon Man Kit, 1992) and *Queen of the Underworld* (*dir.* Sherman Wong, 1993) feature the added attraction of historical verisimilitude. Hong Kong gangster films are also of note for their gender politics. The genre may have taken male

Plate 6   *Project A* (1984)

bonding to new levels of suggestiveness, but it has also, like the martial arts and detective films before it, provided a space for the depiction of strong women warriors. For each of the genre's male icons (Chow Yun-Fat, Andy **Lau**, Shing Fui-On) stands a female counterpart (Jade Leung, Michelle **Yeoh**, Yukari Oshima). Such an encouraging development, however, should not disguise the fact that Hong Kong gangster films remain predominantly boys' own fare.

While Hong Kong gangster films have been popular in Taiwan since the mid-1980s, the genre's influence became visible in mainland China with the release of two 'frenzy' (*fengkuang*) thrillers directed by **Zhou Xiaowen**, an emerging figure of China**'s Fifth Generation**. Zhou's **Desperation** (*co-dir.* Shi Chenfeng, 1987) and *The* **Price of Frenzy** (1988) surprised audiences with their focus on bloodthirsty criminals and the victims' or the police's irrational urge for revenge. With **Bloodshed at Dusk** (*dir.* **Sun Zhou**, 1989) and other similar titles, the new genre quickly established itself as a stalwart of an industry plagued by the fear of financial bankruptcy in an era of economic reforms. What is more interesting, Hong Kong investments soon poured into mainland studios, and co-productions

such as *Presumed Guilty* (*dir.* Zhou Xiaowen, 1993) regularly feature Hong Kong and mainland stars (e.g., **Jiang Wen**) in the 1990s.

See also: detective film; gangster film; martial arts film; westerns

Further reading

B. Ryan (1995), on Hong Kong gangster films and Chineseness; R. Baker and T. Russell (1994), F. Dannen and B. Long (1997), S. Hammond and M. Wilkins (1996), B. Logan (1996), T. Weisser (1997), all with listings of specific titles.

(JS, YZ)

Actress, The
aka *Centre Stage* (Ruan Lingyu)

dir. Stanley **Kwan**
sc. Chiao Hsiung-ping, Qiu-Dai Anping
with Maggie **Cheung**, Tony Kar-Fei **Leung**,
Chin Hong, Carina Lau, Lawrence Ng
Hong Kong: Golden Harvest/Golden Way
Films, 1992

Also known as *Centre Stage*, *The Actress* is ostensibly a **biography** or 'bio-pic' about the great Chinese film star **Ruan Lingyu**. However, the film is formally and thematically so complex a Brechtian example of meta-cinema that it constitutes a radical reworking of both genre and subject matter. On top of that, its mix of unusual scene transitions, flash-forwards, and non-simultaneous voice-overs makes it extremely difficult to segment.

The Actress recounts Ruan's public and private affairs in the years immediately leading up to her premature death. She gives a number of famous performances for Shanghai's Lianhua studios, starring in films like *Wild Flower* (1930), *Little Toys* (1933, both *dir.* **Sun Yu**), *Goddess* (*dir.* **Wu Yonggang**) and *New Woman* (*dir.* **Cai Chusheng**, both 1934). Ruan lives with her mother and adopted daughter, and enjoys a number of other female friendships, such as with the celebrated actress **Li Lili**. However, her personal relationships with her estranged husband, Tang Shichan, and her lover, Chang Damin, cause scandal among high society. Unable to bear the gossip any longer, Ruan commits suicide at the age of twenty-five.

Apart from recounting these events in sumptuous detail, *The Actress* also features colour and black-and-white documentary footage of the 1990s Hong Kong production crew shooting the reconstructions, scenes where director Stanley Kwan interviews his leading stars about the historical figures they are impersonating, extracts from Ruan's original movies, and interviews with her contemporaries from the 1930s Shanghai film industry. For her performance as Ruan Lingyu, Maggie Cheung won a number of prestigious awards, including a Silver Bear for Best Actress at the 1992 Berlin FF.

Further reading

J. Stringer (1997a), on the reconstruction of the bio-pic.

(JS)

adaptations of drama and literature

From its inception at the turn of the twentieth century, Chinese film was intimately related to drama and theatre, as the earliest Chinese designation of film, 'Western shadowplay' (*xiyang yingxi*), clearly demonstrates. Since the 'play' or theatre (as real substance embedded in age-old Chinese tradition) was deemed essential to the film (a new technology imported from the West), early

Chinese filmmakers emphasized not only the performance (*xi*) but also the script (*ben*, literally 'root' or 'base') from which performance derives. Even today, it makes perfect sense to speak of scripts as 'film literature' (*dianying wenxue*) in China, as if the status of literature itself guarantees film's treatment as a serious art form.

Many short features produced in the 1900s–10s were either **filmed stage performances**, such as *Conquering Jun Mountain* (1905), or adapted 'civilized play' (*wenming xi*, a type of modern drama developed under the Japanese influence), such as those produced by **Zhang Shichuan** for Asia Film Company. In the 1920s–30s, several noted dramatists, including **Zheng Zhengqiu**, **Hong Shen**, **Ouyang Yuqian**, **Tian Han** and **Xia Yan**, were actively involved in filmmaking, and it was natural for them to turn to dramatic adaptation. During the same period, many writers of popular 'Mandarin Ducks and Butterflies' fiction also entered the film industry, adapting or reinventing their sentimental or supernatural stories. In the 1940s, adaptation of drama and literature continued as a popular practice. For instance, the film *Night Inn* (*dir.* **Huang Zuolin**, 1947) was adapted from a Chinese play of the same title (written by Ke Ling and Shi Tuo), which was in turn adapted from the Russian writer Gorky's play, *The Lower Depths* (1902).

After 1949, adaptations of literary classics (*mingzhu gaibian*) gradually became a genre in the mainland. *New Year's Sacrifice* (*dir.* **Sang Hu**, 1956), a famous story by Lu Xun, was adapted by Xia Yan, who had adapted Mao Dun's story *Spring Silkworms* (*dir.* **Cheng Bugao**, 1933) while launching a leftist film movement in the early 1930s. By the mid-1980s, one could see an impressive list of literary adaptations: from Cao Yu's, *Savage Land* (*dir.* Ling Zi, 1981), *Sunrise* (*dir.* Yu Benzheng, 1985) and *Thunderstorm* (*dir.* **Sun Daolin**, 1984); from Lao She's *This Life of Mine* (*dir.* **Shi Hui**, 1950), *Camel Xiangzi* (*dir.* **Ling Zifeng**, 1982), *The Teahouse* (*dir.* **Xie Tian**, 1982) and *Drum Singers* (*dir.* **Tian Zhuangzhuang**, 1987); from Lu Xun's *Medicine* (*dir.* Lu Shaolian, 1981), *Regret for the Past* (*dir.* **Shui Hua**, 1981) and *The True Story of Ah Q* (*dir.* Cen Fan, 1981); from Mao Dun's *The Lin Family Shop* (*dir.* Shui Hua, 1959) and *Midnight* (*dir.* Sang Hu, 1981); and from Shen Congwen's *Border Town* (*dir.* Ling Zifeng, 1984) and *A Girl from Hunan* (*dir.* **Xie Fei**, 1986), among others.

Plate 7   *The Lin Family Shop* (1959)

In the early 1980s, adaptations of nativist literature (*xiangtu wenxue*) played a major role in the revitalization of Taiwanese cinema. Adapted from Hwang Chun-ming's stories, the three-part **Sandwich Man** (*dir.* **Hou Hsiao-hsien**, **Tseng Chuang-hsiang**, **Wan Jen**, 1983) was a major early work of New Taiwan Cinema. Literary adaptations proved popular in Hong Kong, too, as evidenced by the numerous adaptations of works by Shen Congwen, Lu Xun, and Ba Jin in the 1950s–60s, such as *Cui Cui* (*dir.* Yan Jun, 1952), *The True Story of Ah Q* (*dir.* Yuan Yang'an, 1958), and *Between Tears and Smiles* (*dir.* **Zhu Shilin**, 1964). Since the mid-1980s, two female writers have attracted most attention: Eileen Chang from 1940s Shanghai – *Love in the Fallen City* (1984), *An Interrupted Love* (1997, both *dir.* Ann **Hui**), and *Red Rose, White Rose* (*dir.* Stanley **Kwan**, 1994); and Lilian Lee (Li Bihua) from 1980s–90s Hong Hong – **Rouge** (*dir.* Stanley Kwan, 1987), *The* **Reincarnation of Golden Lotus** (*dir.* Clara **Law**, 1989), **Farewell My Concubine** (*dir.* **Chen Kaige**, 1993) and *Green Snake* (*dir.* **Tsui Hark**, 1993). In the 1990s, many of the internationally successful films with mainland directors have been based on contemporary literary works, but they sometimes appear to be reinventions rather than adaptations, as is the case with **Zhang Yimou**'s **Ju Dou** (1990) and **Raise the Red Lantern** (1991).

See also: filmed stage performances; leftist film (under Chinese cinema in Historical essays); the musical; New Taiwan Cinema (under Taiwan cinema in Historical essays); theatre and film

Further reading

S. Hoare (1993), a study of Taiwan film and literature; Z. Zhang (1999), a discussion of the influence of teahouse culture on film.

(YZ)

After Separation

(Da saba)

dir. **Xia Gang**
sc. Feng Xiaogang, Zheng Xiaolong
with Ge You, Xu Fan, Zhang Huizhong, Liu Yi
Beijing: Beijing Film, 1992

The film starts inside the airport. Gu Yan bids farewell to his wife, who is going to Canada to study. A man's screaming brings Gu's attention to a woman who lies unconscious on the floor. The man is about to take an international trip and entrusts the woman to Gu. In the hospital, Gu learns that the woman, named Lin Zhouyun, is pregnant and her husband wants her to have an abortion. Back in his apartment, Gu feels lonely and deserted. The trend of going abroad for advanced degrees has left him and many others in an uneasy situation. He wants to talk to Lin, who is nevertheless determined to join her husband in Canada.

A year passes. On the eve of the Chinese New Year, Gu and Lin meet unexpectedly near the telephone booths. They have tried to call their spouses abroad but both have failed. To get over their lone-liness, Gu suggests that they 'play' the roles of husband and wife and enjoy their five-day vaca-tion. While cooking and chatting together, both feel the warmth of family life. A sense of loss dawns on them when they part. Gu and Lin feel close to each other. When the documents arrive for Lin to apply for the Canadian visa, she is rather reluctant to go. Meanwhile, Gu's wife has filed for divorce and hired a Chinese lawyer to bring compensation money to Gu. The lawyer comforts Gu by saying that he himself is in the same kind of situation. The film ends in a farewell scene in the airport. Lin expects Gu to persuade her not to join her husband in Canada. She even pretends she has lost her passport, which Gu finds in his own pocket. With a bitter smile, Gu sees Lin off to the gate, as he did three years ago when his ex-wife departed.

After Separation is a **melodrama** on contem-porary **urban life** in mainland China. Ge You's comic performance makes this sentimental film enjoyable.

(IJS)

Ah Ying

(Qian Defu, Qian Xingcun)

b. 6 February 1900, Anhui province
d. 17 June 1977
Screen writer

Ah Ying was one of the most influential play-wrights of modern China. Besides his involvement in theatre, he wrote screenplays and film criticism. Ah Ying worked as a postman and taught Chinese before enrolling in Shanghai College of Architecture. He joined the CCP in 1926 and was a founding member of the Left League of Writers in 1929. Because of his acquaintance with **Zhou Jianyun**, one of the general managers of Mingxing Film Company, Ah Ying was able to bring a group of leftist filmmakers into the studio in the early 1930s.

Ah Ying contributed greatly to the Leftist Cinema Movement through his activities as a screenwriter. He wrote *The Year of Harvest* (*dir.* **Li Pingqian**, 1933), often regarded as his best work, and co-authored *The Uprising* (*dir.* **Xu Xinfu**, 1933) with Zheng Boqi, *Children of Our Time* (*dir.* Li Pingqian, 1933) with **Xia Yan** and Zheng Boqi, *Three Sisters* (*dir.* Li Pingqian, 1934), and *A Bible for Girls* (*dir.* **Zhang Shichuan** *et al.*, 1934) with Xia

Yan, **Zheng Zhengqiu** and **Hong Shen**. The films Ah Ying scripted or co-scripted are all highly critical of social conditions in China and, by exten-sion, of the KMT regime.

During the Sino-Japanese war of 1937–45, Ah Ying wrote three plays on resistance themes. In addition, he edited a special issue of the liter-ary magazine *Documents* (Wenxian), highlighting Japan's ambitions to take over the Chinese film industry. Partly as a result of such allegations, Ah Ying had to leave Shanghai in 1941 in order to escape arrest. His departure from Shanghai also put to an end his involvement with film-making. His attempts at screenwriting after 1949 were never successful. He died of cancer in 1977 after suffering political persecution during the **Cultural Revolution**.

Further reading
ZDX (1982–6: 1: 76–83), a short biography.

(ZX)

Along the Sungari River

(Songhua jiang shang)

dir./sc. **Jin Shan**
with **Zhang Ruifang**, Wang Renlu
Changchun: Changchun Film, 1947

This is one of the first feature films produced by the CCP. The story is set against the background of the Japanese occupation of Manchuria and focuses on heroic Chinese resistance to Japanese rule.

Niu'er's father runs a highway tavern in Manchuria. Niu'er is particularly fond of a young wagon driver who frequents the tavern, but every-thing changes when the Japanese take Manchuria over. Both Niu'er's parents are killed by the Japanese, and her grandfather and her lover are forced to build a blockhouse for the invaders. Niu'er brings food to the construction site and catches the attention of a Japanese officer. He follows Niu'er home and attempts to rape her, but her lover arrives and kills the perpetrator. The Japanese burn down their tavern in retaliation. Niu'er, together with her lover and grandfather, flees the village. Evading the enemy, they manage to arrive in a mining town after several days on the road. While the young man finds mining work, the grandfather collapses and dies.

The Japanese cruelty towards the Chinese miners causes much resentment among the workers. After a disastrous accident kills over sixty workers, the survivors and families of the victims demand better working conditions. The demonstration turns into a violent conflict with management. The Japanese guards open fire at the crowd. Niu'er and her husband fight back. As they are being chased by the pursuing Japanese soldiers, Chinese resistance forces come to their rescue. In the end, Niu'er and her husband join the guerrillas fighting the Japanese.

(ZX)

animation

Animated film in China includes three types of artistic creation – cartoon, puppet film, and paper-cut film. Drawing on a wealth of fairy tales, folk literature, as well as **legends and myths**, animation offers lovely pictures and imaginative stories and is specially appealing to young audiences.

In the 1920s, the Wan brothers from Nanjing – **Wan Laiming**, Wan Guchan *(b.* 1899), Wan Chaochen *(b.* 1906) and Wan Dihuan – experimented in a cramped Shanghai room and produced the first Chinese cartoon, *Turmoil in a Workshop* (1926). From the late 1920s to the late 1930s, they worked in film studios such as Great Wall (Changcheng), Great China (Da Zhonghua), Lianhua, Mingxing and China Motion Picture Studio (Zhongzhi) of Wuhan, and produced seventeen patriotic short cartoons. It was not until 1941 that they created the first feature-length cartoon, **Princess Iron Fan**, in Shanghai's French Concession. Although the film was a box-office hit in Japanese-occupied Shanghai and was well received in Japan and in Southeast Asia, the Wan brothers had to abandon their animation work in the wake of the Pacific War. After years of sojourn in Hong Kong, the Wan brothers returned to Shanghai in the 1950s.

When the Communists took over Northeast Film Studio, they produced two animations in 1947–8. From 1949 to 1956, twenty-two animations were made, most of them by a special section within Shanghai Film Studio. In 1957, the government established Shanghai Animation Studio as a separate institution, which led to an impressive output of 103 animations in a decade. The new institution successfully brought forth new artistic

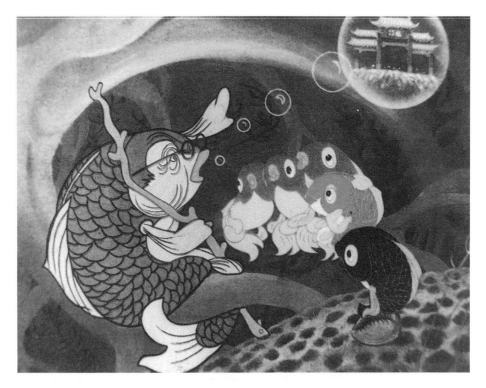

Plate 8   *Little Carps Jump Over the Dragon Gate* (1958)

products: *Zhu Bajie Eats the Watermelon* (*dir.* Wan Guchan, Chen Zhenghong, 1958), the first animated paper-cut film; *Little Duckling* (1960), the first animated folded-paper film; and *Where Is Mama?* (*dir.* Tang Cheng *et al.*, 1961), the first animated ink-and-wash film, which was followed by *The Cowherd's Flute* (*dir.* **Te Wei**, Qian Jiajun, 1963), both paying homage to two prominent Chinese painters, Qi Baishi and Li Keran. Cartoons, however, remained the dominant form. The most successful cartoon of the period was *Uproar in Heaven* (1961–4), a two-part, two-hour feature that took Wan Laiming and his associates four years to complete, and which won Best Film award at the 1978 London FF. After a decade's hiatus during the **Cultural Revolution**, animation production resumed; since the 1980s, regional studios and TV stations have begun making animations of their own. Noticeable among the new productions are *Nezha Conquers the Dragon King* (*dir.* Wang Shuchen, Yan Dingxian, Xu Jingda, 1979) and *Fire Boy* (*dir.* Wang Borong, 1984).

From 1949 to 1984, a total of 254 animations were produced in mainland China, most of them marked by a distinctive, original Chinese style and a high level of artistic achievement. Over twenty animations won prizes at international film festivals: for instance, *Where Is Mama?* won a silver prize at Locarno in 1961, and *Three Monks* (1980) and *Snipe-Clam Grapple* (1983) won two Silver Bears at Berlin in 1982 and 1984, respectively.

In 1996, China launched its first production of computer animation feature, *Uproar in Heaven*, which was directed by **Zhang Jianya**, a **Fifth Generation** director.

Further reading
H. Chen (1989: 2: 103–44), an official account; M. C. Quiquemelle (1991), a historical survey; L. Wan (1986), a memoir.

(YZ)

Apricot Blossom

aka *The Story of Xinghua* (Xinghua sanyue tian)

dir. Yin Li
sc. Shi Ling
with Jiang Liwen, Tian Shaojun, Zhang Guoli, Niu Xingli
Beijing: BFA Youth Film, 1993

This tale of sexual exploitation and moral transgression, modelled after **Zhang Yimou**'s *Ju Dou* (1989), is set in a remote mountain village by the Great Wall. With five thousand yuan, Wanglai purchases a pretty wife, Xinghua (literally 'Apricot Blossom'), but for several years Xinghua fails to bear a child. In his effort to produce a son, Wanglai sexually abuses Xinghua and seeks relations with a mother of three. Xinghua dislikes Wanglai's cruelty and his cunning, dishonest way of doing business. She secretly falls in love with an educated young man named Fulin and becomes pregnant. Wanglai is thrilled at first, but when he learns that the child is not his, he beats up Fulin and destroys Fulin's small tree farm. Xinghua has expected Fulin to stand up against Wanglai, but is greatly disappointed to see Fulin's cowardice.

In spite of his thriving retail shop, Wanglai wants to make more easy money. He hears the rumours that a gold toad is buried somewhere under the Great Wall and brings a group of men to search for it. A thunderstorm strikes that night, and the men only dig up a skeleton under an ancient tower. What is worse, the tower collapses in the rainstorm and kills Wanglai. The film ends with Xinghua's bitter smile, uncertain what she and her baby will face in the future.

(YZ)

Arch, The

(Dong furen)

dir./sc. Tang Shuxuan
with Lu Yan, Qiao Hong, Zhou Xuan
Hong Kong: Film Dynasty Film, 1970

This 16 mm black-and-white experimental film is set in the seventeenth century. Madam Dong is a virtuous widow respected by the villagers. She takes good care of her mother-in-law and her daughter, teaches village children and attends to sick people whenever she can. One year, a team of soldiers are stationed in the village. The captain lives in Dong's compound and admires her grace. While conscious of her own charm, Dong notices that her sixteen-year-old daughter also likes the captain. Meanwhile, the villagers send a plea to the emperor to build an arch of chastity for Dong. When the plea is granted, Dong realizes that she has lost the captain, who marries her daughter and leaves. Her long-time servant also leaves because he does not want to see her feeling miserable all the time. Standing in front of the arch, Dong becomes a kind of tragic heroine.

An early study of female **sexuality**, this film won Best Actress (Lu Yan) and other prizes at the 1971 Taipei GHA.

See also: avant-garde, experimental or exploratory film

(YZ)

Army Nurse
(Nüer lou)

dir. **Hu Mei**, Li Xiaojun
sc. Kang Liwen, Ding Xiaoqi
with Xu Hua, Li Qingqing, Hasi Bagen, Zhao Gang
Beijing: August First Film, 1985

Army Nurse can be called a 'woman's film' in that it contrasts a public discourse which portrays woman as social model with a private discourse which explores woman's inner world. The insertion into the narrative of a woman's subjective perspective and voice forcefully exemplifies the protagonist's divided world and split self.

At age fifteen, Xiaoyu is enlisted in the army as a nurse by her father and sent to an isolated hospital, where the primary concern of the nurses is the care of male patients. The political commissar, Lu, attempts to guide the nurses in their careers and personal affairs. The rhythm of daily life entails mopping floors, distributing medicine, fetching hot water and washing test tubes. One day Xiaoyu meets a male patient, Ding Zhu, to whom she develops a passionate attachment. This unspoken passion (the army forbids dating) surfaces when Ding Zhu asks Xiaoyu to change his bandage. They are alone, and as Xiaoyu unwraps and replaces the bandage around his chest, she feels overpowered by her nearness to him. This surge of emotion moves Xiaoyu to follow the music from Ding's harmonica and to search for his figure each time she passes his ward. When Ding is released from the hospital, Xiaoyu chases him to the bus station, yet cannot express her feelings. Later, Xiaoyu receives a love letter from Ding and runs to the bathroom to read it in private. She barely finishes reading the letter, however, when someone enters. Xiaoyu panics and flushes the letter down a toilet; she is left with only the envelope.

The experience of her first love flows away just like the letter thrown into the toilet, because individuals must choose between personal desire and consensus values. Taking Commissar Lu's advice, Xiaoyu conceals her inner longings and works hard to become an exemplary nurse. While the image track presents Xiaoyu as an honoured model nurse, her voice-over on the sound track speaks of her personal loss and psychological imbalance. At the age of thirty, Xiaoyu is introduced by a friend to a potential husband, whom the Party leader checks and approves. However, the arranged dating and proposed marriage fail to awaken Xiaoyu's emotions. Her feelings of love remain located in the past. On the eve of her wedding day, Xiaoyu returns to her work unit without saying good-bye to the groom. We hear her voice-over as the film ends: 'I've lost so much over the past fifteen years. However, I can still see the longing eyes in the ward looking for me. I'm going back to my patients no matter where I have been.'

Further reading
E. A. Kaplan (1989), a feminist-psychoanalytic reading.

(SC)

art film

A type of film produced not for the commercial market but for artistic or authorial expression. However, an art film may be accessible to a general, educated audience without going to the extreme of formal abstraction or stylistic innovation.

See also: avant-garde, experimental or exploratory film

(YZ)

At the Middle Age
(Ren dao zhongnian)

dir. Wang Qimin, **Sun Yu**
sc. Shen Rong
with **Pan Hong**, Zhao Kui, Da Shichang, Pu Ke, Zheng Qianlong
Changchun: Changchun Film, 1982

This film is adapted from Shen Rong's novella of the same title and deals with the difficulties faced by middle-aged professionals. It works as a subtle criticism of the inadequacies of state policies aimed at this group of people.

Ophthalmologist Lu Wenting suffers heart failure and is taken to the hospital for emergency care. Her department director is greatly saddened by the news and recalls the day eighteen years ago when Lu was first assigned to his department. At that time, Lu, a young girl fresh out of medical school, was still full of energy and spirit, but years of hard work and poor living conditions have worn her down – now she is full of stress and physically burned out. In her recovery room, Lu murmurs that she has been neither a good mother to her two children nor a good wife to her husband. Lu's condition improves with intensive care. Her college friend, Jiang Yafen, together with Jiang's husband, come to say good-bye because they are emigrating to another country: both Jiang and her husband are unhappy with the way doctors and other professionals are treated and have decided to seek a better life elsewhere. But before they board the airplane, Yafen feels a strong sense of attachment to the land she has lived in for the best part of her life. She writes a letter to Lu promising she will one day return. Lu finally recovers and is released from hospital. With her husband's help, she walks home.

In 1982 the film received awards of Best Film and Best Actress (Pan Hong) at China Golden Rooster Awards (GRA), Best Film at Hundred Flowers Awards (HFA) and Best Film from the Ministry of Culture.

(ZX)

audience

At first glance, the film audience in China resembles film audiences elsewhere in the world in that it consists of people from a diverse range of social, cultural and economical backgrounds. But from a comparative perspective, the Chinese film audience differs from film audiences in the West in one fundamental respect; that is, Chinese film audiences have been much more multitudinous and lack a predominant middle-class character. Due to historical circumstance, the development of film in China was not connected to the rise of the middle classes, as happened in many Western countries. Corresponding to the lack of class character of Chinese films is the absence of an overwhelming dominance of film audiences by one social group. Chinese film audiences have always consisted of a multitude of people from a variety of social and economic backgrounds.

Historically, for a long time foreigners residing in China made up an important portion of film audiences in major cities. In fact, in the early days most of the film showings took place in foreign concession areas where Westerners congregated. Not surprisingly, movie theatres were initially built in the International Settlement and French concession in Shanghai to cater to the needs of its international community. This fact accounts for the dominance of foreign films in China in the 1910s–40s.

On the other hand, the early Chinese film audience consisted of two groups: (1) numerous old-fashioned people from the leisure class who resided in the treaty port cities such as Shanghai, Tianjin and Guangzhou; (2) Westernized Chinese who had received foreign-style education and were associated with the foreign establishment. While the old-fashioned types used to frequent teahouses, theatre performances and other traditional entertainment centres and now occasionally relished film as a novelty, the Westernized Chinese saw film as another foreign vogue to be followed closely.

As film's popularity increased and became a major form of mass entertainment for some urban residents by the late 1910s and early 1920s, film audiences began to include people from all social sectors. The process of audience stratification was clearly reflected in the hierarchy of movie theatres and in the types of film programmes tailored to the specific constituents of the various movie theatres. Generally speaking, before the second Sino-Japanese War in 1937, almost all the first-run movie theatres were owned by foreigners and all were located in the foreign concession areas. The admission price of these well-equipped movie houses was beyond the reach of ordinary Chinese. The films shown were mostly foreign imports; only rarely were they Chinese. The audience who frequented these first-run theatres consisted of foreigners living in China and the extremely wealthy Chinese who were associated with the foreign community. These patrons usually went to the movies in fashionable clothing and arrived in automobiles driven by their personal chauffeurs. They represented the most glamorous stratum of the film audience.

Then there were the second-run movie houses that were usually owned by Chinese. Some of them were located in foreign concessions, others in the Chinese quarters. They showed both second-run foreign films and first-run Chinese films, and appealed to a much wider spectrum of the urban population in major metropolises. The audience who went to this type of movie theatre tended to be students, office clerks, civil servants, other salaried employees and their family members. These people came closest to what might be called a Chinese middle class.

Next to them were the truly blue-collar working class, which was largely excluded from the major film establishment. Despite the relative low admission price, the second-run movie theatres were still too expensive for those less fortunate. For them, the only place they could afford was the shabby or run-down neighbourhood movie theatres that were purposely built close to them and tailored to fit their income level. These movie houses were usually much smaller, with poor ventilation and limited seating capacity. However, their audiences only needed to pay a fraction of the cost at a typical first- and second-run movie theatre. The film programme in the neighbourhood theatres also differed from the first- and second-run theatres in two important ways: they seldom showed foreign films and usually selected those domestic productions that fell into the category of entertainment films. The martial arts genre was a major attraction.

While the class factor divided film audiences, other forces, such as gender, age, education, and, occasionally, patriotic sentiment, tended to blur the class boundary. As one film critic pointed out in the 1930s, while men liked sexy and sensuous pictures, women preferred **romance**. Similarly, elderly folks were enthusiastic about historical drama and opera movies, whereas the young audience was usually thrilled by action and adventure films. After the Japanese attacked Shanghai in early 1932, people of all social strata flocked to the movie houses to watch films that showed the heroic resistance by the Chinese Nineteenth Route Army. On those occasions, the shared experience of **nationalism** and patriotism united people from diverse social backgrounds.

Yet, despite film's growing popularity during the 1920s–30s, only a relatively small proportion of China's population was exposed to this new medium. According to an optimistic estimate, there were roughly fifteen thousand people who went to the movies on a daily basis in Shanghai. In Beijing, the number was between six and seven thousand. Since these two cities had the largest number of movie houses in China, and their combined seating capacity made up forty to fifty per cent of the total in the country, these numbers suggest a relative low attendance of movies in the country. Viewed in terms of China's overall population, and compared with the attendance rate in other countries where the population size was much smaller than China, the film audience in pre-1949 China was extremely limited indeed.

Although there were efforts from the film industry and the KMT government to broaden the film audience base, it was not until after 1949 that film really reached the widest possible spectrum of the populace. One of the things the PRC government did after coming into power was to nationalize film production, **distribution** and exhibition. Since part of the Communist ideal is to create a classless society, the party immediately set out to reduce the price difference between movie theatres, making the formerly prestigious and exclusive film theatres accessible to ordinary citizens. The disappearance of the old hierarchy in the exhibition system, along with the continued effort by the government to level off the income gap among the populace, helped to eliminate the social demarcation within the film audience. Meanwhile, the government organized travelling film exhibition teams to bring films to remote villages where people had never been exposed to film before. Although the government sponsored and subsided these activities as a part of its attempt to establish its ideological hegemony, in the process it inadvertently enlarged the basis of the film audience to an unprecedented degree. For the first time, the vast rural population became a part of the film audience, which is one of the major achievements of the CCP regime.

The economic reform since the late 1970s brought many changes to the film industry, including the revival of social stratification among the general population. The increasing gap between the rich and the poor is once again reflected in a divided film audience. As the new hierarchical order in the exhibition business emerges, the first-class movie theatres are frequented by the economically better-off urban dwellers, whereas the second- and third-class theatres become the reserves for the less affluent, a phenomenon that in many ways is reminiscent of the 1920–40s.

See also: action film; dubbed foreign film; filmed stage performances; historical film; martial arts film; theatre and film; Hong Kong cinema; Taiwan cinema (both in Historical essays)

Further reading

L. Lee (1999), a historical look at Shanghai film culture of the 1930s; D. Zhong *et al.* (1997), a study of film audience and film exhibition in 1920s Shanghai.

(ZX)

Autumn Moon

(Qiu yue)

dir. Clara **Law**
sc. Eddie Fong
with Masatoshi Nagase, Li Pui Wai, Choi Siu Wan, Maki Kiuchi
Hong Kong / Japan: Trix Films, 1992

Originally produced as part of a film series entitled *Asian Beat*, *Autumn Moon* is one of the most internationally successful films by Clara Law, arguably Hong Kong's top female director. The film follows the adventures of Tokio, a young Japanese man in Hong Kong, as he cruises the city in search of good food and good sex. One day, while fishing in the bay, Tokio meets Wai, a fifteen-year-old Chinese girl who lives alone with her grandmother, and the two strike up a friendship.

After searching in vain for a good meal, Tokio finally enjoys the cooking of Wai's grandmother. He also learns that his young friend will soon emigrate to Canada, where her parents plan to enroll her in university, and that she feels emotionally undecided about the local boy she is involved with. Tokio himself meets up with Miki, the sister of one of his ex-girlfriends. The two have sex and talk frankly about their life experiences. After grandmother is sent to hospital and then discharged, Wai and Tokio travel to a fishing village to celebrate the Chinese mid-Autumn festival. At night, as if consummating their fleeting friendship, the two laugh and play amid the fireworks.

In its engagement with issues of migration, cultural traditions, sexuality, and the establishment of pan-Asian sensibilities, *Autumn Moon* can stand as representative of Clara Law's prime directorial concerns. The film won a top prize at the 1992 Locarno FF.

(JS)

Autumn's Tale, An

(Qiutian de tonghua)

dir. Mabel Cheung
sc. Alex Law
with Cherie Chung, **Chow Yun-Fat**
Hong Kong: D&B Films, 1987

One of Chow Yun-Fat's own favourite films, this moving love story has elements of a gender-reversed *My Fair Lady* (*dir.* George Cukor, 1964). Jenny comes to New York to visit unfaithful boyfriend, Vincent, and is met by uncouth cousin 'Figurehead' Sam Pang at the airport. Living below her unattractive apartment, Figurehead saves her when she falls asleep with the gas on. He also helps her remodel her apartment and waits in line to surprise her with expensive theatre tickets.

Jenny begins babysitting a teenage girl, Anna, on Long Island while working as a waitress. Her restaurant boss, who has an affair with Anna's mother, tries to seduce Jenny. Figurehead and his friends beat up Jenny's boss, who then fires her. Jenny and Figurehead see an expensive antique watchband, which he decides to buy for her. At the beach, he talks of opening a restaurant on the pier. He invites her to a party without saying that it is his birthday. She talks to Vincent, making a jealous Figurehead leave to fight a gang who are intimidating his friend. Later, Jenny meets Anna and her mother in the park and goes to live with them.

Figurehead buys the watchband, runs to give it to Jenny, and arrives when Vincent is helping her move. Figurehead misunderstands the situation but gives her the watchband anyway. Jenny gives Figurehead a watch, asking him to visit her. Some time later, she tells Anna about the friend she once had who wanted to open the 'Sampan Restaurant'. Anna points in the direction of the pier. Jenny and the now respectable Sam's eyes meet. He says, 'Table for two?' and the image fades to black as she walks up the pier. Chow won Best Actor award at Taipei GHA for this film.

(KH)

avant-garde, experimental or exploratory film

Avant-garde, experimental or exploratory film (*tansuo pian*) does not constitute an artistic phenomenon in China until the 1980s. This is probably due, in part, to a rapid succession of turbulent socio-historical events in the first half of the twentieth century, in part to the strict government control of the film industry in both the mainland and Taiwan during the 1950s–70s, and in part to the lack of private funding – and public interest – necessary for technological and artistic innovation.

The situation changed in the early 1980s when a number of young Taiwan directors attracted international attention with their stylish productions. Prominent in Taiwan's New Wave are **Hou Hsiao-hsien** and Edward **Yang**, whose cinematic studies of Taiwan society are done in a self-reflexive, experimental fashion. Yang's *That Day on the Beach* (1983), set in metropolitan Taipei, makes frequent use of flashbacks and voice-over narration to probe female consciousness and subjectivity, whereas Hou's *A Time to Live, a Time to Die* (1985), set in rural Taiwan, examines generational differences through the eyes of an innocent boy. In the 1990s, the experimental spirit is visible in the works of newer directors, such as *Ming Ghost* (*dir.* Qiu Gangjian, 1990) and *Peach Blossom Land* (*dir.* Stan *Lai*, 1993), both of which favour minimum stage set-ups but use excessive dramatic acting, as if aspiring to a Brechtian conception of theatre.

Starting in the early 1980s, a group of young directors, most of them trained in the West, brought to the Hong Kong film industry technological innovations and stylistic variations. New experiments with special effects pleased the popular audience, and many new productions, such as *Aces Go Places, I-IV* (*dir.* **Tsui Hark**, 1982–5), broke box-office records, generating sequels and imitations. Under enormous commercial pressures, the Hong Kong New Wave may not be as 'avant-gardist' as its Taiwan counterpart, but an experimental impulse is clearly behind such outstanding works as *Days of Being Wild* (*dir.* **Wong Kar-Wai**, 1991) and *The Actress* (*dir.* Stanley **Kwan**, 1992).

The New Wave arrived in the mainland around the mid-1980s. The pioneering **Fifth Generation** works, *One and Eight* (*dir.* **Zhang Junzhao**, 1984), *Yellow Earth* (*dir.* **Chen Kaige**, 1984) and *Horse Thief* (*dir.* **Tian Zhuangzhuang**, 1986), announced to the world that a new cinematic movement was under way in China. These new films signalled a daring departure from the melodramatic norm of leftist film in the 1930s–40s, of **socialist realism** in the 1950s–60s, and of their own contemporaries besieged by an ethos of 'scar literature' (*shanghen wenxue*). The avant-garde nature of the early Fifth Generation films is reflected in their minimum use of plot and dialogue and by their extensive use of natural scenery, disproportionate framing, and unusual point of view. However, since the late 1980s, many Fifth Generation directors have abandoned their avant-garde stances and started making foreign-financed, big-budget commercial films, such as *Li Lianying: The Imperial Eunuch* (*dir.* Tian Zhuangzhuang, 1991) and *Shanghai Triad* (*dir.* **Zhang Yimou**, 1995). The experimental spirit is retained in only a few exceptions, such as *Life on a String* (*dir.* Chen Kaige, 1991), *Sparkling Fox* (*dir.* **Wu Ziniu**, 1993) and *On the Beat* (*dir.* **Ning Ying**, 1995).

See also: leftist film (under Chinese cinema in Historical essays); melodrama

Further reading

H. Chiao (1987, 1988), two collections of Chinese sources on Hong Kong and Taiwan; S. Teo (1994), a brief survey of Hong Kong.

(YZ)

awards

An early prototype of film awards in China can be traced to 1923 when the Education Department of the Beijing government began the practice of recommending what they viewed as good films. Although no award was ever given, it was considered an honour for any film to make it to the list of the official recommendations. Predictably, those recommended films would bring in more profits at the box office as well. Hence, the official list of recommended films was not taken lightly.

After the KMT government unified the country politically in 1927, it set out to centralize film censorship in the early 1930s. While banning undesirable films, the Nationalist film censors continued the practice of recommending films they favoured. If a film was selected by the censors as an official entry in some international film festival, it was viewed as being as prestigious as having won an award already. Such was the case with *Song of the Fishermen* (*dir.* **Cai Chusheng**, 1934), which was one of the biggest box-office hits in Chinese film history. In 1935, the film was selected by the KMT government to represent China at Moscow FF and became the first Chinese film to win an international award.

As far as domestic film awards are concerned, the Nationalist censors drafted a set of criteria to reward good films as early as 1931. But it was not until 1936 that three films won the government's award of Best Film. Jiang Xingde, who wrote the script for *Little Angel* (*dir.* **Wu Yonggang**, 1935), won an award from Jiangsu provincial government in 1934. Although the KMT government began giving film awards during the 1930s, these activities remained irregular and inconsistent. The historical circumstances – the Japanese invasion and the civil war that ensued – did not allow the KMT government the opportunity to develop a system of giving film awards.

It was only after 1957 that the film award began to sink its roots in China. In that year, a total of nineteen films produced between 1949 and 1955 received Best Film Awards administered by the Ministry of Culture of the PRC government. Among the winners there were five first prizes, five second prizes and nine third prizes. Four hundred and eighty-one filmmakers were also honoured with first, second and third prizes. For obvious political reasons, this government-sponsored film award was discontinued for over two decades, but it was resumed in 1980 and has been given on an annual basis since then. In 1986, the administration of this government award was removed from the Ministry of Culture and was placed under the jurisdiction of a committee appointed by the Ministry of Broadcasting, Film and Television (MBFT).

In addition to this government film award, there are two other important awards in mainland China. One of them is the Hundred Flowers Awards (HFA), which was started in 1962 by *Popular Cinema*, a broad-based fan magazine. Unlike the government's Best Film Awards, which not only reflected the official endorsement but has the direct involvement of government officials, the HFA was administered by the magazine's editorial board, and its selection of films and filmmakers in all major categories was determined by the number of votes from participating readers of this magazine and film audiences at large. Unfortunately, only two years into operation, the award was suspended on the eve of the **Cultural Revolution**. The editorial board was accused of defiance of the CCP. It was not until 1980 that the HFA was resumed. Strictly speaking, since the journal's employees are all paid by the government and administratively subject to the leadership of the MBFT, the magazine remains essentially an official publication. Hence, as a film award, it is not really independent of official ideology and the government's influence.

The highest honour for Chinese filmmakers today is no doubt the Golden Rooster Awards (GRA). This award was started in 1981, the year of the rooster according to Chinese zodiac beliefs, by the Association of Chinese Filmmakers. In theory, this organization is a non-official entity and should function like a professional guild for filmmakers. But in the Chinese political context, the organization is highly official because it is sponsored, financed and administered by the government. Nevertheless, the association always manages to maintain as much autonomy as possible. When it comes to giving awards, the GRA selection committee definitely focuses more on the artistic quality of the film than does the government's Best Film Awards (the latter understandably emphasizing ideology more than anything else). In this regard, the GRA stands in contrast with the Best Film Awards. Meanwhile, by relying more on film experts and scholars than on popular votes, the GRA also distinguishes itself from the HFA and brings more prestige to itself. Hence, it continues to be the most highly coveted honour for Chinese filmmakers.

There are several things to be noted about film awards in China. First, film awards appeared in China relatively late. If one counts 1896, the year the first movie was shown in China, as the beginning of Chinese film history, it took four decades before the first film award was given. Even then it was not regularly conducted, neither was there a group of film specialists administering it according to a set of clearly stated criteria.

Another unique feature of Chinese film awards is that they have always been administered by the government. No institution outside the official establishment has ever been involved in giving film awards. As a result, the Chinese film industry never had its equivalent of the Oscars. There have been several explanations for this. One view holds that the general lack of a well-developed civil society in China prevented the film industry from developing its own autonomy and challenging the state's authority in cultural matters. The industry was either too fragmented to take a concerted effort in setting up industry standards, or too preoccupied with survival to be concerned with its independence. During the 1920s, the effort for self-regulation, including promoting certain common standards through award giving, failed because the film industry was too chaotic to discipline itself. In the 1930s, the industry's priority was to minimize the competition from Hollywood by forming an alliance with the KMT government. In return, the government, not the industry, took the lead in promoting films congruous with its political and ideological agendas through award-giving. This legacy of government involvement was interrupted briefly during the war, but was fully revived by the Communists after 1949.

The third noticeable feature of film awards in China is their emphasis on the social function of films. Because the Chinese élite always viewed film as a vehicle for social reform, their judgement of a film's quality was usually based on a film's contribution, or the lack of it, to social well-being. This emphasis on film's social responsibility partly explains why the government always played a major role in film awards. Traditionally, government usually assumed the responsibility of defining morality for the society. Promoting good films and banning bad ones were in keeping with that responsibility. Not surprisingly, for a long period Chinese film awards were more concerned with the overall quality of film than with the various aspects of filmmaking, such as acting, directing, script writing, art design, sound and special effects. In other words, the technical dimensions of film seldom figured prominently in Chinese film awards.

Finally, since the mid-1980s Chinese films have been winning awards at various international film festivals. These awards often pose different standards and are based on different values. They tend to reduce or even challenge the prestige of domestic film awards and further complicate the already complex mechanism of politics involved in film awards.

In Taiwan, the prestigious Golden Horse Awards (GHA) was originally launched in 1957 by a group of studios and media organizations. Although it was a once-only operation, the award coincided with the peak of Taiwanese-dialect films in the late 1950s. In 1962, under the auspices of the KMT Government Information Office, the Taipei GHA was resumed and became an annual event. The official sponsorship gave the GHA a political ambience, but the situation changed in 1984 when the government handed over the administrative powers of this annual award to non-official film organizations in Taiwan, which recommended members of the selection committee. Interestingly, Hong Kong productions have always been counted as domestic titles and for a long time dominated key awards at Taipei GHA. In the mid-1990s, mainland films registered as Hong Kong productions have been allowed to enter the competition, but co-productions between the mainland and Taiwan or Hong Kong are still denied the right of official entry for the GHA.

In Hong Kong, the unofficial Hong Kong Film Awards (HKFA) was started by *Film Biweekly*, but this annual event has attracted influential sponsors in the local media and entertainment industries. Unlike Taipei GHA, the HKFA include films from the mainland, although Hong Kong and Taiwan titles usually win the most prestigious awards such as Best Film and Best Director. Important as it is in Hong Kong and Taiwan, the international reputation of the HKFA has somehow been eclipsed by the annual Hong Kong International FF, which was launched in 1977 and has been consistently supported by Hong Kong City Council.

See also: censorship and film; Chinese film in the West; transnational cinema (both in Historical essays)

Further reading

T. B. Hammer (1991), three English lists of award recipients at China GRA, HKFA and Taipei GHA; J. Zhang and J. Cheng (1995: 1414–51), a comprehensive Chinese listing of domestic and international awards given to films produced in mainland China, Hong Kong and Taiwan.

(ZX, YZ)

Back to Back, Face to Face

(Beikaobei, lianduilian)

dir. **Huang Jianxin**, Yang Yazhou
sc. Huang Xin, Sun Yi'an
with Niu Zhenhua, Lei Luosheng, Li Qiang
Xi'an: Xi'an Film, 1994

A political satire comparable to the director's **Black Cannon Incident** (1985) and **Dislocation** (1986), this film uses the small cultural office in an ancient city as a microcosm for the entire Chinese political arena under the Communist regime. Li Shuangli, the deputy director of the office, is a capable man and has been running the office for years, but his wish to become the real director has long been denied. He casts a vote for himself in an opinion poll, but is criticized by his senior for the 'selfish' act. Since the new director Ma is an inexperienced country bumpkin, Li lures him into a construction project that benefits the contractor and the employees in the office. After several rounds of intrigues, Ma cannot tolerate Li and resigns his position, leaving Li a perfect candidate again.

However, this time Yan, a close associate of Li's senior, takes over the office and works against Li. Because his new leather shoes are damaged by Li's father, Yan beats up the old man and deducts Li's salary. This double blow makes

Plate 9   *Back to Back, Face to Face* (1994)

Li sick. In the hospital, he suddenly realizes that all his political cunning has led him nowhere. He no longer cares about the cultural office and starts plotting to get special permission to have another child, dreaming of having a boy besides his daughter. Meanwhile, the new director Yan is framed in a screening of pornographic video to the public. He runs away and leaves the position of director open again.

Li now accompanies his pregnant wife for walks every day. He does not care if his senior is really serious about offering him the position this time. In a subtle way, the film makes an ironic comment on the shift of emphasis from the socialist **family** to the nuclear family in China of the 1990s.

(IJS)

Bai Yang
(Yang Chengfang)

b. 4 March 1920, Beijing
d. 1996
Actress

Bai Yang was one of the most popular movie stars of the 1930s–40s. Born into a well-to-do family, she lost both her parents when only eleven. In 1931, Lianhua Film Company of Beijing cast her in a supporting role in the silent film *Sad Song from an Old Palace* (*dir.* **Hou Yao**, 1932). However, Bai was offered a three-year contract with Mingxing Film Company in 1936 only after she had established her reputation in the theatre. Her popularity soared after an excellent lead performance in *Crossroads* (*dir.* **Shen Xiling**, 1937). In addition to taking numerous stage roles between 1937–45, Bai also appeared in several films produced by the Nationalist Central Film Studio in Chongqing, all of which purportedly served the war effort.

In the post-war period, Bai starred in almost every major production by Kunlun Film Company. Her performances in *Eight Thousand Li of Cloud and Moon* (*dir.* **Shi Dongshan**), *Spring River Flows East* (*dir.* **Cai Chusheng**, **Zheng Junli**), *Diary of a Homecoming* (*dir.* Yuan Jun, all 1947), *The Sorrows of Women* (*dir.* Shi Dongshan) and *The Lucky Son-in-Law* (*dir.* Yuan Jun, both 1948) won high acclaim.

After appearing in *My Mountains, My Rivers* (1948), Bai made her way to Beijing. Between 1950 and 1962, she starred in a half dozen films. Her performances in *Unity for Tomorrow* (*dir.* Zhao Ming, 1951), *For Peace* (*dir.* **Huang Zuolin**, 1956), *New Year's Sacrifice* (1957), *The World of Love* (1959, both *dir.* **Sang Hu**), *The Story of Jin Yuji* (*dir.* Wang Jiayi, 1959), and *The Life of Dongmei* (*dir.* Wang Yan, 1961) were very popular with audiences. Bai was ranked the most popular film actress in the country in surveys conducted in 1957 by *Beijing Daily* and *Shenyang Daily*. Unfortunately, Bai's film career was cut short due to politics, and she did not make another film after 1962.

Further reading
Z. Chen (1985), a profile; ZDX (1982–6: 1: 24–36), a short biography.

(ZX)

Ballad of the Yellow River
(Huanghe yao)

dir. **Teng Wenji**
sc. Lu Wei, Zhu Xiaoping
with Yu Lin, Duan Xiu, Chi Peng, Cao Jingyang, Ge You
Xi'an: Xi'an Film, 1989

A man's habitual failure to satisfy his romantic desires is played out against the barren landscape and brutal social environment of Northwestern China. In the end, he learns to accept his fate and comes to invest all hope in his adopted daughter.

As a teenager, Danggui attempts to flee his hometown with his sweetheart, but he is caught and brought back for punishment. As he is saved by a man who works as a puller, Danggui also becomes a puller. Years later he falls in love with another woman named Honghua, but Honghua's father has sold her to a man paralyzed from the waist down. Danggui makes another attempt to flee with his woman but is again caught, this time by a group of bandit trackers hired by Honghua's husband. Honghua is returned to her husband and Danggui is severely beaten.

Time passes. One day Danggui, now a middle-aged man, finds a woman dying in the desert with her little daughter. Danggui kills his horse (his only possession) in order to save their lives. They subsequently become a family. Unfortunately, Danggui's happiness does not last very long because the woman, Liulan, is one of the bandit leader's concubines: after the bandit killed two of her babies, she ran away from him with her

Plate 10   *Ballad of the Yellow River* (1989)

daughter Yingzi. On New Year's Day, however, the bandit finds Liulan and abducts her.

Danggui assumes responsibility for raising Yingzi. When she is old enough to get married, Danggui escorts her across the Yellow River. He runs into the bandit, himself now a prisoner, and learns that Liulan is no longer alive. After seeing Yingzi safely across the Yellow River, Danggui walks home by himself along the ancient path.

In 1990 the film obtained awards of Best Director at Montreal FF and Best Film from MBFT.

(ZX)

Banana Paradise

(Xiangjiao tiantang)

dir. **Wang Tung**
sc. Wang Xiaodi
with Niu Chengze, Chang Zhi, Zeng Qingyu
Taipei: CMPC, 1989

Banana Paradise is a satirical portrait of mainland Nationalist soldiers who resettled in Taiwan after 1949. Its title reflects the 'milk and honey' image of Taiwan circulated among the ranks by the Nationalist army. However, the experience of these displaced veterans is one of disappointment and victimization. A soldier-peasant named Menshuan (literally, 'door latch') comes to Taiwan but hopes to return to the mainland before too long. In the meantime, he expects to live easily off Taiwan's tropical bounty. Through a series of misunderstandings, he is mistaken for a spy and imprisoned under the KMT's campaign of White Terrorism. Latch escapes, and hooks up with a woman, Yuexiang, her tubercular friend, and his new-born baby. In one stroke, he manages to escape his political persecution and find a new life by assuming the identity of Yuexiang's friend, who dies of consumption. Clutching obsolete identity papers, they manage to survive as a family. Though largely illiterate, Latch starts his new job as an English translator. With Yuexiang's help, he prospers as a white-collar worker, husband and father. In 1987, when the KMT lifts the ban on visiting relatives in the mainland, Latch must 'reunite' with the parents of the man who succumbed to tuberculosis nearly 40 years earlier. This ironic happy ending is a satire on the absurd consequences of Chiang Kai-shek's authoritarian rule of Taiwan during the 1950s.

Further reading

T. Wang (1991), the director on his film.

(YY)

Battle of Taierzhuang, The

(Xuezhan Taierzhuang)

dir. Yang Guangyuan, Zai Junjie
sc. Tian Junli, Fei Linjun
with Shao Honglai, Chu Guoliang, Jiang Hualin, Liao Junjie, Zhao Hengduo
Nanning: Guangxi Film, 1987

This film is based on a real historical event that took place during the Sino-Japanese war, and is one of the first PRC war films to engage directly with the role played during the war by the Nationalists.

In 1938, the new commander of Japan's military forces in China plans to seize the strategically important central Chinese city of Xuzhou. In charge of Xuzhou's defences is general Li Zongren. One of Li's first moves is to appoint a controversial figure, general Zhang Zizhong. A Chinese warlord in Shandong, Han Fuju, refuses to fight the Japanese and retreats from his position, thus allowing the Japanese to march through an open corridor. In retaliation for Han's treacherous behaviour, Chiang Kai-shek tricks Han into travelling to Kaifeng where he is court-marshalled. Han is later executed in Wuchang. Meanwhile, after occupying Qingdao, the Japanese army moves to Linyi where they meet strong resistance from Chinese armed forces. The battle near Linyi marks the beginning of the battle of Taierzhuang. After severe fighting and heavy casualties on both sides, the Chinese military finally manages to defeat the invading Japanese army.

See also: war film

(ZX)

Beijing Bastards

(Beijing zazhong)

dir./sc. **Zhang Yuan**
with Cui Jian, Li Mai, Wu Lala, Tang Danian
Beijing: *Beijing Bastards* Film Team, 1993

An **independent film** from a rebellious **Sixth Generation** director, *Beijing Bastards* features two pre-eminent rockers in China, Cui Jian (who also served as the film's co-producer) and Dou Wei (with his 'Dream-Making Band'). The minimalist narrative revolves around a Beijing rock band, driven out of their leased building, who have difficulty finding another place to rehearse. The film also includes a few emotional scenes, such as when one band member urges his pregnant girlfriend to have an abortion. Various film segments are connected by random street scenes of Beijing. The bulk of the film consists of rock 'n' roll songs, and the director freely uses semi-**documentary** footage of Cui Jian's concert performances. As in *Dirt* (*dir.* Guan Hu, 1994), rock music seems to be a perfect medium for expressing alienation and discontent for the new generation.

Further reading

C. Berry (1996c), on Zhang Yuan's films; D. Chute (1994), a review of three mainland independent films.

(YZ)

Better Tomorrow, A

(Yingxiong bense)

dir. John **Woo**
sc. Chan Hing Kai, Leung Suk Wah
with **Chow Yun-Fat**, **Ti Lung**, Leslie **Cheung**, Emily Chu, Waise Lee
Hong Kong: Cinema City / Film Workshop, 1986

A reworking of earlier martial-arts themes of brotherhood and loyalty, *A Better Tomorrow* revitalized the career of John Woo by becoming a huge box-office success and by initiating a 1980s cycle of Hong Kong gangster films. The film concerns a leader of the underworld, Ho, who is sent to prison after being double-crossed and then arrested in Taiwan, and his subsequent attempts to go straight. After his release, his old sidekick Mark tries to persuade him to take up their old life again. However, Ho is more concerned to achieve reconciliation with Kit, his brother in the police force, who holds Ho responsible for the death of their father.

Ho's former position as gang leader has now been filled by his old subordinate, Shing, who connives to play brother off against brother. As Kit becomes more estranged from his wife Jacky, Ho sets Shing up for arrest and prepares to let himself be taken in by Kit. In the end, Mark and Shing die violent deaths, while Ho and Kit are reunited at the very moment the elder brother must once again head back to prison.

A Better Tomorrow is now one of the most internationally renowned of modern Hong Kong films. Apart from generating its own sequels – *A Better Tomorrow, II* (*dir.* John Woo, 1987) and *Love and Death in Saigon* (*dir.* **Tsui Hark**, 1989) – its inventive shoot-outs and homoerotic undertones provided stylistic inspiration for North American titles like *Reservoir Dogs* (*dir.* Quentin Tarantino, 1992).

See also: gangster film

Further reading

J. Stringer (1997b), on paradigms of masculinity; T. Williams (1997b), on John Woo's crisis cinema.

(JS)

Big Mill, The

(Da mofang)

dir./sc. **Wu Ziniu**
with Li Yusheng, Liu Zhongyuan
Changsha: Xiaoxiang Film / Hong Kong: Sil-Metropole, 1990

In a small village bordering Hunan and Guangxi provinces, Qingguo, a seventy-three-year-old man, remembers his passionate love for Jiucui as well as how he became a cruel murderer. The film begins and ends with Jiucui's funeral procession, during which Qingguo relives his past. In this prolonged flashback, the old Qingguo occasionally appears to stare at his young counterpart.

At age twenty-three, Qingguo leaves Jiucui to join the Red Army. When he returns from a lost battle, he finds her married to the town's powerful landlord, Liao Baidiao. Liao is paralyzed and obsessed by his desire to father a healthy child, an achievement which would prove his virility and ensure the continuation of his power and blood line. Qingguo and Jiucui meet secretly in a big mill where Qingguo lives in isolation. When he discovers that Liao is responsible not only for the killing of many Red Army soldiers but also for treating Jiucui cruelly, he seeks revenge. He kills Liao's gang of bullies one by one; the mill becomes a macabre site where the corpses of his victims are hidden. Eventually Qingguo kills Liao and takes the pregnant Jiucui to the mill. Qingguo prepares to escape with her, but she is horrified by his cruelty and leaves him. The film returns to the present; Jiucui's funeral is over and the last shot is of the old Qingguo walking alone on the hillside.

Big Mill concerns the Chinese civil war of the 1920s. Battle scenes against the Nationalist army have been a staple of war films in mainland China since the early 1950s, but like other **Fifth Generation** directors, Wu Ziniu concentrates on the psychological make-up of his protagonists and emphasizes the impact of love and desire over social and political issues.

See also: war film

(PV)

Big Parade, The

(Da yuebing)

dir. Chen Kaige
sc. Gao Lili
with Wang Xueqi
Nanning: Guangxi Film, 1985

The Big Parade resembles *Full Metal Jacket* (*dir.* Stanley Kubrick, 1981). The process of military training detailed in Chen's film, however, concerns a different political event: the preparation for China's thirty-fifth national anniversary celebrations. Ostensibly an account of nationalistic pride, the film raises the question of how loyalty to the state can be reconciled with the individual's need for personal expression.

At an isolated air force base a large group of select soldiers undergoes parade training. Dissolves of formation drills and close-ups of marching legs project the dynamic force of collective ideology and military discipline. Scenes of standing at attention for hours in 100-degree heat or collapsing from exhaustion typify the training schedule. Behind the training scenes, however, the emotional lives of the soldiers unfold, each framing perspectives that question concepts of national honour and human nature. Seduced by the idea of patriotism, Xiaoyuan, a new recruit from the countryside, refuses to return home for his mother's funeral. Jiang, embarrassed by his bowlegs, tries to straighten them by wrapping tight bandages around them each night. Another officer conceals his poor health out of fear that he will lose his only opportunity to be promoted. Sixteen-year-old Xiao Liu will marry the girl he loves once he retires from military service. While these soldiers willingly conform to the values and dictates of military life, Lu Chun, an educated man with an individual mind, voices his confusions over the political rhetoric used to justify self-sacrifice.

His is the voice which asks why all possibility for individual expression has been foreclosed.

The film concludes with the honour parade in Tiananmen Square on national day (footage added under the pressure of film censorship). Behind the glorious image remains an unsettling scepticism. Over months of brutal training, these soldiers have covered thousands of kilometres on foot, yet in Tiananmen Square they are required to march just ninety-six steps, the work of a single minute.

See also: censorship and film

(SC)

Big Road
(Dalu)

dir. / sc. **Sun Yu**
with **Jin Yan**, **Zheng Junli**, Han Lan'gen,
Li Lili, **Chen Yanyan**
Shanghai: Lianhua Film, 1934

This silent film, with added soundtrack, is set during the time of the resistance war against the Japanese invasion. Six young male workers and two waitresses in a roadside restaurant experience a political awakening when they participate in the construction of a strategically important road for the Chinese army. They have different characters and come from different social backgrounds. Jin is an optimist in spite of his miserable childhood; Zhang is melancholic and solitary; Luo is a romantic dreamer; Zheng, a student fleeing Manchuria after the Japanese occupation, is an intellectual type; Zhangda is characterized by his physical strength; Xiaoliu used to be a petty thief, but he is redeemed by his friends. As for the two waitresses, Dingxiang is shy and looks up to Moli, who is aggressive and resourceful.

Dingxiang falls in love with Luo, while Moli prefers to remain friends with all six workers. Meanwhile, the Japanese get closer. A rich local landlord betrays the Chinese resistance force by trying to slow down road construction. When they oppose him, he imprisons and tortures them. Thanks to Moli and Dingxiang, they escape and go back to work. The road is finally completed, but Moli and the six workers die in a Japanese bombing. As the only survivor of the group, Dingxiang dreams that her friends are revived and march ahead.

Big Road is a representative work of leftist film of the 1930s which promotes patriotic and socialist ideals. Since its release, the film and its added theme song by **Nie Er**, 'The Song of the Big Road', have enjoyed lasting popularity.

See also: leftist film (under Chinese cinema in Historical essays)

Further reading
C. Berry (1988c), a psychoanalytic reading of desire and sexuality; Y. Zhang (1994c), a critique of Berry's reading.

(PV, YZ)

biography

A type of film focused on the biography of a historical figure; sometimes called 'bio-pic'.

See under: historical film

(YZ)

Bitter Laughter
(Ku'nao ren de xiao)

dir. Yang Yanjin, Deng Yimin
sc. Yang Yanjin, Xue Jing
with **Pan Hong**, Li Zhiyu, Yuan Yao, Bai Mu,
Qiao Qi, **Qin Yi**
Shanghai: Shanghai Film, 1979

This story is set against the background of the **Cultural Revolution** when truth was suppressed and people had to lie in order to survive. A non-conformist journalist stands up and tells the truth, only to be thrown into jail for doing so.

In the winter of 1975, journalist Fu Bin is recalled from a re-education camp and assigned to do a story on how well a group of experts perform in a randomly given test. The test has been organized by the political authorities with the purpose of proving that the experts are not as clever as they are made out to be. One surgeon is tricked by his examiners into making a mistake and becomes a laughing stock. Fu, however, is puzzled by this farce and goes to the mayor to report how the experts' subjection to ridicule has been orchestrated. He is surprised to discover that the mayor himself has choreographed the entire exercise. Yet, when the mayor is then injured in a car accident, he asks the surgeon who flunked the quiz to be in charge of his operation. Fu writes an article revealing the truth, but his wife does not let him submit it for fear of reprisal. Looking for an excuse not to write the report, Fu pretends to be ill. However, he eventually musters enough courage to tell the mayor that he and his followers cannot last long by manipulating other people. Even though the film ends with the protagonist's arrest, Fu himself is no longer tormented by his conscience.

(ZX)

Black Cannon Incident

(Hei pao shijian)

dir. **Huang Jianxin**
sc. Zhang Xianliang, Li Wei
with Liu Zifeng
Xi'an: Xi'an Film, 1985

Among the **Fifth Generation** films, those of Huang Jianxin stand out for taking modernity as both subject matter and style. *Black Cannon Incident*, his first feature, presents an absurd condition where outmoded socialist ideology and newly emergent modern reforms clash in a highly expressive cinematic form.

On a rainy evening, Zhao Shuxin goes to a post office to send a telegram. He never imagines that the phrase 'lost black cannon' and the address '301 cultural relics office' will ruin his professional career. When the message is taken to be a code by the Party vice-secretary, an elderly Marxist lady, Zhao becomes suspect. Montage shots of a telephone, a police car and the telegram receiver signal a political investigation into the 'mysterious telegram'.

An important engineer proficient in German, Zhao once served as interpreter for Hans on a joint-venture project. When Hans comes to China a second time, he is refused permission to work with Zhao. A young interpreter from a travel agency replaces Zhao and unwittingly undermines the project through a number of costly translating mistakes.

Cinematic composition heightens the characters' socio-political alienation and vulnerability. Investigations into the meaning of the telegram and discussions about whether or not to allow Zhao to be an interpreter bring about five party meetings. During these scenes, the use of camera position and *mise-en-scène* is significant. Extreme long shots of the meeting table show party leaders divided on two sides. Above them a giant modern clock ticks relentlessly as the discussion fails to resolve anything. The modernistic setting and contrastive colour scheme – a mark of the director's style – situate the human figure in a world of estrangement.

Hans returns to Germany and the project concludes in a fatal industrial accident. By this time the mystery of the telegram has been solved: Zhao was looking for a Chinese chess piece, called a black cannon, that he left in a hotel room. The farcical narrative and absurd social world of *Black Cannon Incident* is paralleled by the domino game played by two kids at the end of the film.

Further reading
Berry and Farquhar (1994), a critical analysis in relation to East–West influences; H. C. Li (1989), a study of colour and character; P. Pickowicz (1994), a historical study in terms of post-socialism.

(SC)

Black Mountain Road, The

(Heishan lu)

dir. **Zhou Xiaowen**
sc. Zhu Jianxin, Zhou Xiaowen
with Alia, Xie Yuan, Zhao Xiaorui
Xi'an: Xi'an Film, 1990

Few people outside China had heard of Zhou Xiaowen prior to the release of his ***Ermo*** (1994), yet his work compares favourably with that of internationally known **Fifth Generation** auteurs. Some of Zhou's films have spent years on the shelf due to government censorship, while his thrillers have achieved remarkable market success. His camera constantly tracks troubled male subjects and casts them in narratives of violence and **sexuality**. *The Black Mountain Road* is one such film.

Deep in a northern mountain area is a makeshift inn rebuilt from an abandoned Christian church. Here an unnamed woman with her mongrel dog earns a living by serving travelling porters. Food and drink are not enough for these hungry men, and the woman is often the target of sexual attack. Only the dog can save her. Dramatic conflicts ensue after a group of porters kill her one-eyed husband in a violent fight and declare the inn and road their property. The woman is caught between two members of the band, one the masculine, violent 'Big Brother', the other a gentler man. The former wants to possess the woman by force while the latter intends to win her heart. Also serving as cinematographer, the director uses beautiful camera work and *mise-en-scène* to convey the emotionally charged situation.

Caught between their oath of allegiance to each other and their sexual desire for the woman, the two male protagonists struggle to find a balance between identity and sexuality. The female body becomes a site upon which anxieties of male bonding and sexuality are explored. Left behind by the group due to an injured ankle, Big Brother stays at the inn to recuperate. He assumes the position of the woman's husband and rapes her. Returning to the inn, the younger brother offers the woman a truck mirror while she treats the soles of his feet. Through a series of shot/reverse shots, an emotional world opens up without words. The younger brother enters the woman's room, but gazes at her body without daring to touch. As Big Brother reinforces his position as the group's head and the woman's man, the woman gives herself to the younger brother instead. Big Brother punishes her severely for her 'transgression'.

The sexual tension remains unresolved until Japanese troops invade the area. The film then displaces the characters' sexual crisis with a show of national dignity. As they prepare to fight the Japanese, Big Brother relinquishes his claim on the woman. The battle ends tragically, with the inn aflame and the woman dead.

See also: censorship and film; thriller

Further reading

T. Rayns (1995d), on Zhou Xiaowen's films.

(SC)

Black Snow

(Benming nian)

dir. **Xie Fei**
sc. Liu Heng
with **Jiang Wen**, Cheng Lin, Yue Hong, Liu Xiaoning
Beijing: BFA Youth Film, 1989

Based on Liu Heng's novel of the same title, this realistic but pessimistic film of **urban life** opens with a newly released prisoner who walks through the dark side of Beijing to his long deserted home. Li Huiquan was involved in a homicide case years ago when he helped his friend 'Fork' to vent anger against an unfaithful girlfriend. Since both his parents are dead, Li has to make a living by opening a booth selling clothes and shoes in a market. He meets a young singer Zhao Yaqiu (played by a famous pop singer, Cheng Lin) in a

night club and volunteers to escort her home every night she performs. Li likes this innocent girl, but as her reputation grows Zhao has many new fans and becomes egotistic. Cui Yongli, an illegal goods dealer, tries to recruit Li by showing him pornographic videotapes. When Cui sends a prostitute to seduce Li, Li walks away infuriated. After learning that Cui has taken Zhao on a pleasure trip to the south, Li beats Cui up. Fork escapes prison and seeks assistance from Li. Li does not want to betray his former friend, nor does he like to break the law. When Fork leaves on his own, Li withdraws all his savings, purchases a gold necklace and presents it to Zhao. She is now performing in a fancy hotel and declines Li's gift, which Li throws to the roadside in total despair. He gets drunk and walks to a park, where he is mugged by two youngsters and stabbed in the stomach. A night show is just over, and Li stands against a tide of people walking past him. As the lights are turned off, Li falls down to the ground, his blood streaming down. He dies aged twenty-four in the darkness of a deserted park, a victim of a new generation of youth gangs.

A powerful story of disillusioned urban youths, the film was awarded the Silver Bear at the 1990 Berlin FF, perhaps the only mainland urban film to win such high-level international recognition.

Further reading

X. Tang (1994), a critical study of urban space.

(JJS, YZ)

Blood Brothers

(Cima)

dir. **Chang Che**
sc. I. Kuang
with David **Chiang**, **Ti Lung**, Chen Kuan-Tai
Hong Kong: Shaw Brothers, 1972

Blood Brothers is Chang Che's version of an incident in the later years of the Qing dynasty which made a profound impression on Sun Yat-sen. Featuring Chang's leading 1970s actors, David Chiang and Ti Lung, it covers the director's favourite theme of obsolescent heroic values within an alienating social structure and the conflicting tensions affecting people within such an era.

After killing provincial governor Ma Hsin I in combat, Chang Wen Sing surrenders to the authorities. He writes his version of the events in court, which the film replays in flashback. Nine years earlier Chang and blood brother Huong attempted to rob Ma on the road. Although Ma overcame them, he enlisted the young bandits in a scheme to destroy a mountain bandit gang. After achieving this, he became a blood brother to Chang and Huong and then left them to join the Emperor's army. A romantic attachment developed between Ma and Huong's wife.

Several years later, Ma returns as an officer to recruit his blood brothers and their men in his military campaigns. Achieving this through the deaths of many former bandits, Ma then consummates his relationship with Huong's wife and decides to set up the death of his rival. Chang attempts in vain to prevent his blood brother's death. He then takes revenge on Ma, stabbing his adversary, and engaging in a climactic duel. Although the authorities learn the truth, they decide to torture him. But a message from the Emperor ordering them to hand Chang over to Ma's relatives prevents this. Chang dies a bloody ritual death the next day watched by Huong's wife who remembers the past with sadness as images flow on the screen.

(TW)

Bloodshed at Dusk

(Di xue huanghun)

dir. **Sun Zhou**
sc. Sun Yi'an
with Shen Junyi, Gai Lili, Liu Ning
Xi'an: Xi'an Film, 1989

A stylish execution of the **gangster film**, *Bloodshed at Dusk* has most of the ingredients of an **action film**. Newly released from prison, Wei Wenbin wants to kidnap the son of Lu Jianguo, a rich entrepreneur, but because of a mistake he kidnaps the son of a divorced couple, Lu Ye and Xi Juan. Jianguo receives a phone call demanding a ransom of 30,000 yuan. Although his son is safe, he plans to deliver the sum in exchange for peace. The police follow Jianguo to the beach, where Wei realizes his mistake after seeing a poster of the missing boy. He entrusts the boy to his mistress, who releases the boy. But when the boy reaches home, he is caught again and his mother murdered by the criminals. The father Lu Ye chases the murderers in desperation, and a fierce gunfight erupts. With the police's help, Wei and his men are killed, and Lu Ye and his son reunited.

(JJS)

Bloody Morning

(Xuese qingchen)

dir. **Li Shaohong**
sc. Xiao Mao, Li Shaohong
with Hu Yajie, Zhao Jun, Xie Yan, Kong Lin, Lu Hui
Beijing: Beijing Film, 1990

An adaptation of Gabriel García Márquez's *Chronicle of a Death Foretold*, the film shows how the importance assigned to female chastity and family reputation, coupled with turning a blind eye to the law, can lead to tragedy. Moreover, *Bloody Morning* implies that such circumstances can occur in different cultures. The explication of a murder case, using an investigator's voice-over, provides the narrative structure. Only at the end of the film does the audience realize that almost anyone in the village could have prevented the tragedy and that no one, not even the killers, wanted the murder to take place.

The film begins with the scene of the murder and the body of the victim. Through flashbacks and voice-overs, we begin to piece together the fragments of what happened. The victim is a young school teacher, Li Mingguang. The chain of events that costs him his life starts with two girls: Yongfang, his fiancée, and Hongxing, her close friend. In their rural village, Mingguang's school office is the only place where the three can meet and talk. The magazine *Popular Film* allows them to imagine a life beyond that of the local peasants.

Reality is far different from the beautiful images on the magazine covers. In order to afford a wife, the accused killer agrees to marry his sister Hongxing to a rich man: Hongxing's brother can marry the man's handicapped sister in exchange. On her wedding night, Hongxing does not bleed on the bed sheets. Angered that she is apparently not a virgin, her husband sends Hongxing back home. Hongxing's two brothers try to force her to reveal the name of the man to whom she lost her virginity. They suspect Mingguang, and to avenge their humiliation the brothers send out word that they will kill the teacher.

As each witness helps the government inspector collect evidence, we see how well the villagers understood that tragedy was unfolding but attempted to prevent the murder in a most passive way. When the villagers see the two brothers looking for Mingguang, they pass the information on to the village chief and then wait for him to intervene. As Mingguang passes by, the crowd, who know of the danger he is in, pretend that nothing is wrong and greet him as usual. The two brothers publicly kill Mingguang with a knife and an axe. Apparently insane, Hongxing then drowns herself in a lake.

The film attempts not merely to tell the tale of a violent murder, but to shock us with the contradiction between the apparent worthlessness of human life and the emphasis on ethical conventions in Chinese tradition. The use of flashbacks and the juxtaposition of cause and effect creates a sense of absurdity.

(SC)

Blue Kite, The

(Lan fengzheng)

dir. **Tian Zhuangzhuang**
sc. Xiao Mao
with Lu Liping, Pu Quanxin, Li Xuejian, Gao Baochang
Hong Kong: Longwick Film/Beijing: Beijing Film, 1993

From a child's perspective and with a child's voice-over narration unfolds the story of a Beijing family living through the turmoil of the 1950s–60s. Like **Farewell My Concubine** (*dir.* **Chen Kaige**, 1993) and **To Live** (*dir.* **Zhang Yimou**, 1994), *The Blue Kite* exhibits an obsession with the subject of history. The personal and the political intertwine as the film follows the lives of individuals buffeted by the socio-political forces which clash on the national stage.

History, as viewed through the eyes of the child, concerns the 'death of the fathers', with each of three deaths marking a certain historical moment. The death of the boy's first father recalls a time during the anti-rightist movement. Tietou's librarian father, Lin Shaolong, and schoolteacher mother, Chen Shujuan, get married in the days after Stalin's death. The ascendancy of state ideology over domestic life is foreshadowed by the presence of Mao's portrait in the wedding room and by the revolutionary songs that the guests sing. The rectification movement in 1957 brings Shaolong to a labour reform camp, a consequence of his committing the 'anti-revolutionary crime' of voicing his true feelings in response to Mao's call to 'let a hundred flowers bloom'. The news of his death comes in a letter which Tietou is too young

to read. The arrival of Tietou's second father coincides with the absurdities of the Great Leap Forward, a time when people suffer from hunger and disease due to the government's misguided efforts to modernize China. After the death of this father, the boy's mother is remarried to a high-ranking party official, who then falls victim to the violence of the **Cultural Revolution** and dies of a heart attack when assaulted by a mob of Red Guards.

While the death of each father coincides with a cataclysmic moment in modern Chinese history, the surviving woman carries the burden of continuity. In *The Blue Kite*, Tietou's mother marries three times in order to go on living and bring good fortune to her son. After each tragedy, the woman is left to clean up the past and begin life anew. Depicted as a survivor and reservoir of stored sufferings, woman becomes an idealized figure of moral strength.

The Blue Kite is a visually beautiful film, emotionally moving but not overtly melodramatic. The screen space is often divided into a public political sphere and a familial private space. Typically, the camera will frame the family through a doorway shot before slowly leading the viewer further into the inner drama. The metaphor of the blue kite, and the use of a child's narrative voice, reinforce the violent contrast between the oppressive realities of history and the innocence of a child.

See also: melodrama

(SC)

Blush

(Hongfen)

dir. **Li Shaohong**
sc. Ni Zhen, Li Shaohong
with Wang Ji, He Saifei, Wang Zhiwen
Hong Kong: Ocean Film/Beijing: Beijing Film, 1994

Adapted from Su Tong's story, *Blush* re-examines the 1950s campaign to re-educate prostitutes in mainland China. The Communist line on **prostitution** is that prostitutes should be restored to physical and moral health and that the female body should be valued as a site of productive work rather than sexuality and decadence. The film, however, tells a different story. It begins with the army taking some prostitutes to a training school where physical examinations, short haircuts, and bland uniforms will mark their new identities. As Xiao'e weeps at the prospect of a confined collective life, her best friend, Qiuyi, manages to run away. The film then unfolds the two women's different life stories in a parallel structure.

After her escape, Qiuyi hides in the home of Laopu, formerly her rich playboy lover but now a commoner. She sleeps by herself during the day and with Laopu at night. Bored with her new life and unable to tolerate Laopu's mother, Qiuyi seeks refuge in a Buddhist temple, where she shaves her head and tries to become a faithful nun. Already pregnant by Laopu, she has a miscarriage and is cast out of the temple.

Inside the training school, Xiao'e initially complains and then even attempts suicide. After ideological brainwashing, she graduates to the rank of factory worker, but she cannot tolerate manual labour. She marries Laopu and demands a life of luxury. To satisfy her, Laopu steals a large sum of money from his work unit. Meanwhile, Quiyi has married an ordinary old man who owns a teahouse. After Laopu is arrested for his 'crime against the new society', she visits him in prison before his execution. As the film ends, Xiao'e, a supposedly re-educated prostitute, is married once again, leaving her fatherless baby to Qiuyi. Ironically, it is Qiuyi – who escaped the reform process – who has a heart of gold and a love for humanity. In its unglamorized way, *Blush* shows that individual lives and social realities do not always conform to the official line on prostitution.

(SC, YZ)

Boat People
(Touben nuhai)

dir. Ann **Hui**
sc. Tien Kor, Dei An Pang
with George Lam, Season Ma, Andy **Lau**, Cora Miao
Hong Kong/China: Bluebird Film, 1982

Following a television drama (*The Boy From Vietnam*, 1978) and prequel feature film (*The Story of Woo Viet*, 1981), *Boat People* is the third instalment of Ann Hui's 'Vietnamese trilogy'. Shot on location on Hainan Island, the film sparked an international controversy over its politically incendiary subject matter. The movie opens with Akutagawa, a Japanese photojournalist, covering the liberation of Da Nang, Vietnam, in 1975. Three years later

he returns to the country as a guest of the government's Cultural Bureau.

As well as spending time with Communist officials, Akutagawa strikes up a friendship with Cam Nuong, a teenage street urchin, and her two young brothers. One of them, Ah Nhac, is later killed by a land mine. After witnessing the youngsters scavenge from the bodies of execution victims at the nearby 'chicken farm', Akutagawa tries to help them. The journalist had been impressed by the organization of a new economic zone he had been invited to visit. However, he is told by To Minh, an ex-translator for the American army who now plans to escape from Vietnam by boat, that the zone he toured, number 16, is a show model designed to impress visitors: the other zones are much more inhumane. After witnessing further examples of social injustice, Akutagawa resolves to help Cam and her brother escape. Akutagawa is killed in the attempt, but the two young Vietnamese succeed in reaching the boat and put out to sea. A final freeze-frame depicts the two of them looking out across the ocean, an uncertain future ahead.

A commercial and critical event in Hong Kong, *Boat People* was the subject of intense political debate and the precursor of other similarly-themed allegorical narratives. It remains a powerful, if suppressed, document of its time.

Further reading
K. Jaehne (1984), an interview; H. Kennedy (1983), on the politics of the film's reception at the 1983 Cannes FF.

(JS)

Boatman's Daughter
(Chuanjia nü)

dir./sc. **Shen Xiling**
with Xu Lai, Gao Zhanfei, Sun Min, Wang Jiting, Hu Jia
Shanghai: Mingxing Film, 1935

The film concerns the misfortunes of an innocent woman, Ah Ling, who lives with her father in Hangzhou, where they rent a boat transporting passengers across the West Lake. Ah Ling is in love with Tie'er, a factory worker who takes her boat every day and sometimes rows the boat for her father. She helps him with needlework, and the two enjoy their mutual love on a romantic moonlit night.

Ah Ling's peaceful life is disrupted by the appearance of a playboy artist from Shanghai, who wants her to model for his painting and photography. Ah Ling's father refuses at first, but when he becomes seriously ill, Ah Ling is forced to accept the deal. There is no one to help her now as Tie'er has been imprisoned after a strike. Because of her father's debts, Ah Ling is soon sold into **prostitution**. Three months later, Tie'er is released from prison and learns of Ah Ling's fate. He finds her in a brothel and tries to free her, only to be arrested again.

Through its framing sequences at the beginning and end of the film, *Boatman's Daughter* criticizes the hypocrisy of public campaigns against prostitution and laments the widespread moral degradation in contemporary society. The film also emphasizes a sharp opposition between the honest, traditional **rural life** and the corrupt, hostile urban environment – an opposition that constitutes a recurrent theme in Chinese film. The director addresses this theme in his ***Twenty-Four Hours in Shanghai*** (1933) and ***Crossroads*** (1937).

Further reading

Y. Zhang (1999b), a critical study of prostitution and urban imagination.

(PV, YZ)

Border Town

(Biancheng)

dir. **Ling Zifeng**
sc. Li Junpei, Yao Yun
with Feng Hanyuan, Shi Lei, Dai Nan, Liu Kui, Liu Hanpu
Beijing: Beijing Film, 1984

This film is based on Shen Congwen's novella of the same title and tells a simple story of unrequited love. The border town symbolizes a space removed from political life. Indeed, the filmmakers have deliberately avoided making any obvious reference to the specific historical period. The idea is to show that there are things more fundamental to human life than political involvement.

Cuicui is a quiet seventeen-year-old orphan girl who lives with her grandpa in a small town. Two brothers from a wealthy family in the town, Dalao and Erlao, both fall in love with her. Since neither is willing to back off, the two brothers decide to hold a competition: whoever wins

Cuicui's affection through singing can lay claim to her. It turns out that Cuicui prefers Erlao, the younger one. The disappointed Dalao leaves home on a business trip and is killed in an accident. Grandpa becomes troubled by the fact that Dalao's family seems to blame him for his death. When he goes to propose the marriage between Cuicui and Erlao, the latter's parents withhold their consent. The truth is that Erlao's parents have just accepted a marriage proposal from another wealthy family who have offered him a mill as dowry. Although Erlao loves Cuicui and turns down the deal, he is haunted by his brother's death and decides to leave his hometown. Cuicui's grandpa falls seriously ill. Cuicui now has to take over grandpa's job as a ferry man and learn to take care of herself.

The film received Best Director award at the 1985 China GRA as well as a prize from the Montreal FF's selection committee.

(ZX)

Boys from Fengkuei, The

(Fenggui lai de ren)

dir. **Hou Hsiao-hsien**
sc. Hou Hsiao-hsien, **Chu Tien-wen**, Ding Yaming
with Niu Chengze, Chang Zhi, Tuo Zonghua, Lin Xiuling
Taipei: Wanbaolu Film, 1983

Fengkuei is a fishing village in the Pescadore Islands, the largest offshore chain in the Taiwan Straits. Even though Fengkuei offers a lot for city slickers on their weekend vacations, it is just too quiet and boring for its hot-blooded youngsters. The film's main plot line begins with four young men hopping on a boat to an island after they think they have killed someone during a fight with some locals. They land on Kaohsiung, the second largest city in Taiwan, known for its concentrated factory labour and tropical climate. As they are wandering around, a porno theatre tout comes up and tries to sell them some hot stuff. After paying their dues, they climb to the top of an empty building only to find that the 'big colour screen with hot European babes' is, in fact, a view of the city from an unfinished construction site. This disappointing encounter with a city trickster does not stop them from exploring the town. They decide to stay, working in a factory by day and enjoying their youth at night. The story comes to an end when the young men have to go their separate ways as adulthood approaches.

There are many stylistic and narrative innovations· in this movie that reappear in Hou Hsiao-hsien's later films. Accidental violence, death, and the discovery of secrets are some motifs that Hou constantly uses to refer to his own youth as well as to the vagaries of life. The narrative structure is not organized linearly but by a series of seemingly unrelated vignettes, which constitutes the essay-like style of Hou's work. It is the combination of these aspects that defines Hou's unique style, which he continues to refine in later films.

Further reading

G. Cheshire (1993), an excellent analysis of Hou's films; H. Chiao (1993a), an interview with critical comments.

(YY)

Breaking with Old Ideas

(Juelie)

dir. Li Wenhua
sc. Chun Chao, Zhou Jie
with Guo Zhenqing, Bao Lie, Wang Suya
Beijing: Beijing Film, 1975

Breaking with Old Ideas celebrates a radical change in the educational system with the opening of a Communist Labour College to peasants in the 1960s. Two protagonists emerge most prominently in the film. Long Guozheng, a Communist emissary, starts the revolutionary process. Li Jinfeng, one of many peasants who have entered the college, encourages all other students to study hard without forgetting their class origins.

After several conflicts with conservative authorities, Li Jinfeng is about to be expelled. In a trial open to the whole peasant community, she transforms herself from accused to accuser by pointing out the values of the proletarian revolution and by quoting Mao Zedong's teachings. At the end of the film, a message from Chairman Mao arrives in time to support Li Jinfeng and Long Guozheng, and the Labour College thwarts its opponents.

Breaking with Old Ideas is one of a dozen feature films produced during the **Cultural Revolution**. The opposition between good and bad characters is rendered by a set of highly codified devices known as the 'three prominences'. The central hero is prominent among a group of heroes, who are prominent among positive characters, who are always portrayed in bigger profile and in brighter light than the villains.

Further reading

T. Wang (1990), an analysis of film techniques prominent during the Cultural Revolution.

(PV, YZ)

Bridge

(Qiao)

dir. Wang Bin
sc. Yu Min
with Wang Jiayi, Jiang Hao, Du Defu, Lu Ban, **Chen Qiang**, Yu Yang
Changchun: Northeast Film, 1949

One of the first films produced by the CCP, *Bridge* already exhibits some of the key aspects of post-1949 filmmaking in the PRC. These elements include the depiction of popular support for the **Communist revolution** in the late 1940s, the inability of technical experts to solve numerous problems, and the great potential of the masses.

During the civil war a railroad factory is contracted by the CCP to repair a bridge. The chief engineer distrusts his workers' abilities and doubts that the project can be completed on time. Some workers fail to appreciate the significance of the job and show little enthusiasm for the project. A pro-Communist worker, Liang Risheng, takes the initiative in overcoming many of the difficulties encountered during the repairing of the bridge. The workers finally complete the repairs ahead of schedule. In the process, the chief engineer comes to recognize the workers' great potential.

(ZX)

Brighter Summer Day, A

(Gulingjie shaonian sharen shijian)

dir. Edward **Yang**
sc. Edward Yang, Yan Hongya, Yang Shunqing, Lai Mingtang
with Zhang Zheng, Yang Jingyi, Wang Qizan, Lin Hongming
Taipei: CMPC/Edward Yang Film Workshop, 1991

With its title taken from an Elvis Presley ballad, Yang's epic masterpiece delineates the clashing cultures of post-1949 mainland Chinese migrants and their restless, sceptical children. Like *A **Time to Live, a Time to Die*** (1985) and ***Dust in the Wind*** (1986, both *dir*. **Hou Hsiao-hsien**), this film is autobiographical, but it is also based on a true story that shocked Taiwan in 1961. A young man, whose father is being investigated by the authorities, is about to be suspended from high school for his involvement in street gangs. He loses control and murders his girlfriend. The film is a fine characterization of **youth culture** and street gangs in 1960s Taiwan, but the incident is also a pretext for examining the nuances of political, cultural and even musical allegiance among various groups of second-generation mainland sojourners in Taiwan. Four gangs occupy the centre of the narrative, three mainlanders and one native Taiwanese. An alliance is formed between one mainland (youth) gang and the Taiwanese (mostly adult) gang, based upon their mutual admiration for American pop and rock music.

American pop culture is favoured by the younger generation, whereas traditional Chinese culture is the object of weary platitudes by their parents and schoolmasters. This contrast provokes reflections on neocolonialism. The music of Frankie Avalon, Buddy Holly, and Elvis serves as *diegetic* background (narration within the film) for scenes of violence, romance and death. The music is reproduced by these gangs as part of their everyday experience, not merely superimposed by a nostalgic director. When 'Little Elvis,' lead singer of the Little Park youth gang/band, sings, 'Are You Lonesome Tonight?' the poignant coexistence of musical and visual stylization lends a sharp edge to the notion of neocolonialism. *A Brighter Summer Day* is not only an exercise in authorial reminiscence, but an unsettling invitation to mimicry as a form of survival and resistance.

Further reading

S. Teo (1991, 1992), two discussions of the film.

(YY)

Bu Wancang

b. 1903
d. 1974
Director, producer

One of the leading directors of the 1920s–40s, Bu Wancang began his apprenticeship in 1921 under an American cinematographer employed by China Film Company. He became a cameraman himself and worked first for Great China Film Company and then for Mingxing Film Company. He participated in the filming of *The Human Heart* (*dir*. Gu Kenfu, Chen Shouyin, 1924) and *The New Family* (*dir*. Ren Jinping, 1925), both box-office successes. By 1926, Bu was both producer and director at Mingxing, his directorial début being *Innocence* (1926).

After joining Lianhua Film Company in 1931, Bu firmly established his reputation by directing such successful titles as *Love and Responsibility* (1931)**, Three Modern Women** and *Motherly Love* (both 1933). When Shanghai became an 'isolated island' in 1937–41, Bu was involved in the production of costume dramas, all of which carry strong elements of **nationalism**. ***Mulan Joins the Army*** (1939) was based on the life of a legendary patriotic girl who disguised herself as a boy so as to join the army fighting foreign invaders. Ironically, once the Japanese began their occupation of Shanghai's international settlements in 1941, Bu also directed two propaganda films for the Japanese: *Universal Love* (1942) and *The Opium War* (1943). These two titles were denounced by patriotic Chinese as Japanese attempts to justify colonialist policies in China. Such controversy proved damaging to both Bu's political and professional post-war careers. Bu went to Hong Kong in 1948 to work for Yonghua Film Company. He left Yonghua two years later and formed his own Taishan film company. He made a few more films in Taiwan in the early 1960s before retiring.

See also: costume drama; propaganda and film

(ZX)

Bunman: The Untold Story

(Baxian fandian zhi renrou chashao bao)

dir./sc. Herman Yau
with Anthony **Wong**, Danny **Lee**, Shing Fui-On, Parkman Wong
Hong Kong: Golden Princess, 1993

Along with *Doctor Lam* (*dir*. Danny Lee, Billy Tang, 1992) and *Run and Kill* (*dir*. Billy Tang, 1993), *Bunman: The Untold Story* is one of the more gruesome true-life murder dramas to come out of Hong Kong's Category 3 genre. The film starts in 1978 when a man named Leung kills another man, assumes a new identity, and moves on to Macao.

Under the name Wong Chi Hang, Leung tries to secure legal possession of a local restaurant, claiming that the previous owner has moved overseas. Wong kills two employees who know too much – filling, afterwards, the pork buns he serves to his customers with their remains – before the authorities become suspicious. Wong is arrested. While scenes of sickening police torture generate a degree of sympathy for the 'Bunman', a strategically placed flashback then reveals how he hacked the absent restaurateur's entire family to pieces. Wong commits suicide before the Macao police have a chance to prosecute and convict him.

For his performance in *Bunman*, Anthony Wong picked up a Best Actor trophy at the 1993 HKFA. The fact that Wong triumphed over such stiff competition – his rivals included Lau Ching-Wan (*C'est la vie, mon chéri*, *dir.* Derek Yee, 1993), Jackie **Chan** (*Crime Story*, *dir.* Che Kirk **Wong**, 1993), and Ng Hing Kwok (*Temptation of a Monk*, *dir.* Clara **Law**, 1993) – testifies to the inroads that exploitation cinema has made into the Hong Kong mainstream.

See also: Category 3 film

Further reading
J. Stringer (1998a), on Category 3 films.

(JS)

Burning of Red Lotus Temple, The

(Huo shao honglian si)

dir. **Zhang Shichuan**
sc. **Zheng Zhengqiu**
with Zheng Xiaoqiu, Xia Peizhen, Gao Lihen, Tang Jie, **Gong Jianong**
Shanghai: Mingxing Film, 1928

As the most famous early martial arts title, this film led to numerous sequels and imitations. Because of its influence on other films of this genre, its name has become synonymous with martial arts subjects. Originally adapted from a popular knight-errant novel, the film is about adventure, friendship, intrigue and revenge.

Lu Xiaoqing is a skilled martial arts master. After his parents pass away, he sets out to visit other martial arts masters. One day he loses his way and seeks shelter in a temple where he discovers a secret cave. A fight ensues after the monks try to force him to join them, but Lu is

rescued by a passer-by, Liu Chi. After informing the government of the illegal activities in the Red Lotus Temple and going back to investigate the situation, Lu and Liu run into a man named Chang Deqing and tell him what they have discovered in the temple. Unbeknown to them, however, Chang is actually the leader of the temple. As Chang attempts to kill Lu and Liu, a young woman named Gan Lianzhu and her friend Chen Jizhi show up to save Lu and Liu's lives. Gan's mission is to rescue a government investigator who has been kidnapped by the monks and kept in the same cave discovered by Lu. The four form an alliance and arrive at the temple. With the help of the government troops, they kill all but three of the evil monk leaders and rescue the kidnapped investigator.

See also: martial arts film

(ZX)

Burning of the Imperial Palace, The

(Huo shao yuanmingyuan)

dir. **Li Han-hsiang**
sc. Yang Cunbin, Li Han-hsiang
with Zhang Shuyi, **Liu Xiaoqing**, Chen Hua, Tony Kar-Fei **Leung**
Beijing: China Film Co-production/Hong Kong: New Kunlun Film, 1983

This film is based on an actual historical event of 1858–9 when French and English troops marched into Beijing and burned down Yuanmingyuan, the Imperial Palace. The site is preserved now as a reminder of China's humiliating modern history.

A seventeen-year-old girl, Yulan, is chosen to be Emperor Xianfeng's concubine. However, because she is from a clan that does not enjoy close ties with the royal family, she has never been favoured by the Emperor. The Emperor is worried because the throne has no heir: while the Empress has not yet become pregnant, his second wife has only produced a daughter. One day Emperor Xianfeng takes a stroll in the palace gardens. Yulan succeeds in attracting his attention with her singing. From that moment on the emperor starts to visit her frequently and she soon bears him a son. The Emperor is overjoyed and elevates her social status – only the empress now has higher standing.

As the English and French allied troops approach Beijing in a punitive expedition, the court is divided as to what the best response should be. Emperor Xianfeng takes Yulan's advice and sends one of his generals to fight the advancing army. The Chinese military forces, however, suffer a disastrous defeat and the royal family has to flee Beijing. As Emperor Xianfeng continues to indulge himself in the pleasures of a temporary palace and leave many of his responsibilities to Yulan, the French and English troops ransack Beijing. After looting much of the treasure from Yuanmingyuan, the English and French soldiers burn down this architectural wonder of the world.

The film was awarded Best Film prize from the Ministry of Culture in 1983.

(ZX)

C

Cageman

(Long min)

dir. Jacob C. L. Cheung
sc. Ng Chong-chau, Yank Wong, Jacob C. L. Cheung
with Wong Ka Kui, Roy Chiao, Liu Kai-tsi, **Yim Ho**, Lawrence Ah Mon
Hong Kong: Filmagica Productions, 1992

Cageman is a beautifully-acted comedy-drama about the lives of impoverished men who are forced to live in tiny cages in the poorer sections of overcrowded Kowloon. Virtually all the action takes place in Wah Ha's Men's Hostel, a rat-infested tenement block that is due to be demolished by the Urban Council. The local denizens include Mr Koo and his backward son, Prince Sam, the one-hundred-year-old 7–11, Tong Sam, Luk Tung, and Mao, the criminal son of a local police chief, Officer Lam.

The 'cagemen' become the subject of intense media attention when two rival councillors, Tsui and Chow, decide they will exploit a good photo opportunity by spending three days and nights inside the hostel. But both men are also in league with the landlords, and as soon as the visitors move out the building is slated to be demolished. The inhabitants of Wah Ha's are forcibly evicted, cut free from behind their bars, and thrown out on to the street. Some time later, Prince Sam and Luk Tung come across Mao working in his new job at the zoo. The men have exchanged one cage for another.

Cageman was given a Category 3 (adult-only) censorship rating because of its bad language. However, there is nothing exploitative about it. Along with Lawrence Ah Mon's *Gangs* (1988) and *Queen of Temple Street* (1990), Cheung's film stands as one of the most impressive examples of **social realism** in contemporary Hong Kong cinema.

See also: Category 3 film; censorship and film

(JS)

Cai Chusheng

b. 12 January 1906, Shanghai
d. 15 July 1968
Director

Before the arrival of the **Fifth Generation** in the mid-1980s, Cai Chusheng was one of the best known Chinese film directors in the West. His name features in several international publications on the history of cinema.

Cai had a difficult childhood. He had to work as an apprentice in a bank and retail store when only twelve. He found a clerical job in a small film studio in Shanghai in 1927. Later, with **Zheng Zhengqiu**'s help, Cai was transferred to the prestigious Mingxing Film Company where he worked as Zheng's assistant. Cai's career as director took off in 1931 when he joined the newly formed Lianhua Film Company. His first films, *Spring in the South* and *Pink Dream* (both 1932), already give some indication of his undeniable talent. Cai's association with leftist film critics had a profound impact on his filmmaking. While his next film, ***Dawn Over the Metropolis*** (1933), focused on class conflict, social injustice and moral corruption, these themes were carried even further in ***Song of the Fishermen*** (1934), which became the first Chinese film ever to win a major award at an international festival after receiving an honorary prize at the 1935 Moscow FF. During the remainder of the 1930s, Cai continued this vein of social criticism with ***New Woman*** (1934), ***Lost Children*** (1936) and *The Life of Mr Wang* (1937).

Cai went to Hong Kong after the outbreak of the Sino-Japanese war in 1937, co-authored two screenplays on anti-Japanese themes and directed **Orphan Island Paradise** (1939) and *The Boundless Future* (1940). When Hong Hong fell to Japan in 1941, Cai went to Chongqing to join the Nationalist Central Film Studio. Then, soon after the Japanese surrender of 1945, Cai returned to Shanghai and formed Lianhua Film Society, later incorporated into Kunlun Film Company. In 1947, Cai and **Zheng Junli** co-directed **Spring River Flows East**, an immensely popular film that fully sold out its three-month engagement in Shanghai. In the meantime, Cai became further involved with underground Communists. He travelled to Hong Hong again in 1948, this time to escape the Nationalist police, and oversaw the production of *Tears Over the Pearl River* (*dir*. Wang Weiyi, 1949). After 1949, Cai served in the PRC government in numerous administrative capacities. He was appointed director of the committee responsible for artistic activities under the newly organized Film Bureau, of which he also served as deputy chief. He was also a member of the first, second and third National Congress, and President of the All China Filmmakers' Association. Cai became a CCP member in 1956.

Regrettably, Cai's creative activities in the post-1949 period were limited to the production of only one film, *The Waves of the Southern Sea* (1962), and the publication of a few essays on film directing. He was persecuted during the **Cultural Revolution** and died in 1968.

Further reading
ZDX (1982–6: 1: 338–49), a short biography.

(ZX)

Cai Yangming

b. 1939, Yunlin County, Taiwan
Actor, director and screen writer

Cai Yangming started his film career in the early 1960s by serving as screen writer, assistant director and actor. He appeared in over 200 Taiwan dialect films and turned to directing in 1969. In the 1980s, he was one of three Taiwan directors whose films fared well at the box-office. His later works include *Big Brother* (1988) and *Ah Dai* (1992).

(YZ)

Camel Xiangzi, aka Rickshaw Boy
(Luotuo Xiangzi)

dir./sc. **Ling Zifeng**
with Zhang Fengyi, Yin Xin, Yan Bide, **Siqin Gaowa**, Li Xiang
Beijing: Beijing Film, 1982

This film is based on Lao She's novel of the same title and tells the story of a young man whose dreams of a simple and modest life never come true. His hard work and honesty bring him nothing but trouble and tragedy. Hence, the critical thrust is here directed at the unjust society of the 1920s–30s.

A peasant youth, Xiangzi, comes to Beijing in search of work and ends up pulling a rickshaw. He dreams of owning a rickshaw of his own and making an honest living, and after three years of saving his money he indeed does have enough for his own rickshaw. But a local warlord conscripts Xiangzi to work for his troops by using his rickshaw to transport ammunition. The warlord's army suffers a disastrous defeat, and Xiangzi loses his first rickshaw. Unexpectedly, however, he comes across four stray camels, brings them to Beijing, and sells them for thirty-five silver dollars, thus earning the nickname Camel Xiangzi.

The owner of the rickshaw company, Liu Si, has a spinster daughter named Huniu who falls in love with Xiangzi. Although Xiangzi does not love her, he is seduced into sleeping with her. He then tries to avoid her by working for a different employer. His new employer, Mr Cao, is a leftist intellectual. When Cao gets into trouble, Xiangzi is also victimized and loses all his savings. After Huniu tricks Xiangzi into believing that she is pregnant, Xiangzi reluctantly goes back to her. But Liu Si refuses to approve of his daughter's relationship with Xiangzi, which leads to Huniu's estrangement from him. Huniu and Xiangzi formally marry and Huniu genuinely does become pregnant. However, a miscarriage costs her life.

A neighbourhood girl is forced by her father to work as a prostitute. Xiangzi likes her and wants to rescue her from brothel life, but by the time he arrives at the brothel with his savings, she has already committed suicide.

In 1982–3 the film won awards of Best Film and Best Actress (Siqin Gaowa) at both China GRA and HFA, as well as Best Film from the Ministry of Culture.

(ZX)

Cantonese cinema

See under: Hong Kong cinema (in Historical essays)

Capture Mount Hua by Stratagem

(Zhiqu huashan)

dir. Guo Wei
sc. Guo Wei, Ji Ye, Dong Fang
with Guo Runtai, Liu Liu, Fang Hua, **Li Lili**, Hu Peng
Beijing: Beijing Film, 1953

Set in the late 1940s, this **war film** tells the true story of a Communist commando successfully overtaking a strategically important Nationalist stronghold.

After they have seized Mount Hua, a brigade of Nationalist troops control the only path to the mountains. Their aim is to hold on to the fortress and stop the advance of the Communist forces. The CCP send a commando task force to Mount Hua on a mission to take this position back from the Nationalist troops. The commando leader, Liu Mingji, learns that a local pharmacist, Lin Nongsheng, who regularly goes to the mountains to pick herbs, often climbs to the top via a secret pathway, so he and a few soldiers go to Liu's residence to seek him out. However, a group of Nationalist soldiers have already looted the food supplies from Lin's house. Lin runs away after injuring one of the soldiers. When the Communist soldiers arrive, the Nationalist soldiers are just about to kill Lin's mother. That evening, Liu and his men help Lin's mother repair her house: she, in turn, brings Lin out of hiding.

With Lin working for the CCP, Liu's commando unit makes its way to the top of the mountain using a back road. After they surprise the Nationalist guards and take control of one of their positions, the commandos further consolidate their gains by persuading one of the Nationalist units to defect to the CCP side. In the end, Liu and his comrades take control of the whole area and all enemy resistance is eliminated.

(ZX)

Category 3 film

Category 3, introduced in 1989, refers to Hong Kong's adult-only (i.e., banned to under-18s) rating system. Throughout the 1990s, Category 3 films have jostled for position at the domestic box office with a range of other local genres. However, while all Hong Kong movie fads tend to repeat and exploit their attractions, Category 3 leads the way in terms of sex and violence.

Category 3 first gained notoriety with titles such as the gory *Man Behind the Sun* (*dir.* He Chi Chiang, 1990), a tale of human vivisection atrocities in wartime Manchuria, and erotic period dramas like *The Golden Lotus – Love and Desire* (*dir.* **Li Han-hsiang**, 1990). Over the next few years, adult thrillers, ghost, gangster, science fiction and prison quickies became a cultural norm as Category 3 blossomed under the umbrella of looser censorship laws. The genre offered up its own charismatic stars, both male (Simon **Yam**, Anthony **Wong**, Mark Cheng) and female (Chingamy Yau, Pauline Chen, Yung Hung, Amy Yip, Chikako Aoyama). Among the inevitable dross, and despite an all-pervasive misogyny, a fistful of noteworthy releases stand out, including *Cageman* (*dir.* Jacob Cheung, 1992), *Doctor Lam* (*dir.* Danny **Lee**, 1992), *Naked Killer* (*dir.* Fok Yiu Leung, 1992), *Robotrix* (*dir.* Chiany Yu, 1993), and *Sex and Zen* (*dir.* Michael Mak, 1991). Ironically enough, Category 3 elevated itself to a position of respectability at the very moment the Hong Kong film industry was consolidating its international reputation. While Anthony Wong picked up a 1993 Hong Kong Academy Best Actor award for his portrayal of a brutal mass murderer in the true-life *Bunman: The Untold Story* (*dir.* Danny Lee, 1993), soft porn star Veronica Yip made the jump to art-house glamour with her performance in the more mainstream *Red Rose, White Rose* (*dir.* Stanley **Kwan**, 1994).

Category 3 films circulate, mostly on videotape, as cult objects of desire in the West. However, their meaning is tied more to the local context as they appear to speak to the class resentments held by those who have failed to work Hong Kong's economic miracle.

See also: censorship and film; gangster film; ghosts and immortals, film of; science-fiction film

Further reading

S. Stockbridge (1994), a comparative analysis of how Category 3 rape scenes are censored in Hong Kong and Australia; J. Stringer (1998a), a class-based analysis of the genre.

(JS)

censorship and film

Although film was introduced into China as early as 1896, it was not until 1910 that the first film related regulation was issued by the Shanghai Autonomous Bureau under the Qing government, which imposed a ban on showing films in the open field during the summer, because officials disapproved of 'men and women sitting together in the dark'. A year later, the Bureau began to regulate movie theatres as well and issued a seven-article regulation, which stipulated (1) all movie theatres must apply for a licence from the authorities; (2) men and women must be seated separately; (3) no obscene films are allowed; (4) all shows must stop before midnight; (5) violations of (2) (3) and (4) will result in revocation of licence and in other penalties; (6) the police must inspect the movie theatres regularly; and (7) the licence is not transferable.

After the 1911 Revolution, which brought down the Qing dynasty, China entered a period of political disunity. With no central authority effectively governing the country, film censorship was largely in the hands of local governments, particularly the police departments. For instance, in 1921, the police department in Beijing imposed a set of regulations on theatres, including registration with the police, separate seating for men and women, daily submission of programme schedules to the police, reports of tickets sales, and the payment of a certain percentage of sales to the police. The regulations also prohibited the use of film equipment borrowed from foreigners as well as the showing of superstitious and obscene films. According to one contemporary report, the principal deletions during this period fell into two main categories: (a) bathing girls and other presentations of a similar kind, and (b) the representation of Chinese characters in pictures by people of other nationalities which caricatures the Chinese.

In 1924, the Mass Education Department under the Ministry of Education of the Beijing government appealed to the authorities to ban **Yan Ruisheng** (dir. Ren Pengnian, 1921) and *Zhang Xinsheng* (dir. **Zhang Shichuan**, 1922). Both films were based on actual murder cases and attracted large audiences at the time. Two years later, the same department drafted a set of film censorship regulations which aimed at eradicating films that 'disturbed social order, damaged social mores and (in the case of foreign films particularly) were offensive to Chinese sensibility'. However, no specific agency was set up to enforce these regulations.

The first Board of Film Censors was organized in 1923 by the Education Department of Jiangsu province. This was the first government agency in China that was specifically set up to censor films. But it was the Film Censorship Committee of Zhejiang provincial government, instituted in February 1926, that became the model of future film censoring agencies. The initial members of the Zhejiang Film Censorship Committee included sixteen participants from both the bureau of education and the bureau of police. The enlistment of the police enabled the censors to enforce their rulings effectively.

On the whole, governmental control of film before the 1930s was minimal, so much so that some people complained that the policy of 'no support, no interference' was responsible for the 'backwardness' of the Chinese film industry. On many occasions large film studios such as Mingxing Film Company, Shanghai Film Company and the Commercial Press's Film Department, were the champions for film censorship, because they felt that the lack of government regulation was detrimental to the healthy growth of the industry. But the censorship they called for would not focus on the content of films; rather, it would set up production standards. The purpose was clear: by making an issue of technical quality, large studios wanted to eliminate smaller studios, which allegedly produced films of low quality.

In 1927, the Nationalists came into power and founded the Nanjing government. In comparison with the previous warlord regimes, the new government had a much better appreciation of the potential power of motion pictures and took consistent steps to control them. Soon after the Nationalists took over Shanghai in 1927, they moved to set up a film censorship committee to oversee the showing of films in the city. A year later, the Shanghai Board of Film and Theatre Censors was formed. One significant departure from the earlier practice was that, in addition to being concerned with moral implications of films, this new board was more preoccupied with film's political orientation. The rules now curtailed 'deviation from the party's political doctrines'.

In June 1928, the Nanjing government issued *The Thirteen Regulations on Film* in an apparent attempt to achieve a unified national film censorship. Two years later, the Executive Yuan of the Nanjing government drafted a new set of film censorship regulations, known as the *Sixteen Regulations*. On 3 November 1930, the Legislative

Yuan of the government published China's first *Film Censorship Statute*. Unlike all the previous regulations, this statute was the first piece of legislature on film that bore the status of law. Following its publication, the Executive Yuan ordered the Ministry of Education and Interior Affairs to work out a plan to implement the law. In February 1931, the National Film Censorship Committee was established. As the first centralized film censorship institution in China, the committee was comprised of seven members (not including staff and technicians). In addition, a representative from the KMT's Propaganda Department was also on the board. But the educators had a *de facto* control of this committee and often defied the directives from the party. In order better to control the institution, the KMT reorganized it in March 1934 and changed its name to the Central Film Censorship Committee. Meanwhile, the party set up a separate, parallel committee for film script censorship.

The main targets of the Nationalist film censorship could be grouped into four categories. First, any films that had political messages disapproved by the government would be subject to censorship. Most of the leftist films, which exposed social ills, advocated class struggle and were critical of the government, fell into this category. Second, films that were deemed offensive to Chinese dignity would be banned. Many foreign films in which China and Chinese people were presented in negative light were banned on this ground. For instance, *Welcome Danger* (*dir.* Harold Lloyd, 1930) was one of the first victims of the Nationalist film censorship. Numerous American films, including *Shanghai Express* (*dir.* Josef von Sternberg, 1932), *The Bitter Tea of General Yen* (*dir.* Frank Capra, 1933) and *The General Died at Dawn* (*dir.* Lewis Milestone, 1936), to name just a few, suffered the same fate. Third, films that contained elements detrimental to the building of the modern state were strongly discouraged. Many martial arts films, such as *The **Burning of Red Lotus Temple*** (*dir.* Zhang Shichuan, 1928), were banned on the ground that they advocated superstition. Since there was no clear definition as to exactly what superstition meant, films such as *The Ten Commandments* (*dir.* Cecil B. De Mille, 1923), *Frankenstein* (*dir.* James Whale, 1931) and *Alice in Wonderland* (*dir.* Norman Z. McLeod, 1933) were also banned on the charge that they had no scientific basis. Finally, any films that were made in local dialects would be strictly forbidden because such films undermined the Nanjing government's effort to establish Mandarin as the official spoken language in the country.

Due to China's political disunity during the Republican period, Nationalist film censorship was largely confined to regions under Nanjing's control. Provinces like Guangxi and Guangdong were beyond the reach of Nanjing's censors. There films continued to be subject to the censorship rules drafted by the local censors. But the overall trend during the Nanjing period was that the government censors were increasingly assertive in controlling both the production and exhibition of films. Even Guangdong, which used to enjoy a great deal of political autonomy, came under the Central Film Censorship Committee's control after 1936.

The war with Japan changed everything. In July 1937 the Japanese army invaded China, and a few months later Nanjing fell. The Nationalist censorship committee moved with the government first to Wuhan, and then to Chongqing. It still managed to operate for another year, mainly in southern China. As the Japanese bombardment began in 1938, the KMT's Central Department of Propaganda decided to dissolve the censorship committee. It was not until after the war that the KMT government reinstated the institution under the Ministry of the Interior Affairs. But the ensuing civil war never allowed this agency to function fully with the same vigour as it used to during the pre-war period. In 1949 the Nationalists retreated to Taiwan and ended their film censorship on the mainland.

During the first forty years of the PRC period, filmmakers were subjected to the most arbitrary, inconsistent and stringent film censorship because the CCP government never passed a film censorship law and enforced it through an agency. As a result, the criterion for approving or disapproving a film was often dictated by politics at a given moment. Frequently opinions of individual party officials or even personal whims became the rule of the day. From the very beginning the CCP government's policy towards film was unstable and inconsistent. Initially it adopted a rather democratic stand. The earlier directive from the Central Department of Propaganda stated that as long as a film was anti-imperialism, anti-feudalism and anti-bureaucratic capitalism, it should be approved. The party's cultural officials even told the leaders of the film industry in Shanghai in 1949 that censorship was unnecessary, and what was needed was constructive film criticism. Yet within a few months the government changed its position. By December 1949, it decided that although a film script could be exempt from submission for approval, the finished film must be inspected by the authorities before its public release. It further stipulated that a film would be censored or banned if it was deemed to have one of the following features: (1) anti-communism, anti-Soviet Union and anti-people; (2) pro-imperialism or pro-feudalism; (3) pornographic or violating the laws and regulations of the PRC.

However, as one CCP cultural official admitted, because those rules were too broad and subject to different interpretations, it was extremely difficult to enforce them. As happened frequently, whereas some party officials considered a film to be problematic others would see it as a good one. The filmmakers were thus left confused and without protection. In summer 1952 the Minister of Propaganda, Zhou Yang, acknowledged that although in theory his ministry was authorized to decide whether or not to approve a given film, in reality he had to consult with other ministries, even the premier, for a final decision. In an attempt to simplify the matter, the Film Bureau decided that the censorship of film scripts would be handled at the studio level, and the Film Bureau would only inspect the finished films. Two years later, the bureau even proposed that the decision to approve or disapprove a finished film be made by studios. Only special cases would be handled by the central authorities. This model remained effective until the **Cultural Revolution** of the 1960s–70s, when the censorial authority was in the hands of the office of cultural affairs of the state department. Yet even that authority was often compromised when the supreme leader Mao Zedong himself intervened.

In the post-Mao era, the Film Bureau was once again in charge of film censorship. In response to the demand from the industry for a censorship law, the Ministry of Broadcasting, Film and Television published its first film censorship regulation in 1993. Meanwhile, the Bureau set up an office to handle film censorship exclusively. The basic principles of the 1993 document were reaffirmed in 1996 when the State Department issued new Film Administrative Regulations. To date, the pre-production censorship is still handled by the studio, while the post-production censorship is handled by the Film Bureau.

See also: language and film; leftist film (under Chinese cinema in Historical essays); martial arts film; Taiwan cinema (in Historical essays)

Further reading
T. S. Kam (1996), C. Li (1989), both on film censorship in Hong Kong; Z. Xiao (1997, 1999), both historical studies of censorship in the 1920s–30s; M. Yang (1993), with information regarding the Communist censorship in contemporary China.

(ZX)

C'est la vie, mon chéri
(Xin buliao qing)

dir./sc. Derek Yee
with Anita Yuen, Lau Ching-Wan, Carrie Ng, Carina Lau, Sylvia **Chang**
Hong Kong: Film Unlimited, 1993

This deeply affecting, hugely successful **melodrama** steered 1990s Hong Kong cinema away from popular action narratives, and made superstars out of its leading couple. The film concerns the love affair between Min, the twenty-year-old daughter of Cantonese opera performers, and Kit, a down-on-his-luck jazz musician who has just split up with his more successful other half, the pop star Tracy. While trying to establish her own singing career, Min helps pull Kit out of his despondent state. The two enjoy romantic dinners and walks in the hills.

The film switches moods in its second half when the bone cancer that plagued Min in childhood is rediscovered in her body. Min is hospitalized, and her family are forced back into street-singing to make their living. The one character who has provided optimism and support for all around her succumbs to grief and despair. It is now Kit's turn to cheer his partner up. However, in a devastating final scene, Min dies while Kit carries out a final errand for his beloved.

C'est la vie, mon chéri's mixed messages caught a popular mood, and the movie dominated the 1994 HKFA, claiming Best Picture, Director, Screenplay, Actress, Supporting Actor, and Supporting Actress prizes. Newfound superstar, Anita Yuen, later went on to win a second successive Best Actress award for her role in *He's a Woman, She's a Man* (*dir.* Peter Chan, 1994) – a historic double whammy.

See also: action film

(JS)

Chan, Jackie

(Cheng Long)

b. 4 April 1954, Hong Kong
Actor, director, screen writer

Not very much is known about Jackie Chan's early life except that he was entrusted to a Peking opera troupe in Hong Kong after his parents emigrated to Australia in 1962. For the next eight years, Chan and other young members of the 'Seven Little Fortunes' – including Sammo **Hung**, Yuen Biao, Yuen Kwai, Yuen Wah – underwent a rigorous programme of physical training and emotional development (these years are the subject of Alex Law's 1988 film ***Painted Faces***). Chan had been appearing in local movies since age eight, but it was not until the early 1970s that he began to establish his reputation, undertaking stunt work in two Bruce **Lee** showcases, *Fist of Fury* (*dir.* Lo Wei, 1972) and ***Enter the Dragon*** (*dir.* Robert Clouse, 1973).

Chan's big break came at age seventeen. After a first starring role in 1971 he appeared in a flood of movies, including *Hand of Death* (*dir.* John **Woo**), *New Fist of Fury* (*dir.* Lo Wei, both 1976), and *Snake in the Eagle's Shadow* (*dir.* Yuen Woo-ping, 1978). Chan's trademark comic acting style was initiated by *Half a Load of Kung Fu* (*dir.* Chan Chi Hwa, 1978), his image consolidated by classics such as *Drunken Master* (*dir.* Yuen Woo-ping, 1978), *Young Master* (*dir.* Jackie Chan, 1980), and *Wheels on Meals* (*dir.* Sammo Hung, 1984). Chan himself first turned director with *Fearless Hyena* in 1979, although it was not until he signed with Golden Harvest in 1981 that he appeared in some of his best films, such as *Project A* (1984), *Police Story* (1985) and *Armour of God* (1986). The level of stunt work in these and other Jackie Chan movies is simply beyond belief.

Chan's career has taken several twists and turns since the mid-1980s. Hong Kong audiences generally turned their back when he played a yuppie lawyer in ***Dragons Forever*** (*dir.* Sammo Hung, 1988), just as he failed to make much of an impression in North America – both *The Cannonball Run* (*dir.* Hal Needham, 1981) and *The Protector* (*dir.* James Glickenhaus, 1986) were flops. Yet after wonderful appearances in such quality films as *City Hunter* (*dir.* **Wong Jing**), *Crime Story* (*dir.* Che Kirk **Wong**, both 1993) and *Drunken Master, II* (*dir.* Lau Kar-leung, 1994), the Chan cult finally turned global. Now that ***Rumble in the Bronx*** (1994),

Police Story, III: Supercop (1992), and *Police Story, IV: First Strike* (1997, all *dir.* Stanley Tong) have played in malls all across America, there can be little doubt that Jackie Chan is the world's most popular actor.

Since the late 1980s, Chan has been awarded top prizes at Taipei GHA, HKFA, and Asia-Pacific FF. He was elected first president of the Hong Kong Film Directors Association.

Further reading
B. Logan (1996), C. D. Reid (1994), two interviews; S. Fore (1997), on Chan and global entertainment; M. Gallagher (1997), on Chan as a transnational star text.

(JS)

Chang Che

(Zhang Che)

b. 1923
Director, screen writer

An important Taiwan director in the 1950s–60s, Chang Che began his film career as a screen writer for Guotai and Datong film companies in Shanghai in 1947. He wrote and directed the first Mandarin film in Taiwan, *Wind and Cloud on Ali Mountain* (1949), for which he also composed the popular theme song. He went to Hong Kong in the mid-1950s and became the best known director of **martial arts film** with his *One-Armed Swordsman* (1967), the first Hong Kong film to gross over one million local dollars. His *Vengeance* (1970) won him Best Director award at Asia-Pacific FF. He directed about 100 films and helped train a number of young directors and actors, among them **Ti Lung**, David **Chiang** and John **Woo**.

Further reading
Che Zhang (1989), a memoir.

(YZ)

Chang, Sylvia

(Zhang Aijia)

b. 1953, Chiayi, Taiwan
Actress, producer, screen writer, director, singer

A versatile actress in Taiwan and Hong Kong, Sylvia Chang started her screen career at age nineteen hosting a TV variety show. She later joined Golden Harvest in Hong Kong and won Best

Actress at Taipei GHA for *My Grandpa* (1981). She turned to directing at the age of twenty-five and produced a TV series, *Eleven Women* (1982), which brought out some new directing talents. Her second feature film, *Passion* (1986), is about a love triangle involving two friends who love the same man; she wrote, directed and acted in this film with Cora Miao (Miao Jianren), and won Best Actress award at both HKFA and Taipei GHA. Chang's other features include *The Game They Called Sex* (1987), *Sisters of the World Unite* (1991), *Mary From Beijing* (1992) – a romantic **comedy** with **Gong Li** in the cast – and ***Tonight Nobody Goes Home*** (1996). She acted in over eighty films and recorded eleven albums of songs. In the 1990s, she started to play lead roles in films by mainland directors, including *Shadow of Dreams* (*dir*. Lu Xiaowei, 1993).

(YZ)

Chang, Terence
(Zhang Jiacun)

b. 1949, Hong Kong
Producer, director

Despite his low public profile, Chang represents a very significant force as producer and creative partner for John **Woo** and in the Hong Kong cinema's diaspora into Hollywood. After taking architecture coursework at the University of Oregon, he studied filmmaking at New York University. Returning to Hong Kong in 1978, he worked as production manager on two films. He joined Rediffusion Television (RTV) as Administration Officer of the Production Department, supervising all TV production. In 1981, he joined Johnny **Mak**'s company, pro-ducing three films. One of these, *Everlasting Love*, was chosen for the Director's Fortnight section at the 1984 Cannes FF. His only directorial project was in 1985, *Escape from Coral Cove*. As head of Distribution for D&B Films between 1986 and 1988, he launched overseas careers for Brandon Lee, Michelle **Yeoh** (whose manager he later became), and Cynthia Rothrock. As General Manager for **Tsui Hark**'s Film Workshop between 1988 and 1990, he was chief production executive for several films, including John Woo's *The **Killer*** (1989) and King **Hu**'s ***Swordsman*** (1990).

In 1990, Chang, Woo, and Linda Kuk formed Milestone Pictures, producing Woo's *Once a Thief*

(1991) and *Hard Boiled* (1992). He also became manager for **Chow Yun-Fat** and writer Lilian Lee. Chang's partnership with Woo proved extremely fruitful for Hong Kong cinema and has extended successfully to Hollywood. Chang has helped to guide Woo through the difficulties of Hollywood studio politics; additionally, he has assisted other important Hong Kong figures in their transition to the USA.

(KH)

Chang Yi
(Zhang Yi)

b. 1951
Director, screen writer

An active member in New Taiwan Cinema, Chang Yi was a novelist before he turned to screen writing. He shared Best Screenplay award at Asia-Pacific FF with Zhang Yongxiang for *The Pioneers* (*dir*. Chen Yaoxin, 1980). He made his directorial début with an episode in the four-part ***In Our Time*** (1982). His other noted works include ***Jade Love*** (1984) and ***Kuei-mei, a Woman*** (1985), the latter winning Best Director and Best Film awards at Taipei GHA.

See also: New Taiwan Cinema (under Taiwan Cinema in Historical essays)

(YZ)

Chen Baichen
(Chen Zhenghong)

b. 1 March 1908, Jiangsu province
d. 28 May 1994
Screen writer, playwright, fiction writer

A well-known playwright and screen writer, Chen Baichen began writing short stories while still at junior high school. In 1927, he enrolled in Shanghai Liberal Arts University as a literature major. The department of literature was at that time chaired by **Tian Han**, a high-profile leftist intellectual, and through this contact Chen was able to act in *The Melody from a Broken Flute* (1927), written and directed by Tian. By the time Chen wrote his first screenplay in 1947, he had already published ten short stories and a dozen plays.

As a member of the Communist Youth League, Chen was involved in the Left League of the Chinese Writers and other activities encouraged or sponsored by the CCP. During the war he was a visiting professor at the National Drama School and wrote a number of plays critical of the KMT government. After the Japanese surrender, Chen returned to Shanghai where he headed the screen-play committee at Kunlun Film Company. His first script for the studio, *The Lucky Bureaucrat*, was never filmed because of its harsh criticisms of the KMT authorities. The political satire of Chen's co-authored screenplay (with **Chen Liting**) for *Rhapsody of Happiness* (*dir.* Chen Liting, 1947) was particularly appealing to audiences experiencing frustration and disillusionment with the KMT government. ***Crows and Sparrows*** (1949), another film Chen scripted during this period, portrays its KMT officials as corrupt and greedy imbeciles. Its message – that the KMT regime is totally hopeless – came over so loud and clear that the film was not publicly released until 1949.

Chen became a party member in 1950. In 1951 he co-authored, with Jia Qi, *The Rebels* (*dir.* **Zheng Junli**, **Sun Yu**, 1955). During the post-**Cultural Revolution** period, Chen served as chair of the Chinese Department at Nanjing university, and adapted *The Song of a Hero*, a play he had written earlier, into a screenplay in 1978. His last script was *The **True Story of Ah Q*** (*dir.* Cen Fan, 1981), a new adaptation of a famous story by Lu Xun.

See also: adaptations of drama and literature

Further reading

ZDX (1982–6: 2: 227–36), a short biography.

(ZX)

Chen, Joan

(Chen Chong)

b. 1961, Shanghai
Actress

Joan Chen appeared on screen at the age of four-teen when veteran director **Xie Jin** cast her in *Youth* (1976). She entered Shanghai Foreign Languages Institute and made two more films in the mainland, including *Little Flower* (*dir.* Zhang Zheng, 1979), which won her Best Actress award at HFA. She left for the USA in 1981 and studied film at California State University, playing in *Dim Sum: A Little Bit of Heart* (*dir.* Wayne Wang, 1985). Her Hollywood career started when she met producer Dino de Laurentis in the Paramount

parking lot. She played China-doll concubine May-May in de Laurentis's TV movie *Taipan* (1986). The real highlight of Joan's career is her role as Empress in *The Last Emperor* (*dir.* Bernardo Bertolucci, 1987, winner of nine Academy Awards). After a number of little known roles, she attracted public attention in David Lynch's enor-mously popular TV series, *Twin Peaks* (1990), where she played Josie Packard, a mysterious, deadly Asian seductress. Then she appeared in *Heaven and Earth* (*dir.* Oliver Stone, 1993) as a Vietnamese mother who ages from thirty to seventy during the course of the film, and in other titles such as *On Deadly Ground* (*dir.* Steven Seagal, 1994). A familiar presence in Hollywood films by the mid-1990s, Joan made her presence felt in Asia by taking the seductress roles in *The **Temptation of a Monk*** (*dir.* Clara **Law**, 1993) and *Red Rose, White Rose* (*dir.* Stanley **Kwan**, 1994), the latter winning her Best Actress award at Taipei GHA.

Further reading

Asiaweek (1994), a brief mention of her screen roles.

(YZ)

Chen Kaige

b. 12 August 1952, Beijing
Director

One of the best-known directors in the **Fifth Generation**, Chen Kaige comes from a promi-nent film family. His father Chen Huaiai (1920–94) was a famous director in the 1950s–70s, whose works include ***Song of Youth*** (*co-dir.* with **Cui Wei**, 1959), *Haixia* (1975) and dozens of **filmed stage performances**. During the **Cultural Revolution**, Chen Kaige turned against his father's generation, as did millions of other Red Guards. In the late 1960s, he was sent to a rubber plantation in Yunnan province, where he spent three years labouring in the forest. Chen joined the army but remained in Yunnan. He finally managed to return to Beijing in 1975 and worked in a film processing laboratory. After four years of study in the Directing Department of BFA, he was assigned to Beijing Film Studio and worked as assistant to **Huang Jianzhong** on a couple of films.

Chen's first two features were made in Guangxi Film Studio, where he and his classmates **Zhang Yimou** and **He Qun** collaborated on ***Yellow Earth*** (1984) and *The **Big Parade*** (1985). With its new artistic sensibility and historical vision,

Yellow Earth met with torrid enthusiasm at film festivals in Hong Kong, Edinburgh and Locarno and marked the first international success for the Fifth Generation. While negotiating with the authorities over final cuts to *The Big Parade*, Chen accepted **Wu Tianming**'s invitation and made *King of the Children* (1987) for Xi'an Film Studio. Expectation was high for this film based on a novella by Ah Cheng, Chen's workmate back in his Yunnan years, but it failed to win any major international award. In 1987, Chen visited the USA on a scholarship from New York University and stayed there to work towards a film degree. He received financial backing from Europe in 1990 and returned to China to film *Life on a String* (1991), an avant-garde film about two blind musicians travelling around the barren land in search of truth. Turning away from pure art, Chen directed *Farewell My Concubine* (1993), a mainstream film co-produced by Hong Kong and China. The film won him international fame as it took the Palme d'Or at the 1993 Cannes FF; it proved a major commercial success as well, earning millions of dollars in the USA alone.

After that, Chen was sought after in Taiwan and Hong Kong and signed on with Hollywood agent William Morris. However, his next feature, *Temptress Moon* (1995), was a failure in both box-office and film festival circles. Unlike Zhang Yimou, Chen's career is full of ups and downs.

See also: avant-garde, experimental or exploratory film

Further reading
K. Chen (1989–90), an interview with Aruna Vasudev; K. Chen and T. Rayns (1989), the director's own comments; K. Chen (1990), a conversation with Robert Sklar; K. Chen (1991), a memoir; Eder and Rossell (1993: 89–92), with an interview; T. Rayns (1989: 26–32), an insightful analysis; G. Semsel (1987: 134–40), an interview; J. Zha (1995: 79–104), an excellent profile with background information.

(YZ)

Chen Kun-hou
(Chen Kunhou)

b. 1939, Taichung, Taiwan
Director, cinematographer

An important figure in New Taiwan Cinema, Chen Kun-hou entered film circles in 1966 and did various odd jobs before being promoted to the rank of cinematographer. He won Best Cinematography at Taipei GHA for *A Boat in the Ocean* (*dir.* **Lee Hsing**, 1978). He has directed many features since the late 1970s, including *I Came with the Waves* (1979) and *Cool Autumn* (1980). In 1982, Chen joined forces with **Hou Hsiao-hsien** and others to found Evergreen Film Company (Wannianqing). With a budget of five million Taiwan dollars, Chen directed *Growing Up* (1983), a co-production with CMPC that won him Best Director and Best Film awards at Taipei GHA. This nostalgic film of childhood experiences was a box-office hit and set a trend for 'growing-up' films in the 1980s. After *Daddy's Sky* (1984), Chen made *The Season of Fond Memory* (1985), starring Sylvia **Chang** as a practical urban woman who seeks light-heartedly to settle herself in a comfortable marriage. *Marriage* (1985) and *Wandering Youth* (1986) were followed by *Osmanthus Alley* (1987), a glamorous portrayal of a poor village girl who becomes a powerful matriarch in a wealthy household in town.

See also: New Taiwan Cinema (under Taiwan Cinema in Historical essays)

Further reading
R. Chen (1993b: 174–5), a brief entry.

(YZ)

Chen Liting

b. 20 October 1910, Shanghai
Director, screen writer

Like many of his generation, Chen Liting initially became interested in the theatre. He joined the Daxia Theatre Society in 1931 while still an undergraduate at Daxia University. After college, Chen taught for one year at a primary school and wrote a famous play called *Put Down Your Whip*, the simple style and direct message of which proved continuously popular throughout the 1930s and early 1940s.

Chen's earliest association with film came when he contributed reviews to several major newspapers. He also translated a number of Soviet writings on the subject. At a time when Soviet films were largely absent from Chinese screens, Chen's translations made many aware of the existence of an alternative to Hollywood. Chen went to Chongqing in 1941 to join the Nationalist Central Film Studio. By the time the war ended in 1945, he had completed two books: *An Outline History of* the *Film* and *The Rules of the Cinema*. Although both publications drew heavily on Western sources, Chen added his own comments and observations. In 1947, he directed his first film, *The Love of Far Away* (1947). His next title, *Rhapsody of Happiness* (1947), was well received by the critics. Chen's best known directorial work is **Female Fighters** (1949).

During the PRC period, Chen directed two more films, *Inescapable* (1950) and *Work Is Beautiful* (1951). However, most of his creative energy was reserved for his administrative responsibilities. Chen was a member of the National Congress, served as the general manager of Tianma Film Studio from 1957 to 1966, and was in charge of the All China Filmmakers' Association. Upon being rehabilitated after the **Cultural Revolution**, Chen served as deputy director on the committee responsible for artistic quality at Shanghai Film Studio.

See also: theatre and film

Further reading

ZDX (1982–6: 2: 237–44), a short biography.

(ZX)

Chen Qiang

(Chen Qingsan)

b. 11 November 1918, Hebei province
Actor

Chen Qiang established his reputation after playing the evil landlord first in the stage version and then the film adaptation of *The* **White-Haired Girl** (*dir.* Wang Bin, **Shui Hua**, 1950). Legend has it that Chen portrayed this vicious character so well that many people subsequently failed to distinguish between his 'real' self and his theatrical self: audiences threw fruit at him, and a soldier even pointed his gun at him. Chen's success in *The White-Haired Girl* led to other evil roles. His portrayal of a local tyrant who owns a private army and treats the poor brutally in **Red Detachment of Women** (*dir.* **Xie Jin**, 1961) earned him a Best Supporting Actor prize at the 1962 HFA.

However, Chen is also one of the best known comedians of modern China. In film comedies such as *The Adventure of a Magician* (*dir.* **Sang Hu**, 1962) and *What a Family!* (*dir.* Wang Haowei, 1979), Chen handles humorous situations with great versatility and skill. Teaming up with his son,

Chen Peisi *(b.* 1954), himself a comedian turned director, Chen produced a series of films based around the life of an urban youth named Erzi. Titles like *Erzi Runs an Inn* (*dir.* Wang Binglin, 1987) explore changing moralities in the era of economic reform. As a highly respected performing artist, Chen Qiang also served in the 1980s as the secretary of the All China Filmmakers' Association.

See also: adaptations of drama and literature; comedy

Further reading

ZDX (1982–6: 4: 239–49), a short biography.

(ZX, YZ)

Chen Yanyan

b. 12 January 1916, Ningbo, Zhejiang province
Actress

Chen Yanyan was one of the most popular actresses of the 1930s. She grew up in Beijing and spoke beautiful Mandarin, a distinct advantage when the film industry made the transition to sound. Recruited by Lianhua Film Company in 1930, Chen starred in *Southern Spring* (*dir.* **Cai Chusheng**, 1932). Following critical acclaim for this performance, she starred in a string of other influential Lianhua productions, including **Three Modern Women**, *Motherly Love* (both *dir.* **Bu Wancang**, both 1933), **Big Road** (*dir.* **Sun Yu**, 1934), *The Heroine in Besieged City* (*dir.* Wang Cilong, 1936), *Mother's Song* (*dir.* **Zhu Shilin**, **Luo Mingyou**) and *Transition* (*dir.* Zhu Shilin, both 1937). In these films, Chen's girlish looks enabled her to be typecast as young, innocent and helpless. Fans in the 1930s nicknamed her 'the little birdie' (*xiaoniao*). Although Chen later played middle-aged or elderly characters in numerous film made during the 1940s–50s, she is, to this day, remembered mostly for these earlier appearances.

Besides acting, Chen was briefly involved in film production. In 1949, shortly after relocating to Hong Kong, she co-founded Haiyan Film Studio with Wang Hao. Chen starred in several films produced by Shaw Brothers in Hong Kong and CMPC in Taiwan, and received the Best Supporting Actress prize at the 1961 Asian FF for her role in *Misfortune* (1961). She retired from filmmaking in 1972.

(ZX, YZ)

Cheng Bugao

b. 1898, Zhejiang province
d. June 1966
Director

One of the most prolific film directors in China, Cheng Bugao contributed greatly to the development of Chinese cinema during the 1920s–30s. Like most filmmakers of his generation, Cheng never received any formal training. Before starting to direct in 1924, he studied at Zhendan University in Shanghai and wrote regularly about film for newspapers in the city. The disappointing quality of many early Chinese films encouraged Cheng to try his own hand at filmmaking. Cheng joined Mingxing Film Company in 1928 after releasing three early titles and became one of the studio's major directors.

As a humanist, Cheng focused on subject matter that engaged audiences from a wide social strata. Some of his better known early titles include *Divorce* (1928), *The Life of the Wealthy* (1929), *Golden Road* (1930), **Spring Silkworms**, **Wild Torrents** (both 1933), *To the Northwest* (1934) and *The Loyal Warriors* (1935). Although never a committed leftist himself, Cheng made important contributions to the rise of leftist cinema with a number of films highly critical of contemporary social conditions. Both *Wild Torrents* and *Spring Silkworms* are now considered classics of this era.

During the post-war period, Cheng became more politically detached. He went to Hong Kong in 1945–9 and directed several purposefully a-political films. He joined Great Wall Film Company in 1952 and made a few movies before retiring in 1962.

Further reading
B. Cheng (1983), his memoirs of the 1930s.

(ZX)

Cheng Jihua

b. 1921, Hubei province
Critic, historian

Cheng Jihua is best known as the chief co-author of *History of the Development of Chinese Cinema* (1963), the most comprehensive book on pre-1949 Chinese cinema to date. Due to the interruption of the **Cultural Revolution**, the book's second edition did not appear until 1981.

Cheng joined the CCP in 1937, was jailed by the Nationalists in 1941, and became an official in the PRC government after 1949. In 1953, he was appointed chief editor of *Translations on Film Art* (Dianying yishu yicong), a journal exclusively devoted to publishing foreign film scholarship. Cheng served on the editorial board of the academic journal *China Screen* (Zhongguo dianying – later *Film Art* (Dianying yishu)) in 1956. Meanwhile, Cheng also acted as chief editor at China Film Press with responsibility for collecting information on Chinese film history. Cheng was offered a professorship by BFA in 1959. He visited the USA in 1983 and taught courses on Chinese cinema at the University of California, Los Angeles, and other universities. Cheng Jihua is now widely recognized as an authority on Chinese cinema. He has been invited to numerous international conferences and festivals devoted to the subject.

Further reading
ZDX (1982–6: 4: 443–50), a short biography.

(ZX)

Cheng the Fruit Seller

aka *Labourer's Love* (Zhi guo yuan, aka Laogong aiqing)

dir. **Zhang Shichuan**
sc. **Zheng Zhengqiu**
with Zheng Zhegu, Yu Ying, Zheng Zhengqiu
Shanghai: Mingxing Film, 1922

The earliest existing Chinese film, this slapstick **comedy** depicts a fruit seller who devises an ingenious trick to help a doctor win back his patients and who, as a result, can marry the doctor's daughter. The film opens with Cheng attending to his fruit stand, which faces the doctor's small clinic across the street. Cheng expresses his desire for the doctor's daughter by sending her fruit. He even overpowers a couple of hooligans and rescues his sweetheart from danger. However, he has to meet the doctor's condition – making the clinic prosperous – before his marriage proposal can be approved.

Cheng has a sleepless night and comes up with an idea. The second floor of his apartment building is a nightclub where people meet for drinking and gambling parties. Using his carpentry skills, he transforms the stairway into a moveable slide. When the nightclub guests leave, they fall

Plate 11   *Cheng the Fruit Seller* (1922)

from the top of the stairs and injure themselves. One by one, they go to the doctor for treatment. The doctor collects a huge pile of money and agrees to let the fruit seller marry his daughter.

Cheng the Fruit Seller is one of many film projects on which Zhang Shichuan and Zheng Zhengqiu collaborated in the 1920s. It reveals the close links between **theatre and film** in modern China.

Further reading

X. He (1982), an account of Mingxing Company by Zhang Shichuan's widow; Z. Zhang (1999), a critical study of the film.

(PV)

Cheng Yin

(Cheng Yunbao)

b. 21 January 1917
d. 26 April 1995
Director

Cheng Yin's road to filmmaking began after the outbreak of the Sino-Japanese war in 1937, when he became involved in Communist theatrical activities after making the trip to Yan'an. In 1947,

Cheng was assigned to a film team for the first time. After being involved in the production of a number of documentaries, Cheng quickly mastered the craft of directing. As one of the four pillar directors at Beijing Film Studio, Cheng was best known for his war films.

Cheng's biographers usually divide his output into four periods. Representative of his first period (1949–52) are such films as *Steeled Fighters* (1950) and *From Victory to Victory* (1952), the former being the recipient of a Peace Award at the 1951 Karlovy Vary FF and a grand prize from China's Ministry of Culture in 1957. Cheng's films of the second period (1953–66), however, are more varied in quality. While *Girls from Shanghai* (1958) continues his humanistic approach, other films can be more properly labelled propaganda pieces. During the **Cultural Revolution**, Cheng was involved in the adaptation of the model operas *The Legend of the Red Lantern* (1970) and *Red Detachment of Women* (1972). In addition, he also participated in the 1974 remaking of *From Victory to Victory*. During the post-Cultural Revolution period, Cheng directed *The Life of Wei, I-II* (1978–9) and *Xi'an Incident* (1981), the latter title winning him Best Director trophy at the 1982

China GRA as well as a Best Film award from the Ministry of Culture. Cheng served as the president of BFA from 1982 until his death.

See also: adapations of drama and literature; documentary; propaganda and film; war film

Further reading
D. Ma and G. Dai (1994: 117–46), a chapter on Cheng Yin; ZDX (1982–6: 4: 104–12), a short biography.

(ZX)

Cheung, Leslie
(Zhang Guorong)

b. 1956, Hong Kong
Actor, pop singer

One of the most popular film actors in Hong Kong, Leslie Cheung won the first prize in a Hong Kong music competition in 1977 and has had a brilliant career in singing and film acting. He impressed audiences around the world with his sensitive, versatile performances in quality films such as *A **Chinese Ghost Story*** (*dir.* **Ching Siu Tung**, 1987), ***Days of Being Wild*** (**Wong Kar-Wai**, 1991) and ***Rouge*** (*dir.* Stanley **Kwan**, 1987). His homosexual roles in ***Farewell My Concubine*** (*dir.* **Chen Kaige**, 1993) and *He's a Woman, She's a Man* (*dir.* Chan Ho Sun, 1994) convey artistic subtleties and an astonishingly beautiful 'femininity'.

(YZ)

Cheung, Maggie
(Zhang Manyu)

b. 1964, Hong Kong
Actress

One of the most popular film actresses in Hong Kong, Maggie Cheung won Best Actress at Taipei GHA for her role in ***Full Moon in New York*** (*dir.* Stanley **Kwan**, 1989). Later, she won the same title at Berlin FF for portraying the tragic life of **Ruan Lingyu**, a female star of the early 1930s, in *The **Actress*** (*dir.* Stanley Kwan, 1992). She has appeared in countless other films, including ***Song of the Exile*** (*dir.* Ann **Hui**, 1990), ***Days of Being Wild*** (*dir.* **Wong Kar-Wai**, 1991) and *Green Snake* (*dir.* **Tsui Hark**, 1993). Her lead role in *Irma Vep*

(*dir.* Olivier Assayas, 1997) won her critical acclaim in the West.

(YZ)

Chiang, David
(Jiang Dawei)

b. 1947
Actor, director

David Chiang played a prominent role in Hong Kong cinema of the late 1960s and early 1970s in films directed by **Chang Che**, co-starring **Ti Lung**. His parents were both well-known film actors in China. After attending Hong Kong's Chu Hai College, he worked as a martial arts instructor in films and came to the attention of Chang Che and Shaw Brothers in 1966. Chiang co-starred with Ti Lung in *Dead End* (1969) and became the leading actor in *The Wandering Sword* (1970). He then starred mostly in Chang Che films in the early 1970s, often specializing in troubled hero roles. His most notable appearances were in *Vengeance* (1970), *The New One-Armed Swordsman, Duel of Fists* (both 1971), and ***Blood Brothers*** (1972), co-starring Ti Lung. In 1974, he appeared in an English language role in the Hammer/Shaw Brothers co-production *Legend of the Seven Golden Vampires*.

Chiang also directed and starred in *The Condemned* (1976) for Shaw Brothers before branching out as a freelance actor and director in Hong Kong and Taiwan. After directing films with social leanings such as *The Drug Addict* (1974), Chiang often appeared in cameos such as *Yes, Madam!* (1985) and supporting roles as in John **Woo**'s and Wu Ma's salute to Chang Che, *Just Heroes* (1988) and *Once Upon a Time in China, II* (**Tsui Hark**, 1992), playing Sun Yat-sen's assistant. He also continues to direct, his recent films being *The Wrong Couples* (1987), *Will of Iron* (1990) and *Mother of a Different Kind* (1995).

(TW)

Chicken and Duck Talk
(Ji tong ya jiang)

dir. Clifton Ko
sc. Michael **Hui**, Clifton Ko, Ma Wai-hou, Tsim Si-yin, Lau Tin-tsi
with Michael Hui, Ricky Hui, Sylvia **Chang**, Lowell Lo, Lawrence Ng
Hong Kong: Hui's Films, 1988

One of the funniest comedies about Asian cooking since Itami Juzo's *Tampopo* (Japan, 1986), *Chicken and Duck Talk* suggests the need for Chinese modernization while simultaneously showcasing the talents of comedian Michael Hui. The film centres around 'Old Hui's' roast duck restaurant, where dirt reigns supreme and cockroaches are inadvertently served up with the soup. Hui himself is notoriously mean to his family and employees, a point not lost on his successful mother-in-law when she comes to visit.

The opening of an American-style Danny's Fried Chicken store opposite his restaurant presents Hui with a dilemma. How can he keep up with the competition? One by one his customers are seduced away by the glamour of fast food, and even his estranged waiter finds a new job with the rival company. Turning the duck restaurant into a karaoke bar doesn't help; nor do Hui's attempts at television advertising. Hui's traditional cooking methods are no competition against the efficiency of Japanese business techniques and mass production. With all hope gone, Hui's restaurant is finally closed down by a health inspector after rats are found all over the tables – a present from Danny's. In the end, Hui's mother-in-law agrees to renovate, and the restaurant fights back. Employing rigorous training methods, and moving over to specialize in chicken as well as duck, Hui's management leaves Danny's behind. After a fire guts the fast food store, Old Hui even becomes a local hero when he saves the lives of his now defeated rivals.

Michael Hui, together with his brother Ricky, has enjoyed a long and distinguished career in Cantonese **comedy**. *Chicken and Duck Talk* provides a perfect introduction to his prodigious talent.

(JS)

children's film

The term designates films that concentrate on the lives of children and are targeted at young audiences. Rarely self-contained in itself, this genre frequently crosses over to **comedy** and fantasy films. Historically, very few films were specifically made for children during the 1920s–40s. Among exceptions is *An **Orphan on the Streets*** (*dir.* Zhao Ming, Yan Gong, 1949), adapted from Zhang Leping's popular comic strip depicting homeless boy San Mao (three hairs) who wanders along the Shanghai streets and runs into all sorts

of hilarious tragicomic situations. The film's reflection on social problems through a child's eyes appealed to adults as well. Indeed, it proved so popular that as late as 1981 it was drawing large crowds in Hong Kong and Paris, an event that Voice of America radio called 'a San Mao craze'. Indeed, this craze, along with a **nostalgia** for old Shanghai, led to several remakes of San Mao films in mainland China, including *San Mao Runs a Business* (*dir.* **Huang Zuolin**, 1958) and *San Mao Joins the Army* (*dir.* **Zhang Jianya**, 1992).

During the 1950s–70s, children's films were used to teach the history of the **Communist revolution** to the young generation. ***Letter with Feather*** (*dir.* **Shi Hui**, 1954) marked the start of children's war films and was followed by memorable titles such as ***Zhang Ga, a Soldier Boy*** (*dir.* **Cui Wei**, Ouyang Hongying, 1963) and ***Sparkling Red Star*** (*dir.* **Li Jun**, Li Ang, 1974), all featuring smart boy heroes fighting against the Japanese or the Nationalist forces. Films set in the contemporary world would stress the collective spirit and the power of unity, as in *Boy Soccer Team* (*dir.* Yan Bili, 1965). Only a few fantasy films were produced to stimulate children's imagination, as in *The Secret of a Precious Gourd* (*dir.* **Yang Xiaozhong**, 1963) and *Little Dingdang* (*dir.* **Xie Tian**, Chen Wanqian, 1964), both of which are in tune with the legends and fairy tales present in **animation** films. *The Kite* (*dir.* Wang Jiayi, 1958), a fantasy story co-produced with France, marks the first joint production in the mainland.

In 1981, China Children's Film Studio was officially established, temporarily housed under Beijing Film Studio. Its first chief, **Yu Lan**, formerly a popular actress, recruited talents from other studios, among them her son **Tian Zhuangzhuang**, who co-directed *Red Elephant* (1982) with **Zhang Jianya** and Xie Xiaojing. Several women directors worked for Children's Studio, too, and their films won numerous domestic and internationals awards: *Brother Echo* (*dir.* Wang Junzheng, 1982) won an award from the Ministry of Culture, and *Oh! Sweet Snow* (*dir.* Wang Haowei, 1989) won a children's prize at the 1991 Berlin FF. Within a decade, Children's Studio had produced forty-five films and was being praised as the only pure oasis for art films as economic reform had forced other studios to make commercial films since the late 1980s. It is also worth noting that several women directors (e.g., Shi Xiaohua and **Siqin Gaowa**) and **Fifth Generation** directors (e.g., **Peng Xiaolian** and **Wu Ziniu**) made their

Plate 12   *The Kite* (1958)

début with children's films in the 1980s, though not necessarily for Children's Studio.

Children's films are regularly produced in Taiwan. *Cold Ice-Flower* (*dir.* Yang Liguo, 1989), for instance, dramatizes the fate of a poor country boy with a talent for painting who dies without knowing that his picture has won an international prize. Like their mainland counterparts, Taiwan films often portray model teachers with maternal love for their students. Even in films that stress the theme of 'growing up', memorable childhood experiences often dominate the narrative. One example is *Reunion* (*dir.* Ko Yi-cheng, 1985), which contrasts exhausted, depressed modern city-living with innocent childhood memories. In Hong Kong, on the other hand, children's films do not constitute a major genre for a capitalist industry which favours big-budget productions and **mixed genres** of comedy, action and martial arts.

See also: action film; art film; fantasy film; legends and myths; martial arts film; war film

Further reading

Y. Shi (1991), on Children's Film Studio; L. Yu (1985), an overview of mainland films.

(YZ)

China, My Sorrow
(Niupeng)

dir. Dai Sijie
sc. Dai Sijie, Shan Yuanzhu
with Guo Liangyi, Tieu Quan Nghieu
France: Titane Production/Flach Film, 1989

In this unusual film produced entirely in France, the **Cultural Revolution** forms the background to a cinematic study of human nature and the ultimate meaning of life and death. As the film begins, a schoolboy named Tian Ben is caught playing a 'pornographic' tune on a family gramophone to attract the attention of a neighbour's girl. He is caught by the Red Guards and sent to a labour camp in the mountains. There, remote from political centres and exposed to natural elements, Tian gradually and painstakingly learns that sympathy and mutual understanding are irrelevant. Young or old, educated or illiterate, workers in the camp take advantage of each other and show no sign of feelings when their fellow workers are hungry, injured, sick, or dying. A touring Red Guards' propaganda truck, which comes to the wrong place to perform revolutionary shows, only makes the labour camp even more intolerable. Life is reduced to a simple matter of survival. A young boy eats too much one night and dies completely 'satisfied'. No one seems to care, except for a mysterious monk who goes up to the hill top and meditates with a flock of pigeons. In a climactic moment, Tian helps the monk commit suicide, after the latter has performed, all alone in the wilderness, a tragic puppet shadowplay about a bird burning itself to death. The film ends with Tian walking down the hill side, one foot bare, as if he has suddenly glimpsed a revelation of the transcendental meaning of life.

Financed by French and German money, the director used a French cinematographer (Jean-Michel Humeau) and a mixed Chinese and Vietnamese cast. Dai Sijie graduated from Sichuan University in China and studied art (at the Louvre School) and film in Paris. The film was awarded Prix Jean Vigo at Cannes FF.

Further reading

E. Chan (1990), a useful discussion; X. Liao (1994), a post-colonial critique of film representation.

(YZ)

Chinese Ghost Story, A

(Qiannü youhun)

dir. **Ching Siu Tung**
sc. Ruan Jizhi
with Joey **Wong**, Leslie **Cheung**, Wu Ma
Hong Kong: Cinema City / Film Workshop, 1987

A reworking of a traditional tale, *A Chinese Ghost Story* secured Ching Siu Tung's reputation as a director who could combine action, fantasy and **romance** with hi-tech special effects. The film opens with Ning Tsai-Shen, an ineffectual tax collector, taking shelter in the haunted Lan Ro temple. After meeting Yen Che-Hsia, a wandering Taoist swordsman, he falls in love with a beautiful and mysterious woman, Nieh Hsiao-Tsing. Yen informs him that Hsiao-Tsing is a ghost, but Tsai-Shen refuses to believe it. However, the young man soon realizes that his spirit lover is to be married off to Lord Black, the ruler of the Underworld, by an evil ambisexual tree spirit.

After travelling to the Underworld, Tsai-Shen and Yen defeat Lord Black and the tree spirit with the use of Sanskrit magic, but they cannot secure Hsiao-Tsing's reincarnation in human form. After her murder, Hsiao-Tsing's ashes had been buried under the roots of the tree spirit, and the two men are unable to save her by retrieving and reburying her ashes before the sun comes up. As Hsiao-Tsing is now lost forever, Tsai-Shen and Yen can only ride away from her newly planted grave.

An extremely innovative and stylish genre piece, *A Chinese Ghost Story* features astonishing high-wire work, MTV-style pop songs, brief snatches of nudity, and a Taoist priest doing a rap routine. It spawned two Ching Siu Tung-directed sequels (1990, 1991) and countless imitations.

See also: action film; fantasy film

Further reading
D. Edelstein (1988), on the Hong Kong ghost film.

(JS)

Ching Siu Tung

(Cheng Xiaodong)

b. 1953
Director

Ching Siu Tung is the son of Shaw Brothers director Cheung Kung who gave his martial arts-enthusiastic offspring his first job as a stunt man.

He then became one of the most famous exponents of Hong Kong fantasy cinema both as director and choreographer. He is not only known for directing the **Chinese Ghost Story** series but also for choreographing fight sequences in films such as *A Better Tomorrow, II* (1987) and many others.

Ching developed his skills to become a martial arts instructor on *The Fourteen Amazons* (1970), directed by his father. Golden Harvest later offered him the job of directing *Duel to the Death* (1984), a neglected film dealing with the futility of combat. But his work as director of *A Chinese Ghost Story* (1987) and co-director of **Swordsman, II** (1992) and *Swordsman, III: The East is Red* (1993) marked him as the key exponent of Hong Kong New Wave martial arts fantasy cinema. His films are characterized by exciting special effects, such as exhilarating battles (armed and unarmed) with antagonists leaping into the air with the aid of unseen wires, that put Hollywood production values to shame. Ching accomplished many of his major achievements in collaboration with **Tsui Hark** and the Film Workshop.

Ching has also worked on a diverse number of Hong Kong genres such as the time travel romance *The Terracotta Warrior* (1990), the comic book action film *The Raid* (co-directed with Tsui Hark in 1991), and Stephen Chow's satire of Bruce **Lee**'s second film, *Fists of Fury 1991* (1991).

(TW)

Chiung Yao

(Qiong Yao)

b. 20 April 1938
Producer, popular fiction writer

Chiung Yao is a Taiwan woman novelist who specializes in producing tear-jerking romances that focus on issues of **love and marriage** and appeal to women and student audiences. Like Eileen Chang (Zhang Ailing, 1920–96), her Shanghai precursor in the 1940s, Chiung expanded her influence to the film world by having her works adapted for the screen. Song Cunshou *(b.* 1930) directed her *Outside the Window* (1972); **Wang Yin** directed *Whose Belongings?* (1966); and **Lee Hsing** directed *The Silent Wife* (1965). In the 1960s–70s, Chiung twice established her own film companies, Fire Bird (Huoniao) and Superstar (Juxing), and produced film adaptations of her novels. She was very influential in mainland China in the 1980s as several films and TV drama series based on her works were produced to capitalize on the widespread consumption of her romances.

See also: adaptations of drama and literature; romance

(YZ)

Chow, Raymond
(Zou Wenhuai)

b. 1927
Producer

An important producer in Hong Kong, Raymond Chow entered Shaw Brothers in 1957. He established Golden Harvest Film Company (Jiahe) in 1970 and produced several highly profitable Bruce **Lee** films, including *The Big Boss* (1971) and *The Chinese Connection* (1972, both *dir.* Lo Wei). Golden Harvest soon became a giant in the Hong Kong film industry, second only to Shaw Brothers. Later, Chow successfully cooperated with other Hong Kong film producers, such as Michael **Hui** and Jackie **Chan**. He was given an award in the USA in 1980 for his outstanding contribution to international film culture.

(YZ)

Chow, Stephen
(Stephen Chiau, Zhou Xingchi)

Actor

Stephen Chow is one of Hong Kong's most popular movie stars in the 1990s. But his appeal to Western audiences is limited because of his comic speciality in Cantonese *moleitau* (literally 'makes no sense') humour, a technique dependent on verbal puns familiar to local audiences but untranslatable for Westerners. Although often compared to Jim Carrey, Chow is a much more versatile performer capable of different types of **comedy** as well as serious roles. He is the contemporary successor to Michael **Hui**'s brand of comedy.

One of his earliest appearances was in Jet **Li**'s *Dragon Fight* (1988) where he played a goofy deliveryman who stumbles upon Triad cocaine. But Chow also contributed serious performances in Danny **Lee** films such as *Final Justice* (1988) and

Just Heroes (*dir.* John **Woo**, Wu Ma, 1989). In 1990 he replaced **Chow Yun-Fat** as leading star in *God of Gamblers, II* (1990) and the hilarious sequel *God of Gamblers, III: Back to Shanghai* (1992, both *dir.* **Wong Jing**) co-starring **Gong Li**. Chow had already satirized *God of Gamblers* (*dir.* Wong Jing 1989) in *All for the Winner* (*dir.* Correy Yuen, Jeff Lau, 1990). Chow's audiences often witness hilarious parodies of Hong Kong and Western movies as in *Crazy Safari* (*dir.* Billy Chan, 1991), which merges the *Mr Vampire* series with *The Gods Must Be Crazy* (*dir.* Jamie Uys, 1981), and *All's Well, Ends Well* (*dir.* Clifton Ko, 1992), satirizing *Pretty Woman* (*dir.* Gary Marshall, 1990), *Ghost* (*dir.* Jerry Zucker, 1990), *Once Upon a Time in China* (*dir.* **Tsui Hark**, 1991), *Psycho* (*dir.* Alfred Hitchcock, 1960), *The Texas Chainsaw Massacre* (*dir.* Tobe Hooper, 1974) and *Terminator, II: Judgment Day* (*dir.* James Cameron, 1991).

Recently Chow has ventured into **costume drama** territory, playing roles such as the Monkey King in *Chinese Odyssey, I: Pandora's Box* (*dir.* Jeff Lau, 1995) and its sequel as well as legendary Ming Dynasty poet Tang Bohu (Tak Pak Fu) in *Flirting Scholar* (*dir.* Lee Lik-chi, 1993). But he has also successfully parodied James Bond films as mainland agent 007 in *From Beijing with Love* (*co-dir.* Lee Lik-chi, 1995) and the sequel *Forbidden City Cop* (*co-dir.* Vincent Kok, 1996). He also surpassed Jim Carrey in *The Sixty Million Dollar Man* (1995) satirizing both *The Mask* (*dir.* Charles Russell) and *Pulp Fiction* (*dir.* Quentin Tarantino, both 1994). In one scene he turns into a talking toilet trying to avoid being crapped on!

(TW, YZ)

Chow Yun-Fat
(Zhou Runfa)

b. 1955, Hong Kong
Actor

Despite his recent eclipse by Stephen **Chow** as Hong Kong's major star, Chow Yun-Fat will always be associated with the major achievements of the Second New Wave. Educated in a leftist Kowloon school and KMT boarding school, Chow quit at age seventeen to work at a number of jobs before finding fame as a television serial star. Although Ann **Hui**'s *The Story of Woo Viet* (1981) and Leong Po-chih's *Hong Kong 1941* (1984) remain among his earliest fondest performances, Chow's career escalated when John **Woo** cast him to play the doomed, romantic Mark in *A Better Tomorrow* (1986). From then on, Chow's stature rose in the industry as he repeated his successful collaboration with Woo on *A Better Tomorrow, II* (1987), *The Killer* (1989) and *Hard Boiled* (1992).

Although Western audiences tend to associate Chow with Woo, the actor is extremely versatile and has appeared in quite a number of diverse genres. Chow's other successful collaboration has been with Ringo **Lam** who perhaps has extended his acting talents more than Woo. They first worked together on *City on Fire* (1987), with Lam extracting a characteristically darker element from Chow's persona, which he would finally explicitly reveal in the nihilistic *Full Contact* (1992). However, Lam also directed different kinds of performances from Chow in *Prison on Fire* (1987) and *Wild Search* (1990).

Since the mid-1980s, Chow has won Best Actor award several times at Asia-Pacific FF, HKFA and Taipei GHA. In 1989 he was awarded the Outstanding Asian Actor title in the US. However, despite his other remarkable performances in *Love in the Fallen City* (*dir.* Ann Hui, 1984), *An Autumn's Tale* (*dir.* Mabel Cheung, 1987), *All About Ah-Long* (*dir.* Johnny To, 1989), *God of Gamblers* (*dir.* **Wong Jing**, 1989), as well as the Arthurian figure in his farewell to Hong Kong cinema, *Peace Hotel* (1995), he will probably always be remembered as John Woo's romantic killer.

In the 1990s Chow signed up with agent William Morris and appeared in several Hollywood films.

Further reading
P. Fonoroff (1990–1), M. Singer (1988), two profiles.

(TW, YZ)

Chu Tien-wen

(Zhu Tianwen)

b. 1956
Screen writer, fiction writer

One of the most important screen writers in New Taiwan Cinema, Chu Tien-wen was born into a distinguished literary family, her father being a famous writer in Taiwan. She graduated from the English Department of Tamkang University and won several awards for her literary works. Her screen career began in 1983 when she adapted her story for *Growing Up* (*dir.* **Chen Kun-hou**,

1983). She wrote or co-wrote (often with **Wu Nien-chen**) most of **Hou Hsiao-hsien**'s films, including *The Boys from Fengkuei* (1983), *A Summer at Grandpa's* (1984), *A Time to Live, a Time to Die* (1985), *Dust in the Wind* (1986), *Daughter of the Nile* (1987), *A City of Sadness* (1989), *The Puppet Master* (1993) and *Good Men, Good Women* (1995). She twice won Best Screenplay award at Taipei GHA in the 1980s.

See also: New Taiwan Cinema (under Taiwan Cinema in Historical essays)

(YZ)

Chun Miao

(Chunmiao)

dir. **Xie Jin**, Yan Bili, Liang Tingduo
sc. collective
with Li Xiuming, Da Shichang, Bai Mu, Feng Qi, **Zhang Yu**
Shanghai: Shanghai Film, 1975

Chun Miao is one of the propaganda films made during the **Cultural Revolution**. Its ultra-leftist message is that since the old, revisionist and anti-Mao medical establishment does not care about the peasants, it needs to be reformed. The managers of the established hospitals are incompetent, the professional care workers corrupt or evil – therefore, it is imperative that peasants like Chun Miao take over.

In 1965, a little girl from a rural area falls ill. Her mother and Chun Miao rush her to a local clinic, but the chief doctor, Qian Jiren, refuses to help her, recommending that they take her to the major hospital in a nearby city. The girl dies before reaching the hospital. When Chairman Mao places the emphasis of medical care on the rural areas, Chun Miao immediately responds by going to the local medical school to study. The president of the school, Du Wenjie, along with the chief instructor, Qian Jieren, does not take Chun Miao seriously and intentionally makes life difficult for her. A young doctor, Fang Ming, helps her make progress with her study.

Upon her return to the village, Chun Miao begins to practise medicine, but Du confiscates her medical briefcase on the grounds that she does not yet have a licence. Meanwhile Qian conspires with a witch doctor in the village to undercut Chun Miao. After the Cultural Revolution gets under way, Chun Miao puts up posters in the clinic criticizing revisionist medical practices that neglect the needs of peasants. A chronically ill peasant man is brought to the clinic and put under Chun Miao's care. Doctor Qian attempts to murder this patient and blame it on Chun Miao. However, his scheme fails and the clinic falls under the firm control of the revolutionary rebels.

See also: propaganda and film

(ZX)

Chungking Express
(Chongqing senlin)

dir./sc. **Wong Kar-Wai**
with **Lin Ching Hsia**, Takeshi Kaneshiro, Tony Chiu-Wai Leung, Faye Wong
Hong Kong: Jet Tone Productions, 1994

The film that marked Wong Kar-Wai's entry into the international distribution circuit, *Chungking Express* is a freewheeling account of the search for love in Hong Kong in 1994. Dazzlingly shot by the famous Australian cinematographer, Christopher Doyle (Du Kefeng in Chinese), it concerns two romantic policemen and the women they become involved with. The film splits into two halves. In the first, Cop 223 mourns the end of his relationship with his ex-girlfriend, May, and falls in love with a drug dealer in a blonde wig, raincoat and sunglasses, with whom he spends a chaste night. They part. Melancholic because he is unlikely to be paged on his birthday the next day, Cop 223 takes heart when he receives a surprise call from a mysterious woman.

In the second half, Cop 663 loses his air hostess girlfriend, but is happy to be taken in hand by Faye, who works at her uncle's Midnight Express fast food counter. Faye helps Cop 663 recover his passion for life by secretly refurbishing his cluttered flat, letting herself in with the keys his ex-lover left behind. When he finds out, he asks Faye out on a date, but she flies to California instead, leaving him a hand-written boarding pass. The two are reunited one year later when Faye, now an air hostess, walks into the Midnight Express, now owned by Cop 663. She asks where he wants to go, and he replies, 'wherever you go'.

Chungking Express swept the boards at the 1995 HKFA, taking Best Film, Director, and Actor awards (Leung). The film holds out the possibility of making connections in the lonely modern city. Noticeably less alarmist than other pre-1997 titles,

it is still obsessed with time, transit sites, passports and expiration dates.

Further reading
F. Luo (1995: 37–59), on Wong and *fin-de-siècle* decadence; T. Rayns (1995a), an interview; C. Tsui (1995), a critical study of Wong Kar-Wai.

(JS)

City of Sadness, A
(Beiqing chengshi)

dir. **Hou Hsiao-hsien**
sc. **Wu Nien-chen**, **Chu Tien-wen**
with Tony Liang, Xin Shufen, Chen Songyong, Jack Kao, Li Tianlu
Taipei: Era, 1989

Winner of the Golden Lion Award at 1989 Venice FF, *City of Sadness* is the first film from Taiwan to be recognized and celebrated by the Western press. One reason for this is that the film overcame the KMT government's ban on dealing with 'the 28 February Incident', a 1947 political uprising in which more than 10,000 civilians were killed during a military crackdown.

Hou Hsiao-hsien is not interested in turning a historical incident into a thriller or a sensational political tract. Instead, he concentrates on the effects totalitarian rule has on common people, on individuals whose welfare is severely damaged by Japanese imperialism, the corruption of the new KMT regime, and the political suppression that followed the Incident. The Lin family, at the centre of the story, are typical victims of a series of oppressions. As the film begins, with the celebration of Japan's 1945 defeat and the end of colonial rule in Taiwan, the family is notified that the second son, sent to serve in the Japanese army, will never return. The third son, who worked as a secret agent against the Chinese, returns home with a severe mental condition. The youngest son, a deaf-mute photographer, is arrested after the Incident for his involvement with political dissidents. Finally, the eldest son is killed by a mainland Chinese gangster for his refusal to participate in drug smuggling.

The subject matter and the Golden Lion Award combined to make *City of Sadness* a box-office success. However, both audiences and critics were dissatisfied by Hou's representation of the 28 February Incident. They complained that Hou was too preoccupied with poetic realism to give an accurate account of history. This vigorous discussion about the film led to a re-evaluation of New Taiwan Cinema. Despite such criticism, *City of Sadness* is still a masterpiece in which the director perfects his stunning formal style and shows his deep respect for the victims of suffering.

See also: New Taiwan Cinema (under Taiwan Cinema in Historical essays)

Further reading
G. Cheshire (1993), an excellent analysis of Hou's films; H. Chiao (1993a), an interview with critical comments; P. Liao (1993), on rewriting national history; X. Liao (1994), a post-colonial critique.

(YY)

City on Fire
(Long hu fengyun)

dir. Ringo **Lam**
sc. Ringo Lam, Tommy Sham
with **Chow Yun-Fat**, Danny **Lee**, Carrie Ng, Sun Yue
Hong Kong: Cinema City, 1987

An important **gangster film** after John **Woo**'s *A Better Tomorrow* (1986), it inspired many Hong Kong films carrying 'on Fire' in their English titles and was a model for Quentin Tarantino's *Reservoir Dogs* (1992).

When an undercover cop is killed, Ko Chow takes his place, although he has to fight nightmares after a previous betrayal. A gang with Fu as its chief lieutenant robs a jewellery store. Detective Lau and a younger policeman, John, are assigned to the case. After visiting the drunk and embittered Lau, Ko infiltrates the gang, promising guns and ammunition, and is shadowed by John's CID men. Ko's girlfriend, Hung, agrees to marry him, but she gets angry when he postpones their marriage registration. Ko makes a tape of Fu and his friend securing an arms deal in a cemetery, and Fu threatens Ko so as to test his loyalty.

Hung warns Ko to be at the registry office next day at ten. She waits while Ko gets the guns and is picked up by Fu on the way to see their boss, Nam. Hung leaves angrily, bound for Canada with another man. Ko meets Nam and shows interest in joining them. The CID forcibly interrogates Ko until Lau intervenes, argues with John, and reluctantly postpones arresting the gang until after their job. Ko and Fu discuss their lives and become

friends. Hung's letter from the USA asks Ko to take her back to Hong Kong. The heist goes badly: Ko kills a CID man and is himself shot. As Ko dies, he reveals his identity to Fu, who is later arrested. Lau hits John with a brick, blaming him for Ko's death.

Like other contemporary Hong Kong gangster films, *City on Fire* glorifies male bonding in times of crisis and intentionally blurs the line between criminal and police officer.

(KH, YZ)

City Without Night
(Buye cheng)

dir. **Tang Xiaodan**
sc. Ke Ling
with **Sun Daolin**, Lin Shan, Shi Wei, Cui Chaoming, Liu Fei
Shanghai: Jiangnan Film, 1957

This is one of the few Chinese films to take as its subject matter the national bourgeoisie. The story centres on a Chinese industrialist, Zhang Bohan, who successfully resisted the imperialist Japanese economic encroachments of the 1930s, only to be victimized by American capitalists on the eve of the CCP take-over in 1949. While initially resentful of the new CCP policy aiming to promote national industry, he soon reformed himself – after first breaking the tax laws he came to cooperate fully with the state.

During the Sino-Japanese war, Zhang Bohan had returned to China from England after the textile factory run by his father became threatened by a Japanese competitor. Zhang believed that China's future lay in industrial development and he refused to let foreign interests take over his father's factory. By combining the printing facilities of his father's factory with the resources of his father-in-law, Liang Fuquan's, textile factory, Zhang not only saved his father's business from bankruptcy but generated huge profits as well. On the eve of the Nationalist collapse, however, Zhang speculates disastrously in American cotton.

Finally, after the Communist take-over, the PRC government implements a policy encouraging the growth of national industry and protecting the national bourgeoisie, with the result that Zhang's factory expands considerably. However, Zhang tries to avoid paying state taxes and he violates government regulations. When his daughter tries to persuade him to turn himself in, he slaps her in the face, whereupon she leaves home and finds a job to support herself. With the help of his wife and the workers in his factory, he finally admits his mistakes and receives lenient treatment from the government. His daughter returns home and the family is reunited once again.

Viewed with historical hindsight, this film is ironic in that the CCP soon took over all private industries in the late 1950s and subjected all capitalists to one round of political campaign after another, leaving them financially ruined and politically outcast.

(ZX)

Cityscape
(Dushi fengguang)

dir./sc. **Yuan Muzhi**
with Tang Na, Zhou Boxun, Gu Menghe
Shanghai: Diantong Film, 1935

A satire of Shanghai's **urban life**, *Cityscape* presents a story of ambitions, tricks, and lies acted out by a range of characters, including a superficial woman, her two dishonest suitors, her greedy father, and her petulant mother. The story concerns a group of peasants who have just come to Shanghai and are invited by a street storyteller – the film director himself – to look inside a 'film box' (*xiyang jing*, literally 'Western lens', a sort of kinescope). *Cityscape* is what those peasants see inside the film box.

The daughter of a pawnshop owner, Zhang Xiaoyun, loves money and especially what money can buy. She is courted by Li Menghua, a poor, lazy student, and by Wang Junsan, a rich businessman. Trying to win her love, Li ends up ridiculed, whereas Wang appears to be successful. Finally Zhang is pushed by her father into marrying Wang. Shortly after their wedding, Wang falls into poverty when his speculations are devalued and his secretary embezzles his other funds.

Considered the first Chinese musical **comedy**, *Cityscape* opens with the director singing and showing Shanghai and its people to a group of singing and dancing peasants. While the characters themselves do not sing or dance, music is used throughout to enhance the narrative and acting styles.

See also: musical, the

Further reading
S. Tuohy (1999), a study of 1930s film music.

(PV)

comedy

A type of film that incites humour and mirth in the audience, comedy usually features a happy ending. In the early silent period, film comedy was a major genre in China, and filmmakers borrowed freely from Chinese theatre such tricks as twisted facial expression, exaggerated gestures and ridiculous manners to engage the audience. For instance, by mixing mime and slapstick, ***Cheng the Fruit Seller*** (*dir.* **Zheng Zhengqiu**, 1922) reaches a climactic scene where the fruitseller uses his carpentry skills and helps an old physician 'fix' – at dizzying speeds – the twisted necks and legs of a large group of patients. Indeed, the influence of Charlie Chaplin was so extensive in China during that time that some film producers hired a Westerner to play Chaplin in their comedy productions.

With the advent of sound in the early 1930s, film comedy began to develop verbal wit along with humour and farce. Social criticism was integrated into many leftist films, such as ***Crossroads*** (*dir.* **Shen Xiling**) and ***Street Angel*** (*dir.* **Yuan Muzhi**, both 1937), in which comic scenes involving mischief and miscommunications create light moments of laughter and **romance**. In the late 1940s, film satires targeting the corrupted KMT government, such as ***Phony Phoenixes*** (*dir.* **Sang Hu**, 1947), became an outlet for people's frustration over desperate living conditions in post-war Shanghai. On the other hand, sentimentality and tolerance of human follies were playfully combined in a couple of films scripted by the popular woman writer Eileen Chang. ***Long Live the Mistress!*** (*dir.* Sang Hu, 1947), in particular, depends on dialogue to deliver Chang's sophisticated and witty humour in unfolding the battle of the sexes.

During the 1950s–60s, comedy was fully developed into a major genre in mainland China. While some comedies, such as *Before the New Director Arrives* (*dir.* Lü Ban, 1956) and *Big Li, Young Li and Old Li* (*dir.* **Xie Jin**, 1962), poked fun at government bureaucracy (and, predictably, they were soon criticized by the authorities), the majority of new comedies, like *Satisfied or Not* (*dir.* Yan Gong, 1963), urged revolutionary morality in the age of **socialist construction**. ***It's My Day Off*** (*dir.* Lu Ren, 1959), for instance, features a model policeman who keeps helping other people in need and forgetting his own date. After a hiatus of a decade during the **Cultural Revolution**, comedy came back in the late 1970s. Films like *What a Family!* (*dir.* Wang Haowei, 1979) combine humour and laughter to promote government policies (e.g., birth control). Later, in the era of economic reforms, several directors cashed in on the new policy and made comedies on the theme 'It's glorious to get rich first'. The most notable among them are a father–son team, **Chen Qiang** and Chen Peisi *(b.* 1954), who produced a light comedy series on Er Zi, a mixture of farce, satire and slapstick. A more serious attempt had been made by **Zhang Jianya**, whose comedies, such as *San Mao Joins the Army* (1992) and *Mr Wang: Flames of Desire* (1993), aim to capture a distinct Shanghai flavour, something he wishes would be comparable to Woody Allen's comic take on New York City.

Comedies are also popular in Hong Kong and Taiwan. Films by the famous Hui brothers (Michael, Samuel and Ricky) have achieved a unique humour in Cantonese dialect in the 1970s, whereas Stephen **Chow** has taken Hong Kong comedy in a new direction by alternating between sit-com one-liners and schoolboy vulgarity in the 1990s. Indeed, mixed genre has become a must for contemporary Hong Kong films. A typical example is a number of light-hearted moments between serious kungfu fights that make hilarious scenes in *Fong Sai Yuk* (*dir.* Yuan Kui, 1993) both memorable and enjoyable. In Taiwan, *Strawman* (1987) and *Banana Paradise* (1989, both *dir.* **Wang Tung**) focus on innocent and ignorant rural people, and capture the absurd nature of many things that happened in the periods of the Japanese occupation and early KMT rule in Taiwan. Ang **Lee**, on the other hand, attracted international attention with his somewhat moralist urban comedies, *The Wedding Banquet* (1992) and *Eat Drink Man Woman* (1994). More intellectually daring than Lee and Wang is Edward **Yang**, whose *A Confucius Confusion* (1995) experiments with a kind of postmodern view of contemporary **urban life** in Taiwan.

See also: Hui, Michael; kungfu film; mixed genres; theatre and film

Further reading
HKIFF (1985), on the Hong Kong comedy; N. Ma (1987b), a study of 1960s comedy in China; *Shanghai dianying* (1991: 161–88), on comedies produced by Shanghai film studios.

(YZ)

Communist revolution, the

The Communist revolution became a dominant theme in filmmaking even before the CCP completely took control of mainland China in 1949. Under its leadership, Northeast Film Studio produced documentaries of the battles against the Nationalist troops in the late 1940s. After the PRC was founded in 1949, the government persistently used film as an effective mass medium to promote its ideology and to re-educate people of all ages and all regions. In consequence, a concerted, systematic effort at a cinematic rewriting of modern Chinese history was carried on in the 1950s–60s, and several aspects of the Communist revolution received central attention. These include (1) underground Communist activities – especially workers' strikes and student movements – in the Nationalist-controlled areas; (2) peasants' rebellions and guerilla warfare instigated or led by the Communists; and, most important, (3) Communist battles against the Nationalist troops and the Japanese invaders. Among the first category are *The Everlasting Radio Signals* (*dir.* **Wang Ping**, 1958) and *Song of Youth* (*dir.* **Cui Wei**, Chen Huaiai, 1959); among the second category, *Daughter of the Party* (*dir.* **Lin Nong**, 1958) and *Red Guards of Lake Hong* (*dir.* **Xie Tian**, Chen Fangqian, Xu Feng, 1961); and among the third category, *From Victory to Victory* (*dir.* **Cheng Yin**, 1952) and *Tunnel Warfare* (*dir.* Ren Xudong, 1965). During the **Cultural Revolution**, the history of Communist revolution was subject to radical revision by the ultra-leftists headed by Jiang Qing, Mao Zedong's wife, who emphasized in-house power struggles between politically correct and incorrect party factions. However, the supremacy of the Communist party itself has never been challenged. In fact, since the 1980s, memorable films of the Communist revolution have once again dominated the Chinese screen. In addition to an increasing number of **biography** films of top party leaders, such as Mao Zedong, Liu Shaoqi and Zhou Enlai, a series of mega war films were produced in the 1990s to restage the decisive Communist battles which finally drove the Nationalists to the island of Taiwan in 1949.

While focusing on the genre of **historical film** in their glorification of the Communist revolution, mainland Chinese filmmakers continue to eulogize Communist ideology in films on contemporary themes (*see* **socialist construction**). Throughout the 1950s–90s, therefore,

propaganda and film have been closely linked in mainland China, even in the era of economic reforms in the 1990s.

See also: documentary; war film

Further reading
H. Chen (1989), an official mainland account.

(YZ)

Confucius Confusion, A
(Duli shidai)

dir./sc. Edward **Yang**
with Ni Shujun, Wang Weiming, Chen Xiangqi, Wang Bosen
Taipei: Atom Film, 1995

A film's opening often signals a distinct directorial presence. *A Confucius Confusion* has one of the most wonderful openings in all of Chinese cinema. The first sequence starts at a press conference where a Taipei performing artist glides above curious journalists on his roller skates answering questions about his new show. Through such a striking use of *mise-en-scène*, Edward Yang depicts the bizarre world of postmodern Taiwan, where no distinctions can be made between what is authentic and what is fake. It does not take long for the audience to realize that this artist is just a talentless, repulsive poseur possessed of unusual character. One gradually comes to realize that this is a film about fabrication, falsification, denial and reassurance – everything that counts in the world of advertising and commerce.

The story focuses on a woman named Xiao Chi who works in the public relations office of a company owned by her best friend. Almost everyone in the company has an interest in her: her supervisor wants to sleep with her; her best friend suspects her loyalty; her co-workers envy her popularity. Her private life is a mess, too: her selfish boyfriend wants to control her while, at the same time, he is sleeping with her boss; her sister warns her of her naivety but still manages to accuse her of being hypocritical. All the problems related to her work and personal relationships point to universal themes of loyalty, sincerity, and honesty. These themes endow Yang's work with moralistic overtones. And yet this is precisely what makes him an interesting *auteur*. Yang's Confucian upbringing in 'Third World' Taiwan and his experiences in the cosmopolitan USA render his film

unique, full of stunning formal techniques and Confucian clichés.

(YY)

Conquering Jun Mountain
aka *Dingjun Mountain* (Ding Junshan)

dir./sc. unknown
Beijing: Fengtai Photography, 1905

This filmed stage performance was the first film ever made in China by Chinese filmmakers and demonstrated the close link between **theatre and film** in China. The segment of Beijing opera is based on a real historical event that took place during the Three Kingdoms period (AD 220–80).

The King of Wei, Cao Cao, launches an attack against the neighbouring state of Shu, spearheaded by General Zhang He. However, using Prime Minister Zhu Geliang's strategies, the general in charge of Shu's defence, Huang Zhong, defeats Zhang in a counter-attack. After taking one of Cao's supply depots, Shu's army wins a total victory after a final showdown with Cao's invading forces at Jun Mountain.

See also: filmed stage performances

(ZX)

costume drama

One of the most popular genres in Chinese film, costume drama (*guzhuang xi*) refers to a film that is set in imperial China (i.e., before 1911) and features colourful costumes and sets. Costume dramas may be adaptations of literary classics, such as **Romance of the Western Chamber** (*dir.* **Hou Yao**, 1927) and other titles from *The Journey to the West* and *Romance of Three Kingdoms*. It may also be historical films set in ancient times, or be drawn from **legends and myths**, such as **Li Han-hsiang**'s *The Story of Xi Shi, I–II* (1965–6), *The* **Burning of the Imperial Palace** and **Reign Behind a Curtain** (both 1983). Indeed, one may even count opera films as costume dramas, especially titles like **Liang Shanbo and Zhu Yingtai**, which came out in three major productions (*dir.* **Sang Hu**, 1954, Shanghai Film; *dir.* Yan Jun, MP & GI, 1963; *dir.* Li Han-hsiang, Shaw Brothers, also 1963 but renamed as *The Love Eterne*), all enthusiastically embraced by audiences in mainland China, Hong Kong and Taiwan.

Plate 13   *Liang Shanbo and Zhu Yingtai* (1954)

Costume dramas have long been a staple of Chinese film industries in mainland China, Hong Kong and Taiwan. Several waves of costume dramas hit the market: the late 1920s in China, the early 1940s in occupied Shanghai and Hong Kong, and the 1950s–60s in Hong Kong and Taiwan.

See also: adaptations of drama and literature; filmed stage performances; historical film

Further reading

H. Chiao (1993a), on Li Han-hsiang's production in Taiwan; S. Hong (1995), a survey of costume dramas of the late 1920s.

(YZ)

Country Wife, A

(Xiangyin)

dir. Hu Bingliu
sc. Wang Yimin
with Zhang Weixin, Zhao Yue, Liu Yan, Chen Rui
Guangzhou: Pearl River Film, 1983

This film contrasts the lives of two characters: a male chauvinist husband and a traditional wife who adheres to all the feminine virtues prescribed to women. It constitutes a criticism of the patriarchal remnants of contemporary Chinese life.

A country wife, Tao Chun, does everything her husband tells her. Her husband, Yu Musheng, works as a ferry man and is very popular with the villagers. A nearby village has built a train station which Tao is curious about and wants to see, but Yu tells her that she can't go. Yu never takes seriously the pains that Tao frequently experiences around her waist. One day they go to the market to sell their pig. With the money, Tao buys her husband two packets of quality cigarettes and some stationery for her children, yet when she is about to buy herself a jacket Yu orders her to buy some more pig litter instead. Tao falls ill again and is diagnosed with hepatitis. Yu is shocked and shaken. After Tao is released from hospital he takes good care of her. He wants to do something for her to lessen his sense of guilt. Tao tells him that she would like to see the new train station, so the next day Yu carries his wife with the utmost care in a wheelbarrow on a visit to the station.

Typical of **representations of women** on the Chinese screen, this film was awarded Best Film at the 1984 China GRA as well as a second prize from the Ministry of Culture.

(ZX)

criticism

Like film itself, film criticism in China also under-went tremendous changes over the years. In the early days, there were two groups of people who wrote film criticism: (1) film studio employees whose job was to provide publicity articles; and (2) film connoisseurs who wrote mostly personal accounts of their film experience. Strictly speaking, the publicity writings by studio employees were essentially advertisements and can hardly qualify as film criticism. On the other hand, film con-noisseurs' writings resembled, in many ways, tradi-tional Chinese literary criticism, which rarely went beyond a few terse lines of casual remarks on the margins of a poem or a book. Early film criticism seldom delved into in-depth elucidation and was often more judgmental than analytical. The connoisseur film critics usually pointed out what they saw as merits or demerits in a film, but without stating reasons behind their observations.

As the popularity of film increased during the 1920s, so did the number of film **publications**. Professional film critics who had seriously studied film gradually replaced the earlier connoisseurs. Consequently the quality of critical writings about film began to improve. Film critics of the 1920s showed a remarkable sophistication in their under-standing of film and took a diversified approach to film criticism. While some focused on the ideo-logical dimension of film, others situated a given film in its appropriate historical context. Still others were more interested in the technical aspects of film production. The application of foreign film theories and analytical concepts also contributed to the cosmopolitan quality of film criticism of the 1920s. Even though many film publications continued to serve as film studios' publicity agencies, there appeared a small number of independent film magazines that provided outlets for in-depth and serious discussions on film and served as the backbone of mature film criticism in China.

The rise of leftist cinema in the early 1930s brought further changes to film criticism. Until then, very few progressive Chinese intellectuals took film seriously; they generally distanced them-selves from this 'low brow' mass entertainment. Partly inspired by the debate on revolutionary literature in 1928–9, which emphasized the need to bridge the gap between revolutionary ideology and the proletariat, a group of intellectuals from the May Fourth tradition entered the film industry.

Their objective was to popularize politically progressive ideas through the most popular form of modern media. Hence, unlike the film critics of the previous decades who had no particular political agenda, the film critics of the 1930s, particularly the leftist group, had committed polit-ical positions and used film criticism as a way to advance their partisan interest.

While Hollywood films dominated China's film market, the Soviet version of Marxism dominated intellectual discourse on film in the 1930s. The use of Marxist concepts and perspectives were wide-spread in the intellectual community, including those who did not identify with the leftists. As a result, film criticism of this period paid dispropor-tionate attention to the ideological significance of film and often neglected its entertainment value. This type of criticism alienated the audience by not only dogmatically denouncing most of the well-liked popular films, but also ignoring the formal aspects of filmmaking. Although a few people, such as the advocates of soft cinema, opposed this ideological approach to film criticism, they never challenged the leftist dominance of film discourse, which continued throughout the 1930s–40s.

After 1949, the CCP government further downplayed film's entertainment value and stressed its obligation to serve the revolutionary cause. Following the nationalization of the entire film industry, the state also controlled the print media, including all film-related periodicals. Consequently party officials, not film critics, set the tone for film discourse.

Post-1949 film criticism developed several distinctive features. First, political concerns super-seded everything else. Most film criticism dealt with political issues rather than the artistic quality of films. A critic's evaluation of a given film was based, more often than not, on the film's political appropriateness or lack thereof. Since film was expected to inspire the audience and teach people the correct political outlook, the positive charac-ters in the films were looked upon as moral exemplars. In this context, film criticism became a way to give an official version of what is morally right and wrong. When a film fell short of what had been expected of it, it risked being denounced politically. Similarly, if film criticism failed to interpret the film according to the correct line of political thinking, the critic risked ruining his career.

Second, film criticism was conducted not as a scholarly or intellectual exchange of ideas, but was rather carried out as a political campaign. As was often the case, when a high-ranking party official disliked a film a directive would be issued from top leadership and a massive denunciation would ensue. There was no room for further discussion, no chance for filmmakers or critics to argue the case. Scholarly or artistic issues were often dealt with as political, and differences in opinion were taken as deviation from the correct political position. Given this circumstance, writing film criticism became a risky undertaking indeed.

Third, because the emphasis of film criticism was on the political dimension, the expert knowledge of professional film critics and film scholars was rendered irrelevant. At the same time, the state encouraged audiences from the wide social spectrum to voice their opinions of film, on the condition that such opinions be congruous with the party's position. Hence, until the mid-1980s, film criticism in China seemed to have a broader participation from the film audience and was not limited to film scholars. Yet, this seemingly popular nature of film criticism was in fact the result of political manipulation from above, not a genuine or spontaneous mass interest in film from below.

In the post-**Cultural Revolution** period, especially since the mid-1980s, the government has gradually de-emphasized film's political function and has taken a mostly hands-off approach toward film. Unless a film is too explicitly anti-government and anti-party, the authorities no longer interfere in film production and film exhibition. This relatively relaxed political environment has allowed film critics to express individual opinions and observations which may or may not always tally with the party's positions. Meanwhile, the reintroduction of Western film theories and methodologies – the roughly two decades' worth of structuralism, semiotics, psychoanalysis, feminism, neo-Marxism, postmodernism, post-colonialism and the like – has given rise to a variety of new approaches to film criticism. Film scholars and trained experts have once again dominated film discourse. As a result both of such professionalization and of the absence of consistent political sponsorship, mass participation in film criticism has greatly declined. Even though the government still controls all film publications, writings about film during this period have reflected a multitude of voices and positions, and are no longer associated with the hegemonic power of the state alone.

See also: leftist film, soft film (both under Chinese cinema in Historical essays)

Further reading

S. Li (1991), a collection of essays by a leading mainland scholar; S. Lu (1962), recollections of leftist film criticism in the 1930s; Y. Luo *et al.* (1992), a two-volume anthology of Chinese film theory that covers the entire century; G. Semsel *et al.* (1990), English translations of film criticism in China during the 1980s.

(ZX)

Crossroads
(Shizi jietou)

dir./sc. **Shen Xiling**
with **Zhao Dan**, **Bai Yang**, Lü Ban, Sha Meng, Yi Ming, Ying Yin
Shanghai: Mingxing Film, 1937

The story is set in Shanghai in 1937. After graduating from college, four friends have to choose the future direction of their lives. The unemployed Xu attempts to commit suicide but is saved by his friends. Liu leaves the city to join the Communist army's fight against the Japanese. Zhao and Tang remain in Shanghai and dream of their perfect careers: Zhao wishes to become a writer and Tang a sculptor. However, they end up in much less glamourous jobs: while Zhao works as a proofreader at a newspaper, Tang is hired as a window dresser.

Zhao's next door neighbour, Miss Yang, is a female technician in a cotton factory. She works during the day while Zhao does night shifts. Fed up with the cramped space in their dividing room, they exchange nasty written messages. They meet on a bus and subsequently fall in love without realizing that they are neighbours. Zhao is assigned to write articles on social issues and decides to interview Yang. Before long Yang loses her job and decides to go back to the countryside. Her friend, Yao, manages to bring her back to Zhao, but Zhao has also been fired. At this hopeless moment, the news of Xu's suicide shocks everybody. Rather than losing their spirits, Zhao, Tang, Yang and Yao react with strength and optimism. They decide to follow Liu's example and join the fight against the Japanese invasion.

Crossroads analyses Chinese young people's struggle to survive and to achieve their ideals in a hostile city that frustrates and destroys their

Plate 14   *Crossroads* (1937)

dreams. Despite many unresolved problems of **urban life** such as unemployment and the housing shortage, *Crossroads* manages to live up to leftist expectations, and it conveys a strong political message through its positive ending.

See also: leftist film (under Chinese cinema in Historical essays)

Further reading

N. Ma (1989), a critical study of leftist films.

(PV)

Crows and Sparrows

(Wuya yu maque)

dir. **Zheng Junli**
sc. **Chen Baichen**, **Shen Fu**, Wang Lingu, Xu Tao, **Zhao Dan**, Zheng Junli
with Zhao Dan, Wei Heling, **Sun Daolin**, **Wu Yin**, **Shangguan Yunzhu**
Shanghai: Kunlun Film, 1949

In winter 1948, life inside a Shanghai building reflects on a small scale what is happening more generally during the last days of the civil war.

Tenants from different social backgrounds fight their personal wars against Hou Yibo, an evil landlord and high-ranking KMT official. Hou's mistress, Yu Xiaoying, lives on the top floor and supervises three tenant families: the teacher Hua Jiezhi, his wife Yuan Jiajin and their daughter Weiwei; Kong Youwen, who works for a newspaper and is the original owner of the building; and the pedlar Xiao and his wife.

When they learn that Hou intends to sell the building and flee to Taiwan, the tenants try to move somewhere else. Hua thinks he can live in his school, but his Dean, a KMT supporter, manages to have Hua arrested under the pretext of his having instigated strike action. Yuan tries to free her husband by seducing Hou Yibo, but she has to give up when Hou's sexual advances get out of hand. Meanwhile, Hua's daughter has fallen seriously ill and needs penicillin.

The only one who seems to have a good plan is the pedlar's wife. She sells all her valuables (including a small bottle of penicillin) to Yu Xiaoying. The pedlar and his wife then go to the bank to exchange the money for gold. But after having queued up for an entire night they are pushed away and violently beaten up by a gang.

Plate 15   *Crows and Sparrows* (1949)

Events suddenly take a positive turn. Yu's maid, Ah Mei, steals the penicillin for Weiwei, who subsequently recovers. As the KMT troops are defeated in battle, Hou and Yu flee Shanghai, returning the building once again to Kong. Hua is also freed from prison. The film ends with the tenants gathering to celebrate the liberation of the city, the country, and their own selves from evil forces. Promoting Communist ideology, this film has been canonized as a classic example of pre-1949 Chinese film in the mainland.

(PV)

Cui Wei

(Cui Jingwen)

b. 4 October 1912, Shandong province
d. 7 February 1979
Actor, director

Cui Wei was born into a poor peasant family and started working at twelve. Thanks to a helpful relative he was able to attend school, but he was soon expelled due to his political activities. After studying theatre in Beijing for a while, Cui moved to Shanghai in 1935 and participated in the leftist theatre movement. He joined the CCP in 1938 and taught at Lu Xun College of Arts in Yan'an. He was appointed director of the Cultural Bureau of the Central and South China District in 1949.

Cui's involvement with film began in 1954 when he took the male lead in *The Rebels* (*dir.* **Zheng Junli**, **Sun Yu**, 1955). He quit his job as a party bureaucrat to take up a position at Beijing Film Studio in 1955. Cui starred in several other titles, including *The Spirit of the Sea* (*dir.* Xu Tao, 1957), ***New Story of an Old Soldier*** (*dir.* **Shen Fu**, 1959) and *The Legend of the Banner* (*dir.* **Ling Zifeng**, 1960). His excellent performance in *The Legend of the Banner* earned him a Best Actor award at the 1962 HFA.

On top of his work as an actor, Cui also directed or co-directed a number of highly acclaimed films. While ***Song of Youth*** (*co-dir.* Chen Huaiai, 1959) is one of the most celebrated films of the 1950s–60s, ***Zhang Ga, a Boy Soldier*** (*co-dir.* Ouyang Hongying, 1963) is considered by critics one of the best children's films to be produced in China. Cui's adaptation of a traditional opera, *Women Warriors of the Yang Family* (*co-dir.* Chen Huaiai, 1960), won a top prize at the 1962 HFA.

See also: adaptations of drama and literature; children's films; theatre and film

Further reading
D. Ma and G. Dai (1994: 107–16), a chapter on Cui Wei; ZDX (1982–6: 2: 327–38), a short biography.

(ZX)

cultural reflections

Cultural reflections refer to an exciting moment of Chinese film history when filmmakers, together with writers, artists and intellectuals, launched a movement in the 1980s that has been variously described as 'cultural craze' and 'cultural fever'. In terms of film history, the most significant event in this movement is the emergence of the **Fifth Generation** directors, whose awe-inspiring avant-garde films, such as *Yellow Earth* (*dir.* **Chen Kaige**, 1984), *Horse Thief* (*dir.* **Tian Zhuangzhuang**, 1986) and *Red Sorghum* (*dir.* **Zhang Yimou**, 1987), successfully brought international attention to this movement of profound implications in post-Mao China. However, cultural reflections on the roots of the Chinese nation, Chinese civilization, Chinese vitality and Chinese wisdom – reflections undertaken in a depoliticized, fundamentally humanist mode – are not the exclusive enterprise of the Fifth Generation. In fact, several middle-aged filmmakers made a significant contribution to the movement, such as **Wu Yigong** with *Night Rain on the River* (1980), **Xie Fei** with *A Girl from Hunan* (1986), **Zhang Nuanxin** with *Sacrificed Youth* (1985), and **Xie Jin** with *Hibiscus Town* (1986). With several generations participating in this cinematic enterprise, cultural reflections mark a decisive turning point in Chinese film history where party politics no longer controlled every aspect of filmmaking in China.

See also: avant garde, experimental or exploratory film

Further reading
X. Zhang (1997), a book on Chinese modernism; Y. Zhang (1990), on the conceptualization of national roots.

(YZ)

Cultural Revolution, the

The Cultural Revolution, termed more fully, the 'Great Proletarian Cultural Revolution', was launched by Mao Zedong in 1966 in an attempt to consolidate his power by mobilizing millions of Red Guards to revolt against their local governments, and by persecuting tens of thousands of officials and intellectuals. In large measure, Mao succeeded in getting rid of his rivals, but at a cost of victimizing countless people over a chaotic decade. When the Cultural Revolution ended in 1976 with Mao's death, the entire country was left in worst possible shape, physically, intellectually and financially. It took many years for people's wounds to heal, and films of the post-catastrophic period joined forces with literature and the performing arts to help redress the wrongs committed in the decade.

During the Cultural Revolution, feature film productions were suspended for a while, and the only domestic movies people could watch at the time were the filming of Revolutionary Model Operas supervised by Mao's wife, Jiang Qing. Many veteran film people were persecuted and died in prison. For this reason, sentiments ran strong in the immediate post-Cultural Revolution period. Parallel to its literary counterpart, 'scar literature', many films around 1980 re-enact the traumatic experience of social injustice in the decade, directly or indirectly criticizing the CCP from a humanist point of view. For instance, *Reverberations of Life* (*dir.* **Teng Wenji**, **Wu Tianming**, 1979) restages the political persecution of an innocent musician. *In Our Field* (*dir.* **Xie Fei**, 1983) laments the loss of life and meaning in a group of educated youth labouring in the Northeast Wasteland. And *Hibiscus Town* (*dir.* **Xie Jin**, 1986) chronicles a series of irrational political events that plague the life of a small town woman. Indeed, when the mainland production of *Unrequited Love* (1981) was banned for its politically sensitive subject (i.e., persecution of a poet), the script was picked up by **Wang Tung**, a Taiwan director, and a new film was released in 1982. Even Hong Kong directors are fascinated by the Cultural Revolution. They sometimes insert a historical segment in films like *The Reincarnation of Golden Lotus* (*dir.* Clara **Law**, 1989), or devote the entire film to the subject, as in *King of Chess* (*dir.* **Yim Ho**, **Tsui Hark**, 1992).

For China's **Fifth Generation**, the Cultural Revolution constitutes a formative period in their lives, and their experiences as educated youths or army soldiers have inevitably shaped their view of modern Chinese culture and history. It took them almost a decade to confront their experience of the Cultural Revolution in such memorable titles as *Farewell My Concubine* (*dir.* **Chen Kaige**, 1993), *The Blue Kite* (*dir.* **Tian Zhuangzhuang**, 1993), and *To Live* (*dir.* **Zhang Yimou**, 1994). Another noteworthy title is *China, My Sorrow* (*dir.* Dai Sijie, 1989), independently produced outside China. In the 1990s, however, a new generation of filmmakers takes a rather detached, apolitical look at the decade. The best example is *In the Heat of the Sun* (*dir.* **Jiang Wen**, 1994),

which represents the otherwise chaotic years as intensely personal and even pleasurable, to the extent that they coincide with the narrator's sexual fantasies and youthful dreams.

Further reading

C. Berry (1982), an analysis of screen conflicts and characterization; R. Delmar and M. Nash (1976), a survey of titles screened in a London season; I. Mills (1983), on Jiang Ching's crackdown on feature productions; T. Wang (1990), on films produced during the Cultural Revolution.

(YZ)

D

Dan Duyu

b. 1897
d. 1972
Director, producer

Dan Duyu was one of the few Chinese film directors to come out of a strong fine arts background. Before turning to the cinema, Dan studied at the Shanghai Institute of Fine Arts and became famous for painting beauties. His work was widely disseminated through calendars and advertisements. Not surprisingly, Dan brought a proclivity for visual refinement to his filmmaking.

As one of the pioneers of Chinese cinema, Dan was a versatile talent. He founded Shanghai Film Company and took sole responsibility for screenwriting, cinematographic and directorial duties. To reduce production costs, he even cast his own family members in a number of early titles. Dan produced **Sea Oath** (1921), one of the first three feature-length films to be made in China. By the end of the 1920s, Dan had produced seventeen films, including *The Revival of an Old Well* (1923), *Beautiful Concubine Yang*, *The Spider Cave* (both 1927) and *The Intrigue* (1928). In 1931, Dan's Shanghai Film Company merged with Lianhua Film Company, but differences between the two managerial regimes resulted in Dan leaving Lianhua and joining forces with Yihua Film Company instead.

Notable titles Dan directed in the 1930s include *The Ghost in an Old House*, *Oriental Nights* (both 1931), *The Beauty from the Southern Sea*, *Regrets* (both 1932), *The Innocent* (1933), *Body Builders* (1934), *Fairies of the Mortal World* (1935) and *The Musician* (1936).

Dan relocated to Hong Kong after the outbreak of the Sino-Japanese war and worked for Great China Pictures, Asia Pictures and Yonghua Film Company. He retired from filmmaking in 1954 but continued to contribute satirical cartoons to *Hong Kong Daily* (Xingdao ribao).

Further reading

Y. Zheng (1982), on Dan Duyu and his wife, Yin Mingzhu.

(ZX)

Dancing Bull

(Wuniu, aka Wu daban)

dir. Allen **Fong**
sc. Zhang Zhicheng
with Cora Miao, Anthony **Wong**, Lindzay Chan, Fung Kin-Chung
Hong Kong: Dancing Bull Productions, 1991

Apart from offering a powerful argument for the necessity of art's political function, *Dancing Bull* was one of the first films from Hong Kong to thematize the 1989 Tiananmen Square massacre in an unambiguous manner. The film concerns the personal and professional relations between Lisa, an on-the-rise dance choreographer, and Ben, her burnt-out dancing partner. Lisa and Ben establish their own independent dance troupe, but a variety of financial and administrative problems tear them apart. While Lisa gladly accepts funding from a corporate sponsor, Mr Cheng, Ben chastizes her for bowing to the pressures of commercial and political interference.

The couple split up. Ben finds solace in the arms of his old friend, Ah Ching, while Lisa rises to the top of her profession on the back of personal loneliness. Ben and Ah Ching retreat to Lantau Island, marry, and conceive a child. After watching the violent suppression of the democracy movement in Beijing on television, Ben and Lisa reunite professionally so as to produce an agitational piece of modern protest dance on the streets of Hong Kong. As Ah Ching gives birth, Ben attempts to rekindle his romantic ties with Lisa, but Lisa smiles at him before walking away.

Dancing Bull provides an excellent example of Allen Fong's intelligent and provocative exploration of social and emotional dramas. The nod to *Raging Bull* (1980) in the title is just the first of the film's many references to the work of American director Martin Scorsese.

Further reading

A. Fong (1990), the director's reflections on the personal and political nature of his own work.

(JS)

Daughter of the Nile

(Niluohe de nüer)

dir. **Hou Hsiao-hsien**
sc. **Chu Tien-wen**
with Yang Ling, Yang Fan, Li Tianlu, Jack Kao
Taipei: Scholar Film, 1987

This is the first Hou Hsiao-hsien film to feature a female protagonist. Hsiao-yang is the daughter of a workaholic cop who takes his job more seriously than his family. She has to take care of the family in the absence of her long-departed mother. Her elder brother runs a gigolo club and works as a part-time burglar. Hsiao-yang, however, is not the kind of traditional woman whose life only rotates around her family. She is also the leader among a group of her friends. Yet her toughness appears to be an obstacle to gaining the attention of her brother's pal, Yang, who is involved with the mistress of a gangster. Her brother's club is later raided by the police and Yang is shot to death while trying to elope with his lover. Following Yang's death, Hsiao-yang's brother is killed one night while he is out organizing a burglary.

After the box office failure of **Summer at Grandpa's** (1984), *A **Time to Live, a Time to Die*** (1985) and **Dust in the Wind** (1986), Hou cast a pop idol, Yang Ling, in *Daughter of the Nile* to prove that he was capable of making a commercial film. Hou's intentions proved disastrous. He was criticized for a lack of familiarity with urban subjects and for his portrayal of gangsters and illegal activities like male **prostitution**. On the other hand, he disappointed Yang Ling's fans by not giving her enough to do in the film. These complaints suggest that despite the director's concern for box-office profit his artistic integrity remains intact.

Further reading

G. Cheshire (1993), an excellent analysis of Hou's films; H. Chiao (1993a), an interview with critical comments.

(YY)

Daughters of China

(Zhonghua nüer)

dir. **Ling Zifeng**, Zai Qiang
sc. Yan Yiyan
with Zhang Zheng, Bai Li, Xue Yan, Sun Yuezhi, Yu Yang
Changchun: Northeast Film, 1949

This film glorifies Chinese **nationalism** and is based on an event that took place during the Sino-Japanese war. Its most noteworthy aspect is its depiction of Chinese women's direct involvement in combat and the heroic sacrifices made by them in times of war.

After the fall of Manchuria, a peasant woman, Hu Xiuzhi, witnesses the execution of her husband by the Japanese. Seeking revenge, she joins the Manchurian resistance force. Although injured during a battle, she manages to make her way back to her unit. The commander of her all-female squadron is an extraordinary woman, Leng Yun, whose husband had been working as an underground contact for the resistance in the city until his death at the hands of the Japanese. Leng keeps her grief hidden inside her and leads her platoon on a new mission. After blowing up a Japanese ammunitions train, they find that the enemy's troops are taking up positions around their base. As Leng Yun sends warning to headquarters, her squadron tries to distract and trick the Japanese. After heavy fighting and a failed escape attempt, the eight surviving members of the squadron are cornered near a river. Caught between the wild torrents of the river and the pursuing Japanese, they refuse to surrender or be captured. With Hu carrying Leng Yun's dead body, the women warriors walk into the river and are swept away.

(ZX)

Dawn Over the Metropolis
(Duhui de zaochen)

dir./sc. **Cai Chusheng**
with **Wang Renmei**, Gao Zhanfei, Yuan
Congmei, Tang Huiqiu, Han Lan'gen
Shanghai: Lianhua Film, 1933

This film is a good example of leftist cinema. While
presenting the working class in a highly sympathetic light, it portrays the capitalists as decadent,
hypocritical and evil. It also shows the unbridge-
able gap that exists between the two.

A cart puller, Xu Ada, finds an abandoned
baby wrapped in a bundle near a rubbish dump.
A note attached to the bundle reads: 'This
baby's parents can't keep him due to their circumstances. Whoever adopts him, please name him
Qiling. The enclosed money should pay for
expenses related to rearing him.' Unknown to Xu,
the baby's parents are actually watching him
through a luxury apartment window. The mother
of the baby is crying, while her lover, Huang
Menghua, the son of a wealthy family, is trying
to comfort her. It becomes clear that the baby is
their illegitimate child. Huang later leaves this
woman to marry the daughter of another wealthy
family.

Ten years later Xu takes the teenage Qiling to
his workplace to show him the hardships of
working life. Meanwhile, Huang, who is now the
general manager of the company Xu works for,
also brings his son, Huiling, to his office. When
Huang finds out that Qiling is his abandoned
son, he offers Qiling some money to start a business, but unaware of their true relationship,
Qiling declines Huang's gesture of 'kindness'.
Qiling works as a cart puller and continues to live
in poverty while his step-brother, Huiling, squan-
ders his father's money at college on drink and
women. Huang becomes seriously ill and his son
takes over the company. Huiling, however, takes
an interest in Qiling's sister, and to make life
easier, has Qiling thrown in jail. Xu has to work
extra hours to pay for the legal fees and ends up
dying of exhaustion. Qiling's sister is lured into
Huang's residence and raped by Huiling.

Qiling is finally released from jail and comes to
Huang's residence to look for his sister. A mortally
ill Huang beckons Qiling to his room and tells him
of their true relationship. Qiling refuses to have
anything to do with him and walks out with his
sister.

See also: leftist film (under Chinese cinema in
Historical essays)

(ZX)

Day the Sun Turned Cold, The
(Tianguo nizi)

dir. **Yim Ho**
sc. Wang Xingdong, Wang Zhebin
with **Siqin Gaowa**, Tao Chongwa, Ma Jingwu
Hong Kong: Pineast Pictures, 1994

This emotionally unsettling film starts with Guan
Jian, a welder aged twenty-four, who goes to an
urban police station and accuses his mother, Pu
Fengying, of killing his father ten years ago. A
flashback reveals Fengying, a capable woman,
taking care of three children and her husband, a
school principal, in a small village in northeastern
China. One stormy night, Fengying and Jian, then
fourteen, were caught in a dangerous snowdrift but
were rescued by a woodsman, Liu Dagui. Since
then, Dagui became a regular visitor to the Guan's
family, and Jian suspected there was a secret affair
between Dagui and Fengying. Jian became even
more suspicious when his father suddenly fell
sick after threatening to expose the affair. Jian
remembers his mother putting some white stuff
into a chicken soup and, after feeding his father,
dumping the soup on the frozen ground outdoors
even though the children had wanted to taste it.
The father died that evening in a local hospital,
and Fengying was soon married to Liu.

The police investigation creates an unbearable
tension not only between mother and son, but also
among siblings. In an unprecedented way, the
father's grave is dug up, and his body re-examined.
The police eventually determine that the father
died of rat poisoning, a crime later admitted by
both Fengying and Dagui. Jian remains cold when
the two are sentenced to death in court. Before her
execution, Fengying makes a wool sweater, which
she presents to Jian as a souvenir. The film ends
with Jian running through an empty hallway in the
prison and out into the snow-covered wilderness.
He throws the sweater to a passing cart, forever
tormented by the unanswered question: why would
his mother ever murder his father? The viewers,
meanwhile, are tormented by other questions: why
does a son accuse his presumably guilty mother in
the first place? and what moral and political impli-
cation did this 'unfilial' son's accusation carry in

the mid-1990s, when Hong Kong would soon be reunited with the 'motherland'?

Further reading

D. Richie (1996), a commentary on the film.

(YZ)

Daybreak

(Tianming)

dir./sc. **Sun Yu**
with Gao Zhanfei, **Li Lili**, Yuan Congmei
Shanghai: Lianhua Film, 1932

This early leftist film depicts the lives of the working class and their oppression by the capitalists. The victimization of women, in particular, is strongly emphasized. The message conveyed is that the only hope for the oppressed lies in revolution.

A country girl, Lingling, and her lover, Zhang, leave their village and go to Shanghai to look for work. With the help of one of Lingling's relatives they both find employment in a textile factory. One day a foreman harasses Lingling and gets into a fight with Zhang after he tries to protect her. Just as the guards are about to arrest Zhang the general manager arrives in a motor car. As he has evil designs on Lingling, the manager lets Zhang go. Indeed, after Zhang changes jobs and becomes a sailor, the manager rapes Lingling, thus forcing her into **prostitution**. Through flirting with her wealthy patrons Lingling saves money to help the poor. One evening she runs into a man in the street – it is none other than her former lover, Zhang, now a revolutionary army officer sent to Shanghai to collect information. Lingling is excited about Shanghai's impending liberation from the rule of the warlords, but the police come to arrest Zhang, and after helping him escape, Lingling is caught and executed. As the sun rises, cannon thunder emanating from the revolutionary forces can be heard in the background.

See also: leftist film (under Chinese cinema in Historical essays)

(ZX)

Days, The

(Dong Chun de rizi)

dir./sc. **Wang Xiaoshuai**
with Yu Hong, Liu Xiaodong, Lou Ye, Wang Xiaoshuai
Beijing: Yinxiang Film Workshop, 1993

This black-and-white feature is Wang Xiaoshuai's first **independent film**. It opens with a surprisingly frank sex scene and follows Dong and Chun (literally 'winter' and 'spring', played by a real-life artist couple in Beijing), who can see no meaning in their artistic work and find that their relationship is deteriorating daily. Their routine love-making inspires neither of them. Dong, the husband, is depressed because a Hong Kong man refuses to purchase his paintings, while Chun, the wife, is planning to emigrate to the USA. After Chun's abortion, they go to see Dong's family in northeastern China, which provides them with some temporary relief. However, when Chun visits her own family against Dong's will, he becomes increasingly frustrated. One day, he breaks all the glasses in the art school where he works, but he is declared 'normal' by the doctor who examines him. The film ends in spring before the couple's final separation, a spring without much hope.

Like his BFA classmates Guan Hu, **He Jianjun** and **Zhang Yuan**, Wang Xiaoshuai confronts contemporary social problems by examining the intimate moments of his protagonists' personal, existential crisis.

Further reading

D. Chute (1994), a review of three mainland independent films; T. Rayns (1995b), a film review.

(YZ)

Days of Being Wild

(A Fei zhengzhuan)

dir./sc. **Wong Kar-Wai**
with Jacky Cheung, Leslie **Cheung**, Maggie **Cheung**, Andy **Lau**, Tony Chiu-Wai Leung
Hong Kong: Rover Tang and Alan Tang/ In-Gear Film Production, 1991

This major early Wong film is rather enigmatic in its exploration of youthful alienation in the 1960s. Yuddy and Su Lizhen become lovers. She muses about remembering him from 'one minute' of their first meeting. Yuddy is desperate to get news of his mother, who never appears in the film, from his 'guardian' Rebecca, a drunken old woman. A disillusioned, irresponsible youth, Yuddy soon takes up another lover, Mimi, or Lulu. When he first brings her home, his friend Zab visits him.

A policeman, Tide, befriends love-struck Su, asking her to call him at the booth on his beat, but she fails to do so. After his mother dies, Tide travels overseas. Meanwhile, Yuddy kicks Lulu out and Rebecca reveals his mother's whereabouts in the Philippines. Lulu wants to accompany Yuddy but cannot find him, and she gets into a fight with Zab. Yuddy tells us that his mother has refused to see him. Tide waits for his ship in the Philippines and takes in Yuddy, who later stabs a passport forger. Yuddy and Tide fight their way out and board a train, where a stranger shoots Yuddy. Before Yuddy dies, Tide asks him what he was doing at 3 pm on 16 April (the date of Su and Yuddy's meeting). Lulu continues to look for Yuddy and Su keeps on working. The pay phone rings – perhaps Su is finally calling Tide. As the film ends, Smirk, an apparent Yuddy double, gets ready to go out for his own adventure.

The themes of alienation and doubling recur in many of Wong's later films of **urban life**, such as **_Chungking Express_** (1994) and _Fallen Angels_ (1995). All these films are noted for their idiosyncratic treatment of private memory as well as of space and time.

Further reading

C. Stephens (1996b), a brief discussion; F. Luo (1995: 37–59); C. K. Tsui (1995), both critical studies.

(KH, YZ)

Descendants of Confucius, The

(Queli renjia)

dir. **Wu Yigong**
_sc._ Jiao Jian, Zhou Meisen, Yu Aiping, Yang Jiang
with Zhu Xu, Zhao Erkang, Zhang Wenrong, Ning Li
Shanghai: Shanghai Film, 1992

A **melodrama** of generational conflicts in a **family**, this film reflects the changing values in the era of economic reforms in mainland China. Five generations of Confucius' descendants (Kong) live in their ancestor's hometown. Kong Xiangbi, the great-grandfather, is going to celebrate his

ninetieth birthday, but his coffin is sold by Weiben, his great grandson, in exchange for a run-down truck. Dexian, Weiben's father, brings a shovel and breaks the truck's window glass, but is stopped by his own father, Lingtan, a former minister from Beijing. Dexian and Lingtan stare at each other as if they were total strangers. The entire family gathers on the eve of the Chinese New Year. Also present is Annie, a visiting scholar from the USA, who admires the apparent harmony of the extended family.

The next day, Weiban accompanies Annie to tour the cultural relics in their village. He plans to use his truck to make money and then go abroad to study, but his father wants him to return to teach at a local school. In protest, Weiben leaves his wife and baby, announcing that he will follow his grandfather's example and seek his own future away from home. Lingtan, Weiben's grandfather, tests Weiben's determination with a pile of English books. He tells Weiben to pursue his goals step by step. Meanwhile, Dexian is still angry with Lingtan, accusing his father of bringing troubles to the family. He narrates with tears how, after Lingtan left for revolutionary activities elsewhere, his mother was forced to be separated from the Kong family and was not allowed to be buried in the family ground when she died. Weiben returns home and announces that he has sold the old truck. He wants Dexian to understand Lingtan. On the day Lingtan departs for Beijing, his son Dexian is not among the crowd that sees him off. The film ends with Dexian standing alone on a place where his deceased mother used to wait with him for the return of the father – a traditional image full of pathos and sentimentality.

(IJS)

Desperation

(Zuihou de fengkuang)

dir. **Zhou Xiaowen**, Shi Chenfeng
_sc._ Shi Chenyuan, Shi Chenfeng
with Zhang Jianmin, Liu Xiaoning, Jin Lili, Zheng Jianhua
Xi'an: Xi'an Film, 1987

The film starts with Song Ze, an inmate who has killed a cop, escaping to a seaside city, where he asks his former girlfriend to contact Liu Fuxiang, a fellow smuggler. Knowing that Song will demand his share of money from their previous deal, Liu lures Song to a private place in order to kill him by a high-voltage electric wire. In a fierce struggle, Liu himself is electrified. Song tries to get some cash from his father, but his plan to meet his father on the beach is aborted, and he is almost caught when he meets his former girlfriend, who nonetheless persuades him to turn himself in. In desperation, Song packs ten kilograms of TNT in a briefcase and gets on a train. The detective He Lei rides a helicopter in the chase. On board the train, He pretends to be a film worker and engages Song's attention. When the train stops at a local station, He drags Song out of the train, and both fall down on the roadside. The films ends with a spectacular explosion that kills Song and He, but the train and the passengers are safe.

A film modelled after the Hong Kong gangster genre, *Desperation* differs from earlier mainland detective films with its low moral tone and its fast action pace. This successful formula was immediately followed by similar titles from other mainland studios.

See also: detective film; gangster film

(JJS)

detective film

This type of film begins with a persistent search for clues and ends with the solution to a crime. Closely related to **mystery film**, a detective film creates great anticipation and suspense, but distinguishes itself from the former by emphasizing a central character, usually a police agent but sometimes a private detective (or even a journalist). The emphasis on plot or plot complications may lead to scenes of fights and chases typical of an **action film**.

In China, no memorable private detectives of the calibre of Sherlock Holmes have ever emerged in this genre, although several detective films were fashioned on these Western models and were produced as early as the late 1920s. However, for historical and political reasons, the **spy film** has become a more developed sub-genre. In the late 1940s, some films, such as *Code Name Heaven No. 1* (*dir.* Tu Guangqi, 1947), staged the struggles of the Nationalist agents either against the Japanese troops or against Japanese espionage during the war. One particular Japanese agent, Kawashima Yoshiko, who was originally a Manchu princess, emerged as an obsessive figure in Chinese spy films for decades to come. In the late 1980s alone, three films on her legendary espionage career were

produced in Taiwan, mainland China and Hong Kong, including *The Flag Is Flying* (*dir.* **Ting Shanhsi**, 1987) and *Kawashima Yoshiko* (*dir.* **He Ping**, 1989).

Spy films in mainland China serve largely a propaganda purpose of demonizing the Nationalist underground agents or ethnic minority separatists who are plotting with foreign supporters (e.g., the CIA) to explode a time bomb in a city or to disrupt social order in the region. Films such as *Ten o'Clock on the National Day* (*dir.* Wu Tian, 1956), *Secret Guards in Canton* (*dir.* Lu Yu, 1957), ***Visitor on Ice Mountain*** (*dir.* Zhao Xinshui, 1963) and ***Secret Document*** (*dir.* Hao Guang, 1965) aim at boosting the Chinese pride in **nationalism** and inciting an anti-imperialist sentiment. In the 1980s–90s, more detective films were produced in mainland China that focus on crimes and solutions, such as *The Woman Who Disappeared* (*dir.* **He Qun**, 1992) and *Haunted House* (*dir.* **Huang Jianzhong**, 1993) .

In Hong Kong detective films, the need for law and order often engenders a series of conflicts between the undercover agent and his police superiors, who are bureaucratic, corrupt, ignorant, or in any case unreliable. The Hong Kong emphasis on the detective's toughness and individuality frequently results in a kind of male bonding between the cop and the criminal, especially in gangster films of the 1980s. When genre-mixing has been the trend since the 1980s, a crime film (*qi'an pian*) may also carry a Category 3 rating, thus legitimately mixing sex and violence into a spectacular show, as in *Doctor Lam* (*dir.* Danny **Lee**, 1992).

See also: Category 3 film; gangster film; propaganda and film

(YZ)

Diary of a Homecoming
(Huanxiang riji)

dir./sc. Yuan Jun
with Geng Zhen, **Bai Yang**, Lu Si, Yang Hua
Shanghai: Central Film, 1947

Diary of a Homecoming treats the housing problem in Shanghai from a comic perspective. Since the Japanese occupation of Shanghai, Zhao and his wife Yu have been living for eight years in the countryside. When the news of the Japanese surrender reaches them, they decide to move back to the city. On their very first day, they start looking for a place to live, but no rooms are available. They spend the night in their friends' eighth floor apartment. The next day, Zhao and Yu resume their search, only to find they cannot afford anywhere. They have almost given up when a rich lady, Tang, invites the couple to stay with her. She has just had a fight with her lover, Hong, and kicked him out of the house.

This arrangement does not last for very long. Hong comes back to reclaim his house. At this point, the couple also learn that Tang is actually married to Hui, who was arrested as a Japanese collaborator. When the house was expropriated by Hong, Tang became his lover. Things finally explode when Hui's release from prison precipitates a big fight. Zhao, Yu, and Tang move out to live in the small apartment on the eighth floor. The film ends with everyone, including Tang's dog, sleeping peacefully.

(PV)

Difficult Couple, The

(Nanfu nanqi, aka Dongfang huazhu)

dir. **Zhang Shichuan**, **Zheng Zhengqiu**
sc. Zheng Zhengqiu
Shanghai: Asia Film, 1913

This is the first Chinese feature film ever made. It consists of four reels and an all male cast of actors. The film criticizes the traditional custom of arranged marriage.

A matchmaker visits a girl's family and tells her parents about a potential marriage partner. The matchmaker then goes to the man's family and relays to his parents the specific requests from the girl's family. After several visits to each party, the matchmaker works out all the wedding details. Finally, the young couple are brought together to consummate their marriage, even though, up until this moment, they have never actually met each other.

See also: love and marriage

(ZX)

Dirt

(Toufa luanle)

dir./sc. Guan Hu
with Kong Lin, Zhang Xiaotong, Geng Le, Ding Jiali
Hohhot: Inner Mongolian Film/Beijing: Golden Bridge International Trading Co., 1994

A showcase of the **Sixth Generation** in mainland China, *Dirt* is narrated by Ye Tong, a nurse sent by her Guangzhou hospital to take advanced medical training in Beijing. Accompanied by her nostalgic voice-over, Ye Tong meets a group of her childhood friends and is caught in their struggles over conflicting interests and values. Zheng Weidong (his given name literally means 'Defending the East') is a dutiful policeman, who warns Ye not to associate with bad guys like Peng Wei. However, the flamboyant lifestyle of Peng's private rock band attracts Ye. Wearing his hair long, Peng represents those disillusioned, rebellious urban youths who defy social norms. Their practice disturbs the nearby residents, and when Weidong orders them to move out, a fight breaks out and the warehouse is destroyed by a fire.

Ye does not fully appreciate Weidong's sense of duty and justice. One day, Weidong is stabbed by Big Head, an escaped prisoner who used to be their friend and who is accidentally killed when he tries to run away. Ye feels sympathetic for Weidong, and the two make love. The scene cuts to Peng watching a documentary of Premier Zhou Enlai's 1976 funeral in Zheng's house. The house was their childhood hangout years ago. Zheng's sister works in a foreign firm in Beijing after college. She is pregnant and seeks an abortion at first, but changes her mind. A birthday party for Ye turns out an unhappy one because of the tension between Peng and Weidong. Soon afterwards, Zheng's father dies, and Weidong is injured in the head by a mob. The film ends with Weidong sitting in a wheelchair that used to be his father's. He bids farewell to Ye, who thus ponders over her short stay in Beijing: her childhood years are forever lost; all joys and sorrows are quickly forgotten, just as their childhood residential compounds are torn down for the construction of new highrise buildings.

Like ***Beijing Bastards*** (*dir.* **Zhang Yuan**, 1993), *Dirt* articulates a pervasive pessimism felt by many Sixth Generation directors; even the title itself (the Chinese title means 'dishevelled hair') points to an impatient protest. But the fact that Zheng's sister gives birth to a child carries a positive hint of hope – more positive than *Beijing Bastards*. For this reason, the film is one of the few Sixth Generation works that received a positive response from the authorities and was allowed to enter international film festivals.

The director Guan Hu *(b.* 1969) graduated from BFA in 1991 and became the youngest director in Beijing Film Studio. The female lead,

Kong Lin, who had starred in **Bloody Morning** (*dir.* **Li Shaohong**, 1990) and **Raise the Red Lantern** (*dir.* **Zhang Yimou**, 1991), raised a fund of US$10,000 from a Beijing trading company in 1991. After paying about $2,000 for the studio affiliation (so that the film could be distributed in China), the film crew worked for almost four years to bring the project to completion. One of the first Chinese films to feature the MTV style of rock images, *Dirt* relied on a rock band named 'Overload' (Chaozai) for music composition and performance.

(IJS, YZ)

Dislocation

aka *The Stand-In* (Cuowei)

dir. **Huang Jianxin**
sc. Huang Xin, Zhang Min
with Liu Zifeng, Yang Kun, Mou Hong
Xi'an: Xi'an Film, 1986

As with Huang's first film, **Black Cannon Incident**, *Dislocation* uses the science-fiction genre to satirize the workings of bureaucracy. The protagonist, Zhao Shuxin, this time the director of a large department, suffers a series of nightmares. The absurd world that he dreams of signifies China in its socialist heyday, while the everyday world he inhabits represents China's near future. A corrupt social system everywhere undermines technological innovation. Zhao longs for peace of mind and seeks a high tech solution, which unfortunately backfires.

In a skyscraper-filled urban setting, an isolated human figure surrounded by microphones and almost buried by files struggles with a socialist bureaucratic phenomenon: endless and meaningless talks and meetings. The use of red filters and shrill noises on the soundtrack reinforce the sense of unbearable conditions. The character wakes up from this operating room nightmare in which medical staff in black uniforms are attempting to kill him.

Contemplating himself in the mirror inspires Zhao to design a robot. Made in his image, the robot could stand in for him at every boring meeting. The robot should be a mechanical object subject to human instruction by its master. Yet Robot Zhao likes to attend meetings and give talks. It even learns how to smoke and drink. A visual montage of wine cups, cameras, and futuristic buildings, accompanied by the sound of applause,

portrays the world the robot comes to enjoy. Conflicts between human and machine emerge. During a conversation, robot Zhao expresses its concern that humans issue so many rules they then expect others to obey. Director Zhao warns the machine: 'You think too much. That's dangerous'.

The conflicts escalate as the robot becomes addicted to the systemic corruptions of modern living. Away from its master, it dates Zhao's girl-friend, seducing her by offering her Zhao's house key. He humiliates people with threats of violence. When Zhao expresses his desire to assign the robot a job doing work that is too dangerous for humans, the robot rebels by exposing itself in front of its designer. At last, in a final power struggle, Zhao destroys the robot. As Zhao looks again into the mirror, his nightmares begin anew.

See also: science-fiction film

Further reading
P. Pickowicz (1994), a discussion of the film as theatre of the absurd in post-socialist China.

(SC)

distribution

Film as a business started off in China first in the exhibition sector. In the early years, there were hardly any domestic film productions. Film activities centred on showing whatever foreign films were available. As China's film market became increasingly lucrative, foreign capitalists began to invest in building a distribution network. By the mid-1920s, six major foreign film distributors controlled more than thirty theatre houses in the country. Forty more distribution companies were scattered around Harbin, Andong, Dalian, Tianjin, Beijing, Shanghai and Hong Kong. Some of those distributors had the exclusive rights to deal with films produced by a certain company. For instance, Pathé's productions, along with films produced by Warner Brothers, Charlie Chaplin and Harold Lloyd, were handled by Pathé's distributor in China. Similarly, Paramount productions were handled by its China distributor, Far Eastern Company. The situation in which Westerners controlled film distribution ended in 1941 when the Pacific War broke out. The Japanese, who had already gained control of film distribution in Northern and Central China, then further centralized its control through their United China Film Company (Huaying).

As domestic film production expanded, Chinese filmmakers began to resist foreigners' control of the movie houses by developing their own distribution network. In 1926, Mingxing Film Company took control of seven theatre houses and formed its own monopoly on film distribution in eastern China. In the north, **Luo Mingyou** built on his success in film exhibition and organized a distribution network that monopolized film distribution throughout Northern China. It was this distribution network that served as the backbone of Lianhua Film Company in the early 1930s. In the south, Tianyi Film Company maintained its strong hold as the main supplier of films to South China and Chinese communities in Southeast Asian countries. Although these distribution networks did not break foreign dominance of the film market, they provided the domestic filmmakers with a considerable breathing space.

After World War II, the KMT government confiscated the Japanese-controlled China Film Company. In so doing, the Nationalists also took over the huge distribution network China Film Company had built during the war. Naturally, when the Communists came into power in 1949, they inherited a well established and highly centralized film distribution system. In October 1949, the Film Bureau under the Ministry of Culture set up a Distribution Department within the bureau, in charge of all film distribution in the country. Unlike the previous film-distributing agencies, the new department was not associated with any film studios, neither was it an independent agency. In other words, the PRC government first nationalized film distribution in the country before nationalizing film production. Between 1949 and 1953, the distribution department underwent some reorganization and eventually became China Film Distribution Company with branch offices in every province. This basic operation model remained unchanged until late 1980s.

Since film was understood by the CCP as a vehicle for propaganda and not for entertainment, from the very beginning the PRC government used distribution as an effective means to achieve political objectives. Through its control over the distribution network, the new regime effectively drove American films out of China's market by late 1950. Meanwhile, in order to promulgate its ideology, the government subsidized numerous film screenings with admission free or at a discount price, and made efforts to reach the audience in rural and remote mountain areas. After 1958, film distribution in China was guided by three principles. First, film exhibition must serve the political needs of the party. For instance, when Mao Zedong issued a statement in 1963 supporting African Americans during their civil rights movement, China Film Distribution Company released *Tamango* (*dir.* John Berry, 1957), a film about the slave trade, to support Mao's position. Second, politically significant films would be given more publicity, more screenings, and shown in better theatres. Third, films should be ranked according to their political correctness or artistic quality and programmed accordingly. By the time the **Cultural Revolution** began in 1966, most of the films made before 1966 were banned. There were in circulation only eight films, all of stage performances of the revolutionary operas. Sometimes people were required by the authorities to go and see these movies time and again. Naturally the government would bear the entire cost.

With the economic reform under way after 1979, drastic changes took place in the film industry. In 1980, a new regulation changed the earlier practice where film studios received a flat fee of 700,000 yuan for every film they produced from China Film Corporation, the state-owned distribution and exhibition monopoly company. Now, the flat fee was replaced with a fee per print sold, which meant the studios had to be responsive to both the box office and the government's cultural and ideological needs. In other words, through its control over the distribution–exhibition monopoly, the government continued to have a tight grip on film studios.

By the early 1990s, that model began to change, too. In 1994, the Ministry of Broadcasting, Film and Television finally annulled the rule that required film producers and studios in China to sell their films to China Film Corporation. Instead, film studios and producers can deal with anyone who is interested in purchasing their films. Since China Film Corporation no longer has control over numerous provincial or regional distributors, a fierce competition for the exclusive rights to distribute certain films has appeared. The film producers have been greatly benefited from this change. As for China Film Corporation, although it has lost its monopoly over domestic distribution, it is still the only authorized importer of foreign films. In 1995, it brought ten major Hollywood productions on a box-office split arrangement. The huge popularity of those Hollywood films translates into high profitability for China Film Corporation, but it also carries a potential threat to the domestic film industry, especially when film attendance has consistently decreased for a decade since the late 1980s. To maintain a balance, the PRC government carefully limits the number of foreign films to be imported each year.

See also: Chinese film in the West; foreign films in China; Taiwan cinema (all in Historical essays)

Further reading

C. Berry (1996a), a report on the reform in the mainland film industry.

(ZX)

Doctor Bethune

(Bai Qiuen daifu)

dir. **Zhang Junxiang**
sc. Zhang Junxiang, Zhao Tuo
with Tan Ningbang, Cun Li, Ying Ruocheng, Yang Zaibao, **Tian Hua**
Shanghai: Haiyan Film, 1964

This film is based on the life of a Canadian doctor, Norman Bethune, and is designed as a tribute to the contribution he made to the Chinese resistance against the Japanese between 1937 and 1945.

Canadian surgeon Norman Bethune heads a travelling medical team that assists wounded soldiers in the CCP base areas. One day, while he is performing surgery, the Japanese invade. While his guards urge him to leave, Bethune insists on finishing the operation because his patient is in mortal danger. Minutes after he and his team leave the makeshift operating room, it is hit by a bomb. As an internationally renowned surgeon, Bethune is also responsible for the training of many Communist medical workers during his stay in China. His professionalism and devotion to the cause of Chinese resistance earn the high respect of people who have worked with him. During an operation he accidentally cuts himself and subsequently dies of an infection.

The story of Bethune became famous after Mao Zedong wrote an article and urged the Communists to learn from him.

(ZX)

documentary

In the current Chinese system of classification, documentary (*jilu pian*) stands in close affinity to, if not altogether subsuming, the newsreel (*xinwen pian*). In the late Qing period, an Italian filmmaker shot some documentaries in Shanghai and Beijing. During the Republican revolution in 1911–12, two documentaries were produced: *The Wuhan Battle* and *The Shanghai Battle*. When the film department of the Commercial Press was established in 1918, it distinguished between the documentary of natural scenery (*fengjing pian*) and the newsreel of current events (*shishi pian*). By the 1920s, film studios were making documentaries intermittently, the most notable being **Li Minwei**'s films of Sun Yat-sen, the earliest Republican leader (produced by Minxin Film Company) and the documentaries of the May Thirtieth Strikes in Shanghai (produced by Youlian and Changcheng). In the early 1930s, Lianhua Film Company established an educational and documentary film department which managed ten branches in major Chinese cities as well as in Hong Kong, Singapore and the Philippines. Over 150 documentaries were made and shown in movie theatres without extra charge to patrons. Two interesting titles from Lianhua are *A History of the Resistance War*, which chronicles the battle against the Japanese at Shanghai in January 1932, and *Scenes from the South Seas*, which documents the overseas Chinese and local customs in Southeast Asia. These two films were screened in Europe and North America in the 1930s.

During the Sino-Japanese War of 1937–45, newsreels of wars and patriotic events were produced by the studios under Nationalist control, by Northwest Film Company under Yan Xishan, and by the small Communist film teams in Yan'an and Anhui. In Manchuria and occupied Shanghai, the pro-Japanese governments also sponsored documentary production. Later, when the Communists took over Northeast Film Studio, they dispatched film teams and documented their major battles with the Nationalist troops who were forced to retreat to Taiwan in 1949. In Taiwan, the KMT government restructured Taiwan Film Studio, Agricultural Film Studio, and CMPC and continued to produce newsreels and documentaries. Many of their productions won international awards, such as *Taiwan Agriculture* (1956), *Taiwan Industry* (1972) and *Confucius* (1976).

In the mainland, documentary production was shifted from Northeast Studio to the newly established Beijing Film Studio, which filmed the Korean War and the achievements of **socialist construction**. In 1953, Central News Documentary Film Studio was founded in Beijing, which has remained at the centre of documentary production in the mainland ever since. Documentary films covered a wide range of subject matter. Apart from usual topics like national news, military life, natural scenery and sports events, new subjects were explored, such as *The Artist Qi Baishi* (1955), a biography of the famous painter, and *Superfluities* (1955), an investigative report on bureaucracy. Many veteran feature film directors, such as **Sang Hu**, **Shen Fu**, **Tang Xiaodan** and **Zheng Junli**, also participated in documentary filmmaking. Documentaries of ethnic minorities became an indispensable means of promoting solidarity within the nation. By and large, all documentaries produced in the 1950s–80s faithfully reflected Communist policy and were integral to the state's propaganda machine. In the 1980s, noticeable changes occurred in the realm of artistic expression. First-person narration was introduced, new camera angles experimented with, and personal experience emphasized. But as far as the official line was concerned, it was business as usual.

A fundamental change in mainland documentary production took place in the early 1990s when a group of independent filmmakers arrived on the scene. Considered the first such film of its kind, **Wu Wenguang**'s *Bumming in Beijing – The Last Dreamers* (1990) documents a community of underground artists and writers who drift from various provinces to the capital city. Hao Zhiqiang's *Big Tree Village* (1994), winner of the Earth Watch Award, captures the environmental damage caused by sulphur mining in a remote area in Sichuan province. Many new independent documentaries were shot on a budget of less than US$1,300 and were circulated outside the official distribution network. Another important figure in independent filmmaking is **Zhang Yuan**, whose *The Square* (1995) is a documentary of daily scenes in Beijing's Tiananmen Square. The government's 1994 ban on his third feature, *Chicken Feathers on the Ground*, is the subject of yet another independent documentary, *Discussions Caused by a Film Being Stopped* (1994), an hour-long video shot by Ning Dai, Zhang's wife and the only female on the official blacklist. Ning's film was screened at the 1994 Human Rights FF in New York.

See also: ethnic minorities, film of; independent film; propaganda and film; war film.

Further reading

H. Chen (1989: 2: 3–67), an official mainland account; Y. Du (1978: 47–72), a brief survey; L. Jaivin (1995), a report on the defiant independent filmmakers.

(YZ)

Dong Cunrui

(Dong Cunrui)

dir. Guo Wei
sc. Ding Hong, Zhao Huan, Dong Xiaohua
with Zhang Liang, Yang Qitian, Zhang Ying, Zhou Diao
Changchun: Changchun Film, 1955

This **war film** tells the story of a martyr who gave his life in order to save his comrades. It pays tribute to Dong at the same time as it glorifies the **Communist revolution** and provides a model for the audience to imitate.

A young army reserve Dong Cunrui and his friend Guo Zhenbiao want to join the Eighth Route Army under the CCP, but their applications are turned down because they have not yet reached the legal age of entry. Before a local party branch leader is killed by the Japanese he leaves his party membership dues to Dong and asks him to give it to the party. Using this as a letter of introduction, Dong's second request to join the army is granted.

Years later Dong has become a CCP member fighting the Nationalists. During the battle to liberate Longhua, Dong and his team are assigned to blow up the enemy's block houses and so clear a path for the attacking forces. Dong finishes the job and is about to leave the area when a machine gun located above a bridge appears to block the path of the marching Communist soldiers. Dong manages to get underneath the bridge, but cannot find a suitable spot to place the dynamite. With time slipping away and more comrades being killed by enemy fire every second, Dong finally uses his own arm as support for the dynamite. He lights the fuse and blows up the bridge.

This film obtained Best Film award from the Ministry of Culture in 1957.

(ZX)

Dragons Forever

(Feilong mengjiang)

dir. Sammo **Hung**
sc. Gordon Chan
with Jackie **Chan**, Sammo Hung, Yuen Biao, Yuen Wah, Deannie Yip
Hong Kong: Golden Harvest/Paragon Films, 1988

After *Project A* (*dir.* Jackie Chan, 1984) and *Wheels on Meals* (*dir.* Sammo Hung, 1984), *Dragons Forever* is the third Hong Kong **action film** to feature the combined talents of kungfu stars Jackie Chan, Sammo Hung, and Yuen Biao. It also represents a stepping stone in Chan's career in that it helped bridge the gap between his earlier martial arts and later crime-busting personas.

Chan plays a seedy lawyer, Johnny Lung, who is hired by a Hong Kong chemicals plant to thwart the owners of a local fish farm who are prosecuting the industrialists for environmental crimes. Johnny falls in love with one of his adversaries, May, and reneges on his commitment to his client, Wah Hua. He then enlists the help of a professional burglar, Tung Te-Piao, and a shady gun-runner, Fei, but the three men don't see eye to eye and fight continually. Finally getting their act together, May, Johnny, Tung, and Fei unite to infiltrate the chemicals plant. Once inside they find that it is really a cover for a narcotics operation. A final showdown leaves everyone bruised and battered, but the villains are defeated, Johnny and May are together, and the three men remain friends of sorts.

There may be little to distinguish between good Jackie Chan movies, but *Dragons Forever* includes a number of his very best fight scenes. The final confrontation in a drug refinery is marked by some inventive set designs and much bone-crunching stunt work. There is also the added bonus of two great celluloid villains, played by Yuen Wah and Benny 'The Jet' Urquidez.

See also: kungfu film

(JS)

Dream in Paradise
(Tiantang chunmeng)

dir. **Tang Xiaodan**
sc. Xu Changlin
with Shi Yu, Lu Ming, Lan Ma, **Shangguan Yunzhu**, **Wang Ping**
Shanghai: Central Film, 1947

Upon hearing the news of the Japanese surrender in August 1945, the architect Ding Jianhua and his wife Shulan dream of returning to Shanghai, building a house and starting a new life. When

Plate 16   *Dream in Paradise* (1947)

they move to the city, they are welcomed by Ding's friend, Gong, who offers to host the couple and Ding's mother. Gong has become rich helping the Japanese and now hopes to exploit Ding's connections with the government. But Ding's connections do not turn out to be so powerful, and Gong's attitude changes. He asks Ding and his family to move into a small attic room. Ding cannot find a job, and Shulan is about to give birth to her baby.

In desperation, Ding gives Gong all he has, including his new-born son and a blueprint of his dream house. Shulan believes that the baby has been taken to an orphanage, but when she finds out the truth, she tries to get her baby back. Gong's wife, who feels no affection for the baby, is ready to return him to Shulan, but Gong wants to keep him. After a violent fight, Gong leaves his wife and claims the baby for whom – he reminds Ding – he has already paid. Ding finally agrees to give their son to Gong, who promises to take good care of him. Gong and the baby will live in Gong's new house. The film ends with a shot of Ding, his wife, and his mother on a street, looking at their dream house that now belongs to someone else.

(PV)

Drive to Win

(Sha Ou)

dir. **Zhang Nuanxin**
sc. Zhang Nuanxin, Li Tuo
with Chang Shashan, Guo Bichuan, Lu Jun, Li Ping
Beijing: BFA Youth Film, 1981

This is one of the early avant-garde films produced after the **Cultural Revolution**. Although the protagonist, Sha Ou, never has the chance to taste the sweetness of victory herself, she is portrayed as a winner in life. The emphasis is on the process of achieving rather than the attainment of a goal itself. In the end, all Sha's personal sacrifices are vindicated when her team wins the gold medal for the country. The rather conventional message reiterated here is that the interests of the group should take priority over those of the individual.

Sha Ou injures herself during training shortly before her national volleyball team is to go abroad for an international game. But she insists on being included in the squad and works hard to recover, supported by her understanding mountain-climbing husband. Although Sha finally

participates in the game, her team loses the match. Sha is deeply troubled by the defeat. Shortly afterwards her husband is killed in an avalanche. Stricken with grief, Sha visits the ruins of the Imperial Palace in Beijing, where she and her husband used to take walks. At this location she is reminded of her country's humiliating modern history and is inspired to think beyond individual gains and losses. Sha comes to devote herself to the training and coaching of the next generation of Chinese women volleyball players. A few years later Sha is paralysed due to over-work. But as she sits in a wheelchair watching the Chinese beating the Japanese in a thrilling televised game, she can no longer hold back tears of joy.

For its daring exploration of new film techniques and its message of **nationalism**, the film was awarded a special award at the 1982 China GRA and Best Film award from the Ministry of Culture in 1981.

See also: avant-garde, experimental or exploratory film

(ZX)

Drum Singers

aka *Travelling Players* (Gushu yiren)

dir./sc. **Tian Zhuangzhuang**
with Li Xuejian, Zhuxu, Tan Mingdi
Beijing: Beijing Film, 1987

An adaptation of Lao She's novel, the film tries but fails to reproduce Lao She's signature style – 'Beiping taste'. *Drum Singers* departs from the emphasis on cinematic form of Tian's **Horse Thief** (1986) and the historical nostalgia of *The Blue Kite* (1993).

During the war, a family of four flees from Beijing to Chongqing. The family's survival depends on the father Fang Baoqing and the daughter Fang Xiulian, two distinguished drum singers. The film does not dwell on the popular storytelling art of drum singing, but rather on the **family**, especially Fang's two daughters. The adopted Xiulian is a talented singer. On stage she wins acclaim and makes money for the family, while at home her stepmother belittles her, following the old belief that an artisan is nothing but a servant for the rich. An old local landlord is attracted to Xiulian and offers to take her as a concubine. Xiulian's stepmother favours the opportunity to trade Xiulan for wealth, but

Xiulian's father opposes the marriage. Later, Xiulian meets an intellectual who encourages her to attend school. In school, however, other girls humiliate her. Frustrated, Xiulian begins to date a young student and tries to live on her own. Xiulian is finally seduced by a KMT officer who leaves when she is ready to give birth to their child.

The story of Fang's other daughter speaks of woman's fate in the old society from a different angle. Dafeng is not a singer, nor is she educated; she allows her parents to dictate her life. Her mother arranges a marriage to the landlord's assistant, but this man abandons Dafeng for his first wife. Dafeng then marries a musician simply to maintain the status of wife. Xiulian and Dafeng follow different downward paths to similar circumstances, a theme in many of Lao She's stories.

After observing his daughters' difficult lives, the father can find no meaning in the profession of drum-singing. The film ends with a close-up of the same passenger liner which had earlier brought the family to Chongqing now taking them back to Beiping.

See also: adaptations of drama and literature

(SC)

dubbed foreign film

Dubbed foreign film is a special type of production in mainland China which involves the translation of foreign scripts into Chinese and dubbing by professional actors and actresses. The translated dialogue has to conform to the original length, and the entire dubbed film is re-presented as if originally manufactured with a Chinese soundtrack.

Film dubbing started in 1948, when Northeast Film Studio produced a Chinese version of the Soviet film *An Ordinary Soldier*. In the subsequent years, Shanghai Film Studio joined forces with Northeast Studio to establish a team of film dubbing specialists. In 1950–3, the two studios produced over 180 foreign, mostly Soviet, films, and these dubbed films had a sizeable impact on audiences. In 1952 alone, 300 million people saw dubbed films, including *Lenin in October* and *Lenin in 1918*, two Soviet features that were screened over and over again during the 1950s–60s. In 1957, Shanghai Film Dubbing Studio was established. In the next decade, dubbed films covered a wider selection, ranging from film adaptations of world literary classics (by Dickens, Mark Twain,

Shakespeare, Stendhal, Tolstoy, Dumas *père*) to original features from Africa, Asia, Europe, and Latin America. Many technical innovations which later benefited the dubbing of Chinese films in minority languages were carried out in this period. During the **Cultural Revolution**, only a few dubbed films were produced, among them *Flower Girl*, a North Korean tear-jerker which provided a much needed emotional outlet for the Chinese audience. From 1969 to 1984, film dubbing resumed at its normal rate and over 200 films were released to the public, including Chaplin's comedies, *Rebecca* (dir. Alfred Hitchcock, 1940), and *Les Misérables*. In addition, Shanghai and Changchun also produced a number of dubbed foreign TV drama series (like *Robin Hood*), and the dubbing of Chinese features in English or French is reportedly under way. In the 1990s, foreign films and TV dramas are frequently dubbed in Mandarin as well as minority languages. Dubbed big-budget Hollywood films, such as *Forrest Gump* (dir. Robert Zemeckis, 1994) and *Broken Arrow* (dir. John **Woo**, 1996), proved immensely popular in China during the mid-1990s.

See also: comedy; foreign films in China (in Historical essays); language and film

Further reading
H. Chen (1989: 2: 145–62), an official historical account.

(YZ)

Dust in the Wind
(Lianlian fengchen)

dir. **Hou Hsiao-hsien**
sc. **Wu Nien-chen**, **Chu Tien-wen**
with Xin Shufen, Wang Jingwen, Li Tianlu
Taipei: CMPC, 1986

It is common knowledge in Taiwan that many young men lose their girlfriends while away fulfilling their military obligations. But for Wu Nien-chen, the most influential scriptwriter to date in Taiwan, losing a close girlfriend means more than simply being 'out of sight, out of mind'. *Dust in the Wind* is based on Wu's autobiography. While in the army, the protagonist Yuan writes several times a week to his girlfriend. However, just as he is about to complete his service, his girlfriend marries the man who has been delivering the mail to her.

Yuan is the son of a miner who lives with his family in a town located in northern Taiwan. After his father loses a leg in an accident at work, Yuan, as the eldest son, goes to work in Taipei to help the family. Like most of Hou's films, *Dust in the Wind* is about people who live on the margins of society and who experience tragedy on a daily basis. For example, what happens to a poor worker whose borrowed motor cycle is stolen? This plot line is transposed into the film in homage to the Italian neo-realist classic *Bicycle Thief* (*dir.* Vittorio De Sica, 1947). Like De Sica's jobless worker, Antonio, Yuan intends to steal another bike. Yet unlike De Sica, Hou does not let his protagonist suffer public humiliation; he simply ends the scene with the girlfriend pulling Yuan away from the target. This scene strengthens Hou's emphasis on forgiveness. Just as Yuan never begrudges poverty, he decides not to create another victim out of his own misfortune. As the film nears its end, Yuan forgives his 'betraying' lover by giving her his best wishes.

Further reading
G. Cheshire (1993), an excellent analysis of Hou's films; H. Chiao (1993a), an interview with critical comments.

(YY)

E

Early Spring in February
(Zaochun eryue)

dir./sc. **Xie Tieli**
with **Sun Daolin**, Fan Xuepeng, Xie Fang,
Shangguan Yunzhu
Beijing: Beijing Film, 1963

This film is based on a short story of the same title by the leftist writer Rou Shi. Set in the 1920s, the story focuses on how Xiao Jianqiu's search for a good society leads him to become a revolutionary.

Xiao accepts a teaching position offered him by a friend, Tao Mukan, who runs a school in a small town. Soon after Xiao's arrival in the town, he learns that the widow of his best friend, Li, who was killed during the Northern Expedition, also lives there and is having financial difficulties supporting herself and her daughter. Xiao feels sympathy for Mrs Li's situation and offers to pay for the girl's schooling. Yet his relationship with Mrs Li becomes the subject of gossip in the town, causing Xiao much stress. The only person who understands and supports him is Tao's younger sister. However, Miss Tao's affection for Xiao makes one of her suitors, Mr Qian, extremely jealous. Although Xiao loves Miss Tao, he decides to marry Mrs Li because he feels she needs him more, especially after her son dies of an illness. But the personal attacks which follow in the wake of his marriage drive Mrs Li to suicide. An emotionally devastated Xiao realizes that the only solution to the miseries of people like Mrs Li lies in the reformation of the whole society. He leaves the town in order to join the revolutionary movement.

The film's focus on individuals' emotions and its positive representation of intellectuals were exceptional in mainland filmmaking of the 1950s–60s.

See also: representations of intellectuals

(ZX)

Eat Drink Man Woman
(Yinshi nannü)

dir. Ang **Lee**
sc. Ang Lee, Hui-Ling Wang, James Schamus
with Sihung Lung, Yun-Wen Wang, Kuei-Mai Yang, Sylvia **Chang**, and Winston Chao
Taipei: CMPC/Good Machine, 1994

Retired widowed master chef, Mr Chu, lives in Taipei with his three grown-up daughters. The eldest, schoolteacher Jia-Jen, has converted to Christianity after a past bitter romance. Jia-Chien is an airline executive while the youngest, Jia-Ning, works part time in a fast food restaurant. Every evening Chen cooks lavish meals for his daughters despite the fact that he has lost his taste for food. Jia-Chien wishes to leave home to live in an apartment bloc under construction, Jia-Ning becomes attracted to her girlfriend's rejected boyfriend, while Jia-Jen's romantic feelings awaken towards school coach Ming Dao. The mother of Jia-Jen's old friend, Jin-Rong, returns from the USA. Jin-Rong is going through a bitter divorce.

One evening Jia-Ning announces she is pregnant and moves out to live with her boyfriend. Jia-Chien loses her savings when she discovers the fraudulent nature of the company building her apartment. Though attracted to her handsome colleague Li Kai, she believes he betrayed Jia-Jen until he states her sister invented the story. Jia-Jen becomes the next daughter to move out after announcing her marriage to Ming Dao. Jia-Chien becomes disillusioned when she discovers her artist boyfriend Raymond has betrayed her. She decides to reject a promotion to Holland when she believes her father is ill. To everyone's surprise, however, Chu announces his intention to marry Jin-Rong.

The film ends with Jia-Chien back in her father's kitchen preparing a meal for him. Now a prospective father again, Chu finds that Jian-Chien's meal has reawakened his lost taste buds.

Further reading

W.M. Dariotis and E. Fung (1997), a critical study of Ang Lee's films; CMPC (1994), a script with other material.

(TW)

education film

See under: science and education film

Eight Thousand Li of Cloud and Moon

(Ba qian li lu yun he yue)

dir./sc. **Shi Dongshan**
with **Bai Yang**, Gao Zheng, Tao Jin
Shanghai: Kunlun Film, 1947

This film stands as one of the representative titles of the post-war period, many of which are highly critical of social realities in China under the Nationalists.

A young girl named Lingyu lives with her relatives in Shanghai. After the outbreak of the Sino-Japanese war, she decides to join a travelling theatre troupe because she finds their performances inspirational and effective in mobilizing the masses for the war effort. While travelling with the troupe, Lingyu learns about real life, acquires acting skills and falls in love with a colleague, Libin. Despite the hardships the troupe members have to endure, they feel it has all been worth it when they see the impact their work has on audiences. After the troupe arrives in Chongqing, Lingyu runs into the cousin who had earlier tried to stop her from leaving Shanghai. He seems to be well connected and lives a luxuriant life, but his affection for Lingyu is not reciprocated. Lingyu and Libin are married on Victory Day. Afterwards they go back to Shanghai and live temporarily with Lingyu's relatives, but before long they become disgusted with the social injustices and inequalities surrounding them. With the help of friends, Libin finds a school teaching job and Lingyu becomes

Plate 17   *Eight Thousand Li of Cloud and Moon* (1947)

an investigative reporter. Her exposures make her cousin uneasy because he is himself involved in a number of illegitimate deals. But Lingyu refuses to be lobbied by her relatives on his behalf. One evening she is hit by a car and taken to the hospital. Her friends come to see her, but no one knows if she will survive.

(ZX)

Emperor's Shadow, The

(Qin song)

dir. **Zhou Xiaowen**
sc. Lu Wei
with **Jiang Wen**, Ge You, Xu Qing
Hong Kong: Ocean (Dayang) Film, 1996

An epic **historical film** by a latecomer in the **Fifth Generation**, this film of love, friendship and revenge opens with a breathtaking scene by a Yellow River cliff. Yingzheng, the dying First Emperor, who unified China in the second century BC, orders a large set of musical instruments to be thrown into the water. The film then cuts to the miserable days Yingzheng spends in his childhood as a hostage in a rival state. He enjoys the friendship of an upstart musician, Gao Jianli. After Yingzheng conquers all other warring states, he wants Jianli to compose a theme song that glorifies his achievements. A captive from a conquered state who bears the sign of a slave on his forehead, Jianli refuses to serve Yingzheng. To end Jianli's hunger strike, Yingzheng's favourite daughter volunteers to help. She succeeds with her charming voice, and then requests that the musician be her music tutor. The princess has been paralysed since her childhood. During their first lesson, Jianli rapes the princess out of revenge, but her paralysis is miraculously 'cured' as a result. The camera captures her graceful figure as she runs cheerfully to her father.

Yingzheng pardons Jianli's sin but forces him to compose the music. The Emperor is building his great palace, and his soldiers have beheaded thousands of captives who refuse to work. Jianli is greatly shocked by Yingzheng's ruthless display of his imperial power and composes a sorrowful song. Meanwhile, Yingzheng marries the princess off to the son of his top general in order to strengthen his power base. Before her departure, the princess stops to bid farewell to Jianli, who is sad when he sees the 'slave' sign that the princess has put on her own forehead. At a palace ceremony, the theme song is played to thousands who attend. Suddenly, Jianli tries to hit Yingzheng, who draws out his sword and kills the attacker. The news soon comes to Yingzheng that the princess was murdered by her angry husband on her wedding night. In revenge, Yingzheng orders that all family members and relatives of his devoted general be executed. By this time, the First Emperor has lost his favourite daughter, his childhood friend and several of his top generals who helped him conquer other states.

Further reading
T. Rayns (1995d), on Zhou Xiaowen's films.

(YZ)

Enchanted by Her Long Braid

(Da bianzi de youhuo)

dir. Cai Yuanyuan
sc. Cai An'an
with Ning Jing
Macao: Cai Brothers/Zhuhai: Brothers Film and TV/Guangzhou: Pearl River Film, 1996

Adapted from a novel by the Macao writer Li Qi, this film features a Portuguese actor in a story of interracial marriage set in the Portuguese Colony of Macao.

Back in the 1930s, Atoshinto is urged by his father, who runs a shipping business, to attend a party at the mansion of a wealthy young widow. On his way, Atoshinto runs into a Chinese lion dance and is surprised to find that the leading performer is a young woman with a long braid. Enchanted by her smile, he ventures to the Chinese quarter and becomes transfixed when he catches sight of her by the public well. The woman goes up to this 'foreign devil' and spreads water on him.

Atoshinto is madly in love, for he has been driven away by the woman several times in the Chinese community. One day, he finds out that the new Chinese woman who brings water to his house is none other than Ah Ling, his beloved woman. He starts courting her in public, and Ling is moved by his honesty. One night, Atoshinto is caught by Ling's neighbours after his secret tryst with Ling, but Ling uses force to save Atoshinto and declares that he is her 'man'. Ling is nonetheless prohibited from entering her Chinese community for dating a foreigner. After refusing to part with Ling, Atoshinto is also driven away by his angry father.

The two lovers rent a room and start a new life, which turns out to be extremely difficult at first. Atoshinto fails to find work and becomes irritable. Ling cannot tolerate his abuse and leaves him. After working as a coolie on the harbour, Atoshinto lands on a decent job. He returns to seek Ling, who almost sells her long braid for cash. The two lovers are formally married in a church. On a rainy evening, Ling has a difficult labour, and Atoshinto runs to the Chinese quarter to beg Ling's adoptive mother for help. The baby of this interracial marriage is born, and the Chinese community celebrates the event with a banquet.

A **melodrama** marked by a strong **nostalgia** for the colonial culture of bygone days, this film also presents female **sexuality** as an exotic object of the male gaze.

(YZ)

Enter the Dragon
(Longzheng hudou)

dir. Robert Clouse
sc. Michael Allin
with Bruce **Lee**, John Saxon, Jim Kelly, Shih Kuen
Hong Kong: Warner Brothers, 1973

Enter the Dragon was Bruce Lee's solo attempt to enter the American market. It is a mixed product and compares unfavourably with his other Hong Kong movies. Although Lee complained about Clouse's inability to understand the appropriate camera angles for martial arts sequences, the film does contain some of his most exciting combat performances. Conscious of the difficulties of launching an Asian star in the Hollywood market, the producers hedged their bets by featuring minor American co-stars such as John Saxon and Jim Kelly. However, the film also reprises well-known Hong Kong cinematic characteristics such as featuring Lee as a Shaolin Temple graduate, and presenting Sammo **Hung**, Jackie **Chan**, and Angela **Mao** Ying in cameos, as well as starring Kwan Tak-Hing's old adversary, Shih Kuen, from the Wong Fei-hung series – beginning with *The True Story of Wong Fei-hung* (*dir.* Wu Pang, 1949) – as Lee's antagonist. But Shih Kuen is now more of a Dr No and Rotwang figure (complete with artificial hand) indebted to *Metropolis* (*dir.* Fritz Lang, 1926).

The film opens with Lee demonstrating his Shaolin Temple martial arts skills. A British official recruits him to investigate the activities of Han, a crime boss who lives on a mysterious island. Since Lee's sister died in an encounter with Han's men, he takes on the assignment and joins the martial arts tournament held on the island. Also present are Vietnam veterans Roper and Williams who have fled the USA for different reasons. Han kills Williams and recruits Roper into his gang, but Roper refuses to kill Lee. A large-scale fight ensues. Lee chases Han into a hall of mirrors before finally dispatching him.

(TW)

Ermo
(Ermo)

dir. **Zhou Xiaowen**
sc. Lang Yun
with Alia, Liu Peiqi, Ge Zhijun, Zhang Haiyan
Shanghai: Shanghai Film/Hong Kong: Ocean Film, 1994

In the era of economic reforms, a country woman named Ermo believes the idea of **modernity** means the ownership of a large-screen television. Her cunning and insistent pursuit of this dream generates a clash between socialist values and emerging consumer culture. As she struggles with new ideas and experiences, the film examines the ways country people comprehend modern life in this period of political and economic transitions. The director's keen observations and fresh cinematic style make the film enjoyable.

The journey to modernity starts with a spatial transition from village to town. The film opens with Ermo selling twisted noodles. The shots of her kneading dough with her bare feet and of extruding noodles through a manual press convey fascinating visual and sexual images. Her neighbour, Xiazi (literally, 'a blind'), drives her to a town where she peddles noodles for a higher price and notices a 29-inch television set that even the county head cannot afford. She stays in town, makes twisted noodles for a restaurant and earns extra money from selling her blood. She begins to buy new clothes for her husband and her son, and then a bra for herself – something she has never seen before. Ermo realizes her sexual powers and has relations with Xiazi.

Disgusted with his wife's overweight figure and her failure to bear a son, Xiazi calls her a slack-assed, fat pig. For Xiazi, an ideal woman should be able to run a business as well as produce baby boys; in other words, she should embody traditional virtues while achieving success in the modern world. The contrast between two male characters further reinforces the clash between an old system and newly emergent lifestyles. Ermo's husband, the former village chief, is presented as a relic of the past, politically powerless and sexually impotent. He knows his diminished social status, but still claims family authority by ordering Ermo around the household. Xiazi, on the other hand, is an entrepreneur who owns an old truck and a television. His pursuit of wealth serves as catalyst in Ermo's transformation from a village woman to a modern consumer. Xiazi clings to some traditional beliefs, however, and judges women according to their reproductive record. The film places all characters at the intersection of tradition and modernity.

The television set not only drives Ermo's ambition but also opens a window to global representations of modern life. The television screen allows villagers to see the world. As a crowd watch a dubbed Western soap opera in a store, Ermo naively asks why the foreigners speak Chinese. Near the end, Ermo saves enough money. A two-shot places Ermo and the television together on the family bed with an audience of villagers gathered around. The composition suggests that either the television or Ermo might be the primary object of fascination. The film ends with an international weather forecast while Ermo and her family are fast asleep. Ironically, Ermo's journey to modernity ends with the image of snow dots flickering on the television screen.

The film won a Special Jury Prize at the 1994 Locarno FF.

Further reading

T. Rayns (1995c,d), two pieces on Zhou Xiaowen.

(SC)

ethnic minorities, film of

A special genre of Chinese cinema, the film of ethnic minorities concentrates on the life of non-Han people in China who usually reside in geopolitically peripheral areas like mountain or border regions. Although an early attempt at depicting minority people can be traced back to the 1930s, when the small studio production *Romance in Yao Mountains* (*dir*. **Yang Xiaozhong**, 1933) offered a voyeuristic glimpse of the primitive lifestyle of the Yao tribes, the generic features of this type of film were not recognizable until *Storm on the Border* (*dir*. **Ying Yunwei**, 1940), which represents the solidarity between Han and Mongolian in their joint fight against Japanese invaders.

After the Communists took over the mainland film industry, the genre became fully instituted in the 1950s. The newly classified fifty-five 'ethnic minorities', who have markedly different cultural traditions, were officially claimed as an inseparable part of the Chinese nation and were thereby subject to centralized state power. Most films of ethnic minorities made by state-run studios in the 1950s–60s reflect the government's insistence on Han cultural hegemony. This insistence manifests itself in several ways: one is to represent minority peoples as wholehearted participants in **socialist construction**, as in *Five Golden Flowers* (*dir*. Wang Jiayi, 1959) and *Daji and Her Fathers* (*dir*. Wang Jiayi, 1961); another is to present them fighting side by side with the Han people against their 'common' enemies, such as evil landlords in *Third Sister Liu* (*dir*. Su Li, 1960) or the Tibetan separatists in *Serfs* (*dir*. Li Jun, 1963). The theme of class struggle, crucial to the discourse of **socialist realism**, finds its way into many films of ethnic minorities from different genres, such as the **musical** fairy tale *Ashma* (*dir*. **Liu Qiong**, 1964) and the **comedy** about a legendary Muslim hero *Effendi* (*dir*. Xiao Lang, 1980).

According to official figures, many ethnic minorities were represented on film during the 1950s–60s, including the Uighur, the Tibetan, the Mongolian, the Zhuang, the Dai, the Li, the Miao, the Dong, the Korean, the Qiang, the Tajik, and others. Many films deal with the **Communist revolution**, while some are intertwined with elements of spy films, like *Menglongsha Village* (Menglongsha, *dir*. **Wang Ping**, Yuan Xian, 1960) and *Visitor on Ice Mountain* (*dir*. Zhao Xinshui, 1963). These films invariably emphasize the heroism of Communist soldiers who rescue the exploited or persecuted minority peoples from their cruel tribal chiefs. To make the chiefs truly culpable they are shown collaborating with foreign forces. Other than by class-consciousness, solidarity among the Han and the minorities seems to be best achieved through joint efforts to defend the nation's border regions.

On the other hand, however, this genre offered filmmakers a rare opportunity during the 1950s–60s to explore subjects otherwise forbidden or deemed dangerous by Communist censorship.

As love or romance increasingly became taboo in films about the Han people, especially in their **urban life**, ethnic minorities were 'recruited' to satisfy the Han urban viewers' desire for the exotic and the erotic. By showing young minority men and women singing intimate love songs and dancing in colourful costumes, the Han film-makers subtly explored issues in cultural rather than political terms, such as the relationship between Chinese film and traditional folk music and landscape painting. In cases like *Third Sister Liu*, the aesthetic seemed to triumph over the ideological.

After a decade's hiatus, ethnic minorities returned in the late 1970s. In the 1980s, new films in this genre experimented with different styles but still conformed to the basic pattern of Han cultural hegemony. In some cases, the narrative focus shifts from the exoticized ethnic other to the problematic Han self. Unlike the beautiful landscapes (e.g., the scenic Li River) in many previous films, which offer excessive visual pleasure at a time of the overpoliticization of everyday life, the landscape in some new films appears more uncanny than exotic – uncanny in that it both attracts the Han viewers' visual attention and blocks their efforts at comprehension. In **On the Hunting Ground** (1985) and **Horse Thief** (1986, both *dir.* **Tian Zhuangzhuang**), not only is the life of minority people registered in an apparently documentary style, without any authorial commentary, but the sound track is punctuated by Mongolian and Tibetan dialogue utterly unintelligible to Han audiences. In Tian's case, the Hans' presumption to be the sole interpreter of minority culture and history is implicitly challenged, if not subverted, and the gap between the Han and the minorities is represented as insurmountable.

A similar questioning of the possibility of integrating Han and minority cultures is undertaken in **Sacrificed Youth** (*dir.* **Zhang Nuanxin**, 1985). Although the Han girl puts on the Dai dress and attracts a young Dai hunter, she ultimately fails to become an integral part of the Dai community, for she runs away from the village and returns years later, only to find the idyllic Dai world wiped out by a massive landslide. *Sacrificed Youth* presents the Dai as an object of feminized beauty that will satisfy Han people's **nostalgia** for lost innocence and will enable them to confront the taboo issue of **sexuality**. Evoked as a pure other, the Dai community constitutes an imaginary stage for the Han people's recovery of subjectivity, for the reclamation of their lost connection to nature, and for reflection on the traumatic experiences of the **Cultural Revolution** from individual perspectives.

Compared with other contemporary films in this genre, those by Tian and Zhang constitute the exception rather than the norm. Films that glamorize the exotic beauty of minority peoples continue to appear on the market. Regularly featuring love triangles and spy intrigues, their plots present an endless parade of enticing smiles, fancy hairstyles, elaborate costumes, melodious songs, erotic dances, and other imaginable or unimaginable visual treats, such as transvestism in *Love Song in the Valley* (*dir.* Wu Guojiang, Huang Yan'en, 1981). As if feminine beauty itself is not attractive enough, some films add violence (bloody revenges, murders, suicides, etc.) and include a love–hate relationship between lovers, thus making minority peoples yet more exotic. *The Strange Marriage* (*dir.* **Lin Nong**, 1981) and *Ruthless Lovers* (*dir.* Chen Guojun, 1986) are among these films which reveal a more masculine – constructed as brutal, primitive, and uncivilized – side to minority cultures, a practice which may be traced back to *Serfs*.

In contemporary mixed genre films from Hong Kong (e.g., martial arts-cum-**historical film**), minority people again constitute the spectacle of exoticism and the erotic. In *Swordsman* (*dir.* **Ching Siu Tung**, 1990), poisonous snakes and snake-like women among the 'barbarous' Miao tribes are offered up as spicy treats for urban audiences. In Taiwan, the status of indigenous peoples has been an issue in the cinematic rewriting of Taiwan history since the late 1980s. In the mainland, as more and more minority directors start their careers in regional studios (like Inner Mongolian and Tianshan), it remains to be seen whether they will be allowed to develop their ethnic identities and to transform the genre.

See also: censorship and film; martial arts film; mixed genres; music and film; painting and film; spy film

Further reading

P. Clark (1987b), an informative background piece; S. Donald (1995), a critique of ethnic and gender identities; E. Yau (1994b), a theoretical essay on non-Han women; Y. Zhang (1997a), a critical study of nationhood and ethnicity.

(YZ)

Evening Bell

(Wan zhong)

dir. **Wu Ziniu**
sc. Wu Ziniu, Wang Yifei
with Tao Zeru, Liu Ruolei, Ge Yaming
Beijing: August First Film, 1988

An intense psychological study, *Evening Bell* represents a new type of mainland **war film** that focuses on individuals' reactions to the war. In the autumn of 1945, after Japan has declared surrender, a team of five Chinese soldiers are in charge of burying dead soldiers in the battle field. They discover a secret Japanese ammunition warehouse inside a mountain cave. Thirty-two Japanese soldiers have been cut off from the outside world and have almost starved to death. The Chinese soldiers leave some food for them outside the cave. When they come out to devour the food, a Chinese woman runs out from the cave screaming, and this triggers a tension between the two sides. The woman dies of exhaustion, and several angry Chinese soldiers want to take revenge by gunning down the Japanese. But the commander negotiates with the Japanese, who eventually deliver the bodies of three other Chinese from the cave. The next morning, the Japanese soldiers agree to lay down their weapons and surrender. An officer kills himself by cutting open his belly, while another officer goes insane and sets fire to the cave. A huge explosion destroys the warehouse. In the barren battle field, the Chinese lead the Japanese captives away.

A **Fifth Generation** director noted for his war films, Wu Ziniu makes effective use of sound and visual images to convey the unbearable impact of the war. The film won the Silver Bear at the 1989 Berlin FF and other international prizes.

Further reading

W. Liu (1988), an interview with the director.

(IJS)

exile

One of the most frequently recurring themes in Chinese film, exile refers to a state of physical dislocation that inevitably results in emotional devastation and social alienation. The case of physical dislocation occurs in early films mainly because of wars, as in **Spring River Flows East** (*dir.* **Cai Chusheng**, **Zheng Junli**, 1947), or natural disasters (e.g., drought and floods), which force peasants into exile in the city, as in many 1930s films. The sense of exile is particularly acute in many Taiwan films, which dramatize the existential crisis of those mainlanders, especially veteran soldiers, who are estranged in the island and feel emotionally devastated. *Lao Mo's Second Spring* (*dir.* Li Youning, 1984), for instance, tells the bitter-sweet story of two of these exiled mainlanders, and *Two Sign-Painters* (*dir.* Yu Kanping, 1990) doubles the sense of exile with a young Taiwanese's tragic struggle to adapt to modern **urban life**. In an opposite direction, a group of mainland productions in the 1980s elaborate the experience of educated urban youths who were sent to the remote countryside (e.g., northeast wasteland, northwest grassland and deserts, and southeast jungles) during the **Cultural Revolution**.

In Hong Kong productions, **Song of the Exile** (*dir.* Ann **Hui**, 1990) studies a dislocated family composed of a mother of Japanese origin, a daughter who graduates from London and grandparents who stay in the mainland. **Days of Being Wild** (*dir.* **Wong Kar-Wai**, 1991), on the other hand, focuses on a disoriented present and an uncertain future, thereby creating an overwhelming sense of internal exile in an urban locale that can no longer be called one's home. Wong Kar-Wai's emphasis on the transitional nature of life in the post-modern city is shared to a certain degree by **Wu Wenguang**'s documentaries on exiled mainland artists, especially in *At Home in the World* (1995) where he records the transnational aspects of the life of Chinese diasporas.

(YZ)

F

family

Family narratives have long been a staple of the Chinese film industry. In the 1920s, **Zheng Zhengqiu** insisted on filming family drama as a means to attracting traditional Chinese audiences over to the new form of entertainment. Even in his comedies such as ***Cheng the Fruit Seller*** (1922), the conception of family takes up a focal point. Zheng's influence on the 1930s was both immediate and pervasive, as a new generation of filmmakers proceeded to produce serious films in keeping with time-honoured Confucian dictates on the family, such as obedience of the son to the father or of the wife to the husband. In ***Song of China*** (*dir.* **Fei Mu**, **Luo Mingyou**, 1935), for instance, the countryside is where traditional family values are preserved, while the city is where the young and the innocent are corrupted. Patriarchal values were taken for granted in the 1930s–40s, even in cases where the patriarch is absent or leftist ideas are prominent. Films such as ***Spring River Flows East*** (*dir.* **Cai Chusheng**, **Zheng Junli**, 1947) and ***Myriad of Lights*** (*dir.* **Shen Fu**, 1948) unmistakably promote family values, in spite of their obvious affiliation with leftist ideology.

In the 1950s–70s, the conception of family drastically changed in mainland China. Although the extended family was still portrayed in a positive light, it was the 'socialist family' that was most favoured by the Communist government. Families of different backgrounds and different regions were supposedly connected to one another and formed a giant revolutionary family, with Mao Zedong as the god-like supreme patriarch. From the propagandist ***Revolutionary Family*** (*dir.* **Shui Hua**, 1961) to the ultra-leftist ***Breaking with Old Ideas*** (*dir.* Li Wenhua, 1975), the socialist family has become an amorphous entity that includes everyone and everything and leaves practically no space for individuality and privacy. Ironically, by the end of the **Cultural Revolution**, the concept of the socialist family had proven quite detrimental to, if not entirely destructive of, family in the traditional Chinese sense. In the vacuum of a revolutionary aesthetic, the humanist conception of family emerged; it emphasized mutual understanding and support. While *The* ***In-Laws*** (*dir.* Zhao Huanzhang, 1981) reverts to a modified version of Confucian ethics in **rural life**, *Neighbours* (*dir.* Zheng Dongtian, Xu Guming, 1981) looks to the urban neighbourhood as a small-scale but functional unit of support.

In the course of the 1980s, concepts of family dramatically changed: from socialist family and neighbourhood to extended family and nuclear family. **Love and marriage** became a popular theme, and **romance** was almost everywhere to be seen. By the early 1990s, however, family dissolution (in the form of divorce or extra-marital affairs) emerged as a new trend, but this time families are destroyed not by ultra-leftist ideology but by internal conflicts. *No One Cheers* (*dir.* **Xia Gang**, 1993) presents this comic situation in the modern city: a couple continue to live together after their divorce and share frustrations caused by their respective new dates. In ***After Separation*** (*dir.* Xia Gang, 1992), both marriage and divorce have become so meaningless to two urbanites that they enjoy playing the game of living together as husband and wife.

In a similar trajectory, Taiwan films underwent ups and downs in their configurations of family. ***Home, Sweet Home*** (*dir.* **Pai Ching-jui**, 1970) and *A Boat in the Ocean* (*dir.* **Lee Hsing**, 1978) clearly manifest an emphasis on the Confucian concept of family, especially on the roles of virtuous wife and caring mother. In ***That Day on the Beach*** (1983) and *A* ***Confucius Confusion***

(1995, both *dir.* Edward **Yang**), family dissolution is construed as not only acceptable but almost inevitable. Indeed, what may appear alarming to traditionalists when viewing *Vive l'amour* (*dir.* **Tsai Ming-liang**, 1994) is not that the new generation are anti-family rebels, but that they are a bunch of urban drifters who care nothing about the traditional family.

In Hong Kong, where urban **youth culture** reigns supreme, family drama does not compete well with popular genres such as gangster and martial arts films. Nevertheless, a few memorable titles, especially those by the New Wave directors, have caught critical attention: *Father and Son* (*dir.* Allen **Fong**, 1981), *Song of the Exile* (*dir.* Ann **Hui**, 1990) and *The Day the Sun Turned Cold* (*dir.* **Yim Ho**, 1994). In a sense, these titles continue a tradition of Hong Kong filmmaking in the 1950s, when film realism – as exemplified by **Zhu Shilin** – meant a serious treatment of **urban life** that deeply involves one's family.

See also: comedy; gangster film; martial arts film; representations of women; woman's film

Further reading
C. Tang (1992a,b), two studies of Zheng Zhengqiu; Y. Zhang (1994b), a study of rural–urban differences in family structures.

(YZ)

Family Portrait

(Sishi buhuo)

dir. **Li Shaohong**
sc. Liu Heng
with Li Xuejian, Song Dandan, Ye Qun
Beijing: Beijing Film/Hong Kong: Era, 1992

An unusual combination of urban film and psychological drama, *Family Portrait* explores the relations between past and present. As we watch the characters view a series of slides, a voice-over pieces together the narrative fragments. The photographs are of a mother who passed away before the present events take place. Viewing the photographs is Xiaomu, a motherless boy in search of his father. A caller from the Children's Welfare School asks Cao Depei, a professional photographer, to claim his 'son'. It is not until then that Cao learns that his ex-wife, who died of cancer, bore him a son. Travelling home by train, Cao ponders how to break this news to his present

wife, with whom he has a six-year old boy. While Cao returns to the city, Xiaomu secretly follows him.

In a basement darkroom, Cao looks at old slides of Xiaomu's mother. The two figures in the photos, both dressed in the style of educated youth during the **Cultural Revolution**, recall the time when Cao and his ex-wife loved each other. As the slide projector moves from image to image, Cao's relationship with the woman on the screen comes into focus. Cao temporarily hides Xiaomu in the basement. Once alone, Xiaomu turns on the projector, finds the images of his mother, and reaches out to her on the screen.

Conflict ensues when Xiaomu is introduced to Cao's new family. Xiaomu attends Cao's 'second' son's birthday dinner, which ends with a fight. While trying to visit Xiaomu in the basement, Cao's wife happens across the slides of Xiaomu's mother. She is moved emotionally but does not say anything to Cao. Meanwhile, Xiaomu has left a farewell note and headed back to his mother's home town. Cao is overwhelmed by the loss of his son. The film ends with Cao and his wife reaching a mutual understanding. As Cao calls to remind her to attend his first photo exhibition, she responds by suggesting that they buy bunk beds for the two boys.

The film won Best Film prize at the 1992 Locarno FF.

(SC)

Family Scandal

(Jiachou)

dir. **Liu Miaomiao**, Cui Xiaoqin
sc. Le Meiqin, Zhang Tingji
with Li Wannian, Wang Zhiwen, He Bing, Wu Dan
Beijing: BFA Youth Film/Yinchuan: Ningxia Film, 1994

Co-directed by the youngest female member of the **Fifth Generation**, this tale of moral transgression is set in Southern China in the 1920s. Zhu Huatang owns all pawn shops in an ancient city and enjoys wealth and prosperity. His only regret is that he fails to control his son, Huizheng. Spoiled by his mother, Huizheng hates his strict father but loves his money. He likes Fang, a maid growing up with him in the household. Tian Qi, a smart servant of their age, also loves Fang and works hard to marry her. But Huatang takes Fang as his concubine and lets Tian be in charge of his warehouse.

Soon Huatang discovers that a piece of his prized treasure is missing and suspects Huizheng. In anger, Huizheng seduces Fang and makes her pregnant. She persuades him to elope with her, but Huizheng is not committed. Huatang comes in and shoots Huizheng, who is injured but manages to escape. Huatang takes Tian as his adopted son and lets him run the business for five years. Meanwhile, Huizheng has become a politician and uses his influence to curb his father's business development. The pawn shop business declines rapidly as a result. In a series of brutal acts, Tian murders Huizheng, takes away Huatang's treasure and exchanges it for a sum of money necessary for reviving the business. Before he dies, Huatang stares at Tian, who has changed from an honest servant to a cold-blooded businessman.

(YZ)

fantasy film

A type of film that features improbable or impossible characters and events. It works to appease human fears and anxieties on the one hand and to satisfy the desire for wish-fulfilment in a world of magic and wonder on the other. Fantasy film can be subdivided into **science-fiction film**, **horror film**, adventure tales, and romantic fairy tales, the latter two often mixed in **children's film**. In the Chinese context, films of ghosts and immortals represent special types of fantasy film that perennially appeal to audiences.

See also: ghosts and immortals, film of

(YZ)

Far from the War

(Yuanli zhanzheng de niandai)

dir. **Hu Mei**
sc. Li Baolin
with Huang Zongluo, Liu Qiang, Zhu Lin
Beijing: August First Film, 1987

A rare glimpse at the psychological effects of war from a **Fifth Generation** woman director, this film follows Gu Meng, a retired army officer, who lives in two different worlds simultaneously. In reality, he stays with his son's family, and his daily routine includes playing with his grandson. In his fantasy world, however, Gu often tries to figure out what happened to him years ago in World War II. Through numerous flashbacks, Gu's past is reconstructed piece by piece: at sixteen, he killed a Japanese soldier who attempted to rape a woman named Chen Yunhua; together Gu and Chen joined the Communist army and fell in love; in a battle Chen lost her eyesight and was transferred to her home town. Gu has never been able to track her down, but a recent news report of her donation of ten thousand yuan to a local school rekindles Gu's passion. Gu finds it difficult to communicate his feelings to his son, an instructor at a military school, and even more so to his daughter-in-law. He secretly withdraws all his pension and departs for Chen's native village in Shandong province. Learning that Chen died a year ago, Gu donates his money to the local school. His son finds him in the village, and the two return to the city, where Gu feels much better because he has contributed his share to society.

(JJS)

Farewell My Concubine

(Bawang bieji)

dir. **Chen Kaige**
sc. Lilian Lee, Lu Wei
with Leslie **Cheung**, Zhang Fengyi, **Gong Li**
Hong Kong: Tomson Film, 1993

The classical opera piece 'Farewell My Concubine' narrates a love story between the King of Chu and his favoured concubine, Yu Ji. Chen's film follows the life-long drama of two opera actors – Xiaolou and Dieyi – who play the roles of king and concubine. Their on-stage roles as inseparable lovers and off-stage lives as companions, however, are tested by the trauma of China's social upheavals. As the film ponders the question of whether it is possible to remain true to anything or anyone under the pressure of difficult circumstances, it also examines how social and operatic conventions can transform a biological male into a cultural female.

The gender reconstruction begins with the metaphor of castration. A prostitute unable to raise her nine-year old son Xiao Douzi takes him to an opera school where he attracts the teacher's attention with his effeminate features. Xiao Douzi is denied admission due to a sixth finger on his right hand. In order to move her son from a brothel into an opera school, the mother takes a knife and chops off the extra finger. Once admitted, Xiao Douzi is forced to accept the role of female impersonator by his opera master, who repeatedly uses corporal punishment. Life at the opera school comprises training in acrobatics, martial arts and singing. Confused by his biological maleness and assigned female role, Xiao Douzi constantly botches his lines when taking the role of a young maiden. Instead of saying 'I am by nature a maiden, not a boy,' he repeats, 'I am by nature a boy, not a girl'. Each time he fluffs the line he is beaten up. Years of physical 'correction' and psychological trials inculcate in Xiao Douzi a new gender identity.

Xiao Douzi becomes a talented female impersonator skilful in the art of costume and make-up. Beyond his transformation in appearance, he undergoes a change in personality and starts to think and act like a woman. His identity fuses with that of the theatrical mask he wears, but the insular world of opera is shattered by the turbulence of life in China. Xiaolou and Dieyi react differently to the intrusion of the outside world on their professional and personal lives. When Xiaolou marries a prostitute named Juxian, Dieyi strives to keep their partnership and friendship intact. The deep bonds between the two actors survive the years of the Japanese occupation and the civil war. During the **Cultural Revolution**, they are forced to betray each other and their artistic integrity. The film ends years later on their rehearsal for a reunion performance. At the climactic moment in the opera, Dieyi actually does kill himself with the king's sword, finally merging art and life and subsuming his identity to that of the celebrated concubine Yuji.

The film won Golden Palm at the 1993 Cannes FF.

Further reading

E. A. Kaplan (1997), a psychoanalytic reading of the film; W. Larson (1997), a critical analysis of the film; J. Lau (1995), a study of transnational Chinese cinema; M. Tessier (1993), a brief discussion.

(SC)

Fate in Tears and Laughter

(Ti xiao yinyuan)

dir. **Zhang Shichuan**
sc. Yan Duhe
with **Hu Die**, Xia Peizhen, Wang Xianzai, **Gong Jianong**, Zheng Xiaoqiu
Shanghai: Mingxing Film, 1932

Based on a popular sentimental novel, this film depicts a tragic romantic story that explores the dark social realities of warlord rule. The studio spent a fortune in its legal disputes over the right to film this novel, generating a good deal of publicity in the process. However, the results at the box office were still disappointing.

Fan Jiashu studies in Beijing and stays with his cousin. While Xiugu, the daughter of his street performer friend Guan Shoufeng, has fallen in love with him, he has a crush on a singer named Fengxi. Guan falls ill but cannot afford to see a doctor. Fan immediately offers financial help, which further impresses Xiugu, but the latter decides to bury her feelings after learning that Fan is really in love with Fengxi. Fan's cousin does not approve of Fan's romance with Fengxi and tries to turn his attentions to He Lina, a girl from a wealthy family. However, Fan has no interest in He. Although Fan asks Guan to take care of Fengxi while he visits his sick mother in Hangzhou, Fengxi's uncle actually marries her to a local warlord while Fan is away. Fengxi's mother tries to stop this by asking Guan for help. Guan sneaks into the general's mansion, but is disappointed to observe Fengxi giving in to the general's demands.

When Fan returns to Beijing he is shocked to find that Fengxi has married the warlord as a concubine. As Fan withers in depression, Xiugu disguises herself as a maid and sneaks into the general's residence to see Fengxi. Convinced that Fengxi is still in love with Fan, Xiugu arranges a rendezvous for them. During their meeting, Fan asks Fengxi to flee Beijing with him, but she refuses to go, fearing the general will catch them. Disappointed, Fan leaves her.

The general learns of Fengxi's tryst with Fan and is enraged. He begins to abuse Fengxi and turn his attentions to Xiugu. Xiugu plays with the general and dupes him into going with her to a remote area where she kills him. By now Fengxi has been institutionalized. Although Guan and Xiugu manage to free her from the mental hospital, she no longer has any recollection of Fan or anybody else. Guan sends Fan a note asking him to meet him and Xiugu at a Western Hill residence. When Fan goes there, he finds He Lina waiting for him.

(ZX)

Fate of Lee Khan, The
(Yingchunge zhi fengbo)

dir./sc. King **Hu**
with **Li Lihua**, Angela Mao, **Hsu Feng**, Bai Ying
Hong Kong: King Hu Film Productions/Golden Harvest, 1973

This is the last film of King Hu's 'inn' trilogy, the others being *Come Drink With Me* (1966) and *Dragon Gate Inn* (1967). Like *The Valiant Ones* (1975), it opens with actual portraits of the main characters accompanied by a commentary giving the historical background for their activities. The film is set in 1366 in the final years of the Yuan Dynasty when Mongol invaders ruled the land.

He'nan Baron Lee Khan and his sister, Wan Erh, travel to Shanxi province to obtain a war map stolen from the revolutionary camp. The scene changes to Spring Inn where Wendy and her companions, Peony, Peach, Lilac, and Chili pose as waitresses. During the film's first part the action is choreographed according to Hu's favourite Chinese chequers metaphor wherein a battle for space occurs between the patriots and their enemies. Eyeline matching shots and camera movements predominate. Chinese nationalists Wang Shih Cheng and Sha Yun Hsan arrive to aid the women.

The second part begins with Lee Khan's arrival and with *mise-en-scène* and fixed camera positions now characterizing the next phase of the Chinese chequers strategy. Khan now has the map but his deputy, Tsao, is also a Chinese patriot and reveals his identity to the resistance group. After an unsuccessful attempt to obtain the map, a fight breaks out between both groups. As in *Dragon Gate Inn*, space changes from interior to exterior landscape. Peony finally obtains the map from Lee Khan, but at the cost of her death and that of most of the patriots except Wendy, Wang and Tsao.

(TW)

Fei Mu

b. 1906, Shanghai
d. 1951
Director

Acclaimed as one of the most accomplished of all Chinese directors, Fei Mu spent his childhood in Beijing. After graduating from a French school, Fei worked as an accountant for a mining company in Hebei province. Besides his knowledge of French, Fei was self-taught in English, German, Russian and Italian. Before being hired as chief editor for the information department of North China Film Company in 1930, Fei contributed film reviews to numerous newspapers and journals in Beijing. He also co-published, with **Zhu Shilin**, a film magazine entitled *Hollywood* (Haolaiwu).

Fei moved to Shanghai in 1932 where he was offered a position as director by Lianhua Film Company. His critically acclaimed début, *City Night* (1933), concerns class tensions between workers and capitalists and exhibits an unmistakable sympathy for the working poor. Following this success, Fei directed *Life* and *A Nun's Love* (both 1934). His ***Song of China*** (*aka Filial Piety, co-dir.* **Luo Mingyou**, 1935) glorified traditional family values and was intended to help promote the ideology of the New Life Movement. The film was taken to the USA and re-edited for a limited release. Fei proceeded to *Wolf Hunting* (1936), a film that deals implicitly with the increasing Japanese aggression against China. Fei's last film, ***Spring in a Small Town*** (1948), presents its triangular love story with great conceptual and technical maturity. Many critics consider this film to be one of the best art films produced before 1949, a Chinese equivalent to *Citizen Kane* (*dir.* Orson Welles, 1941).

Fei suffered from chronic health problems and had very poor eyesight. He died in 1952, three years after moving to Hong Kong and co-founding Longma Film Company with Zhu Shilin and Fei Luyi.

See also: art film

Further reading
A. Zhang (1987), on Fei Mu's film art.

(ZX)

Female Fighters

aka *Three Women* (Liren xing)

dir. **Chen Liting**
sc. **Tian Han**
with Huang Zongying, Sha Li, **Shangguan Yunzhu**, Zhang Yi, **Zhao Dan**
Shanghai: Kunlun Film, 1949

In *Female Fighters*, three women are brought together through different emancipatory experiences. The film opens with the rape of a poor worker, Jin Mei, by two Japanese soldiers. A woman involved in the underground resistance, Li Xingqun, comforts Jin Mei after the rape. Meanwhile, Li's friend, Liang Ruoying, a superficial bourgeois woman, listens to the radio and expresses anti-Japanese feelings to her collaborationist husband.

This is the beginning of a series of hardships for Jin Mei and Ruoying. Jin Mei loses her job and is forced into prostitution in order to make a living after her husband is blinded by bullies. Ruoying gets into trouble while helping her ex-husband, Zhang Yuliang, who is involved in anti-Japanese activities. Zhang's heroic spirit gradually changes and strengthens Ruoying, but when she is abandoned by her second husband she becomes desperate and thinks about killing herself. At the same time, Jin Mei tries to commit suicide because her husband finds out that she has become a prostitute. Jin Mei is saved, and the three women meet in Li Xingqun's school. Thanks to Xingqun's teachings, Ruoying and Jin Mei understand that they should not feel ashamed or hopeless but should face their common oppressors with courage.

Female Fighters is a good example of how Chinese film uses the woman's body as a symbol of oppression, and of how women of various class backgrounds are called upon to join the cause of national salvation.

(PV, YZ)

femininity

Femininity refers to the construction of femaleness or womanhood on screen. Historically, the earliest type of such constructions is the Confucian concept of womanhood, which consists of obedience to father and husband, courtesy to relatives and family friends, and self-censorship of one's speech and manners. This traditional type of femininity translates most famously into an array of dutiful daughters, virtuous wives and caring mothers that has populated the Chinese screen in various regions, including Taiwan and Hong Kong, for several decades. **Hu Die** in *Twin Sisters* (*dir.* **Zheng Zhengqiu**, 1933) and **Ruan Lingyu** in *Little Toys* (*dir.* **Sun Yu**, 1933) are just two classic icons of such 'virtuous' femininity.

Contrary to the Confucian construction, a type of bourgeois femininity emerged in the 1930s, especially in films set in Shanghai. Defined by a modern, Western lifestyle, which includes such necessary ingredients as jazz music, ballroom dancing, cocktails and the latest fashion, this 'decadent' femininity is simultaneously delivered to the voyeuristic gaze of the audience and condemned in moralist terms. From *Three Modern Women* (*dir.* **Bu Wancang**, 1933) to *Spring River Flows East* (*dir.* **Cai Chusheng**, **Zheng Junli**, 1947), bourgeois ladies appear on a regular basis and openly flaunt their sexuality on the screen.

Also during the 1930s–40s, a new type of femininity was constructed in leftist films, which prefer the asexual revolutionary woman to the sexy bourgeois lady. Cast in the role of a revolutionary intellectual or a self-conscious factory worker, this new woman typically identifies herself with proletarian masses, volunteers in a workers' evening school, and participates in strikes and demonstrations. In their newly constructed asexual image (often dressed in blue factory uniform and without makeup), new revolutionary women join forces with their male comrades in creating a new world of justice and equality for all. This asexual type of femininity was carried to an extreme by ultra-leftist ideology during the **Cultural Revolution**, when nearly all positive female protagonists on stage or on the screen were resolutely cut off from any possible sexual relations.

In the late 1940s, a number of humanist films presented a new, more complicated type of femininity. The protagonists in *Long Live the Mistress!* (*dir.* **Sang Hu**, 1947) and *Spring in a Small Town* (*dir.* **Fei Mu**, 1948), for instance, combine an independent spirit and a sexual awareness with an incredible amount of resourcefulness in dealing with the traditional family situation. Without disrupting the patriarchal order, they make their desires felt and triumph over despicably weak male characters around them. In a sense, these strong women figures are a prototype of the beautiful, strong-willed protagonists in **Zhang Yimou**'s films, such as *Red Sorghum* (1987), *Ju Dou* (1989) and *Raise the Red Lantern* (1991).

Except for the revolutionary type, other constructions of femininity sketched above are also found in Taiwan and Hong Kong. In Hong Kong, one sometimes meets a type of femininity more sensuous than the bourgeois lady. In *Rouge* (*dir.* Stanley **Kwan**, 1987) and *The **Reincarnation of Golden Lotus*** (*dir.* Clara **Law**, 1989), female protagonists live in a kind of fantasy world where their sexual desires are completely satisfied. The influence of this new type of sensuous femininity is visible in mainland productions of the 1990s, too. *Yesterday's Wine* (*dir.* **Xia Gang**, 1995), for instance, dwells excessively on a teenage girl's lingering passion for a married neighbour. Contrary to both the 1930s and the 1960s, such display of sexual desire no longer provokes outright condemnation or immediate state censorship.

See also: censorship and film; representations of women; sexuality; woman's film

Further reading
J. Dai (1995), on the Communist discourse of 'femininity'; S. Fore (1993), on Clara Law's film; Y. Wei (1997), on Zhang Yimou's films.

(YZ)

Fifth Generation, the

The term applies to the group of film directors who began making films in the mid-1980s. Most of them are members of the first graduating class of BFA in the post-**Cultural Revolution** period. Although **He Ping**, **Huang Jianxin**, **Sun Zhou**, **Zhang Zeming**, **Zhou Xiaowen** and a few others were not from the 1982 class, they are often considered as members of the Fifth Generation because their films share certain common traits.

As a group, the Fifth Generation filmmakers were all born in the 1950s and grew up amidst the political turmoil of the 1960s. None of them had an uninterrupted pre-college education. Unlike typical Chinese students today, members of the Fifth Generation had already acquired a variety of occupational experiences before they entered BFA. Their post-graduation successes also follow a similar pattern: all making directorial débuts in minor studios in interior China and establishing their names through international media.

The first film of the group, *One and Eight* (*dir.* **Zhang Junzhao**, 1984), was produced by

Guangxi Film Studio in Nanning, which also released the internationally acclaimed *Yellow Earth* (*dir.* **Chen Kaige**, 1984). Meanwhile, **Wu Ziniu** directed *Secret Decree* (1984) in Xiaoxiang Film Studio in Changsha, Huang Jianxin directed *Black Cannon Incident* (1985) in Xi'an Film Studio, and **Tian Zhuangzhuang** directed *On the Hunting Ground* (1985) in Inner Mongolian Film Studio. While these films frequently ran into problems with government officials, they also failed to engage Chinese film audiences at large. Indeed, until **Zhang Yimou**'s *Red Sorghum* (1987) won the Golden Bear at Berlin FF in 1988, the audience for the Fifth generation's films was limited to intellectuals and college students.

Individual differences are obvious among the members of the Fifth Generation. But as a whole, these directors present a new vision of Chinese reality, current or historical, that is often incongruous with the official ideology. They hold a critical view of traditional Chinese values and offer their critique of that tradition from a humanistic perspective. Aesthetically, they reject the primacy of literary qualities found in so many films of the previous generations and attach greater importance to cinematic qualities. They put a great deal of emphasis on audio-visual elements in film making. By discarding **melodrama** as a main structuring principle, they have revolutionized Chinese cinematic language and have brought Chinese film to international attention.

Since the late 1980s, films by the Fifth Generation directors have been increasingly financed by overseas capital and have been widely distributed abroad. Typically, the narratives of these films are set in rural China in some unspecific period of time and expose the backwardness of the traditional ways of Chinese life. This obsession with rural China is also reflected in a few women directors of the Fifth Generation, such as **Li Shaohong**, **Liu Miaomiao** and **Peng Xiaolian**. As a result, many Chinese critics accused the Fifth Generation directors of exaggerating the dark side in China, making their films specifically for international film festivals, while entirely ignoring their Chinese audience at home. Regardless of whether or not such accusation is fair or valid, the fact remains that many Fifth Generation filmmakers have been increasingly removed from mainstream filmmaking in China.

In the 1990s, significant exceptions to what has been construed as characteristic of the Fifth Generation are found in a number of popular films directed by the later comers in this group, such as **He Qun** (with his **gangster film**), **Xia Gang** (with his urban **melodrama**) and **Zhang Jianya** (with his **comedy**). The output of these less-known directors, together with the obvious changes in leading figures like Tian Zhuangzhuang and Zhang Yimou, will certainly challenge a monolithic view of what the Fifth Generation stands for.

Further reading
R. Chow (1995), a critical book on a few Fifth Generation films; P. Clark (1989), a study of the strategy of reinventing China; K. Eder and D. Rossell (1993), with profiles and interviews; P. Hitchcock (1992), a theoretical essay on the aesthetics of alienation; N. Ma (1987a), a close reading of some of the earlier of the new films; T. Rayns (1989), an informative survey of major figures; G. Semsel (1987), with useful background information; X. Zhang (1997), a book on film modernism.

(ZX, YZ)

film education

The beginning of film education in China can be traced to the early 1920s. As movies became more and more popular and film studios sprang up all over the country, numerous film schools were set up to meet the industry's demand for trained personnel. In fact, many film studios themselves were involved in recruiting, training and selecting film talents. By the mid-1920s there were no fewer than fifteen film schools in China. The credibility of these schools, like the great number of film studios of these days, varied greatly.

Three of them stood out among the rest. Mingxing Film School was founded in 1922 and managed by Zheng Zhegu (1880–1925). As one of the forerunners in film education, Mingxing Film School produced a whole generation of filmmakers who would play a crucial role in the development of Chinese film. Students at Mingxing Film School had the opportunity to participate in filmmaking while learning the basics. Mingxing's box-office hit, *Orphan Rescues Grandfather* (dir. **Zhang Shichuan**, 1923), cast several students from the school.

Another well-respected film school was China Film School, which was established in 1924 in Shanghai and attached to China Film Company. The founder of the company, Zeng Huantang, personally supervised the school's daily routines.

Its faculty included well-known directors, actors and script writers such as **Hong Shen**, Gu Kenfu (?–1932) and **Bu Wancang**. One of the leading female movie stars during the 1920s–30s, **Hu Die**, graduated from this school. Among the three majors offered at China Film School, film directing was conspicuously absent; instead, the school emphasized acting, cinematography and script writing.

Finally, Changming Film School was established in Shanghai in 1924. The founders of the school, Wang Xuchang and Xu Hu, were returned students from France. Unlike their colleagues in other film schools, Wang and Xu implemented correspondence teaching as the primary pedagogical method and recruited some leading figures in the film industry to serve on the faculty. The general manager of Mingxing Film Company, **Zhou Jianyun**, director **Cheng Bugao** and script writer/editor Chen Zuiyun all taught in this school. Even more significant than its contribution in training filmmakers, the school's effort in drafting textbooks for its students inadvertently led to an early synthesis of film discourse in China.

During the 1930s, while some film studios continued to run film schools on the side – for instance, Lianhua Film Company opened its training institute in Beijing and graduated future movie stars like **Bai Yang**, Wang Bin (1912–60) and Yin Xiuqin (1911–79). Film education also became a part of the university curriculum. In January 1935, Daxia University in Shanghai offered the first film-related class. Besides showing educational films to his students, the instructor also frequently took students to visit film studios, exposing them to the actual process of filmmaking. In September 1936, **Sun Shiyi** set up a special programme in Wuxi, which was devoted to film and broadcasting. **Ouyang Yuqian**, **Situ Huimin**, **Tian Han**, Wan Guchan (b. 1900), Xu Xingzhi (1904–91), Yang Jiming (1905–91) and **Yuan Muzhi** all taught classes there as visiting faculty. Two years later, Jinling University created a film department in Chengdu which specialized in film education and had Luo Jingyu (1911–70) and Qu Baiyin (1910–79) briefly on its faculty.

In November 1937, the Japanese-controlled Manchurian Motion Pictures set up an actor training school. The school expanded rapidly and by 1940 it had added departments of directing, cinematography, script writing and sound recording. Its enrolment was open to both Chinese and Japanese. Because of the school's close association with the Japanese, a number of Japanese filmmakers taught classes there.

In Shanghai, there were two Chinese-run film schools during the war. Zhang Shichuan founded Datong Acting Institute in 1938. It was located in the foreign concession area of Shanghai and served as a talents-recruiting agency for Datong Film Company. In addition, Golden Star (Jinxing) Film Company also had a Training School for Theatre and Film. Its instructors included Zhou Jianyun, **Huang Zuolin** and Yao Xinnong. Ouyang Shafei *(b.* 1924), a leading female star of the 1940s, **Xie Jin**, an important film director in the PRC period, and Ding Li, a well-known director and script writer, were all former students at the training school.

Besides these Chinese-run film schools, there was also the Academy of Movie Arts, China, which was founded and managed by a German couple, Julius Jack Fleck and Louise Fleck. Julius Fleck was an internationally known film director and had made numerous films before going to China and setting up this academy in January 1940. In contrast to the Chinese film schools, Fleck's academy excluded directing, script writing and general theory of motion pictures from its curriculum and focused almost exclusively on the skills of acting. Its course offerings included dialogue, voice training, posture training, body movements, make-up, screen acting, song and dance, and acting internship. Unfortunately the academy was short lived, as it closed soon after the outbreak of the Pacific War.

Even before its victory in 1949, the CCP had already been involved in training film personnel. While short-term classes offered in Yan'an in 1944–5 focused on technical aspects of motion pictures, management classes at Northeast Film Studio in 1949 gave about 650 students rudimentary knowledge about film administration. These people later served in the key positions of the Communist-controlled film industry. After the founding of the PRC in 1949, the new government paid particular attention to training filmmakers loyal to the party.

The founding of Beijing Film Academy (BFA) in 1956 marked the beginning of a new era for film education in China. The academy was built on the former Beijing Film School established in 1951. In 1952, the PRC government rearranged the higher education system in the entire country. As a result, all film departments from other schools and universities were combined with Beijing Film

School. Hence, the school became the best staffed and best equipped training centre for filmmakers. In preparation for upgrading the school to a four-year college, the government sent a delegation to the Soviet Union, studying the way film education was conducted there. When the academy was officially launched on 1 June 1956, it was clearly modelled after Moscow Film School. Four Soviet film experts were invited to China to teach courses at the academy. The academy initially had only three departments: directing, acting and cinematography. Later, departments of film literature, art design and film technology were added. Over the last forty years, the academy has always been at the centre of film education in China. Among its many graduates, **Chen Kaige**, **Tian Zhuangzhuang**, **Xie Fei** and **Zhang Yimou** have become internationally recognized *auteurs*.

A major development in film education during the 1980s was that film-related classes were once again offered by colleges and universities throughout the country. In 1983, a national conference to promote film education in colleges and universities was held. Participants of the conference later formed an association devoted to the cause. By 1991, many universities had set up divisions or departments of film and/or television education. China Eastern Normal University and Beijing Normal University were the two pioneers in instituting film education on university campuses. At the post-graduate level, MA degrees on cinema studies have been offered by the post-graduate programmes at BFA, the China Research Centre of Film Art and the China Research Institute of Arts, all in Beijing.

Film education at the undergraduate level has long been under way in Hong Kong and Taiwan. Among noted institutions that offer regular film courses are Hong Kong Baptist College – once with Lin Niantong (1944–90), a leading film scholar, on its staff – as well as National Taiwan University, National Chengchi University and Fu Jen Catholic University in Taipei. But as of 1997, film studies majors are offered only at National Taiwan College of Arts at both undergraduate and MA levels.

(ZX, YZ)

filmed stage performances

Filmed stage performance *(wutai yishu pian)* is to be distinguished both from the **musical**, which is normally shot on location, and from the film adaptation of drama, which may differ drastically from the stage version in content as well as in form.

This typical Chinese genre developed from an age-old Chinese tradition that has linked **theatre and film** throughout the twentieth century. Significantly, the first Chinese feature, ***Conquering Jun Mountain*** (1905), is a recording of a Peking opera scene played by the leading star of the time, Tang Xinpei. It proved a huge success. Other opera stars soon joined in this new venture: Yu Jusheng and Zhu Wenying in *Green Rock Mountain* and Yu Zhenting in *The Leopard* (both 1906), both produced by Fengtai Photography Shop in Beijing; and Mei Lanfan in *Chunxiang Disturbs the School* and *Fairy Maidens Spread Flowers* (both 1920), both produced by the film department of the Commercial Press. When the first sound film, ***Sing-Song Girl Red Peony*** (*dir.* **Zhang Shichuan**, 1930), was produced by Mingxing Film Studio in Shanghai, the filmmaker deliberately incorporated four Peking opera scenes. The film delighted filmgoers in major Chinese cities as well as overseas audiences. In the 1930s–40s, Tianyi, Lianhua, Minhua, Qiming and other companies continued to produce films of traditional operas, only three of which were released in their entirety. One such complete production is *Remorse at Death* (*dir.* **Fei Mu**, 1948), the first Chinese colour film produced by Yihua Film Company, featuring Mei Lanfang in the lead role.

In the 1950s–60s, the mainland government greatly supported the genre. In 1960–3, forty such films were produced, almost one third of the total feature output for this period. By official count, over twenty varieties of traditional operas, and their leading actors/actresses, were represented. These include, under Peking opera, *Wu Song* (1963) with Gai Jiaotian and *Boar Forest* (1962) with Li Shaochun and Yuan Shihai; under Shanghai opera, *Dream of the Red Chamber* (1962) with Xu Yulan and Wang Wenjuan; under Kunqu, *Startling Tour in the Garden* (1960) with Mei Lanfang and Yu Zhenfei; under Huangmeixi, *Cowherd and Fairy Maiden* (1963) with Yan Fengying and Wang Shaofang; under Cantonese opera, *Guan Hanqing* (1960) with Ma Shizeng and Hong Xiannü. Some of these films were extremely popular and were still being shown in the 1980s in both China and other Southeast Asian markets.

The influence of mainland productions of stage performances exerted a profound impact on opera movies in Hong Kong. By the early 1960s, Huangmeixi (literally 'yellow plum opera') had become the most popular genre in Hong Kong and Taiwan. Following the success of a mainland title, ***Liang Shanbo and Zhu Yingtai*** (*dir.* **Sang Hu**, 1954), Shaw Brothers released *The Love Eterne* (*dir.* **Li Han-hsiang**, 1963) to compete with MP & GI's production, *Liang Shanbo and Zhu Yingtai* (*dir.* Yan Jun, 1963). In fact, the filming of this classic love story can be traced back to earlier ventures in Hong Kong, such as a Tianyi production in 1935, *Liang Shanbo's Second Meeting with Zhu Yingtai* (*dir.* Chen Pi, 1952), another Cantonese version directed by Wang Tianlin in 1955, *The Tragic Story of Liang Shanbo and Zhu Yingtai* (*dir.* Li Tie, 1958), and finally a Chaozhou dialect version in 1963.

See also: adaptations of drama and literature

Further reading

HKIFF (1987), on Cantonese opera movies.

(YZ)

Plate 18   *Chunxiang Disturbs the School* (1920)

Fire on the Plain

(Liaoyuan)

dir. **Zhang Junxiang**, Gu Eryi
sc. Peng Yonghui, Li Hongxin
with Wang Shangxin, Wang Xiyan, Wei Heling,
Zhu Xijuan
Shanghai: Tianma Film, 1962

By presenting the history of a labour movement
as a tortuous path from failure (when it is a spontaneous uprising) to success (when it comes under
the leadership of the CCP), the film portrays the
Communists as the saviour of the Chinese working
class and thus glorifies the **Communist revolution**.

At the turn of the century, the coal miners in
Jiangxi go on strike. They demand the payment
of their overdue salaries and the improvement
of working conditions. But their demands are
met with violent repression. The leaders of the
strike are arrested and executed by the authorities.
The hardship for the miners continues. After the
founding of the CCP in 1921, Lei Huanjue, a
Communist, is sent to mobilize the workers. Lei
runs an evening school for the workers and raises
their class consciousness in his classes. Meanwhile,
he publishes articles in the newspaper to reveal
the injustice at the coal mine. On the eve of the
national labour movement of 1923, Lei instigates
another strike which forces the management to
yield to the workers' demands.

(ZX)

Five Girls and a Rope

See under: *Wedding Maidens, The*

Five Golden Flowers

(Wu duo jinhua)

dir. Wang Jiayi
sc. Zhao Jikang, Wang Gongpu
with Mo Zijiang, Yang Likun, Zhu Yijin, Wang
Suya, Tan Shaozhong
Changchun: Changchun Film, 1959

Five Golden Flowers is a musical **comedy** based on
a series of misunderstandings caused by five
women having the common name of Jinhua
(Golden Flower). The story is set during the Great
Leap Forward of the late 1950s when farmers
worked hard to increase production in people's

communes. In Yunnan, a Bai ethnic minority
youth, Ah Peng, falls in love with Jinhua; they
promise to meet at the Butterfly Spring in a year's
time. When the date arrives, she does not show
up, so Ah Peng starts looking for her. Since he
does not know the girl's surname he keeps on
running into other Jinhuas, thus creating a series
of amusing misunderstandings.

Ah Peng meets a foundry worker Jinhua, a
tractor driver Jinhua, a stockyard worker Jinhua,
and a manure collector Jinhua. It is at the wedding
of this last Jinhua that Ah Peng finally meets the
girl of his dreams. She turns out to be the vice-
president of the commune. The reunion of Ah
Peng and Jinhua is celebrated by song at the
Butterfly Spring, with other Jinhuas and their
lovers gathering for a final chorus.

This film provides a good example of the
ethnic minorities genre, which celebrates official
discourses on the solidarity between Han Chinese
and other ethnic minorities. It also presents
minority people as enthusiastic participants in
socialist construction.

See also: ethnic minorities, film of; musical, the

Further reading
P. Clark (1987b), a survey of films of ethnic
minorities; Y. Zhang (1997a), a critical study of
nationhood and ethnicity.

(PV, YZ)

Fong, Allen

(Fang Yuping)

b. Hong Kong, 1947
Director

Educated at Baptist College in Hong Kong,
University of Georgia and University of Southern
California in the USA, Allen Fong is one of Hong
Kong's original New Wave directors. Fong first
attracted attention for his television work, and had
two of his entries for the celebrated series *Below
Lion Rock* screened at international film festivals.
Both of these 1977 entries (*Wild Children* and *Song
of Yuen Chow-Chai*) prefigure the realistic aesthetic
Fong would go on to develop in his feature films.

Apart from its status as a key New Wave text,
Fong's first release, *Father and Son* (1981) harked
back to Wu Hui's 1954 film of the same title, thus
sparking off a debate among Hong Kong critics of
the two films' relative merits. The movie exhibits
the kind of sensitivity to relationships and social

Plate 19   *Ah Ying* (1983)

surroundings that were then developed in a sequel, *Ah Ying* (1983). This touching story concerns the eponymous heroine, a twenty-two year old fish-seller who aspires to be an actress, and is shot in a style that recalls the great Japanese director Ozu Yasujiro. The film also made impressive use of its non-professional cast, synchronized sound recording, and regional dialects. The 1986 drama *Just Like the Weather* came next. Confirming Fong's lack of interest in mainstream genres, the film told the very individual story of a young couple who are faced with the decision of whether or not to emigrate from Hong Kong. Finally, after time spent acting for Asian American director Wayne Wang, Allen Fong re-emerged at the end of the decade with one of the most important and timely films to come out of the Chinese democracy movement, ***Dancing Bull*** (1991).

Fong's first three films won him Best Director and Best Film awards at HKFA. In the 1990s he directed films in the mainland, such as *Hay Stall KTV* (1996) for Fujian Studio.

Further reading

A. Fong (1990), the director's thoughts on his own films; J. Kowallis (1997), a comparison of Fong and Stan Lai.

(JS)

Fong Sai Yuk

(Fang Shiyu)

dir. Corey Yuen
sc. Kay On, Chan Kin-chang, Tsui Kang-yung
with Chiu Man-Cheuk, Paul Chu Kong, Sibelle Hu, Jet **Li**, Michelle Reis, Josephine **Siao**
Hong Kong: Eastern Productions, 1993

This kungfu **comedy** is a major example of the 1990s martial arts revival in Hong Kong. It opens as the Qing Emperor orders a special commissioner to terminate the Red Flower society. Governor Tiger Lu brings his wife Siu Wan and daughter Ting Ting to Canton, where Ting Ting falls in love with Fong Sai Yuk. Also in Canton are Fong's mother, a trained martial artist, and his strict scholastic father.

Lu sponsors a kungfu competition to find Ting Ting a husband. At a critical moment in their fight, Sai Yuk deliberately loses so as to avoid injuring Siu Wan. Dissatisfied with her son's performance, Fong's mother disguises herself as his nonexistent brother, Tai Yuk, and wins the competition, whereupon Siu Wan falls in love with Tai Yuk. Learning that Tai Yuk has escaped, Lu forces Sai Yuk to take his place as groom. Although in love, Sai Yuk and Ting Ting are not aware of each other's true identity. Fong Sai Yuk later discovers that his father is a member of the Red Flower society. A spectacular fight between the commissioner and Sai Yuk ensues, with the latter rescuing his father and escaping unharmed. At Lu's house Sai Yuk and Ting Ting agree to get married. The commissioner comes to their wedding but they cannot conceal their identities from him any longer. Siu Wan is mortally wounded and Mr Fong captured in the resulting fight.

Sai Yuk goes to town to retrieve the body of a friend who has been killed by the commissioner's guards. Siu Wan learns of Tai Yuk's true identity as she dies in her arms. After Sai Yuk fights the commissioner, the townspeople help him save his father. Fong's mother, Ting Ting, and Lu now join the fight. At a critical moment, the head of the society comes flying through the air to kill the evil commissioner. Finally, Sai Yuk and Ting Ting go off with the society while Lu and the Fongs leave together.

See also: kungfu film; martial arts film

(KH)

For Fun

(Zhao le)

dir. **Ning Ying**
sc. Ning Dai, Ning Ying
with Han Shanxu, He Ming, Huang Wenjie, Huang Zongluo
Beijing: Beijing Film/Hong Kong: Vanke Film & TV, 1992

Adapted from Chen Jiangong's novel of the same title, *For Fun* depicts the lives of a group of amateur Peking opera performers who seek to enjoy their retirement years in Beijing. Old Han used to be the doorkeeper at an opera theatre. On the day of his retirement, he entrusts his job to two apprentices and returns home sadly. He cannot tolerate the lonely days: at a park his sharp criticism of a group of senior citizens practising arias drives everyone away. Later, on his initiative, the senior citizens organize a cultural centre and start to meet regularly, but Han still bosses people around and finds fault with everybody. Such tensions cause much unhappiness, but Han eventually realizes that he is now a retired person himself and that he needs to enjoy fun and friendship as others do.

For Fun is characterized by a personal, **documentary** film style that boasts a fresh sense of humour, a strong humanism and natural performance. Western critics have compared the film to French 'nouvelle vague' classics and to the fables of Federico Fellini. It was the first contemporary Chinese urban film to be greeted with widespread enthusiasm in the West. The film was a major international hit: in 1993 alone, it was screened at over twenty film festivals (Hong Kong, Berlin, Montreal, Spain, Tokyo, Nantes, Toronto, London, Turin, Mannheim, etc.) and won numerous top awards. Many Western countries have bought distribution rights. *For Fun* marks a new development in Chinese urban cinema.

(YZ)

Fourth Generation, the

This term, like that of '**Fifth Generation**', refers mainly to film directors and does not usually include actors and other people working on the technical side of film production.

In the Chinese genealogy of film directors, the Fourth Generation refers to the group of film directors who learned the craft of filmmaking in the late 1950s and early 1960s. Many of them graduated from BFA just before the **Cultural Revolution**. Although the term may not have a precise definition, its usage has been consistent and not in the least confusing in Chinese film studies. The Fourth Generation includes roughly all filmmakers between the Third Generation of directors who started directing films in the early 1950s and the Fifth Generation who graduated from BFA in the early 1980s. Hence, the characteristics of the Fourth Generation must be understood in relation to the two generations immediately before and after it.

As compared with the Third Generation, members of the Fourth Generation were generally better educated and most of them had formal training in filmmaking. They spent their formative years in post-1949 China and grew up predisposed to Marxist ideology. In contrast to the Fifth Generation, although the Fourth Generation also experienced disillusionment with socialist China, politically they are much less rebellious against the establishment than their Fifth Generation colleagues. Members of the Fourth Generation remain essentially reformers at heart and oppose drastic change.

Aesthetically, their film training in the 1960s was largely limited to the Soviet style of film craftsmanship. Unlike the generations before them who had exposure to Western films in the 1920s–40s, the Fourth Generation had no contact with Western culture until the early 1980s. Hence, they show much less fascination with the kind of technical novelty developed in the West since the 1960s and tend to be on the conservative side when it comes to experimenting with new film techniques.

The Fourth Generation's films stay close to the humanistic tradition of the 1930s–40s and follow a rather conventional narrative strategy. Among the representatives of this generation, **Huang Jianzhong**, **Huang Shuqin**, **Teng Wenji**, **Wu Tianming**, **Wu Yigong**, **Xie Fei** and **Zhang Nuanxin** are all well known both in China and overseas. Since the early 1990s, as enthusiasm for the Fifth Generation waned, the reputation of the Fourth Generation has been on the rise. Many directors of the Fourth Generation are extremely productive, even when they hold important administrative and educational positions.

Further reading

S. Toroptsev (1992), a brief discussion of the Fourth Generation; F. Xie (1990), an informative essay from a key Fourth Generation director.

(ZX)

From Victory to Victory

(Nanzheng beizhan)

dir. **Cheng Yin**, **Tang Xiaodan**
sc. Shen Ximeng, Shen Mojun, Gu Baozhang
with Feng Zhe, **Zhang Ruifang**, Chen Ge,
Tang Huda, Xiang Kun
Shanghai: Shanghai Film, 1952

This **war film** is based on one of the CCP's successful military campaigns against the Nationalists during 1945–9. It glorifies the **Communist revolution** by contrasting the heroism, determination, self-sacrifice and good coordination of the CCP armed forces with the factionalism, arrogance and lack of popular support of the Nationalist troops.

As the Nationalist troops advance into Northern China, the CCP command orders a strategic retreat, a decision which meets with resistance from the rank and file who want to confront

the enemy. While Major Gao has to convince his soldiers of the wisdom of the central military committee, Zhao Yumin, the woman guerila leader of the region, tries to explain to the villagers why they need to retreat. The Nationalists are fooled into thinking that they have wiped out the CCP forces and continue to advance into the trap set by the CCP forces. After the Nationalist division realizes it is being encircled, it tries to blow up a dam to stop the CCP troops from attacking it. But the attempt is foiled by Zhao and her guerila force. In the end, the Nationalist troops suffer a disastrous defeat and many of their high-commanding officers are captured by Communist soldiers.

The film was remade into a colour feature during the **Cultural Revolution**.

(ZX)

Full Moon in New York

(San'ge nüren de gushi, aka Ren zai Niuyue)

dir. Stanley **Kwan**
sc. Zhong Acheng, Qiu-Dai Anping
with Sylvia **Chang**, Maggie **Cheung**, **Siqin Gaowa**
Hong Kong: Scholar Film, 1989

In this powerful examination of how the feelings of **exile** affect three Chinese women in the most populated city in the world, the director strikes a balance by following a representative each from the mainland, Hong Kong and Taiwan. Zhao Hong is newly married to a Chinese American, who loves his wife but does not understand her concerns. Zhao wants to work and bring her mother to New York, but her husband does not want their cosy private life to be disturbed. Zhao meets Huang Xiongping, an actress devoted to the performing arts. Huang has tried to get important stage roles and blames her failures on a widespread discrimination against the Chinese in the USA. Huang and Zhao eat dinner at a restaurant run by Li Fengjiao. Li is a typical Hong Kong businesswoman, familiar with all money-making tricks such as stock market and real estate speculations. Li's father is worried that she is still single, but Li is actually a lesbian and has a lover named Stella. The three Chinese women feel a strong cultural tie binding them together, but their different backgrounds, tastes and lifestyles also create conflicts among them. One rainy night they get drunk and walk along the streets, shouting and singing together – a rare image of sisterhood in Chinese film that overrides historical and geopolitical differences.

The film won Best Film, Best Screenplay, Best Actress (Maggie Cheung) and other top prizes at the 1989 Taipei GHA.

Further reading
W. Law (1993), a profile of the director.

(JS, YZ)

G

Game of Death

(Siwang youxi)

dir. Robert Clouse
sc. Jan Spears
with Bruce **Lee**, Kim Tai Yong, Gig Young,
Dean Jagger, Hugh O'Brian
Hong Kong: Golden Harvest, 1978

Game of Death may actually be the first postmodernist **martial arts film** in an accidental sense in which the referent has no coherent reality. Bruce Lee died after completing only several scenes of combat footage for the second film of his proposed Tang Lung series. Golden Harvest's Raymond **Chow** immediately recruited Robert Clouse, director of ***Enter the Dragon*** (1973), to make a feature film using the surviving footage. He did this by having Kim Tai Tong, a Korean 'lookalike', portray Lee's character, Billy Lo, in dimly lit and abruptly edited scenes throughout the film. Golden Harvest also used another twenty minutes of Lee's surviving footage in *Game of Death, II* (1981), directed by Ng See-Yuen, also featuring Kim Tai Yong as the Lee clone. *Game of Death* is remarkable less as a cinematic achievement than for its attempt to mix clone and star together in a fabricated posthumous production.

The plot uses one of the rumours about Lee's death for its premise. A triad organization (run by whites!) infiltrating the entertainment industry demands money from Billy Lo. When he refuses they arrange his murder. However, Billy survives and after some plastic surgery takes his revenge on the mob. On his way to confront a gang leader, Dr. Land, Billy (now represented by the original Bruce Lee) confronts three martial artists: a Korean, a Japanese, and a seven-foot Afro-American Hakim. Originally the scene was designed to pit Tang Lung's superior Chinese martial arts against other national variations. This does not exist in either the Hong Kong or American versions. The former credits Lee, Clouse, and Sammo **Hung** as co-directors.

(TW)

gangster film

A type of film that features conflicts between the police and criminals or among different factions of criminals, usually in a violent way.

See also: action film

(YZ)

Garlands at the Foot of the Mountain

(Gaoshan xia de huahuan)

dir. **Xie Jin**
sc. Li Zhun, Li Cunbao
with Lu Xiaohe, Tang Guoqiang, He Wei, Gai Ke, **Siqin Gaowa**
Shanghai: Shanghai Film, 1984

Set against the Sino-Vietnam war of 1979, this film focuses on the sacrifices of ordinary soldiers and their families and subtly criticizes the corruption and selfishness of some of the high ranking commanders and their family members.

A captain, Liang Sanxi, is finally granted a short leave to visit his family, but he wants to wait for the newly appointed political advisor to arrive first so that he can help the newcomer settle in. The newcomer is Zhao Mengsheng, son of a high ranking military commander. Zhao is only using this new assignment as a stepping stone on his way back to the city and he has little interest in the position. Zhao's disappointing performance as an officer forces Liang to delay his visit home.

The Sino-Vietnamese war breaks out and all military leave is cancelled. Yet, at the same time, Zhao receives his transfer papers allowing him to work in a department far removed from the front. To pacify his comrades' resentment, Zhao decides to stay. However, his mother calls the commanding general of Zhao's unit and asks the general to keep Zhao out of harm's way. The general, who also has a son serving in Liang's unit, turns down her request. During a military operation in Vietnam, Liang, along with the general's son and a number of other soldiers, is killed in action. After the war, as Zhao goes over their personal belongings, he finds a note from Liang listing all the debts he owes and asking his mother and wife to pay them back. Zhao is further moved when Liang's mother and wife come to pay Liang's debts with his burial money and their meagre savings. He assembles his soldiers and salutes the two women with a military honour.

In 1984 the film was granted awards of Best Screenplay and Best Actor at China GRA; Best Film and Best Actor at HFA; and Best Film by the Ministry of Culture.

(ZX)

Ge Lan
(Grace Chang, Zhang Yuying)

b. 1934, Shanghai
Actress

Ge Lan was fond of Peking opera in her childhood and once appeared on stage with the famous actor Yu Zhenfei. In 1949 she moved with her family from Shanghai to Hong Kong, where she attended an acting workshop organized by Taishan Film Company in 1952. She starred in over thirty films, most notably *Wild, Wild Rose* (*dir.* Wang Tianlin, 1960) and **Star, Moon, Sun** (*dir.* Yi Wen, 1961). She was particularly famous for 'song-and-dance films', a type of Hong Kong **musical** popular in the 1950s–60s. *Mambo Girl* (*dir.* Yi Wen, 1957) and *Because of Her* (*dir.* Yi Wen, Wang Tianlin, 1963) won her immense popularity. In 1959, Ge Lan was invited by NBC Radio to join a song-and-dance tour in the USA and became the first Chinese singer-dancer-actress to issue a solo record there.

(YZ)

genre films

Genre films refer to films with distinctive genre features. A group of films sharing similar storylines, character types, themes, settings, moods and film techniques are classified by convention into a film genre. The most popular film genres in China are **comedy**, gangster (or action), martial arts (also called kungfu or swordplay), ghosts and immortals, war, and historical (including **biography**) films, while the detective, spy, horror, the **musical**, science-fiction and **Westerns** are among the less developed genres. Also endearing to Chinese audiences are **animation**, **children's film** and **filmed stage performances** (or opera movie), while art and independent films began to draw critical attention in the 1980s. Generic features, however, are not exclusive to any given genre, and many popular films now carry features of **mixed genres**.

See also: action film; art film; detective film; gangster film; ghosts and immortals, film of; historical film; horror film; independent film; kungfu film; martial arts film; science-fiction film; spy film; swordplay film; war film

(YZ)

ghosts and immortals, film of

Somewhat comparable to **fantasy film** in the West, films of ghosts and immortals (or ghost films for short) constitute a major portion of commercial film in China since the late 1920s. Due to the immense popularity of traditional Chinese narratives of ghosts and immortals, which were very much part of the audience's daily life through attendance at a variety of theatrical shows or storytelling performances, Chinese filmmakers adapted many of these narratives and provided new visual dimensions to familiar stories and memorable characters, such as Monkey King in *The Journey to the West*.

The appeal of ghost-like characters to Chinese audiences was already evident in **Zhuangzi Tests His Wife** (*dir.* **Li Beihai**, 1913), the first Hong Kong short feature that creates special visual effects to represent the other-worldly ambience of the original fable. Since then, ghost stories have remained a fascinating genre in Chinese filmmaking, in spite of being subjected to a crack-down by the KMT government in the early 1930s and by the the Communist regime in the 1950s–70s.

Relatively free from government regulations, Hong Kong has remained a major production site for ghost stories, some of which are often remade. A few recent titles will suffice to illustrate the appeal of this genre to a broad range of audiences: *Mr Vampire* (*dir.* Ricky Lau, 1985) for fans of **mystery film**, *Rouge* (*dir.* Stanley **Kwan**, 1987) for fans of **melodrama**, *A Chinese Ghost Story* (**Ching Siu Tung**, 1987) for fans of **martial arts film**, and *Ming Ghost* (*dir.* Qiu Gangjian, 1990) for fans of **art film**. It is noteworthy that while Hong Kong and Taiwan consistently make ghost films, only a limited number of such stories are released in mainland China, and they are often classified under other genre terms, such as **costume drama** and mystery film.

Indeed, the prototypes of immortals in this genre come largely from costume drama, which features an array of supernatural beings, ancient generals and court ladies. Beginning with *Wonder of Wonders* (*dir.* Xu Zhuodai, 1927), films of ghosts and immortals have been mixed with martial arts features. Many martial arts heroes have been endowed with the magic powers of the immortals, and the ways in which they leap into the air and fly in the clouds frequently blur the distinction between immortals and kungfu masters. The mixed generic nature of films of ghosts and immortals is best exemplified in *Green Snake* (*dir.* **Tsui Hark**, 1993), where two snake spirits compete with a Buddhist monk by using both their supernatural power and sexual appeal. Clearly, special effects and mythical story line remain two major attractions of this genre.

Further reading
HKIFF (1989), on Hong Kong ghost films; S. Hong (1995), a survey of commercial films in the 1920s.

(YZ)

Girl Basketball Player No. 5
(Nü lan wu hao)

dir./sc. **Xie Jin**
with **Liu Qiong**, Yu Mingde, **Qin Yi**, Cui Chaoming, Xiang Mei
Shanghai: Tianma Film, 1957

Under the Nationalist regime a basketball player, Tian Zhenhua, falls in love with Lin Jie, the daughter of Tian's boss, who is also the owner of Tian's basketball team. Lin's father accepts a bribe and orders his players to lose a game against a team of foreign sailors. Tian is motivated by a sense of national honour and refuses to obey the order: as a result, the Chinese team wins the match. But Tian is beaten up afterwards by a gang hired by Lin's father. Meanwhile, Lin is forced to marry someone else.

Years later, Lin Jie leaves her abusive husband and works as a teacher to support herself. Tian, on the other hand, becomes the chief coach for a female basketball team after 1949. Tian takes a special interest in No. 5, Lin Xiaojie, because of her proven abilities as a great player. Xiaojie is injured during a training session and taken to the hospital. When Tian goes to visit her, he runs into Xiaojie's mother, who is no other than his former sweetheart, Lin Jie. As the two lovers rekindle their old flame, player No. 5, Xiaojie, is admitted into the national team for an overseas game.

This **sports** film promotes **nationalism** and the wisdom of collectivity.

(ZX)

Girl from Hunan, A
(Xiang nü Xiaoxiao)

dir. **Xie Fei**
sc. Zhang Xian
with Na Renhua, Ni Meiling, Liu Qing, Deng Xiaoguang
Beijing: BFA Youth Film, 1986

This film reflects critically on China's patriarchal traditions and the question of female **sexuality**. It shows how women in traditional Chinese society are both the victims of inhumane marriage practices and active participants in the victimization of others.

A teenage girl, Xiaoxiao, is married to Chunguan while he is still a toddler. As the custom dictates, she is expected to help her mother-in-law bring Chunguan up and leave the consummation of their marriage until later. Soon Xiaoxiao grows into a mature woman and falls in love with Huagou, a hired labourer working for her mother-in-law. Their illicit affair is overshadowed by the execution of a widow in the village who is caught having an affair with a man. Xiaoxiao becomes even more scared when she realizes she is pregnant. She suggests to Huagou that they flee, but he runs away, leaving Xiaoxiao to fend for herself. She also tries to run away, but is brought back to her mother-in-law who is persuaded that putting Xiaoxiao to death will only result in the household being haunted by her vengeful ghost. So she decides to spare Xiaoxiao's life.

Years later Xiaoxiao's son is a toddler, while her husband is a young student in town. During one of Chunguan's home visits he witnesses two wedding preparations: one for Xiaoxiao's toddler son and one for him and Xiaoxiao – it is time for them to consummate their marriage. Chunguan runs away in disgust.

In 1988 the film was awarded the Golden Panda at a film festival in France as well as the Don Quixote prize at San Cervantes FF in Spain.

See also: love and marriage

Further reading

E. A. Kaplan (1991), a feminist-psychoanalytic reading.

(ZX)

Girl in Disguise
(Huashen guniang)

dir. Fang Peilin
sc. Huang Jiamo
Shanghai: Yihua Film, 1936

The plot twists of this exemplary soft film centre on the confusions of gender identity. The story begins with the wife of a wealthy Singapore Chinese giving birth to a baby girl. The girl's father names her Liying. However, knowing that the girl's grandfather in the mainland will not welcome a granddaughter, Liying's parents send a telegram to Shanghai explaining that they have had a boy, thus making the old man extremely happy. Eighteen years later, the grandfather urges Liying's parents to bring 'him' to Shanghai, so the couple disguise the girl as a boy and send 'him' to see 'his' grandpa. During Liying's stay in Shanghai, one of the girls, Zhu Naifang, falls in love with 'him', while Liying herself falls in love with a young man named Lin Songpo. As he does not realize that Liying is a 'she', Lin turns his attention to another woman, Li Airong. But Li is a lesbian and is infatuated with Zhu. One day two of Liying's friends come from Singapore to visit her. Liying sneaks out of her grandfather's house and goes off with her friends, this time dressed as a girl. Lin sees the girls in the park and is quite taken by Liying's beauty, yet he fails to recognize her as Liying.

Liying's grandpa is very disappointed to discover that she is not in fact a boy. Another telegram arrives from Liying's parents in Singapore announcing that this time they really have produced a baby boy. The grandpa cheers up again and sends Liying to bring her brother to Shanghai. A nephew of the old man, Zhaohuan, wants to drive a wedge between Liying's father and grandfather so that he can take over the family business. As Liying arrives at Shanghai's pier with her baby brother, a thief hired by Zhaohuan steals the baby by substituting a baby girl in its place. Thinking that Liying's parents are deceiving him once again, grandpa gets upset. He now sends Zhaohuan to Singapore to attend to family business and orders Liying's father to return to Shanghai. Liying learns about Zhaohuan's scheme and disguises herself as a man in order to visit the thieves' hide-out. By using her charm, Liying manages to rescue her baby brother and have the thieves arrested.

The film was a huge box-office success and led to a number of sequels. As late as 1956, Hong Kong's Yihua Company released another sequel to the film, which was directed by Chen Huanwen.

See also: soft film (under Chinese cinema in Historical essays)

(ZX)

Girls from Shanghai
(Shanghai guniang)

dir. Cheng Yi
sc. Zhang Xian
with Zhao Lian, Tao Baili, An Rang, Li Keng, Liu Zhao
Beijing: Beijing, 1958

In this film about socialist construction, a young technician, Lu Ye, overcomes his self-centred attitude with the help of Bai Mei, a girl from Shanghai. Lu lives a celibate life and is entirely devoted to his job at the construction site. When a group of girls from Shanghai join the work team, Lu and his friends fear that the urban visitors will disrupt their lives and work. However, despite their love of singing and dancing, the girls are serious workers. One of them, Bai Mei, is the construction site inspector. While observing her work, Lu's attitude changes from indifference to deep respect. They gradually fall in love.

Lu wants to experiment with a new building method. He is so self-confident that he does not listen to Bai Mei, who advises him to be more careful and discuss his ideas with his superiors first. Because she is concerned with the effect of Lu's new method, she decides to inform Lu's superiors herself. As a result she is criticized and sent away from the construction site. But her warnings turn out to be prophetic. Lu's method fails and results in heavy losses. He feels guilty and works hard to make amends. However, he ends up hospitalized because of stress and fatigue.

Bai Mei tries to visit him before starting work at a new construction site, but the two miss each other: when Bai reaches the hospital Lu has already left; when Lu goes to the railway station Bai's train has already departed. Bai sends a letter to Lu, who realizes that their mutual understanding is now stronger than ever. The last scene finds Lu happily back at work, wanting now to serve the socialist cause and not his personal ambitions. This film illustrates how socialist concerns are given priority over **romance** in mainland Chinese films of the 1950s–70s.

(PV)

Go Master, The

(Yi pan meiyou xiawan de qi)

dir. Duan Jishun, Junya Sato
sc. Li Hongzhou, Ge Kangtong
with **Sun Daolin**, Huang Zongying
Beijing: Beijing Film/Tokyo: Toko Tokuma, 1982

A joint production between China and Japan, this film is set against the background of the Sino-Japanese war. While emphasizing the atrocities the Japanese military committed in China, the film also shows the friendship between the peoples of the two countries.

In the mid-1920s, a Chinese Go master, Kuang Yishan, is invited by a friend to go to Beijing with his eight-year-old son to participate in a national competition. The sponsoring warlord, General Pang, is offended when Kuang refuses to indulge him on the chess board. That evening a Japanese Go master Sunpo is impressed by Kuang's skill and visits him for a friendly game. When he notices the great potential of Kuang's son, he offers to take him as his student. However, before they can finish the game, General Pang's guards take Kuang away to jail. It is only through Sunpo's help that Kuang is finally released.

Ten years later, Kuang sends his son Aming to Japan to study Go with Sunpo. Before long,

Aming marries Sunpo's daughter and wins a national Go championship. After the Sino-Japanese war breaks out, the Japanese authorities try to pressure Aming into adopting Japanese citizenship: when he refuses, they have him killed.

Back home, Kuang's wife and daughter are both killed by the Japanese because Kuang refuses to play Go with them. They even cut off two of Kuang's fingers, prohibiting him from playing Go ever again. Sunpo, who has been drafted to China, witnesses all of these events.

After the war, Kuang goes to Japan to look for his son but he fails to find him. In 1956, Sunpo visits China as a member of a Japanese Go delegation. He brings with him his sister and grandchild, Aming's daughter. When the two old friends meet again, they resume their interrupted game of thirty years earlier.

The film was awarded a special prize from the Ministry of Culture in 1982 and at the 1983 China GRA. It also won the first prize at the 1982 Montreal FF as well as a Best Film award from the Japanese government.

(ZX)

God of Gamblers

(Dushen)

dir./sc. **Wong Jing**
with **Chow Yun-Fat**, Andy **Lau**, Joey **Wong**, Ng Man Tat
Hong Kong: Win's Film, 1989

With Hong Kong capitalism facing an uncertain future after 1997, it is not surprising that the city's film industry should find the arbitrary fates dealt out by gambling to be such appealing subject matter. *God of Gamblers*, an eclectic action-**comedy** that quotes everything from *Battleship Potemkin* (*dir.* Sergei Eisenstein, 1925) to *Rain Man* (*dir.* Barry Levinson, 1988) was a box-office smash in 1989.

The film concerns an attempt by Ko Chun, the 'god of gamblers', to defeat a villainous rival, Chan Kam Shing. Initiating a cross and double-cross narrative chain, Ko bumps his head, loses his memory, and is found by two local down-and-outs, Knife and Jane, who nurse him back to health. Ko is also protected by his assigned bodyguard, Dragon. When Ko recovers his memory after bumping his head again, he discovers that his partner, Yee, is responsible for the death of his girlfriend, so he has Yee killed. In the end, Ko defeats Chan at the card table and manages to manoeuvre him out of international waters so that the Hong Kong police can arrest him. Ko and Knife become partners with the promise that they will next take on the casinos of Las Vegas.

The phenomenal success of *God of Gamblers* led to a surge of Hong Kong gambling films in the early 1990s. For his part, director Wong Jing immersed himself in the genre as if there was no tomorrow, helming *God of Gamblers, II* (1990), *God of Gamblers III: Back to Shanghai* (1992, with superstars Stephen **Chow** and **Gong Li**) and *God of Gamblers' Return* (1995 – the only sequel to feature the inimitable **Chow Yun-Fat**).

See also: action film

(JS)

Goddess

(Shennü)

dir./sc. **Wu Yonggang**
with **Ruan Lingyu**, Zhang Zhizhi, Li Keng
Shanghai: Lianhua Film, 1934

A Shanghai prostitute tries to free herself from a greedy, evil pimp. She confronts not only this violent man who takes all her money and keeps her subject to his will, but also an oppressive society that discriminates against her child.

A school principal is the only person willing to help her out. He agrees to allow her child to attend his school, but the objections from parents grow so strong that he has to resign his position upon the child's expulsion. The prostitute decides to leave the city and start over again somewhere else. When she realizes that her pimp has stolen all her savings to pay for his gambling habit, she kills him with a wine bottle. She is arrested and sentenced to twelve years in prison. However, this tragic ending is lightened by her subsequent meeting in her cell with the principal, who promises to take care of her son.

Goddess contains one of Ruan Lingyu's greatest performances. Using **prostitution** as a symbol of oppression and victimization, the film is regarded as a classic of the silent Chinese cinema, comparable to the best contemporary films from the West.

Further reading

R. Chow (1995: 23 6); a brief discussion of visuality; W. Rothman (1993), a comparative study of melodrama; Y. Zhang (1999b), a critical discussion of prostitution and urban imagination.

(PV, YZ)

Gong Jianong

(Robert Kung)

b. 23 February 1902, Nanjing
d. 27 October 1993
Actor

One of the most popular male stars of the 1920s–30s, Gong Jianong graduated from Southeastern University with a major in physical education. He landed a clerical job at Great China Film Company in 1925, but made his début appearance in *Innocence* (*dir.* **Bu Wancang**, 1926) for Minxin Film Company a year later. Within twelve months he had transferred again, this time to Mingxing Film Company. Before this studio was dissolved in 1938, Gong starred in approximately sixty films. His popularity reflects changing attitudes towards **masculinity** in the 1930s, a time when film audiences tired of traditional effeminate male images in favour of the kind of athleticism embodied by Gong.

During the Sino-Japanese war, Gong worked for several studios in Shanghai and directed *A Lonely Soul of the Dark Night* and *An Exotic Corpse* (*co-dir.* **Zhang Shichuan**, both 1941).

Gong always avoided leftist filmmakers and remained pro-Nationalist to the end. In the late 1940s, he worked in the Nationalist army's theatre troupe and then moved on to Taiwan, where he starred in more than a dozen titles before retiring in the early 1970s. The ROC authorities in Taiwan presented Gong with a lifetime Achievement Award in 1981. Gong was honoured again at the 1993 Taipei GHA for contributions made to the development of Chinese cinema.

Further reading

J. Gong (1967), three volumes of memoirs.

(ZX)

Gong Li

b. 31 December 1966, Shenyang, Liaoning province
Actress, singer

Born in northeastern China and raised in Ji'nan, Shandong province, Gong Li graduated from high school in 1983 and twice failed her college entrance examinations. She worked in a bookstore and took lessons from Yin Dawei, a stage director with Ji'nan military drama troupe. She entered the Central Drama Academy in Beijing in 1985 and not long after was chosen by **Zhang Yimou** to play the lead in *Red Sorghum* (1987), which won the Golden Bear at Berlin FF. Gong Li subsequently starred in many other Zhang Yimou films, such as *Code Name Puma* (1988), *Ju Dou* (1989), *Raise the Red Lantern* (1991), *The Story of Qiuju* (1992, for which she was awarded Best Actress at the 1992 Venice FF), *To Live* (1994) and *Shanghai Triad* (1995). This successful partnership secured both of their international reputations. In addition, Gong Li appeared in a number of films from Hong Kong and Taiwan, including *The Empress Dowager* (*dir.* **Li Hanhsiang**, 1988–9), *The Terracotta Warrior* (*dir.* **Ching Siu Tung**, 1990), *Mary from Beijing* (*dir.* Sylvia **Chang**, 1992) and *The Great Conqueror's Concubine* (*dir.* Xian Jiran, 1994). Her acting in *Farewell My Concubine* (1993), *Temptress Moon* (1995, both *dir.* **Chen Kaige**) and *The Soul of the Painter* (*dir.* **Huang Shuqin**, 1993) is particularly noteworthy. The Oscar-winning American director Oliver Stone has reputedly asked her to play Jiang Qing, Mao Zedong's wife, in his feature *The Story of Mao Zedong*. In 1996, Gong Li also started out on a singing career.

Further reading

Baoguang Chen (1993), a short biography.

(YZ)

Good Men, Good Women

(Haonan haonü)

dir. **Hou Hsiao-hsien**
sc. **Chu Tien-wen**
with Lim Giong, Annie Shizuka Inoh, Jack Kao
Tokyo: Team Okuyama/Taipei: Liandeng Film, 1995

In this last film of his Taiwan trilogy, Hou Hsiao-hsien focuses on the political suppression in the 1950s known as White Terrorism. Based on a novel about Zhong Haodong and Jiang Biyu, a left-wing couple who devoted their lives to nationalist and socialist causes in the 1940s–50s, Hou's film does not hesitate to express sympathy for Chinese nationalists. But Hou also refers to the present context in his attempt to represent the left-wing movement in Taiwan history. Hou chooses to do this through the presentation of a complex and difficult narrative form. Liang Jing, a hostess/actress, is to play Jiang Biyu in a film called 'Good men, good women', and the film is preceded by Liang's first-person narration of entries from her diary. In episodic accounts, Liang tells of her grief over her gangster boyfriend, Ah Wei, who died of gunshot wounds. Meanwhile, she receives bizarre faxes of pages from her own diary. She believes that these faxes are evidence that Ah Wei's spirit is overseeing her life. On the other hand, visual images supplement her writing by depicting her wild days with Ah Wei as well as the production of the actual film.

In tandem with Liang's story, Hou also wants us to be aware that there is a serious film being made. Finished film stock from 'Good men, good women' is fed at intervals between Liang Jing's narration. Piece by piece, the story of the revolutionary couple – Zhong Haodong and Jiang Biyu – comes into being, as do the histories of the Taiwanese contribution to the war against the Japanese in the 1940s and socialist subversion of the KMT in the 1950s. As the film crew finishes shooting in Taiwan, Liang informs us that Jiang has died and will now never have the opportunity to see the film of her life.

By interrogating a real life event (i.e., Jiang's death) via two levels of historical narration, Hou is not afraid to express his political views and experiment with a new narrative style. The reception of the film was unexpectedly negative, partly because of Hou's sympathy with the leftist-nationalist tradition in Taiwan, and partly because of his juxtaposition of a slut and her small time gangster boyfriend with a celebrated political duo.

(YY)

Good Morning, Beijing

(Beijing nizao)

dir. **Zhang Nuanxin**
sc. Tang Danian
with Ma Xiaoqing, Wang Anquan, Jia Hongsheng, Jin Tiefeng
Beijing: BFA Youth Film, 1990

The film opens in the early morning, when Ai Hong and Wang Lang ride a bicycle to the terminal station for bus 99. They meet a new bus driver Zou Yongqiang. The work day starts. While

Wang is busy taking tickets and answering questions, Ai is absent-minded and cares little about her job. One winter day, Ai does not ride the bike with Wang, and Wang feels rather bitter when he sees Ai talking to Zou in the station. Ai's admiration for Zou does not last long, though. One Sunday, while window-shopping with Zou, Ai desires beautiful clothes but cannot afford them. She wants to quit her job and make big money, but Zou disapproves of her plan. After they break up, Zou is upset and hits a man while driving. Meanwhile, Ai meets Chen Mingke, a fashionable, self-acclaimed overseas student. Chen takes her to night clubs and buys a gold necklace and a 'boombox'. Intoxicated by her new lifestyle, Ai soon forgets her job and her old friends. However, when she finds herself pregnant, she goes to Chen and realizes that he is but a private entrepreneur.

A year later, Ai brings her huge bags of goods on board bus 99. At a bus stop, Zou and Wang help her to unload the bags, and they meet her husband Chen. The sun rises again and shines on the city of Beijing, where the young people go in different directions and pursue their different dreams.

This is a fairly positive film about **urban life** in contemporary China. As in most films of the 1990s, it is marked by a multiplicity of values and a tolerance of human follies.

Further reading

X. Tang (1994), a critical study of the film.

(IJS)

Good Woman

(Liangjia funü)

dir. **Huang Jianzhong**
sc. Li Kuanding
with Cong Shan, Zhang Weixin, Wang Yijia, Liang Jian
Beijing: Beijing Film, 1985

Like *A **Girl from Hunan*** (*dir.* **Xie Fei**, 1986), this film studies female **sexuality** and offers a cultural critique of the unjust and inhumane aspects of traditional Chinese life. It also glorifies the CCP's liberation of women from the yoke of the 'feudal' past.

In a remote part of China, marriage practices follow the pattern of matching older women with younger men. An eighteen-year-old girl, Yu Xingxian, is married to a six-year-old boy, Yi

Shaowei. Yu's widowed mother-in-law, Wuniang, is a kind woman and treats her well. One of Wuniang's nephews, Kaibing, comes to help them with some farm work and falls in love with Yu. A few villagers want to punish them, but Yu announces her intention to divorce Yi and marry Kaibing. Armed with the protection of the new marriage law promulgated by the CCP, Yu and Kaibing are saved from persecution by the villagers. Although Yu feels attached to Wuniang, who has been both understanding and supportive, she decides to begin a new life by leaving both her and the boy.

The film was awarded top prizes in 1986 at both Karlovy Vary FF and the Atlantic FF held in Spain. It also won, among others, the Critics Award at the 1987 FF held in India.

Further reading

E.A. Kaplan (1991), a feminist-psychoanalytic reading.

(ZX)

Goodbye, South, Goodbye

(Nanguo zaijian, nanguo)

dir. **Hou Hsiao-hsien**
sc. **Chu Tien-wen**
with Lim Giong, Annie Shizuka Inoh, Xu Guiyin, Jack Kao
Tokyo: Team Okuyama/Taipei: Liandeng Film, 1996

This film of **youth culture** features good punk music, a road movie motif, lavish costumes and the stunning landscapes of southern Taiwan. This is also the most pessimistic film Hou Hsiao-hsien has ever made. The story concerns three gang members, the leader Xiao Kao, his pal Ah Beng, and Beng's girlfriend Xiao Mahua. Different from their leader, Ah Beng and Xiao Mahua are carefree punks who are always getting high and into trouble. As the three of them travel to Ah Beng's home town in the south to help out with an illegal land deal, Ah Beng fights with his cousin, a well-connected local cop, who mobilizes his people in town to kidnap the three hoodlums from Taipei before they can complete the transaction. Xiao Kao's big brother then comes to the rescue and talks the cop into releasing his 'three little friends'. At the end of the film they are released, but just when they get on the road to Taipei Ah Beng crashes his car into a rice paddy, killing Xiao Kao.

In the mid-1990s, *fin-de-siècle* sentiments dominated Hong Kong culture as the date of its reunion with China approached. The cultural élites in Taiwan, on the other hand, seemed to accept this historic event with few misgivings. *Goodbye, South, Goodbye* can be read as a symptom of millennial anxieties. Beyond this, the film also reveals Hou's continuous fascination with the **gangster film**. No other Taiwanese director takes a more romantic or sincere view of this subculture than Hou. After the poor reception of his **Good Men, Good Women** (1995), Hou wanted to make a film with contemporary appeal, and *Goodbye, South, Goodbye* succeeded in drawing large male audiences, many of them sporting dragon tattoos similar to those worn by Xiao Kao in the film.

(YY)

Growing Up
(Xiaobi de gushi)

dir. **Chen Kun-hou**
sc. **Hou Hsiao-hsien**, **Chu Tien-wen**, Din Yaming, Xu Shuping
with Zhang Chunfang, Cui Fusheng, Yu Liso, Niu Chengze
Taipei: CMPC, 1983

Growing up is the simple yet profound story of a little boy, Xiaobi, who refuses to accept his mother's marriage to a much older man. When his mother marries his stepfather, Xiaobi develops from a quiet little boy into a lively, somewhat rowdy teenager. His antagonism toward his stepfather does not change even though the stepfather treats him like his own son. Tensions finally explode when the stepfather scolds Xiaobi for his bad behaviour in school. Xiaobi fights back by rejecting his stepfather's authority. Infuriated by such ungratefulness, the stepfather takes it out on his partner, who has been quietly playing the role of dutiful wife and mother. The mother feels that all her efforts have been in vain and so kills herself, with the result that Xiaobi and his stepfather are reconciled. Later, when Xiaobi finishes junior high school and starts to attend an army academy, his rebellion finally comes to an end.

The film is narrated by a playmate of Xiaobi's, an eyewitness to all events. By using an objective narrative point of view, the film detaches itself from the main characters. As one of the cornerstones of New Taiwan Cinema, *Growing Up* is marked by a realistic style, humour, and sympathy for the protagonists. It also marks the high point of the partnership between director Chen Kun-hou and his early collaborator Hou Hsiao-hsien, who later became Taiwan's most internationally renowned film *auteur*. In turn, growing up became a major theme in the Taiwanese cinema of the 1980s.

See also: New Taiwan Cinema (under Taiwan cinema in Historical essays)

(YY)

Gu Changwei

b. 12 December 1957, Xi'an, Shaanxi province
Cinematographer

An active member of the **Fifth Generation** filmmakers, Gu Changwei was a classmate of **Zhang Yimou** in the Cinematography Department of BFA. Upon graduation in 1982, he was assigned to Xi'an Film Studio and served as cinematographer on many award-winning films. He has to his credit **Magic Braid** (*dir.* Zhang Zien, 1986), **King of the Children** (1987), **Farewell My Concubine** (1993, both *dir.* **Chen Kaige**), **Red Sorghum** (*dir.* Zhang Yimou, 1987), *Presumed Guilty* (*dir.* **Zhou Xiaowen**, 1993) and **In the Heat of the Sun** (*dir.* **Jiang Wen**, 1994), among others. He is considered one of the best cinematographers in mainland China in the 1990s, and won a top prize at the 1988 China GRA.

(YZ)

Guerrillas on the Plain
(Pingyuan youji dui)

dir. Su Li, Wu Zhaodi
sc. Xing Ye, Yu Shan
with Guo Zhenqing, Wang Enqi, Zhang Ying, Liang Yin
Changchun: Changchun Film, 1955

Set during the Sino-Japanese war, this **war film** depicts the heroic Chinese resistance to Japanese invasion and emphasizes the contribution made by Communist guerrilla forces to the war effort.

Guerrilla leader Li Xiangyang is assigned to harass Japanese troops guarding the county seat. As Li and his comrades help the peasants in Li Village hide their grain, a landlord named Yang sneaks out of the village and reports Li's activities to the Japanese. But by the time the Japanese arrive, Li and the villagers have already left. The Japanese search for the entrance to the underground tunnels where the grain is stored. Li's guerrillas attack a nearby Japanese block house to distract the enemy, but the Japanese commander sees through the scheme and refuses to leave the village. As the Japanese finally locate an entrance to the underground tunnel, Li and his men blow up a Japanese ammunition train. Trying to outmanoeuvre Li, the Japanese take the village by surprise and force the villagers out from the tunnels. It is not until Li's forces attack the county that the Japanese commander decides to leave the village, but not before committing heinous atrocities. In revenge, Li's men sneak into the county, execute the landlord who betrayed the villagers, and confuse the Japanese by creating disturbances all around them. Finally, they ambush the Japanese troops on their way to loot the Li village and annihilate the whole squadron.

(ZX)

He Jianjun
(He Yi)

Independent filmmaker

A noted figure of the **Sixth Generation**, He Jianjun studied in a special directing class at BFA in 1985. He served as an assistant director on **Fifth Generation** landmarks *Yellow Earth* (1984) and *King of the Children* (1987, both *dir.* **Chen Kaige**). Like his classmate **Wang Xiaoshuai**, Jianjun did not belong to any government unit. His first independent film, *Red Beads* (1993), is about a young man who tries to understand the nature of the madness that afflicts a female patient at a Beijing mental hospital. To further his exploration of the sense of a tormenting existential crisis in modern urbanites, Jianjun made *Postman* (1995). Focusing on an introverted postman who secretly opens people's letters and intervenes in others' lives, the film touches on a wide spectrum of social and psychological issues, such as homosexuality, incestuous feelings, extramarital affairs and suicide. Both of Jianjun's films were independent productions that had to be smuggled out of China for screenings at international film festivals.

See also: independent film

Further reading
D. Chute (1994), a review of three mainland independent films.

(YZ)

He Ping

b. 1957, Beijing
Director

He Ping started working for Science and Education Film Studio in 1980, where he made documentaries as well as **filmed stage performances**. In 1987 he was transferred to Xi'an Film Studio and directed *We Are the World* (1988) and *Kawashima Yoshiko* (1989). His Chinese Western, *The Swordsman in Double-Flag Town* (1990), is a spectacular, highly stylish **martial arts film**. His next feature, *Red Firecracker, Green Firecracker* (1994), is a lush pictorial account of sexual repression and moral transgression. The film comes across as a reinvention of *Ju Dou* (*dir.* **Zhang Yimou**, 1990), set in a town by the surging Yellow River, and decorated with fantastic fireworks displays. The film won top prize at the 1994 Hawaii FF and is distributed in the USA by October Films of New York. He's rising international fame secured him, for the first time, a handsome Hong Kong investment (US$1.2 million), with which he made *Sun Valley* (1996), a Chinese Western **swordplay film** about the transformation of a bloodthirsty psychotic under the care of a sensitive village widow.

See also: documentary; Westerns

(YZ)

He Qun

b. 1956, Beijing
Director, screen writer, art designer

A newly emerging figure from the **Fifth Generation**, He Qun was the art director for *One and Eight* (*dir.* **Zhang Junzhao**, 1984) and *Yellow Earth* (*dir.* **Chen Kaige**, 1984). He had a miserable childhood: at age two his father, a sculptor and lecturer at the Central Arts and Crafts Academy in Beijing, was branded a Rightist and sent to a labour camp in northeastern China. During the **Cultural Revolution**, He Qun worked as a welder in the suburbs of Beijing for six years but still found time to write and paint. Like **Zhang Yimou**, he experienced setbacks before finally being admitted to the Art Department of BFA in 1978. After graduation, He was assigned to Guangxi Film Studio, where he collaborated with his classmates on several ground-breaking films, including *The **Big Parade*** (*dir*. Chen Kaige, 1985). He continued to win critical acclaim for his art direction of such films as ***Widow Village*** (1988) and *The **Wedding Maidens*** (1990, both *dir*. Wang Jin). He Qun turned director in 1988. *Mutiny* (1988), a **war film**, and *Westbound Convict Train* (1989), a **gangster film**, show He's ability to combine commercial appeal and artistic achievement. Made for US$300,000 by Pearl River Film Studio and Nanyang Company of Hainan, *Steel Meets Fire* (1991) depicts legendary heroes fighting the Japanese and earned a net profit of over $250,000. He also directed a **comedy**, *Conned-Once Restaurant*, and a **detective film**, *The Woman Who Disappeared*, both produced by Fujian Film Studio in 1992. His attention to ordinary people finds its best expression in *Country Teachers* (1993), a moving story of dedicated teachers working in a poor mountain village school, which was awarded Best Film by MBFT in 1994.

Further reading

X. Luo (1994b), a biographic sketch.

(YZ)

Herdsman, The

(Mu ma ren)

dir. **Xie Jin**
sc. Li Zhun
with Zhu Shimao, Niu Ben, Cong Shan, **Liu Qiong**
Shanghai: Shanghai Film, 1982

By telling the story of a man who is wrongly labelled a Rightist, but well received by the herdsmen, this film criticizes the political excesses of the radical CCP and shows how, despite the injustices suffered, the man's love for his country remains uncompromised.

In the fall of 1980, a wealthy overseas Chinese, Xu Jingyou, comes to China to look for his son Lingjun. When the two meet, Xu offers to bring his son, who works as a herdsman in north-western China, to the USA. However, Lingjun is not interested.

The film flashes back to thirty years earlier when Xu left his wife and son during a business trip to the USA. Soon after he left, his wife died of an illness and Lingjun became orphaned. While working as a secondary school teacher, Lingjun was labelled a Rightist and sent to a labour camp where he became so depressed that he even attempted suicide. But the villagers made him feel welcome. During the **Cultural Revolution**, they sheltered him from further political persecution. In 1972, a young woman refugee from Sichuan came to the village. Lingjun helped her and later married her. In 1979, he was cleared of the Rightist charge and reinstated in his teaching job. Now, with a loving wife, an adorable son, and many friends in the village, Lingjun is quite content with his life. However, his father's arrival brings back unpleasant memories. After careful consideration, he decides to stay in China.

The film was awarded the prize of Best Film at the 1982 HFA and by the Ministry of Culture.

(ZX)

Heroic Sons and Daughters

(Yingxiong ernü)

dir. Wu Zhaodi
sc. Mao Feng, Wu Zhaodi
with **Tian Fang**, Guo Zhenqing, Zhou Wenbin, Pu Ke
Changcun: Changchun Film, 1964

This **war film** glorifies personal sacrifice in the name of revolution and proposes a new definition of **family** based on shared revolutionary values.

During the Korean war a young soldier, Wang Cheng, sneaks out of the hospital and asks his commander to send him to the front. The commander realizes that Wang is the son of an old friend of his. Wang's request is granted and he fights bravely at the front. During one battle, however, Wang is killed in action.

A military performance troupe stages a show based on Wang's life so that other soldiers can learn from Wang's example. The leading star of the show is Wang Cheng's younger sister, Wang Fang. The commander discovers that Wang Fang is his daughter. Years earlier, when he worked underground for the CCP in Shanghai, he and his wife were arrested by the Nationalist police. His friend, Wang Fubiao, who is Wang Cheng's father, adopted their daughter. His wife was later executed by the Nationalists and all contact with Wang was lost. The commander decides not to reveal the truth to Wang Fang for the time being, lest her performance be affected.

Wang Fang is wounded during an enemy air raid and subsequently sent back to China. A month later, Wang has recovered and returns to the front. Her foster father, Wang Fubiao, also comes to Korea as a member of a visiting delegation. When the three of them meet, Wang Fubiao tells Wang Fang who her real father is.

(ZX)

Hibiscus Town

(Furong zhen)

dir. **Xie Jin**
sc. Zhong Acheng, Xie Jin
with **Liu Xiaoqing**, Xu Songzi, **Jiang Wen**, Zhang Guangbei, Zhu Shibin
Shanghai: Shanghai Film, 1986

This film offers a critical re-examination of the CCP's radical politics. It shows how the lives of innocent, honest and hard-working people are ruined by political campaigns and the hypocrisy and twisted psychology of Mao Zedong's willing executioners.

Hibiscus town's 'beauty queen', Hu Yuyin, opens a bean curd shop, and the business does extremely well. But its success and, particularly, the new house Hu is soon able to buy, makes Li Guoxiang, the general manager of the state-run eateries, extremely jealous. During a political campaign, Li leads an investigative team to the town and labels Hu a rich peasant. While Hu's husband is forced to commit suicide, the other two local party officials, Gu Yanshan and Li Mangeng, who have been supportive of Hu, are removed from their posts. A lazy man, Wang Qiushe, now fills the senior position in town.

Li herself becomes the object of political persecution once the **Cultural Revolution** begins. Meanwhile Hu is sentenced to sweep the streets with a rightist named Qin Shutian. The two gradually fall in love and hold a secret wedding. After Hu's pregnancy becomes apparent, they request Wang's permission for them to get married. Wang considers the affair between Hu and Qin a crime and sentences Qin to ten years in jail and Hu three years probation. When the Cultural Revolution ends, Qin is released from jail and reunites with

Hu. With the change in the CCP policy, Hu reopens her bean curd shop.

In 1987 the film received awards of Best Film and Best Actress (Liu Xiaoqing) at China GRA; Best Film, Best Actor (Jiang Wen) and Best Actress at HFA; Best Film from MBFT; and the Crystal Ball from Karlovy Vary FF.

Further reading
N. Browne (1994), a critical study in terms of political melodrama; A. Kipnis (1996/7), a historical study of the film.

(ZX)

Hills of No Return, The

(Wuyan de shanqiu)

dir. **Wang Tung**
sc. **Wu Nien-chen**
with Yang Guimei, Chen Bozheng, Zhang Ce
Taipei: CMPC/Jiacheng Film, 1992

This three-hour-long feature film chronicles the miserable life of a group of Taiwan miners in the Japanese occupation period. The film opens with two unemployed brothers who are on their way to a gold mine and are scared to find human remains on the hillside. They stay with a widowed mother, who curses because more foolish men have come to sacrifice themselves for the Japanese owners. The two brothers work very hard, and the elder brother helps the widow take care of her children from time to time.

Working conditions in the mine are dangerous, and accidents occur from time to time. The widow makes extra money by prostituting herself to the miners. One day, the elder brother drives away the customers waiting outside, and the widow is angry for losing money. She plans to earn enough money to purchase a plot of land on the plain and leave this mountain village which has claimed the lives of her husband and others who fathered her children. The widow and the elder brother enjoy each other's attentions, but soon he is killed in an accident. The widow gathers the villagers together and tearfully vows that she will take the miner's ashes to her new home outside the mountains. She and her children leave with all the belongings they can carry and walk down the hills of no return.

This extremely sad film seems to be expanded from a reference in ***Dust in the Wind*** (*dir.* **Hou Hsiao-hsien**, 1986) and resembles *A Borrowed Life* (*dir.* Wu Nien-chen, 1993) in many details. In

1993, it won Best Film award at the first Shanghai FF, Best Actress (Yang Guimei) at Singapore FF, and Best Screenplay at Asia-Pacific FF.

(JJS)

historical film

A type of film that represents a historical event or figure by recreating authentic costumes and settings and delivering them on the screen. The emphasis on the visual dimensions of authenticity, however, does not prevent an often highly fictional treatment of historical material, which depends heavily on the director's ideological and cultural preferences. There is a long tradition of fictional narratives of historical events and figures in China, and these narratives, such as *Romance of Three Kingdoms* (Sanguo yanyi) and *Heroes from the Marshes* (Shuihu zhuan), provide the filmmakers with a rich source for cinematic adaptations that would appeal to general audiences.

Historical films frequently deal with important military and political events. Examples in mainland China include the first Sino-Japanese war in *Naval Battle of 1894* (*dir.* **Lin Nong**, 1962) and a Nationalist military coup in *Xi'an Incident* (*dir.* **Cheng Yin**, 1981). In Taiwan and Hong Kong, *Eight Hundred Heroic Soldiers* (1975) and *Blood-stained Yellow Flowers* (1980, both *dir.* **Ting Shan-hsi**) deal with courageous Nationalist soldiers and the Republican revolution, respectively, while *Hong Kong 1941* (*dir.* Leong Po-chih, 1984) depicts the fall of the city to the Japanese troops. It is clear from these examples that historical films dealing with military events usually fall into the category of war films.

Similarly, historical films that depict major historical figures often merge into **biography** films. In mainland China, *Lin Zexu* (*dir.* **Zheng Junli**, Chen Fan, 1959) and *Qiu Jin* (*dir.* **Xie Jin**, 1983) are both set in the late Qing period when corrupt officials ruined the entire country. In Hong Kong, a film bearing the same title, *Qiu Jin* (*dir.* Tu Guangqi, 1953), had been released by Xinhua Film Company, and another version of *Qiu Jin* (*dir.* Ting Shan-hsi, 1972) was separately produced in Taiwan. While mainland and Taiwan productions tend to prefer events in modern Chinese history, presumably for the purposes of promoting **nationalism** and the Communist or the Nationalist revolution, Hong Kong productions (as well as Taiwan titles invested in by Hong Kong producers) tend to focus on ancient historical figures. Hong Kong costume dramas, in this sense, can be regarded as historical films as well, especially those films that depict famous emperors, kings, generals and concubines. Indeed, if one combines all productions in the mainland, Taiwan and Hong Kong, a long list of important figures in Chinese history have made their screen appearances, some several times (e.g., Emperor Qianlong, Empress Dowager Cixi, Sun Yat-sen and Mao Zedong).

When the production of a historical film becomes elaborate and involves a huge sum of money and a great number of people, the result is sometimes called an 'epic film'. On the other hand, when meticulous attention is given to the authenticity of costumes, manners and settings in a historical film, the result may be termed a 'period film'. These two terms can refer to the same films, as in the case of **Li Han-hsiang**'s famous costume dramas in Taiwan and Hong Kong, *The Story of Xi Shi, I–II* (1965–6), *The Burning of the Imperial Palace* and *Reign Behind a Curtain* (both 1983). Recent mainland counterparts to Li's epics include *The Emperor's Shadow* (*dir.* **Zhou Xiaowen**) and *Warrior Lanling* (*dir.* Hu Xuehua, both 1996), which restage the spectacular shows of the accomplishments of the First Emperor and a legendary king through breathtaking scenes and dramatic actions.

See also: Communist revolution; costume drama; war film

Further reading

S. Su (1996), on distortions of facts in historical films of the 1990s; ZDYYZ (1984), an official mainland account.

(YZ)

Home, Sweet Home

(Jia zai Taibei)

dir. **Pai Ching-jui**
sc. Zhang Yongxiang
with Wu Jiaqi, Zi Lan, Gui Yalei, **Ko Chun-hsiung**
Taipei: CMPC, 1970

The film opens with a scene in the air. A group of overseas students travel home from the USA to Taipei and feel excited. Xia Zhiyun has an agriculture degree and now brings home his

Chinese-American wife. They visit their parents' farm and fall in love with the idyllic landscape. He Fan has not finished his degree because he had a part-time job washing dishes in a restaurant. He has been writing letters to Juanjuan, and plans to marry her on this trip. However, when he tours the scenic 'Sun-Moon Pond', Fan meets Xia Zixia, who has been hoping that her brother Ziyun will take her to the USA.

Wu Daren's plan for this trip is different from others'. Since he has found a job as a hydraulic engineer in the USA and fallen in love with an American girl, he plans to get a divorce in Taipei. He stays in a hotel, but is soon moved when he learns that, in his absence, his wife has worked hard to raise their son, support Wu's younger brother and take care of his paralysed father. When he is invited by his former classmate to visit the new hydraulic constructions, Wu feels that Taiwan needs him more. He decides to stay and live in his 'sweet home'. Meanwhile, Zhiyun and his wife have also decided to stay in Taiwan. In order to fulfil her American dream, Zixia wants to marry He Fan. After the wedding, He Fan is bound for the USA again and feels uncertain of his future before the departure.

This film provides an example of Taiwan's propaganda film done in the form of **melodrama**. It won Best Screenplay and Best Actress (Gui Yalei) awards at the 1970 Asia–Pacific FF.

See also: propaganda and film

(IJS)

Homecoming
(Si shui liu nian)

dir. **Yim Ho**
sc. Yim Ho, Kong Liang
with **Siqin Gaowa**, Josephine Koo, Xie Weixiong, Zhou Yun
Hong Kong/China: Bluebird Film/Target Films, 1984

One of the first Hong Kong films of the 1980s openly to confront the implications of 1997, this Hong Kong–Mainland co-production stimulated an extended debate among Chinese critics of its themes and aesthetic techniques. The film opens with the arrival of Coral, a lonely Hong Kong businesswoman, in the small village in South China where she grew up. Apart from visiting the grave of her recently-deceased grandmother,

Coral meets a number of her childhood friends. These include Pearl, who is now headmistress of the village school, and Pearl's husband, Tsong.

Despite the closeness the three friends still enjoy, emotional problems begin to emerge. After being separated in the 1960s, the rural Chinese workers and the urban denizen from Hong Kong find it difficult to establish common ground again twenty years later. Things come to a head after Coral persuades a local village chief, Uncle Zhong, to allow the schoolchildren to make a trip to Guangzhou. There, the two female friends reach an understanding of each other's lives. While Coral enjoys independence in Hong Kong, she is being sued by her own sister, her business is failing, and she has had two abortions out of loveless affairs. Pearl enjoys the affections of her husband and daughter, Beannie, but she has turned into a party cadre, and she feels that her life lacks spice. The two friends part on the understanding that they may or may not meet each other again in the near future.

Despite the attention *Homecoming* received from critics in both Hong Kong and the mainland, and even with the interest of subsequent titles like *Buddha's Lock* (1987), **Red Dust** (1990), and *The Day the Sun Turned Cold* (1994), director Yim Ho remains largely unappreciated outside Asia.

Further reading
C. Li (1994), E. Yau (1994a), two critical studies.

(JS)

Hong Kong 1941
(Dengdai liming)

dir. Leong Po-chih (Liang Puzhi)
sc. Chen Guanzhong
with **Chow Yun-Fat**, Cecilia Yip, Alex Man
Hong Kong: D&B Films, 1984

Along with Ann **Hui**'s **Boat People** (1982) and *Love in the Fallen City* (1984), this film was one of the first from Hong Kong to propose the return to China in 1997 as an allegory of invasion and occupation. The film is told in flashback narration by Hsia Nan, who in 1941 is the sickly nineteen-year-old daughter of a local merchant. Nan is in love with her childhood friend, Huang Ko Chiang, but her father intends to marry her off to another man.

As the British colonialists prepare to flee the approaching Japanese army, Nan and Chiang meet a sharp-witted fellow traveller named Yeh Chien Fei. However, while a chain of events brings the three friends closer together, Nan increasingly feels torn between her love for the two men. When the Japanese enter the city, Fei procures immunity papers by pretending to be a local collaborator, and he uses them to rescue Chiang from a life of slave labour. As Nan nurses Chiang back to health, Fei decides to leave Hong Kong so that he will not come between his two friends. Before this can happen, though, all three are confronted by a Japanese officer whom they are then forced to kill. Nan, Chiang, and Fei finally reach a boat and set off on the open sea. When a Japanese patrol pulls up alongside, Fei sacrifices his life so that his two friends can complete their journey in safety. Much later, after outliving Chiang, the elderly Nan recounts the story of the two men in her life.

Actor Chow Yun-Fat won prizes at 1985 Asia-Pacific FF and Taipei GHA for his performance in the film. Director Leong Po-chih later used the film as a model for his epic *Shanghai 1920* (1991).

(JS)

Hong Shen

(Hong Da)

b. 31 December 1894, Changzhou, Jiangsu province
d. 25 August 1955
Screen writer, director, actor

One of the most important filmmakers from China, Hong Shen was initially interested in theatre. After graduating from Qinghua University in 1916 and being awarded a scholarship to the USA, Hong was expected to study ceramics. Instead he pursued theatre at Harvard University and did a brief internship at the Boston Institute of Performing Arts before returning to China in 1922. Hong became involved with the China Film Company while still employed at a tobacco firm. His earliest contribution to the movies was a script entitled *The Story of Shen*. Though never filmed, it was the first full-length screenplay to be completed in China.

In 1925, Hong was offered a script consultant position at Mingxing Film Company. He scripted, directed and starred in *The Young Master Feng* (1925), *Love and Gold* (1926) and *The Mistress's Fan* (1928). His films, mostly about the Chinese bourgeoisie, have more psychological depth than other

titles of the period. Hong took a radical turn in the early 1930s. In addition to producing three scripts highly critical of social conditions, he directed *Oppression* (1933), thus establishing his work as an important feature of leftist cinema. Before 1937, Hong was one of the most solicited of all Chinese screen writers, contributing thirteen screenplays for Mingxing, Lianhua, Xinhua and Yihua studios.

Besides being a screen writer and director, Hong was also a film critic and a social activist. In 1930 he led protests against Harold Lloyd's *Welcome Danger*, which at the time was considered offensive to Chinese sensitivities. His name also figured prominently in the later campaign to thwart American investors' attempts to build an Oriental Hollywood in China, as well as in protests against a German–Japanese co-production, *The New Land*, in 1937. After 1937, Hong devoted his creative energies to writing for the theatre and directed only one more film, *Weakness, Thy Name Is Woman* (1948).

See also: theatre and film

Further reading
ZDX (1982–6: 1: 214–21), a short biography.

(ZX)

Hope in the World

(Xiwang zai renjian)

dir./sc. **Shen Fu**
with Lan Ma, **Shangguan Yunzhu**, Zhang Gan, Zhao Yuan
Shanghai: Kunlun Film, 1949

In occupied Shanghai, Professor Ye Gengbai and his family are persecuted for their anti-Japanese activities. Ye's wife, Tao Jinghuan, is desperate because she has received no news of her husband since he was arrested three years earlier. Their son Yusheng and his fiancée Huang Minghua are also involved in underground resistance and must flee Shanghai, but Yusheng does not want to leave his mother with his younger siblings.

One night a sickly woman arrives and informs them of Ye's fate. The woman's husband had been arrested at the same time as Ye and had subsequently died in prison. She tells them that Ye is still alive and that his only companion is a little bird, but unfortunately the woman dies before she can reveal the location of the prison. Ye gets in touch with his family shortly afterwards by sending the bird as a messenger. However, Jinghuan's reply letter gets intercepted by the prison chief, who then decides to free Ye and have him followed by Lei Dianchen. Lei rents an apartment in the same building as the Yes'.

Yusheng and Minghua are also being followed by another spy, Li Lü. One evening, Yusheng kills a man who attacks him backstage in the theatre where they perform patriotic plays. Yusheng and Minghua throw the corpse into the river and are about to make their getaway, but Li sees everything and tries to have them arrested. In a desperate attempt to save his son, Jinghuan shoots Li. When Lei arrives and discovers Li's corpse, Ye assumes responsibility for the murder and is arrested once again. Ye courageously faces his fate, secure in the knowledge that Yusheng and Minghua have escaped and are free to continue their resistance activities.

(PV)

horror film

A type of film that deliberately induces feelings of fright and terror in the viewer. For reasons yet to be determined, in spite of its occasional successes the horror film has never been a popular genre in China. One possible explanation is that the Chinese rarely enjoy watching deformed figures, at least not as a central character throughout a film. Another possibility is that the potentially disrupting or terrifying power of a ghost in the horror film is often reduced by the tradition of an aesthetic association of ghost characters (many of them beautiful and kind-hearted loners) in Chinese narratives.

The first and most successful attempt at the horror genre in China is Xinhua Film Company's *Singing at Midnight* (*dir*. **Ma-Xu Weibang**, 1937). With combined press publicity and aggressive marketing efforts, the film established Ma-Xu Weibang as the first Chinese director of the genre. The handsome box-office returns from the film led the director to make other horror titles, such as *Walking Corpse in an Old House* and *The Lonely Soul* (both 1938), as well as a sequel to *Singing at Midnight* (1941). The fascination with the success of this first horror film is evident in the film's several remakes: in the 1960s by Shaw Brothers, in the 1980s by Shanghai Film Studio (*dir*. Yang Yanjin, 1985), and in the 1990s by Mandarin Films in Hong Kong, with a different English title, *The Phantom Lover* (*dir*. Ronny Yu, 1995). Back in the late 1940s, imitations of *Singing at Midnight*, such as *Haunted House No. 13* (*dir*. Xu Changlin, 1948), also turned out quite successful.

While the horror film has never been popular in mainland China and Taiwan, some elements of horror creep into detective films, such as *Silver Snake Murder Case* (*dir*. **Li Shaohong**, 1988), as well as into films of ghosts and immortals. In Hong Kong productions like *A **Chinese Ghost Story*** (*dir*. **Ching Siu Tung**, 1987), demonic tree and animal spirits perform the horror function in a title that may otherwise be classified as a **costume drama** or **martial arts film**.

See also: detective film; ghosts and immortals, film of

(YZ)

Horse Thief

(Dao ma zei)

dir. **Tian Zhuangzhuang**
sc. Zhang Rui
with Tseshang Rigzin, Dan Jiji
Xi'an: Xi'an Film, 1986

A remarkable early **art film** from the **Fifth Generation** director, *Horse Thief* reflects Tian's concern for marginal cultures in central China and his obsession with cinematic form. The film dwells on the role of religion in the lives of the Tibetan people and renders ancient tradition with striking visual beauty. A Chinese projection of a non-Chinese minority, the film does not offer a commentary on Tibetan religion so much as an evocation and critical examination of repressed cultural forces.

Horse Thief examines the place of religion in Tibetan society. Religious scenes and the depiction of one family's struggle for survival form the basis of the narrative. Poor Rorbu has to steal horses occasionally so as to provide for his family, even though this act of necessity violates his religious faith. The opening 'heaven burial' sequence – wherein the dead are exposed to vultures for the purpose of rebirth – foreshadows Rorbu's own fate, but his sincere worshipping of the mountain God displays his profound faith. A Buddhist believer and yet a horse thief, Rorbu is driven out of his tribe for the crime of highway robbery.

Now isolated from the community, Rorbu endures his son's death through illness. To purge their sins, he and his wife perform one hundred thousand prostrations to Buddha. The depth of this religious devotion is stunningly represented through a series of dissolves, wherein religious symbols are superimposed onto the human body. In a temple, after turning the wheel for visions of enlightenment, Rorbu and his wife are blessed with the birth of another son.

However, their life remains difficult, especially when pestilence spreads across the land. Rorbu sells his only horse and looks for any kind of work. Finally, in order to survive, he must steal another horse. Rorbu's wife and baby try to join the community before snow traps them in for the winter. Shots of blood on the snow and Rorbu's abandoned knife suggest that he has now perished.

(SC)

Hou Hsiao-hsien

(Hou Xiaoxian)

b. 1947, Guangdong province
Director, screen writer, producer, actor

One of the best known directors from New Taiwan Cinema, Hou Hsiao-hsien followed his Hakka (Kejia) family to Taiwan and settled near Kao-hsi-ung (Gaoxiong) in 1949. After graduating from the film programme at National Taiwan College of Arts in 1972, he entered the film industry and worked as assistant and screen writer for many years. He directed *A Cute Girl* (1980), *Cheerful Wind* (1981) and *Green, Green Grass of Home* (1982), but did not attract critical attention until his *The Son's Big Doll*, an episode in the three-part film *Sandwich Man* (1983). Since then, the influence of nativist literature has been very apparent in Hou's work, such as *The Boys from Fengkuei* (1983), which won Best Picture award at the 1984 Nantes FF, and *A Summer at Grandpa's* (1984). These films also represent two recurrent and interrelated themes pursued in Hou's subsequent work: first, a traumatic experience of **urban life**, especially in relation to urbanization and its socio-psychological consequences; second, growing up in Taiwan's multi-lingual, multi-cultural society. In the first category, the lyrical film *Dust in the Wind* (1986), marked by Hou's characteristic long takes, demonstrates his superb rendering of the rural–urban divide by following the adventures of two innocent young villagers in Taipei, while *Daughter of the Nile* (1987) captures the prevalent mood of urban disillusionment by portraying a displaced family torn apart by alien forces. In the second category, *A Time to Live, a Time to Die* (1985), which won the Critics Award at the 1986 Berlin FF, chronicles in a semi-autobiographic fashion the daily life of an extended mainland family now living in Taiwan, and it examines change from the viewpoint of an innocent child.

Hou's insistence on using various dialects (Cantonese, Hakka, Taiwanese or Fukienese, and Shanghainese) is best exemplified in his acknowledged masterpiece, *A City of Sadness* (1989), which dramatizes the different ways four Taiwanese brothers react to the KMT regime when it takes control of Taiwan away from the Japanese in the mid-1940s. This epic film offers a passionate look at the sensitive issue of Taiwanese identity and it won the first Golden Lion ever awarded to a Chinese film at Venice FF. As the second of his 'Taiwan Trilogy', *The Puppet Master* (1993) continues Hou's investigation of Taiwan history, this time by focusing on the Japanese occupation period. By portraying a puppet artist's total immersion in traditional Chinese culture, Hou aims to offer a corrective to the prevailing thread of materialism in contemporary Taiwan. This is carried even further in the last film of the trilogy, *Good Men, Good Women* (1995), which describes how a political prisoner released in 1987 finds modern society completely alienating. Hou's film did not do well at the box office; so he went ahead to film *Goodbye, South, Goodbye* (1996), a study of gangster culture in Taiwan, and hoped he would attract more audiences.

Besides directing and screen-writing, Hou has also acted in films like *Taipei Story* (*dir*. Edward Yang, 1985) and served as production manager on *Raise the Red Lantern* (*dir*. **Zhang Yimou**, 1991). He is supportive of many young directors in Taiwan. In 1988, the New York FF's World Critics Poll voted him one of the three directors who will lead world cinema in the coming decades.

See also: New Taiwan Cinema (under Taiwan cinema in Historical essays)

Further reading

G. Cheshire (1993), an excellent analysis of Hou's films; H. Chiao (1993b), an interview with critical comments; J. Yip (1997), on Hou's historical vision.

(YZ)

Hou Yao

b. 1903, Guangdong province
d. 1942, Hong Kong
Director, screen writer, critic

Hou Yao was an early filmmaker whose writings helped lay the foundations for Chinese cinema. A graduate of Nanjing Advanced Normal School, Hou became a member of the well-known Association for Literary Study in 1922. In 1924, he took a position as screen writer and director at Great Wall Film Company, and later worked for Minxin and Lianhua as well. His famous films of this period include a **melodrama** of **love and marriage**, *Revived Rose*, an adaptation of classical drama, *Romance of the Western Chamber* (both 1927) and a **costume drama**, *Mulan Joins the Army* (1928).

Hou synthesized the aesthetic principles embodied in early Chinese filmmaking through the publication of his *Methods of Scripting Shadowplays* (Yingxi juben zuofa, Shanghai: Taidong shuju, 1926). An early exposition of 'shadowplay theory', this book continues to be of interest to contemporary scholars.

Hou moved to Hong Kong in 1933. While working as an editor, he founded Wenhua Film Company, which merged with Nanyang Film Company in 1938. Between 1938 and 1942, Hou produced a number of highly nationalistic propaganda films, such as *The Will to Resist*, *The Last Minute Call* (both 1938) and *Storms Over the Pacific* (1939). Such patriotism irritated his enemies. Hou was murdered by the Japanese in 1942, shortly after the outbreak of the Pacific war.

See also: adaptations of drama and literature; propaganda and film

(ZX, YZ)

Hsu Feng

(Xu Feng)

b. 1950
Actress, producer

Hsu Feng became known for her roles in a number of films directed by King **Hu**, such as *Dragon Gate Inn* (1967), *A Touch of Zen* (1970), *The Fate of Lee Khan* (1973), *The Valiant Ones* (1975) and *Raining in the Mountain* (1979). She has acted in more than fifty films and twice won Best Actress

at Taipei GHA: for *The Assassin* (1976) and *The Pioneers* (1980). She established Tomson Film Company (Tangcheng), which has produced high quality art films such as *Five Girls and a Rope* (*dir.* Yeh Hong-wei, 1991; see under **Wedding Maidens**), **Farewell My Concubine** (*dir.* **Chen Kaige**, 1993), and **Red Firecracker, Green Firecracker** (*dir.* **He Ping**, 1994), and distributed mainland independent productions like **Beijing Bastards** (*dir.* **Zhang Yuan**, 1993).

See also: art film; independent film

Further reading
M. Tessier (1992), a profile with an interview.

(YZ)

Hu Die

(Butterfly Wu)

b. 1907, Shanghai
d. 1989, Canada
Actress

One of the most popular stars of the 1920s–30s, Hu Die spent most of her adolescence in northern China, in cities such as Beijing, Tianjin and Yingkou. As a result of this she could speak perfect Mandarin Chinese, a fact which proved most beneficial when the silent film industry made the transition to sound.

After graduating from Zhonghua Film School in 1924, Hu starred in twenty films before signing a contract with Mingxing Film Company in 1928. She remained a leading actress and starred in almost all the studio's major productions. Her numerous box-office hits for Mingxing include such **Zhang Shichuan** films as *The White Cloud Pagoda* (*co-dir.* **Zheng Zhengqiu**), *The **Burning of Red Lotus Temple*** (both 1928), **Sing-Song Girl Red Peony** (1930), the first Chinese talkie, and *Orchid in the Deep Valley* (1934). Although never a leftist herself, Hu starred in several films with a strong leftist bent. One of Hu's most popular performances was in a double role, **Twin Sisters** (*dir.* Zheng Zhengqiu, 1933).

As the highest paid actress of the 1930s, Hu's popularity among movie fans was peerless. Her closest rival was **Ruan Lingyu**, the leading actress at Lianhua Film Company, but whereas Ruan appealed most to well-educated audiences, Hu's followers came from a much wider social stratum. In 1933 one of Shanghai's fan magazines, *The Star*

Plate 20   Hu Die, the movie queen

Daily (Mingxing ribao), cast a readers' ballot to find the 'Queen of Chinese Cinema': Hu won hands down.

In recognition of her achievements, Hu was selected to join the delegation travelling to an international film festival held in Moscow in 1935. The delegation consisted mostly of influential men from the Chinese film industry. Hu was the only movie star in the group. When the festival was over, the delegation made a detour through Europe before returning to China. Since both Chinese film and Chinese film stars were novelties to the Europeans, Hu attracted a good deal of public attention. One year later, upon her return to China, she published a book detailing her experiences and observations on that trip.

Between 1937 and 1941 Hu lived and worked in Hong Hong. After Hong Kong fell in 1941, she refused to work for the Japanese and fled to Chongqing. Hu was briefly engaged in business activities after the war, but soon resumed acting. She retired in 1967 and lived in Canada until her death.

Further reading

D. Hu (1988), a memoir.

(ZX)

Hu, King (Hu Jinquan)

b. 29 April 1931, near Beijing
d. 14 January 1997, Taipei
Director, actor, screen writer

An important Hong Kong director in the 1960s–70s, King Hu attended Beijing National Art Institute and was stranded in Hong Kong in 1949 when the Communists took over China. He did various jobs in the 1950s, including one at the Voice of America, and worked as actor and art designer for Longma, Great Wall and Shaw Brothers before turning to film direction in the early 1960s. His Come Drink with Me (1966) paved the way for the new Hong Kong **martial arts film**, with its trademark humour and carefully choreographed action. He went to Taiwan and served as production manager for Lianban Film Company. His noted works include Dragon Gate Inn (1967), winner of the Best Screenplay award at Taipei GHA; A **Touch of Zen** (1970), winner of the Technical Superiority Prize at the 1975 Cannes FF; and Legend of the Mountain (1979), winner of the Best Director award at Taipei GHA.

Further reading

J. Hu and L. Zhong (1979), an extended interview; T. Rayns (1976), a brief profile.

(YZ)

Hu Mei

b. 1956, Beijing
Director

One of the best known female directors of the **Fifth Generation**, Hu Mei comes from an intellectual family. During the **Cultural Revolution** her father, a conductor for an army symphony orchestra, was imprisoned by the Red Guards, and her grandfather, a painter, died after being interrogated. In 1975 Hu Mei joined the army and performed in a song and dance troupe. She studied in the Directing Department at BFA between 1978 and 1982 and upon graduation was assigned to August First Film Studio. **Army Nurse** (1985), a psychological film she co-directed with Li Xiaojun, her male classmate, addresses the issue of female subjectivity by dramatizing the inner life of an army nurse torn between her personal feelings and her social obligations. In its emphasis on gender experience (enhanced by female voice-over), this lyrical film is closer to **Sacrificed Youth** (dir.

Zhang Nuanxin, 1985) than to other Fifth Generation films of the time. *Far from the War* (1987), Hu's second feature, continues her psychological quest. It portrays a Yan'an veteran who increasingly lives in a fantasy world. Through an elaborate series of fragmented flashbacks, he gradually remembers a moment of real passion in his life. After making *The Gunslinger Without a Gun* (1988), Hu Mei left August First Studio and became an independent TV producer. Hu Mei is fond of psychological books and has reportedly read Simone de Beauvoir, Marguerite Duras and Freud.

Further reading

W. Bao (1983), a profile; C. Berry (1988b: 32–41), an informative interview; T. Rayns (1989: 32–5), a brief discussion.

(YZ)

Hu Xueyang

b. July 1963, Mohe, Heilongjiang province
Director, actor

One of the earliest **Sixth Generation** filmmakers to direct within the studio system, Hu Xueyang entered the Directing Department of BFA in 1985 and was assigned to Shanghai Film Studio in 1990. After a short film, *Recollections of Childhood*, he directed *A Lady Left Behind* (1991), a **melodrama** tracing the emotional life of a Chinese wife whose husband has gone overseas. The film won a Golden Pyramid at the 1992 Cairo FF. Hu's second feature is *The Drowned Youth* (1994), in which he plays a tennis instructor who is seduced by the young wife of a businessman and tormented by his desire for her. Like other directors of his generation, Hu is interested in **youth culture** and individual expression.

(YZ)

Huang Baomei

(Huang Baomei)

dir. **Xie Jin**
sc. Chen Fu, Ye Ming
with Huang Baomei
Shanghai: Tianma Film, 1958

In this film promoting **socialist construction**, the title character of the true-life docudrama, Huang Baomei, plays herself. The rest of the cast also comprises women workers from Shanghai's textile industry – none of whom are professional actors.

Huang Baomei is a model worker from Shanghai No. 17 Textile Factory and the forewoman of her department. When her co-worker, Zhang Xiulan, complains that her work station is too old to be efficient, Huang trades her new machine for Zhang's. After Huang demonstrates that she can maintain the highest production record even on Zhang's machine, Zhang is convinced that she needs to work harder. Huang learns from the newspaper that Shanghai's No. 7 Textile Factory has more efficient means of dealing with production problems. She immediately goes there to learn new methods and bring the knowledge back to her colleagues. To increase productivity she organizes team work competitions. But when her rival team runs into difficulty she goes to help them, even though her team members disapprove. In the end, Huang's team still manages to win the competition.

(ZX)

Huang Jianxin

b. 1954, Xi'an province
Director

A close associate of the **Fifth Generation**, Huang Jianxin served in the army and studied Chinese literature at Northwest University in the mid-1970s. Upon graduation, he worked as a script editor at Xi'an Film Studio, where he was acquainted with **Wu Tianming** in the early 1980s. In 1983 he attended a special two-year directing class at BFA. He returned to make his first feature, ***Black Cannon Incident*** (1985), a highly acclaimed political satire that ridicules party bureaucracy. The film portrays an eccentric engineer as an anti-hero, an ultimate loser, who finds himself in the film's sequel, ***Dislocation*** (1986), in a surreal high-tech environment. Promoted to the rank of director, this new type of intellectual designs a robot double of himself who can be sent as a stand-in to endless, meaningless political meetings. Both films are characterized by Huang's daring experiments with colour, composition, and camera angles. ***Transmigration*** (aka *Samsara*, 1988), a film adapted from Wang Shuo's novel about a group of disillusioned Beijing youth, completed Huang's first 'urban trilogy' on political culture in contemporary China.

In 1989 Huang visited the Australian Film, Radio and Television School in Sydney. He returned to Xi'an Studio to direct **Stand Up, Don't Bend Over** (1992), which was followed by the Hong Kong-financed **Back to Back, Face to Face** (1994). Both films returned Huang to his earlier satirical stance, exposing the ever-present influence of the 1960s–70s ideological brainwash, but they lack the adventurous spirit that characterizes Huang's previous films. Huang also directed *The* **Wooden Man's Bride** (1993), a Chinese Western executed in a visual style reminiscent of **Red Sorghum** (*dir.* **Zhang Yimou**, 1987). This voluntary departure from his usual style, however, did not win Huang any major international prize, so he proceeded to two other urban features, *Signal Left, Turn Right* (1995) and *Surveillance* (1996), both focusing on seemingly trivial matters that bother ordinary urbanites.

See also: Westerns

Further reading

J. Huang (1991), an interview with Chris Berry; P. Pickowicz (1994), an excellent study of Huang and post-socialism; T. Rayns (1989: 35–9), a brief discussion.

(YZ)

Huang Jianzhong

b. 29 December 1943, Indonesia
Director

Huang was born into an overseas Chinese family. In 1948, his parents left Indonesia and brought him to China, where he finished his pre-college education in Beijing. By chance he was enrolled in film school at Beijing Film Studio in 1960. After many years as assistant director, Huang made his directorial début with *As You Wish* (1982). Although he does not officially belong to the **Fifth Generation**, his films share certain features with the work of that group. His **Good Woman** (1985) won the top award at the 1986 Karlovy Vary FF and the Atlantic FF in Spain. It also won the Critics Award at the 1987 International FF in India, not to mention some less prestigious prizes.

Within China, Huang enjoys a reputation as one of the most talented directors. While his *Questions for the Living* and *Two Virtuous Women* (both 1987) veer towards the avant-garde and were well received by critics, *Dragon Year Cops* (*co-dir.* Li Ziyu, 1990) and *Spring Festival* (1991) were both

politically correct populist works, the winners of top awards at HFA and from MBFT. Huang has remained prolific throughout the 1990s, directing *God of the Mountain* (1992) and many other films.

Further reading

K. Eder and D. Rossell (1993: 94–7), with an interview.

(ZX)

Huang Jun

b. 1958, Ruijin, Jiangxi province
Director, screen writer

The earliest figure from the **Sixth Generation** to direct feature films, Huang Jun spent his childhood in the impoverished mountain area in Jiangxi province and worked for two years as a farm-hand and soldier. He entered the Department of Industrial Economic Management at Chinese People's University in Beijing in 1985 and, upon graduation, miraculously passed the entrance examinations to be admitted as a graduate student of film theory at BFA. He wrote and directed his first film, *Childhood in Ruijin*, a semi-biographical account of children in his home town in 1990. While Jiangxi Film Studio released only twenty-eight prints of the film, it was, ironically, banned by the Jiangxi authorities and was not shown in the province until after it had won an award at China GRA. Huang's second feature, *The Prostitute and the Raftsmen* (1993), is a co-production between Jiangxi and Changchun studios which dramatizes life-and-death struggles during the Sino-Japanese war. Huang also co-wrote and directed *Living with You* (1994) for Fujian Film Studio, a sympathetic treatment of urban housing problems told within the terms of a love triangle. Apart from directing, Huang is busy writing screenplays.

Further reading

K. Eder and D. Rossell (1993: 97–8), with a brief interview; W. Zhao (1994), a biographic sketch.

(YZ)

Huang Shaofen
(Huang Ke)

b. 2 May 1911, Guangdong province
Cinematographer

Regarded as one of the best directors of photography in China, Huang Shaofen moved at the age of fourteen to Shanghai, where he worked as an apprentice cinematographer at Minxin Film Company. He joined Lianhua Film Company in 1929 and became the studio's most prominent cameraman. Huang was involved in most, if not all, of Lianhua's major productions, such as *Memories of the Old Capital*, **Wild Flower** (both *dir.* **Sun Yu**, both 1930), **Three Modern Women** (*dir.* **Bu Wancang**, 1933) and **Song of China** (*dir.* **Fei Mu**, **Luo Mingyou**, 1935).

During the Japanese occupation of Shanghai, Huang turned down a request from the Japanese-controlled United China Film Company to serve as chief cinematographer on a propaganda film, *The Sorrow of Spring River* (*dir.* Dao Yuanhao, Yao Feng, 1944). As a result, he was deprived other work opportunities until after the war.

In the post-war era, Huang was involved in the production of a number of films, including **Phony Phoenixes**, **Night Inn** (both *dir.* **Huang Zuolin**, both 1947) and *Bright Sky* (*dir.* Cao Yu, 1948).

After 1949, Huang continued to work as a cinematographer, first for Shanghai United Film Studio and then for Shanghai Film Studio. He was the chief cameraman on *The Point of Departure* (*dir.* Zhang Ke, 1954), **Girl Basketball Player No. 5** (*dir.* **Xie Jin**, 1957), **Lin Zexu** (*dir.* **Zheng Junli**, Chen Fan, 1959), **Spring Comes to the Withered Tree** (*dir.* Zheng Junli, 1961) and **Sentinels Under the Neon Lights** (*dir.* **Wang Ping**, Ge Xin, 1964).

See also: propaganda and film

Further reading

ZDX (1982–6: 1: 313–17), a short biography.

(ZX)

Huang Shuqin

b. 9 September 1940, Guangdong province
Director

One of China's most talented woman directors, Huang Shuqin is the daughter of **Huang Zuolin**, a famous director of the 1940s. She grew up in Shanghai and graduated from the Directing Department at BFA in 1964, but her career developed slowly due to the **Cultural Revolution**.

Huang worked as assistant to **Xie Jin** on two films, *The Cradle* (1979) and *The* **Legend of Tianyun Mountain** (1980). Her own début, *Contemporary People* (1981), won critical acclaim. She

has subsequently directed several award-winning titles. While *Forever Young* (1983) received an honourable mention at an international film festival held in the former Soviet Union in 1984, *Childhood Friends* (1984) won the Ministry of Culture's Best Film award in 1985. Huang's **Woman Demon Human** (1987), reputedly the first truly 'feminist film' in China, was awarded Best Screenplay at the 1988 China GRA, a top prize from the Fifth Film and Video Festival in Brazil, and an award from a French festival in 1989. Inspired by the success of this film, Huang continued to highlight issues of gender in her next film, *The* **Soul of the Painter** (1994), which is based on the life of Pan Yuliang, an extremely controversial female Chinese painter who studied in France.

Besides films, Huang has also directed a hit television series, *Fortress Besieged* (1990). The programme earned Huang several awards, including a Golden Bear from the First International TV Show Festival and a second prize in the Best Television Programmes Competition in China in 1991. After directing another popular TV series on the marriage problems experienced by educated youth, *Evil Fates* (1995), Huang completed a highly acclaimed **children's film**, *I Have My Daddy, Too* (1996).

Further reading

J. Dai (1995), a brief discussion of Huang; J. Dai and M. Yang (1995), a critical interview ; S. Huang (1995), the director's own commentary; L. Xiao (1992), a profile.

(ZX, YZ)

Huang Yu-shan

b. 1954, Penghu, Taiwan
Director, screen writer

Perhaps the only notable woman director working in Taiwan in the late 1980s, Huang Yu-shan graduated from the Department of Western Languages and Literatures at Chengchi University in 1976 and completed her MA in Chinese at New York University in 1982. Since then she has made several **documentary** films, including *A-Sun, the Painting of Wu Shieng Sun* (1985) and *Women Who Have Changed Taiwan* (1994). Her feature début was *Autumn Tempest* (1988); *Twin Bracelets* (1990) won her critical recognition. *Peony Birds* (1993) explores mother–daughter relationships, privacy and other taboo subjects of contemporary life.

(YZ)

Huang Zuolin

(Zuolin)

b. 24 October 1906, Tianjin
d. 1 June 1994
Director, playwright

An accomplished film director of the 1940s, Huang received solid training in traditional Chinese literature and was well versed in Confucian classics. At the age of ten he was sent by his parents to a church school, but he never became a devoted Christian.

Huang travelled to England in 1925 and earned a degree in political economy at Birmingham University in 1927. After returning to China in 1929, he found employment at a commercial firm while teaching part time at several local universities. Intellectually, Huang remained dissatisfied because his real interest lay in theatre. He returned to England to study drama at Cambridge University, earning an MA in literature in the process. He rounded up his studies in 1937, returned to China, and devoted himself to the resistance theatre movement.

Huang's involvement with film began in 1947 when Wenhua Film Company offered him a job as director. His début, ***Phony Phoenixes*** (1947), was such an immediate success that it was even dubbed into English to meet the demand from overseas buyers. Huang's second film, ***Night Inn*** (1947), based on *The Lower Depths*, a play by the revolutionary Russian playwright Maxim Gorky, deals with the hardships and frustrations experienced by people from the lower social strata. Huang's third film, *The Watch* (1949), was an adaptation of a short story by a Soviet writer. In this film, Huang not only cast a large number of non-professional actors; he also used hidden cameras to enhance the realistic effect. This innovative approach was well received by critics.

Yet Huang's major passion remained the theatre. After directing *Erosion* (1950), in which his wife Danni played the female protagonist, he retired from filmmaking to resume writing and directing stage plays. It was not until the late 1970s that he returned to direct a rather mediocre film, *The Man Who Lost His Memory* (1978). Two years later, he directed *Mayor Chen Yi* (1980).

See also: adaptations of drama and literature; theatre and film

Further reading

P. Pickowicz (1993b), a historical study of *Night Inn*; ZDX (1982–6: 7: 408–19), a short biography.

(ZX)

Hui, Ann

(Xu Anhua)

b. 23 May 1947, Liaoning province
Director

Ann Hui moved to Macao in her childhood, earned an MA degree in comparative literature from Hong Kong University, and studied filmmaking at London International Film School. After working extensively in television during the late 1970s, she made her feature film début in 1979 as part of Hong Kong cinema's New Wave.

Hui's first two titles, a thriller called *The Secret* (1979) and a ghost drama called *The Spooky Bunch* (1980), deserve their page in Chinese history: never before had major productions such as these been written, produced and directed solely by women. Her next two films, ***Boat People*** (1982) and *The Story of Woo Viet* (1981), engage politically with the plight of Vietnamese refugees, the former winning her Best Film and Best Director awards at HKFA. After shooting her own adaptation of Eileen Chang's best-selling novel *Love in the Fallen City* (1984), Hui started work on an ambitious two-part historical epic, finally released in 1987 as *The Romance of Book and Sword*. Mixing costume with contemporary drama and realism with fantasy, these six titles alone provide evidence of immense talent.

While Ann Hui may be one of Hong Kong's top women directors (along with Clara **Law**, Sylvia **Chang**, and Mabel Cheung), she has never called herself a feminist. However, her habitual use of melodramatic conventions and sly gender inversions complement the creative links she has forged with female actors. Hui's association with Maggie **Cheung** on the autobiographical ***Song of the Exile*** (1990) is particularly memorable; the film won top prizes at 1990 Asia–Pacific FF and one Italian festival. In recent years, Hui has continued to work in both film and television. A 1991 thriller, *Zodiac Killers*, may have disappointed the critics, but Ann Hui tends to bounce back when least expected. For example, her ***Summer Snow*** (1994) won Best Film, Director, Screenplay, Actor, Actress, and Supporting Actor categories at the fifteenth HKFA. From there, she proceeded to another adaptation of Eileen Chang, *An **Interrupted Love*** (1997), a story of love and betrayal set in old Shanghai, co-produced with mainland studios.

See also: adaptations of drama and literature; fantasy film; ghosts and immortals, film of

Further reading

A. Hui (1990), K. Jaehne (1984), two interviews.

(JS)

Hui, Michael

(Xu Guanwen)

b. 1942

Actor, director, producer

An active figure in the Hong Kong film industry, Michael Hui first made his name as a **comedy** actor in *The Warlord* (*dir.* **Li Han-hsiang**, 1972). With brothers Samuel (Xu Guanjie, *b.* 1948) and Ricky (Xu Guanying, *b.* 1946) he established his own company to produce such films as *Games Gamblers Play* (1974). The Huis subsequently broke into the Japanese market-place with *The Private Eyes* (1976), while their *Security Unlimited* (1981) set an all-time box-office record for both domestic and foreign films in Hong Kong. Hui has also contributed screenplays to such comedies as **Chicken and Duck Talk** (1989).

(YZ)

Hung, Sammo

(Hong Jinbao)

b. 1950, Hong Kong

Actor, director, producer

Though lesser known internationally than Jackie **Chan**, Sammo Hung is an endearing martial arts hero to Hong Kong audiences. He and Chan survived years of hardship and poverty until they became screen superstars. Just as Chan tends to incorporate comic elements from folk tradition into his action films, Hung draws extensively on Chinese legends and myths and uses the familiar figures of ghosts and immortals to frame his kungfu films.

Born into a family from Jiangsu province, Hung adopted 'Sammo' as a nickname derived from the Cantonese pronunciation of a popular cartoon character San Mao (three hairs). He enrolled in Yu Zhanyuan's China Drama Academy at the age of ten and studied Peking opera for eight years. As senior member of The Seven Little Fortunes group, he assisted Yu in instructing his fellow students and eventually became the school's manager of martial arts. His first film appearance was in *Education of Love* (1961).

In 1970 Golden Harvest hired Hung as martial arts instructor on *The Fast Sword*. He soon built up an impressive record in this field working on (and often appearing in) King **Hu** films such as *The **Fate of Lee Khan*** (1973) and *The Valiant Ones* (1975). Hung also briefly appeared with Bruce **Lee** in **Enter the Dragon** (1973) as well as the unfinished **Game of Death** (1978; the Hong Kong version credits him as co-director). Hung directed the martial art sequences in *The Skyhawk* (1974) featuring Kwan Tak-Hing as Huang Fei-Hong, and later appeared with him in the title role of *The Magnificent Butcher* (1980).

In 1977, Hung directed his first film, *The Iron-Fisted Monk*, followed by *Enter the Fat Dragon* (1978), *Warriors Two* (1978), *Knockabout* (1979) and *The Victim* (1980). Although he became identified with **comedy** kungfu and attempted a different career path with *Eastern Condors* (1986), audiences often prefer to see him in lighter roles as in *Close Encounters of the Spooky Kind* (1980) and *Pedicab Driver* (1990).

See also: action film; kungfu film

(TW, YZ)

I

Iceman Cometh

aka *Time Warriors* (Jidong qixia)

dir. Fok Yiu Leung
sc. Johnny **Mak**, Stephen Shiu
with Yuen Biao, Yuen Wah, Maggie **Cheung**
Hong Kong: Golden Harvest/Johnny Mak
Productions, 1989

A rough transposition of the Western **fantasy film** *Highlander* (*dir.* Russell Mulcahy, 1986), *Iceman Cometh* typifies the creative genre-mixing that often characterizes good Hong Kong action films. The narrative opens during the time of the Ming Dynasty, with the evil Feng San raping and killing the Emperor's cousin. As punishment for his negligence, Feng Sau Ching, head of the Royal Guard, is ordered to capture the villain before he takes possession of a black jade Buddha that can activate a time wheel. After a blistering sword fight, the two men topple off a mountain cliff.

In 1989, a group of explorers discover San and Sau Ching's preserved bodies. Seizing the opportunity to make money, they take both corpses to Hong Kong, where the time-travellers are soon thawed out. Sau Ching wanders Kowloon as an illegal immigrant until he is employed by Polly, a local prostitute. Polly uses Sau Ching's fighting skills to extort money from her customers. One night the Royal Guard learns from an old Cantonese movie that his master's dynasty was violently usurped. When he then discovers that Feng San is also in Hong Kong, Sau Ching vows to avenge the Emperor. As San tries to use the time wheel to transport modern military hardware back to ancient China, Sau Ching fights and kills him. Believing that Sau Ching has returned to his own century, Polly is overjoyed to find that he has decided to stay on with her in Hong Kong after all.

Iceman Cometh makes brilliant use of the talents of Yuen Biao and Yuen Wah, two stalwarts of the famous Peking opera troupe the 'Seven Little Fortunes', whose work is often overshadowed by that of their more famous friends, Jackie **Chan** and Sammo **Hung**.

See also: action film

(JS)

In-Laws, The

(Xi ying men)

dir. Zhao Huanzhang
sc. Xin Xianling
with Ma Xiaowei, Hong Xuemin, Wen Yujuan, Mao Yongming
Shanghai: Shanghai Film, 1981

This film deals with ethical issues in a contemporary rural **family**. It reaffirms many of the traditional virtues ascribed to women by contrasting Xue Shuilian, a considerate, giving and unselfish daughter-in-law, with Qiangying, who is portrayed as a demanding, fussy and unreasonable person. The film can be read in many ways as prescribing proper conduct for an extended Chinese family.

A peasant woman, Xue Shuilian, who is married to Chen Renwu, the second son of the Chen family, experiences interpersonal conflicts within the family. Xue's sister-in-law, Qiangying, asks her husband to buy her a pair of pants resembling those worn by Xue. A few days later the younger sister of Xue's husband, Renying, brings home a piece of cloth given to her by her boyfriend. But Qiangying assumes her mother-in-law is favouring Renying. To appease Qiangying, the mother-in-law borrows money to buy some of the same material for Qiangying. Xue quietly offers to buy her sister-in-law a piece of cloth.

Qiangying, however, is not satisfied with what she has acquired and pressures her husband into splitting with his parents' household. Meanwhile, she conspires with a neighbouring matchmaker to arrange a marriage for Renying. Renwen, Qiangying's husband, is so enraged by the way Qiangying conducts herself that he slaps her in the face. As a result, Qiangying walks out and stays with her parents. During Qiangying's absence, Xue takes on the responsibility of caring for Qiangying's two children, feeding the livestock and doing her farm work. One day, Qiangying misses her children and comes back to take another look at them. When she realizes what Xue has done for her she feels ashamed of herself. She admits her wrongdoing and peace is restored to the household.

In 1981 the film received awards of Best Film at HFA and Best Film from the Ministry of Culture.

Further reading

C. Berry (1991b), a discussion of sexual difference and the viewing subject.

(ZX)

In Our Time

(Guangyin de gushi)

dir. Tao Dechen, Edward **Yang**, **Ko Yi-cheng**, **Chang Yi**
with Lan Shengwen, Shi Anni, Sylvia **Chang**, Li Liqun
Taipei: CMPC, 1982

This four-part film ushered in the New Wave Taiwan film in the early 1980s. *Little Dinosaurs* (*dir.* Tao Dechen) tells the story of an introspective boy, Mao, who is afraid of talking to others. Only a girl named Fang understands him, and they enjoy peaceful days together. But soon Fang's family emigrate to the USA, leaving Mao alone with his toy dinosaurs. *Desires* (*dir.* Edward Yang) follows a teenage girl also named Fang, who grows up with an imaginative boy. Fang is secretly in love with a college student, only to find out later that he is the boyfriend of her elder sister. *Leap Frog* (*dir.* Ko Yi-cheng) features an ambitious college student who has a wide range of interests and participates in lots of extracurricular activities. From time to time he feels uncertain about his real goals but finally finds his real self in a swimming competition. *Show Your ID* (*dir.* Chang Yi) dramatizes the predicaments of modern **urban life**. One day, a

young couple move to their new apartment. The wife goes to work and is refused entry because she forgets to bring her ID. Meanwhile, the husband is suspected of being a thief simply because he stays home alone, and is beaten up by an angry crowd.

In Our Time makes a fresh start by focusing on ordinary people and their seemingly uneventful lives. It foreshadows several recurring themes (e.g., **nostalgia** for childhood and growing up in the countryside) in New Taiwan Cinema.

See also: New Taiwan Cinema (under Taiwan cinema in Historical essays)

(IJS)

In the Heat of the Sun

(Yangguang canlan de rizi)

dir./sc. **Jiang Wen**
with Jiang Wen, Xia Yu, Ning Jing, Tao Hong, **Siqin Gaowa**
Hong Kong: Dragon Air (Ganglong) Film/ Taiwan: Xiehe Film, 1994

This directorial début from a famous mainland actor has attracted much critical attention. While most critics praise Jiang's sophisticated film language and his creative imagination, others are reluctant to endorse his iconoclastic view of the **Cultural Revolution**.

The film opens with Ma Xiaojun, a naughty son of an army officer who is away most of the time. Living with his mother, Ma is free to play all kinds of tricks in and out of his middle school. A new schoolteacher is angered by the unruly behaviour of the army kids, but no one cares. The kids form separate gangs and fight each other. Meanwhile, Ma cultivates a habit of prying open various locks. He damages a condom in his father's locked drawer, which leads to the birth of his younger brother a year later. Then he ventures to break into people's apartments without ever being caught. One day, he hides under a bed when a pretty teenage girl unexpectedly returns to her room. Ma learns that her name is Mi Lan and later introduces her to his group. He even climbs up a tall smoke-stack to demonstrate his prowess. The phallic icon betrays Ma's stirring sexual desire for Mi Lan: he wanders on the rooftops like a lone wolf when she disappears from his 'surveillance'. He enjoys pouring a kettle of warm water over her head to help her wash her hair. In a bizarre dream sequence, he is bothered by diarrhoea and finds no private place in a farm field while Mi Lan chases him with an alarm clock.

Mi Lan, on the other hand, favours an older friend of Ma's. The tension between Ma and his rival gets out of control when they celebrate Mi Lan's birthday. Ma is beaten – or is he? The self-questioning tone in Ma's voice-over narration puts his own memory to test. Anyway, he is estranged by his group, and the story ends with Ma being repeatedly kicked back into a swimming pool by his friends when he tries to climb up. With this allusion to the violence of the Cultural Revolution, the film completes the initiation of a teenager into adulthood. What is ironic, however, is the film's 'epilogue' in black and white, where old Mr. Ma (played by the director) is riding in a black limousine and commenting on the new scenes of Beijing.

The film won the award of Best Actor (Xia Yu) at the 1995 Taipei GHA.

(IJS, YZ)

In the Wild Mountain

(Yeshan)

dir. Yan Xueshu
sc. Yan Xueshu, Zhu Zi
with Du Yuan, Xin Ming, Yue Hong, Xu Shouli
Xi'an: Xi'an Film, 1985

In this film about **rural life** in the era of economic reforms, veteran Hehe is not considered a good farmer by his villagers because he is not content with the traditional way of life and always wants to do something different. His attempts at making bricks and raising fish have both failed disastrously. His wife Qiurong is finally tired of him, and the two decide to separate for the time being. Hehe finds a temporary shelter at Huihui's house and starts a new business making bean curd. Huihui is a traditional peasant whose only regret is that his wife Guilan has not produced a child. Guilan is sympathetic to both Qiurong and Hehe. She particularly enjoys having Hehe around, because he tells her stories about the outside world he saw while serving in the military. Hehe's bean curd business fails again. He decides to seek employment in the city. Before leaving, he asks Huihui to take care of Qiurong. Huihui helps Qiurong wholeheartedly, but refuses to be Hehe's business partner in his silk cocoon venture. It is Guilan who offers Hehe her personal savings as start-up money. Just as they seem to be near success, a natural disaster wipes out Hehe's silkworm business. Meanwhile, rumours among the villagers

about the relationship between Guilan and Hehe enrages Huihui. He beats Guilan, which results in their divorce. At the film's end, Huihui marries Qiurong and Guilan marries Hehe. The two couples continue their different approaches to life.

The film won Best Film award from MBFT in 1985; Best Film, Best Director, Best Actress (Yue Hong) and other prizes at the 1986 China GRA; a grand prize at the 1986 Nantes FF; and a Catholic award at the 1987 Berlin FF.

Further reading

N. Ma (1993), a critical study of the film's melo-dramatic presentation.

(ZX)

In Their Prime

(Tamen zheng nianqing)

dir. **Zhou Xiaowen**, Fang Fang
sc. Li Pingfen
with Hong Yuzhou, Wang Gang, Yue Hong, Yang Shengli
Xi'an: Xi'an Film, 1986

The film opens with a squad of nine Chinese soldiers moving to a cave amid intense gunfire and artillery shells. It is during the unpopular Sino-Vietnamese border war in the 1970s. The soldiers endure the heat and humidity inside the cave for three months. The army sends two men to bring them water and letters from their families. In a skirmish, a soldier is captured by the Vietnamese but rescued by his fellow soldier. Another Chinese soldier runs into a Vietnamese woman carrying a baby. He does not want to harm them, but when he turns away the woman shoots him. The soldiers grow more and more irritated by the deteriorating conditions inside the cave. A soldier dies while delivering water to them.

Frequent flashbacks bring the viewer to Beijing, where a year before the squadron leader met Yan Pingping, a pregnant woman whose husband had died in the war and who had been instructed to have an abortion. Waiting outside the operation room, Yan changes her mind and decides to keep her child. In the empty hallway of the Museum of the History of Military Revolutions, Yan cries and screams, while the squad leader tries to persuade her to have the operation, but their voices are turned into unintelligible echoes.

Back at the front, the order to retreat finally comes. On the way, a soldier is killed by a landmine. The rest of the squad carry his body and fight their way through waist-deep red mud. The film ends with the squad leader and Yan browsing through tombstones and looking for the lost soldier.

In terms of subject matter, this film resembles *Shanggan Ridges* (*dir.* Sha Meng, Lin Shan, 1956), a mainland **war film** that glorifies the Chinese soldiers holding their position in a similar cave during the Korean War. Not much of heroism or **nationalism** is found in Zhou's film, though. Because of its humanitarian values and its anti-war message, *In Their Prime* has been banned from release in mainland China.

(JJS, YZ)

independent film

Independent filmmaking did not start in mainland China until the late 1980s, when a group of young people began shooting films and videos outside the government studio system. Among these independents are Duan Jinchuan, Hao Zhiqiang, **He Jianjun**, Ning Dai, Shi Jian, **Wang Xiaoshuai**, Wen Pulin, **Wu Di**, **Wu Wenguang**, **Zhang Yuan**, and the documentary-filmmaking collective SWYC (Structure, Wave, Youth, and Cinema), which consists mainly of employees from China Central TV. Working outside or on the margins of government-controlled facilities, these independents frequently circulate their work on videotape and sometimes exhibit it overseas. Inevitably, they have run into trouble with the government. In April 1994, an official ban was placed on any future work produced in the mainland by many such independents, but defiant filmmakers like Wu Wenguang and Zhang Yuan continue to work on their projects.

In Taiwan, Huang Mingchuan is said to have pioneered genuinely independent production with his début feature *The Man from Island West* (1990). Critical response to the film was so positive that Huang proceeded with *Bodo* (1994), a re-examination of army life in Taiwan from a distinctively unofficial angle. In Hong Kong, independent short films started in 1966 with the College Cine Club. Since the 1980s, independent filmmakers in Hong Kong have produced numerous documentaries and animated films, and Allen **Fong** has been an enthusiastic supporter of the movement. The independents explore the concepts of social realism and the alternative cinema, and exhibit their productions at film festivals.

See also: documentary; censorship and film

Further reading
C. Berry (1995a), on mainland independent films; G. Cheshire (1994), a report on the ban on mainland independents; D. Chute (1994), a review of three mainland independent films; M. Huang (1990, 1994), two books on Huang Mingchuan and Taiwan independent filmmaking; L. Jaivin (1995), a report on the defiant independent filmmakers; S.N. Ko (1995), on Hong Kong independent short films.

(YZ)

Interrupted Love, An
(Bansheng yuan)

dir. Ann **Hui**
sc. Xiao Mao
with Wu Qianlian, Ge You, Anita **Mui**, Li Min
Hong Kong: Guotai Film/Tianshan Film/
Shanghai: An's Visual Communications, 1997

A **melodrama** based on Eileen Chang's novel, this film is set in 1930s Shanghai. Manzhen, a pretty factory worker, falls in love with Shen Shijun, an ambitious man who seeks an independent career in Shanghai. Manzhen's sister Manlu is a socialite; for security, she agrees to be a concubine to Zhu Hongcai.

Shen's mother urges Shen to marry his rich cousin Shi Cuizhi, but Shen is not interested in her. One day Shen invites his friend Xu Shuhui to Nanjing. Xu and Shi like each other, but Xu's poor family background prevents their union. Soon Shen's father dies in Nanjing, and Shen has to leave Shanghai and takes over his father's business. He and Manzhen exchange letters, but no longer feel as passionate as before. Left alone, Manzhen becomes a new target for Zhu, her sister's playboy husband. Zhu has blamed Manlu for not bearing any child for him. To please Zhu, Manlu sets up a trap whereby Manzhen is raped by Zhu and later gives birth to a son. When Shen comes to Shanghai to visit Manzhen, her room is empty. Shen's cousin Shi also comes to Shanghai to look for Xu, but Xu has gone to the USA. Shi and Shen meets in Nanjing and gradually fall in love.

Manzhen eventually escapes from Manlu and Zhu, but Shen and Shi are already married by then. When he meets Manzhen again years later, Shi wants to resume their interrupted love, but Manzhen says the past cannot be relived.

This typical **romance** reflects a **nostalgia** for old Shanghai in both Hong Kong and China.

(YZ)

It's My Day Off

(Jintian wo xiuxi)

dir. Lu Ren
sc. Li Tianji
with Zhong Xinhuo, Zhao Shuyin, Ma Ji, Li Baoluo, **Shangguan Yunzhu**
Shanghai: Haiyan Film, 1959

An educational **comedy** that promotes **socialist construction**, the film shows a series of altruistic actions performed in a single day by the policeman Ma Tianmin. Because Ma is a bachelor, his chief's wife, Yao Meizhen, volunteers to be his match-maker. She arranges for Ma to go on a date on his day off with a postal worker, Liu Ping. On his way to meet Liu, Ma becomes involved in a series of accidents. He helps out an old farmer who came to Shanghai to sell his pigs but who can no longer find his way to the market because the city has grown so rapidly. Ma feeds the pigs and has the farmer taken to the market place by truck. As a result, Ma misses his first date with Liu.

Yao arranges a second date at the movie theatre. This time Ma has to take care of a little child who has suddenly fallen ill. By the time the child is safely at home, Ma has missed his second appointment with Liu. Yao gives Ma another chance. He is invited to have supper at Liu's house and to meet her family. On his way to her house, Ma has to return a lost purse to its owner. When he finally arrives at Liu's house, everybody is disappointed with what they take to be his rude behaviour. However, Ma is forgiven when Liu's father recognizes Ma as the policeman who helped him and his pigs. Ma's chief also turns up to explain how Ma had been delayed by his attention to duty. As a result of these accounts, all tensions are defused and a happy ending secured.

By showing how all members of the new socialist society possess a good heart, *It's My Day Off* praises the sense of solidarity inspired by the **Communist revolution** and combines it with traditional virtues (such as matchmaking) in a spirit of mediation and goodwill.

Further reading

N. Ma (1987b), a study of 1960s comedies.

(PV)

J

Jade Love
(Yuqing sao)

dir./sc. **Chang Yi**
with Yang Huishan, Lin Dingfeng
Taipei: Tianxia Film, 1984

Jade Love is adapted from a famous story by the renowned writer Bai Xianyong. Set in the late 1930s, it depicts a woman struggling with her sexuality in a patriarchal society. Yuqing is a beautiful widow who works as a nanny for Rongge, the young master of a rich family in a provincial town. Outside the young master's mansion, she has her own private life: she keeps an invalid young lover, Qingsheng, in a back alley attic.

Rongge soon finds out about Yuqing's secret life. Like his nanny, he is deeply attracted to Qingsheng. He then interposes himself in the already tangled relationship between Yuqing and Qingsheng by taking Qingsheng out for a taste of a 'real' man's life. For the first time in his life, Qingsheng watches Peking opera and falls in love with an actress. After vowing his love to the actress, Qingsheng asks Yuqing for his freedom. When she realizes that she can no longer keep him in their secluded attic, she knows it is time to act. When Rongge wakes up in the middle of the night on New Year's Eve, he rushes to the attic only to find a perplexed Yuqing wielding a knife and stabbing Qingsheng's body repeatedly. She then kills herself, a smile on her face as she dies.

As the most controversial entry in the best film category at Taipei GHA, *Jade Love* was severely criticized for its 'indecent' portrayal of sexuality. The sharp contrast between Yuqing's volcanic desire and her obedient yet dignified demeanour remains an emblematic image of woman in Chinese literature, and Chang Yi's treatment of the story provides Taiwanese cinema with a memorable screen image.

(YY)

Jiang Wen

b. 1963, Beijing
Actor, director, screen writer

One of the best-known mainland actors since the 1980s, Jiang Wen impresses audiences with his independent spirit and his sense of humour. He was raised in a soldier's family and entered the Central Drama Academy in Beijing at the age of seventeen. He admires **Shi Hui**, especially his performance in ***This Life of Mine*** (1950). Jiang's screen début was as Pu Yi, China's last emperor, in *The Last Empress* (*dir.* Chen Jialin, 1985). Since then he has appeared in numerous films, taking a range of challenging roles from emperor, intellectual and peasant to ex-prisoner and detective. He has worked with famous directors on *A Woman for Two* (*dir.* **Ling Zifeng**, 1988), ***Hibiscus Town*** (*dir.* **Xie Jin**, 1986), ***Red Sorghum*** (*dir.* **Zhang Yimou**, 1987), ***Black Snow*** (*dir.* **Xie Fei**, 1989), ***Li Lianying: the Imperial Eunuch*** (*dir.* **Tian Zhuangzhuang**, 1991), *Presumed Guilty* (*dir.* **Zhou Xiaowen**, 1993), and the immensely popular 21-part TV drama *A Native of Beijing in New York* (1994). He twice won Best Actor award at HFA and was invited by the State Department on a one-month tour of the USA in spring 1992 as 'an outstanding young talent'. With financial backing from Hong Kong and Taiwan, he adapted Wang Shuo's novel *Ferocious Animals* and directed ***In the Heat of the Sun*** (1994), a nostalgic account of the passionate lives lived by a group of Beijing youth during the **Cultural Revolution**.

Further reading

X. Luo (1994a), a biographic sketch.

(YZ)

Jin Shan

(Zhao Mo)

b. 9 August, 1911, Hunan province
d. 7 July, 1982
Film actor and dramatist

A famous actor of the 1940s, Jin Shan had a difficult childhood. His father died when he was only two months old. During his adolescence, he had to drop out of school several times and was abused by his stepfather. He went to Shanghai in the late 1920s and joined the CCP in 1932. Jin was an active participant in the leftist theatre movement during the 1930s. In 1936, he made his first film appearance in Xinhua Film Company's *The Night of the Debauch* (*dir.* **Shi Dongshan**, 1936). But what really established Jin's reputation was his superb performance in *Singing at Midnight* (*dir.* **Ma-Xu Weibang**, 1937).

Jin's most important achievements since the late 1940s include his two films as director: *Along the Sungari River* (1947) tells the story of an uprising by Chinese miners against the Japanese, while *Storm* (1959) is based on the real-life story of a Communist lawyer who defended several accused workers during the warlord period. Jin's portrayal of this latter character was widely praised by film critics.

Further reading

ZDX (1982–6: 2: 131–42), a short biography.

(ZX)

Jin Yan

(Jin Delin)

b. 8 April 1910
d. 27 December 1983
Actor

One of the most popular stars of the 1930s (nicknamed the 'Chinese Valentino'), Jin Yan was born into a Korean doctor's family in Seoul. Jin's family moved to China in the wake of the Japanese occupation of Korea; Jin took his new name during his school years in Tianjin.

Jin travelled to Shanghai in 1927 and was admitted into Minxin Film Company's training programme. Within a year he had appeared in two films. By 1929 Jin was playing male lead in several swordplay films. After he joined Lianhua Film Company in 1930, he starred in almost every major production released by the studio. According to a poll conducted by a Shanghai newspaper, Jin was the most popular actor with Shanghai audiences. In fact, he was voted 'King of the Screen' by his fans in 1932.

Among Jin's numerous films are *Wild Flower* (1930), *Big Road* (1934, both *dir.* **Sun Yu**), *Love and Responsibility* (1931), *Three Modern Women*, *Motherly Love* (both 1933), *The Golden Age* (1934, all *dir.* **Bu Wancang**), *The New Peach Blossom Fan* (*dir.* **Ouyang Yuqian**, 1935) and *The Pioneers* (*dir.* **Wu Yonggang**, 1936). Many of these films were written or directed by leftist filmmakers. Yet despite Jin's association with the leftists – which resulted in physical threats after his name appeared on the blacklist of an ultra-right wing Nationalist group – Jin was merely an artist with a social conscience: he never joined the CCP, not even after the CCP came to power in 1949.

Jin's film career began to go downhill after the Sino-Japanese war broke out in 1937. During an eight year stretch he made only one title, *The Sky Rider* (*dir.* Sun Yu, 1940), for the Nationalist Central Film Studio. After briefly flirting with his childhood dream of becoming an architect, and a failed attempt at business, Jin returned to Shanghai once the war ended. He starred in three films produced in the city between 1945 and 1949.

Although Jin made a comeback in the 1950s, starring in *The Return of Spring* (*dir.* Xu Tao, 1950), *The Point of Departure* (*dir.* Zhang Ke, 1954), *Mother* (*dir.* **Ling Zifeng**, 1956), and *Eagle in the Storm* (*dir.* Wang Yi, 1957), his film career was cut short in 1958 by a serious illness. He made no more appearances after that date.

See also: swordplay film

Further reading

ZDX (1982–6: 1: 161–8), a short biography.

(ZX)

Ju Dou

(Ju Dou)

dir. **Zhang Yimou**, Yang Fengliang
sc. Liu Heng
with **Gong Li**, Li Baotian, Li Wei
Japan: Tokuma Shoten Publishing Co., 1989

Ju Dou addresses the familiar subject of how Chinese social conventions repress personal desires. Set in a small village in northern China in the 1920s, the film depicts the triangular relationship between a young wife, her elderly husband, and her lover. The old and cruel dye-house owner, Yang Jinshan, purchases a beautiful young woman, Ju Dou, who might bear him a male heir and work for him in the house. Jinshan is sexually impotent and abuses Ju Dou each night. Her loud cries of torment arouse the sympathy of Tianqing, the owner's adopted nephew. The 'horse riding' scene – with Jinshan mounted on a saddle on the back of the almost naked Ju Dou, her mouth gagged and hands tied – is striking. The old man's mistreatment and the young man's secret passion lead Ju Dou to undress in front of the voyeuristic Tianqing. As a result, 'aunt' and 'nephew' consummate their affair and produce a son, Tianbai, whom Jinshan mistakenly believes to be his own.

Illicit relations unfold under the roof of the dye house and within the walls of the courtyard. An expressionist colour scheme – with the red water of the dye vat and the bright colours of the hanging fabric – visualizes the lovers' passion, while the use of *mise-en-scène* and camera framing tightly suggests their social confinement. The victimizer, now paralysed after a stroke, becomes the victim as Jinshan watches his wife and nephew openly enjoying their affair. However, the lovers come to suffer both psychologically and physically for their transgression. The angry son, confused about his true paternity, accidentally drowns his symbolic father and wilfully kills his biological father. With no escape from feudalism's omnipresent power, Ju Dou starts a fire in the dye-house, thus sending her longed-for liberation up in smoke. The film's exposition of repressed subjectivity and sexuality demonstrates how any system of representation is both a sociocultural construct and a semiotic apparatus.

In 1991 *Ju Dou* won Best Film award at Chicago FF and was nominated for Best Foreign Film at the Oscars. It immediately became the model for several other Chinese films about sexual repression and moral transgression.

Further reading

W.A. Callahan (1993), a discussion of cultural politics; J. Lau (1991b, 1994), two studies of cultural interpretations of the film; S. Cui (1997), an analysis of gender meanings constituted in cinematic representation.

(SC)

Juvenile Delinquents

(Shaonian fan)

dir. Zhang Liang
sc. Wang Jingzhu, Zhang Liang
with Lu Bin, Jiang Jian, Zhu Manfang
Shenzhen: Shenzhen Film, 1985

One of the few Chinese films to deal with youth problems, *Juvenile Delinquents* calls for a more tolerant and receptive attitude towards juveniles and suggests that troubled youth actually craves love and understanding.

A journalist, Xie Jiexin, is sent to a juvenile rehabilitation centre to do a story. She observes Fang's violent behaviour, Xiao's trouble-making techniques, and Shen's sincere attempts to reform himself. One day Fang plans to escape by pretending to have swallowed a pair of small folding scissors. But he becomes ashamed when he sees how the people around him demonstrate genuine concern for his safety in their rush to save his life. He confesses his scheme to the supervisor and willingly accepts a penalty. Everyone in the centre except for Fang and Xiao has family members appear on visiting day. Disheartened over being abandoned by his parents, Fang swallows the folded scissors for real. He is immediately taken to the hospital and saved from danger. Xie and the centre's supervisor both persuade Fang's father to pay Fang a visit. When he does come to see Fang in the hospital, his son is touched and resolves to change his ways. Meanwhile, Shen's good behaviour earns him an early release: he subsequently passes the college entrance examination and goes to university. Xie decides to write a story calling for all people to pay attention to the youth problem. Ironically, just as she arrives home, she sees the police taking away her own son.

In 1985–6 the film was granted Best Film award from both HFA and MBFT.

Further reading

C. Berry (1988a), a brief discussion of the film in terms of realism.

(ZX)

K

Killer, The

(Diexue shuang xiong)

dir./sc. John **Woo**
with **Chow Yun-Fat**, Danny **Lee**, Sally Yeh,
Chu Kong
Hong Kong: Golden Princess, 1989

The Killer has done more than any other film to
introduce Western audiences to the contemporary
Hong Kong action cinema. Setting new standards
in gunfight choreography, the film attracted
Hollywood notices with its unique mix of **melodrama** and mayhem. The story concerns Jeff, an
assassin with a conscience, who accidentally blinds
a singer, Jennie, during a hit in a night club.
Tormented by guilt, Jeff is convinced by Sydney,
his old partner, to take on one more job. Betrayed
after its completion, Jeff finds himself pursued
by both a gangland leader, Johnny Weng, and a
rogue police inspector, Lee.

After Jeff's unsuccessful attempt to assassinate
Weng, Jeff and Sydney's reconciliation, and the
death of Randy, Lee's partner, the killer and
the police inspector meet and start up a friendship. They are tracked to an isolated church,
whereupon a blazing gunfight ensues. In the end,
Jeff, Sydney, and Weng meet violent deaths, while

Plate 21   *The Killer* (1989)

Jennie is left blind and alone. Lee cries for the loss of his gangster friend as he prepares to meet the wrath of his superiors.

The Killer consolidated John Woo's reputation as one of the world's most accomplished action directors and provides the supreme example of Chow Yun-Fat's stylish charm. Although a promised North American remake never materialized, the film continues to circulate widely in the West on video and laser disc.

See also: action film

Further reading

J. Sandell (1994), on masochism and homoeroticism; J. Stringer (1997b), on masculinity.

(JS)

King of Masks, The

(Bianlian)

dir. **Wu Tianming**
sc. Wei Minglun
with Zhu Xu, Zhou Renyin
Beijing: BFA Youth Film/Hong Kong: Shaw Brothers Film, 1996

The first film he directed after having left mainland China in 1989 and taken up residency in the USA, *The King of Masks* demonstrates Wu Tianming's mastery of film art. Set in a small town in China, the film tells of an old artist's quest for an heir. 'The king of masks' has inherited the family magic of changing operatic faces. He plays in the market and lives on a boat with his monkey. A locally famous opera actor wants to learn his trick, but the king says he can only pass it on to his son. The problem is that, being a poor old man, he does not have a son. He goes to an auction and purchases a boy who catches his attention. The king is happy that from then on the boy will cook for him and clean the boat – but he soon finds out that the 'boy' is a girl in disguise.

Driven away by her master, the girl remains faithful and manages to escape from the kidnappers along with a small boy, whom she delivers to the boat. The king cannot believe his eyes when he sees the boy, as if his prayer to Buddha were answered. However, the boy turns out to be the son of a rich family in town, who got lost while watching an opera. The police locate the boy and arrest the king. To show their toughness against crime, they sentence him to death.

The girl realizes her fatal mistake. After visiting the master in his death cage, she starts her crusade to save the king's life. She kneels down on the steps outside the actor's house overnight. The actor is moved by the girl and speaks to a local military commander, who, however, refuses to intervene. As a last resort, the girl hangs herself from the roof of the theatre, pleading for help, in the middle of an opera show. She drops down and is rescued by the actor. Publicly shamed, the commander finally agrees to talk to the local police, and the innocent king is released. He no longer holds gender bias and teaches the girl his family secret of changing masks.

A tribute to Confucian morality, the film won awards for Best Director at China GRA and Best Film at Zhuhai FF in China, as well as Best Director and Best Actor (Zhu Xu) at Tokyo FF, all in 1996.

(YZ)

King of the Children

(Haizi wang)

dir. **Chen Kaige**
sc. Zhong Acheng
with Xie Yuan, Yang Xuewen, Chen Shaohua, Zhang Caimei
Xi'an: Xi'an Film, 1987

This film exemplifies Chen Kaige's persistent inquiry into the relations between culture and self. Set in the **Cultural Revolution**, the narrative concerns the educational meanings that can be acquired from nature. Both philosophically and artistically ambitious, the film failed in its attempt at domestic and international recognition – a fact that points to the director's estrangement from his audience. Chen Kaige's penchant for allegory and psychological exploration hinders viewers' engagement with the film.

Lao Gan, an educated youth, is selected as a village-school teacher, or the king of children in Chinese colloquial terms. The teacher's duty is to copy hypocritical political texts on to the blackboard, which the students, having no textbooks, then write down. The students do not understand what they are writing, nor does Lao Gan know how to teach official doctrine. Wang Fu, the best student in the class, questions Lao Gan's ability to teach and offers to show him how.

The film's inquiry into the meaning of education locates its answers in the primitive simplicity of the students' natural surroundings. A series of shots/reverse shots show Lao Gan gazing into the distance taking in the ancient forests and natural sounds. He soon leads his class away from their obedient copying and back to their inner natures. Education becomes a process of re-connection with what is natural, what is free from the constraints of rules and regulations. Lao Gan's explanation of the term 'to live', for instance, is that 'one needs food and drink' – that is why the Chinese character for this concept includes a water radical and the word 'tongue'.

The spatial connections between classroom and landscape further signal a relation between human desire and the Taoist concept of emptiness. When Lao Gan offers to teach a cowherd how to read and write it is the cowherd who silently re-educates him, simply by being a natural man. Lao Gan is eventually asked to resign from his post because of his heterodox teaching style. His final words to his students warn of the dangers of copying, even copying from the dictionary.

Further reading

J. An (1994), a discussion of Taoist principles and Chinese landscape painting; K. Chen and T. Rayns (1989), a script of the film; R. Chow (1995: 108–41), a critique of the ideology of gender; X. Zhang (1997), an analysis of autobiographical and allegorical aspects.

(SC)

Ko Chun-hsiung

(Ke Junxiong)

b. 1943, Kaohsiung, Taiwan
Actor

Ko Chun-hsiung started acting in the early 1960s in Taiwan-dialect films and won Best Actor award several times at Asia-Pacific FF and Taipei GHA. He appeared in over 170 films, most notably *Lonely Seventeen* (1967) and ***Home, Sweet Home*** (1970, both *dir.* **Pai Ching-jui**), *Martyrs* (1974) and *Eight Hundred Heroic Soldiers* (1975, both *dir.* **Ting Shan-hsi**), and *My Grandpa* (1981).

(YZ)

Ko Yi-cheng

(Ke Yizheng)

b. 1946
Director, screen writer and actor

Ko Yi-cheng graduated from the film programme at the School of International Journalism and received an MA in Film from Columbia College in California in 1980. He returned to Taiwan and started to teach, write screenplays and act. He played various roles in such films as ***Rapeseed Woman*** (*dir.* **Wan Jen**, 1983) and ***Taipei Story*** (*dir.* Edward **Yang**, 1985). His directorial début, *Leap Frog*, the third episode in the four-part ***In Our Time*** (1982), signalled the beginning of New Taiwan Cinema. He later directed *The Child with a Sword* (1983), *I Love Mary* (1984), *Reunion* (1985), *Our Sky* (1986) and *Babies* (1991).

See also: New Taiwan Cinema (under Taiwan cinema in Historical essays)

(YZ)

Kuei-mei, a Woman

(Wo zheyang guole yisheng)

dir. **Chang Yi**
sc. Xiao Sa, Chang Yi
with Yang Huishang, Li Liqun
Taipei: CMPC, 1985

The metaphor of the suffering woman is commonly used in Taiwanese cinema to critique women's oppression under patriarchy. *Kuei-mei, a Woman*, however, glorifies women's suffering as the ultimate means of preserving family order. Kuei-mei, the protagonist, loses her fiancé during the civil war in the 1940s and follows the KMT government to Taiwan after the Communist takeover of the mainland. She later marries a widower with three children and starts a new life.

The marriage does not bring Kuei-mei happiness; on the contrary, it brings her a series of hardships. On top of raising several small stepchildren and her own twins, she has to endure her husband's adultery, gambling and alcoholism. When his affair is discovered and his gambling debts become overdue, Kuei-mei begins to take command. She finds a new job for herself and her husband in Japan and leaves her two children with relatives in Taiwan. After working hard for several years in Japan, Kuei-mei returns home with a bounty of gifts, a faithful husband, and enough money to open a restaurant of her own.

Now financially and maritally secure, Kuei-mei has to confront yet another problem, namely her pregnant stepdaughter. The determined mother drags her self-destructive stepdaughter to the abortion clinic out of her old conviction that she knows what is best for her children. As Kuei-mei approaches her sixties she begins to suffer from cancer. Awaiting death in the hospital, she has yet to put her mind at rest. When her elder son returns from Japan for a family reunion she divides her property equally among the children, proving once again that she is a caring mother. Along with **Rapeseed Woman** (*dir.* **Wan Jen**, 1983), *Kuei-mei, a Woman* is perhaps the most powerful portrait of Taiwanese women's experience. Kuei-mei's endurance over an historic period of time gives her story a truly epic sweep.

(YY)

kungfu film

A type of film that features extensive kungfu or martial arts fights.

See also: martial arts film

(YZ)

Kwan, Moon

(Guan Wenqing)

b. 1896
d. 1995, USA
Director, producer

A noted figure in early Chinese cinema, Kwan Moon grew up in Guangdong province and went to study at a college in Washington D.C. He served as Hollywood's cultural advisor before returning to China in 1920. He trained film actors and actresses in Canton and Hong Kong in addition to teaching classes in make-up. In 1933 he co-founded Grandview Film Company with Zhao Shushen in San Francisco and produced several patriotic films. He established Shanyue Film Company in 1937 and subsequently directed about fifty Cantonese films, earning the nickname 'poetic director'. He moved to the USA and lived there till his death.

See also: Cantonese cinema (under Hong Kong cinema in Historical essays)

Further reading
W. Guan (1976), a memoir.

(YZ)

Kwan, Stanley

(Guan Jinpeng)

b. 1957, Hong Kong
Director

Stanley Kwan studied mass communication at Baptist College and worked with the television station TVB before gaining precious industry experience in the early 1980s as assistant director on Ann **Hui**'s **Boat People** (1982) and *The Story of Woo Viet* (1981). With the support of actor **Chow Yun-Fat** and scriptwriter Qiu Gangjian, Kwan turned his first film, *Women* (1985), into a box-office success. An ambitious second film about the damaged emotional lives of a number of young professionals, *Love Unto Waste* (1986), was a flop, although it did demonstrate the director's ability to play with narrative expectations and to get compelling performances from a stable of talented actors. The film also attracted generous festival notices.

Kwan hit the big time with his third feature, the highly original ghost drama **Rouge** (1987). A critical and box-office success, the film won Best Film and Best Director awards at HKFA and provoked stylistic comparison with a range of Hollywood masters, such as George Cukor, Max Ophuls and Josef von Sternberg. However, a follow-up title, **Full Moon in New York** (1989), failed to consolidate Kwan's reputation, although it won a top prize at Taipei GHA. Like Mabel Cheung's An **Autumn's Tale** (1987), another account of life in New York's Chinatown, Kwan's film was taken to be an aesthetic and imaginative retreat. No such criticism pertains to Kwan's next film, however. The **Actress** (1992) is a formally innovative bio-pic about the Chinese silent film star **Ruan Lingyu**. It won numerous international awards and spellbound festival audiences with its dazzling production designs. After shooting a number of short titles which confirm Kwan's identification with female characters, the director stabilized his erratic career with the release of a sixth feature film, *Red Rose, White Rose* (1994), a melodrama based on Eileen Chang's story, as well as *Yang Yin: Gender in Chinese Cinema* (1996), a study of gender in Chinese cinema commissioned by the British Film Institute.

See also: ghosts and immortals, film of

Further reading
M. Atkinson (1996), T. Rayns (1990), two career overviews; W.M. Law (1993), with Kwan's comments on his own work.

(JS)

L

Lai, Stan

(Lai Shengchuan)

b. 1954, Washington, D.C., USA
Director

After moving to Taipei with his parents in 1966, Stan Lai returned to the USA, where he won several prizes and earned a Ph.D. in Theatre Arts from the University of California at Berkeley in 1983. He was appointed as a professor at National Taiwan College of Arts and started his distinguished career in experimental theatre, producing critically acclaimed stage plays, *We All Grew Up This Way*, *The Passers-By* (both 1984), and many others. In 1987, he turned to opera and directed *The Journey to the West*, which *Time* magazine considers to be a fantastic 'postmodern opera', replete with prototypical imagery and ancient symbolism. In 1988, Lai won the ROC's National Prize for Art and Literature for his *Peach Blossom Land* (1986), an experimental drama that creates order out of disorder by juxtaposing two disparate plays of absurd, comic and sentimental stories. His Performance Workshop soon became a centre of cultural events in Taipei, and Lai was selected as one of the ROC's 'Ten Outstanding Youths' in 1989.

Lai's film début, **Peach Blossom Land** (1993), is noted for its bold innovation and visual style. The film won him a Caligari prize at Berlin FF, a silver prize at Tokyo FF, and Best Film award at Singapore FF. His successful film début was followed by *The Red Lotus Society* (1994), another highly complex film that questions corruption, hypocrisy, and a greed for wealth and power prevalent in contemporary Taiwan society. In this regard, Lai comes close to other famous Taiwan film directors such as **Tsai Ming-liang**, **Hou Hsiao-hsien** and Edward **Yang**.

Further reading

H. Chiao (1994), an interview on his films; H. Hong and H. Yue (1992: 195–8), on Lai's theatre career; J. Kowallis (1997), on Lai and postmodernism.

(YZ)

Lam, Ringo

(Lin Lingdong)

b. 1955, Hong Kong
Director

After secondary school, Ringo Lam joined a television station training course as an actor before deciding to work as assistant producer. Dissatisfied with television, he decided in 1978 to study film at York University in Toronto for three years. He began working at Cinema City in 1981 and directed his first film when Carl **Mak** offered him *Esprit d'amour* (1983) starring **Chow Yun-Fat**. After directing *Aces Go Places, IV* (1985) Carl Mak produced Lam's breakthrough film, *City on Fire* (1987), leading to a successful collaboration with Chow on *Prison on Fire* (1987), *Wild Search* (1990), *Prison on Fire, II* (1991), and *Full Contact* (1992).

Although Lam has worked in other genres such as **romance** and **comedy**, his films of **urban life** are more pessimistic than John **Woo**'s. *City on Fire*, *Full Contact*, the historical epic *Burning Paradise* (1994), and his Hollywood début *Maximum Risk* (1996) are all characterized by a dark visual style associated with the worlds of film noir and naturalism. These films often depict doomed characters facing a hostile universe whose survival is tentative at best. While John Woo dramatizes a world torn between heroic Chinese values and rapacious capitalism, Ringo Lam's cinematic landscape presents the latter as completely victorious, casting individual survival into doubt. Lam's venture into Hong Kong cinema's familiar Shaolin Temple world in *Burning Paradise* showed that environment already contaminated by dangerous dehumanizing forces that would become more powerfully manifest in his later urban films. However, the *Prison on Fire* films present an optimistic 'better tomorrow', in terms both of the protagonist's resilience and his comradeship with mainland Chinese prisoners.

(TW)

language and film

It seems common sense that Chinese films carry standard Mandarin (or Beijing) dialogue, but back in the 1930s things were quite different. In the silent era, actors and actresses who did not speak perfect Mandarin could appear comfortably in front of the camera without worrying about their heavy accents. As sound films began to emerge in the early 1930s, however, several stars had to take lessons to learn the standard or 'national language' (*guoyu*) promoted by the KMT government. In the 1930s, under the pressures of the Shanghai industry, the government even attempted to ban Cantonese-dialect films produced in Hong Kong and Guangdong (Canton). The ban did not work, due in part to the local resistance and in part to the ensuing wars. In the 1930s–40s, Cantonese films were produced in large quantity in Hong Kong; in fact, they were far more popular than a handful of Mandarin-dialect films, and commanded a large Southeast Asian market. Hong Kong's Cantonese and Mandarin film industries developed on separate routes in the 1950s–70s, and they rarely mixed until the 1980s. Now, as a standard money-saving strategy, synchronized-sound recording is abandoned and two sets of soundtrack are regularly dubbed for most productions, while English (and sometimes Chinese) subtitles are supplied to the videotape versions.

Some sources mention the production of films in Amoy (Fukienese) and Swatow (Chaozhou) dialects in Hong Kong, but Fukienese – most familiarly known as Taiwanese – was frequently used in Taiwan in the 1950s. Although Taiwanese-dialect films declined in the 1960s–70s, the dialect was given prominent place again in New Taiwan Cinema films, especially those by **Hou Hsiao-hsien**. In their search for Taiwan identity and experience, Taiwanese dialect appears to be an important tool for many Taiwan filmmakers.

Local or provincial dialects are rarely used in mainland productions. Sometimes it sounds unreal and unnatural when minority characters speak to each other with a perfect Beijing accent in films of ethnic minorities. Until the 1980s, however, Mandarin has prevailed in the Chinese soundtrack. By the mid-1980s some filmmakers tried to achieve a higher level of realism by mixing dialect or minority language in their films, such as **Sacrificed Youth** (*dir.* **Zhang Nuanxin**) and **On the Hunting Ground** (*dir.* **Tian Zhuangzhuang**, both 1985). Since then, inclusion of dialects or heavy local accents has become more acceptable. In *The* **Story of Qiuju** (*dir.* **Zhang Yimou**, 1992) and **Ermo** (*dir.* **Zhou Xiaowen**, 1994), peasant women's heavy accent constitutes an exotic ethnic sign for urban Chinese as well as Western viewers.

Polyglot, or the mixture of several languages and dialects, in Taiwan and Hong Kong has also received critical attention. The use of Mandarin, Taiwanese, Hakka, and Shanghainese in *A* **City of Sadness** (*dir.* Hou Hsiao-hsien, 1989) conveys more acutely the sense of helplessness in local Taiwanese in their dealings with the KMT government and Shanghai businessmen in the late 1940s. The mixing of Cantonese, Mandarin (spoken alternatively with a Taiwan and a Beijing accent), Japanese and English in **Chungking Express** (*dir.* **Wong Kar-Wai**, 1994), on the other hand, symbolically marks Hong Kong as a transit place for its residents as well as its visitors.

See also: censorship and film; dubbed foreign film; ethnic minorities, film of; New Taiwan Cinema (under Taiwan cinema in Historical essays)

Further reading

T. S. Kam (1993), on Cantonese dialect as cultural resistance; Z. Xiao (1999), a discussion of the ban on Cantonese-dialect films in 1927–37.

(YZ)

Lau, Andy
(Liu Dehua)

b. 27 September 1961, Hong Kong
Actor, singer

One of the most famous singers in Hong Kong, Andy Lau attended a training programme organized by Television Broadcasts Ltd (Hong Kong) in 1981 and starred in television dramas. Since the mid-1980s he has had numerous concert performances and has released several albums, including a 1990 hit, *Can It Be Possible?*

Lau's film début was ***Boat People*** (*dir.* Ann **Hui**, 1982). Since then he has appeared in a wide variety of roles, such as a gangster in *As Tears Go By* (1988) and a cop in ***Days of Being Wild*** (1991, both *dir.* **Wong Kar-Wai**). Among his other films are *Lai Shi, China's Last Eunuch* (*dir.* Jacob Cheung, 1988), ***God of Gamblers*** (*dir.* **Wong Jing** 1989), *Zodiac Killers* (*dir.* Ann Hui, 1991), *Drunken Master, II* (*dir.* Lau Kar-leung, 1994). Diligent as he is, Lau has managed to cut down on his movie output since the mid-1990s.

Further reading

F. Dannen and B. Long (1997: 104–7), a profile with a selected filmography.

(YZ)

Law, Clara
(Luo Zhuoyao)

b. Macao, 1957
Director

One of the 'second wave' Hong Kong directors who made their feature débuts in 1988 (cf. **Wong Kar-Wai**, Lawrence Ah Mon, Alex Law), Clara Law is also among the handful of internationally respected women directors associated with the settlement's film industry (cf. Ann **Hui**, Sylvia **Chang**, Mabel Cheung). Born in Macao, trained in London, and based for many years in Kowloon, Law chose **comedy** as the subject of her first film. Although a patchy divorce farce, *The Other Half and the Other Half* (1988, scripted by her collaborator/partner Eddie Fong) explores many of the themes that dominate her later films, such as the politics of sex, migration, and identity.

Law's next film, *The **Reincarnation of Golden Lotus*** (1989), was successful domestically and distributed widely in North America. Written by Lilian Lee, its narrative moves audaciously among the worlds of ancient China, the **Cultural Revolution** and modern Hong Kong. *Farewell, China* (1990) returns to the migration thematic to tell a powerful story of a Chinese couple whose lives take a turn for the worse once they set their sights on North America, while ***Autumn Moon*** (1992) includes a formally bold use of camcorder imagery. The flatulent historical drama *The **Temptation of a Monk*** (1993) came next. However, after

providing a short entry for the feminist portmanteau film *Erotique* (1994), Law returned to the fuller exploration of cultural movement with *Floating Life* (1996), a story of Asian displacement set in Australia, where Law and her family now live.

Further reading

S. Fore (1993), on the politics of melodrama in *The Reincarnation of Golden Lotus*; T.S. Kam *et al.* (1994–5), an interview.

(JS)

Lee, Ang
(Li An)

b. 1954, Taipei
Director, screen writer

One of the first Chinese-born directors to achieve fame in both Asia and the West, Ang Lee graduated from National Taiwan College of Arts in 1975 and studied drama directing at University of Illinois and film production at the New York University. After winning awards for his student work in 1985, he spent six years writing screenplays before getting the chance to direct *Pushing Hands* (1991). A study of interracial marriage and the generation gap in a Chinese American **family**, this Taiwan production won him the awards of Best Director at Taipei GHA and Best Film at Asia-Pacific FF. *The **Wedding Banquet*** (1992), a hilarious **comedy** about the triangular relationship between a gay couple (Taiwanese and American) and a mainland Chinese woman in the USA, secured Lee's international reputation when it received the Golden Lion at Berlin FF and earned large box-office profits in the West. His next feature, ***Eat Drink Man Woman*** (1994), a mix of comic and serious reflections on life, was nominated for Best Foreign Film award at the Oscars. These three films constitute Lee's 'Father knows best' trilogy, which examines from a humanist perspective the conflict between traditional Chinese and modern Western values in an urban setting. With a reputation for making quality commercial films, Lee entered Hollywood and directed *Sense and Sensibility* (1995) for Columbia, winning the Golden Bear at the 1996 Berlin FF. The film features an entirely Western cast and won an Oscar for Best Screenplay Adaptation. He proceeded to *The Ice Storm* (1997), a 20th Century Fox production about life on the US East Coast. Lee was voted 1995 Best Director by the American Film Critics Association.

Further reading

CMPC (1994), the script of *Eat Drink Man Woman* with an interview; W.M. Dariotis and E. Fung (1997), on Lee's images of Chinese diasporas; D. Lee (1994), a profile with an interview.

(YZ)

Lee, Bruce
(Li Xiaolong)

b. 1940, San Francisco, USA
d. 1973
Actor, director

An internationally known martial arts expert, Bruce Lee was born into a Chinese family and grew up in Hong Kong, where he appeared as a child actor in several films. After studying philosophy at the University of Washington, he starred in numerous American TV shows, including *Batman* and *Green Hornet*. He opened a training centre and taught his own branch of martial arts. In the early 1970s, he became a popular action star in Hong Kong kungfu films and enjoyed a worldwide reputation. He died shortly after writing and directing **Return of the Dragon** (1973). His other notable films include *The Big Boss* (1971) and *The Chinese Connection* (1972). He died suddenly while filming **Game of Death**, which was completed using added footage and released posthumously in 1978.

See also: martial arts film

Further reading

A. B. Block (1974), a book-length study; H. Chiao (1981), on his influence on kungfu film; C. Zhu (1995), a biography.

(YZ)

Lee, Danny
(Lee Sau-yin, Li Xiuxian)

b. 1954, Hong Kong
Actor, producer, director

Danny Lee began as a contract player at Shaw Brothers in 1971. Between then and 1978 he appeared in over forty swordplay roles, as well as

Plate 22   *The Big Boss* (1971)

such films as *Inframan* (1976) and *King Ape* (1975). He continued to act after leaving Shaw Brothers and began directing in 1979. In 1984, he won the Best Actor Awards in Hong Kong and Taiwan for *The Law with Two Phases* (Gongpu), which he also wrote and directed. This film established Lee's 'cop' image and cemented his reputation as an expert director of gangster films. He formed his own successful production and distribution company, Magnum Films, in 1989.

Lee's name became well-known to Western viewers when he appeared in John **Woo**'s landmark *The **Killer*** (1989) as the deeply conflicted and emotional police inspector who finds friendship with **Chow Yun-Fat**'s contract killer. But Lee is more than an accomplished Hong Kong character actor; his performances have matured, becoming more subtle and emotionally effective. He has been able to lend an unexpected individual dimension to the normally stereotypical roles of policeman and gangster, notably in Ringo **Lam**'s 1987 film *City on Fire*. Lee has the distinction of having played more variations on the cop role than just about any other Asian or Western actor, and he has done so with intelligence, conviction, and a special magnetism. His directing, too, is often quite effective and nicely stylized, for example in *Twist* (1995).

See also: gangster film

(KH)

Lee Hsing

(Li Xing)

b. 1930
Director, screen writer

An important director in the formative years of Taiwan cinema, Lee Hsing graduated from the Education Department at Taiwan Normal University and started directing Taiwanese dialect films in the late 1950s. In the 1960s he became famous for his works of 'wholesome realism' (*jiankang xieshi zhuyi*), such as *Head of Street, End of Lane* (1963), *Oyster Girl* and *Beautiful Duckling* (both 1964). His other notable works include *The Silent Wife* (1965), winner of Best Screenplay award at Asia-Pacific FF; *Execution in Autumn* (1972), winner of Best Film and Best Director awards at Taipei GHA; *A Boat in the Ocean* (1978), winner of Best Director award at Asia-Pacific FF; and *Good Morning, Taipei* (1979), which featured **Hou**

Hsiao-hsien as screen writer and **Chen Kun-hou** as cinematographer. By the mid-1990s, Lee had directed forty-nine feature films and two documentaries, most of which promote traditional **family** values and feature good father figures. In 1990 he served as chair of the executive committee of Taipei GHA.

See also: documentary

Further reading
R. Huang (1994: 389–91), a brief entry.

(YZ)

Lee Tsu Yung

(Li Zuyong)

b. 1903
d. 1959
Producer

A wealthy Shanghai businessman, Lee Tsu Yung started out in the film business in partnership with Chang Shin-Kuan, who owned such companies as Far East, Great Wall and New Xinhua in the postwar period. They established Yonghua Company in Hong Kong and produced many quality films, like *The Cremation* (*dir.* **Zhang Junxiang**, 1948) and *Sorrows of the Forbidden City* (*dir.* **Zhu Shilin**, 1948). Unfortunately, Yonghua was plagued by bad luck, including fire and numerous financial problems. By the early 1950s, it increasingly had to depend on the International Film Distribution Company for financial support.

(YZ)

leftist film

See under: Chinese cinema (in Historical essays)

Legend of Tianyun Mountain, The

(Tianyunshan chuanqi)

dir. **Xie Jin**
sc. Lu Yanzhou
with Shi Weijian, Zhong Xinghuo, Wang Fuli, Hong Xuemin
Shanghai: Shanghai Film, 1980

This is one of the first films to deal with the injustices of the anti-Rightist campaign of the late 1950s. In Xie Jin's typical fashion, the complex historical issues are presented in personal terms of love, jealousy, revenge and human weakness.

Two female college graduates, Song Wei and Feng Qinglan, take part in a scientific expedition. Song and the expedition team leader, Luo Qun, fall in love. Song joins the CCP and is transferred to a party cadre school. Yet just as the two are about to get married, the Anti-Rightist Campaign starts up and Luo is labelled a Rightist. Under political pressure, Song breaks her engagement with Luo and marries Wu Yao, who is in charge of the campaign. Luo is sentenced to a life of hard labour in a remote village.

Feng has long had a secret crush on Luo. Now that Luo has fallen from his pedestal, Feng comes to stay with him and, against all opposition, marries him. The two live through many years of hardship until the end of the **Cultural Revolution**. Now both Song and her husband serve as high-ranking party officials in the district where Luo is serving his sentence. While Song attempts to rectify the wrongs committed against Luo in the 1950s, Wu opposes the move, which leads to their divorce. Eventually, through Song's efforts, Luo is cleared of all false charges. But Feng does not live long enough to share the news with him. When Song comes to visit Luo, she sees Luo in silent mourning in front of Feng's tomb.

In 1980 the film was granted awards of Best Film and Best Director at China GRA; Best Film at HFA; Best Film from the Ministry of Culture; and Best Film at the 1982 HKFA.

(ZX)

legends and myths

Legends and myths in traditional Chinese oral and written narratives provide Chinese filmmakers with a rich source of original stories. In several film genres, legends and myths appear in large numbers. In the mid-1920s, many martial arts films surprised audiences with their cinematic representations of legendary heroes and heroines. With special film techniques, these films made kungfu experts literally fly in the air and travel on clouds. So popular was the genre at the time that *The **Burning of Red Lotus Temple*** (*dir.* **Zhang Shichuan**, 1928) ran up to eighteen parts by 1931. The second wave of martial arts films came in the early 1940s in occupied Shanghai, and after that Hong Kong became a major production site for the genre, exporting its products to Taiwan,

Southeast Asia and the West. The legendary Wong Fei-hung (Huang Feihong), for instance, appeared and reappeared in Hong Kong films. Among the most famous recent titles are ***Once Upon a Time in China*** (*dir.* **Tsui Hark**, 1991) and its sequels.

Among other genres that frequently draw from traditional Chinese legends and myths are films of ghosts and immortals, films of ethnic minorities, and **animation** films. The original stories of ***Third Sister Liu*** (*dir.* Su Li, 1960), *Ashma* (*dir.* **Liu Qiong**, 1964) and *Effendi* (*dir.* Xiao Lang, 1980), for example, are drawn from folktales and local legends, and they all demonstrate folk wisdom that appears so endearing to general audiences nationwide. The same is true for many animation titles, such as ***Princess Iron Fan*** (*dir.* **Wan Laiming**, Wan Guchan, 1941), *Zhu Bajie Eats the Watermelon* (*dir.* Wan Guchan, Chen Zhenghong, 1958), *Nezha Conquers the Dragon King* (*dir.* Wang Shuchen, Yan Dingxian, Xu Jingda, 1979) and *Fire Boy* (*dir.* Wang Borong, 1984).

See also: ethnic minorities, film of; ghosts and immortals, film of; kungfu film

(YZ)

Letter with Feather

(Jimao xin)

dir. **Shi Hui**
sc. **Zhang Junxiang**
with Cai Yuanyuan, Jiang Rui, Tian Long, Shu Shi, Zhou Boxun
Shanghai: Shanghai Film, 1954

This children's **war film** glorifies the patriotism of a teenage boy during the war with Japan. The protagonist's heroic deeds are meant as an example for Chinese youth to follow.

Haiwa is a twelve-year-old boy whose father is a guerrilla leader. One day, Haiwa takes an urgent letter to an Eighth Route Army unit. The importance of the letter is indicated by the three feathers attached to it. So, as a cover, Haiwa pretends to be a shepherd. A Japanese patrol catches him, but he has cleverly hidden the letter under a sheep's tail. As the Japanese slaughter Haiwa's sheep, he manages to save the one with the letter. During the night, he sneaks away from the enemy's camp while the Japanese soldiers are sleeping, but in the process of retrieving the letter, he falls into Japanese hands again. The Japanese want him to work as their guide. Haiwa takes advantage of the opportunity and brings them to a wrong location where the Eighth Route Army ambush the Japanese and have Haiwa rescued. With the information provided in the letter Haiwa brings, the Chinese soldiers knock off an enemy block house and capture the Japanese commander.

The film received Best Film Award at the 1955 Edinburgh FF as well as a prize from the Ministry of Culture in 1957.

See also: children's film

(ZX)

Leung, Tony Kar-Fei

(Liang Jiahui)

b. 1958
Actor

A popular Hong Kong film actor, Tony Kar-Fei Leung won Best Actor award at HKFA for his role in ***Reign Behind a Curtain*** (*dir.* **Li Han-hsiang**, 1983). He has appeared in *The **Burning of the Imperial Palace*** (*dir.* Li Han-hsiang, 1983), *Prison on Fire* (*dir.* Ringo **Lam**, 1987), *The **Actress*** (*dir.* Stanley **Kwan**, 1992) and numerous other films.

He should be distinguished from another popular Hong Kong actor, Tony Chiu-Wai Leung (Liang Chaowei), who has appeared in titles such as *A Bullet in the Head* (1989), *Hard Boiled* (1992, both *dir.* John **Woo**) and ***Chungking Express*** (*dir.* **Wong Kar-Wai**, 1994).

(YZ)

Li Beihai

(Lai Pak-hoi)

b. 1889
d. 1950
Director, actor, producer

Li Beihai played in the first Hong Kong short feature, *Stealing the Roast Duck* (*dir.* Liang Shaobo, 1909), an Asia Films production. With his brother **Li Minwei** he directed ***Zhuangzi Tests His Wife*** (1913) for their own Huamei Company. When Minxin Company was organized, Li Beihai directed *Rouge* (1925), the first feature length film from Hong Kong. In 1930 he managed the Hong Kong branch of Lianhua Film Company for **Luo**

Mingyou. In 1933 he established Zhonghua Company and directed Hong Kong's first partial-sound film, *Conscience*, and full-sound film *An Idiot Disturbs the House*. He left the film industry in 1935 after directing a number of other titles.

(YZ)

Li Chenfeng

(Lee Sun-fung)

b. 10 April 1909, Guangdong province
d. 21 May 1985
Director, screen writer

A well-known Cantonese film director, Li Chenfeng worked in his teens as a ticket collector in a movie house in Guangzhou (Canton). In 1929, he was enrolled in a theatre school attached to Guangdong Theatre Institute. His stage activities began in 1931 when, together with two friends, he formed a theatre group called 'Times Theatre'. In 1937 he co-authored a screenplay. After other successful screenplays, he started his prolific directing career with a Cantonese film, *Waiting for the Moon* (1949). By 1978, he had helmed approximately eighty Cantonese films, eight Mandarin films and ten films in Swatau dialect. His representative works include *Spring* (1953), *Cold Night* (1955), *A Loner in the Crowds* (1960) and *Miss Su* (1962).

See also: Cantonese cinema (under Hong Kong cinema in Historical essays)

(ZX, YZ)

Li Han-hsiang

(Li Hanxiang)

b. 18 April 1926
d. 1996, Beijing
Director

One of the most prolific and legendary of Chinese directors, Li Han-hsiang studied Western painting at Beiping National Art Institute and left the mainland for Hong Kong in 1949. He did various odd jobs for Lee Tsu Yung's Yonghua Company before serving as assistant on *Cui Cui* (*dir.* Yan Jun, 1952). After his directorial début in 1954, Li rapidly became a leading director at Shaw Brothers and made several award-winning films renowned for their authentic sets and elaborate *mise-en-scène*. His film adaptations of Huanmeidiao opera were popular in Hong Kong and won him a Best Director award at Asia-Pacific FF. The **costume drama** *The Love Eterne* (1963) was based on a classical Chinese love story and received, among others, Best Film, Best Director and Best Actress awards at Taipei GHA.

In 1963 Li broke away from Shaw Brothers to establish Guolian Film Company in Taiwan. He directed big-budget films such as *The Story of Xi Shi, I–II* (1965–6), which broke Taiwan's box-office record for domestic features and won him Best Film and Best Director at Taipei GHA. His high profile on the island encouraged private film companies and local talent and gradually turned Taiwanese cinema away from heavy-handed political indoctrination. Mismanagement, however, soon left Li bankrupt and he returned to Hong Kong to direct comedies and soft-porn films such as *The Warlord* (1972) and *Golden Vase Beauties* (1974).

In 1982, he travelled to Beijing and directed two co-productions, *The **Burning of the Imperial Palace*** and ***Reign Behind a Curtain*** (both 1983). Both films proved immensely popular in Hong Kong and the mainland and returned Li to his favourite subject – historical stories centred on imperial court intrigues, as in *The Empress Dowager, I–III* (1988–9). Li died while directing a film in Beijing in 1996, thus ending one of the most remarkable careers in the history of Chinese cinema. All Li's major works are melodramas with strong sensual and visual appeal. His complicated relationships with the governments of Hong Kong, Taiwan and the mainland illustrate the complexity of links between filmmaking and politics in contemporary China.

See also: adaptations of drama and literature; comedy; historical film; melodrama

Further reading
W. Bao (1983), on Li's two costume dramas; H. Chiao (1987: 85–9), a brief discussion; H. Chiao (1993a), a book on Li Han-hsiang and his Taiwan company; H. Li (1984), a three-volume memoir.

(YZ)

Li, Jet
(Li Lianjie)

b. 1963, Beijing
Actor

A popular **kungfu film** actor, Jet Li was known as Li Lianjie when he won the national championship at the age of eight in mainland China, a title he held for five consecutive years. His screen début was *Shaolin Temple* (*dir.* Zhang Xinyan,

Plate 23   *Shaolin Temple* (1982)

1982). He moved to Hong Kong and starred in numerous martial arts films, including **Once Upon a Time in China** (*dir.* **Tsui Hark**, 1991), **Fong Sai Yuk** (*dir.* Yuan Kui) and *The Tai-chi Master* (*dir.* Yuan Heping, both 1993). Li's best screen roles are those of legendary heroes of **masculinity** and moral integrity who rescue suffering victims and defeat evil victimizers (foreign as well as domestic). By contrast, his contemporary roles, as in *The Bodyguard from Beijing* (*dir.* Yuan Kui, 1994), are not generally successful. In the mid-1990s, Li started playing in Hollywood films, one of them being *Black Mask* (1997).

See also: martial arts film

(YZ)

Li Jun

b. 1922, Shanxi province
Director

A noted mainland director of the 1960s–70s, Li Jun went to Yan'an in 1938 and worked for various CCP propaganda offices and military units. On the basis of directing a successful play in 1951, Li was transferred to August First Film Studio. After making a number of documentaries, Li began directing feature films in 1959. His **Serfs** (1963) exhibits a remarkable aesthetic realism and won a Golden Eagle award at the 1981 Manila FF. During the **Cultural Revolution**, Li co-directed **Sparkling Red Star** (1974) with Li Ang. Despite its heavy political message, the film was beautifully crafted.

One of Li's best post-Cultural Revolution films is *The Call of the Front* (1979), the story of a wounded soldier's love affair with the peasant woman who cares for him. Its dramatic tensions centre on the soldier's conflicting needs; he wants to stay with the woman but also yearns to return to the battlefield. The film was critically acclaimed for its psychological insights. It won Best Film award from the Ministry of Culture in 1979 and was voted one of the ten best Chinese films by the 1982 HKFA.

See also: documentary

Further reading
ZDX (1982–6: 5: 210–6), a short biography.

(ZX)

Li Lianying: The Imperial Eunuch
(Da taijian Li Lianying)

dir. **Tian Zhuangzhuang**
sc. Guo Tianxiang
with **Jiang Wen**, **Liu Xiaoqing**
Beijing: Beijing Film/Hong Kong: Skai Film, 1991

While Bernardo Bertolucci's *The Last Emperor* (1987) transforms the Forbidden City in Beijing into an historical spectacle for an international audience, Tian's *Li Lianying* offers a portrayal of the Empress Dowager Cixi and the famous eunuch Li Lianying. Characterization is given precedence over the presentation of history. Although viewers might feel narratively confused about certain events, marvellous acting well conveys the Empress's power and the eunuch's servility.

The film describes how the Qing Empire was fragmented under a female ruler. Cixi approaches national affairs as she does family business. In 1885, when the newly established Chinese navy faces serious challenges from the Western forces, she appropriates military expenditure by sending Li to build her a summer palace. Not satisfied with Li's performance, she abruptly removes him from his post. Her message is clear: if someone brings her a moment's unease, she will respond with a lifetime punishment.

The 1890s see China caught between ancient tradition and Western influence. China's ambiguous response to modernity is ironically suggested by Cixi's interest in, and ignorance of, Western practices. In one scene a group of young eunuchs dressed in Chinese robes and with long braids hanging down their necks perform ballroom dancing and the tango. In another scene, a Western violinist performs while Cixi asks the musician what a violin is.

In 1898, the goal of remaining Chinese while still adopting certain Western practices moves the Qing court in the direction of reform. Two intellectuals, Kang Youwei and Liang Qichao, submit proposals to Emperor Guangxu, an idealistic youth. But Cixi confines Guangxu to the palace and executes the radicals. At Guangxu's behest, Li is willing to risk his life to help the Emperor meet his beloved princess. Cixi later orders Li to throw the princess, who is three months pregnant with the Emperor's child, down a well.

In 1900, foreign invasions and internal chaos force Cixi to flee for her life from Beijing. The film doesn't dwell so much on national upheavals as on Cixi's interaction with common people during her escape. At a large family residence, the Empress and an old granny enjoy a conversation together. Before she dies in the palace in 1909, Cixi is carried on Li's back and dreams that the granny is her mother.

The complex figures of Cixi and Li cast shadows on numerous rulers in China's history. In the relation between the Empress and her eunuch we see the fallen, rotten fruit of a patriarchal, imperial system.

(SC)

Li Lihua

b. 17 July 1924, Shanghai
Actress

Daughter of Li Guifang, a famed actress of Peking opera, Li Lihua began her film career in Japanese-occupied Shanghai and attracted public attention for her performance in a Guohua production, *Tang Bohu Picks Qiuxiang* (*dir.* Yue Feng, 1940). In the post-war period, she starred in Wenhua's **comedy Phony Phoenixes** (*dir.* Cao Lin, 1947) and other films before moving to Hong Kong. She

Plate 24   Li Lihua, a Hong Kong star

was frequently cast in films produced by Great Wall, Longma, Yonghua and Shaw Brothers, and became the best-known actress in the 1950s–60s. She won Best Actress award twice at Taipei GHA for *Between Tears and Smiles* (*dir.* **Zhu Shilin**, 1964) and *Storms over the Yangtze River* (*dir.* **Li Han-hsiang**, 1969), and once at Asia-Pacific FF for *Famed Forever* (*dir.* Yan Jun, 1964). Of the more than 120 films in which she appeared, *The* **Fate of Lee Khan** (*dir.* King **Hu**, 1973) may be most familiar to Western audiences.

Further reading

L. Li (1969), a memoir.

(YZ)

Li Lili

(Qian Zhenzhen)

b. 2 June 1915, Tongcheng, Anhui province
Actress

Li Lili first appeared in film at age eleven when she starred with her mother and uncle in *Invisible Swordsman* (*dir.* Qian Zhuangfei, 1926). The film was written and directed by Li's father, an underground Communist. When the Nationalists purged the Communists in 1927, Li's father fled Shanghai. Li was adopted by the owner of a dance troupe, Li Jinhui, and changed her name to Li Lili.

As one of the most popular film stars of the 1930s, Li's appeal was, so some critics claim, based on her **sexuality**. She was sometimes dubbed the Chinese Mae West. Certainly her movie roles accentuate her sensuality. In *Revenge by the Volcano* (*dir.* **Sun Yu**, 1932), she played a good-hearted dancer working in a club frequented by sailors. In **Daybreak** (*dir.* Sun Yu, 1932), she played a pro-revolution prostitute. She wears shorts for most of the duration of **Queen of Sports** (*dir.* Sun Yu, 1934). Interestingly, most of these films were written and directed by leftist filmmakers.

After Shanghai fell to the Japanese in 1937, Li transferred to Wuhan and starred in *The Patriotic Family* (*dir.* Yuan Congmei, 1938), a China Film Company production. She also travelled to Hong Kong to appear in **Orphan Island Paradise** (*dir.* **Cai Chusheng**, 1939). During the filming of **Storm on the Border** (*dir.* **Ying Yunwei**, 1940), Li visited Yan'an, the site of the wartime Communist headquarters. Li starred in two more films on resistance themes, *To Die a Heroic Death* (*dir.* He Feiguang, 1943) and *Blood on the Cherry* (1944).

After 1949 Li was employed by Beijing Film Studio and starred in ***Capture Mount Hua by Stratagem*** (*dir.* Guo Wei, 1953). She studied film acting at BFA, and has been teaching in the Acting Department there since her graduation.

Further reading

ZDX (1982–6: 2: 355–62), a short biography.

(ZX)

Li Minwei

(Lai Man-wai)

b. 1893, Japan
d. 1953, Hong Kong
Producer, director, actor

One of the founding fathers of Chinese cinema, Li Minwei spent most of his life in Hong Kong, where he bought his first camera at the age of fourteen. He was a member of Sun Yat-sen's revolutionary society in the 1900s and came to believe in the potential of theatre to raise the consciousness of the masses. He formed a drama group and staged plays with revolutionary messages.

Li produced his first film, ***Zhuangzi Tests His Wife*** (*dir.* **Li Beihai**, 1913) for Huamei (literally 'China-America'), the first film company in Hong Kong jointly owned by the Americans Mr Brodsky and Mr Vanvezer. Li Minwei wrote the script and acted with his wife, Yan Shanshan (1896–1952), who subsequently became the first film actress in China. In 1921, he formed Minxin (literally 'new people') Film Company in Hong Kong and produced many documentaries, including some about Sun Yat-sen, which, unfortunately, have not survived the ensuing war years. Li's first attempt at feature film production fell flat after his application for a licence to expand his studio was denied by the British authorities on the grounds that Li was connected to the revolutionaries.

Li moved his studio to Shanghai and made his first feature, *Rouge* (1925). The cast for this film consisted mainly of his own family members: Li himself also starred. The film was shown in Hong Kong for one week and earned some profits. Li expanded his Minxin business to Shanghai in the mid-1920s, employing directors **Bu Wancang**,

Ouyang Yuqian and **Hou Yao** in the process. In addition to overseeing production, Li also ran a film school in 1928. His negotiations with **Luo Mingyou** resulted in the founding of Lianhua Film Company, with Li himself serving as manager of one of the three company branches. By 1936, Luo Mingyou had lost control of Lianhua and was pressured into forsaking his managerial interests. Li then resigned from his own post at the studio in support of his colleague.

After the Sino-Japanese war broke out, Li returned to Hong Kong and reorganized Minxin Film Company and Minxin Theatre. Although his work was interrupted by the Japanese occupation of Hong Kong between 1941 and 1945, he resumed his business in Hong Kong after the war and then joined Yonghua Film Company in 1947.

See also: documentary; theatre and film

Further reading

M. Li (1993), a brief recollection; ZDX (1982–6: 1: 327–33), a short biography.

(ZX, YZ)

Li Pingqian

(Li Chunshou)

b. 1902, Hangzhou, Zhejiang province
d. 18 November 1984
Director, screen writer

Li Pingqian was one of the most prolific film directors in China. He studied sociology at Hujiang University, but left school in 1919 without completing his studies. Li attended a film school run by Mingxing Film Company in 1920 and, upon graduation, worked as an assistant cinematographer. He co-founded Shenzhou Film Company with Wang Xuchang in 1924 and starred in *You Can't Look Back* (*dir.* Qiu Qixiang, 1924). Li's directing début was *The Sister* (1926). In 1927, after his company went bankrupt, Li joined Tianyi Film Company. When he joined Mingxing Film Company in 1932, Li had already made several dozen films. His directing talents were further exhibited in his Mingxing films, *Children of Our Time* and *The Year of Harvest* (both 1933). Clearly, Li was one of the most in-demand film directors of the 1930s.

Japanese bombing destroyed Mingxing Film Company in 1937. Like other studio employees, Li had to be on the constant lookout for new jobs, and he subsequently found wartime work at Yihua, Xinhua, Huaxin, Huacheng, United China (Huaying) and China United Film (Zhonglian). After directing a few films for Cathay and Wenhua companies in the late 1940s, Li moved to Hong Kong and began making Cantonese films for Yonghua, Great Wall and other companies in the 1950s–60s. His total film output exceeds 100 titles.

(ZX)

Li Shaohong

b. July 1955, Suzhou, Jiangsu province
Director

A female director from the **Fifth Generation**, Li Shaohong attracted critical attention with her controversial ***Bloody Morning*** (1990), a seemingly clinical but emotionally torturing analysis of tribal relationships and blood revenge in a remote mountain village. Completed a year after the Tiananmen Incident, the film contains a graphic scene where two peasants butcher a schoolteacher in front of a nonchalant crowd in broad daylight. It was banned from export until 1992, when it was screened at the Montreal and other film festivals and won a Golden Balloon at Nantes.

Li Shaohong joined the army in December 1969 at age fourteen and studied in the Directing Department at BFA between 1978 and 1982. She worked as assistant director for three years and waited three more years before directing her first assignment at Beijing Film Studio, *The Silver Snake Murder Case* (1988). This controversial **detective film** contains terrifying scenes and was reportedly the first to be designated 'adult only' due to its violence. However, it was a huge commercial success with 198 prints sold, the second highest record for Beijing Studio. In spite of the ban on her equally violent *Bloody Morning*, Li proceeded with ***Family Portrait*** (1992), an **art film** financed by Taiwan's Era International to test the mainland market. With remarkable psychological insight, this film depicts a father confused and 'lost' in the midst of modern **urban life**. It was initially released in a run of only forty-seven prints but won the critics' award for best film at Locarno FF. Li Shaohong purchased the right to Su Tong's novel and directed ***Blush*** (1994), a cinematic study of **prostitution** reform in the mainland, which won a Silver Lion at Berlin FF. In 1996, Li

was reportedly working on a twenty-episode TV series, *Thunderstorm*, an adaptation of Cao Yu's famous play.

Li Shaohong's mother used to be a film director; her husband, Zeng Nieping, serves as cinematographer on all her films. She admires Chinese films of the 1930s–40s and likes directors such as David Lynch and Kurosawa Akira.

See also: adaptations of drama and literature

Further reading
K. Eder and D. Rossell (1993: 99–103), with an interview; B. Reynaud (1994–5), a biographical sketch; D. Zhang (1993), an informative biography.

(YZ)

Li Shizhen
(Li Shizhen)

dir. **Shen Fu**
sc. Zhang Huijian
with **Zhao Dan**, Shu Shi, Gu Yelu, Zhong Xinghuo, Shu Xiuwen
Shanghai: Shanghai Film, 1956

This **biography** film is based on the life of the real historical figure Li Shizhen. The story focuses on the social injustices suffered by Li as well as the difficulties he overcame in writing the famous *Encyclopedia of Herbs*. Implicit in the narrative are criticisms of the old 'feudal' society.

Li Shizhen is a highly respected doctor in the Ming Dynasty. At one time he saves the life of a prince. When asked what he would like to have as a reward, Li requests that he be allowed to revise the *Encyclopedia of Herbs*, but after the request is rejected by the emperor, Li decided to go back to his home village to work on the project by himself. Although the local gentry are cynical about his efforts, the villagers support him. Li and his student, Pang Xian, climb numerous mountains and classify hundreds of herbs. During one of these investigative journeys, Li meets a man named Wei and the two become good friends. One day, Wei falls off a cliff in an attempt to save Li's notebook. Li refuses to be discouraged by the tragedy and finally manages to complete the project after thirty years of perseverance.

(ZX)

Li Shuangshuang

(Li Shuangshuang)

dir. Lu Ren
sc. Li Zhun
with **Zhang Ruifang**, Zhong Xinghuo, Zhang Wenrong, Zhao Shuying
Shanghai: Haiyan Film, 1962

In this film about social changes in socialist China, Li Shuangshuang is elected the leader of women's team because of her ability and her sense of fairness. Her husband, Xiwang, does not like to get involved in public affairs, but Li reveals to the villagers that Xiwang is a good book-keeper. As a result, Xiwang is appointed the village accountant. Reluctant to offend his friends, Xiwang credits Jin and Sun more than they deserve. Li finds out about this and criticizes Xiwang publicly. Greatly embarrassed, Xiwang leaves home and goes to work in the transportation team.

Sun's daughter, Guiying, is in love with a man of her village, Erchun. But her parents have promised her to a man from the city. In desperation, Guiying asks Li for help. Li is sympathetic and goes to tell the man from the city that Guiying is already engaged. Upset by Li's interference, Guiying's parents accuse her and make a scene in front of Li's home. Xiwang happens to come home at that moment. He does not like Li getting involved in other people's business and leaves home again to show his unhappiness. But Li is supported by the rest of the villagers. Because of her able leadership, they have a good harvest that year. Xiwang has a change of heart and comes home to apologize to his wife. Incidentally, he reveals that Sun and Jin are engaged in illegal activities. Li immediately criticizes him for not stopping them. Upon hearing this, Xiwang walks out of the house again. But to Li's delight, this time he stands up against them and criticizes their wrongdoing.

The film received the awards of Best Film, Best Screenplay and Best Actress (Zhang Ruifang) at the 1963 HFA.

Further reading

C. Berry (1991b), a discussion of sexual difference and the viewing subject.

(ZX)

Liang Shanbo and Zhu Yingtai

(Liang Shanbo yu Zhu Yingtai)

dir. **Sang Hu**, Hu Sha
sc. Xu Jin, Sang Hu
with Yuan Xuefen, Fan Ruijuan, Zhang Guifeng
Shanghai: Shanghai Film, 1954

This adaptation of a Chinese opera is based on a well-known legend about two lovers whose romantic yearning for each other is thwarted by the 'feudal' custom of arranged marriage.

The daughter of a gentry family, Zhu Yingtai, is determined to go to school just as men do. She disguises herself as a man and goes to Hangzhou. On her way there, she meets a young man named Liang Shanbo and takes an instant liking to him. The two become good friends and study together for the next three years. Zhu gradually falls in love with Liang, but Liang remains unaware that Zhu is a woman. Zhu's father urges her to go home and she reluctantly says good-bye to Liang. She gives him hints that should make him realize the truth about her, but Liang doesn't pick them up. Only after she has left does Liang learn from the wife of their tutor that Zhu is a woman and that she is in love with him. Liang immediately goes to Zhu's home to propose, but Zhu's father has already engaged his daughter to a man from another family. Liang and Zhu meet again in great sadness: not long afterwards, Liang dies of depression. Upon hearing this news, Zhu decides to commit suicide. On her way to her wedding ceremony, Zhu stops by Liang's tomb and mourns his death. Suddenly, a clap of thunder explodes and the tomb opens up. As soon as Zhu jumps in it closes once again. The thunder ceases. A rainbow appears in the sky. Liang and Zhu turn into a pair of butterflies dancing among the flowers.

The film received an award for musicals at the 1954 Karlovy Vary FF and an award at the 1955 Edinburgh FF, as well as Best Film from the Ministry of Culture in 1957. It exerted a great impact on opera movies in Hong Kong during the 1960s.

See also: filmed stage performances; legends and myths; love and marriage; musical, the

(ZX)

Lianhua Symphony

(Lianhua jiaoxiang qu)

Eight episodes:
(1) *dir.* **Situ Huimin**, *sc.* **Cai Chusheng**
dir./sc. (2) **Fei Mu**; (3) Tan Youliu; (4) **Shen Fu**;
(5) He Mengfu; (6) **Zhu Shilin**; (7) **Sun Yu**; (8)
Cai Chusheng
with (1) Mei Xi; (2) Li Zhuozhuo, **Chen
Yanyan**; (3) **Zheng Junli**, Bai Lu; (4) Liu
Jiqun, Han Lan'gen, Yin Xiucen; (5) Li Qing; (6)
Li Lili; (7) Shang Guanwu; (8) Wang Cilong
Shanghai: Lianhua Film, 1937

This omnibus film includes eight episodes which
deal with social iniquities and the resistance
against the Japanese. In (1) 'Two Dimes'
(Liangmao qian), a poor man is condemned to
eight years in prison because he has transported
some illegal goods on his wheelbarrow in order
to earn two dimes. In (4) 'Three Men's Destiny'
(Sanren xing), three good-hearted ex-convicts are
sent back to prison again immediately after their
release because they take responsibility for the
death of a man killed by his abused wife. In (6)
'Ghosts' (Gui), a young peasant girl who fears
ghosts realizes the danger she faces comes from
evil people not imaginary spirits. In (5) 'A Scene
Under the Moon' (Yuexia xiaojing), a young man
who fled Manchuria after the Japanese invasion
comes to Shanghai to look for his father, fails to
find him, and becomes a thief. One night he tries
to rob the jewellery shop where his father works
as a custodian, but after this brief and accidental
reunion, the son is arrested and taken away.

The remaining episodes present allegories of
the resistance against the Japanese and their
collaborators. In (2) 'Spring Boudoir's Dreams'
(Chungui duanmeng), two girls dream that an evil
spirit burns a leaf of Chinese flowering crab-apple
(*haitang*) and then tries to attack them, but they
react bravely and shoot him. In (3) 'A Stranger'
(Mosheng ren), a greedy old man helps a bandit
who turns out to be the murderer of the old man's
son. When he realizes this, he burns his money
and joins other villagers in their pursuit of the
bandit. In (7) 'Hallucinations of a Crazy Man'
(Fengren kuangxiang qu), a poor farmer is locked
up in a mental hospital when he tries to fight his
oppressors. In (8) 'The Five Little Ones' (Xiao
wuyi), Li is cheated by He, who pretends to be his
friend. He connives to make Li's five children fight
amongst themselves and finally kidnaps Li's

youngest daughter. The children finally realize
He's evil nature and, joining up with a number of
other children, manage to free their little sister.
The villain is beaten up, thrown into the river, and
kicked out of the community by this symbolic,
miniature mass movement.

Lianhua Symphony is an interesting experiment
which gave Lianhua's promising young directors
a good chance to display their talents.

(PV)

Life

(Rensheng)

dir. **Wu Tianming**
sc. Lu Yao
with Zhou Lijing, Wu Yufang, Gao Baocheng,
Qiao Jianhua
Xi'an: Xi'an Film, 1984

In this typical film about **rural life**, a young
man's search for a better life becomes entwined
with his romantic involvement with two women:
one modern and the other traditional. In the end,
he loses both.

A young rural school teacher, Gao Jialin, has
to give up his decent teaching job and work as
a farmer because a corrupt local party official
has managed to replace Gao with his own son.
Qiaozhen, the village beauty queen, tries to
comfort him. Events soon take a dramatic turn.
One of Gao's uncles is appointed head of the
Labour Bureau in the county government and
offers Gao a position as reporter at the local radio
station. Qiaozhen, who loves Gao dearly, intu-
itively senses that Gao's career opportunity
threatens their relationship and makes Gao
promise he will not abandon her. The anchor
woman of the radio station, Huang Yaping, was
Gao's former high-school classmate and has
always secretly admired Gao's talents. Before long
Huang splits with her boyfriend, Zhang Kenan,
and begins to date Gao. Although Gao still loves
Qiaozhen he can't resist Huang, particularly when
she promises to find him a job in the city.
Qiaozhen is heartbroken when Gao ends their
relationship, and decides to marry a man she does
not even care for. Meanwhile, Huang's lobbying
efforts on Gao's behalf succeed in getting Gao sent
to the city. However, the mother of her former
boyfriend reports this act of favouritism to the
authorities, and Gao is subsequently sent back to

his village. While all the villagers are critical of his conduct, particularly his break-up with Qiaozhen, Qiaozhen continues to love him in her own quiet way.

The film was awarded Best Film and Best Actress prizes at the 1985 HFA.

(ZX)

Life of Wu Xun, The

(Wu Xun zhuan)

dir./sc. **Sun Yu**
with **Zhao Dan**, Huang Zongying, Zhou Boxun, **Wu Yin**
Shanghai: Kunlun Film, 1950

This film is based on the exploits of a real historical figure, Wu Xun, who devoted his life to the promotion of free education for peasant children. It was widely criticized in the early 1950s and became the first notorious victim of CCP film censorship policies.

After his father dies, Wu Xun and his mother are reduced to poverty. While working as a hired labourer, Wu is short-changed by his employer because he can't read. His friend, Zhou Da, is thrown into jail because he stands up for Wu. Wu's girl friend, Xiaotao, who works as a maid for a landlord and his family, is sold by her employer to another man. In protest, she commits suicide. Having witnessed these tragedies, Wu concludes that the only way poor people can empower themselves is through education. He decides to raise funds and set up free schools for children from impoverished families. To this end he saves, begs, and even appeals to the wealthy landlords for help. Finally, his free school is established. However, his friend, Zhou Da, who has since become a peasant rebel leader, considers that Wu's belief in the power of education to change everything is too naive. Zhou proposes open rebellion against the establishment.

The Emperor learns of Wu's free school and rewards Wu with official titles, uniforms and other commemorative awards. But Wu refuses to accept those official honours by pretending to be insane and thus unable to go through with the ceremony. As Wu continues his efforts to establish free education for the poor, the peasant rebels led by Zhou sweep through the prairies.

See also: censorship and film

(ZX)

Life on a String

(Bianzou bianchang)

dir./sc. **Chen Kaige**
with Liu Zhongyuan, Huang Lei, Xu Qing
Germany: Serene Production, 1991

As with his ***Yellow Earth*** (1984) and ***King of the Children*** (1987), Chen Kaige here pursues philosophical themes in an experimental style. Perhaps his most enigmatic and least popular film, it invokes dialectical concepts of salvation and despair, reality and illusion, substance and emptiness, and invites audiences to view the action symbolically.

Two blind musicians, a master and his disciple, travel across a rural landscape in the sincere belief that they will one day be able to see the world. The old musician is driven by his master's pronouncement that when he breaks the 1,000th string on his banjo a medical prescription that might cure his blindness will be released. The itinerant musician has believed in this prophecy for sixty years. His music is reputed to possess the power to resolve human conflict, and the musician is venerated by local people wherever he goes. Meanwhile, his young disciple falls in love with a village girl. Distraught because it is impossible for her to marry the young musician, the girl kills herself. The master instructs his student that a blind man's life must be based around music not women.

When the 1,000th string finally breaks, the prescription turns out to be nothing but a piece of blank paper. Realizing that his wish for salvation has been a cruel joke the master ends his life. The young disciple continues to journey but with his own banjo now holding a letter from the girl he loves rather than a supposed cure for blindness. Perhaps he will be able to finally read the letter on the day he snaps the 1,000th string.

Chen again employs spectacular images of the Yellow River and Loess Plateau to signify ancient belief in the natural order of things. The combination of folk and modern music enhances the visuals and adds resonance to the protagonists' quest.

See also: avant-garde, experimental or exploratory film

(SC, YZ)

Lin Ching Hsia

(Brigitte Lin, Lin Qingxia)

b. 1954, Taipei
Actress

One of the most popular actresses in Hong Kong and Taiwan, Lin Ching Hsia made her début in Taiwan with *Outside the Window* (*dir.* Song Cunshou, 1972) while she was still in high school. Her performances in *Eight Hundred Heroic Soldiers* (*dir.* **Ting Shan-hsi**, 1975) and *Red Dust* (*dir.* **Yim Ho**, 1990) won her Best Actress awards at Asia-Pacific FF and Taipei GHA. She has appeared in over 100 films, including such major Hong Kong productions as *Peking Opera Blues* (*dir.* **Tsui Hark**, 1986*)*, *Swordsman, I* (1990) and *Swordsman, II* (1992, both *dir.* **Ching Siu Tung**), *The East Is Red* (1993) and *Chungking Express* (*dir.* **Wong Kar-Wai**, 1994). A long-time screen icon in Hong Kong and Taiwan, Lin specializes in delivering graceful and enigmatic images of female machismo, cross–dressing, and a form of gender-bending that eventually merges into androgyny and transexualism. After her marriage in 1994, she bid farewell to the film world and retired to San Francisco.

Further reading

H. Hampton (1996), an excellent essay on her screen images.

(YZ)

Lin Dai

(Linda Lin)

b. 26 Dec. 1934, Nanning, Guangxi province
d. 17 July 1964
Actress

Lin Dai studied music at Guangxi Academy of Art before moving to Hong Kong with her father Cheng Siyuan. She entered Great Wall and Yonghua companies and became famous for her performance in *Cui Cui* (*dir.* Yan Jun, 1952). She won Best Actress award four times at Asian Film Festivals, for *Diau Charn of the Three Kingdoms* (*dir.* **Li Han-hsiang**, 1958), *Smiling Beauty* and *Lingering Passion* (both *dir.* Tao Qin, 1961). She committed suicide in 1964, one of several Hong Kong film actresses tragically to end their own lives.

Further reading

X. Xiao (1964), a biography.

(YZ)

Lin Family Shop, The

(Lin jia puzi)

dir. **Shui Hua**
sc. **Xia Yan**
with **Xie Tian**, Lin Bin, **Yu Lan**, Chen Shou
Beijing: Beijing Film, 1959

Adapted from Mao Dun's famous story, this film constitutes a graphic exposition of the CCP's view of the national bourgeoisie. Zhang Bohan is both the victim of foreign imperialist-capitalist economic oppression and the victimizer of the Chinese working class and even minor business. Such an ambivalent position matches the mix of sympathy and cynicism evidenced by Zhang's character.

Mr Lin manages a family shop in a town only a few hundred miles from Shanghai. His business is negatively affected by a number of factors: Japanese encroachment, corrupt domestic politics and historical circumstances. His daughter is ridiculed in school by her classmates for wearing a dress made of Japanese-manufactured materials. The town's chamber of commerce takes advantage of popular anti-Japanese sentiment among the populace to ban the sale of Japanese goods. Lin, though, continues to offer bribes so that he can sell Japanese products with a label claiming they are made in China. After the Sino-Japanese war breaks out, Lin's creditor from Shanghai demands that his loan be paid back immediately. In an effort to come up with the money, Lin has to squeeze the farmers renting his land. Meanwhile, his illegal sale of Japanese goods finally lands him in jail. After his assistant manager bails him out, Lin decides to flee, but not before promising his daughter to his assistant manager. While the major creditors of Lin's business are able to seize his property for collateral, the small creditors become the real victims of his bankruptcy.

(ZX)

Lin Feng-chiao

(Lin Fengjiao)

b. 1953, Taipei
Actress

Lin Feng-chiao began screen acting at the age of seventeen and earned critical acclaim for her performance as a devoted wife in *A Boat in the Ocean* (1978). She won Best Actress award at Taipei

GHA for *Story of a Small Town* (1979). Notable among her seventy-odd films are *Our Land, Our People* (1978), *Good Morning, Taipei* (1979) and *China, My Native Land* (1980). All the films listed here were directed by **Lee Hsing**.

(YZ)

Lin Nong

b. 1918, Sichuan province
Director

A mainland director whose interests lie in **historical film** and films of ethnic minorities, Lin Nong studied agriculture and forestry during his youth. The outbreak of the Sino-Japanese war in 1937 aroused his patriotic feelings. In 1939, he travelled to Yan'an, the wartime Communist headquarters, and enrolled in Lu Xun College of Art, concentrating on drama.

Lin's film career began when he was transferred to the newly-founded Northeast Film Studio, the predecessor of today's Changchun Film Studio. Lin's directing début was *An Accident* (1953). Since then he has directed over a dozen films, including such well known titles as *The Mysterious Traveller* (1955), *Bonfires in the Border Village* (1957), *Daughter of the Party* (1958), ***Naval Battle of 1894*** (1962), *The Besieged City* (1963) and *The Strange Marriage* (1981).

Among Lin's successes, *The Naval Battle of 1894* is perhaps most representative of his aesthetic taste and personal style. Lin's proclivity for depicting major historical events has sometimes brought him political trouble. For example, his *The Besieged City* deals with one of the crucial moments of the civil war, namely the battle between the Communist and Nationalist troops over the city of Changchun. Many historians consider that this event, which was a turning point in the Northeast Campaign, sealed the fate of Chiang Kai-shek's regime. Naturally, any film representing this episode of the civil war was bound to catch the attention of high ranking party officials, such as then Premier Zhou Enlai. Zhou approved the film, but suggested some revisions. After following Zhou's suggestions, the filmmakers thought they would be safe from further interference by state authorities. But, as the inner party power struggles between Zhou and his political rivals intensified during the **Cultural Revolution**, Lin's film became the first victim. It was banned because it had received Zhou's endorsement.

Lin has not been very productive in the post-Cultural Revolution period, directing no more than three films since 1978.

See also: ethnic minorities, film of

(ZX)

Lin Zexu

(Lin Zexu)

dir. **Zheng Junli**, Qin Fan
sc. Lu Dang, Ye Yuan
with **Zhao Dan**, Han Fei, Gao Bo, **Qin Yi**, Wen Xiying
Shanghai: Haiyan Film, 1959

Based on actual events that took place during the Opium War, this **historical film** promotes Chinese **nationalism**. Particularly noteworthy is the role played in this film by the Chinese masses, including women. Their determination to resist foreign encroachment contrasts positively with the capitulation of the court.

Emperor Daoguang sends Commissioner Lin Zexu to Canton to take charge of the anti-drug campaign. Upon his arrival, Lin disguises himself as a merchant to collect information about the opium trade so that he can observe at first hand the problems caused by the drug. When foreigners refuse to turn in their opium, Lin blockades their residence. One of them tries to sneak out with the help of a Chinese official but is caught by local Chinese fishermen. Using this event as a bargaining card, Lin pressures Yu Kun into coughing up the money needed for the improvement of the coastal defences. Meanwhile, the British ambassador to China, Eliot, tells the opium dealers to turn their goods over to Lin, promising them that the British government will compensate them for their losses.

After Lin destroys the opium, the British government sends a fleet of warships. Taken by surprise by this turn of events, the Chinese Emperor gives in to British demands. Lin is removed from his post and sent into exile. Qi Shan replaces Lin and demolishes the coastal defenses as a gesture of goodwill to the British. But the local people continue their resistance to the foreigners. As Lin goes on his journey of exile, the Canton militia ambush a British patrol squadron and annihilate them.

Almost forty years later, *The Opium War* (*dir.* **Xie Jin**, 1997), a film that dramatizes the same historical events, was released in both mainland

China and Hong Kong in celebration of the handover of Hong Kong to Chinese rule.

(ZX)

Ling Zifeng

b. 1917, Beijing
Director

A highly respected veteran director in the mainland, Ling Zifeng grew up in a scholarly family. His father, an educator, was well versed in several foreign languages, and his two sisters were both artists. Ling himself enrolled in Beiping Academy of Arts in 1933, first as a Western art major, then as a student of the Department of Graphic Design, and finally as a graduate from the Sculpture Department. He held a solo exhibition of his work while still a student.

Ling's film career took off from his interest in theatre. As a stage designer and make-up artist, he worked for numerous theatrical troupes. In the late 1930s, Ling had the chance to play minor roles in several films produced by the Nationalist China Motion Picture Studio. It was not until 1948, however, that he began directing at Northeast Film Studio under the Communist leadership. His début, ***Daughters of China*** (1949), earned critical acclaim and won a Peace and Freedom award at the 1950 Karlovy Vary FF. His next film, the epic *The Legend of the Banner* (1960), is considered by many critics to be one of the best films produced in the PRC. To date, though, Ling's own favourite is ***Camel Xiangzi*** (1982), an adaptation of Lao She's famous novel. In this film Ling recreates the ambiance of old Beijing, taking full advantage of his childhood memories of the city to render the story in a realistic style. Ling's two other film adaptations were also warmly received: ***Border Town*** (1984), an idyllic tale from Sheng Congwen, and *A Woman for Two* (1988), another study of old Beijing.

A prolific director, Ling contributed to the ethnographic film trend of the early 1990s with ***Ripples Across Stagnant Water*** (1991), a beautifully executed period piece.

See also: adaptations of drama and literature; theatre and film

Further reading

D. Ma and G. Dai (1994: 157–78), a chapter on Ling Zifeng; ZDX (1982–6: 4: 372–80), a short biography.

(ZX, YZ)

Little Toys

(Xiao wanyi)

dir./sc. **Sun Yu**
with **Ruan Lingyu**, Yuan Congmei, **Li Lili**,
Luo Peng, Han Lan'gen
Shanghai: Lianhua Film, 1933

In the late 1920s a village woman's life is shaken by a series of tragedies indirectly caused by the development of the capitalist economy and the outbreak of war. A mother of two, Ye earns her living by making small toys which her husband sells in the town. During a battle between warlords, her husband is killed, her son Yu'er is lost, and her village is practically destroyed. Ye and her daughter, Zhu'er, move to Shanghai and resume their business, but they can barely compete with the more modern and sophisticated toys produced overseas.

Ye and her fellow workers help the Chinese troops fighting against the Japanese invasion of Shanghai. Zhu'er and her boyfriend are both killed. Left completely alone, Ye sells her toys in the street. One day she meets again the son she had lost years before. Yu'er now lives with a rich businessman who had bought him from a child trader. Mother and son meet without realizing the other's true identity. Not long after, frightened by some firecrackers which remind her of the bombing, Ye starts yelling at people urging them to wake up, react, and fight. Her final message is clear. The tragedy of her life was not fated: those who fail to act against foreign invasion must share the blame for what transpires.

This early film promotes **nationalism** and patriotism at a time when China faced the threat of economic, cultural and military imperialism.

(PV)

Liu Miaomiao

b. 1962, Guyuan, Ningxia, Hui autonomous region
Director

The youngest director from the **Fifth Generation**, Liu Miaomiao comes from an ethnic Hui (Muslim) family. After graduating from the Directing Department of BFA in 1982, she was assigned to Xiaoxiang Film Studio, where she directed *Stories of the Voyage* (1985) at age twenty-three. Within a decade she had a number of feature films to her credit, including *Women on the Long March* (1987), which captures the inner feelings of women soldiers in the Red Army, and *The Boxer* (1988), as well as over thirty TV dramas. *An Innocent Babbler* (1993), directed for Children's Film Studio on a low budget, tells how a tongue-tied schoolboy matures through the hardships his family experiences in an impoverished village. Liu received no salary for her work on the film but liked it so much that she borrowed money to bring it to Venice FF, where it won her the Golden Congressman Award. She then turned to **melodrama** with *Family Scandal* (1994), a tale of rape, suicide and revenge co-directed with Cui Xiaoqin for Youth Film Studio. Channel Four Television in Britain has reportedly commissioned Liu to direct a low-budget romance between a Western army general and a Chinese woman.

Further reading
D. Yun (1994), a biographic sketch.

(YZ)

authorities in 1952 due to Liu's pro-PRC activities. Back in China, Liu starred in three major 1950s productions: *The Caravan* (*dir.* Wang Weiyi, 1954), *The Spirit of the Sea* (*dir.* Xu Tao) and *Girl Basketball Player No. 5* (*dir.* **Xie Jin**, both 1957). Liu did not appear again on the screen for another two decades, when he returned in *The Herdsman* (*dir.* Xie Jin, 1982).

Liu began directing films as early as 1950 and was particularly interested in **filmed stage performances**. His *Rebel Song* (1956) and *The Daughter-in-Law* (1959) were both adapted from traditional Chinese operas. His best-known work to date is probably *Ashma* (1964), a well crafted **musical** that won a top prize at the 1982 FF for musicals held in Spain.

See also: propaganda and film

Further reading
ZDX (1982–6: 7: 131–43), a short biography.

(ZX)

Liu Qiong

b. 16 October 1913, Beijing
Actor, director

A veteran actor of the 1940s, Liu Qiong used to be a student at Shanghai Law School, located near the site of the old Lianhua Film Company. He became acquainted with several Lianhua people (e.g., **Jin Yan** and **Wu Yonggang**) who regularly used the school's basketball facilities. Through their patronage, Liu cameoed in *Big Road* (*dir.* **Sun Yu**, 1934) and other Lianhua productions.

During the Japanese occupation of Shanghai, Liu was invited by the Japanese-controlled United China Film Company to star in two propaganda films, *The Opium War* (*dir.* **Bu Wancang**, 1943) and *The Sorrow of Spring River* (*dir.* Dao Yuanhao, Yao Feng, 1944). In a gesture of patriotic defiance, he turned both requests down and started to devote himself to theatre instead. He resumed his film career after the war, playing an ancient general named Wen Tianxiang in *The Spirit of the Nation* (*dir.* Bu Wancang, 1948). In this **costume drama**, Liu gave one of his best and most memorable screen performances.

Between 1948 and 1952, Liu worked for Hong Kong companies such as Yonghua, Great Wall and the Fiftieth Film Company. Liu and his wife were expelled from Hong Kong by the British

Liu Xiaoqing

b. 1951, Sichuan province
Actress

Regarded by many as one of the best actresses in China, Liu Xiaoqing has starred in several dozen films and won numerous awards since 1976. She grew up in an unhappy family: her parents divorced just before she was born, and her mother remarried when Liu was only three years old. At first, Liu was a stage actor with an army troupe. Her first opportunity in movies came when the August First Film Studio invited her to act in *Sea Gull*, a remake of the 1959 film of the same title. Although the film was eventually abandoned for political reasons, Liu then landed a role in *The Great Wall of the South China Sea* (1976). Her performance attracted much attention and led to more offers from major studios throughout China.

Liu was awarded Best Supporting Actress at 1980 HFA for her performance in *What a Family!* (*dir.* Wang Haowei, 1979). Her career peaked when she won successive Best Actress prizes at the China GRA, in 1987 for her performance in *Hibiscus Town* (*dir.* **Xie Jin**, 1986), and in 1988 for her portrayal of an uninhibited woman in *Savage Land* (*dir.* Ling Zi, 1981).

Unfortunately, Liu has been a prime target of star gossip, and her autobiography, *Going My Own*

Way (Zou wo ziji de lu, 1983), provoked much controversy. Since the mid-1980s, Liu has become more involved in business ventures, fuelling rumours that she is the wealthiest woman in China.

Despite announcing in 1988 that she would retire from filmmaking, Liu has continued to take starring roles, most notably in the high-profile film series *Dream of the Red Chamber* (*dir.* **Xie Tieli**, 1988–9), and in other costume dramas co-produced with Hong Kong, such as *Li Lianying: The Imperial Eunuch* (*dir.* **Tian Zhuangzhuang**, 1991).

See also: costume drama

Further reading

X. Liu (1992), a memoir.

(ZX)

Long Arm of the Law
(Shenggang qibing)

dir. Johnny **Mak**
sc. Phillip Chan
with Lin Wei, Wong Kin
Hong Kong: Johnny Mak Workshop/Bo Ho Films, 1984

This grittily realistic film is influenced by Italian neo-realism and tough crime dramas like *The French Connection* (*dir.* William Friedkin, 1971). In 1983, Tung, the leader of a mainland gang, takes the train from Kowloon Station. His men retrieve weapons in an alley and wait for him. Together they plan to pull a big jewel robbery in Hong Kong and then 'retire' after its completion. They cross the border by convincing Hong Kong police they are members of a drum troupe headed for Buddha's birthday celebrations.

Once outside their well-protected target, their car is checked by the police and a gunfight ensues. The gang escapes and makes plans to try again. Tung meets his 'middleman', Tai, and tells him that they must postpone the job. Tai will pay Tung $50,000 to kill 'Fatso', an undercover policeman. Tung and his men shoot Fatso at a skating rink at the mall, but Tung is furious when he finds out that he has been set up to kill a cop. Suspecting Tai, the police question him fruitlessly about Tung's 'O' gang. Tung and some of his friends truss Tai up in a car and set it on fire. They then rescue him and demand more money. Tai shows

the police a video of the Fatso hit, thus betraying the gang.

The men hit the jewellery store again, but things go wrong. When the police chase them a guard is killed. Tai goes to meet the gang, but the transmitter in his car is discovered. As Tung is about to shoot Tai, a police helicopter opens fire, killing Tai and wounding one of the men. Some of the gang escape to Kowloon's Walled City. However, after being betrayed they are all shot dead by members of the Special Police Force.

Long Arm of the Law is one of the earliest Hong Kong films to examine seriously the Hong Kong–mainland relationship and the city's then-imminent return to mainland China. The emphasis on survival skills has special resonance in the context of 1997 anxiety.

Further reading

C. Li (1994); E. Yau (1994a), two critical studies.

(KH, YZ)

Long Live the Mistress!
(Taitai wansui)

dir. **Sang Hu**
sc. Eileen Chang
with Jiang Tianliu, **Shi Hui**, Zhang Fa, **Shangguan Yunzhu**
Shanghai: Wenhua Film, 1947

In this family **melodrama**, the protagonist is a strong woman who deals with a troublesome, unfaithful husband and tries to save their marriage by fixing his messy life. Tang Zhiyuan is a weak husband who pretends to love his wife Chen Sizhen, borrows money from her rich father, and takes a mistress when he himself makes money. In spite of her husband's infidelity, Chen tries to please her mother-in-law and sister-in-law, and skilfully helps Tang get rid of his now more demanding and oppressive mistress. Victimized by patriarchy, Chen nevertheless learns to use the system to her own advantage. She reverses her victim role and wins out on all fronts.

Written by the most famous woman writer of the 1940s, this film preserves the witty dialogue and delicate psychological twists that characterize the stories of Eileen Chang. It initiated a cycle of family melodramas popular in Hong Kong and Taiwan since the 1960s.

(PV, YZ)

Lost Children

(Mitu de gaoyang)

dir./sc. **Cai Chusheng**
with Ge Zuozhi, **Shen Fu**, Chen Juanjuan,
Zheng Junli, Li Zhuozhuo
Shanghai: Lianhua Film, 1936

This film narrates the adventurous story of a young boy who feels more at home with his beggar friends than as the adopted son of a wealthy family. It contrasts the hypocrisy and decadence of rich people with the virtue and genuine human compassion shown by the poor.

An orphaned teenage boy named Sanzi sneaks on to a ship bound for Shanghai where he becomes a beggar. A wealthy man, Shen Cihang, throws a big party to celebrate his birthday. When Sanzi and his beggar friends show up at Shen's residence, they are driven away. One day Shen falls into the river and is saved from drowning by Sanzi. After Shen recovers, he finds that Sanzi resembles his own deceased son and decides to make Sanzi his heir. Sanzi attends school with other children from wealthy families. After overhearing Sanzi's snobbish classmates making fun of the child's past, Shen begins to regret his adoption.

One day Sanzi runs into Shen's wife having a tryst with her lover. Afraid that Sanzi may tell her husband, Mrs Shen accuses Sanzi of stealing her jewellery and kicks him out of the house. An old house-servant who speaks up for Sanzi is also fired. The servant then takes care of Sanzi and his homeless friends. However, the old man dies of a heart attack on Christmas Eve while trying to entertain those children.

Now without an adult guardian, Sanzi and his friends begin to roam the streets again. One day they steal some bread from Shen's charity agency and are chased by the police to an unfinished skyscraper. With nowhere to run, the children cry out to the metropolis below them.

(ZX)

love and marriage

Often treated together, love and marriage have been two favourite themes in Chinese cinema from its very beginnings. As in the West, cinematic representations of love and marriage in China have changed over time. From the 1910s to the 1990s, focus on the themes shifted from a questioning of arranged marriage approved by parents to a search for the idea of love based on mutual understanding, from love (or desire) as an expression of individuality and freedom to marriage as necessary fulfilment of one's social (or even political) obligations. Defined in this entry as heterosexual love between young people, love frequently leads to marriage in films with happy endings. However, it is love without marriage and marriage without love that have attracted most attention from Chinese filmmakers.

While making *The* **Difficult Couple** (*dir.* **Zhang Shichuan**, 1913), one of China's earliest short features, **Zheng Zhengqiu**, the screenwriter, deliberately sought to ridicule elaborate marriage rituals in China. In so doing, he not only made marriage ceremonies a fascinating screen spectacle, but also created – perhaps without his knowledge – a subject of intense ethnographic interest. This interest has been made all the more visible by a group of recent Chinese films, such as **Raise the Red Lantern** (*dir.* **Zhang Yimou**, 1991), *The* **Wooden Man's Bride** (*dir.* **Huang Jianxin**, 1993) and **Red Firecracker, Green Firecracker** (*dir.* **He Ping**, 1994). Back in the 1910s–20s, what increasingly concerned Chinese filmmakers was the new generation's reaction to the age-old Confucian concept of a hierarchical **family** structure, which rigidly defines the social and familiar roles of husband and wife but leaves little room for their mutual consideration. The result of the Confucian system is an apparently stable family in which the young respect the old and the female obeys the male – a stability, nevertheless, often achieved on the basis of loveless marriages. Like their counterparts in literature and drama, Chinese films of the 1920s–30s frequently criticize the practice of arranged marriages. In films such as **Sea Oath** (*dir.* **Dan Duyu**, 1921), *Little Darling* (*dir.* Zheng Zhengqiu), *The Love Story* (*dir.* **Shi Dongshan**, both 1926) and **Revived Rose** (*dir.* **Hou Yao**, **Li Minwei**, 1927), one also encounters a growing sympathy for the younger generation's pursuit of genuine love against parental or societal restrictions.

By the 1930s, the concept of modern love seemed to have triumphed over – though by no means eliminated – traditional practices (e.g., arranged marriage and concubinage). In many films about **urban life**, the love story of career women was critically examined. **Wild Flower** (*dir.* **Sun Yu**, 1930) and **New Woman** (*dir.* **Cai**

Chusheng, 1934), for instance, provide two different endings for career women in the city: a happy one where the woman gives up her career and becomes a virtuous housewife, and a tragic one where the woman continues to pursue her career and is eventually destroyed by an evil society. As hinted in *New Woman*, socio-economic conditions in the city were rather antagonistic to the young generation's ideas of love and marriage in the 1930s. Not only was the love between two young people destroyed in ***Boatman's Daughter*** (*dir.* **Shen Xiling**, 1935); a marriage based on genuine love was ruthlessly crushed in ***Plunder of Peach and Plum*** (**Ying Yunwei**, 1934). Indeed, the prospects of love grew darker and darker in urban films from the mid-1930s onwards. Just as the otherwise cheerful protagonists in ***Crossroads*** (*dir.* Shen Xiling, 1937) fail to prevent an unemployed college schoolmate from committing suicide in Shanghai, young protagonists in ***Street Angel*** (*dir.* **Yuan Muzhi**, 1937) cannot save a miserable prostitute from being killed by urban gangsters.

An alternative to the pursuit of fated love was provided for the younger generation in several leftist films in the 1930s. Increasingly, young people were urged to channel their libidinal desire into a passion for revolution and national salvation. In films like ***Three Modern Women*** (*dir.* **Bu Wancang**, 1933) and ***Big Road*** (*dir.* Sun Yu, 1934), heterosexual love is reconfigured as inconsequential or incompatible with the public cause, while marriage is either pushed to the background or dropped entirely from the story. Although it was still inconsistent during the 1930s–40s (as evident in a discussion of marriage below), this marginalization of love became dominant in mainland China during the 1950s–70s, when sexual love between individuals was forced to expand or be 'elevated' into a kind of 'spiritual' love for the community, the country and the CCP. One example is ***It's My Day Off*** (*dir.* Lu Ren, 1959). While it is supposed to tell of a young policeman who goes to meet his date for the first time (as arranged by the wife of his superior), this **comedy** evades the question of sexual love altogether and, instead, shows the audience again and again how much the policeman 'loves' serving people in need. Indeed, except for some films of ethnic minorities, such as ***Five Golden Flowers*** (*dir.* Wang Jiayi, 1959) and ***Third Sister Liu*** (*dir.* Su Li, 1960), films about love affairs became increasingly a rarity in the 1960s. By the early 1970s, love was

regarded as a tabooed subject and was conspicuously absent in 'revolutionary' titles, like ***Breaking with Old Ideas*** (*dir.* **Li Jun**, Li Ang) and ***Chun Miao*** (*dir.* **Xie Jin**, Yan Bili, Liang Tingduo, both 1975).

After the **Cultural Revolution**, the issue of love was treated as a pressing case of humanism in mainland China. *The Corner Forsaken by Love* (*dir.* Zhang Qi, Li Yalin, 1981) dramatizes the tragic results of repressing and persecuting love and desire in a rural village during the 1960s–70s. The lingering fear of expressing one's feelings of love is further depicted in ***Under the Bridge*** (*dir.* Bai Chen, 1983), in which the male protagonist has to overcome social prejudice to openly date a neighbour who has a child out of wedlock. In the 1980s–90s, the themes of love and marriage were used not only to criticize ultra-leftist ideology of the 1970s, but also to confront various types of social problems in contemporary society. Both *The Invisible Web* (*dir.* Wang Haowei, 1981) and *Backlit Pictures* (*dir.* Ding Yinnan, 1982) are highly critical of parents' interference in children's marriage choices. *Who Is the Third Party?* (1988) and *The World of Women* (1992, both *dir.* Dong Kena) seriously examine the effects of a loveless marriage and the threat an extra-marital affair poses to society in general. Whereas divorce was frequently dismissed as a viable option in resolving marriage problems in the 1980s, it has gained more and more acceptance in the films of the 1990s. In *The* ***Days*** (*dir.* **Wang Xiaoshuai**) and *No One Cheers* (*dir.* **Xia Gang**, both 1993), divorce no longer seems to cause traumatic feelings to the parties involved, and love has almost become an elusive entity beyond the protagonists' comprehension.

Contrary to the majority of films in the 1980s–90s that treat love and marriage as social problems, a few mainland films represent love as a fundamentally sexual experience, detached from any consideration of marriage. In *Savage Land* (*dir.* Ling Zi, 1981), sexual love between the male and the female protagonists intensifies their desire for a bloody revenge. In both *The Wooden Man's Bride* (1993) and *Red Firecracker, Green Firecracker* (1994), the female protagonist's passionate love for a young workman empowers her to transgress the social norms and seek her sexual fulfillment. Clearly no longer a tabooed subject, sexual love has become all the more fascinating if it is presented as illicit or forbidden, as in the case of Zhang Yimou's ***Ju Dou*** (1989), where an 'aunt' has sex with a 'nephew' and gives birth to a son

Plate 25   *No One Cheers* (1993)

(or 'brother'), and *Raise the Red Lantern* (1991), where the Third Mistress sleeps with her doctor outside the master's compound. In films such as these, sexual love in a repressive society has furnished a new visual icon to the Western fascination – or obsession – with the *ars erotica* of an ancient culture.

It is obvious by now that, as far as love and marriage are concerned, mainland Chinese films of the 1990s are characterized by multiplicity and tolerance. Across a broad spectrum, we have near one extreme an implicit confirmation of Confucian ethics in The **Descendants of Confucius** (*dir*. **Wu Yigong**, 1992), a study of changing values in four generations of Confucius' descendants in the era of economic reforms. Near the other extreme, we have **Yesterday's Wine** (*dir*. Xia Gang, 1995), a **melodrama** devoted to a re-enacting of the transformation of a teenage girl into a fully grown sexual being. Her illicit – and almost 'incestuous' – love for a married neighbour and his long-separated American son is narrated in a sentimental voice-over and enhanced by beautiful visual images (including a house by the Californian beach).

To a certain extent, *Yesterday's Wine* is reminiscent of the melodramas of **Chiung Yao** (*b*. 1938).

Melodrama became a popular narrative genre in Taiwan in the 1960s–70s, dwelling excessively on issues of love and marriage as well as insurmountable generation gaps. Films based on Chiung Yao's novels, such as *Whose Belongings?* (*dir*. **Wang Yin**, 1966) and *Outside the Window* (*dir*. Song Cunshou, 1972) captured the imagination of Taiwan's younger generations. Yet they are not unique in Chinese film history because this tradition of family drama can be traced back to Shanghai films of the late 1940s. **Long Live the Mistress!** (*dir*. **Sang Hu**, 1947), scripted by Eileen Chang, perhaps the most worshipped female Shanghai writer in Taiwan, shows how skilful a housewife is in dealing with her husband's extra-marital affair without bringing serious damage to the marriage. **Spring in a Small Town** (*dir*. **Fei Mu**, 1948) reveals a housewife's sexual desire for a former lover and her determination to preserve the integrity of the marriage in the end. **Sorrows and Joys of a Middle-Aged Man** (*dir*. Sang Hu, 1949) provides a sympathetic look at the emotional life of a retired schoolteacher. He does not like to be a dependant in his son's house, marries a woman young enough to be his daughter, and becomes a teacher and the father of a newborn child again.

Another type of Shanghai film of the late 1940s has also influenced productions in Hong Kong and Taiwan. The emotional traumas suffered by families during wars and other adverse times were dramatized in Shanghai films such as *Eight Thousand Li of Cloud and Moon* (*dir.* **Shi Dongshan**) and *Spring River Flows East* (*dir.* **Cai Chusheng, Zheng Junli**, both 1947), in Hong Kong films such as *Tears Over the Pearl River* (*dir.* Wang Weiyi, 1949) and *Between Tears and Smiles* (*dir.* **Zhu Shilin**, 1964), as well as in Taiwan films such as *The Silent Wife* (1965), *A Boat in the Ocean* (1978, both *dir.* **Lee Hsing**), and *Home, Sweet Home* (*dir.* **Pai Ching-jui**, 1970). In these films, love and marriage are represented as something that ties the family together and enables them to survive hard times.

In the 1980s–1990s, multiplicity characterizes Hong Kong and Taiwan films as much as it does mainland productions. For rebellious urban protagonists in *Days of Being Wild* (*dir.* **Wong Kar-Wai**, 1991) and *Vive l'amour* (*dir.* **Tsai Ming-liang**, 1994), sexual love has more to do with identity crisis than with plans for marriage. In Edward **Yang**'s *That Day on the Beach* (1983) and *Terrorizer* (1986), identity crises, especially those experienced by female protagonists, are examined together with loveless marriages they go through. In *Eat Drink Man Woman* (*dir.* Ang **Lee**, 1994), three daughters exemplify three different attitudes toward love and marriage (i.e., a spinster's asceticism, a career woman's random choice, and a schoolgirl's naivety), but they are all surprised by their conservative father's marriage with a divorced mother of their age, who is pregnant by their father by the end of the film. Indeed, the title *A Confucius Confusion* (*dir.* Edward Yang, 1995) is an apt metaphor for multiple – and often 'confused' – takes on the themes of love and marriage in contemporary Chinese film productions, where the remnants of Confucian ethics still constitute a significant cultural force against which new ideas and values continue to be formulated and tried out.

See also: ethnic minorities, film of; representations of women; romance; sexuality; woman's film; youth culture

Further reading

R. Chen (1995: 36–54), a report on Taiwan films.

(YZ)

Lü Sushang

b. 13 July 1915, Zhanghua, Taiwan
d. 9 Nov. 1970
Director, screen writer, historian

After graduating from high school, Lü Sushang organized Yinhua Pictures and worked in film distribution. In 1938 he studied film in the Art Department of Japan University and in other Japanese schools. He returned to Taiwan in the early 1940s to became a celebrated live interpreter (*bianshi*) for silent films. Before writing screenplays and directing films in the 1950s he pursued a successful career in the police force. He published *History of Taiwan Cinema and Drama* (1961) and other books.

Further reading

S. Lü (1961), a Taiwan film history.

(YZ)

Luo Mingyou

b. 1900, Hong Kong
d. 1967, Hong Kong
Director, producer

One of the most influential producers of the 1930s, Luo Mingyou was the founder of Lianhua Film Company and owner of a chain of movie theatres throughout north China. Luo studied law at the prestigious Beijing University in 1918 and became interested in film. Tired of frequenting the expensive movie houses run by foreigners, Luo decided to manage one himself. In 1919, with the support of his parents and his brother-in-law, Luo renovated a tea house into a 700-seat cinema. His admission fees were significantly lower than those of rival theatres.

Although Luo's movie house was destroyed by fire after only six months in operation, this first taste of business kindled his ambitions. A year later, he rebuilt the movie house. He gradually expanded his enterprise and took over several theatres owned by foreigners in Beijing and Tianjin. In 1927 Luo formed North China Film Company (Huabei), which came to control most of the film exhibition and **distribution** circuits in north China.

Dismayed by the poor quality of domestic films and inspired by the arrival of sound, Luo decided to produce movies himself. In 1930, by combining North China with two film studios in Shanghai, he formed Lianhua Film Company. During its heyday, Lianhua had headquarters in Hong Kong, three production studios in Shanghai, and training schools for actors in both Beijing and Shanghai. Along with Mingxing and Tianyi, Lianhua established a solid base for filmmaking in China.

The Manchurian Incident of 1931 sent the studio into a downward spiral because it cost Luo his distribution networks in north China, the basis for his production activities in Shanghai. To make matters worse, one of Lianhua's three studios was totally destroyed when the Japanese attacked Shanghai in 1932. Lianhua never recovered from these setbacks.

Politically, Luo was loyal to the KMT government and served the regime without reservation. Under Luo's management, Lianhua made *Little Angel* (*dir.* **Wu Yonggang**) and ***Song of China*** (*dir.* **Fei Mu**, Luo Mingyou, both 1935) in support of the New Life Movement. Lianhua also signed a contract with the KMT government to make newsreels. Ironically, though, Lianhua also churned out a large number of leftist films, such as ***Three Modern Women*** (*dir.* **Bu Wancang**, 1933), ***Big Road*** (*dir.* **Sun Yu**) and ***Goddess*** (*dir.* Wu Yonggang, both 1934).

After the war, Luo became a devout Christian and lived in Hong Kong until his death.

See also: documentary

Further reading
ZDX (1982–6: 1: 183–90), a short biography.

(ZX)

Ma-Xu Weibang

(*aka* Xu Weibang)

b. 1905
d. 1961
Actor, director

One of the most accomplished directors of the 1940s, Ma-Xu Weibang studied at Shanghai Institute of Arts, where he also taught after graduation. He left the institute in 1924 to take on a number of acting roles at Mingxing Film Company. Although he began directing as early as 1926, Ma-Xu had to wait a decade for his first hit movie. **Singing at Midnight** (1937), made for Xinhua Film Company, mixes elements of **thriller**, mystery and **romance** into the first Chinese **horror film**, and its enormous success led to a 1941 sequel. Riding the crest of the wave, Ma-Xu then made two more horror titles, *Walking Corpse in an Old House* and *The Lonely Soul* (both 1938). During the Japanese occupation of Shanghai, Ma-Xu was involved in the production of the highly controversial film *The Opium War* (*dir.* **Bu Wancang**, 1943). He moved to Hong Kong after the war and directed *The Haunted House* (1949), a film many critics regard as his best. But Ma-Xu quietly disappeared from the film world after directing a remake, *Revived Rose* (1953). His filmography numbers thirty-three titles.

See also: mystery film

(ZX)

Magic Braid

(Shen bian)

dir./sc. Zhang Zien
With Wang Yawei, Xue Shouli, Chen Baoguo
Xi'an: Xi'an Film, 1986

This **martial arts film** can be read metaphorically. A Chinese expert loses his magic braid in a battle with the foreigner whose modern rifles overpower his martial arts skills. Before long, however, he has transformed himself into a sharpshooter of foreign-made pistols and can claim that the magic powers are still with him.

Sha'er makes a living selling bean curd. One day a local thug named Glass Flower insults him in the marketplace and is taught a lesson by Sha'er. Glass Flower then brings several martial arts masters back for revenge, but they are all defeated by Sha'er using his braid as a magic weapon. Finally, Glass Flower brings a Japanese samurai to beat Sha'er. But the Japanese is no match for Sha'er either. Because of his victory over the samurai, Sha'er becomes a national hero and is showered with gifts and banners by people in the city of Tianjin. He then marries the girl next door.

By 1900, the Boxers have invited him to join their cause. Sha'er accepts their invitation and fights bravely against the allied troops, but a bullet shatters his braid and he comes home devastated. Years later, Glass Flower returns with a pistol and goes to Shaer's house to settle their old score. But Sha'er has now turned himself into a two-handed sharpshooter. After observing Shaer's shooting skills, Glass Flower can only beg for mercy.

(ZX)

Mah-jong

(Majiang)

dir./sc. Edward **Yang**
with Virginie Ledoyen, Tang Congsheng, Ke Yulun, Zhang Zheng, Wang Qizan
Taipei: Atom Films, 1996

Following his urban **comedy** *A Confucius Confusion* (1995), Edward Yang continues to explore the issue of existential crisis in Taiwan's younger generation in his distinctively modernist – or some would say 'post-modernist' – fashion.

As the Chinese game 'mah-jong' requires four players, the film features four teenagers, Red Fish, Luen Luen, Hong Kong and Toothpaste, whose bizarre names already suggest their anti-traditional attitude. Indeed, as the film progresses, they prove themselves to be excellent players in the modern theatre of Taipei, and their games of making money and chasing women are as adventurous and as meaningless as their own lives. The battle of the sexes seems of particular appeal to these young adventurers. They first attempt a 'symbolic' gang-rape of a naive girl Alison, but one of them, Hong Kong, is later turned into an object of desire by three wealthy and 'lusty' women.

As in Yang's masterpiece **Terrorizer** (1986), a mysterious woman appears in this new urban drama, but this time she is a French woman named Marthe, whose entrance in the Hard Rock Café at the beginning of the film points both to Taipei's transnational cultural links to the West and the persistence of boundary markers such as Chinese vs. foreign or urban vs. rural. What have inevitably disappeared in the film, at least inasmuch as delinquent teenagers are concerned, are traditional values and ideologies, which seem no longer capable of imposing rules of the game in the jungle of the modern city.

Further Reading

H. Chiao (1996a), an interview with Yang regarding the film.

(YZ)

Mak, Carl

(Mai Jia)

b. 29 Feb. 1944
Director, producer

An active figure in the Hong Kong film industry, Carl Mak grew up in Guangdong province and moved to Hong Kong in 1958. He studied electrical engineering in the USA and worked for a telephone company in New York City in 1969. After taking film courses at New York University in 1971–3, he returned to Hong Kong to set up Pioneer Film Company (Xianfeng) in 1975 and Garbo Films (Jiabao) in 1978. He initiated the popular mixed genre of kungfu **comedy** and wrote, directed and acted in *Tiger and Frogs* (1978).

In 1980, he teamed up with Dean Shek (Shi Tian, *b.* 1950) and Raymond **Wong** to form Cinema City (Xin yicheng), which proved a successful venture when *Aces Go Places*, *I-III* (*dir.* **Tsui Hark**, 1982, 1983, 1984) broke all-time box-office records in Hong Kong and earned Carl the accolade of Best Actor at the 1982 Hong Kong Academy Awards.

See also: Kungfu film; mixed genres

Further Reading

J. Lent (1990: 102–105), a brief mention of Cinema City.

(YZ)

Mak, Johnny

(Mai Dangxiong)

b. 2 Dec. 1949
Director, screen writer, producer

Unlike many of his contemporaries with advanced professional training, Johnny Mak failed to complete his college education, signing up for a year-long programme in TV acting instead. He worked in the media and became an executive producer of several popular quality dramas. He established the Johnny Mak Film Workshop in 1981 and directed **Long Arm of the Law** (1984), a **gangster film** in the Hollywood docudrama mould. Its realistic portrayal of character interrelationships helped him win Best Director award at Taipei GHA.

Further Reading

H. Chiao (1987: 77–81), a brief discussion.

(YZ)

Mama

aka *The Tree of the Sun* (Mama)

dir. **Zhang Yuan**
sc. Qin Yan
Distributed by Xi'an Film, 1991

One of the first independent films produced in the mainland, *Mama* tells of a Beijing librarian (Qin Yan) who takes care of her autistic son while fighting the indifference, if not outright prejudice, of society at large. Shot in black and white, the film conveys a simple but touching message. The story is based on Qin Yan's own experiences with a special-needs child. Zhang Yuan incorporates his video interviews with autistic people into the narrative in order to achieve a greater authenticity. The film was registered with Xi'an Film Studio, which provided distribution but no financial support. In 1992 the film was screened at Human Rights FF in Seattle and at Asian American FF in Washington, DC, USA.

See also: independent film

(YZ)

Mandarin movies

See under: Hong Kong cinema (in Historical essays)

Mao, Angela

Mao Ying

b. 1952, Taiwan

Actress

Angela Mao Ying personified the archetypal martial arts heroine of Hong Kong cinema of the 1970s as much as Cynthia Khan and Michelle **Yeoh** do in the 1990s. Angela performed as an opera player before entering films, starting her fighting roles as early as age five. Her most famous performance was as the female martial arts lead in *Yang Paifen* where the role called for her to deflect twelve spears in succession by using only her foot. Discovered by director Huang Feng (*b*. 1919), she signed a five-year contract with Golden Harvest in 1970 and often appeared in many films directed by Huang Feng and Luo Wei (*b*. 1918), frequently co-starring with Carter Huang and Sammo **Hung** (who also functioned as martial arts director).

Although earlier critics assumed her roles reflected the growing influence of Western Women's Liberation, they were really contemporary cinematic expressions of women warriors in Chinese history and literature. Her initial starring role was in the first Golden Harvest production, *Angry River* (1970), directed by Huang Feng, in which she played the avenging daughter of a murdered martial arts teacher. In the next Golden Harvest production, *The Invincible Eight* (1970), she joins her eight brothers in avenging the death of their parents and disguises herself in male attire by carrying a fan concealing a lethal weapon. But in *Lady Whirlwind* (1971), she decides to waive her

revenge against the man responsible for abandoning her pregnant sister when she learns of his fight against an opium and gambling syndicate. She also played a female revolutionary in King **Hu**'s *The Fate of Lee Khan* (1973) as well as a Chinese student fighting wicked Japanese in 1934 Korea in *Hapkido* (1972). Ironically, her best-known appearance for Western viewers is as Bruce **Lee**'s sister in *Enter the Dragon* (1973) – a cameo that does little justice to her kungfu abilities.

See also: martial arts film

(TW)

marriage

See under: love and marriage

martial arts film

Also known as the kungfu or **swordplay film**, the martial arts film is one of the most popular genres in China. Although Western audiences first experienced the Hong Kong martial arts film with the 1971 release of *King Boxer* (or *Five Fingers of Death*, *dir*. Cheng Chang Ho) in Britain and the USA, the genre has a much more prestigious history in mainland China. A number of early silent films, such as *An Empty Dream* (*dir*. Ren Pengnian, 1922), *A Chivalrous Boy* (*dir*. Fu Shunnan, 1924) and *A Female Knight-Errant* (*dir*. **Shao Zuiweng**, 1925) borrowed from Chinese **legends and myths** and experimented with special visual effects of the new medium. Together these films paved the way for the rise of an immensely popular genre, represented then by *The Burning of Red Lotus Temple* (*dir*. **Zhang Shichuan**, 1928), the first of an unprecedented eighteen episodes in all. During 1928–31, over 250 swordplay films were produced, many of them bearing in their titles 'burning' (*huoshao*) as a magic word.

The first phase of martial arts films established certain genre features: legendary heroes and heroines, black-and-white characterization, dramatic conflicts, suspense and plot complications, as well as solution by way of kungfu competitions. Although condemned by critics as unrealistic and escapist (in the sense that they did not address real-life issues directly), martial arts films reflected popular sentiments and a plebeian value system. Between 1937 and 1949 two waves of refugee

Plate 26   *Drunken Master* (1978)

directors from Shanghai brought the genre to Hong Kong. But it was not until interest declined in old swordplay films that Cantonese Hong Kong martial arts films really developed. They were characterized by an emphasis on realistic combat sequences as opposed to the fantastic heroism of the earlier films. In 1949 appeared the first of what would become a series of more than eighty films, *The True Story of Wong Fei-hung* (*dir.* Wu Pang), featuring Kwan Tak-Hing in the title role.

The series began when director Wu Pang read a newspaper article stating that his Cantonese opera composer friend Wu Yixiao had been a disciple of Wong Fei-hung. Immediately the legend became a fact, and Kwan Tak-Hing began a new film career in which he became identified with the legendary character. Wu directed most of the series and scripted the first four films. The films stressed martial arts expertise rather than spectacle, with Kwan demonstrating filial Confucian virtues in opposition to the villain usually played by Shih Kien (Shi Jian, *b.* 1913).

In 1965 Cantonese films lost ground to a resurgence of Mandarin cinema in Hong Kong catering to Southeast Asian and Taiwanese markets after cultural changes in mainland China. This development, along with the rise of the Shaw Brothers

studio, accompanied the publication of martial arts novels inspiring renewed interest in the fantastic aspects of combat. In 1961 Yue Feng (*b.* 1910) directed *The Swallow* with future King **Hu** associate Han Ying-Chieh working as martial arts instructor. Three years later, *The Golden Eagle*, *Treasure Island* and the Shaw Brothers' *Tiger Boy* (*dir.* **Chang Che**, starring **Wang Yu**, Lo Lieh) stimulated the growth of new-style martial arts films. Although the Shaw Brothers produced new versions of the *Burning of Red Lotus Temple* series, King Hu's *Come Drink With Me* (1966) represented a distinctive addition with Han Ying-Chieh's Peking opera-influenced martial arts techniques. King Hu soon moved to Taiwan where he directed a series of artistic versions of the genre, such as *Dragon Gate Inn* (1967), *A **Touch of Zen*** (1970), *The **Fate of Lee Khan*** (1973), *The Valiant Ones* (1975), *Raining in the Mountain*, and *Legend of the Mountain* (both 1979), featuring breathtaking views of the Taiwan landscape and dealing with issues of heroism and spirituality versus a politically corrupt world. These films, often featuring actors such as Shih Chun, **Hsu Feng**, and Roy Chiao, were set in the Ming Dynasty period, the last imperial dynasty ruled by the Han Chinese.

Meanwhile the Shaw Brothers studio took a different direction from King Hu. In 1967, Chang Che's *One-Armed Swordsman* (starring Wang Yu) broke box-office records, leading to the director's temporary ascendence as the producer of violent and fantastic martial arts films often featuring masochistically disturbed heroes. Director and star collaborated again in *Golden Swallow* (1968), featuring the heroine of King Hu's *Come Drink With Me*, until Wang Yu decided to leave Shaw Brothers to become actor-director in films such as *One-Armed Boxer* (1971) and *Beach of the War Gods* (1973). Chang replaced Wang with two young actors, **Ti Lung** and David **Chiang**, who would feature in several historical and modern films such as *Vengeance* (1970), *The New One-Armed Swordsman*, *Duel of Fists* (both 1971) and ***Blood Brothers*** (1972). In 1974 Chang left Shaw Brothers and set up his own quasi-independent studio in Taiwan, making a number of films dealing with the legendary Shaolin Temple of the Qing Dynasty, such as *Heroes Two*, *Men from the Monastery* (both 1973) and *Shaolin Martial Arts* (1974).

While fantastic elements dominated most martial arts films at this time, the Golden Harvest films of Bruce **Lee** represented a return to the more realistic combat depictions of Kwan Tak-Hing's films. Although Lee and Kwan differed enormously, both shared an interest in realistic techniques. Lee based his *Jeet Kune Tao* formula on the *Win Chung Fist* method he learned at the age of thirteen. This derived from a martial art deliberately designed for females and those with small bodies, making size unimportant. In his films, Lee rejected any use of special effects to promote his realistic combat technique, making himself a heroic representative of Chinese in both past and present. In his first Hong Kong box-office success, *The Big Boss* (*dir.* Lo Wei, 1971), he defends oppressed Chinese values in contemporary Thailand. *Fist of Fury* (*dir.* Lo Wei, 1972) places Lee's character in pre-war China against allegorical representatives of enemy cultures such as Japan and Russia, while *Return of the Dragon* (*dir.* Bruce Lee, 1973) sees him protecting his countrymen in modern Rome against a Mafia boss using Korean and American martial artists. All Lee's films championed his special fighting technique. The surviving footage of Lee later used in *Game of Death* (*dir.* Robert Clouse, 1978) was originally designed to illustrate this in fights against Korean, Japanese, and American martial artists.

The genre went into decline after Lee's death and did not really recover until the 1978 merger of **comedy** with martial arts in the films of Jackie **Chan** and Sammo **Hung**. **Tsui Hark**'s *Zu-Warriors of the Magic Mountain* (1982) saw the return of the spectacular and fantastic. In 1990, Wong Fei-hung returned to cinematic glory with Tsui's ***Once Upon a Time in China*** series, featuring a younger actor (Jet **Li**) situated in the legendary master's actual era in allegorical representations of fears concerning 1997. The combat scenes were more fantastic than realistic, but allegorical associations were more than real for contemporary audiences. Real and fantastic associations within the genre finally mixed.

Jet Li, a mainland martial arts champion who became famous with his screen début in *Shaolin Temple* (*dir.* Zhang Xinyan, 1982) and moved to Hong Kong to star in numerous kungfu features, is a good illustration of the close cooperation between mainland China and Hong Kong. Although, when *A Mysterious Giant Buddha* (*dir.* Zhang Huaxun, 1980) was first released in mainland China, film censors and critics were rather suspicious of this long repressed genre, martial arts films soon gained such popularity that many studios started making them. Like their Hong Kong and Taiwan counterparts of the 1960s–70s,

most mainland productions emphasize high moral integrity and real combat scenes. Some films even build in the theme of patriotism or **nationalism** by staging fights between Chinese experts and foreign competitors, as in *The Undaunted Wudang* (*dir.* Sun Sha), *Pride's Deadly Fury* (*dir.* Zhang Huaxun, both 1983), and *Magic Braid* (*dir.* Zhang Zien, 1986). To capitalize on the mainland market, Hong Kong producers invested in many co-productions of this genre in the 1980s–90s. More recently, a number of Hong Kong and mainland young directors also contributed their highly stylized variations to the genre, such as **He Ping** with *The **Swordsman in Double-Flag Town*** (1990) and *Sun Valley* (1996), Clara **Law** with *The **Temptation of a Monk*** (1993) and **Wong Kar-Wai** with *Ashes of Time* (1994). From its early silent phase to its contemporary full-coloured production, the martial arts film has remained a staple of the industry and one of the most popular genres in China.

See also: action film; historical film; martial arts film

Further Reading

H. Chiao (1981), on Bruce Lee; V. Glaessner (1974), a study of the kungfu genre; L. Jia (1995), on martial arts films of the 1930s–40s; M. Mintz (1978); S. Lau (1980), both on martial arts films; H. Rodriguez (1997), on the Wong Fei-hung series; S. Teng (1996d), kungfu films from Bruce Lee to Jackie Chan; M. Yang (1995), a dissertation on contemporary films.

(TW, YZ)

masculinity

Masculinity denotes the kind of qualities pertaining to the male character who has strong physical and intellectual powers and cares very little about his emotions. Historically, masculinity first surfaced in China in martial arts films, such as *The **Burning of Red Lotus Temple*** (*dir.* **Zhang Shichuan**, 1928), in which legendary knights errant roam about the country and right wrongs by resorting to physical fights. In the 1930s, however, leftist films began to replace the previous emphasis on the physical with a new emphasis on the intellectual. Informed by leftist ideology and rising patriotic sentiments, a new conception of masculinity sought to transform effeminate male characters who had populated love stories of the earlier decades into genuine revolutionary fighters. In keeping with this conception, not only were male characters urged not to indulge in **romance**, but 'new women' were also asked to renounce their gender difference and participate in the movement of national salvation as the intellectual equals of their male 'comrades'. The resulting cinematic masculinization of both male and female characters is best exemplified in the **war film**, an emerging genre in the late 1930s. In films such as *Protect Our Land* (*dir.* **Shi Dongshan**) and *Eight Hundred Heroic Soldiers* (*dir.* **Ying Yunwei**, both 1938), army soldiers and civilian volunteers fight battles against all odds and, if necessary, sacrifice their lives to defend the country.

In the 1940s–60s, war films continued to be produced in mainland China and Taiwan, and masculinity became an all too political concept. Since the resurgence of the martial arts film in Hong Kong in the 1960s, however, the type of masculinity characterized by both a high moral order and a detachment from romantic sentiments again dominated the screen. *Dragon Gate Inn* (*dir.* King **Hu**), *One-Armed Swordsman* (*dir.* **Chang Che**, both 1967) and *Return of the Dragon* (*dir.* Bruce **Lee**, 1973) presented a series of martial arts heroes whose combat skills appealed to the audience and paved the way for the rise of a new type of masculinity in gangster films of the 1980s. With its high-speed chases and beautifully choreographed gun fights, *The Killer* (*dir.* John **Woo**, 1989), and numerous films like it, portray a chaotic world where the only thing that matters is no longer the question of law and order but male bonding (often between the undercover agents and the criminals). The ideal image of masculinity in the Hong Kong screen, therefore, shifted from Bruce Lee (the martial art hero) to **Chow Yun-Fat** (the lone killer).

In mainland China, it is interesting that neither the war nor the kungfu genre produced an ideal screen figure of masculinity (although **Zhao Dan**'s roles in some historical films may come close to such an ideal). Rather, it is the legendary 'Grandpa' (played by **Jiang Wen**) in *Red Sorghum* (*dir.* **Zhang Yimou**, 1987) that captured the public imagination of a new type of masculinity that depends on a primitive lifestyle, vulgar language and rude behaviour. Jiang Wen went on with his mostly masculine roles as an ex-prisoner in *Black Snow* (*dir.* **Xie Fei**, 1989) and a macho detective in *Presumed Guilty* (*dir.*

Zhou Xiaowen, 1993). In general, the concept of masculinity seldom occupies mainland and Taiwan directors unless it is defined in the political sense (i.e., in connection with images of war heroes and revolutionary martyrs).

See also: gangster film; historical film; kungfu film; martial arts film

Further Reading
J. Sandell (1996), J. Stringer (1997b), T. Williams (1997a, b), all on John Woo; Y. Wang (1989b), Y. Zhang (1990), both on *Red Sorghum*.

(YZ)

melodrama

A critical term hardly translatable in Chinese (*tongsu ju* being a possible equivalent), melodrama is used to refer to a type of Chinese film characterized by moral polarization, prolonged human suffering, excessive emotionalism, exaggerated expression, extravagant representation and extreme suspense. Apart from traditional theatre, sentimental butterfly fiction popular in the 1900s–20s provided Chinese filmmakers with a rich resource of stories of human tragedy. Silent films of the late 1920s and the early 1930s, like those by **Zheng Zhengqiu**, **Shi Dongshan** and **Sun Yu**, had already contained many melodramatic elements outlined above. With the advent of sound, sorrowful tunes (i.e., 'melo – from *melos*' – the musical component of the melodrama) added much to the attraction of those films that elaborate the fate of miserable rural and urban people, as in *Plunder of Peach and Plum* (*dir.* **Ying Yunwei**, 1934) and *Boatman's Daughter* (*dir.* **Shen Xiling**, 1935).

The melodramatic tradition continued in the late 1940s, especially in epic films such as *Spring River Flows East* (*dir.* **Cai Chusheng**, **Zheng Junli**, 1947), and was further carried on in Taiwan and Hong Kong in the 1950s–70s. Films about the separation of **family** members during the wars became a stalwart in this genre. Also popular in the period is the melodrama that depicts **romance** involving young people and their conflicts with parents regarding **love and marriage**. **Chiung Yao**'s films, in this case, are melodramatic in nature, and were immensely popular in Taiwan. Films like these may be termed 'family melodrama'.

In mainland China a different type of melodrama, sometimes termed 'political melodrama', developed in the aftermath of the **Cultural Revolution**. The best example of this is the so-called '**Xie Jin** model', a type of film that dwells excessively on innocent victims' traumatic experiences of political persecution so as to invoke in the viewer an acute sense of injustice as well as a profound feeling of sympathy. Political melodramas were particularly popular in China from the late 1970s to the mid-1980s.

See also: film adaptations of drama and literature; theatre and film

Further Reading
N. Browne (1994), N. Ma (1994), two studies of Xie Jin's melodramas; E. Kaplan (1991), on melodrama and images of women in mainland productions of the 1980s; P. Pickowicz (1993a), an excellent historical survey of the genre from the 1930s to the 1980s.

(YZ)

mixed genres

As defined in **genre films**, a group of films sharing similar story lines, character types, themes, settings, moods and film techniques are classified by convention into a film genre, such as action, **comedy**, martial arts, ghosts and immortals, historical and war films. Since the 1980s, especially in Hong Kong, it has become increasingly popular for filmmakers to cross the genre lines and create mixed genres that appeal to the audience's desire for new visual sensations and new narrative formulas. Comic kungfu films and romantic gangster films are among the most popular in the 1990s.

See also: action film; gangster film; ghosts and immortals, film of; historical film; kungfu film; martial arts film; war film

(YZ)

modernity

A critical term referring to the experience of a fundamental break from traditional ways of life and the attendant feelings of anxiety over existential problems and of uncertainty about the future. The theme of such 'experiential' modernity is typically expressed in two narrative paradigms: one involving a shift from the traditional to the modern, and the other a sharp contrast between **rural life** and **urban life**.

The first paradigm was already visible in **Zheng Zhengqiu**'s films of the 1920s, which criticized traditional practices and prejudices such as arranged marriage and chaste widowhood. The second paradigm emerged in the early 1930s, when Chinese filmmakers began to examine the impact of modernization on a country with thousands of years of history. Invariably the city was imagined as a place of crime, corruption and degradation, whereas the countryside was depicted as the place where the prodigal son would return to cure himself of urban disease. This polarized representation remained consistent in most films of the 1930s–40s, such as ***Song of China*** (*dir.* **Fei Mu**, **Luo Mingyou**) and ***Boatman's Daughter*** (*dir.* **Shen Xiling**, both 1935), in spite of the fact that their directors and screen writers might have rather different political affiliations.

While the urban–rural contrast became less pronounced in the mainland after 1949, it was used again and again in Taiwan films during the 1950s–70s to represent an idealized integration of the traditional and the modern, especially in propaganda films such as ***Oyster Girl*** and *Beautiful Duckling* (both *dir.* Li Jia, **Lee Hsing**, both 1964), which aimed to promote the government's modernization policy. Interestingly, as far as a drive for modernization is concerned, mainland films of the 1980s resemble their Taiwan counterparts in several ways. Icons of modern life dominate the screen: skyscrapers, Boeing jets, luxury cars, futuristic offices, five-star hotels, karaoke bars, big-screen TV sets, hi-fi sound equipment and what not. Under the sheer display of such material emblems of modernization, however, many directors in mainland China, Taiwan and Hong Kong, like **Li Shaohong**, **Xie Fei**, **Sun Zhou**, **Hou Hsiao-hsien**, Edward **Yang**, **Tsai Ming-liang**, Ann **Hui**, Stanley **Kwan** and **Wong Kar-Wai**, continue to explore all nuances of modernity as experienced by a great variety of people.

See also: propaganda and film

Further Reading
P. Pickowicz (1991), on tradition and modernity in the 1930s.

(YZ)

Mr Vampire

(Jiangshi xiansheng)

dir./sc. Ricky Lau
with Lam Ching Ying, Chin Siu Ho, Moon Lee,
Pauline Wong, Ricky Lau
Hong Kong: Bo Ho Films/Golden Harvest,
1985

Sammo **Hung**'s production of *Mr Vampire* remains
one of Hong Kong's best-loved kungfu ghost
comedies. It features excellent performances, a
catchy theme song, and an intriguing range of new
generic features, such as hopping vampires and
high-kicking vampire hunters.

The movie concerns the exploits of a *fengshui*
master, Uncle Kau, and his two young assistants,
Man Choi and Chou. After Kau is asked to
exhume the mortal remains of Mr Yam's father,
strange things start to happen. The dead man's
spirit returns in vampire form and local townspeople, including Yam himself, start turning up
dead. While a bumbling police officer tries to
pin the blame for the murders on Kau, Yam's
daughter Ting Ting has to fight off the affections
of Man Choi. In turn, Chou is targeted by a female
ghost who seduces him one dark night. After
extended chase and fight scenes, the vampire
corpses are finally defeated and Uncle Kau gets
the better of the female ghost. However, Chou
insists that he let her go because she had earlier
saved his life. Kau does so, and she acknowledges
her true feelings for Chou by flying off to the spirit
world rather than bring him more trouble in the
here and now.

The colourful sets, atmospheric **horror film**
trappings, and excellent comedy and kungfu stunts
brought *Mr Vampire* a large international audience.
It also revitalized the career of Lam Ching Ying,
who before turning vampire hunter had been a
successful martial arts star. Like other innovative
genre hybrids from Hong Kong, the movie generated a number of sequels and imitations.

See also: comedy; ghosts and immortals, film of;
kungfu film; martial arts film

(JS)

Mui, Anita

(Mei Yanfang)

b. 10 October 1963, Hong Kong
Actress, singer

Anita Mui is as well known for her singing talents
as for her acting performances in Hong Kong
cinema. Her veteran Chinese opera singer mother
began training her at the age of four. By eight, she
began singing in nightclubs to support her family.
At nineteen, she won the top prize in a television-
sponsored singing contest in 1982. Mui's first film
was *Last Song in Paris* (1982). She gradually built
up expertize in action, **comedy** and dramatic
roles.

In 1987 she won Best Actress award at HKFA
and Taipei GHA for her role in **Rouge** (*dir.*
Stanley **Kwan**, 1987) as a ghostly 1930s prostitute
who returns to seek her lost lover in 1980s Hong
Kong. It typified the quintessential romantic
persona appearing in her better roles. Tsui Hark's
A Better Tomorrow, III (1989) introduced her to
action cinema. She played another mysterious
femme fatale but one who teaches **Chow Yun-
Fat**'s Mark to fire a gun and gives him the
iconographical raincoat and dark glasses characterizing John **Woo's** doomed romantic hero. In
Shanghai, Shanghai (1990), she displayed her skill in
martial arts along with Sammo **Hung** and Yuen
Biao, as well as performing superbly as 'Wonder
Woman' in the comic-book styled *The Heroic Trio*
and its apocalyptic sequel *The Executioners* (both *dir.*
Johnny To, 1993).

Mui's comic talents appear to good advantage
in *Fight Back to School, III* (1993), a Stephen **Chow**
satire of *Basic Instinct* (*dir.* Paul Verhoeven, 1992),
where she performs the Sharon Stone role. She
stole *Drunken Master, II* (*dir.* Lau Kar-leung, 1994)
from Jackie **Chan** in the role of his feisty
stepmother. But Chan's American breakthrough,
Rumble in the Bronx (*dir.* Stanley Tong, 1994)
merely used her as a comic 'patsy.' Mui used her
pop music persona as gender-bender 'Asian
Madonna' to good effect in *Who's the Woman, Who's
the Man* (*dir.* Peter Chan, 1996).

See also: action film

Further Reading
F. Dannen and B. Long (1997: 118–20), a profile
with a selected filmography.

(TW)

Mulan Joins the Army
(Mulan congjun)

dir. **Bu Wancang**
sc. **Ouyang Yuqian**
with Chen Yunshang, Mei Xi, Liu Jiqun, Huang Naishuang, Han Lan'gen
Shanghai: Huacheng Film, 1939

Based on a famous Chinese legend that promotes filial piety, the film shifts its focus to the resistance of foreign invasion, a theme befitting the historical context in which the film was produced.

During the Northern Dynasties (386–581 AD), the northern tribes invade China. An old soldier, Hua, is in poor health, but is urged by the government to join the service. Hua's daughter, Mulan, who has been practicing martial arts with her father since childhood, disguises herself as a boy and joins the army in her father's stead. In time, Mulan demonstrates her extraordinary qualities and is promoted to sergeant. During an enemy attack, the commanding Chinese general is shot by an arrow. Before he is taken away, he authorizes Mulan to take over his position. Under Mulan's leadership, the Chinese troops launch a counter attack and drive the enemy into retreat. Mulan's best friend Liu discovers Mulan's true gender identity, but keeps it a secret. At the victory celebration the emperor rewards both of them with promotions. But Mulan declines her appointment and asks to be retired so that she can take care of her ageing parents. Liu requests that he be sent to attend to the wounded general. After the emperor grants their requests, Mulan resumes her feminine identity and marries Liu.

In spite of its theme of **nationalism**, the film caused a big stir when it was shown in Chongqing in 1939. Some people resented the film because it was made in Shanghai, a city under Japanese control. In one incident, the film was burned by the audience and a riot ensued.

See also: legends and myths

(ZX)

music and film

Film music is a complex and under-studied area in Chinese film. Since the first Chinese short feature, **Conquering Jun Mountain** (1905), was a filming of Peking opera excerpts, one may expect traditional Chinese music to play a major part in early sound films. But the case turned out differently. Although the first talkie, **Sing-Song Girl Red Peony** (*dir.* **Zhang Shichuan**, 1930), carried a strong Chinese flavour by focusing on the life of a traditional sing-song girl, and background music played by traditional Chinese instruments (e.g., *erhu* and *pipa*) were added to silent films as late as 1935, as in **Song of China** (*dir.* **Fei Mu**, **Luo Mingyou**, 1935), many sound films in the early 1930s featured an extensive array of Western music. Apart from a small number of popular theme songs in a distinctive Chinese style, such as the 'Song of the Fishermen' and the 'March of the Volunteers' (the latter adopted as the national anthem of the PRC after 1949), the soundtrack of most films in the 1930s are filled with typical Western genre music, ranging from arias, fantasies, nocturnes and sonatinas, to humoresque, waltz and even jazz. For some films focusing on bourgeois life in Shanghai, like *A* **New Year's Coin** (*dir.* Zhang Shichuan, 1937), Western music flows naturally in and out of the dance hall and piano parlour. But for rural films, Western music often leaves an impression of unreality and spoils the harmony between the image track and the soundtrack. For instance, against the picturesque scenes of West Lake in Hangzhou, the viewers of **Boatman's Daughter** (*dir.* **Shen Xiling**, 1935) are greeted by pieces of Western music played by piano and violin. The apparent reason for such an extensive, oftentimes indiscriminate, use of Western music in the mid-1930s is that many composers at the time had just completed their education in Western music and had yet to develop their own styles in music composition.

Experiments with film music developed very fast, however. Background sound was given a symbolic role in **Plunder of Peach and Plum** (*dir.* **Ying Yunwei**, 1934), and original scores for background music – together with original theme songs – were written specifically for **Cityscape** (*dir.* **Yuan Muzhi**, 1935), which was marketed as the first musical **comedy** in China. By the late 1940s, music had become an integral part of a majority of Chinese feature films. It is not until the 1950s–60s, however, that a concerted effort to compose film music with Chinese 'national' characteristics was launched in mainland China. Folk songs and regional music were collected and adapted for the screen, especially in the genres of ethnic minorities and of the **musical**, and a number of theme songs, such as those from **Five**

Golden Flowers (*dir.* Wang Jiayi, 1959) and *Third Sister Liu* (*dir.* Su Li, 1960), were popular for a long time. Theme songs from many films in the 1980s–90s continue to engage audiences nationwide; yet increasingly these songs are no longer characterized by a traditional Chinese style, but by a variety of popular styles from Taiwan and Hong Kong, as is obvious in *Black Snow* (*dir.* **Xie Fei**, 1990). By comparison, *Swan Song* (*dir.* **Zhang Zeming**, 1985) and *The True Hearted* (*dir.* **Sun Zhou**, 1992) seem to be elegies to traditional music.

Film music in Taiwan and Hong Kong did not go through a phase of conscientious search for national or regional characteristics. For some reasons, music does not constitute a major target in the search for Taiwan's rural identity by its New Wave directors. A nostalgic look at the decline of traditional puppet shows in *The Puppet Master* (*dir.* **Hou Hsiao-hsien**, 1993), for instance, remains largely an individual effort. What has received more attention from Taiwan filmmakers are the influences from the West, such as that of Elvis Presley on Taiwan's youngsters in *A Brighter Summer Day* (*dir.* Edward **Yang**, 1991), or that of modern show business on local, inarticulate Taiwan people in *Papa, Can You Hear Me Sing?* (*dir.* Yu Kanping, 1983). In fact, in the 1950s–60s the Broadway type of musicals were produced in Taiwan and Hong Kong, and titles such as *Mambo Girl* (1957) and *Mad About Music* (1963, both *dir.* Yi Wen) proved immensely popular.

See also: ethnic minorities, film of; nostalgia

Further Reading
P. Fonoroff (1997: 188–99), beautiful stills with captions on Hong Kong musicals; S. Tuohy (1999), a study of 1930s film music.

(YZ)

musical, the

In contrast to **filmed stage performances** (*wutai yishu pian*), which have fascinated Chinese audiences throughout the century, the musical is not a major genre in Chinese cinema, except during the 1950s–60s in Hong Kong. In terms of emphasis, the Chinese musical can be subdivided into three categories: 'the sing-song film' (*gechang pian*), 'the song-and-dance film' (*gewu pian*) and 'the musical' (*yinyue pian*).

Historically, 'the sing-song film' emerged first during the period when Chinese filmmakers attempted to produce sound films. The producers of *Sing-Song Girl Red Peony* (1930) and many other films of the early 1930s had recordings of theme songs ready for sale by the time films were screened in the first-run theatres. Like Hollywood musicals, Chinese sing-song films also feature pretty women smiling, singing and dancing away on the screen. This was the type of musical that prevailed in Hong Kong during the 1950s–60s. Films like *Peach Flower River* (1955) and *Princess of a Hundred Flowers* (1957), both directed by Wang Tianlin and featuring Zhong Qing (*b.* 1933), were box-office hits, and for a while popular wisdom had it that no film was worth watching if it did not feature a beautiful song. Female stars dominated Hong Kong film of the 1950s, and their male counterparts functioned as mere foils to their charming voices. Although the fashion switched to **martial arts film** in the 1970s, as late as 1983 a Taiwan production, *Papa, Can You Hear Me Sing?* (*dir.* Yu Kanping, 1983), was still attempting to capture the glamour of sing-song films.

By coincidence, the 1950s–60s also witnessed a sing-song film boom in mainland China. In an over-politicized climate, musicals provided enchanting audio-visual treats for audiences at the same time as they offered filmmakers a rare opportunity to be stylistically innovative. *Third Sister Liu* (*dir.* Su Li, 1960), for instance, combines a series of melodious folk songs with picturesque scenes of the Li River near the famous resort in Guilin. The exotic appeal of musicals like *Third Sister Liu* and *Ashma* (*dir.* **Liu Qiong**, 1964), the latter based on an ethnic folk tale, also derived from their representation of China's minorities as people who like to sing love songs and seek romantic affairs, two pursuits severely criticized, if not absolutely forbidden, in the Han cultural context of the time. Of course, most mainland musicals had to incorporate politically correct messages, such as class struggle and solidarity among the Han and ethnic minorities, but judging from the lasting popularity of their theme songs, audiences enjoy musicals less for their political indoctrination than for the pleasure of entertainment. When *Tang Bohu Picks Qiuxiang* (*dir.* **Li Pingqian**, 1962), a Hong Kong musical about the legendary womanizer Tang Bohu, hit mainland markets in the late 1970s, it was warmly received partly because many of its songs recall those in *Third Sister Liu*, both films being derived from the

Plate 27   *Third Sister Liu* (1960)

folk-music tradition of Southern China (*jiangnan*). Its success might be attributed to the same regional-musical appeal – *huaguxi*, 'flower-drum play' – that helped *Red Guards of Lake Hong* (dir. **Xie Tian**, Chen Fangqian, Xu Feng, 1961) become so popular despite its thematic focus on the **Communist revolution**.

For the closest equivalent to Hollywood or Broadway musicals, however, one has to turn to several elaborate productions of 'song-and-dance films' from Hong Kong during the 1950s–60s. *Mambo Girl* (dir. Yi Wen, 1957), for instance, features **Ge Lan** performing the latest fashions in exotic dance. She was so popular that, after her marriage in 1960, she had to appear in a farewell feature – the title expressive of her fans' feelings: *Because of Her* (dir. Yi Wen, Wang Tianlin, 1963) – before she was allowed to retire. Another memorable example of this sub-genre is *Smiling Beauty* (dir. Tao Qin, 1961), which won Best Actress and Best Music awards at Asia-Pacific FF as well as Best Director and Best Music at Taipei GHA. Indeed, during this period both Cantonese and Mandarin musicals were immensely popular and entertaining. In contrast to these Hong Kong productions, mainland song-and-dance films try to propagate official ideology. A film of large-scale song-and-dance ensembles, *The East Is Red* (dir. **Wang Ping**, 1965) presents an 'epic' re-enactment of the Communist revolution.

Finally, 'the musical' in the Chinese context often focuses on the life of an individual musician or composer and plays out the conflict between Western and traditional or regional Chinese music. The quest for indigenous Cantonese music in ***Swan Song*** (dir. **Zhang Zeming**, 1985), for instance, articulates a **nostalgia** for a tradition lost during the **Cultural Revolution**. Interestingly, Western music appears not only as a vital force but also as a means of individual expression in a variety of contemporary features – it signifies political protest in ***Reverberations of Life*** (dir. **Wu Tianming**, **Teng Wenji**, 1979) and cultural resistance in ***Rock 'n' Roll Kids*** (dir. **Tian Zhuangzhuang**, 1988). Although not conceived as musicals, **Sixth Generation** films like ***Beijing Bastards*** (dir. **Zhang Yuan**, 1993) and ***Dirt*** (dir. Guan Hu, 1994) use rock music to forge an identity for social outcasts during a period of existential crisis in **urban life**.

See also: adaptations of drama and literature; ethnic minorities, film of; music and film; theatre and film

Further Reading

L. Qiu and M. Yu (1995: 1: 109), a brief entry on Ge Lan; P. Fonoroff (1997: 180–99), an informative introduction with beautiful photos.

(YZ)

My American Grandson

(Shanghai jiaqi)

dir. Ann **Hui**
sc. **Wu Nien-chen**
with Wu Ma, Wong Kwan-yuen, Carina Lau
Shanghai: Shanghai Film/Taipei: Golden Tripod, 1991

Ann Hui is on familiar ground with this film, having explored the theme of cultural conflict in her masterly *Song of the Exile* (1990). This **melodrama** about cultural differences between the USA and China concerns Ku, a widower who lives in a Shanghai apartment house feeling sad about growing old.

Ku's son telephones him from the USA. He will send Ku's teenage grandson, Ming, to Shanghai while he and his wife travel to Germany. Before long the spoilt Ming has become angered over cultural differences between America and China. Dong, a young man living in Ku's house, becomes disgusted by Ming's lack of respect for Ku, even though the old man has gone out of his way to make his grandson feel comfortable. Ku also shows Ming the school where he used to teach.

Ming is a surly student and tells his teachers that their precepts of traditional culture are stupid. He is soon telephoning his parents, pleading to be taken back home. After falling into a pond, Ming is cared for by some villagers whose honest and simple ways he comes to respect. Once Ku has come to collect him again, the two refuse to speak for days before Ming finally feels remorse: now they become the best of friends.' Dong learns American ways from Ming and tries to get over his frustration at not having won the love of Ku's niece. Increasingly attracted to each other, Ku and his neighbour, Mrs Mo, listen to music and do not even hear the phone when Ming's parents telephone for him to come back home. Now a transformed character, Ming is sad to leave Shanghai, although Ku has to grin and bear the fact of his grandson's return to America.

(KH)

My Memory of Old Beijing

(Chengnan jiushi)

dir. **Wu Yigong**
sc. Yi Ming
with Shen Jie, Zheng Zhenyao, Zhang Fengyi, Zhang Min
Shanghai: Shanghai Film, 1982

This film depicts a series of events and personalities of old Beijing as witnessed through the eyes of a young girl. It is one of the few films from the PRC that conscientiously seeks a lyrical or poetic style.

Yingzi, a six-year-old girl, is brought to Beijing by her parents during the 1920s. Her first friend in this new environment, Xiuzhen, is a traumatized young woman obsessed with finding her daughter. Xiuzhen's college-student husband had been taken away by the police years earlier without anyone learning of his subsequent whereabouts. After she gave birth to a baby girl with a mole on her neck, her in-laws abandoned the baby without even consulting her first. Xiuzhen then grew mentally disturbed. Yingzi soon learns that one of her playmates, Xiao Guizi, has a mole on her neck, and so she brings them together. Xiuzhen is overjoyed and decides to look for her husband. But she and Guizi are run over by a passing train.

Yingzi is greatly saddened. Before long she meets a new friend, a young man who steals in order to be able to put his brother through school, but because Yingzi unintentionally reveals his secret hide-out to a plain-clothes policeman, the young man is arrested.

At the age of nine, Yingzi turns her attention to her nanny, Song. At first she does not understand why Song leaves her own children at home to take care of her. She later learns that Song's own son drowned a few years earlier and her daughter was sold by her husband. Song now works to support herself and her husband. Yingzi's father dies of a lung disease and her family has to relocate again. As she says goodbye to Song and to the neighbourhood she has spent the last three years in, tears fall down her cheek.

The film was awarded the Golden Eagle at the 1983 Manila FF.

(ZX)

Myriad of Lights

(Wanjia denghuo)

dir. **Shen Fu**
sc. Shen Fu, **Yang Hansheng**
with Lan Ma, **Shangguan Yunzhu**, **Wu Yin**,
Shen Yang, Gao Zheng
Shanghai: Kunlun Film, 1948

This film reveals the poverty obscured by Shanghai's glamorous facade. Hu Zhiqing is employed in a trading company whose manager, Qian Jianru, is his former classmate. Hu, his wife Youlan, and their daughter can barely make ends meet. What is more, Hu's mother arrives from the country with brother Chunsheng and his wife. They have left their poor village because they think life in Shanghai will be easier for them.

Crowded into a small apartment, Zhiqing realizes life has become too difficult for him. His salary is never enough, Youlan is expecting another child, and the only other income coming in is the little money Chunsheng earns by shining shoes in the street. The situation gets worse when Hu loses his job after opposing Qian's business practices. One day, Chunsheng is beaten up by a rich customer who turns out to be Qian. When Youlan tries to talk Qian into giving Hu another chance, Hu's mother unexpectedly shows up and attacks Qian harshly for having beaten Chunsheng. Youlan's mediation fails and the two women start quarrelling. As a result, Youlan leaves the house and has a miscarriage. Hu's mother decides to go back to the country, but she has no money for the ticket. In her desperation, she finds comfort in her niece, Ah Zhen, a factory worker.

Meanwhile, Hu is mistakenly accused of stealing a purse on a bus. Escaping from the crowd who chase him, he is hit by a car and taken to the hospital. He stays there for several days, while his wife and mother – now reconciled – look for him everywhere. When Hu finally comes back, he finds everybody gathered around Ah Zhen. They all promise each other that they will be strong and fight together against hard times. In this film, the opposition between honest **rural life** and corrupt **urban life** is displaced by generational and class conflicts.

(PV)

mystery film

A type of film unravelling the complicated process of solving a case of high complexity. Closely related to **detective film**, such a film normally consists of the discovery of a crime, the search for clues, and the arrest of the criminal. A mystery film, however, pays more attention than a detective film to its eerie atmosphere, its prolonged suspension and its irrational events, as well as the crime's psychological and emotional impact on the protagonists and the audience. The tradition of Chinese ghost stories has been frequently utilized in this genre, as in *The Ghost in an Old House* (*dir.* **Dan Duyu**, 1931) and *Walking Corpse in an Old House* (*dir.* **Ma-Xu Weibang**, 1938). Sometimes political elements are added to enhance the plot, as in *Haunted House* (*dir.* **Huang Jianzhong**, 1993). Occasionally the mystery in question may be a medical case, as in *Arc Light* (*dir.* **Zhang Junzhao**, 1988), where a mental patient's irrational, highly mysterious questioning leads a doctor to question the normality of the rational world itself.

See also: ghosts and immortals, film of

(YZ)

myths

See under: legends and myths

N

Narrow Street

(Xiao jie)

dir. Yang Yanjin
sc. Xu Yinhua
with Guo Kaimin, **Zhang Yu**
Shanghai: Shanghai Film, 1981

The film is a powerful condemnation of the political radicalism of the **Cultural Revolution** and shows how ordinary people were victimized during a decade of turmoil.

A blind man, Xia, tells the film director a story. During the Cultural Revolution, Xia was a technician. One day, he met Yu, a young boy who seemed to be vulnerable. The two soon became good friends. During a trip, Xia discovered that Yu was a girl. The reason she disguised herself as a boy was that she had earlier been bullied by the Red Guards who shaved her hair. Xia was sympathetic and wanted to help her. He went to steal a wig from a theatre troupe for Yu, but was caught and suffered a severe beating. Xia lost his sight as a result. When he came out of the hospital, he went back to the little alley to find Yu, but she was no longer there. Xia and the director imagine several scenarios for Yu: perhaps she has become a fallen woman; or again she may have become a violinist. In fact, Yu has become a factory worker and has been looking for Xia. One day they accidentally meet on a train, and the film ends with their reunion.

(ZX)

nationalism

Nationalism refers to the ideology of a nation – in the sense both of 'nation-people' and of 'nation-state'. For thousands of years, the Chinese thought of their country as the Middle Kingdom, situated squarely in the centre of the world. The year 1895 is significant in that it marks both the invention of cinema and the Chinese defeat in the first Sino-Japanese war. Due to this immense national humiliation, many intellectuals started promoting the idea of nationalism at the turn of the century.

The concept of nation-people is reflected in many of **Zheng Zhengqiu**'s early films, which emphasize education as an effective means of strengthening the nation. In the 1930s, a number of different interpretations of nationalism competed on the screen. For the KMT government, the national tradition, in particular Confucian ethics, was most important to the project of nation-building. Some filmmakers participated in the Nationalist-sponsored New Life Movement and produced ethical films such as **Song of China** (*dir.* **Fei Mu**, **Luo Mingyou**, 1935) and *Little Angel* (*dir.* **Wu Yonggang**, 1935). For radical leftist intellectuals, on the other hand, it was Communist ideology that would eventually save the nation from foreign imperialists. Leftist films of the 1930s–40s, such as **Three Modern Women** (*dir.* **Bu Wancang**, 1933), **Big Road** (*dir.* **Sun Yu**, 1934), **Spring River Flows East** (*dir.* **Cai Chusheng**, **Zheng Junli**, 1947) and **Crows and Sparrows** (*dir.* Zheng Junli, 1949), placed a great emphasis on national salvation and solidarity among the people in troubled times, although they also promoted the idea of class struggle, sometimes quite explicitly.

The 1950s–70s was the period of state-building in both mainland China and Taiwan. The nation-state became a sacred idea that could override other ideological or political concerns. Propaganda films that promote government policies played a major role in the period. Historical and war films were produced not only to enhance the image of a strong nation resisting the Japanese invasion, but also to establish the position of either the KMT or the CCP as the legitimate leader of the Chinese people in the Republican revolution or the **Communist revolution**. Meanwhile Hong Kong productions looked back to a national tradition of legendary martial arts heroes and heroines who help preserve justice at the local level and exemplify the Confucian idea of moral integrity.

In the 1980s, renewed attention to the nation-people occurred in China and Taiwan at the same time. The mainland filmmakers, especially the **Fifth Generation** directors, sought to rediscover or reconstruct national culture and 'national roots' by way of cultural reflection. In the works of **Chen Kaige**, **He Ping**, **Zhang Yimou** and **Zhou Xiaowen**, one sees a new kind of cultural nationalism that resists Communist ideology in the name of the nation-people. Similarly, Taiwan New Wave directors moved quickly to reconsider what it means to be Taiwanese and what constitutes Taiwan's identity. **Hou Hsiao-hsien**'s *A City of Sadness* (1989), for instance, re-examines the issue of nationhood and national history from a distinctively Taiwanese perspective. Together with his colleagues like **Wang Tung** and **Wu Nien-chen**, Hou contributed to the rise of a new type of Taiwanese nationalism.

For obvious political reasons, the effects of Chinese nationalism on China's ethnic minorities have rarely been scrutinized in film productions. Most mainland films in this genre take the official position and champion the solidarity of all peoples in China. Whether or not other nationalities will be allowed to articulate their identities *vis-à-vis* the dominant Han culture remains to be seen.

See also: cultural reflections; ethnic minorities, film of; historical film; propaganda and film; war film

Further Reading

C. Berry (1992), a problematic thesis on race; C. Berry (1994a), a comparative study of the mainland and Taiwan; J. Ma (1993), on early forms of cinematic nationalism; G. Semsel *et al.* (1990: 97–140), Chinese debates on film's 'national form'; J. Weakland (1971), a discussion of invasion and resistance; Y. Zhang (1997a), a critique of nationhood and ethnicity.

(YZ)

Naval Battle of 1894

(Jiawu fengyun)

dir. **Lin Nong**
sc. Xi Nong *et al.*
with Li Moran, Wang Qiuying, Pu Ke, Zhou Wenbin, Pang Xueqin
Changchun: Changchun Film, 1962

On the eve of the first Sino-Japanese war in 1894, the commander of the Chinese North Sea Fleet, Ding Ruchang, and the captain of the cruise ship Zhiyuan, Deng Shichang, request that their fleet be allowed to patrol along the route used by two Chinese transportation ships. But their request is rejected by Li Hongzhang, then Prime Minister of China, with the result that the two Chinese transports are sunk by the Japanese navy, along with one of the two escort ships. The captain of the other escort ship, Fang Boqian, orders his sailors to hang out the white flag and prepare to flee. Refusing to carry out this order, they fire on the pursuing Japanese ship without Fang's approval. The Japanese ship sustains great damage and turns away.

Back at the base, Fang claims credit for disabling the Japanese ship during the battle and is received as a war hero. But Deng learns the truth from a sailor whom Fang had fired from his ship and who then reveals Fang's white flag episode at the victory celebration banquet. Ding and Deng go to Tianjin to see Li Hongzhang, bringing with them a petition signed by sailors and local people. They arrive at the residence when Li is in the middle of dinner with a group of Western diplomats. He hopes to avoid war with Japan through the mediating efforts of the Western powers. Deng overhears the conversation and is taken aback by the way the Western powers pressure Li into appeasing the Japanese.

When Li sends for Deng, Deng wastes no time lashing out at the hypocrisy of the Western diplomats. Deng's impropriety costs him his position as captain. Only after the court reluctantly decides to go to war with Japan is Deng reinstated by the navy. During one confrontation with the Japanese, Deng's ship manages to cause serious damage to the enemy's flag ship. But just as Deng tries to sink the Japanese ship he runs out of ammunition. The Japanese ship now turns around with the intention of capturing Deng's ship. Deng orders his crew to ram the enemy, but instead they are sunk by an incoming torpedo.

This **war film** promotes Chinese **nationalism** and narrates China's humiliating confrontation with imperialism at the turn of the century.

(ZX)

New Story of an Old Soldier

(Laobing xinzhuan)

dir. **Shen Fu**
sc. Li Zhun
with **Cui Wei**, Gao Bo, Gu Yelu, Chen Shu
Shanghai: Haiyan Film, 1959

This film tells the story of a military veteran's transition to civilian life. Its most significant moments concern the tensions between the veteran and his colleague and employees. While his colleague is portrayed as a conservative and the young people as undisciplined, the veteran is presented as the most loyal to the party and, therefore, as representative of what is correct – even though he is at times a little rigid.

In the late 1940s, the battle between the Communists and the Nationalists over Manchuria has just come to an end. A Communist veteran, Zhan, requests to work in the civilian sector and run a farm at the Manchurian frontier. An agricultural expert, Zhao Songyun, is appointed to assist Zhan in the management of the farm. Not long after they start the enterprise, a group of urban unemployed, including Zhan's son, Yunsheng, come to join them. Zhan is eager to start planting a grain harvest so that they can support the CCP's fight against the Nationalists. Zhao, however, insists that the virgin Manchurian land needs at least a year of cultivation before it is ready to produce food. The young men and women working on the farm side with Zhan, but Zhan returns this support by imposing numerous restrictions on their activities, including a ban on dancing and romantic relationships, and hence generates a good deal of resistance from the young people. A plague sweeping across the farm endangers the crops. As a result, many leave to seek opportunities elsewhere.

Zhao resents Zhan's authoritarian style of leadership and takes his case to the governor. Acting on this pressure from above, Zhan tries to improve himself. Some bandits make an attempt to loot the farm, but they are defeated by the guards and workers led by Zhan. By the end of the year, the workers have successfully built their first generator. The news that the CCP has taken Beijing without bloodshed arrives just as Zhan's son and five other farm workers are getting married. In the meantime, Zhan moves on to a new post and new challenges.

(ZX)

New Taiwan Cinema

See under: Taiwan cinema (in Historical essays)

New Woman

(Xin nüxing)

dir. **Cai Chusheng**
sc. **Sun Shiyi**
with **Ruan Lingyu**, **Zheng Junli**, Yin Xu, Wang Naidong
Shanghai: Lianhua Film, 1934

Inspired by the real-life suicide of an actress named Ai Xia, this film is strongly critical of social injustice, particularly the treatment of women in 1930s China. But its negative portrayal of journalists caused controversy – one of the factors which, according to some, contributed indirectly to the suicide of Ruan Lingyu not long after the film's release.

Wei Ming is a music teacher in a girls' school. Before she came to Shanghai she had a love affair with a man who later left her after she became pregnant. In her spare time Wei writes fiction, and one of her novels, *The Tomb of Love*, is being considered by a publisher. The chief editor first rejects her manuscript without even reading it, but after learning that the author is a woman, and a pretty woman at that, he decides to publish it with her photo on the cover. Meanwhile a member of the board at her school, Dr Wang, whose wife happens to be Wei's former classmate, makes a pass at Wei and, when rejected, uses his powers of influence to make the school principal fire her. Wei's financial situation deteriorates further when her sister brings her sick daughter to Shanghai. The hospital refuses to help the child unless Wei pays the deposit. In a desperate attempt to save her daughter's life, Wei is talked into 'selling' herself for one night. But when she is led into the inner chamber of a brothel, the customer she finds sitting there is none other than Wang! Humiliated and outraged, Wei explodes in hysteria and attacks Wang. The news that Wei was seen in a brothel is leaked by Wang to a journalist. The scandalous story soon appears in the newspapers. Wei, having just lost her daughter, is devastated by the vicious attacks and commits suicide.

Further Reading

K. Harris (1995), a historical study of the film; Y. Zhang (1994a), a critique of gender politics in the 1930s.

(ZX)

New Year's Coin, A

(Yasui qian)

dir. **Zhang Shichuan**
sc. **Xia Yan**
with Gong Qiuxia, Hu Rongrong, Li Minghui, **Gong Jianong**
Shanghai: Mingxing Film, 1937

The plot rotates around a silver coin which Mr. He gives to his granddaughter, Rongrong, as New Year 'lucky money'. After Rongrong spends the money on firecrackers the coin travels through all segments of 1930s Shanghai society, revealing economic crisis and social inequalities. The coin acquires different values in each owner's hands. For a poor lady it is a precious coin to be saved in a bank; for a gangster it is the means to pay prostitutes. For Xiuxia, Rongrong's cousin, it provides a means of paying a friend's overdue rent. This decision symbolizes Xiuxia's desire to leave her miserable dance-hall life and redeem herself by joining the ranks of workers. The film ends with Mr. He giving more money to Rongrong as a New Year's gift, but this time it is a dollar bill not a silver coin.

Written by the underground Communist Xia Yan, the film emphasizes the contrast between the rampant poverty of the urban slums and the decadent lifestyle of bourgeois households. To avoid government censorship, the film lists **Hong Shen** instead of Xia Yan as its screenwriter. However, because it features extensive song and dance, and the child star Hu Rongrong (nicknamed the 'Chinese Shirley Temple'), the film has not been

given as much attention as other contemporary leftist films by official mainland film historiography.

See also: censorship and film

Further Reading

Y. Zhang (1996: 126–8), a brief discussion of urban perception.

(PV, YZ)

New Year's Sacrifice

(Zhufu)

dir. **Sang Hu**
sc. **Xia Yan**
with **Bai Yang**, Wei Heling, Li Jingpo
Beijing: Beijing Film, 1956

This adaptation of Lu Xun's short story of the same title concerns the tragic life of a woman in traditional Chinese society.

Xianglin's widow overhears that her mother-in-law is going to sell her, so she runs away. She finds a job as a maid in Mr Lu's residence in a town far away from her deceased husband's village. Just as she begins a new life there, she is kidnapped by several men sent by her mother-in-law and brought back to be sold to a farmer named He Laoliu. The widow refuses to marry He and attempts suicide. Gradually, however, she learns that He is an honest man and the two of them finally get married. Their baby boy, Amao, arrives a year later. Yet their happiness proves short-lived. First, He dies of exhaustion. Then their son is killed by a wolf. The landlord then takes the house back because He's widow cannot afford to pay the rent. The now homeless widow goes back to Mr Lu and resumes her duties as a housemaid. Although at first people feel some sympathy for her, they soon grow tired of her repetitive stories. Her employer finds her eccentricity a potential threat to the household and fires her. The widow becomes a beggar. She collapses in the street on New Year's Eve.

The film won a special prize at the 1957 Karlovy Vary FF, as well as the Silver Cap at the 1958 International Film Week held in Mexico.

(ZX)

Plate 28   *New Year's Sacrifice* (1957)

newsreel

See under: documentary

Nie Er

(Nie Shouxin, Hei Tianshi)

b. 14 February 1912, Kunming, Yunnan
province
d. 17 July 1935
Composer

One of the best-known composers for leftist films
of the 1930s, Nie Er began his music training at
the age of ten. He became a political activist at
college, joined the Communist Youth League in
1928, and narrowly escaped arrest in 1930.

After working as a shop clerk for a year,
Nie found employment in Li Jinhui's Bright
Moon Song and Dance Troupe. However, as Li's
emphasis on entertainment conflicted with Nie's
political ideals, Nie left the troupe and headed for
Beijing, where he was to acquaint himself with a
number of important leftist intellectuals. Nie wrote

film reviews in his spare time. His criticism of *Pink
Dream* (*dir.* **Cai Chusheng**, 1932) so impressed
the director that the two became good friends. In
1933, Nie joined the CCP and was recruited into
Lianhua Film Company. In the space of two years
Nie composed scores for seven films. The 'March
of the Volunteers', a theme song he wrote for
Children of Troubled Times (*dir.* Xu Xingzhi, 1935),
became one of the most popular tunes of the
1930s: the song, with revised lyrics, was adopted·
as the PRC national anthem in 1949.

In 1935, on his way to the Soviet Union, Nie
made a stop over in Japan and was killed there in
an accident at the age of twenty-three.

Further Reading

ZDX (1982–6: 1: 289–96), a short biography.

(ZX)

Night Inn
(Ye dian)

dir. **Huang Zuolin**
sc. Ke Ling
with Zhang Fa, **Zhou Xuan**, Tong Zhiling,
Shi Yu, **Shi Hui**
Shanghai: Wenhua Film, 1947

This Chinese adaptation of Maxim Gorky's play *The Lower Depths* is one of the classic leftist films of the post-war period.

Mr Wen's tavern shelters a prostitute, a pickpocket, a pedlar, a street performer, and a dustman. Yang, the pickpocket, generously distributes his loot to his friends in the inn. He had earlier been involved with Mrs Wen, but he now falls in love with her sister, Xiaomei – causing the jealous Mrs Wen to abuse Xiaomei. Mrs Wen confides her frustrations to her former lover, Mr Fang, who suggests that she free herself from her husband by murdering him and avenge herself on Yang by selling Xiaomei to the brothel.

One of the tenants, Mrs Lai, is seriously ill and can't afford to pay her rent. Mr Wen goes after her ruthlessly. Mrs Lai gives Mr Wen a gold ring she has treasured for many years because it was given to her by her former employer as a reward for a decade's service, but Mr Wen points out that the ring is only gold-plated and hence worthless. Upon hearing this, Mrs Lai passes out. Yang wants to find a decent job so as to be worthy of Xiaomei's love. After being rejected by several potential employers, he finally lands a position at a blacksmith's. Mrs Wen proposes to Yang that he kill her husband in exchange for Xiaomei, but Yang declines the offer. Mrs Wen then kills her husband by poisoning his tea. Yang is arrested as the suspect and sentenced to ten years in prison. Xiaomei is raped by a man hired by Mrs Wen and is sold to the brothel. In the end, Fang confesses the scheme to the police and both he and Mrs Wen are arrested. Xiaomei commits suicide.

See also: leftist film

Further Reading
P. Pickowicz (1993b), a historical study of the process of stage and film adaptations.

(ZX)

Night Rain on the River
(Bashan yeyu)

dir. **Wu Yonggang**, **Wu Yigong**
sc. Ye Nan
with **Zhang Yu**, Li Zhiyu, Zhang Min, Mao Weihui, Zhong Xinghuo
Shanghai: Shanghai Film, 1980

Critical of the political excesses of the **Cultural Revolution**, this film depicts the hardship and injustice suffered by ordinary people during these years.

The poet Qiu Shi is taken out of jail and escorted by two secret agents, Liu Wenying and Li Yan, to the city of Wuhan. They board a passenger ship and encounter numerous people victimized by the radical politics of the 'Gang of Four'. Among those who share a room with them are a peasant girl who has been pressured into marrying a stranger in order to pay her family's debts, an old lady whose son has been lost in a conflict between warring factions, a traumatized Beijing Opera singer terrified of any reference to politics, and a little girl who seems to be searching for something. Unbeknown to Qiu Shi, the little girl is actually his daughter. When Qiu was arrested six years earlier, the girl had not yet been born: Qiu's wife died of depression a short while after the delivery. Also unbeknown to Qiu, a rescue operation is under way. The participants in this operation all resent the Gang of Four and view Qiu's imprisonment as an outrage. The only person who does not take part in this operation is Liu Wenying. Liu has been indoctrinated to believe that Qiu is a counter-revolutionary and that the Cultural Revolution has brought the Chinese people a better way of living. But what she witnesses during the journey changes her mind about many things, particularly about Qiu. After freeing Qiu, she confronts Li and asks him to have her arrested for letting Qiu go. Li throws the handcuffs in the river and welcomes her as a participant in the rescue mission.

The film gained awards of Best Screenplay and Best Actress (Zhang Yu) at the 1981 China GRA, and Best Film from the Ministry of Culture in 1980.

(ZX)

Ning Ying

Director, screen writer

A newly emerging figure from the **Fifth Generation**, Ning Ying grew up in a well-educated family playing the violin. She enrolled in the Recording Department at BFA in 1978–82 and studied editing and directing in the Rome Film Laboratory Centre in 1985–6. She served as assistant director on Bertolucci's *The Last Emperor* (1987) and returned to work in Beijing Film Studio in 1987. Her first film as director was a Hollywood-style **comedy**, *Someone Happened to Fall in Love with Me* (1990), but since 1989 she had been working on an adaptation of a Chen Jiangong novel about a group of Beijing retirees with her sister, Ning Dai, a graduate of the Screenplay Department at BFA and an active independent filmmaker. Their effort paid off, as *For Fun* (1992) brought Ning Ying critical recognition in 1993, winning a Young Cinema Gold Prize at Tokyo and a Golden Balloon at Nantes. The film's documentary style and humanism are taken to be expressive of 'New Urban Cinema', a new direction for Chinese features, and its successful financing, production and distribution was labelled the '*For Fun* phenomenon'.

With monetary awards from international festivals, Ning Ying began shooting *On the Beat* (1995), another Beijing film based on a Chen Jiangong novel, which uses a non-professional cast and depicts the daily routine of two ordinary Beijing policemen. Despite a few hilarious scenes, it remains the closest Chinese equivalent to films of the Italian neo-realist movement. The film won the Silver Mongolfière at the 1995 Nantes FF.

See also: independent film

Further Reading

W. Li (1994), a biographic sketch; J. White (1997), on Ning Ying's urban realism.

(YZ)

nostalgia

A strong feeling for something valuable that is irretrievably lost, nostalgia is a theme that characterizes many Chinese films produced in mainland China, Taiwan and Hong Kong during the 1980s–90s. Contrary to the patriotism of the 1920s–30s and the idealism of the 1950s–70s, mainland filmmakers fell back on nostalgia from time to time in the 1980s as they slowly recovered from the traumatic experiences of the **Cultural Revolution**. One example is the female protagonist in *Sacrificed Youth* (*dir.* **Zhang Nuanxin**, 1985), who yearns for a natural, beautiful way of life symbolized by an idyllic village in the Dai ethnic minority region; yet her yearning is in vain because near the end of the film a massive mud-slide wipes out the village and leaves her overwhelmed by feelings of loss and nostalgia. The nostalgia for wasted or 'sacrificed' youth is also articulated in the mid-1990s, but with historical hindsight even the Cultural Revolution has become coloured by subjective emotion. While a nostalgia for the simplicity of life and youthful idealism permeates *A Mongolian Tale* (*dir.* **Xie Fei**, 1995), a different mode of remembrance takes over *In the Heat of the Sun* (*dir.* **Jiang Wen**, 1994), which refigures the Cultural Revolution as a time for fun and, alas, for youthful innocence forever lost.

In Taiwan, *In Our Time* (*dir.* Edward **Yang** *et al.*, 1982) and other early New Wave films set the tone of nostalgia for the peaceful rural community in one's memory. *Growing Up* (*dir.* **Chen Kun-hou**, 1983) started a trend of nostalgic films that carry a whole generation back to their youthful dream in the country, a dream recreated in *A Time to Live, a Time to Die* (*dir.* **Hou Hsiao-hsien**), *Reunion* (*dir.* **Ko Yi-cheng**, both 1985) and other films about a group of school-children 'growing up' in the natural surroundings. Parallel to a pervasive nostalgia for lost childhood in Taiwan, a nostalgia for the lost city and its lost culture is strongly presented in Hong Kong films since the mid-1980s, a turning point when its denizens realized their fate of returning to China after the British rule expired in 1997. Both *Rouge* (1987) and *The Actress* (1992, both *dir.* Stanley **Kwan**) look back to the 1930s as a time when people were more heroic and more committed to their ideas. As shown in *Love in the Fallen City* (*dir.* Ann **Hui**, 1984), as far as individuals are concerned, the past emerges in one's nostalgic recollection as both glamorous and trivial, both monumental and inconsequential. Nostalgia, in this sense, constitutes nothing but a cinematic image, an elusive object hovering above the screen and waiting for the viewer's sympathetic identification.

See also: ethnic minorites, film of

Further Reading

R. Chow (1993), a theoretical reading of nostalgia; F. Luo (1995: 60–75), on Hong Kong nostalgic films.

(YZ)

Old Well

(Lao jing)

dir. **Wu Tianming**
sc. Zheng Yi
with **Zhang Yimou**, Liang Yujin, Lu Liping
Xi'an: Xi'an Film, 1987

This film can be read as an allegory of China's search for **modernity**. The internationally acclaimed director Zhang Yimou takes the male lead in his only major screen appearance to date. In the process of devoting himself to finding water for his villagers, the protagonist's personal life is sacrificed to the greater needs of the collective.

Sun Wangquan is one of three youths with a high school diploma in Old Well, a village plagued by a shortage of water. The villagers have been trying unsuccessfully for generations to find a well, and Sun himself has now become a participant in the continuous search for water. Although Sun is in love with his high school classmate Qiaoying, his father and grandfather have accepted a dowry from a young widow in the village because this money needs to be used to find a wife for Sun's younger brother. Sun's attempt to flee the village with Qiaoying is frustrated by his grandpa. He reluctantly marries the widow.

Sun plays an important role during a feud with another village over the ownership of a dry well and becomes the village hero. He is then given the opportunity to receive further technical training in town. Upon returning to the village, he and Qiaoying lead an exploration to locate a water source, but the two become trapped in an underground cave after an accident. Believing that they are going to die, they share their secret feelings for each other. A timely rescue by the villagers saves their lives, but one of their friends is killed.

By this time they have located a well, but do not have sufficient funds actually to dig. During a fund-raising event, Sun's grandfather donates his coffin, his wife brings her sewing machine, and Qiaoying, who is about to be married to a man from the town, instructs her sister to bring all her wedding gifts. In the end, the villagers finally succeed in digging a well that can produce enough water to sustain the village.

The film received the following awards: Special Jury Award at the 1987 Hawaii FF; Best Film, Best Director and Best Actor (Zhang Yimou) at the 1988 China GRA; Best Film and Best Actor at the 1987 HFA; Best Film from MBFT; and the Grand Prize at the 1988 Tokyo FF.

Further Reading

H. Chiao (1990b), a collection of relevant materials on the film; Y. Wang (1988), a psychoanalytic reading of the film.

(ZX)

On the Hunting Ground

(Liechang zhasa)

dir. **Tian Zhuangzhuang**
sc. Jiang Hao
with Autegen Bayaer, Laxi, Bayanertu
Hohhot: Inner Mongolian Film, 1985

An avant-garde film that helped usher in China's **Fifth Generation**, this first solo directorial début brought Tian Zhuangzhuang both reputation and notoriety. The Chinese title means the rules of the game on the hunting ground, but it is only partially understandable to most Chinese audiences. Tian's **documentary** style and his use of the Mongolian language make this film even harder to comprehend.

The hunting rules are handed down from generation to generation, and every year before the hunting season the Mongolians gather in front of a valley conducting rituals and reviewing their rules. Then gunshots are heard, and goats and rabbits are seen running everywhere. At dusk, cheerful hunters return with their game. Wangsen Zhabu is found poaching and, as a form of punishment, must kneel down and receive his mother's thrashing. Taogetao, Wangsen's brother, takes revenge against the betrayer and secretly lets wolves into Bayasi Guleng's sheep farm. The angry Bayasi goes to the mountain alone to fight the wolves. Wangsen informs his friends of Bayasi's danger, and together they go to the rescue. Bayasi and his wife thank Wangsen and sing songs for him at their family banquet.

The next year, Bayasi steals his friend's game and feels uneasy. Taogetao's tent catches fire, but no one is hurt. Taogetao confesses his wrongdoing the year before, and Bayasi also admits his faults. Together they kneel down in self-punishment, and the hunting brothers become friends again.

Although lip service to the collective **family** is still noticeable, Tian's film differs from previous films of ethnic minority in that it no longer identifies itself with government propaganda.

See also: avant-garde, experimental or exploratory film; ethnic minorities, film of; propaganda and film

(IJS)

Once Upon a Time in China

(Huang Feihong)

dir. **Tsui Hark**
sc. Tsui Hark, Yuen Kai-chi, Leong Yiu-ming, Tang Pik-Yin
with Jet **Li**, Yuen Biao, Rosamund Kwan, Jacky Cheung, Kent Cheng
Hong Kong: Golden Harvest/Film Workshop, 1991

Films about folk hero Wong Fei-hung (Huang Feihong) are a staple of Hong Kong popular cinema, and Jet Li's embodiment of the character in *Once Upon a Time in China* provides only the most recent in a long line of cultural models. It is the end of the nineteenth century, and China is under the sway of the Western powers. In the city of Foshan, Wong and his disciples organize a local militia, dispense herbal medicines, and practice

their kungfu skills as a way of defending their country. However, Wong's enemies are many – they include both foreigners and unscrupulous Chinese slave traders, a street performer, Yan Zhendong, and the Sha He gang.

On the other hand, Wong's followers include Porky the butcher, Buck-toothed Su, a British-educated doctor Liang Kuan, who starts out as Wong's rival but eventually becomes a disciple, and Thirteenth Aunt Shisan Yi, who is secretly in love with Wong. A series of skirmishes and set-ups initiates a number of fights between the opposing camps. Yet both Wong's friends and his foes find themselves powerless in the face of such lethal modern technologies as the cannon and the gun. After a spectacular final confrontation between Wong and Yan Zhendong on top of a mountain of bamboo ladders, Yan is shot dead by Western bullets.

Wong Fei-hung's latest big screen incarnation has spawned four direct sequels – of which Tsui Hark's *Once Upon a Time in China, II* (1992) is the most distinguished – as well as numerous derivatives, such as *The Last Hero in China* (*dir.* **Wong Jing**, 1993), and *Once Upon a Time: A Hero in China* (*dir.* Tang Chi Li, 1992).

See also: kungfu film

Further Reading
K. Lo (1993), on martial arts technologies; H. Rodriguez (1997), on the moral economy of the earlier Wong Fei-hung series.

(JS)

One and Eight

(Yi ge he ba ge)

dir. **Zhang Junzhao**
sc. Zhang Ziliang
with Tao Zeru, Chen Doming, Lu Xiaoyan, Xie Yuan.
Nanning: Guangxi Film, 1984

The first landmark piece from the **Fifth Generation**, *One and Eight* is a genuine collaborative effort involving three 1982 graduates from BFA: Zhang Junzhao (directing class), **Zhang Yimou** (cinematography) and **He Qun** (art design). Based on Guo Xiaochuan's narrative poem, the film departs from the norms of the mainland **war film** by portraying bandits and other Communists' prisoners as capable of heroism.

Plate 29 *One and Eight* (1984)

While being transferred across land to the location of their trial, a chain-gang comprising three bandits, three army deserters, a Japanese spy, a landlord (the titular eight) and Wang Jin, a wrongly accused Communist officer, are surrounded by Japanese troops. At one point, they are about to be executed as they are only an added burden for their escorts. However, as fighting breaks out and the Communists begin to lose the battle, the chain-gang volunteers to fight with them. Most of the men are killed in the fierce fighting and only a few manage to escape. The film ends with Wang Jin silhouetted against a savage landscape, carrying a wounded comrade on his shoulders.

The film's emphasis on individuality and personal feeling is as remarkable as the fresh visual images contributed by Zhang Yimou. For example, Zhang uses natural lighting, decentred composition, and a monochromatic colour scheme to achieve the look of woodcuts. The result is a new film language that prioritizes visuality over narrative. *One and Eight* took two years to clear the workings of film censorship. Among the seventy changes eventually made, the most notable concerns the fate of a female army nurse who was originally shot dead by a bandit to prevent her rape by the Japanese. In the final version, however, she is saved by the bandit at the cost of his own life. The film had a limited release and was banned from export until 1987.

See also: censorship and film

Further reading
N. Ma (1987a: 73–7), a critical analysis.

(YZ)

opera movie

See under: filmed stage performances

Orphan Island Paradise
(Gudao tiantang)

dir./sc. **Cai Chusheng**
with Li Qing, **Li Lili**, Li Jingpo, Lan Ma
Hong Kong: Dadi Film, 1939

This is one of the few Mandarin films produced in Hong Kong during the Sino-Japanese war, in which elements of traditional horror, **thriller** and suspense are blended with nationalistic and anti-Japanese themes.

A young lady travels to Shanghai in the hope of finding her fiancé. Although she does manage to locate him, it emerges that he is infatuated with a dancing girl and fraternizing with traitors and Japanese. The dancing girl turns out to be a member of an underground resistance organization. She is in love with the group leader, and together they assassinate several notorious traitors: their activities are supported by the newspaper boys and street pedlars who report them. During a New Year's party, members of the resistance organization elude the enemy's security checks and successfully execute a few more high profile traitors. The dancing girl and the group leader decide to sacrifice their love for each other to the greater good of the resistance by each taking on a new assignment.

See also: horror film; Mandarin movies (under Hong Kong cinema in Historical essays)

(ZX)

Plate 30   Poster for *An Orphan on the Streets* (1949)

Orphan on the Streets, An

aka *The Winter of Three-Hairs* (San Mao liulang ji)

dir. Zhao Ming
sc. **Yang Hansheng**
with Wang Longji, Guan Hongda, Wang Gongxu
Shanghai: Kunlun Film, 1949

Based on the famous serial comics by Zhang Leping, this film is critical of the neglect of children under the KMT regime and shows the hardship those homeless children had to endure. Symbolically, their liberation by the Communists implies that the CCP brings Chinese people a brighter future.

San Mao wakes up in the morning and goes to steal food with other homeless children like himself. A street gang recruiter wants him to join the gang, but San Mao turns him down. To support himself, he polishes shoes, sells newspapers and picks garbage. One day he finds a wallet in the street. But when he returns it to the owner, the man accuses him of pickpocketing and beats him badly. San Mao decides to sell himself. He puts a 'for sale' sign on his back and walks the streets. A childless wealthy lady wants to adopt him and brings him home. San Mao is bathed, dressed in a Western suit, and given a new name 'Tom'. However, he resents the discipline and rigid 'civility' of the rich, and misses the freedom he once enjoyed on the street. At the party his foster mother throws for him, San Mao feels edgy about all the attention paid to him. He is further embarrassed when a little girl greets him with a kiss, leaving her lipstick on his cheek. Following a series of mishaps at the party, San Mao throws off his new clothes, leaves the lady's mansion, and joins his beggar friends in the street. As the Communist soldiers enter Shanghai, San Mao and his friends are among the cheering crowd.

Further Reading
M. Farquhar (1995), a discussion of Zhang Leping's comic version.

(ZX)

Orphan Rescues Grandfather

(Guer jiu zu ji)

dir. **Zhang Shichuan**
sc. **Zheng Zhengqiu**
with Wang Hanlun, Wang Xianzai, Zheng

Xiaoqiu, Zheng Zhegu
Shanghai: Mingxing Film, 1923

According to some sources, this successful early Chinese film saved its studio from bankruptcy and helped the Chinese film industry as a whole get on its feet. The film's message is simple: education is the source of good and therefore worth investing in.

The wealthy Yang Shouchang lives happily with his son Daosheng and daughter-in-law, Yu Weiru. One day Daosheng has an accident while out horse riding and dies of his injuries. Daosheng's cousin Daopei, who has long coveted Yang's wealth, now seizes the opportunity to request that Yang adopt him as his heir. Before long Daopei has moved in with Yang and Yu Weiru. Daopei's friend Lu Shoujing is also brought in to work as a household manager. Lu tries to seduce Yu, but the latter spurns him. When Lu finds out that Yu is carrying her late husband's baby, he warns Daopei that the birth of this grandchild will reduce his chances of inheriting Yang's wealth. Through a cunning scheme, the two accuse Yu of infidelity and Yang expels Yu from the house. Yu goes home to live with her father and soon gives birth to a baby boy. But Yu's father dies and she has to support the baby by herself.

In the meantime, Daopei and Lu squander Yang's money and Yang becomes deeply depressed. While visiting the school built with money he had earlier donated, Yang comes across a well-mannered student named Yu Pu – the boy is none other than Yang's own grandson. Not knowing Yu's true identity, Yang invites him for a visit. A little while later, Yang discovers how Daopei has been spending his money, but puts the blames on Lu's bad influence. When Yang tries to get rid of Lu, Lu and Daopei plot to murder Yang so that Daopei can inherit Yang's wealth. Just as Daopei is about to strike, Yu Pu arrives and rescues Yang. Daopei confesses to Yang on his deathbed how he fabricated the story about Yu Weiru's infidelity. Yu's true identity is now revealed and the family is reunited. Yang asks Yu Weiru to forgive him and gives half of his wealth to his daughter-in-law. But Yu feels that, as it is the school that taught her son good values, she should give half of her inheritance money to the building of more free schools, thus enabling poor children to have the opportunity to better themselves.

(ZX)

Osmanthus Alley

(Guihua xiang)

dir. **Chen Kun-hou**
sc. **Wu Nien-chen**, Ding Yamin
with Lu Xiaofen, Lin Xiuling, Ren Dahua
Hong Kong: Golden Harvest Film/Taipei: CMPC/Scholar Film, 1987

A **melodrama** on a woman's fate, the film opens with a sad scene in which Tihong and her brother bury their father in the rain. Four years later, she is sixteen and is courted by a fisherman. But another unexpected blow comes and his brother dies on the sea fishing. To change her fate, Tihong agrees to be married into a rich household in town. Her husband is good to her, but he dies of an illness when their son is five and Tihong only twenty-three.

Left alone to herself in the osmanthus alley, Tihong fights for her position in the extended family by hiring her own cousin as manager of the household. She also pleases her rival, the uncle, by hiring a local opera troupe to perform in their house. Courted by a flirtatious actress, she neglects her duties. When her maid reminds her of her vulnerable position, Tihong quickly cuts herself off from the actress and punishes her son for playing with a man servant. After the uncle's death, Tihong becomes the matriarch of the family. She sends her son to study in Japan and takes up opium-smoking. A handsome servant rekindles Tihong's desire and they have sex. Although she is shocked to find herself pregnant, she is quick to frame the servant in a case of jewellery theft and asks the police to arrest him. With her maid's help, she covers up her pregnancy and visits her son in Japan, where the baby is born and is adopted by a Japanese couple.

Tihong lives alone till the age of sixty-five. The film ends with her sitting in a rocking chair. Her former fisherman suitor returns to conduct a ritual ceremony for the dead on the sea. But as an old lady, Tihong does not care about anything, her life already predestined from the beginning.

The film won Best Actress award (Lu Xiaofen) at the 1988 Asia-Pacific FF.

Further Reading
Y. Zhang (1994b), a critical study of the urban–rural antithesis.

(JJS, YZ)

Our Field

(Women de tianye)

dir. **Xie Fei**
sc. Pan Yuanliang, Xie Fei, Xiao Jian
with Zhang Jing, Lei Han, Lü Xiaogang,
Lin Fangbing, Zhou Lijing
Beijing: BFA Youth Film, 1983

Our Field depicts the lives of five educated youths during the **Cultural Revolution** and follows their continuous search for meaning during the subsequent years.

Five high-school graduates from Beijing are assigned to Manchuria for 're-education'. Qi, Xiao, Qu, Ning and Xi all live together and become good friends. While Qi is initially somewhat disillusioned with the revolution after her own parents are branded 'counter-revolutionaries', she later regains her faith. Xiao has overseas relatives whom he hopes will help him travel abroad. But his letters to them are all returned and he becomes depressed. In a desperate attempt to· improve their diet, Qu steals game from a local villager and gets into trouble, but after learning of their situation, the villagers forgive Qu and offer their help. The hard living conditions in Manchuria wear Ning's patience and resolve down. She decides to marry someone so that she can leave. While all around her lose hope, Qi retains her high spirits and idealism. However, she dies on duty while trying to put out a forest fire and is buried in Manchuria. Xi graduates from college. When he runs into Qu and Ning, they both persuade him to find a job in Beijing. But after thinking hard and long, Xi decides to go back to Manchuria to join Xiao, who has already moved back there.

(ZX)

Ouyang Yuqian

(Ouyang Liyuan)

b. 1 May 1889, Hunan province
d. 21 September 1962
Director, actor, screen writer, playwright

One of the most talented screenwriters of the 1920s–40s, Ouyang Yuqian was born into a wealthy family. At the age of fifteen, he went to Japan for his secondary education and later enrolled in Meiji University. He studied acting against his parents' will, eventually becoming a Peking opera singer. Ouyang joined the South China Drama Society (Nanguo jushe) and went on to make a significant contribution to the development of spoken drama in China.

In 1926, Ouyang joined Minxin Film Company, starred in *Innocence* (*dir.* **Bu Wancang**, 1926), and directed *Three Years Later* (1926) and *The Singer in Exile* (1927). He went to Canton in 1929 to study drama. In 1932 he toured France, England, Germany and the Soviet Union. Upon his return to China in 1933, Ouyang was involved in the Fujian Uprising and had to seek refuge in Japan after the uprising was suppressed by the KMT government.

After directing *The New Peach Blossom Fan* (1935), Ouyang took charge of Mingxing's script department in 1935. His films of this period include *The Story of Lingzi* (1936) and *Extravaganza* (1937). The latter was a satire on the decadent and meaningless lives lived by members of high society. Ouyang also took on administrative responsibilities for several patriotic organizations in the mid-1930s. His screenplay for ***Mulan Joins the Army*** (*dir.* Bu Wancang, 1939) was based on a legend about a girl who disguised herself as a boy so as to become a member of the resistance force opposing invaders during the Song Dynasty (960–1279).

Ouyang was engaged in theatre activities in the hinterland during the Sino-Japanese war. He wrote two screenplays and directed several films in Hong Kong after the war. In the post-1949 period, Ouyang devoted his energies primarily to the study of theatrical art and the training of a new generation of performing artists. After making several opera movies in 1950, Ouyang retired from filmmaking.

See also: filmed stage performances; legends and myths

Further Reading

Y. Ouyang (1984), a memoir; ZDX (1982–6: 2: 259–69), a short biography.

(ZX)

Oyster Girl

(Kenü)

dir. Li Jia, **Lee Hsing**
sc. Zhao Qibin, Liu Changbo
with Wang Mochou, Wu Jiaqi, Gao Xinzhi
Taipei: CMPC, 1964

An example of Taiwan's 'wholesome realism', this film turns attention to ordinary people in rural areas. Oyster girl Ah Lan lives alone with her alcoholic father. Her mother died years ago, and Lan has been working hard to support her father and her younger brother. She loves fisherman Jinshui, but gambler Ah Huo often harasses her. Huo's girlfriend is jealous and picks a fight with Lan in the oyster farm.

Dr. Su is elected head of the village. Huo is angry because his candidate loses. He attacks Dr. Su, who is rescued by Jinshui. Jinshui and Lan sit on a rock and talk about their marriage. The rising tide cuts off their route home, and they swim to a nearby raft. Jinshui dries Lan's clothes by a fire, and the two spend the night together. When Jinshui asks for Lan's hand, her father demands a high payment for dowry, so that Jinshui must go fishing again to raise the money. Meanwhile Lan is pregnant and has to stay with her aunt in another village to avoid rumours back home. She works so hard there that she experiences a difficult childbirth. After an operation, she is still in a critical condition. Jinshui returns and rushes to the hospital, where he gives blood to Lan. She recovers, and the two get married.

Under Dr. Su's leadership the village organizes a co-op and builds a processing plant and a market. Lan joins hundreds of oyster girls on the sea, and they sing cheerful songs of their happy life in the fishing village.

Plate 31   Poster for *Oyster Girl* (1964)

The film praised the KMT government's agricultural policy in Taiwan. It won Best Film award at the 1964 Asia-Pacific FF.

(JJS)

P

Pai Ching-jui

(Bai Jingrui)

b. 1931
Director

An important director in the formative years of Taiwan cinema, Pai Ching-jui has made more than thirty films since the 1960s. Among those highly acclaimed are *Lonely Seventeen* (1967) and *My Bride and I* (1969), both winners of Best Director award at Taipei GHA, as well as ***Home, Sweet Home*** (1970), winner of Best Film award at Taipei GHA. Most of Pai's films are family melodramas that promote Confucian ethics. In 1990, he directed the first co-production between the mainland and Taiwan, *The Man Married to the Imperial Court* (1990).

See also: melodrama

(YZ)

Painted Faces

(Qi xiaofu)

dir. Alex Law
sc. Alex Law, Mabel Cheung
with Sammo **Hung**, Zhong Jinren, Zhang Wenlong, Huang Jianwei
Hong Kong: Shaw Brothers Film, 1988

A sentimental tribute to a group of Hong Kong kungfu superstars with an operatic background, this semi-autobiographical film recaptures the early life of Sammo Hung, Jackie **Chan** (Cheng Long) and Yuan Biao and demonstrates the close linkage between **theatre and film** in China.

Naughty boy Long is too poor to attend a regular school, so his mother sends him to a Peking opera school. Under Master Yu's strict training, Long learns all kinds of basic skills. San Mao is a model student and takes charge of all children in the school. They go to perform in a local theatre and become more and more fascinated with the stage.

Years later, teenagers San Mao, Long and Ah Biao face their new life. San Mao falls in love with a young Cantonese opera player and leaves the school because of Master Yu's intervention. After Long and other students explain the situation to Master Yu, San Mao returns. As time goes by, the attendance in theatre decreases. To make a living, students have to do stunts for filmmakers. Master Yu decides to dissolve the school and emigrate to the USA. Before his departure, he tells his students to stay together and do the best they can. Ten years later, San Mao, Long and Biao have all become stars in the film industry.

In 1988, the film won awards of Best Film, Best Director and Best Screenplay at Taipei GHA, and Best Actor (Hung) at HKFA and Asia-Pacific FF. It also won a Silver Hugo at the 1989 Chicago FF.

(IJS)

painting and film

The relationship between film and painting, especially traditional Chinese painting, is a subject that has attracted scholarly attention. Some have borrowed concepts from traditional Chinese aesthetics (e.g., 'emptiness' and 'free imagination') and studied typical uses of frame composition, landscape structure, long takes and flat lighting in Chinese films. From this aesthetic perspective, ***Spring Comes to the Withered Tree*** (*dir.* **Zheng Junli**, 1961) is said to recreate, by cinematic means, the visual quality of traditional scroll painting. Even King **Hu**'s martial arts films, such as *A* ***Touch of Zen*** (1970) and *Legend of the*

Mountain (1979), have appeared to embody a certain kind of Chinese aesthetic. Many scholars have also noted the Taoist influence on the landscape structuring in several **Fifth Generation** films, especially *Yellow Earth* (1984) and *King of the Children* (1987, both *dir.* **Chen Kaige**), while others have pointed out the wood-block effect achieved in *One and Eight* (*dir.* **Zhang Junzhao**, 1984).

See also: martial arts film

Further Reading
C. Berry and M. Farquhar (1994), on film's relationship with painting; D. Hao (1994), Z. Ni (1994), two studies of the influence of traditional Chinese painting on filmmaking; N. Lin (1985, 1991), on the impact of classical Chinese aesthetics on film language and film theory; C. Woo (1991), on the relationships between poetry, painting and film.

(YZ)

Pak Yin

(Bai Yan)

b. 1920
d. 1987, Hong Kong
Actress, producer

A famous Hong Kong film actress in the 1940s–50s, Pak Yin made her screen début with *The Beautiful Country* (1937). Her performances in **Tang Xiaodan**'s *Behind the Shanghai Front* (1938) and **Li Chenfeng**'s *Spring* (1953), *Cold Night* (1955) and *The Orphan* (1960) earned her the title 'Queen of southern China'. She co-owned Union Film Enterprises (Zhonglian) and Shanlian Film Company, which produced *All These Pitiable Parents* (1960) and other social dramas. She left the film industry in 1964 and authored two film-related books.

Further reading
Y. Bai (1955), an autobiography.

(YZ)

Pan Hong

b. 4 November 1954, Shanghai
Actress

One of the most accomplished mainland actresses of the 1980s–90s, Pan Hong received a formal training in performance at the Shanghai Institute of Drama between 1973 and 1976, was assigned to Shanghai Film Studio, and made her first film appearance in *A Slave's Daughter* (*dir.* Zeng Weizhi, 1978). ***Bitter Laughter*** (*dir.* Yang Yanjin, Deng Yimin, 1979) brought her to the attention of the critics. After starring in *Lady Du* (*dir.* Zhou Yu, 1981), Pan became recognized as one of the most talented film actresses in China. In 1983, she received her first Best Actress award at China GRA for ***At the Middle Age*** (*dir.* Wang Qimin, **Sun Yu**, 1982): she won the same title again in 1988 for *The Well* (*dir.* Li Yalin, 1987) and in 1994 for her portrayal of a woman stockbroker in *Shanghai Fever* (*dir.* Li Guoli, 1993). In addition, Pan was honoured with a Best Actress award at the 1994 HFA and by MBFT. Such awards are fitting testament to Pan Hong's peerless acting talents.

(ZX)

Papa, Can You Hear Me Sing?

(Da cuo che)

dir. Yu Kanping
sc. Raymond **Wong**, **Wu Nien-chen**, Ye Xueqiao
with Sun Yue, Liu Ruiqi, Jiang Xia, Li Liqun
Taipei: Cinema City, 1983

This **melodrama** tells the sad story of a mute veteran mainland soldier who makes a living by collecting empty bottles and other junk in Taipei. In 1958, he finds an abandoned baby girl in a rich residential district and names her Ah Mei. His wife is angry and leaves him. The mute has a hard time bringing up the baby, but he entertains her by blowing pretty tunes. His kind neighbours help him liberally.

Mei graduates from high school and becomes a popular singer. A young composer teaches her how to improve her singing. Soon a businessman offers Mei a contract to sing on a tour to Southeast Asia. The mute is caught in a dilemma: he wants Mei to have a bright future but is afraid of the dangers it involves. To get her father out of poverty, Mei signs the contract, which brings her fame but not freedom. She has a busy performing schedule and cannot come home to visit her father. On a rainy night, the mute lies on his bed listening to the radio. Mei sings a sentimental tribute to her father. A neighbour rushes to the theatre and drags Mei away. The mute dies at home in old age, and the film ends with Mei's beautiful voice filling the soundtrack.

In 1983, the film won awards of Best Actor at Taipei GHA and Best Music at HKFA.

(IJS)

Peach Blossom Land

(Anlian taohua yuan)

dir./sc. Stan **Lai**
with **Lin Ching Hsia**, Jin Shijie, Li Liqun
Taipei: CMPC, 1993

This avant-garde film marks the beginning of a cinematic adventure by the most famous stage director in contemporary Taiwan. The film consists of two interrelated and interrupted stage plays, *Secret Love* and *Peach Blossom Land*. The first is a sentimental story of two lovers, Yun Zhifan and Jiang Binliu, who exchange their feelings in Shanghai, lose communication during the war, get married respectively in Taiwan, and find each other in their old age. The second is a creative adaptation of a classic Chinese myth about the carefree life in a secluded paradise. Unlike the original myth, the fisherman finds Peach Blossom Land a place not so much of harmony and perfection as of human follies (e.g., dishonesty and adultery).

Shot entirely indoors, the film relies on a minimum use of stage sets but extensive dialogues. The director creates some lively moments when two theatre crews fight for their reserved time on stage by removing each other's stage sets. There is no illusion of reality in either story, and the film directly invites viewers to participate in the making and unfolding of both.

The film won an award at the 1993 Tokyo FF.

See also: avant-garde, experimental or exploratory film; drama and literature

Further Reading
H. Chiao (1994), a profile of the director; H. Hong and H. Yue (1992), a book on the film; J. Kowallis (1997), a postmodern reading of the film.

(YZ)

Peking Opera Blues

(Dao ma dan)

dir. **Tsui Hark**
sc. To Kwok-Wai
with **Lin Ching Hsia**, Sally Yeh, Cherie Chung, Mark Cheng

Hong Kong: Cinema City/Film Workshop, 1986

A staple of Hong Kong retrospectives and North American video outlets, *Peking Opera Blues* helped establish popular Cantonese cinema's international reputation during the late 1980s. The film is set in China in 1913 and opens with General Tsao taking charge of the city palace after General Tun has been ousted from power. The former's daughter, Tsao Wan, returns from studying overseas so as to continue her pro-democratic guerilla activities against her father. In the process, she meets Ling Pak Hoi, a young revolutionary, Sheung Hung, a gold-digging musician, Pat Neil, daughter of the owner of the Peking Opera House, and Tung Man, a soldier. The five form an unlikely alliance. However, their plan to steal some incriminating documents from General Tsao at a Peking opera performance is foiled by an army of violent tax collectors.

After a series of separations, betrayals, and rescues, the five friends finally achieve their revolutionary goal. Both generals are killed and the documents find their way into Tsao Wan's hands. However, nothing much happens as a result. An end title tells us that the warlords are at it once more: war has broken out, the country has split in two, and the democratic revolution must start all over again.

Peking Opera Blues is an excellent example of Tsui Hark's directorial style, which mixes action, **comedy**, and cynical political comment with dynamic editing and sound/image relationships. As a narrative about the confusions experienced by modern China at moments of intense social change, it is bracketed by his earlier *Shanghai Blues* (1984) and later **Once Upon A Time In China** (1991).

See also: action film

Further Reading
L. Lee (1994), on parody and allegory; J. Stringer (1995), on allegory and gender politics.

(JS)

Peng Xiaolian

b. 1953, Shanghai
Director, screen writer

One of the female directors from the **Fifth Generation**, Peng Xiaolian spent nine years in the countryside during the **Cultural Revolution** before she entered the Directing Department of

BFA in 1978. Upon graduation in 1982, she started to work for Shanghai Film Studio. Her first assignment was a **children's film**, *Me and My Classmates* (1985), which describes how **sports** events help to unite middle-school students. Her major feature is ***Women's Story*** (1987), a profeminist work about female consciousness and sisterhood in the age of mainland economic reform. She wrote the script and revised it six times before acquiring permission to shoot the film. In 1989, Peng visited the USA on a scholarship and stayed to work towards a MFA degree at New York University. Already an accomplished fiction writer in the mainland, she writes about Chinese immigrants in the USA and has made a few student films based on these new experiences.

Further Reading

C. Berry (1988b, 1993b), two interviews.

(YZ)

Phony Phoenixes

(Jia feng xu huang)

dir. **Huang Zuolin**
sc. **Sang Hu**
with **Shi Hui**, Lu Shan, **Li Lihua**, Yan Su
Shanghai: Wenhua Film, 1947

This film is a light **comedy** about two con artists who try to trick each other into marriage but then actually fall in love in the process.

The general manager of Dafeng Company, Zhang Yiqing, suffers terrible losses on the stock market. When he reads in a personal column that a wealthy young woman, Miss Fan, is looking for a husband, he gets an idea of how to recuperate. An acquaintance of his, Yang Xiaomao, is a handsome young man and skilled barber. Zhang persuades Yang to respond to the advertisement and promises to help him in every way he can. In return, he hopes to have access to some of Miss Fan's money if Yang succeeds in marrying her. Yang agrees. With a new suit and a fake diamond ring borrowed from Zhang, Yang pretends to be a student, just returned from England, who is now general manager of Dafeng Company. It turns out, however, that Miss Fan is also a con artist. She has recently become a widow and is now looking to marry a rich man who can support herself and her baby. After a few meetings and dinners, Yang and Fan are both anxious to tie the wedding knot.

Then they discover the truth about each other. After exchanging accusations and recriminations, they realize that they actually have a lot in common and so decide to get married for real. Miss Fan lands a job at her husband's barber shop and both learn to live a decent life through honest work.

(ZX)

Pioneers, The

(Chuangye)

dir. Yu Yanfu
sc. Zhang Tianmin *et al.*
with Zhang Lianwen, Li Rentang, Chen Ying
Changchun: Changchun Film, 1974

This film promulgates Mao Zedong's policy of self reliance. It reflects some of the doctrines prevalent during the **Cultural Revolution** among representatives of the correct party line. The film became entangled in political factionalism of the time, and only a personal intervention by Mao himself spared some of those involved in its production from further persecution.

A worker representative, Zhou Tingshan, is determined to find an oilfield for China and so free the country from its dependence on foreign oil. He wants to do this by relying solely on Mao's writings rather than on material conditions. The chief executive of the oil company, Hua Chen, who has known Zhou for ten years, encourages him to stand firm because the deputy chief executive, Feng Chao, holds a different point of view. Feng does not believe in the potential of the workers' revolutionary spirit and he blindly worships all things foreign. His ally, chief engineer Zhang Yizhi, lacks imagination and does everything by the book. At a critical moment, a 'friendly' country withdraws all its technical support, thus making things extremely difficult for the company. At the same time, Feng disrupts the exploration of new oilfields by deliberately staging an accident. An investigation of Feng subsequently exposes him as a traitor. Zhang is shocked and begins to change his strategy. He and his workers finally succeed in finding a rich oilfield, and so manage to free China from its dependency.

(ZX)

Plunder of Peach and Plum

aka *Fate of Graduates* (Taoli jie)

dir./sc. **Ying Yunwei**
with **Yuan Muzhi**, Chen Bo'er, Tang Huaiqiu,
Zhou Boxun
Shanghai: Diantong Film, 1934

An effective early sound film, *Plunder of Peach and Plum* narrates the tragic fate of Tao Jianping, a victim of society's iniquity and corruption. The film begins when Tao (a homophone for 'peach') is about to be executed and meets his school principal in his cell. Tao tells him how his life went wrong despite all his efforts. His narration begins on the day of his graduation. Married to Li Lilin, Tao starts working for a shipping company from which he is later fired when he is too honest to ignore a violation of the safety laws.

While Tao looks for other jobs, his wife Li (a homophone for 'plum') decides to work as a secretary. Things improve when Tao also finds a job in a construction company, but he loses it because again he refuses to break safety laws. Shortly afterwards, Li is sexually harassed by her boss. She escapes unharmed, but the incident causes a serious row between the couple. Tao picks up a very low-paying job in a factory; they move to progressively cheaper apartments. After their baby is born Li falls down the stairs and ends up seriously ill. In order to buy her medicine, Tao asks for an advance on his salary but he is refused. Although Tao steals the money anyway, Li dies soon after. After her death things only get worse. Not having any food for his child, Tao abandons her in an orphanage. As soon as he gets home, the police come to arrest him for theft. Tao is then held responsible for the death of a police officer who is killed in the ensuing chase.

After Tao is executed, the film ends with the famous 'Graduation Song' (lyric by **Tian Han** and music by **Nie Er**), which encourages the students to become the élite of society, but which is also an ironic commentary on Tao's tragic life. This tragedy of **urban life** is implied in the film's title, which plays on the Chinese connotation of 'peaches and plums' (*tao li*) to represent students as the hope for a better future.

See also: representations of intellectuals

(PV, YZ)

Price of Frenzy, The

(Fengkuang de daijia)

dir. **Zhou Xiaowen**
sc. Zhou Xiaowen, Lu Wei
with Wu Yujuan, Li Qing, Xie Yuan, Chang Rong
Xi'an: Xi'an Film, 1988

The second of the director's 'frenzy' gangster films that set a trend in mainland China in the late 1980s, this film is a bit softer than his ***Desperation*** (1987) because of its focus on female psychology. The film opens with a soft-porn scene in a women's public shower room, where a middle-school girl, Lanlan, has her first period. One rainy night, she is tricked into a stolen car and raped by Sun Dacheng, an unemployed muscular man. Lanlan's sister Qingqing, a hospital nurse, vows to take revenge. She traces a magazine found in the abandoned car to the book stand owned by her admirer Li Changwei, and furiously tears at his soft-porn books and magazines. Qingqing's divorced parents arrive from other cities, but the sisters detest them for their irresponsibility. Taking the investigation into her own hands, Qingqing leads Lanlan every day along the streets, examining male drivers and taking hundreds of pictures. Her obsession with revenge causes a medical incident in the hospital.

Meanwhile, Zhao, an old policeman, suspects a car repair shop in a tower on the hilltop. After Zhao's visit, the owner Sun Dasheng realizes his brother's criminal act and arranges for him to escape. They go out to withdraw money. When Dacheng browses through the book stand, he is recognized by Lanlan from behind the window. Li rushes out to grab Dacheng but is knocked down by the car. Qingqing hangs on to the car, and the police join the chase. Dasheng is captured, but Dacheng points his gun to Qingqing's head and leads her up to the tower. Zhao points his gun to Dacheng's head and follows upstairs. The two hostages and their capturers face one another on the top of the tower. Suddenly, Qingqing pushes Dacheng to the wall and kicks him over. The rapist falls from the tower and dies instantly. Justice is served, but Qingqing is arrested. Lanlan's life will never be the same.

See also: gangster film

Further Reading

E. Rashkin (1993), a critical study of the film.

(JJS)

Princess Iron Fan

(Tieshan gongzhu)

dir. Wan Laiming, Wan Guchan
Shanghai: United China Film, 1941

The first feature-length **animation** in China, the film is based on an episode from the classic novel *Journey to the West*. Sun Wukong, the monkey king, escorts his master Tripitaka in a pilgrimage to India and defeats demons and monsters headed by Princess Iron Fan near the Flaming Mountain. Produced in the French Concession of Japanese-occupied Shanghai over a period of sixteen months, the film contains patriotic messages that were easily picked up by audiences at the time. It played for forty-five consecutive days in three Shanghai theatres and was exported to Singapore and Indonesia.

Further Reading

M.C. Quiquemelle (1991: 178–80), a succinct summary.

(YZ)

propaganda and film

Film and propaganda have long been connected in China, and many hold the Communists respon-sible for this close – and often counter-productive – connection. But the fact of the matter is that long before the Communists took over mainland China in 1949, the Nationalists had imposed their share of ideological restriction in the film industry. The New Life Movement (*Xin shenghuo yundong*), for instance, was a political campaign sponsored by the KMT officials in the 1930s in order to promote Confucian ideology and Chinese **nationalism**. The campaign left its mark on feature films such as ***Song of China*** (*dir.* **Fei Mu**, **Luo Mingyou**, 1935) and *Little Angel* (*dir.* **Wu Yonggang**, 1935). From the late 1930s to the early 1940s, many **documentary** and feature productions from the Nationalist-controlled studios in Chongqing were propagandist in nature, presenting the Nationalist troops as actively engaged in battles against the Japanese invaders. The Nationalist propaganda legacy was carried on in Taiwan, where the KMT government reorganized its film studios and

Plate 32   *Princess Iron Fan* (1941)

heavily invested in the production of propaganda films in the 1950s–70s. Sometimes called 'policy films' (*zhengce pian*) by Taiwan historians, these propaganda films promote nationalist and anti-Communist sentiments, praise government achievements in rural reforms and military education, and portray the Nationalist troops as the major force in the resistance war against Japan. Such examples include *Never to Part* (*dir.* **Xu Xinfu**, 1951), *Oyster Girl* (*dir.* **Lee Hsing**, 1964), *Martyrs* (*dir.* **Ting Shan-hsi**, 1974) and *The Spirit of the Huangpu Military Academy* (*dir.* Liu Jia-chang, 1978).

The Communists, on the other hand, did nearly the same type of propaganda work, though its scale and effects are surely more widespread and far-reaching. The origins of Communist interest in film propaganda can be traced to the leftist film movement in the 1930s, which won over many liberal filmmakers through its rhetoric of national salvation and patriotism. The sensitive political and economic conditions in the 1930s, however, made it necessary for the leftists to disguise whatever political message they wanted to convey behind an 'artistic' appearance, which often included **romance** and **melodrama**. As a result, many leftist films were quite popular at the time, and a few of them, such as *Crossroads* (*dir.* **Shen Xiling**, 1937), were even voted among the all-time best in the Nationalist-controlled areas during the 1940s.

The Communist policy on propaganda films became more and more rigid in the mainland from the 1950s, and all film productions had to conform to the politically correct line of thought. While almost all newsreels served the purposes of propaganda during this period, a large number of feature productions were devoted to the **Communist revolution** and biographies of heroes and model workers, like *Dong Cunrui* (*dir.* Guo Wei, 1955) and *Huang Baomei* (*dir.* **Xie Jin**, 1958). However, since the CCP policies changed from time to time, it had placed the filmmakers in a rather impossible position in which they had to anticipate what would be interpreted as correct in a few years after a film was released to the public. This impossible position made filmmakers an easy target in a series of political campaigns, and many veteran directors, such as **Sun Yu** and **Shi Hui**, had to live under an enormous pressure to transform or 'reform' themselves and their artistic sensitivities. Political criticism and persecution of filmmakers became more fierce during the

Cultural Revolution, when propaganda was practically the only thing that mattered in film as well as in everyday life.

The 1980s saw the beginning of a general relaxing of political control on filmmaking in mainland China, but this did not mean that film was free from propaganda. Quite the contrary, films had to stay within the narrow parameters of the politically correct, and any outright defiance of the CCP authorities would lead to immediate censorship troubles. One case is *Unrequited Love*, a film about political persecution in the Cultural Revolution: it was banned from release by the CCP in 1981, but a different version of the film was made in Taiwan in 1982. Propaganda films have continued to be made in the 1990s, especially war and historical films. To strengthen their ideological control of the masses, the Communists agencies frequently distribute tickets free of charge and require people to view certain propaganda films. With press publicity largely controlled by the government, propaganda films, such as those about the CCP founders (e.g., Mao Zedong and Zhou Enlai), the Communist battles against the Japanese and the Nationalist troops, and the Communist martyrs and war heroes who sacrificed their lives for the revolution and the country, enjoy huge box-office successes and exert considerable impact on audiences, especially on the younger generations.

See also: biography; censorship and film; documentary; historical film; war film

Further Reading

R. Huang (1994), a book on propaganda films in Taiwan.

(YZ)

prostitution

Prostitution is a recurring theme on the Chinese screen. In the 1920s–40s, there was a real-life connection between the world of prostitution and that of the film. Some actresses (e.g., Xuan Jinglin, 1907–92) were former prostitutes, and their income from filmmaking activities helped them extract themselves from prostitution. Indeed, up to the 1930s, a popular association of actresses with prostitutes was still so strong that when Ai Xia (1912–34) and **Ruan Lingyu**, two famous actresses of the time, were exposed as having had romantic relations with several men, they could not tolerate public pressures and committed suicide in despair.

Like their real-life counterparts, prostitutes are represented as victims of social prejudice as early as the 1920s, as in *A Shanghai Woman* (*dir.* **Zhang Shichuan**, 1925). In the 1930s, films like *Daybreak* (*dir.* **Sun Yu**, 1932), *Goddess* (*dir.* **Wu Yonggang**, 1934) and *Boatman's Daughter* (*dir.* **Shen Xiling**, 1935) would depict prostitutes as possessing a heart of gold and would hold an evil society responsible for ruining their lives. In times of war, prostitutes became a symbol of national humiliation, as portrayed at the beginning of *Female Fighters* (*dir.* **Chen Liting**, 1949) when a poor woman is raped by two Japanese soldiers. In the early 1950s, prostitution was used in *Sisters, Stand Up* (*dir.* Chen Xihe, 1951) as part of the Communist propaganda effort to demonstrate the power of the new society in transforming former prostitutes into independent workers. This myth of successful prostitution reform, however, is questioned decades later in *Blush* (*dir.* **Li Shaohong**, 1994), which reveals a former prostitute's yearning for the good old days and her 'degradation' beyond ideological salvation.

In the 1960s–70s, prostitutes as central protagonists disappeared almost entirely from the screen in mainland China, but they returned in the 1980s with unprecedented glamour. While mainland and Taiwan productions such as *Intimate Friends* (*dir.* **Xie Tieli**, Chen Huaiai, Ba Hong, 1981), *A Flower in the Rainy Night* (*dir.* **Wang Tung**, 1983) and *The Prostitute and the Raftsmen* (*dir.* **Huang Jun**, 1993) still preserve the image of a kind-hearted, self-sacrificing prostitute, a few Hong Kong titles prefer gorgeous-looking courtesans who flaunt their **sexuality** openly. *Rouge* (*dir.* Stanley **Kwan**, 1987) and *Farewell My Concubine* (*dir.* **Chen Kaige**, 1993) replace miserable street-walkers with talented courtesans, thus representing prostitution as an icon of a glamorous culture lost forever. It is interesting to compare the male directors' emphasis on physical beauty in the above titles with a female director's focus on individual psychology in *The Soul of the Painter* (*dir.* **Huang Shuqin**, 1993). In any case, prostitution has been used and is still being used to represent certain cultural and ideological values cherished by generations of Chinese filmmakers.

See also: propaganda and film; representations of women

Further Reading
Y. Zhang (1999b), a critical survey of the theme.

(YZ)

Protect Our Land
(Baowei women de tudi)

dir./sc. **Shi Dongshan**
with Wei Heling, Shu Xiuwen, Dai Hao
Chongqing: China Motion Picture, 1938

One of the few features films made during the Sino-Japanese war, *Protect Our Land* calls for Chinese people to make a concerted effort to fight the Japanese. Particularly noteworthy is the notion that the concerns of the national interest should take precedence over those of the family.

Liu Shan's home is destroyed by the Japanese during the Manchurian Incident of 1931. He flees Manchuria and builds a new home in a small town in the southern part of China. But just as he begins to enjoy a peaceful life, the Sino-Japanese war breaks out and the small town becomes a battle field. Refusing to help the Chinese troops dig trenches, the locals all want to flee the area.

Plate 33   *A Flower in the Rainy Night* (1983)

However, Liu persuades many of them to stay and fight the Japanese invaders. Liu's brother is lured by a traitor into working for the enemy by directing Japanese bombers to their flight targets. When Liu fails to stop him, he has to kill his own brother. Led by Liu, the townspeople and the Chinese troops charge towards the Japanese line.

See also: nationalism

(ZX)

publications

This entry discusses film magazines alone and does not include other publications on film, such as critical, historical or textual studies, bibliographies, biographies, film synopses, memoirs and yearbooks.

Film publications appeared in China as early as 1921. In that year, *Film Magazine* (Yingxi zazhi) was published in Shanghai, and *Film Weekly* (Dianying zhoukan) made its début in Beijing. By January 1922, *Film Journal* (Dianying zazhi) was also launched in Beijing. Although all of them proclaimed that their purpose was to promote the development of Chinese film, the actual contents of those magazines were devoted mostly to discussion of foreign films. This, in part, was because the majority of films shown in China in those days were of foreign origin and there were very few domestic productions.

The first film magazine exclusively devoted to domestic productions was *Morning Star* (Chenxing), which was published in late 1922. It focused on Mingxing Film Company's productions and had a special issue for every new release. In many ways, this was the first studio-sponsored trade publication. The spectacular success of *Orphan Rescues Grandfather* (dir. **Zhang Shichuan**) in 1923 sparked a new enthusiasm in film among Chinese entrepreneurs. Following the boom of film studios was the mushrooming of film magazines and newspaper columns devoted to film-related topics.

Those earlier film magazines fell into three groups: film studio's publicity materials, scholarly journals for serious discussion of film, and tabloid stories about filmmakers' private lives. But the difference among them is only a matter of degree. Sometimes the so-called 'serious' magazines also carried publicity materials for studios, or sensational stories about film personalities. By all accounts, the most respectable film magazine

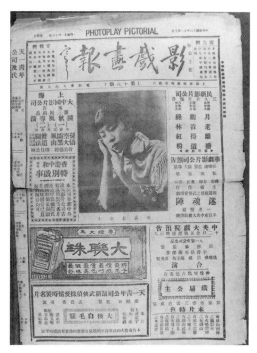

Plate 34   Front cover of *Photoplay Pictorial* (Dec. 1927)

in the late 1920s was *Film Monthly* (Dianying yuebao). It was published by Liuhe Film Company and edited by Guan Jian and Shen Hao. Many leading writers, directors and critics, such as **Hong Shen**, **Ouyang Yuqian**, **Tian Han** and **Zheng Zhengqiu**, contributed to in-depth discussions of film. By 1930, another influential film magazine, *Movie Life* (Yingxi shenghuo), was launched. Unlike *Film Monthly*, *Movie Life* was an independent publication, not sponsored or associated with a particular studio.

To some degree, the success of leftist cinema in the early 1930s was attributed as much to leftist-controlled film magazines and newspaper columns as to the actual number of leftist films produced. A group of underground Communist intellectuals effectively controlled the public forum on film by either publishing their own journals or infiltrating existing major film publications. *Film Art* (Dianying yishu), *Mingxing Monthly* (Mingxing yuebao), *Yihua Weekly* (Yihua zhoubao), *Stage and Screen* (Wutai yinmu) and *Film and Theatre* (Dianying xiju) were all in the hands of leftist-oriented editors. One film journal that directly opposed the leftist monopoly on film discourse was *Modern Cinema* (Xiandai dianying). First published in March 1933 and edited by Liu Na'ou (1900–40) and Huang Jiamo, *Modern Cinema* was more concerned with the visual quality of motion pictures and opposed the subjugation of cinema to moral or political interference. But at a time when China was in a national crisis in the face of increasing Japanese aggression, *Modern Cinema*'s detached aestheticism seemed to have little relevance to China's immediate needs.

Among the large number of film periodicals that mushroomed in the early to mid-1930s, the two longest-running film magazines were *Movietone* (Diansheng), which spanned from May 1932 to late 1939, and *The Chin-Chin Screen* (Qingqing dianying), which published its first issue in April 1934 and lasted until 1950. Both magazines were news oriented, but slightly tilted toward gossip and sensationalism. Perhaps because of that, they had a larger readership than both the polemic leftist film journals and the high-brow approach to film as represented by *Modern Cinema*.

After Shanghai fell to the Japanese, the popularity of movie magazines continued. In the foreign concession area there were no fewer than fifty film periodicals in circulation. One major feature of the 1940s was that there appeared truly independent film magazines that were not in any way sponsored, supported or even associated with a particular film studio. The thematic orientations of the movie magazines of this period ranged from anti-Japanese propaganda and discussion of European or American films to gossip about film personalities. As the Japanese moved into the concession area following their attack on Pearl Harbour, the majority of the film magazines ceased publication.

Between 1941 and 1945 there were about thirty periodicals that published articles dealing with films. Among them, only about ten were exclusively focused on film. Of course, the Japanese brought their own film journals to Shanghai. *East Asian Cinema* (Dongya yingtan) and *Japanese Movie News* (Riben yingxun) both served as advocates for the ideology of Greater East Asia Co-prosperity. In Chongqing, due to the shortage of film stock supplies, film production virtually came to a halt by late 1942. But intellectual discourse on film continued. *China Screen* (Zhongguo dianying), *Cinema Today* (Jinri dianying), *Film Chronicle* (Dianying jishi bao), and *Sino-Soviet Culture* (Zhong Su wenhua) were the main venues of film-related discussions.

The end of the war brought the revival of film journals in many cities. A total of over seventy titles were published between 1945 and 1949. In 1946 alone, thirty film-related magazines were published. One striking change in the post-war film magazines, as compared with the previous decades, was the sharp increase of interest in American films. About one-third of film periodicals were exclusively devoted to coverage of Hollywood's new releases, personalities, and gossips. Another third of the film magazines of this period divided contents between foreign and domestic films. Only about one-third of film periodicals focused on Chinese films. This was due to the fact that American films made a comeback in the post-war era and the KMT government was eager to please the US government.

After 1949, the number of film magazines in mainland China dropped drastically. Most film publications from the pre-1949 period discontinued after 1949. A few of them lasted until the end of the 1950s. The reason was simple: most of those film magazines could not meet the needs and requirements of the PRC government to use public forums as vehicle for political indoctrination. In their place, the government published its own film magazine. While Shanghai Municipal government published *Popular Cinema* (Dazhong dianying) in 1950, China's Film Management Company sponsored *New Cinema* (Xin dianying). Meanwhile, the Film Bureau edited a series called *Translated Texts on Film* (Dianying yishu yicong), which focused on Soviet film theory. Two other film journals were also noteworthy in the 1950s: *China Film* (Zhongguo dianying) and *International Cinema* (Guoji dianying). They were merged into *Film Art* (Dianying yishu) in 1959, which has remained to date one of the most academic film magazines in China. Two film studios, Beijing and Changchun, published *Film Script* (Dianying chuangzuo) and *Film Literature* (Dianying wenxue) respectively, each focusing on the studio's own productions.

All film journals were closed down during the **Cultural Revolution** (1966–1976), and it was not until 1979 that many of them re-emerged. Meanwhile, more new journals were launched in the 1980s, many associated with particular film studios. Among them, Shanghai's *Scripts* (Dianying xinzuo), August First's *August First Film* (Bayi dianying), Xi'an's *Northwest Film* (Da xibei dianying) and Pearl River's *Screenplays* (Yinmu juzuo) command special attention. During the 1980s, film publications showed a further divide between those designed for serious film scholars, such as *Contemporary Cinema* (Dangdai dianying), *World Cinema* (Shijie dianying) and *Film Culture* (Dianying wenhua), and those for movie fans. Needless to say, as elsewhere in the world, magazines in the second category enjoy a much larger readership.

Three leading film magazines deserve further elaboration below. The first of them, *Popular Cinema*, has the longest history and enjoys the largest readership in China. First issued on 16 June 1950 in Shanghai, the magazine was devoted primarily to domestic films, but a significant amount of space was allocated to discussions of Soviet films. In fact, the front cover of the first issue was a scene from a Soviet Film titled *The Son of the Regiment*. Initially, the magazine was edited by Mei Duo and Wang Shizhen. Starting with the first issue of 1952, the magazine incorporated *New Cinema*. While Mei Duo remained editor-in-chief, the journal changed its page layout and improved print quality. Meanwhile the headquarters of the editorial board was relocated to Beijing. In 1956, the management merged with the newly established China Film Publishing House, but the magazine continued to be one of the best-selling periodicals in China. As the political climate began to change in the mid-1960s, the journal became essentially the CCP's vehicle for political campaign. After its sixth issue was published in 1966, the magazine was closed down. It was not until 1979 that *Popular Cinema* re-emerged. The new editor-in-chief was Lin Shan. Within two years, its annual sale reached 960 million copies. In some places, local post offices had to impose a quota system to limit the number of subscribers. Although since the late 1980s the number of subscribers has dropped significantly, *Popular Cinema* still has the largest readership among all film magazines.

The second leading magazine in China is *Film Art*. First published in 1959, this monthly magazine was born out of the merger between *China Film* and *International Cinema*. As one of the leading scholarly journals devoted exclusively to film, *Film Art* published many critical essays on film studies. After the third issue of 1966, it ceased publication for the next thirteen years because of the interruption of the Cultural Revolution. In 1979, it was reissued, but changed to a bimonthly. In terms of the administrative hierarchy, the editorial board of *Film Art* is subject to the leadership of the Association of Chinese Filmmakers. Since the journal does not have mass appeal, it has been heavily subsidized by the government. With the transformation of the film industry under way in the 1990s, the future of this magazine remains uncertain.

The third leading magazine is *Contemporary Cinema*. First published in July 1984, this bimonthly is sponsored by the China Research Centre of Film Art in Beijing. The editorial board consists of scholars associated with this institution. Since its début, the magazine has quickly become one of the most important forums for serious film **criticism**. Its special columns address issues of film theory, film history, contemporary cinema and foreign films, among others. Occasionally it also publishes film scripts or synopses.

In Taiwan, one of the leading film magazines is *Film Appreciation* (Dianying xinshang). Established in January 1983 by the government-run Taipei Film Library, the magazine covers a wide range of topics in film criticism, film history and film theory, including structuralism, semiotics and avant-garde film art. It also examines issues concerning film education, the film industry and film technology. *Influence* (Yingxiang dianying zazhi), another important film magazine in Taiwan, was founded in November 1989 by a private company and recruited several influential film critics, such as Peggy Hsiung-Ping Chiao (b. 1953) and Huang Jianye (b. 1954), on its editorial board. It carries articles on new releases, box-office returns, major figures and other special forums.

In Hong Kong, the leading film magazine is *Film Biweekly* (Dianying shuangzhou kan), first established in 1979. It carries film reviews, interviews, studio and theatre reports, as well as other relevant entertainment news. One of the most significant contributions the magazine makes to the development of Chinese film is its organization of the annual Hong Kong Film Awards (HKFA).

See also: leftist film (under Chinese cinema in Historical essays)

(ZX, YZ)

Puppet Master, The
(Xi meng rensheng)

dir. **Hou Hsiao-hsien**
sc. **Wu Nien-chen**, **Chu Tien-wen**
with Li Tianlu, Lim Giong, Yang Liyin, Xin Shufen
Taipei: Era, 1993

In the 1990s, Li Tianlu is one of Taiwan's most famous living puppet masters. A **biography** film about his life during the Japanese occupation, *The Puppet Master* is the second in Hou's 'family album' trilogy on Taiwan history. Domesticity is a prominent issue in *The Puppet Master*, which deals with the youth, apprenticeship, professional accomplishments and romantic complications of Li's life between 1909 and 1945. Li's development as an artist and (occasionally unfaithful) husband and father, played out under the heavy hand of Japanese rule, parallels the development of political consciousness in Taiwan. With *A City of Sadness*, Hou's acclaimed account of the tumultuous uprisings of post-colonial, post-war Taiwan, Li's story gives way to that of his many successors. In depicting typical scenes of Taiwanese family life, Hou again employs understated sequence shots of long duration and camera distance. This distancing connects Hou's cinematography with Li's puppet mastery and prompts reflection on how stylization can displace overt political comment.

The film's evocative Chinese title, 'Drama, Dream, Life', suggests a rich layering of personal, familial, communal and national aspirations, narrated through semi-documentary sequences reminiscent of the studio interviews in *Reds* (*dir.* Warren Beatty, 1981) and *The Thin Blue Line* (*dir.* Errol Morris, 1988). Li's wry, sometimes excruciatingly funny memories punctuate the historical representations. His commanding presence reminds the audience that in the name of a semibiographical historical chronicle, the film is actually showing the performances of not one but several masters. The vividness of Li's memories, the staging of a colonial people's deference to their long-time masters, and the judicious interweaving of artifice, politics and authenticity help give Hou's film its complex structure.

Further Reading
N. Browne (1996), a critical study of the film; G. Cheshire (1993), an excellent analysis of Hou's films; H. Chiao (1993b), an interview with critical comments.

(YY)

Plate 35   *The Puppet Master* (1993)

Q

Qin Yi

(Qin Dehe)

b. 1922, Shanghai

Actress

A well-known actress of the 1940s–60s, Qin Yi entered the world of film through a series of accidents. Travelling to Wuhan in 1937 with the intention of joining the army, the 'reality shock' she subsequently experienced in a former warlord unit turned her youthful idealism into bitter disillusion. She attempted to quit but was arrested as a deserter by the Nationalist military police. Although the fall of Wuhan in 1938 saved her from a military trial, Qin was stranded in Chongqing, the wartime capital of China. She was 'discovered' while staying at a local YCWC shelter by veteran directors **Shi Dongshan** and **Ying Yunwei**, and on the basis of their introductions, found employment at Nationalist China Motion Picture Studio. Although Qin remained with the studio only briefly and never had the opportunity to take a leading role, this exposure to filmmaking served as an initiation. After she left the studio, Qin worked for several years in the theatre and won critical acclaim.

After the war Qin starred in *Loyal Family* (*dir.* **Wu Yonggang**, 1946), *The Love of Far Away* (*dir.* **Chen Liting**, 1947) and *Mother* (*dir.* **Shi Hui**, 1949). After 1949 she appeared in more than a dozen films, mostly in supporting roles. Two of these are available in the West, *Railroad Guerrillas* (*dir.* Zhao Ming, 1956) and *Lin Zexu* (*dir.* **Zheng Junli**, Cen Fan, 1959).

Further Reading

ZDX (1982–6: 6: 333–44), a short biography.

(ZX)

Queen of Sports

(Tiyu huanghou)

dir./sc. **Sun Yu**
with **Li Lili**, Bai Lu
Shanghai: Lianhua Film, 1934

In this early **sports** film, a rich girl is admitted to a school of physical education and learns the value of altruism in the world of athletic competition. Even though initially enthusiastic about training, she is immature and unaware of the difficulties that lie ahead. Her natural talent wins her several championships and enables her to become a queen of sports. With the press, her fans and handsome boys taking notice, she becomes intoxicated by success. However, she gradually loses interest in training and is subject to criticism from her coach. When one of her team-mates dies after being forced to take part in a race when seriously ill, she come to realize that competitive athletics involves a lot of hard work and pain. She abandons competition so as to devote herself to the promotion of all sports activity.

(PV)

Questions for the Living

(Yi ge sizhe dui shengzhe de fangwen)

dir. **Huang Jianzhong**
sc. Liu Shugang
with Chang Lantian, Lin Fangbing, Jun Wu, Ji Yuan
Beijing: Beijing Film, 1987

Apparently inspired by the aesthetics of surrealism, the narrative of this avant-garde film focuses on a ghost's visits to guilty souls, as well as on the moral 'landslide' of 1980s China.

An actor, Ye Xiaoxiao, witnesses a pickpocket in action and tries to stop him. But no one else comes forward to help him: even the victim refuses to claim his wallet. The thief, encouraged by the onlookers' passivity, stabs Ye several times, but after the murder Ye's ghost refuses to leave. An old man suggests to the ghost that he interview each person present during the incident.

One of the passengers on the bus is a martial arts master, Zhao Tiesheng. At the time of the stabbing, he not only refused to stand up and help Ye, but positively enjoyed the exciting spectacle. Now, faced with Ye's ghost, he is deeply ashamed of himself. Ye's friend, a scriptwriter, was also present that day. Although he did shout for the driver to go 'straight to the police', he was scared of the thief. The ghost's visit makes him feel guilty. The victim initially distorted the truth by reporting the incident to the police as a gang fight. Under the ghost's scrutiny, however, he finally admits his cowardice and selfishness. One of the passengers on the bus, a four-year-old girl, tells the truth, and with clues provided by her the police are finally able to make an arrest.

The film switches frequently from the real and the imaginary worlds and is marked by images of surrealist colours and shapes as well as of primitive rituals.

See also: avant-garde, experimental or exploratory film

(ZX)

R

Rainclouds Over Wushan

(Wushan yunyu)

dir. Zhang Ming
sc. Zhu Wen
with Zhang Xianmin, Zhong Ping, Wang Wenqiang
Beijing: Beijing Film/Eastern Land Cultural Enterprise, 1995

This directorial début from a member of the **Sixth Generation** seeks a new film language that bridges traditional and modern aesthetics. Set in the famous Three Gorges, where a new dam project will make a huge reservoir out of the surrounding mountain area, the film follows Mai Qiang, a reticent signal man aged thirty, who works at a beacon by the Yangtze River. Mai's friend thinks Mai is too lonely and needs a woman in his life, but Mai does not like the woman his friend introduces to him. He has repeatedly encountered a woman with a sweet smile in his dreams.

Chen Qing is a young widow living with her son. She works at a inn and is often despised by people around her. The inn manager tries to protect her, but Chen does not like the way he acts. She longs for a change in her life and seems to hear someone calling her from time to time.

One day, Mai gets drunk and meets Chen. Surprised that he has found the woman in his dreams, Mai forces her to have sex with him. After the act, Chen's sorrowful weeping makes Mai extremely ashamed, and he leaves her all the money he has with him. The incident is reported to the police and Mai is arrested. But Chen saves Mai by declaring that she consented to the sexual act, and the rape incident is thus turned into a case of moral indecency for Chen. Mai admires Chen's courage and realizes how much pressure she has undergone. He makes up his mind and goes to propose marriage to her.

The film was entirely shot on location in a small mountain town. It carries very little dialogue. The director graduated from the Directing Department at BFA with an MA degree.

(YZ)

Raise the Red Lantern

(Da hong denglong gaogao gua)

dir. **Zhang Yimou**
sc. Ni Zhen
with **Gong Li**, Ma Jingwu, He Saifei, Cao Cuifeng, Jin Shuyuan
Beijing: China Film Co-production, 1991

The stage for dramatic action in this film of astonishing visual beauty is set by the power relations which link a master and his four wives. The film opens on a close-up of Song Lian, a young college student who has agreed to be a feudal patriarch's fourth concubine. On arrival at master Chen's mansion, she finds a sealed-off world where concubines live a life of complete servitude.

Much of the narrative action centres on the master's daily selection of one concubine with whom to spend the night, a decision which is signalled by the ritual lighting of red lanterns outside the chosen woman's apartment and the giving of a foot massage. The first wife has stopped competing for the master's attention in view of her advanced age and the fact that she has already borne him a male heir. The three remaining women, however, strive to undermine each other's authority as they jostle fiercely for favour. The master's power extends through the whole household, even though the viewer hardly ever sees him represented directly.

The women's need to attract the master sexually displaces their resentment over gender oppression. Song Lian senses the underlying power currents on her wedding night when Third Mistress feigns illness to lure the master back to bed. Realizing that security can only be had once she also has borne him a male heir, Song Lian fakes pregnancy. Unfortunately, the subsequent nights of red lanterns and foot massages are short-lived as her jealous maid soon reveals the deception. The lanterns outside Song Lian's apartment are then covered forever with black hoods.

Third Mistress Meishan is a former opera singer whose remarkable voice articulates her inner feelings. She sings on the rooftops and ventures outside the household to take the family doctor as a lover. After her betrayal by Second Mistress, however, Meishan is gagged, bundled to an isolated room on the roof of the compound, and hung. Song Lian witnesses the abduction and confronts the murderers before descending helplessly into madness. At the film's end, a Fifth Mistress arrives to take her place. The visual treatment of master Chen's compound and the interweaving of complex narrative threads create a suffocating world where women are trapped by the rule of male law.

The film won several top prizes in Belgium, China, Italy, the United Kingdom and the USA.

Further Reading

Q. Dai (1993), a criticism of Zhang's misuse of Chinese culture; S. Fong (1995), an analysis of female voice and madness; J. Lee (1996), an analysis in Confucian and feminist terms.

(SC)

Rapeseed Woman

(Youma caizi)

dir. **Wan Jen**
sc. Liao Huiying, **Hou Hsiao-hsien**
with Chen Qiuyan, Su Mingming, **Ko Yi-cheng**
Taipei: Wanbaolu Films/Ming Yi, 1983

Rapeseed Woman depicts the life of a Taiwanese nuclear family from the early 1960s to the 1980s. Wenhui, the protagonist, is the daughter whose point of view we share in a sprawling five-part story. These episodes represent different periods from her life and they chart a movement towards greater liberation and control. Vignettes from Wenhui's early life show how patriarchal relations

affect her mother, Xiaoqin, with whom Wenhui identifies after witnessing her father's brutality. The patriarchal roles enforced in this part of the film have a political valency due to the lingering Japanese colonial presence in Taiwan at this time. The film changes direction when Xiaoqin becomes head of the family and moves the family to Taipei – significantly, it is here that she becomes calculating, greedy and 'patriarchal'.

Wenhui now receives little more consideration and respect from her mother than she did when living in the countryside with her father. In the meantime, the latter has found work in the Philippines, which enables the family's fortunes to improve. Nevertheless, Wenhui's mother abuses and exploits her, forbidding her to date boys as she begins her adolescence. As she enters young adulthood and begins a successful career, the daughter–mother relationship is continually strained until the moment Wenhui finally breaks free. This high quality **melodrama** is brought to a curious, ambiguous, resolution: by deciding to forgive her mother's acquiescence in the patriarchal order, Wenhui simultaneously devalues her own hard-won victories.

(YY)

Rebel of the Neon God

(Qingshaonian Nezha)

dir./sc. **Tsai Ming-liang**
with Chen Zhaorong, Wang Yuwen,
Li Kangsheng, Ren Changbin
Taipei: CMPC, 1992

Rebel of the Neon God is the début feature of Tsai Ming-liang, a Malaysian-Chinese immigrant who came to Taiwan at the age of twenty before working in television and assisting on several theatrical features. Tsai's cool, stylish vision of Taipei's nocturnal *demi-monde* begs comparison with the work of the most influential independent director from Hong Kong – indeed, Tsai's style might be termed '**Wong Kar-Wai**-like'.

The film concerns generational conflict. The protagonist, Xiaokang, lives with his parents despite being unable to accept their world of middle-class aspiration and acquisition. The parents themselves are driven to distraction by the pressures of life in Taipei, from which they withdraw through occult Taoism and other emotional escape routes. As a result, Xiaokang spends most of his time hanging out on the street with his delinquent friends Ah Zi and Ah Bing, drifting through video arcades, roaring over rain-slicked Taipei roads, and picking up casual liaisons like Ah Gui, a cheerfully promiscuous girl who frequents roller-skating rinks.

The characters' aimless urban wandering may constitute the action but it cannot provide a clear plot line. As they have been defined by the cold, glossy surfaces of Taipei prosperity – superficially alluring but lacking depth and meaning – Xiaokang and his friends do not initiate anything. Tsai's bright, seductive and predatory style revels in its own lack of substance, and this lack mirrors the absence of purpose in the characters' own lives – their selves remain lost in the blinding glare of a Benetton shop window.

See also: independent film

Further Reading

C. Stephens (1996a), a perceptive analysis of Tsai's work.

(YY)

Reconnaissance Across the Yangtze

(Du jiang zhencha ji)

dir. **Tang Xiaodan**
sc. Shen Mojun
with **Sun Daolin**, Qi Heng, Kang Tai, Chen Shu, Li Lingjun, Zhong Shuhuang
Shanghai: Shanghai Film, 1954

In this **war film** that glorifies the **Communist revolution**, Li and his reconnaissance team are sent by the CCP's military command to investigate the Nationalist defence build-up on the northern side of the Yangtze River. Li and his men swim across the Yangtze at night to make contact with Sister Liu, who is the leader of the guerilla force. Despite heightened security patrols, members of the reconnaissance team are able to disguise themselves as Nationalist army officers or labourers. After they successfully steal documents containing information about the enemy's defence lay-out, they are trailed by an opposing security force. Several members of the reconnaissance team give their lives to protect their comrades. Finally, one of them manages to swim across the Yangtze River to deliver the documents to the high command.

With the aid of the information provided by the reconnaissance team, the Communist army is able to attack the enemy's defence with pin-point accuracy. The Operation Crossing the Yangtze is a total victory. As Li's unit moves further south, he says good-bye to sister Liu.

The film won the Best Film award from the Ministry of Culture in 1957. It was remade into a colour feature during the **Cultural Revolution**.

(ZX)

Red Cherry

(Hong yingtao)

dir. Ye Daying (Ye Ying)
sc. Jiang Qitao
with Guo Keyu, Xu Xiaoli
Beijing: BFA Youth Film/Moscow: Moscow Film, 1995

This co-produced **war film** has Chinese and English subtitles and features a mixed soundtrack of Chinese and Russian. Set in the Soviet Union during World War II, the film traces the story of two Chinese orphans whose lives are devastated by the war. In 1940, Chuchu and Luo Xiaoman are sent to Moscow International Orphanage, an institution that educates the orphans of persecuted Communists and revolutionaries. In an oral examination, the two recite stories in Russian of their happy families in China. When the teacher asks Chuchu to tell her true story, she admits in tears that her father was arrested by the Nationalist agents and cut into two pieces in front of her while she was not allowed even to cry.

The two orphans have a good time in Moscow, but the war soon forces the orphanage to evacuate. Chuchu and many girls are captured by the Germans and undergo a great deal of suffering. A crippled German officer imprisons Chuchu in a castle and tortures her so that she agrees to let him make an elaborate tattoo of the Nazi eagle on her back. The tattooing takes a long time to complete. By the time the eagle is embodied as a life work of art on Chuchu's smooth skin, she has become almost insane.

Meanwhile, Luo is stranded in the besieged city of Moscow and witnesses how an innocent Russian girl keeps talking to her dead mother in bed. Luo befriends the girl and helps an agency deliver death notices to the surviving family members. When he finds out that a group of German captives work in a construction site every day, he hides himself in a nearby damaged building and throws stones at them. One day, some Germans chase him inside the building. Instead of running home, Luo leads the German deep into the building and sets fire to gasoline barrels. The Russian girl cries as the entire building bursts into flames and explodes.

After the war, the Soviet doctors try in vain to remove the tattoo on Chuchu's back. She returns to China and lives in shame until 1990.

The film was a box-office hit in spite of its predominant Russian dialogues. With an unprecedentedly high investment of two million US dollars, the film raked in over six million. In addition, it won Best Film award at the 1996 China GRA.

(IJS)

Red Crag

(Liehuo zhong yongsheng)

dir. **Shui Hua**
sc. Zhou Gao
with **Yu Lan**, Zhang Ping, Xiang Kun, Hu Peng, **Zhao Dan**
Beijing: Beijing Film, 1965

Adapted from a novel, *Red Crag*, by Luo Guangbin and Yang Yiyan, this film glorifies martyrdom in the **Communist revolution**. It portrays a group of underground Communists in southwestern China and their heroic struggle against the Nationalists on the eve of 1949.

On her way to make contact with the local guerrillas, Jiang sees a severed head hanging over the city wall. The victim turns out to be her husband, the guerrilla leader who was executed by the Nationalists. The barbaric scare tactics only reaffirmed Jiang's hatred for the Nationalists. Because of a defector's betrayal, the CCP's underground network in the city of Chongqing is in danger. One of the ringleaders, Xu Yunfeng, is arrested. Jiang is also arrested as she escorts a shipment of weapons to the guerrilla. Despite being tortured by the KMT secret police, Jiang refuses to give her inquisitors any information, which earns her the respect of her fellow jail-mates. With the help of a prison cook, who turns out to be an undercover Communist, the prisoners plan a break-out. As the Communist army comes close to the city, the KMT secret service has Xu and Jiang executed. Many prisoners manage to escape

to safety, while others are ruthlessly gunned down by the Nationalist soldiers.

(ZX)

Red Detachment of Women

(Hongse nianzi jun)

dir. **Xie Jin**
sc. Liang Xin
with Zhu Xijuan, **Wang Xin'gang**, **Chen Qiang**
Shanghai: Tianma Film, 1961

On tropical Hainan Island a group of courageous women carry on the Communist war against the Nationalists. Wu Qionghua joins the group and becomes a proud leader after having suffered humiliation, pain and loss. The evil landlord Nan Baitian had killed her father and taken Wu as his slave. She tried to escape but was always caught and harshly punished. She was eventually freed by Hong Changqing, a Communist agent disguised as a rich overseas Chinese arms dealer.

Wu joins a female detachment of the Red Army led by Hong. However, obsessed by her desire to get revenge against Nan, she is injured and puts her comrades in danger. She transforms her personal hatred into class solidarity through Communist education. After Hong is murdered by Nan, Wu leads her detachment in a successful offensive. She kills Nan, takes over Hong's position, and carries on marching forward into battle.

This is one of Xie Jin's early popular films. A ballet version was produced by Pan Wenzhan and Fu Jie in 1971 and an opera version directed by Cheng Ying a year later. With their depiction of good smoothly triumphing over evil, both are typical products of the **Cultural Revolution**.

(PV, YZ)

Red Dust

(Gungun hongchen)

dir. **Yim Ho**
sc. San Mao, Yim Ho
with **Lin Ching Hsia**, Maggie **Cheung**, Qin Han, Yim Ho
Hong Kong: Tomson/Beijing: China Film Co-production/Changchun: Changchun Film, 1990

This **melodrama** of lovers' misunderstandings and war-time separations is set in the mid-1940s.

Shen Shaohua attempts suicide but does not die after her father disapproves of her marriage with Xiaojian and locks her in their house. She leaves her home town when her father dies, and becomes a fiction writer. Politically insensitive, she falls in love with Zhang Nengcai, a Japanese collaborator. After the war Zhang goes into hiding, and when Shaohua finds him in a village he is living with a widow. Shaohua is greatly depressed and stays with her friend Yuefeng. Soon Yuefeng and her boyfriend participate in an anti-government demonstration and are killed in the crack-down. Meanwhile, Zhang is wrongly accused of being an underground Communist. Shaohua tries to rescue him but gets herself injured in a car accident.

Before the Communist takeover in 1949, a rich merchant wants to take Shaohua to Taiwan and exchange two gold bars for two boarding passes for a ship. At the last minute, Shaohua lets Zhang go on board. After forty years of separation, Zhang returns to the mainland in search of his lost love. Shaohua has long been dead, and Zhang only gets a copy of her novel.

The film won Best Film, Best Director, Best Actress (Lin Ching Hsia) and other prizes at the 1990 Taipei GHA.

(YZ)

Red Firecracker, Green Firecracker

(Paoda shuangdeng)

dir. **He Ping**
sc. Da Ying
with Ning Jing, Wu Gang
Xi'an: Xi'an Film/Hong Kong: Wong's Co., 1994

In this fascinating tale of sexual repression and moral transgression set in the early twentieth century, the director outsmarts **Zhang Yimou** by using spectacular firecracker explosions and the surging Yellow River as symbols of uncontrollable sexual energy.

The film opens with a migrant painter Niu Bao crossing the Yellow River to find a job in a small town. The rich household which owns a large firecracker business is managed by Chunzhi, a pretty young woman who conceals her gender identity by dressing as a man. Surrounded by the ingratiating butler and foremen, Chunzhi lives an

uneventful life until she catches sight of Niu, who is hired to paint fortune pictures on the doors inside the compound. Man Dihong, a suspicious foreman, leads Niu to a deserted room and warns him not to go about freely. An explosion erupts and kills a worker, and the man responsible is severely punished. Niu is amazed to see how emotionless Chunzhi is in handling the accident.

However, Chunzhi soon makes her affection for Niu clear. She dresses herself in beautiful female attire and attracts Niu. In spite of others' warning, Chunzhi has trysts with Niu inside the compound, and the old butler hires a local team performing a ritual of exoneration. After being beaten up, Niu leaves town to learn the tricks of playing with firecrackers. Months later, in a public competition with Man, Niu demonstrates his prowess and performs breath-taking tricks with firecrackers. All of a sudden, a giant firecracker explodes between Niu's legs and makes him sexually crippled. He is carried away from the town on a stretcher. The film ends with Chunzhi, already pregnant, announcing that she will give birth to her child, regardless of what others will say.

The film won a grand prize at the 1994 Hawaii FF.

(YZ)

Red Sorghum

(Hong gaoliang)

dir. **Zhang Yimou**
sc. Chen Jianyu, Zhu Wei, Mo Yan
with **Gong Li, Jiang Wen**
Xi'an: Xi'an Film, 1987

After serving as cinematographer on several **Fifth Generation** films, Zhang Yimou directed *Red Sorghum* as his feature début. Its first-person narration introduces a nostalgic story about the life and death of a family ancestor as a means of recovering the past. The film opens with a voice-over and a series of shots of a marriage procession. Against a barren setting, eight boisterous carriers are tossing a bride as she rides in a red sedan. The carriers' masculine vitality contrasts both with the bride's fear and helplessness and with the wretched state of the leprous old winery owner she is fated to marry. The bride discreetly gazes on the bare-chested bodies of the men who transport her, thus foreshadowing her liberation from the bondage of an arranged marriage.

The wedding party is confronted by a masked bandit as it passes through a sorghum field. The head sedan carrier rescues the bride and leads his men in the murderous counter-attack against the abductor. Later, on a return trip to her family, the bride is again kidnapped in the sorghum field by a masked man, but this time it turns out to be the sedan carrier himself. Against a drum-laden soundtrack, the man tramples the sorghum plants into a bed for sexual union.

The sexual encounter in the field produces a son, the narrator's father. The sedan carrier kills the winery owner and marries the girl, and the two of them join in the spirited collective life of winery workers. After the Japanese invasion, however, the sorghum field is transformed into a scene of death. The local people are forced into labour trampling the sorghum plants to build a road. To instil fear in the workers, the Japanese order a village butcher to flay Luohan, a former winery worker who has become an underground Communist. The woman urges the men to avenge Luohan's death. Against a soundtrack of wedding music the ambush (filmed in slow motion) of a Japanese truck follows. The woman is shot as she brings food to the men, her blood and the wine pouring into the sorghum field. As an eclipse of the sun turns the entire screen red, the film ends with a drum beating, the sorghum plants swaying, and the son chanting a ritual folk song to his dead mother.

The leitmotifs of sorghum and wine symbolize life and death, birth and renewal, body and humanity. A subjective search for a national soul through the allegorical re-imagining of one family's past brings together history, legend and memory.

Further Readings

H.C. Li (1989), a study of colour and character; M. Shao (1989), a mainland reading; Y. Wang (1989b), an exploration of masculinity and femininity; X. Zhang (1997), a discussion of ideology and utopia; Y. Zhang (1990), on body images and national allegory.

(SC)

Red Swan

(Hong tian e)

dir./sc. Gu Rong
with Xu Songzi, Xu Yajun, Xing Minshan, Dong Zhizhi
Nanning: Guangxi Film/Nanhai Film, 1996

Marketed as the first Chinese ballet feature in wide screen and synchronized-sound recording, *Red Swan* opens with Qiao Danying, a famous ballet artist, who reminisces about her life on stage. In 1954, Qiao works very hard to meet the high expectations of her Soviet teacher, and her successful performance in *Swan Lake* earns her fame. Her dance partner Zhong Xueyang courts her, but she prefers Zhu Tong, who has just returned from the Soviet Union. After marrying Lin Hong, Zhong is still jealous of Qiao. One night, he makes a mistake and drops Qiao off the stage. Zhong is suspended from performance for one year, but he does not admit his mistake.

Qiao recovers from the incident but cannot play the lead role in *Swan Lake*. Instead, she is invited to work on **Red Detachment of Women**, a revolutionary ballet with a distinctive Chinese style. She plays the female lead and wins a standing ovation from the audience. But Zhong has lost his bid for the male lead and plots to take revenge. The **Cultural Revolution** starts in 1966, and Zhong becomes a local commander of the Red Guards. He imposes heavy physical duties on the pregnant Qiao on the one hand and lures Qiao's husband Zhu to seek divorce on the other. Qiao and other artists are sent to the countryside. She has a miscarriage after Zhong forces her to dance on a concrete floor.

In 1976, Qiao returns to the city and meets her ex-husband, who has become an alcoholic in his attempt to forget his 'sins'. Meanwhile, Zhong has been arrested for his criminal acts during the Cultural Revolution. His wife signs the divorce paper and leaves for France. When the old theatre is set for demolition, Zhu walks by and is overcome by remorse. The explosion brings down the theatre, and no one knows what has happened to Zhu.

The film ends with Qiao's reunion with her former Soviet teacher: the two embrace in tears. This political **melodrama** reflects a **nostalgia** in the 1990s for the Soviet cultural influence of the 1950s–60s.

(YZ)

Regret for the Past

(Shang shi)

dir. **Shui Hua**
sc. Zhang Yaojun, Zhang Lei
Beijing: Beijing Film, 1981

Based on Lu Xun's short story of the same title, this film offers a critical reflection on the May Fourth Movement of 1919. By focusing on the tragic result of a love affair, the film shows the limits of free love, a key notion of the 1920s.

In the post-May Fourth period, a petty bureaucrat named Juansheng works in the Education Bureau. Despite his enlightened views on many subjects, Juansheng does not have the courage to break free from traditional patterns of life. His sense of emptiness and loneliness soon evaporate, however, when he falls in love with Zijun, an independent-minded modern woman. Zijun's parents oppose her relationship with Juansheng, but she ignores their reproaches and marries him. The two indulge in the joys of love.

The honeymoon period doesn't last long, however. Juansheng finds Zijun's interest in trivial matters an increasing disappointment. He tries to think of ways to rejuvenate their relationship, but ultimately fails to find any solutions. After he becomes unemployed, the couple are driven further apart by economic hardship. Zijun realizes that Juansheng looks upon her as a burden and she feels disheartened. She wants to leave him, but has nowhere to go except back to her parents. After her health deteriorates rapidly because of emotional stress, she dies of an unknown disease. Juansheng is greatly saddened, but carries on his search for a meaningful life.

The film was awarded Best Film prize from the Ministry of Culture in 1981.

(ZX)

Reign Behind a Curtain
(Chuilian tingzheng)

dir. **Li Han-hsiang**
sc. Yang Cunbin, Li Han-hsiang
with Tony Kar-Fei **Leung**, **Liu Xiaoqing**, Chen Hua
Beijing: China Film Co-production/Hong Kong: New Kunlun Film, 1983

A sequel to the director's *The* **Burning of the Imperial Palace** (1983), this film is set after the Qing court signed the unequal treaties with the European powers. Emperor Xianfeng stays in his summer palace north of Beijing and indulges in wine and women. Soon he is confined to bed by an illness. Sushun advises the emperor to kill Concubine Ci to prevent future troubles, but the

Emperor refuses. Instead, he entrusts his young son to Sushun and seven other ministers. He also gives an imperial seal to Ci, instructing her to defend the Qing court with the Empress.

After Emperor Xianfeng dies, Ci plots with a prince and asks an official to propose this solution: 'The prince holds the court, while the Empresses reign behind the curtain'. The eight ministers fiercely oppose the proposal. They secretly hire assassins to kill Ci on her way to Beijing, but the prince's troops come first and arrest them. In 1861, the six-year-old Emperor Tongzhi mounts the throne. Sushun is beheaded in a Beijing marketplace, and his supporters are either executed or imprisoned. The two Empresses take charge of the court, and Ci – better known thereafter as Empress Dowager Cixi – rules China with an iron fist for forty-eight years.

This **costume drama** was popular in both China and Hong Kong. The stories of Dowager Cixi have also been told in other films, such as *Two Empress Dowagers* (*dir.* Wang Xuexin, 1987) and **Li Lianying: The Imperial Eunuch** (*dir.* **Tian Zhuangzhuang**, 1991).

(IJS)

Reincarnation of Golden Lotus, The
(Pan Jinlian zhi qianshi jinsheng)

dir. Clara **Law**
sc. Lilian Lee
with Joey **Wong**, Eric Tsang, Wilson Lam
Hong Kong: Golden Harvest/Friend Cheers, 1989

This modernized adaptation of a famous episode in two traditional Chinese novels is a pro-feminist story of female desire, female **sexuality** and female revenge. It begins in a supernatural setting and then proceeds to 1966 Shanghai, where little Lotus's tight socks recall Golden Lotus's bound feet and the book *Golden Lotus* is burned for its counter-revolutionary theme. Years later Lotus's ballet troupe director rapes her and accuses her of seduction. She meets Wu Long, who mirrors the lover of her 'past' life. In the 1980s a rich baker, Wu Dai, marries her and brings her to Hong Kong. He hires his friend Wu Long as family chauffeur.

One night Lotus tries to seduce Wu Long in his car, nearly causing a crash. After initially embracing her he pulls away confusedly. She goes to a night club and is picked up by the cocaine-sniffing Siu. A mysterious fortune-teller tells Lotus of her past and she makes the connection with the present. She experiences visions of Siu's death. Wu Long, who killed Lotus's historical-fictional counterpart, finds her and Siu together and warns her not to cheat on Wu Dai again.

When he finds his wife reading about Golden Lotus, Wu Dai vaguely recalls the story but misses its relevance to his own life. He takes fifty aphrodisiac pills given him by Siu and loses consciousness. Not long after, Wu Long accuses Lotus of poisoning Wu Dai. Exactly as in her previous visions, Wu Long throws Siu out of an upstairs window while Wu Dai unexpectedly awakens unharmed. When Wu Long is injured after chasing Lotus in her car, she drives him in the direction of the hospital. The pages of *Golden Lotus* fly on to the car as Wu Long slowly dies. Her desire for revenge now fulfilled, Lotus releases the wheel and embraces her dead lover. Their car disappears out of the frame before exploding in a ball of flames.

See also: adaptations of drama and literature

Further Reading
S. Fore (1993), a critical analysis; T.S. Kam *et al.* (1994–5), a brief discussion.

(KH, YZ)

representations of intellectuals

The 'intellectual' (*zhishi fenzi*) is a term used in modern China to refer to anyone who has received college – or sometimes even secondary or vocational – education. Unlike its traditional counterpart, the literatus, denoting a scholar versed in Confucian classics and talented in literature and arts, the intellectual conjures up the image of a modern person who applies his or her knowledge directly to improve the world. In this sense, the word 'intellectual' carries a strong sense of commitment to social issues and a possibility of political participation.

In the 1920s–30s, the intellectual often appeared on the Chinese screen as a schoolteacher whose role closely resembled that of the traditional scholar. While the grandfather in ***Song of China*** (*dir.* **Fei Mu**, **Luo Mingyou**, 1935) represents the wisdom of the Confucian patriarch whose personal integrity holds the **family** together against all

odds, the principal of a Shanghai vocational school in ***Plunder of Peach and Plum*** (**Ying Yunwei**, 1934) comes closer to the modern meaning of intellectual in that he prepares his students to enter the world of commerce and industry and to work for a modernized China. The contrastive endings in these two films make an ironic comment on the fate of intellectuals in modern China: whereas the first film ends with the grandfather's vision that his grandson will take over his orphanage and continue his welfare mission by bringing up another generation of 'educated' youngsters, the second film ends with the execution of one of the 'brightest' of the next generation, whose social status is degraded step by step, from a petty bourgeois through a miserable worker to a prosecuted criminal.

In the 1930s, the tragedy of the young intellectual in *Plunder of Peach and Plum* was meant not just as a condemnation of evil urban society that seeks money at the cost of morality, but also as a warning to the younger generation that they must not pursue their own dream of **love and marriage** without participating in a public cause of some kind. Increasingly, in leftist films such as ***Three Modern Women*** (*dir.* **Bu Wancang**, 1933), *Children of Troubled Times* (*dir.* Xu Xingzhi, 1935) and ***Crossroads*** (*dir.* **Shen Xiling**, 1937), young intellectuals were urged to join forces with the working classes and contribute to the cause of national salvation. Those who care only about their own feelings and well-being are symbolically 'punished' on the screen, often by losing their loved ones, and sometimes by committing suicide themselves. Interestingly, very few young intellectuals were given a happy life in leftist films of the 1930s–40s. In ***Diary of a Homecoming*** (*dir.* Yuan Jun) and ***Dream in Paradise*** (*dir.* **Tang Xiaodan**, both 1947), their dreams of living a decent life in Shanghai after the war are repeatedly crushed by evil forces beyond their control.

In the late 1940s, ***Sorrows and Joys of a Middle-Aged Man*** (*dir.* **Sang Hu**, 1949) is an exceptional film because it provides a fairy tale-like ending to the life of an intellectual – significantly no longer young but miraculously still 'productive'. After devoting his early life to teaching at a local school, the father retires and lives with his son, a successful banker in Shanghai. Bored with his dependent life, the father falls in love with a teacher young enough to be his daughter, and transforms his tomb site (a gift from his son) into a new school, where he and the young woman start a new life with a new-born boy. Obviously influenced by Confucian ideology, respected figures of middle-aged schoolteachers appeared again and again in mainland China and Taiwan, for instance in *A Boat in the Ocean* (*dir.* **Lee Hsing**, 1978) and *Reunion* (*dir.* **Ko Yi-cheng** 1985). Although *The **Life of Wu Xun*** (*dir.* **Sun Yu**, 1950) was criticized in China specifically for its ideological connection with Confucianism, what is ironic is that four decades later *Country Teachers* (*dir.* **He Qun**, 1993), a similar film emphasizing the enduring spirit of teachers in a poverty-stricken mountain village, was endorsed publicly by the Communist regime. Indeed, in the figure of schoolteacher one sees a long tradition of cultural respect that sometimes overrides ideological or political differences.

However, politics did make a great deal of difference in representations of intellectuals in mainland China. In the 1950s–60s, all intellectuals were required to transform their petty bourgeois consciousness and identify themselves with the new regime and with the masses of workers, peasants and soldiers, who were exalted as the real heroes of the **Communist revolution** and **socialist construction**. By the 1960s, fewer and fewer films would portray intellectuals as main protagonists, and those that did were severely criticized in the early years of the **Cultural Revolution**, a period when knowledge was equated to counter-revolution. College professors, schoolteachers, doctors and engineers were given mostly negative portrayal in the 1960s–70s, at best as characters who gradually change their ideological position under 'correct' political guidance. In films such as ***Breaking with Old Ideas*** (*dir.* Li Wenhua, 1975), intellectuals are depicted as not only useless when facing real-life problems, but also as potentially dangerous in that they make their students forget or even 'detest' their rural origins.

In the wake of a decade-long, nationwide political persecution of intellectuals during the Cultural Revolution (so disastrous that many veteran filmmakers died), mainland films in the late 1970s and the early 1980s responded in an extremely emotional way to such human disasters, often presenting the persecuted intellectuals as central characters. ***Reverberations of Life*** (*dir.* **Teng Wenji**, **Wu Tianming**, 1979) features a blacklisted musician, and *Unrequited Love* (1981, banned in the mainland) follows an exiled poet. In keeping with the government's new policy of four modernizations, intellectuals and scientists were given

unprecedentedly positive portrayal in the 1980s, as in ***At the Middle Age*** (*dir.* Wang Qimin, **Sun Yu**, 1982) and ***Black Cannon Incident*** (*dir.* **Huang Jianxin**, 1985).

The wheel of fortune turned again in the late 1980s, when economic reforms had created a class of *nouveaux riches* and intellectuals had lost much of their political and 'commercial' values on the screen. The devaluation of intellectuals is treated with a particularly sinister tone in several films based on Wang Shuo's novels. ***Transmigration*** (*dir.* Huang Jianxin), *The **Trouble Shooters*** (*dir.* Mi Jiashan, both 1988) and *Half Flame, Half Brine* (*dir.* **Xia Gang**, 1989) portray female college students as naive and vulnerable, male professors and scientists as unfaithful and hypocritical, and a would-be writer as vainglorious and despicable. In *Shanghai Fever* (*dir.* Li Guoli, 1993), an architect is carried away by a desire to outsmart his wife in stock speculation and he attempts to commit suicide by jumping from the top of a hotel when he has lost his friend's money. From a morally upright school master to a money-crazed architect, representations of intellectuals on the Chinese screen cut across a wide spectrum and are influenced by dominant economic and political forces over time.

(YZ)

representations of women

As the work of women directors is included under the category **woman's film**, this entry deals only with male representations of women. Ever since 1913, when actress Yan Shanshan first appeared with her husband **Li Minwei** in a Hong Kong short, ***Zhuangzi Tests His Wife*** (*dir.* **Li Beihai**, 1913), Chinese women have appealed to the male imagination. And women remain the object of attraction, obsession, and sometimes scandal in various kinds of films by male directors.

Images of women in Chinese cinema can be divided into several types. Among the traditional types are the dutiful daughter, the virtuous wife, the caring mother, and the old grandmother. Among the modern types are the aspiring career woman, the pleasure-seeking bourgeois lady, the ascetic factory worker, and the androgynous revolutionary cadre.

Historically, traditional women received most attention during the 1910s–20s and they were portrayed largely within the domain of the extended Chinese **family**. With the influx of modern ideas, the time-honoured system of arranged marriage came under an increasing amount of criticism, as in *The **Difficult Couple*** (*dir.* **Zhang Shichuan**, 1913). After the May Fourth New Culture Movement of the late 1910s, the patriarchal figure who pursues his own interests over his children's feelings was usually presented in a negative light, whereas the younger generation were seen as more and more determined to seek their own happiness: for example, in *Good Brothers* (*dir.* Ren Pengnian, 1922), where two brothers are reunited with their sweethearts after many trials and misunderstandings. In some cases the young girl was even given the chance to find a man of her own liking. In ***Cheng the Fruit Seller*** (*dir.* Zhang Shichuan, 1922), the dutiful daughter, who takes care of her ageing father, is depicted as freely 'displaying' herself in the public sphere (her father's clinic), thus arousing the hard-working fruit seller's desire. To please the audience, the dutiful daughter is married off happily by the end.

The fate of the virtuous wife, however, is another story. In *Little Darling* (*dir.* **Zheng Zhengqiu**, 1926), the wife has to endure prejudice simply because she has remarried and supports a child from her previous marriage. In *Conflict Between Love and Lust* (*dir.* Wang Cilong, 1930), the wife has to tolerate her husband's taking of a new wife and wait for the prodigal to return in the end. As demonstrated in a number of other films like these, women were inevitably victimized by patriarchal society, but their victimization elicited sympathy from enlightened male filmmakers who identified woman's virtue as consisting of, among other things, tolerance, patience and understanding.

Also exemplifying tolerance and patience is the figure of the old grandmother, who occupies a special position in the extended family. Functioning as the ultimate source of courage, perseverance, and wisdom, the grandmother usually leads the family in their survival of hard and miserable times. From ***Spring River Flows East*** (*dir.* **Cai Chusheng**, **Zheng Junli**, 1947) and ***Myriad of Lights*** (*dir.* **Shen Fu**, 1948) to *Sowthistle* (*dir.* Li Ang, 1965), the old grandmother remains an endearing figure for audiences. In terms of her moral strength and ability to pull the family together against all odds, there is no equivalent image to the powerful figure of the grandmother in Chinese cinema.

In the 1930s, modern women began to dominate the screen. As a new social figure, the career woman was featured briefly in ***Wild Flower*** (*dir.* **Sun Yu**, 1930) and ***New Woman*** (*dir.* **Sun Shiyi**, 1934), briefly because her career success – in music or literature – inspired such anxiety in male representation that it had to be terminated in one way or another. In accordance with this line of thinking, the opera singer in *Wild Flower* has to lose her voice in order to marry her artist husband, and the writer in *New Woman* has to attempt suicide and die in a hospital after failing to save her daughter's life. In both films, career success does not bring happiness or self-fulfilment to the modern woman – it brings calamity and death instead.

Indeed, death and disease were ominously associated with women in the 1930s, especially in the case of the educated, apparently independent new woman. Significantly, some of these committed suicide in an ultimate protest against a male-dominated society that held no place for their survival. In spite of their modern knowledge, they were sexually harassed by their bosses, mistreated or abandoned by their husbands, and tormented by their inability to provide for their children, who consequently died of disease or in accidents. Like the woman writer in *New Woman*, the secretary in *Women* (*dir.* **Shi Dongshan**, 1934) commits suicide after her child is killed in a fire at home while she is away. In ***Plunder of Peach and Plum*** (*dir.* **Ying Yunwei**, 1934), the secretary escapes her boss's attempted rape only to die a few days after giving birth to her child. The fate of these screen images of career women seemed to crystallize in the real life tragedy of **Ruan Lingyu**, who committed suicide (as does the character she plays in *New Woman*) in 1935 out of protest at the injustices she suffered in Shanghai, a modern city that treated her personal life as a lurid scandal. Since the mid-1930s Ruan Lingyu has been an obsession in Chinese film circles. For instance, *The **Actress*** (*dir.* Stanley **Kwan**, 1992), a Hong Kong film based on her life, exhibits a good deal of **nostalgia** for the film world of the 1930s.

As the screen writer **Tian Han** later revealed about ***Three Modern Women*** (*dir.* **Bu Wancang**, 1933), the career woman was judged by leftist filmmakers to belong to the petty-bourgeoisie and her fate, therefore, depended entirely on whether or not she would join the urban proletariat and identify herself with **nationalism**. The telephone operator in *Three Modern Women* thus signifies a shift in ideological emphasis from the career woman to the factory worker in leftist film. Educated factory workers, who often assume the role of volunteer instructors in workers' evening schools, appear throughout the 1930s–40s, as in *New Woman*, *Myriad of Lights*, and *Female Fighters* (*dir.* **Chen Liting**, 1949). They are increasingly portrayed as free from immediate family relations, emotionally independent of male comrades, and intellectually superior to many, if not all, other characters. **Love and marriage** were no longer their prime concerns. In the 1950s–60s the configuration of this type of intellectual but ascetic woman continued, as in *Stage Sisters* (*dir.* **Xie Jin**, 1965), and culminated in the extreme figure of the androgynous revolutionary cadre during the period of the **Cultural Revolution**. With their plain factory or army uniforms, characters such as Fang Haizhen in *On the Docks* (*dir.* Xie Jin, **Xie Tieli**, 1972, 1973) are hardly distinguishable from their male counterparts. In a sense, this type is configured less as a woman (a gender-specific human figure) than as a revolutionary (a de-gendered, desexualized ideal).

The preponderance of de-gendered, desexualized women in the 1960s–70s, however, does not mean that Chinese cinema refused its audiences visual pleasure. On the contrary, voyeurism had been a component of the Chinese screen since as early as the late 1920s, if not earlier, when popular actresses like **Hu Die** and Ruan Lingyu were elevated to positions of stardom. Perhaps the figure who best embodies urban attraction (and corruption in the leftist interpretation) is the bourgeois lady who populated films of the 1930s–40s. She is usually dressed in the latest fashion, owns a luxury car, frequents theatres and dance halls, and pursues a romantic life. As the camera lingers excessively and lovingly on her sensual body and her fancy outfits, she emerges as a quintessential modern figure, the classic object of the male gaze and male desire. With a little variation, the bourgeois lady may appear as 'traditional' as she is modern. In *Long Live the Mistress!* (*dir.* **Sang Hu**, 1947), the wife proves her virtue by allowing her husband an extramarital affair and then scheming to win him back; in her final victory, she re-establishes herself as the focus of male desire.

Another popular figure of urban attraction in the 1930s is the dancing girl. She performs spectacularly on stage or in nightclubs but is concomitantly perceived· to be an erotic object available for service to male patrons – a situation hinted at by the end of *A New Year's Coin* (*dir.* Zhang Shichuan, 1937). As a modern woman, the dancing star functions very much like the woman athlete, another attractive urban figure whose healthy, well-developed body is on full display to the public, as in *Queen of Sports* (*dir.* Sun Yu, 1934). However, in moral terms, the dancing star comes closer to a traditionally more 'depraved' figure – the prostitute. In the 1920s–30s, **prostitution** was a major theme in Chinese film. By and large, the prostitute was projected as a symbol of oppression and exploitation, an object who elicits sympathy and a concern for social justice. This kind of moral imperative runs through films like *A Shanghai Woman* (*dir.* Zhang Shichuan, 1925), *Goddess* (*dir.* **Wu Yonggang**, 1934), and *Street Angel* (*dir.* Yuan Muzhi, 1937), and it is consistent with the general image of woman as victim in other Chinese films, from *A Blind Orphan Girl* (*dir.* Zhang Shichuan, 1925), through *The White-Haired Girl* (*dir.* **Shui Hua**, 1950) and *New Year's Sacrifice* (*dir.* Sang Hu, 1957), to *Hibiscus Town* (*dir.* Xie Jin, 1986) and *The Woman from the Lake of Scented Soul* (*dir.* **Xie Fei**, 1992).

The woman question has been the subject of unprecedented attention in Chinese cinema since the early 1980s. The female body is reconfigured as the classic locus of **sexuality** in a variety of films from the mainland, Hong Kong, and Taiwan: *The Corner Forsaken by Love* (*dir.* Zhang Qi, Li Yalin, 1981), *Jade Love* (*dir.* **Chang Yi**, 1984), *A Girl From Hunan* (*dir.* Xie Fei, 1986), *Osmanthus Alley* (*dir.* **Chen Kun-hou**, 1987), *Rouge* (*dir.* Stanley Kwan, 1987), *Raise the Red Lantern* (*dir.* **Zhang Yimou**, 1991), and *Farewell My Concubine* (*dir.* **Chen Kaige**, 1993). The sexual desire of the young girl or the young widow and the 'perverse' sexuality of the prostitute or the concubine has invariably captured the male imagination. On the pretext of challenging Confucian morality and political repression, filmmakers of the 1980s–90s unravel a dazzling parade of feminine beauty. **Femininity**, which was rarely explored in the early decades – with a few exceptions, like *Spring in a Small Town* (*dir.* **Fei Mu**, 1948) – is presented appreciatively, either through stylist flamboyance (e.g., the opium-smoking scene in *Rouge*) or through the dramatization of hedonistic delight (e.g., the foot-massage scene in *Raise the Red Lantern*). As embodied by Joan **Chen**, **Gong Li**, **Lin Ching Hsia**, Anita **Mui**, or Joey **Wong**, this gorgeous new screen image – exuding a seductive sexuality, an exquisite femininity – represents a variant of the *femme fatale*, a figure who simultaneously arouses the male's desire to pursue and possess her and his anxious wish to escape the danger and destruction brought in her wake. Two good examples of this type are the female protagonists of *Ming Ghost* (*dir.* Qiu Gangjian, 1990) and **Shanghai Triad** (*dir.* Zhang Yimou, 1995). From an historical perspective, we might conclude that this new feminine – and often sexually aggressive – embodiment of Chinese womanhood departs radically from the masculinization of women that occurred in earlier decades.

One quality that often distinguishes male from female cinematic productions is the latter's emphasis on the subjectivity of female characters. With the exception of *Spring in a Small Town*, **That Day on the Beach** (*dir.* Edward **Yang**, 1983) and a few other titles, subjectivity is hardly an issue in many films directed by men, because they are more concerned with the body than with the mind of their female characters. As soon as they attempt to enter the woman's mind they seem to fall back on the age-old stereotype of the virtuous woman who, perhaps more than the seductive *femme fatale* and the masculinized revolutionary cadre, remains the dominant image of Chinese womanhood. From **Little Toys** (*dir.* Sun Yu, 1933) and *Spring River Flows East* to *The* **Herdsman** (*dir.* Xie Jin, 1982) and *A* **Country Wife** (*dir.* Hu Bingliu, Wang Jin, 1983), virtuous women of different ages and social status have continued to populate the Chinese screen, especially in films about **rural life**. This observation also applies in the case of men's films from Taiwan; virtuous women have appeared consistently in such films as **Home, Sweet Home** (*dir.* **Pai Ching-jui**, 1970), **Rapeseed Woman** (*dir.* **Wan Jen**, 1983) and *A* **City of Sadness** (*dir.* **Hou Hsiao-hsien**, 1989).

See also: leftist film (under Chinese cinema in Historical essays)

Further Reading
J. Dai (1995), a feminist survey of post-1949 mainland films; T. Rayns (1987), a comparative study of China, Hong Kong and Taiwan; E. Yau (1989), a feminist reading of 1980s mainland films; E. Yau (1990), a study of post-1949 mainland films; Y. Zhang (1994a), an analysis of three 1930s films; Y. Zheng (1997), on images of women in new Chinese cinema.

(YZ)

Return of the Dragon
(Menglong guo jiang)

dir./sc. Bruce **Lee**
with Bruce Lee, Nora Miao, Chuck Norris, Robert Wall
Hong Kong: Cathay/Golden Harvest, 1972

Return of the Dragon was Bruce Lee's only film as actor-director-scenarist. It was intended to be the first of a series featuring his character Tang Lung, who would also have featured in **Game of Death** (1978) if Lee had lived. The Chinese title, *Fierce Dragon Crosses River*, matches the innovative credit titles showing a Chinese boat crossing an ocean from China to Rome. Lee's character is an innocent abroad naive to Western ways. The initial scenes (censored in the US version) show Tang, the comic object of the Western gaze, breaching cultural etiquette by squatting in an airport urinal and later incompetently ordering the wrong dishes at a restaurant and mistaking a hooker for a lady. The film is a variation of *The Big Boss* (1971), where Lee's naive character helps a family friend defend her restaurant from the Italian Mafia and later taking on the 'hired guns', who possess various national martial arts skills, with his own special brand of the same.

As in most Lee films, the plot is fairly basic and only exists as a showcase for its star's skills. Tang Lung arrives in Rome to help Chen Ching defend her restaurant against the mob. Although Chen regards Tang as an embarrassment, retired manager Uncle Wang welcomes him. After various defeats, the Mafiosi hire martial arts champion Colt to kill Tang. The film moves to the gladiatorial combat in the Roman Coliseum where Tang defeats (and reluctantly kills) his opponent in the contest. Tang discovers Uncle Wang is a traitor and flees from his bullets before the police arrive and shoot him. After family funerals, Tang leaves for the airport.

(TW)

Reverberations of Life
(Shenghuo de chanyin)

dir. **Teng Wenji**, **Wu Tianming**
sc. Teng Wenji
with Shi Zhonglin, Leng Mei, Fu Qinzeng, Xiang Kun
Xi'an: Xi'an Film, 1979

Set against the background of the political demonstrations of 1976, this film condemns the authoritarian rule of the Gang of Four, but also represents complex political divisions in personal terms.

In the spring of 1976 a violinist, Zheng Changhe, actively participates in political protests against the Gang of Four. His activities are monitored by Wei Li, who remains loyal to the the Gang. Wei is in love with a girl named Xu Shanshan, although she has a crush on Zheng. At a concert attended by Xu, Zheng performs his own composition commemorating the late premier Zhou Enlai. Xu is impressed both by Zheng's performance and by his political stance. Wei convinces Xu's mother of the political risks her daughter will face if she continues to associate with Zheng, by pointing out that the musician is now barred from performing in public. While Xu's mother tries to prevent her daughter from having a relationship with Zheng, Xu's father supports her. On 5 April, as hundreds of thousands of people gather to protest in Tiananmen Square, Wei seeks Zheng's arrest. At the same time, Zheng is violating the terms of the ban imposed on him by giving a concert at Xu's residence. Such defiance of the Gang of Four's political power is met with ruthless opposition. Only after the Gang are arrested is Zheng able to give another public performance of his work.

The film received Best Film award from the Ministry of Culture in 1979.

(ZX)

Revived Rose

(Fuhuo de meigui)

dir. **Hou Yao**, **Li Minwei**
sc. Hou Yao
with Lin Chuchu, He Neng, Li Minwei
Shanghai: Minxin Film, 1927

An early example of Chinese **melodrama**, the film tells a complicated love story. Xiuyun is courted by Xiaoxing, a promising young painter. When Xiaoxing gives her his painting, 'Revived Rose', Xiuyun breaks into tears. Xiaoxing does not know the reason until later, when he goes to celebrate the wedding of his idiotic cousin and is shocked to find Xiuyun to be the bride. Xiuyun is the victim of an arranged marriage, and so is Xiaoxing. He resists his father's order to marry another girl and is exiled to Hong Kong as a result.

Xiuyun attempts suicide on her wedding night but is saved by her husband. After negotiations, her marriage is dissolved. She becomes a governess, but is soon fired when the family hears the rumours about her. To escape social pressures back home, she goes to Hong Kong. A Hong Kong girl named Ruoyun loves Xiaoxing, but he still misses Xiuyun. Xiuyun places a newspaper advertisement looking for Xiaoxing. When she sees him going out with Ruoyun, she feels extremely depressed. After leaving a suicide note, she goes to the beach. When he finds the note, Xiaoxing drives to the beach and rescues Xiuyun from the sea. The film ends with the two suffering lovers looking at each other in tears.

(YZ)

Revolutionary Family

(Geming jiating)

dir. **Shui Hua**
sc. **Xia Yan**, Shui Hua
with **Yu Lan**, **Sun Daolin**, Wen Xiying, **Tian Fang**, Yu Yang
Beijing: Beijing Film, 1961

To glorify the **Communist revolution**, this film depicts those underground Communists who, despite hardship and personal sacrifice, remain loyal to the party.

A peasant girl, Zhou Lian, is married to a revolutionary college student, Jiang Meiqing: they have three sons. Even though Zhou loves Jiang dearly, she initially has little understanding of what he actually does. Gradually, however, she becomes enlightened and begins to participate actively in the revolution. After her husband, who turns out to be a Communist, is arrested and killed by the Nationalists, Zhou is transferred to Shanghai, where she works for the CCP as an underground contact. Meanwhile, her oldest son, Liqun, finishes his studies in the Soviet Union and returns to China. Both Zhou and Liqun's true identities are discovered and they are arrested by the Nationalist police. Desperate for information about the CCP network in Shanghai, Zhou's inquisitors threaten to kill her son if she does not cooperate. However, as Zhou values the revolutionary cause more than her personal feelings she refuses to yield any information. Liqun is executed. After the outbreak of the Sino-Japanese war, Zhou is released through an amnesty programme: the CCP and the

Nationalists have agreed to free all political prisoners through the formation of the Second United Front. Zhou, along with her two remaining children, travels to Yan'an, where the headquarters of the Communist base areas are located.

The film was granted Best Film award at the 1962 HFA. Yu Lan, who played the female lead, won Best Actress award at the 1961 Moscow FF.

(ZX)

Ripples Across Stagnant Water

(Kuang)

dir. **Ling Zifeng**
sc. Han Lanfang
with Xu Qing, You Yong, Zhao Jun, Cheng Xi
Hong Kong: Skai (Shijia) Film/Chengdu: Emei Film, 1991

Executed by a veteran mainland director, this film tells a tale of sexual and moral transgression. Its Chinese title carries a number of meanings: 'turbulent (currents)', 'wild (passion)' or 'arrogant (character)'. All this finds a perfect embodiment in a pretty country woman. She longs for **urban life** and is married to a dumb and cowardly shop owner Cai Xingshun, so she is called Sister Cai. Xingshun's parents are dead, and he counts on his cousin Luo Desheng, a powerful local man, for protection. When customers try to take advantage of Sister Cai, Luo comes and beats them up. The two become intimate.

One day in the spring, Sister Cai plays with her son and feels bitter when she sees Luo return from a trip with a prostitute named Liu. Liu loves Luo and wants to give up prostitution. She follows Luo's instructions and fools around with a landlord named Gu Tiancheng in the gambling house. Soon Gu loses all his money to Luo and leaves the town. Liu notices the passion between Luo and Sister Cai and arranges for the two to meet in the lantern festival. They run into Gu and his friends, and a fight breaks out when Gu insults Sister Cai. Gu loses his daughter in the chaos and becomes seriously ill. He is cured by a foreign doctor and is converted to Christianity.

Meanwhile, the Boxer Rebellion sweeps across the region, and Gu's business is closed due to his association with the missionaries. The event turns around when Beijing is taken over by the foreign powers. In revenge, Gu uses his missionary connections and accuses Luo and Cai of being

Boxers. When the Qing soldiers come to arrest Luo, he has already escaped, but Cai is imprisoned, severely beaten, and their shop closed. Gu goes to the countryside to investigate Luo's whereabouts and is bewitched by Sister Cai's beauty and charm. He wants to marry her, but she consents only on condition that her husband will be released and she will be allowed to meet freely with Luo. Gu puts these marriage agreements in writing, and the film ends with Sister Cai bringing her son to the prison, waiting for Cai's release.

(IJS)

River Without Buoys, The

(Meiyou hangbiao de heliu)

dir. **Wu Tianming**
sc. Ye Weilin
with Li Wei, Hu Ronghua, Tao Yuling
Xi'an: Xi'an Film, 1983

This film contrasts the freedom, harmony and peace enjoyed by the boatmen who drift on the river with the oppressive, highly politicized and chaotic world endured by those who live onshore. It can be read as a critique of the radical politics of the CCP.

A boatman, Pan Laowu, has worked for thirty years on the Xiao river enjoying the life of a drifter. During the **Cultural Revolution**, he and his two friends Shi Gu and Zhao Liang manage to stay out of trouble. Shi's sweetheart Gaixiu is being forced by a corrupt local official to marry someone else. In defiance of the local official's authority, Pan allows her to seek refuge on his boat. He also takes on to his boat a former party official who is currently being persecuted. Though fearful of the consequences of taking these two people on board, Zhao eventually accepts them as well.

When Pan goes to buy some medicine in town, he runs into his former girl friend, Wu Aihua, who is now a beggar. Years earlier, after Pan's boat capsized in the river and he was thrown deep into debt, he decided not to see Wu again so that she would not be dragged down with him. Now, however, their reunion brings back memories of the past. Pan helps her settle down and asks her to buy some medicine for the party cadre, while he goes back to his boat, promising that he will come back for her. On his way back, however, a wild torrent threatens the lives of all on board. Pan manages to save everyone from harm, but is himself swept away in the process. The next day, Zhao, Shi and Gaixiu look for Pan along the river, calling out his name as they go.

In 1984 the film was awarded a second prize from MBFT and an award at Hawaii FF.

(ZX)

Rock 'n' Roll Kids
(Yaogun qingnian)

dir. **Tian Zhuangzhuang**
sc. Liu Yiran
with Tao Jin, Ma Ling, Shi Ke
Beijing: Beijing Film, 1988

After his two controversial avant-garde titles, the director made this entertainment film as if to please audiences and critics alike. This film of urban **youth culture** features a promising dancer Long Xiang, who is bored with his routines in a dance troupe and wants to go independent. His girlfriend Yuanyuan persuades him not to quit his professional career, for they both have worked hard to attain their current leading positions in the troupe. Long, however, does not change his mind. He meets an ambitious fashion designer, Luo Dan, who hires him to train her models. Soon Luo's fashion show wins a top prize, and Long's solo dance is also highly acclaimed. Luo likes Long very much, but Long still misses Yuanyuan. When he visits Yuanyuan again, she is already engaged to someone else.

In his depression, Long runs into Xiaoxiao, a cheerful young woman. Long comes to a city park at night and admires street kids' free-style rock 'n' roll and break dances. To Luo's disappointment, Long resigns his fashion training position. He brings Xiaoxiao to a campus, where dancers and singers join college students in a celebration. Long stays at Xiaoxiao's place. The next morning, Xiaoxiao prepares breakfast while Long is still asleep, and leaves him the key to her room when she departs for work. Long wakes up. After losing Yuanyuan and leaving Luo, he seems happy to accept Xiaoxiao, a fellow traveller on the road to an uncertain future.

See also: avant-garde, experimental or exploratory film

(JJS)

romance

A type of film that elaborates a heterosexual love relationship in a positive way. Always emotional and at times sentimental, a film romance can also be a **melodrama** that subjects the characters to a series of trials and tribulations, without necessarily providing a happy ending for the lovers. Except for the 1950s–70s in mainland China when love was almost a tabooed subject, film romances have been popular throughout the century, as also in Hong Kong and Taiwan. Such romances may be film **adaptations of drama and literature**, like *Romance of the Western Chamber* (*dir.* **Hou Yao**, 1927), *Lonely Seventeen* (*dir.* **Pai Ching-jui**, 1967), *Regret for the Past* (*dir.* **Shui Hua**, 1981) and *Red Rose, White Rose* (*dir.* Stanley **Kwan**, 1994). They may also be rendered in other genres, such as the **comedy**, ethnic minorities or **martial arts film**, and thus result in **mixed genres** like romantic comedy and romantic thriller.

See also: ethnic minorities, film of; love and marriage; representations of women; sexuality

(YZ)

Romance of the Western Chamber
aka *Way Down West* (Xi xiang ji)

dir./sc. **Hou Yao**
with Lin Chuchu, Ge Cijiang, Li Dandan
Shanghai: Minxin Film, 1927

An adaptation of a classic drama of **love and marriage**, the film is set in the Tang dynasty. After the prime minister dies, his wife, daughter and son escort his coffin to their home town. They stay in Pujiu Temple. One day, while the daughter Yingying takes a walk with her maid Hongniang, they run into a young scholar Zhang Junrui, who is on his way to the capital to take the civil service examinations. He is enchanted by Yingying's beauty and stays in the temple's western chamber. That night, Zhang overhears the conversation between Yingying and Hongniang on the other side of the wall, and recites a poem to express his admiration. Yingying responds with her own poem.

The bandit chief Sun Feihu hears of Yingying's beauty and arrives with five thousand soldiers. In the besieged temple, Yingying's mother is out of her wits. She promises that anyone who can drive away the bandits will marry Yingying. Zhang asks a monk to deliver a letter to his friend, an army general, who immediately comes to the rescue. Yingying's mother thanks Zhang with a large sum of money, but says that Yingying has been engaged to someone else. Zhang is disappointed and falls ill. Hongniang thinks of a good way to bring the lovers together. Zhang plays a stringed instrument and sings of his sorrows at night, and Yingying is greatly moved. With Hongniang's help, the two first exchange love letters and poems, and then meet secretly in the western chamber. When Yingying's mother discovers the secret a month later, she reluctantly agrees to the marriage on condition that Zhang has to pass the examinations with high honours.

Zhang parts with Yingying in tears. Suddenly, the bandit Sun comes and takes away Yingying. Zhang chases and kills Sun with his pen-brush, which has magically become as long and sharp as a spear. Zhang happily embraces Yingying, who then turns out be to his servant boy. It is a dream after all.

See also: adaptations of drama and literature

Further Reading
K. Harris (1999), an excellent analysis of the film.

(YZ)

Rouge
(Yanzhi kou)

dir. Stanley **Kwan**
sc. Lilian Lee, Qiu-Dai Anping
with Anita **Mui**, Leslie **Cheung**, Alex Man, Emily Chu
Hong Kong: Golden Harvest/Golden Way Films, 1987

One of the most distinctive and internationally successful films to come out of Hong Kong in the 1980s, *Rouge* plays with the conventions of the ghost film and the Hollywood-style **melodrama**. The movie oscillates between two time frames as it tells the story of Fleur, a courtesan from the 1930s, and her romance with her young lover, Twelfth Master Chan Chen-Pang. The two had made a double suicide pact in 1934, but only Fleur makes it to the next world. She returns to Hong Kong in 1987 in search of her still-mortal lover.

Plate 36   *Rouge* (1987)

Enlisting the help of two local journalists, Yuen and his girlfriend Ah Chor, Fleur places advertisements in the local newspaper hoping to be reunited with Chan. As each day passes, the ghost becomes weaker and weaker, and her relationship with the two humans becomes more and more strained. In turn, Yuen and Ah Chor compare their love for each other with the passion shared between Fleur and Chan and find their own emotional life wanting. Fleur eventually locates Chan, but is saddened to find that he is now a failed opera actor and opium addict who hangs around movie sets in search of petty work. As a film crew shoots a Hong Kong ghost drama, Fleur returns the rouge locket Chan gave her fifty-three years earlier and walks away, determined not to wait for him any longer.

Rouge offers multiple attractions – a compelling double narrative, an intriguing ghost theme, and lush production designs. It established Stanley Kwan's directorial career and has been slated for a Hollywood remake.

See also: ghosts and immortals, film of

Further Reading
R. Chow (1993), on nostalgia; D. Eng (1993/4), on a failed Oedipal drama; L. Lee (1994), on parody and allegory.

(JS)

Ruan Lingyu
(Ruan Agen, Ruan Yuying)

b. 26 April 1910, Shanghai
d. 8 March 1935, Shanghai
Actress

Ruan Lingyu was one of the most accomplished stars of the 1930s. Her tragic death in 1935 and her well-attended public funeral received coverage in major newspapers around the world – a rare event in the film business.

Ruan exhibited her talents at an early age. In 1926, she was recruited by Mingxing Film Company and soon made her first appearance in *Marriage in Name* (*dir.* **Bu Wancang**, 1927). After starring in four films for Mingxing, she joined Great China - Lily Film Company and made another six titles. Among these, *Amorous Lesson* (*dir.* **Li Pingqian**, 1929) represents the best of Ruan's early performances.

Ruan joined Lianhua Film Company in 1930 and had an astonishing success with the studio's first release, *Memories of the Old Capital* (*dir.* **Sun Yu**, 1930). As a result, Ruan became Lianhua's major asset. She began to expand her range of characters, playing a patriotic worker in ***Three Modern Women*** (*dir.* Bu Wancang, 1933), a devoted mother in ***Little Toys*** (*dir.* Sun Yu, 1933) and a freelance writer in ***New Woman*** (*dir.* **Cai Chusheng**, 1934). Many of Ruan's contemporaries suggested that her superb technical skills grew out of her ability to transform her own life experiences into her character portrayals. Some pointed out the parallels between her own unhappy life and the lives of those she played on-screen. Indeed, throughout her short career, Ruan played rape victims in at least two movies and committed suicide four times. Her characters were often sick, sad, depressed or doomed. Yet people who worked with her remembered Ruan as a talented, easy-going and cooperative colleague.

In contrast to her professional success, Ruan's private life was a series of disasters. Her father died when she was only five. To support the family, Ruan's mother worked as a maid for the Zhang family. Years later, the youngest son of the family, Zhang Damin, became interested in Ruan and proposed marriage. But because Zhang's parents

Plate 37   Ruan Lingyu, a tragic star

disapproved of the couple's different social standing, the marriage was never made official. Ruan and Damin began to fall out not long after their wedding and soon separated. Without a legal divorce, however, Ruan discovered that when she began to live with her new lover, a wealthy merchant named Tang Jishan, she was technically guilty of adultery – a crime in Chinese law of the time. Zhang tolerated this for a while so long as Ruan paid him off. But when Ruan tried to break with him completely, he pressed charges against her, leading to a ruling obliging Ruan to appear in court. The affair was sensationalized by the newspapers in Shanghai. In despair, Ruan Lingyu committed suicide. When tens of thousands of people attended her funeral procession in the city, even the *New York Times* reported the phenomenon.

In death as in life, Ruan continues to inspire fascination and love. In addition to several TV dramas, a biographical film *The **Actress*** (*dir.* Stanley **Kwan**, 1992) attempted to recapture the glamorous lifestyle of 1930s Shanghai.

See also: biography

Further Reading
K. He *et al.* (1986), a biography; ZDX (1982–6: 1: 111–19), a short biography.

(ZX, YZ)

Rumble in the Bronx

(Hong fan qu)

dir. Stanley Tong
sc. Jackie **Chan**
with Jackie Chan, Anita **Mui**, Francoise Yip, Bill Tung
Hong Kong: Golden Harvest, 1994

Originally titled *Red Indian Territory* (Hong fan qu), *Rumble in the Bronx* is Jackie Chan's fifth attempt to break into the American market after the ignominious failures of *The Big Brawl* (*dir.* Robert Clouse, 1980), *The Cannonball Run* (1981), *The Cannonball Run, II* (1983, both *dir.* Hal Needham) and *The Protector* (*dir.* James Glickenhaus, 1986). Shot in Vancouver (substituting for New York), the film's eventual success owed much to Chan's determination to maintain control by making it primarily for the Southeast Asian market.

The American version opens with vacationing Hong Kong policeman Kevin arriving in New York for his uncle's wedding. They begin conversing in Cantonese before the dialogue changes to American dubbing. Bill sells his supermarket and Kevin finds himself protecting its new owner from marauding bikers as well as gangsters in search of missing diamonds. Eventually, Kevin enlists the bikers as allies against the gangsters.

Rumble's plot is mixed and wastes Anita Mui in a thankless role. But it has other redeeming features. After Kevin's fight with the street gang, he criticizes them for falling into the dehumanizing stereotypes the system wishes them to perform and hopes that they will drink tea with him one day. The Hong Kong version has Kevin excitedly speaking in Cantonese so that the biker leader needs the aid of a Chinese member to interpret Kevin's words. Anita Mui also has more scenes in the Cantonese version, which has Uncle Bill and his Afro-American bride perform a touching Chinese theatrical number complementing the American song seen in the stateside version. The Cantonese version also contains a scene of Kevin pledging his fidelity to his Hong Kong girlfriend. This impresses the biker leader's girlfriend, who becomes attracted to him.

(TW)

rural life

For the majority of Western audiences, images of China are closely associated with certain kinds of rural landscapes: chimney smoke rising from a remote mountain village, a barefooted farmer guiding a water buffalo ploughing through a paddy field, or chatty women rinsing clothes by a river with children playing around. Invariably, rural images seem to fix China in a timeless frame, giving it at once an aura of great tradition and a sense of backwardness. On the Chinese screen, rural life, which covers a wide spectrum of social and familiar activities to be enumerated below, is generally portrayed in a much more positive light than **urban life**. In fact, a rural–urban contrast runs deep in the Chinese imagination and constitutes a recurrent theme in many rural films.

In the course of the century, several prevalent rural configurations have emerged on the Chinese screen: a stronghold of tradition, an idyllic site, a place violated by modern technology, a cradle of revolution, a reserve of primitive passions, and so on. In ***Song of China*** (*dir.* **Fei Mu**, **Luo Mingyou**, 1935), the rural **family** is believed to be the centre where Confucian virtues persist, hence its Chinese title 'Filial Piety' (*tianlun*); moreover, the rural is meant to be China, hence its export English title. In the film, the son and the daughter seek modern life in the city and are judged as 'corrupt' and unfilial. It is through the grandson, who was once delighted to meet an old shepherd and his sheep in his grandparents' village, that the family members are reunited in the end.

In **Border Town** (*dir.* **Ling Zifeng**, 1984), it is an old ferryman and his granddaughter who conjure up an idyllic landscape. They live under a pagoda by a mountain river and view life as unfolding in a cyclical pattern. In *Border Town* and earlier films like **Third Sister Liu** (*dir.* Su Li, 1960), peaceful rural landscapes are displayed as if they are part of a traditional scroll painting. Idyllic pictures of rural life are also found in many Taiwan films, especially those by **Hou Hsiao-hsien**. The simplicity of life and the innocence of the mind are two qualities that are evoked with **nostalgia** against the background of a natural environment of mountains, rivers and fields.

Notwithstanding idyllic images in cinematic representation, the rural community could not avoid facing challenges from the modern world. Since the 1930s, rural people are often shown to be driven into bankruptcy by modern technology. In **Spring Silkworms** (*dir.* **Cheng Bugao**), **Little Toys** (*dir.* **Sun Yu**, both 1933) and **Song of the Fishermen** (*dir.* **Cai Chusheng**, 1934), traditional means of production are replaced by the industrialized ones, and rural people are often uprooted and displaced to urban areas. In their efforts to reveal miserable living conditions in the countryside, leftist films have exposed natural and human disasters that plagued rural people, such as flood, drought, famine, banditry and warlordism. Films like **Wild Torrents** (*dir.* Cheng Bugao, 1933) and **Big Road** (*dir.* Sun Yu, 1934) have introduced the idea of class struggle and thus led to a new image of the countryside as a cradle of revolution.

The image of the cradle of revolution has been fully developed in mainland China since the 1950s. From the guerilla warfare against the Japanese and the Nationalist troops to the land reform under Communist leadership, the vast rural areas in China provide an excellent stage for revolutionary activities. War films such as **Guerrillas on the Plain** (*dir.* Su Li, Wu Zhaodi, 1955) and **Tunnel Warfare** (*dir.* Ren Xudong, 1965) chronicle a **Communist revolution** that was strategically based on the countryside. *The* **White-Haired Girl** (*dir.* Wang Bin, **Shui Hua**, 1950) and other films dramatize class struggles between peasants and landlords. **Li Shuangshuang** (*dir.* Lu Ren, 1962), *The* **In-Laws** (*dir.* Zhao Huanzhang, 1981), and countless other films praise the achievements of **socialist construction** that affect billions of rural people. In the Communist era, the rural has been gradually transfigured from a place of changelessness to one of profound change.

In the 1980s, several mainland directors departed from the mainstream propaganda film and explored the ways such profound changes in the rural area affected individuals and their families. While largely framed in the rural–urban antithesis, **Wu Tianming**'s *Life* (1984) and **Old Well** (1987) reveal some kinds of deeply entrenched rural mentalities, especially with regard to **love and marriage**, that simply refuse to give way to modern ideas. **In the Wild Mountain** (*dir.* Yan Xueshu, 1985), however, presents a more optimistic view of the countryside. It follows two couples through their divorce and re-matches them by dividing the two conservative farmers from the two reform-minded ones, thus achieving a new order of peace and satisfaction.

Indeed, satisfaction at an individual level has received a great deal of attention since the late 1980s. With a new awareness of desire and **sexuality**, films such as *A* **Girl from Hunan** (*dir.* **Xie Fei**, 1986), **Red Sorghum** (*dir.* **Zhang Yimou**, 1987) and *Widow Village* (*dir.* Wang Jin, 1988) represent rural China as a rich reserve of primitive passions. Images of exotic rituals and fertile soils in these new rural films have attracted the Western gaze and created a new kind of 'ethnographic' interest in the immense rural landscape that is still known as China.

See also: painting and film; propaganda and film; war film

(YZ)

S

Sacrificed Youth

(Qingchun ji)

dir./sc. **Zhang Nuanxin**
with Li Fengxu, Guo Jianguo, Yu Ji,
Feng Yuanzheng
Beijing: BFA Youth Film, 1985

Unlike many other films critical of the political
repression of the **Cultural Revolution**, *Sacrificed
Youth* examines this period from a cultural perspective. The film's juxtaposition of Han and ethnic
Dai people highlights what has gone 'wrong' with
mainstream Han culture.

During the Cultural Revolution, a woman
student from Beijing named Li Chun is sent to a
Dai village in southwestern China for re-education. Initially she has difficulty fitting in with the
local people. But her host family – the granny,
the uncle and the big brother – are extremely kind
to her and help her in any way they can. Gradually
Li adapts herself to the new environment and
discovers her **femininity** after dressing herself
like a Dai girl. Meanwhile, her medical knowledge
also saves the life of a Dai boy who otherwise
would have become a victim of superstition. On a
market day, Li meets a young man named Ren
Jia from a nearby village who is also from Beijing.
The two immediately fall in love. Soon afterwards
Li finds out that the big brother from her host
family is also in love with her, but she is repelled
by his straightforwardness and his somewhat
violent manner. After careful consideration, she
transfers to another village to avoid the uncomfortable situation. Years later, Li goes to revisits
the Dai village before going to college. But the
village has been wiped out in a landslide. Her host
family and Ren Jia are all gone.

Further Reading

E. Yau (1994b), a study of ethnicity and cultural
representation; Y. Zhang (1997a), a discussion of
ethnicity and nationhood.

(ZX)

Sandwich Man

(Erzi de da wan'ou)

dir. **Hou Hsiao-hsien, Tseng Chuang-
hsiang, Wan Jen**
sc. **Wu Nien-chen**
with Chen Bocheng, Yang Liyin, Cho Shengli,
Jiang Xia, Jing Ding, Chen Qi
Taipei: CMPC, 1983

The omnibus work *Sandwich Man* consists of three
short films. The first, *The Son's Big Doll* (*dir.* Hou
Hsiao-hsien), concerns a poor man whose job is to
masquerade as a clown, walking around town
advertising movies for the local theatre. He does
this so often that his newborn son comes to recognize him only when wearing his clown suit and
make-up: when he shows up one morning in ordinary street clothes his son, having no idea who he
is, cries out as his father tries to cuddle him.

The second film, *Xiao Qi's Hat*, is Tseng
Chuang-hsiang's directorial début. A young
employee is sent by his company to the countryside to sell a high-tech Japanese cooker. Unlike his
partner, who is concerned about the product's
sluggish sales, the young man is more interested
in finding out about a little local girl named Xiao
Qi who always wears a hat. As he gradually wins
Xiao Qi's trust, he is ever more curious to take off
her hat – when he eventually does so he sees a big
patch of burnt skin on the top of her head. He
leaves town after his partner is killed demonstrating the cooker.

The Taste of the Apple is the last but least 'alienating' film of the three. Directed by Wan Ren, this melodramatic film builds on the sarcasm and irony of the original myth of the psychology of Third World poverty in the 1950s. A poor labourer is hit by a car driven by an American colonel and loses his leg. To compensate, the colonel and the American Embassy offer him money together with the chance for his deaf-mute daughter to receive a free education in the USA. At the hospital, as the whole family eats apples for the first time in their lives – courtesy of the colonel – the overwhelmed father announces that he would not mind losing his other leg if it would bring more such good fortune.

Sandwich Man and ***In Our Time*** (*dir.* Edward **Yang** *et al.*, 1982) are regarded as the two films that inaugurated New Taiwan Cinema. However, *The Sandwich Man* is stylistically and thematically more indicative of the movement's characteristics. The filmmakers adaptation of Hwang Chunming's novella points to the critical direction in which the New Wave was to move: namely, towards the critique of Taiwan's modernization and political–economic dependence on the First World. Moreover, the cinematography and general visual sense of all three parts exhibits a deeper awareness of the necessity of creating a heterogeneous national cinema.

See also: New Taiwan Cinema (under Taiwan cinema in Historical essays)

Further Reading

G. Cheshire (1993), an excellent analysis of Hou's films; H. Chiao (1993b), an interview with critical comments.

(YY)

Sang Hu

(Li Peilin)

b. 22 December 1916, Shanghai
Director, screen writer

An important director in the 1940s–50s, Sang Hu was born into a paper merchant's family. His father was a Beijing opera fan. Through his influence, Sang became interested in traditional Chinese theatre at an early age. After his parents died, he had to work as an apprentice in a stock exchange firm to support himself.

In 1934 Sang discontinued his courses in journalism at Hujiang University and took a job from the Bank of China. By coincidence, he met Zhou

Xinfang, a well-known Beijing opera singer, and the two became good friends. Zhou introduced Sang to **Zhu Shilin**, one of the most accomplished film directors at the time. It was Zhu who initiated Sang into film making.

Sang started writing the script for *Soul and Flesh* (1941). It was also the first time he used his pen name, Sang Hu. Following the success of *Soul and Flesh*, Sang wrote four more film scripts before the end of the war. But not until he joined Wenhua Film Company in 1946 did Sang begin directing films. During his days at Wenhua, he wrote the script for ***Phony Phoenixes*** (*dir.* **Huang Zuolin**, 1947), and directed *Lingering Passion*, ***Long Live the Mistress!*** (both 1947) and ***Sorrows and Joys of a Middle-Aged Man*** (1949).

After 1949 Sang worked for Shanghai Film Studio and directed two award-winning films, ***Liang Shanbo and Zhu Yingtai*** (1954) and ***New Year's Sacrifice*** (1957). Sang was also one of the few film directors who were allowed to make films during the **Cultural Revolution**. Since 1979 he has directed four films, two of which, *Twins Come in Pairs* (1979) and *The Stamp Collector* (1984), won top prizes from the Ministry of Culture in 1979 and 1984.

See also: theatre and film

Further Reading

ZDX (1982–6: 6: 391–403), a biographic sketch.

(ZX)

science and education film

Also known as 'education film', science and education film was officially established as a genre in mainland China during the 1950s. Its aims are to promote science and technology, report new developments and educate the masses by using easy-to-understand language and theory. The genre covers a wide range of subjects, such as agriculture, astronomy, biology, evolution, geology, genetic engineering, military sciences, medicine, pharmacy and telecommunications. Many popular films in this genre present vivid pictures of animals (e.g., pandas and snakes), insects (e.g., bees and butterflies), plants (e.g., bamboos), as well as deserts and seas. Some films also introduce cities like Beijing, or newly discovered artefacts like the Dunhuang murals.

(YZ)

science-fiction film

Science-fiction film, like the science-fiction story, is an underdeveloped genre in China. There are few Chinese features comparable to the highly sophisticated and immensely popular Western explorations of space travel, alien invasion and futuristic societies. In mainland China, a near equivalent to the depiction of a futuristic society is *Dislocation* (*dir.* **Huang Jianxin**, 1986), wherein a robot takes on human weaknesses and acts against its inventor's will. Even here, however, the director emphasizes the efficiency and potential disaster of the high-tech society in which the robot operates rather than the contaminating effects of party bureaucracy. In Hong Kong, science-fiction elements are sometimes incorporated into gangster **comedy** films, such as in *Aces Go Places* (*dir.* **Tsui Hark**, 1982), where a mock 'star wars' is fought out between police and gangsters using miniature space weapons. In spite of the genre's box-office appeal, only a few full-scale science-fiction films have been produced, such as *Robotrix* (*dir.* Jamie Luk, 1993) and *The Wicked City* (*dir.* Mak Tai Kit, 1992).

See also: gangster film

(YZ)

Sea Oath

(Haishi)

dir./sc. **Dan Duyu**
with Yin Mingzhu, Zhou Guoji, Dong Liansheng
Shanghai: Shanghai Shadowplay, 1921

One of the first three Chinese long features, *Sea Oath* consciously imitates Hollywood **melodrama** by treating **love and marriage** as an issue of life and death. Fuzhu falls in love with a poor painter, Zhou Xuanqing. They vow that if one of them breaks faith, he or she must die by drowning in the sea. Meanwhile, Fuzhu is courted by her rich cousin. Gradually she enjoys the luxury and agrees to marry her cousin. In the middle of their wedding in a church, Fuzhu remembers her promise to Xuanqing and runs away from her cousin. Xuanqing is still angry with her. Fuzhu feels ashamed and jumps into the sea. Xuanqing follows her and rescues her from the sea. He is now sure of her true love. The two get married and live happily ever after.

(YZ)

Secret Document

(Mimi tuzhi)

dir. Hao Guang
sc. Shi Chao, Zheng Hong and Hao Guang
with **Tian Hua**, **Wang Xin'gang**, Shi Wei, Xing Jitian
Beijing: August First Film, 1965

This **detective film** offers a Chinese version of James Bond, with less romance but more politics. It exhibits a sense of genuine paranoia – enemies lurk around every corner waiting to strike – and is noteworthy for the fact that all prime suspects in this spy case are educated Chinese.

At a crowded train station a scientist, Li Hua, loses his briefcase containing secret documents. A woman investigator, Shi Yun, is assigned to the case. The day after the incident occurs, the briefcase is returned to Li by Dr Gu Zhongru and his student Jin, who had earlier decided to pick it up after seeing a man dumping it. While money and other valuables in the briefcase are missing, the secret documents seem to be intact. Upon closer examination, however, Shi concludes that the documents have been photographed. A number of clues lead Shi to her prime suspect, a chef named Ye. Meanwhile, Shi's husband, Chen Liang, who is working on a different case, provides a further tip: a female musician named Fang Li, whom Chen has been assigned to investigate, seems to be in contact with Ye. But just as they try to find out more about Ye, Dr Gu recognizes Ye as the person who earlier threw the briefcase away and takes him to the police. Doctor Gu's conduct makes Shi suspicious. When Fang asks Chen to take her and Gu to Shenzhen, Shi realizes they are planning to ambush Chen and herself after crossing the border. Shi finds the roll of film containing the secret documents in one of Gu's shoes.

(ZX)

Sentinels Under the Neon Lights

(Nihongdeng xia de shaobing)

dir. **Wang Ping**, Ge Gan
sc. Shen Ximeng
with Xu Linge, Gong Zipei, Tao Yuling
Shanghai: Tianma Film, 1964

This film centres on how the new masters of Shanghai, in this case Communist soldiers, resist the city's corrupting forces. Although it features a happy ending, it also offers a realistic depiction of the problems the CCP faced during its initial years in power.

A squadron stationed in Shanghai encounters a series of problems. Lieutenant Chen Xi is fascinated by the city's cosmopolitan lifestyle. When his wife visits him from the countryside, he finds her unsophisticated and boring. A new recruit from the city, Tong Anan, does not take military rule seriously: when criticized, he quits. Meanwhile, Sergeant Zhao Dada cannot get used to city life and begins to miss the front line. The political commissar Lu Hua and the captain of the squadron try to raise the class consciousness of their soldiers and so cultivate their sense of responsibility. Indeed, the soldiers soon learn of the city's hidden dangers when a group of Nationalist agents attempts to murder Tong's sister. The squadron captures the underground Nationalists during the New Year festivities. After the Korean war breaks out, Chen, Tong and Zhao all request to be transferred to the front.

(ZX)

Serfs

(Nongnu)

dir. **Li Jun**
sc. Huang Zongjiang
with Wang Dui, Baima Yangjie, Xiao Duoji, Qiong Da, Ciren Duoji
Beijing: August First Film, 1963

The setting is Tibet. Jampa (Qiangba) is the son of two serfs who were killed by their master after Jampa was born. He grows up with his grandmother and is forced to serve as a human horse for the master's son, Namchal (Langjie). Jampa gradually becomes more introverted: before long he has resolved not to speak to other people any more. Believed mute, his only two friends are Gezong (Gesang) and Gezong's sister Lamka (Landuo).

Jampa gets in touch with Chinese soldiers who help him recover from Namchal's cruel treatment. This contact brings him hope that his slave condition might be brought to an end. Jampa, Gezong, and Lamka decide to escape to join the Chinese Liberation Army. Gezong and Lamka succeed, but Jampa is caught and handed over to the living Buddha Thubtan (Tudeng), who takes him as his lama. Thubtan pretends to support the Chinese but actually works with Namchal as a Tibetan separatist. When Namchal escapes during a major revolt against serfdom, Jampa is forced to follow him and serve, once more, as a human horse. This time, however, Jampa rebels by engaging him in a violent struggle. He is saved by a Chinese soldier who dies in the rescue. Jampa then returns to unmask Thubtan's acts of betrayal. He is knocked down and almost burned to death in a fire set by Thubtan, but he survives to expose the weapons Thubtan has hidden in the temple. The film ends with a convalescent Jampa uttering his first words after years of silence – he mouths the name Chairman Mao while gazing at a portrait of the leader on the wall.

Serfs is a unique film of ethnic minorities which does not glamorize minority peoples by stereotyping them in scenes of song and dance. Instead, it shows how the bloody reality of class struggle extends beyond ethnic boundaries, and seeks to prove that the **Communist revolution** benefits the entire Chinese nation, not just the Han majority.

See also: ethnic minorites, film of

Further reading
P. Clark (1987b), a survey of films of ethnic minorities; Y. Zhang (1997a), a critical study of nationhood and ethnicity.

(PV)

sexuality

Sexuality refers not just to sex itself but to a whole range of ideas and rules that attempt to regulate sexual activities. In traditional China, Confucian ideology dominated public perceptions of sexuality and dictated patriarchal values to both men and women. Within the **family** system, a man was allowed to have wives and concubines, whereas a woman must remain perpetually chaste and virtuous, obeying her parents before marriage, her husband when married, and her grown-up son after her husband's death. The strict hierarchical power structure worked to preserve the stability of the family and to ensure the continuity of family names by restricting sexuality to its productive function. Over centuries, however, an alternative type of sexuality was tolerated outside the confines of the family system. Male literati, merchants and officials would seek pleasure in houses of

prostitution or other entertainment quarters, and talented courtesans were permitted – and, indeed, encouraged – to flaunt their sexuality and to enhance their patrons' pleasure by providing wine, song and good companionship. A virtuous wife and a talented courtesan: these two images of female sexuality have survived from traditional China and have appeared consistently on the Chinese screen.

In the 1920s, **Zheng Zhengqiu** addressed several issues related to women's virtues and chastity in his family dramas on **love and marriage**, widowhood and prostitution. Female sexuality became a bigger issue in the 1930s, when male filmmakers of various ideological persuasions tried to figure out their 'appropriate' responses to the emergence of these 'new women': the naive, sentimental student, the charming, coquettish dancer, the cunning, decadent bourgeois lady, the independent career woman, and the ascetic, strong-willed factory worker. Competing answers were presented in a variety of films, such as **Wild Flower** (*dir.* **Sun Yu**, 1930), **Three Modern Women** (*dir.* **Bu Wancang**, 1933), **New Woman** (*dir.* **Cai Chusheng**, 1934), **Girl in Disguise** (*dir.* Fang Peilin, 1936) and *A New Year's Coin* (*dir.* **Zhang Shichuan**, 1937). In the 1940s, filmmakers continued to probe questions of female sexuality, and sometimes they touched on male sexuality as well. While **Spring River Flows East** (*dir.* Cai Chusheng, **Zheng Junli**, 1947) criticizes the decadent, irresponsible sexual life of its male protagonist (who has been corrupted by two bourgeois ladies), **Sorrows and Joys of a Middle-Aged Man** (*dir.* **Sang Hu**, 1949) seems to admire a retired schoolteacher's pursuit of happiness by marrying the daughter of his former colleague.

In the 1950s–70s, while sexuality as a subject was prohibited in mainland productions, films in Taiwan and Hong Kong continued to explore moral issues related to female sexuality, chastity, widowhood and so on. While *The Silent Wife* (*dir.* **Lee Hsing**, 1965) and **Home, Sweet Home** (*dir.* **Pai Ching-jui**, 1970) depict the virtuous wife who takes care of her ageing parents-in-law and brings up the child in her husband's absence, *Outside the Window* (*dir.* Song Cunshou, 1972) reveals the potential dangers of an inappropriate sexual relation. In Taiwan and Hong Kong as well as in mainland China, graphical sexual scenes began to appear on the screen in the 1980s. Just as in **Osmanthus Alley** (*dir.* **Chen Kun-hou**,

1987), a widow who has sexual relations with a male servant quickly covers up the scandal by firing the man, so in *Passion in Late Spring* (*dir.* Chen Yaoxin, 1989), a passionate ex-widow who wants to elope with her lover is caught, beaten up, incarcerated and eventually transformed by her husband into a smiling, obedient and dutiful wife. In both films, it is the Confucian idea of a decent family that ultimately triumphs over temporary eruptions of passion and disorder.

Similar tales of sexual transgression and physical punishment were dramatized in mainland China in the 1980s. In *The Corner Forsaken by Love* (*dir.* Zhang Qi, Li Yalin, 1981), a village girl who has sex with her lover before marriage commits suicide after her lover is arrested and imprisoned for the 'transgressive' act. In **Bloody Morning** (*dir.* **Li Shaohong**, 1990), another village woman goes insane and commits suicide after her husband discovers on their wedding night that she is not a virgin and sends her back to her parents' family. In films like these, adultery is not even an issue, but virginity is nonetheless perceived as a crucial matter in conservative rural areas. What came to be an encouraging sign since the early 1980s is that more and more films appeal to tolerance with regard to sexual transgression. Focusing on the fate of a girl who is married to a child husband and who later falls in love with another man, both *A* **Girl from Hunan** (*dir.* **Xie Fei**, 1986) and **Good Woman** (*dir.* **Huang Jianzhong**, 1985) manage to provide a more or less happy ending: instead of being drowned in the lake, the girl in the first film gives birth to a boy and legitimately stays in the house; in the second film, the girl is divorced from her child husband and departs with her lover.

Unlike films of the early 1980s, which are permeated with a heavy moral ambience, since the late 1980s a number of mainland titles treat sexual transgression and adultery more as a fascinating cinematic image than a serious ethical issue. Primitive passions keep erupting and exploding in films such as *Two Virtuous Women* (*dir.* Huang Jianzhong, 1987), **Red Sorghum** (1987), **Ju Dou** (1989, both *dir.* **Zhang Yimou**), *The* **Black Mountain Road** (1990), **Ermo** (1994, *dir.* **Zhou Xiaowen**) and *The* **Wooden Man's Bride** (*dir.* **Huang Jianxin**, 1993). Interestingly, regardless of their historical settings (either in the 1930s or the 1990s), all these films portray a rural woman who 'bewitches' a man with her uninhibited sexuality.

Plate 38   *A Girl From Hunan* (1986)

What is missing in these spectacular displays of female desires, however, is the woman's intellectual response to sexuality – an issue cleverly foreclosed by these films' choice of rural women as central characters. Only in a few films by female directors does one find a more serious attempt to comprehend the meaning of transgressive sexuality to female characters themselves. While **Sacrificed Youth** (*dir.* **Zhang Nuanxin**) and **Army Nurse** (*dir.* **Hu Mei**, both 1985) contemplate the political impact of asexuality on a generation of urban Chinese women, **Woman Demon Human** (1987) and *The* **Soul of the Painter** (1994, both *dir.* **Huang Shuqin**) present two career women who are in charge of their own sexuality. Other films by both male and female directors, such as **Strange Circle** (*dir.* Sun Sha, 1986) and **Women's Story** (*dir.* **Peng Xiaolian**, 1987), venture to examine the question of sisterhood by focusing on intimate female relationships. One film, **Sunshine and Showers** (*dir.* **Zhang Zeming**, 1987), is said to touch on the question of homosexuality.

As a theme, homosexuality did not receive serious cinematic attention until the 1990s.

Farewell My Concubine (*dir.* **Chen Kaige**, 1993) presents a tragic story of a gay actor who endures a series of humiliations, persecutions and betrayals, only to commit suicide when things are supposed to get better. *He's a Woman, She's a Man* (*dir.* Peter Chan, 1994) follows a fan who disguises herself as a man in order to get closer to a pop singer, and whose ambiguous sexuality prompts the singer to examine his own identity. While this Hong Kong **comedy** of transvestism is reminiscent of an earlier 'soft film' in Shanghai, **Girl in Disguise** (1936), another Hong Kong production, **Swordsman, II** (*dir.* **Ching Siu Tung**, 1992), features the transexualism of a martial arts hero who has transformed himself into a woman. *Happy Together* (*dir.* **Wong Kar-Wai**, 1997), on the other hand, concerns two modern-day Chinese gay men stranded in the alien land of Argentina. Transvestism and homosexuality are treated in other Hong Kong titles, often in the comedy genre. In Taiwan, a gay film *The* **Outcasts** (*dir.* Yu Kanping, 1986) was made before *The* **Wedding Banquet** (*dir.* Ang **Lee**, 1992) seriously confronted the issue. Hints of homosexuality are found in other Taiwan productions, as in **Vive**

l'amour (*dir.* **Tsai Ming-liang**, 1994). In the mainland, independent filmmaker **Zhang Yuan** directed *East Palace, West Palace* (1997), reputedly China's first 'gay film'.

In spite of recent developments, male sexuality seems to be of relatively little interest to Chinese filmmakers, except when the sensitive issue of homosexuality is implicated. On the contrary, female sexuality remains an intensely fascinating subject, and films on this subject continue to appear on the Chinese screen.

See also: femininity; martial arts film; masculinity; representations of women; woman's film

Further Reading
C. Berry (1996b), a critical discussion of homosexual films; M. Chang (1999), on images of movie stars in the 1920s–30s; R. Chow (1995), a theoretical study of mainland films; S. Cui (1997), on *Ju Dou*; S. Stockbridge (1994), on sexual violence in Hong Kong films; Y. Zhang (1999a), on films and film culture of the 1920s–40s.

(YZ)

Shangguan Yunzhu

(Wei Junluo)

b. 1920, Jiangyin, Jiangsu province
d. 1968
Actress

A famous actress of the 1940s–60s, Shangguan worked in a portrait gallery in Shanghai. Since many of the studio's customers were filmmakers, she developed a fascination with acting. She enrolled in Guanghua Drama School in 1940 and was employed by Xinhua Film Company upon graduation.

Shangguan made her first film appearance in *Fallen Rose* (*dir.* Wu Wenchao, Wen Yimin, 1941) and adopted Shangguan Yunzhu as her name. In the post-war period, she played major roles in *Dream in Paradise* (*dir.* **Tang Xiaodan**) and *Long Live the Mistress!* (*dir.* **Sang Hu**, both 1947). Her excellent performances in these titles impressed critics and producers alike. Shangguan's association with leftist filmmaking began when she starred in *Spring River Flows East* (*dir.* **Cai Chusheng, Zheng Junli**, 1947), *Myriad of Lights* (1948) and *Hope in the World* (1949, both *dir.* **Shen Fu**).

During the PRC period, Shangguan continued to be recognized as one of the most versatile and talented film actresses. Her performances in *It's My Day Off* (*dir.* Lu Ren, 1959), *Spring Comes to the Withered Tree* (*dir.* Zheng Junli, 1961), *Early Spring in February* (*dir.* **Xie Tieli**, 1963) and *Stage Sisters* (*dir.* **Xie Jin**, 1965) give a fair indication of the wide variety of characters she was capable of portraying. Rumour has it that she had a brief romance with Mao Zedong before the **Cultural Revolution**, an affair that caused her death.

Further Reading
ZDX (1982–6: 7: 10–21), a short biography.

(ZX)

Shanghai Triad

(Yao a yao, yao dao waipo qiao)

dir. **Zhang Yimou**
sc. Bi Feinian
with **Gong Li**, Li Baotian, Li Xuejian, Wang Xiaoxiao
Shanghai: Shanghai Film, 1995

Shanghai Triad is a **gangster film** set in 1930s Shanghai. Narrated from the point of view of the character Shuisheng, it opens on a number of generic cues: an establishing shot of a crowded dock, a close-up of a truck full of illegal goods, a shadowy warehouse where underworld figures in overcoats make deals and shoot each other.

Shuisheng is brought from the countryside to serve Jewel, a leading nightclub showgirl and mistress of the clan's godfather. On-stage she is a Hollywood-style harlot, a leggy singer costumed in red feathers. Off-stage, however, her life is dictated by the gangsters as her privileges have been bought at the cost of virtual enslavement to the boss. Shuisheng is the accidental witness to Jewel's outbursts of frustration and her aborted affair with a younger clan member. The camera follows the boy's gaze as it provides a voyeuristic peek into Jewel's private life. Musical numbers are an integral part of the narrative as Jewel's stage numbers mimic her real-life predicament. For example, while she is usually only allowed to sing the godfather's favourite numbers, especially 'Beautiful Flowers and the Round Moon', she sings the song 'Pretender' when betrayed by her lover.

A bloody gang feud forces the godfather's retreat to an isolated island, the kind of natural location Zhang Yimou loves to include in his films. Jewel experiences a limited freedom on the island. The only inhabitants, a widow and her young daughter, remind Jewel of the beauty and simplicity of her lost childhood. She comes to feel motherly affection for the girl – as they sing the children's song 'Row, row, row to my grandma's bridge', Jewel finds meaning in her life.

But this moment of self-realization is soon eclipsed by horror. The godfather discovers his henchman's betrayal, kills him, and buries Jewel alive for having had a sexual affair with the man. The film ends with Shuisheng hanging upside down from the mast of the boat as the gang departs the island. The godfather has also executed the widow and taken her daughter away, promising the girl a life as beautiful as Jewel's had been. From Shuisheng's point of view, the world has now turned upside down.

Although *Shanghai Triad* reaches heights of cinematic beauty, its characters are somewhat flat, its action rather prosaic.

Further Reading

S. Kraicer (1997), a brief discussion.

(SC)

Shao Zuiweng

(Shao Renjie)

b. 1896, Ningbo, Zhejiang province
d. 1979
Producer, director, screen writer

An important figure of early Chinese cinema, Shao Zuiweng graduated from Shenzhou University in 1914. He worked briefly as a lawyer for a district court in Shanghai, took a managerial position in a bank in 1921, and was in partnership in several small businesses. He turned to theatre management in 1922 and was in charge of Happy Stage (Xiao wutai) – among the people who worked for him were **Zhang Shichuan**, **Zhou Jianyun** and **Zheng Zhengqiu**, the three founders of Mingxing Film Company. The spectacular success of Mingxing's ***Orphan Rescues Grandfather*** (*dir.* Zhang Shichuan, 1923) inspired Shao to form his own film company, Tianyi, in 1925. He served as general manager as well as director, while his brothers (better known in the future as the Shaw Brothers) took responsibility for accounting and distribution.

Tianyi's first release, *A Change of Heart* (*dir.* Shao Zuiweng, 1925), brought in huge profits. A shrewd businessman, Shao could predict what audiences would like. He was one of the first filmmakers in China to draw extensively on a rich source of traditional literature as well as on **legends and myths**. His success in early **genre films**, such as **costume drama**, ghosts and immortals, and swordplay, inspired many studios to imitate his work.

Tianyi was also among the first filmmakers to make the transition to sound. Unlike many of his colleagues, Shao had confidence in the direction the medium was taking. As a result, he was the producer of one of the first Chinese sound films, *A Singer's Story* (*dir.* **Li Pingqian**, 1931).

As a canny businessman, Shao was never interested in using film as a vehicle for moral or political purposes. When other major studios churned out leftist films in the early 1930s, Tianyi remained politically indifferent and continued to produce 'entertainment' films.

Besides his Shanghai operations, Shao always maintained a business interest in Southeast Asia. When the Sino-Japanese war broke out, he was quickly able to relocate his film studio to Hong Kong and transfer most of his business operations to Southeast Asia, where the studio's name was changed from Tianyi to Nanyang (South Sea). Along with his brothers, Shao built a film empire that was to dominate filmmaking in Hong Kong and Southeast Asia for decades to come.

See also: ghosts and immortals, film of; Shaw, Run Run; swordplay film

Further Reading

ZDX (1982–6: 1: 191–5), a short biography.

(ZX)

Shaw, Run Run

(Shao Yifu)

b. 1907
Producer

Born into a wealthy Shanghai textile manufacturing family, Run Run Shaw entered Tianyi Film Company (run by his elder brother **Shao Zuiweng**) in 1925, starting out as a cinematographer and screenplay writer. In 1957 he left Singapore, where he had owned theatres exhibiting films produced by Runme Shaw, and took over at Shaw Brothers in Hong Kong. Run Run built a 46-acre studio complex known as 'Movie Town' in 1961 and turned Shaw Brothers into the largest, most influential film company in Hong Kong between the early 1960s and the mid-1980s. The company produced on average thirty films a year, several of which won top prizes at Asian Film Festivals; it also employed trend-setting directors such as **Chang Che**, King **Hu** and **Li Han-hsiang**, and expanded its distribution network to Japan and Europe. For his contribution to world cinema, Run Run Shaw was twice awarded Queen's medals, in 1974 and 1977.

Further Reading

Y. Du (1978: 152–68), a history of fifty years of Shaw Brothers; J. Lent (1990: 97), a brief discussion of Shaw Brothers.

(YZ)

Shen Fu

(Shen Aijun, Shen Baiming)

b. 23 March 1905, Tianjin
d. 27 April 1994
Director

An important director of the 1940s, Shen worked in many jobs before becoming a filmmaker. He once took an apprenticeship in a photo shop and served in a military band. In 1924, he became an actor at Bohai Film Company in Tianjin, where he wrote, directed and played a role in *A Big Briefcase* (1926). Although this first movie was hardly well received by audiences, Shen was not discouraged. He continued his film education by sitting in movie houses studying the work of great masters like Charlie Chaplin.

Shen joined Lianhua Film Company in 1933 and edited the studio's publication, *Lianhua Pictorial* (Lianhua huabao). He wrote and directed *The Way Out* (1933), which was banned by the Nationalist Film Censorship Committee for its overt criticism of social and economic conditions: the film was eventually released with numerous changes. In 1936, Shen Fu scripted *Wolf Hunting* (*dir.* **Fei Mu**, 1936) and turned his hand to comedy.

After the war Shen went to Beijing, worked as the deputy manager of Nationalist Central Film Studio's branch in the city, and made two films, *The Holy City* (1946) and *Pursuit* (1947). He was eventually removed from his post when he refused to make an anti-Communist film. Back in

Shanghai, Shen joined Kunlun Film Company, where he wrote and directed ***Myriad of Lights*** (1948) and wrote ***Crows and Sparrows*** (*dir.* **Zheng Junli**, 1949).

During the PRC period, Shen directed six films, among which ***Li Shizhen*** (1956) and ***New Story of an Old Soldier*** (1959) are considered most representative of his later work. After the **Cultural Revolution**, Shen served in several important administrative positions.

See also: censorship and film

(ZX)

Shen Xiling

(Shen Xuecheng, Ye Shen)

b. 1904, Hangzhou, Zhejiang province
d. 19 December 1940
Director, screen writer

An important director of the 1930s, Shen Xiling studied textile colouring technology before turning to fine arts. In Japan, he took an internship at a theatre working as stage designer. Shen returned to China in 1928 and was involved in leftist theatre activities. Meanwhile he also worked as a window dresser after the two art schools he held teaching positions at were shut down by the authorities.

In 1931, Shen was offered a job as stage designer by Tianyi Film Company. He wrote his first screenplay, *The Protest of Women*, but his request to direct the film was turned down by the studio. Shen joined Mingxing Film Company and directed *The Protest of Women* in 1933. His next feature, ***Twenty-Four Hours in Shanghai*** (1933), ran into censorship problems with both the foreign concessions and the Nationalist Film Censorship Committee. While the film was eventually passed with several cuts, Shen refused to release the truncated version. The studio, worried about possible financial losses, insisted on screening the film publicly, whereupon Shen decided to quit in protest, only to be persuaded into staying on by friends. During the rest of his tenure at Mingxing, Shen helped produce the box-office hit, ***Twin Sisters*** (*dir.* **Zheng Zhengqiu**, 1933), co-directed *A Bible for Girls* (*co-dir.* **Zhang Shichuan** *et al.*, 1934) and directed three classics of the 1930s: *Homesick*, ***Boatman's Daughter*** (both 1935) and ***Crossroads*** (1937).

Shen eventually left Mingxing and joined Lianhua Film Company in 1937. One of the promises Lianhua made to him was to allow him to direct *The **True Story of Ah Q***, an adaptation of Lu Xun's well-known short story. However, the Sino-Japanese war made the completion of this project impossible. After Shanghai fell in 1938, Shen went to Chongqing, where he was appointed an honorary director by Nationalist Central Film Studio and directed *Children of China* (1939). Unfortunately, Shen died of typhoid fever in 1940 before he could finish two other projects.

See also: adaptations of drama and literature

Further Reading
ZDX (1982–6: 1: 84–91), a short biography.

(ZX)

Shi Dongshan
(Shi Kuangshao, Kuang Shao)

b. 29 December 1902, Hangzhou, Zhejiang province
d. 23 February 1955
Director

An important director of the 1920s–40s, Shi Dongshan entered Shanghai Film Company as a stage designer in 1921. He played minor roles in *The Revival of an Old Well* (*dir.* **Dan Duyu**, 1923) and other titles. In 1925, when the studio was deep in debt, its management established a best screen-play award so as to help overcome the threat of financial ruin: Shi's *Flirting with Disaster* won the top prize, and he was asked to direct the film.

Shi's earlier films, such as *The Love Story* (1926), display an obsession with visual qualities and a distancing from socio-political issues. After he joined Lianhua Film Company, however, Shi changed his style and directed more political films. Even the titles are suggestive: *Facing the National Crisis, Struggles* (both 1932). As Shi became further involved in leftist activities during the 1930s, his films became more critical of the KMT regime. In 1934, Shi accepted an invitation from Yihua Film Company to direct *Women* and *Lost Innocence* (both 1934), titles that clearly exhibit his concern for social reform. Shi continued in this direction with *The Night of the Debauche* (1936) – an adaptation of *Inspector General*, a famous novel by the Russian writer Gogol – and *Marching Youth* (1937).

After the outbreak of the Sino-Japanese war, Shi made a number of propaganda films, such as ***Protect Our Land*** (1938), *Good Husband* (1939)

and *The Victory March* (1941). After the war, Shi went back to Shanghai and co-founded Kunlun Film Company with several friends. His ***Eight Thousand Li of Cloud and Moon*** (1947) and *The Sorrows of Women* (1948) were both released by Kunlun.

In the post-1949 period Shi made one feature, *New Heroes and Heroines* (1951) and co-directed a **documentary**, *Opposing Biological Warfare* (1952), with **Cai Chusheng**.

See also: adaptations of drama and literature; propaganda and film

Further Reading
ZDX (1982–6: 1: 15–23), a short biography.

(ZX)

Shi Hui
(Shi Yutao)

b. 1915, Tianjin
d. 1957
Actor, director

One of China's best actors, Shi Hui left behind an important legacy of screen performances. In a brief career, he starred in fifteen titles and directed three.

Shi had a difficult childhood and took numerous odd jobs before becoming an actor. In 1940 he moved to Shanghai and took his first movie role in *The Chaotic World* (*dir.* Wu Renzhi, 1941), a film banned by the Japanese after the Pacific War. Shi's best post-war performances include **Phony Phoenixes** (*dir.* **Huang Zuolin**, 1947), ***Long Live the Mistress!*** (1947) and ***Sorrows and Joys of a Middle-Aged Man*** (1949, both *dir.* **Sang Hu**).

In the late 1940s Shi gradually shifted his attention to screenplay writing and directing. Amongst his work as director, ***This Life of Mine*** (1950) best represents his acting style, while ***Letter with Feather*** (1954) won a top prize at the 1955 Edinburgh FF; *The Heavenly Match* (1955), a filmed stage performance, became a box-office hit in Hong Kong and started a decade-long trend there for opera movies.

Unfortunately Shi's career was cut short by the Anti-Rightist Campaign of 1957. He was labelled a Rightist by the authorities and subject to public denouncement and humiliation. In protest, he committed suicide.

See also: filmed stage performances

Further Reading

G. Barmé (1983), a profile; ZDX (1982–6: 2: 67–77), a short biography.

(ZX, YZ)

Shui Hua

(Zhang Yufan)

b. 23 November 1916, Nanjing
d. 16 December 1995
Director

A noted director of the 1950s–60s, Shui Hua attended law school at Fudan University in the early 1930s and studied briefly in Japan. He returned to China and joined the resistance theatre movement. He went to Yan'an in 1940 and became a CCP member in 1942. While teaching at Lu Xun College of Arts, he was involved in theatre activities in the area. His directorial début, The **White-Haired Girl** (1950), was an adaptation of a famous stage play in Yan'an.

Shui's films are known for their fine craftsmanship and meticulous attention to detail, and they have garnered numerous awards. The White-Haired Girl received a special honour at the 1951 Karlovy Vary FF and an award for Best Film made between 1949–55 from the Ministry of Culture in 1957; The **Lin Family Shop** (1959) received critical acclaim at a film festival in Portugal, and **Revolutionary Family** (1961) won Best Screenplay at the 1962 HFA. Finally, **Regret for the Past** (1981), an adaptation of Lu Xun's famous short story, earned Best Film award in 1981 from the Ministry of Culture.

See also: adaptations of drama and literature; theatre and film

Further Reading

D. Ma and G. Dai (1994: 1–105), a long chapter on Shui Hua; ZDX (1982–6: 4: 17–26), a short biography.

(ZX)

Siao, Josephine

(Xiao Fangfang)

b. 1947
Actress

A versatile film actress, Josephine Siao began her film career at age seven and won a Best Child Actress award at the age of nine at a Southeast Asian film festival. Since then she has been active in Cantonese cinema. In 1961–7, she starred in a great number of martial arts films.

Siao did not get a regular education in her childhood years, because of her tight filming schedule. In 1968 she saved money and went to study at a university in New Jersey, graduating with an MA degree in five years. She returned to the screen, co-directed Jumping Ash (1976) and produced The Spooky Bunch (dir. Ann **Hui**, 1980) while acting in both. She starred in, as well as co-wrote and co-directed, The Secret (dir. Ann Hui, 1979), which helped to pave the way for the Hong Kong New Wave. By the mid-1990s, Siao had appeared in over 100 films. Her performance in **Summer Snow** (dir. Ann Hui, 1994) won her Best Actress award at Berlin FF. Some of her other memorable roles are to be found in **Fong Sai Yuk** (dir. Yuan Kui, 1993) and Stage Door (dir. Shu Kei, 1996).

See also: Cantonese cinema (under Hong Kong cinema in Historical essays); martial arts film

(YZ)

Sing-Song Girl Red Peony

(Genü Hongmudan)

dir. **Zhang Shichuan**
sc. **Hong Shen**
with **Hu Die**, Wang Xianzai, Xia Peizhen, **Gong Jianong**
Shanghai: Mingxing Film, 1930

Sing-Song Girl Red Peony is renowned as one of the first sound films to be produced in China. It was a box-office success and was remade in the 1940s.

Although sing-song girl Red Peony is married to an abusive husband, traditional teaching about woman's virtue dictates that she stays with him no matter what. As a well-known actress, Red Peony brings home a respectable income, but it is never enough to keep up with her husband's extravagant spending. After the cumulative effects of depression damage her voice, she gradually fades from the spotlight. Meanwhile, her husband continues to squander the money away and cause problems for the family. After one of his attempts to sell their daughter is thwarted by Red Peony, he tricks his daughter into going to a brothel and manages to sell her to the brothel owner. One of Red Peony's suitors learns of this and brings her daughter back home after paying a huge sum of money. At the same time, Red Peony's husband is arrested on an involuntary manslaughter charge. Despite all that he has done, Red Peony forgives him and visits him in prison before going on a performance tour. She even appeals to her friends to lobby for her husband's early release. Finally, her husband's conscience is awakened and he reforms himself.

(ZX)

Singing at Midnight

(Yeban gesheng)

dir./sc. **Ma-Xu Weibang**
with **Jin Shan**, Hu Ping, Shi Chao, Gu Menghe
Shanghai: Xinhua Film, 1937

The basic story line of this Chinese **horror film** resembles *The Phantom of the Opera* (*dir.* Rupert Julian, 1925). However, by situating the story in the context of warlordism, *Singing at Midnight* injects a heavy dose of social criticism.

A travelling performance troupe stays in an old theatre building where the male lead, Sun, receives help from a 'ghost' during his rehearsals. The supposed ghost later reveals himself to Sun as a well-known revolutionary who, in order to avoid political persecution, had changed his name to Song and taken up acting as a career. Ten years earlier, he had fallen in love with the town's beauty, Miss Li, thus making a local thug who also took an interest in Li extremely jealous. The thug deformed Song's face. Not wanting to be seen in public with such a grisly appearance, Song pretended to be dead and asked his loyal servant to arrange a fake funeral. Upon hearing this news, Li was too traumatized to maintain her sanity. Song now feels guilty about what happened to Li and keeps her company by singing for her in the middle of the night. Hence, the theatre building is believed to be haunted.

After telling his story, Song begs Sun to act like him and visit Li, hoping this may help Li recover. And when Sun does so, Li indeed mistakes him for Song and shows signs of recovery. Meanwhile, Song helps Sun's troupe stage a new show. The local thug who had earlier victimized Song is now interested in Lüdie, the troupe's female lead and Sun's lover. In a final showdown, Lüdie is shot while trying to protect Sun. Song comes out of hiding and kills the thug. But the crowd mistakenly perceive Song to be the evil-doer and chase after him. The police also learn of his past revolutionary activities and try to arrest him. Surrounded by his pursuers, Song commits suicide by jumping into the river. As Sun and Li mourn Song's death, they can hear him singing once more.

The film was a huge box-office success and led to remakes in Shanghai and Hong Kong, some as late as the 1990s.

(ZX)

Siqin Gaowa

b. January 1950
Actress, director

Siqin emerged as one of the best film actresses of the 1980s–90s after her astonishing performance in *The Call of the Front* (*dir.* **Li Jun**, 1979), where she played a peasant widow who falls in love with the wounded soldier she takes care of. After receiving an award from the Ministry of Culture, Siqin joined the August First Film Studio. Two years later, she received Best Actress awards at China GRA and HFA for her portrayal of a prickly spinster in *Camel Xiangzi* (*dir.* **Ling Zifeng**, 1982). Siqin's acting talents have also been recognized outside China: in 1985, for example, she won Best Actress award at HKFA for her performance in *Homecoming* (*dir.* **Yim Ho**, 1984).

Siqin married a Swiss businessman and emigrated to Sweden in 1986. She has, however, continued to star in such highly acclaimed films as *Full Moon in New York* (*dir.* Stanley **Kwan**, 1989), *The Woman from the Lake of Scented Soul* (*dir.* **Xie Fei**, 1992), *An Old Man and His Dog* (*dir.* **Xie Jin**, 1993) and *The Day the Sun Turned Cold* (*dir.* Yim Ho, 1994). In addition to appearing in numerous Hong Kong films, Siqin has also directed a **children's film**, *The Private Teaching Company* (1989).

(ZX, YZ)

Situ Huimin

(Situ Zhu)

b. 16 February 1910, Guangdong province
d. 4 April 1987
Director

A noted filmmaker of the 1930s–40s, Situ Huimin was born into an overseas Chinese Christian family. In 1923, his parents brought him back to China and enrolled him in high school in Guangzhou. However, much to his parents' dismay, Situ joined an organization called the Anti-Christian League and he became a member of the Communist Youth League in 1925. Situ joined the CCP in 1927 and fled to Japan as a political refugee a year later due to his role in a failed uprising against the Nationalists. While in Japan he studied graphic design, cinema and electronics. In 1929, Situ was arrested by the Japanese police and jailed for six months for involvement in anti-war activities.

Situ returned to China in 1930. He worked as an evening school teacher and graphic designer before being hired, in 1932, as a stage designer by Tianyi Film Company. One of Situ's most important contributions was his role in bringing sound technology to the Chinese film industry. Situ Huimin and his associates manufactured the first Chinese recording machine in 1933, thus breaking a monopoly previously held only by foreigners. It was also through Situ's initiative that the Society for the Study and Research of Motion Picture Technology was founded.

Because of Situ's connection with Communist intellectuals, his Diantong Film Company acted as a shelter for many leftist filmmakers: Situ himself directed **Xia Yan**'s script for *Goddess of Liberty* in 1935, for example. After Diantong was forced to close by the Nationalist authorities in 1936, Situ worked for Lianhua Film Company as director as well as sound technician. He directed three films on anti-Japanese themes in the late 1930s. After the war, he went to the United States and took film classes at Columbia University. While doing an internship in Hollywood, he became acquainted with Charlie Chaplin and several other American filmmakers. In 1947 he made a **documentary** about Chinese folk dance which won a prize at the 1948 Edinburgh Festival of Documentary Cinema. Situ briefly worked for RKO before returning to China in 1952.

During the **Cultural Revolution**, Situ was stripped of all his official positions as well as the possibility of making more films. He was rehabilitated in 1975 and served as Deputy at the Ministry of Culture, Vice-President of All China Filmmakers' Association and Director of the Institute of Science and Technology for Motion Pictures.

Further Reading

ZDX (1982–6: 1: 53–64), a short biography.

(ZX)

Sixth Generation, the

The 'Sixth Generation' refers to the group of filmmakers who emerged in the early 1990s. They were mostly born in the 1960s and experienced the **Cultural Revolution** in their early childhood. All Sixth Generation directors received formal training at BFA. But unlike the **Fifth Generation** directors who had engaged in a variety of occupations before studying film at college, members of the Sixth Generation went straight to BFA after high school or college, as in the case of graduate students like **Huang Jun** and Zhang Ming (*b.* 1961). As a result, they share a common emphasis on personal experience and emotions.

Most films by this group show little interest in the grand notion of history or in current issues of morality, politics and society. They tend to offer young people's personal accounts of their adolescent experiences, which are intentionally detached from contemporary politics and social reality. Many films this group made in the early 1990s are financed by foreign money, and only a few of them were officially distributed in China. For this reason, the Sixth Generation has sometimes been regarded as representing underground film in China.

Zhang Yuan, one of the leading figures of this group, completed ***Beijing Bastards*** (1993), a semi-documentary study of a Chinese rock star as a symbol of rebellion. The 'unofficial' screening of this film at Tokyo FF caused the Chinese government to protest in the festival. Shot in black and white, **Wang Xiaoshuai**'s *The Days* (1993) depicts the relationship between two artists, a husband and a wife, who struggle before their divorce. The narrative style of Wang's film gives the flavour of a personal diary. Another noted director of the group is **He Jianjun**. His *Red Beads* (1993) is about the fantasy world of a patient in a psychiatric hospital. He's second film is a twenty-minute short, *Self Portrait*, which shows practically nothing but his own paintings.

Although these highly stylized and ideologically disruptive films have received critical acclaim at international film festivals, at home there is hardly an audience for them. In this regard, they are even less popular in China than the early avant-garde Fifth Generation films. However, by the mid-1990s, there were unmistakable signs that many Sixth Generation directors had begun to shift toward a more socially concerned position. Guan Hu's ***Dirt*** (1994), for instance, addresses a broader range of social issues than Zhang Yuan's *Beijing Bastards*, although the two are equally concerned with rebellious rock musicians and their quest for freedom and independence. Films by less, or no longer, rebellious members of this group, such as *The Drowned Youth* (*dir.* **Hu Xueyang**), *Living with You* (*dir.* Huang Jun), *Weekend Lovers* (*dir.* Lou Hua, all 1994), ***Rainclouds Over Wushan*** (*dir.* Zhang Ming), *Falling in Love* (*dir.* Li Xin), *This Is How Steel Is Made* (*dir.* Lu Xuechang), *No Visit After Divorce* (*dir.* Wang Rui), *Postman* (*dir.* He Jianjun) and *Yellow Goldfish* (*dir.* **Wu Di**, all 1995), further demonstrate the Sixth Generation's ability to tackle social issues from distinctively personal perspectives and to connect themselves to a larger base of Chinese audiences. The fact that a few of these films have won international film **awards** through official channels indicates the promise of the new group.

Indeed, by the mid-1990s a generation with two faces seems to have appeared. On the one hand, Zhang Yuan has continued to be defiant of government censorship. Distributed overseas, his independent films are among the most controversial of all Chinese films in the 1990s. On the other hand, many new directors are willing to speak to the domestic audience. Working inside or outside the studio system in China, the Sixth Generation directors are struggling to define their political positions as well as their personal styles. The future direction of this group of twenty- and thirty-somethings remains uncertain and unpredictable.

See also: censorship and film; independent film

Further Reading
China Screen (1997), a series of profiles of the Sixth Generation filmmakers; X. Han (1995), an informative study of the Sixth Generation by one of their professors at BFA; T. Rayns (1993), a report on some early films by the group.

(ZX, YZ)

social problems, film of

Because of the Chinese tradition of emphasizing the educational function of entertainment, films that deal with social problems are often considered to form a special category. However, since social problems cover a wide range of topics, and since films of other genres often address similar social issues, there is hardly any way to fix a set of generic features for films of social problems. Even profit-oriented commercial films may take social problems rather seriously.

Historically, films of social problems started in the 1920s, when **Zheng Zhengqiu** addressed several social issues such as arranged marriage, **prostitution** and women's education in his family dramas. In the 1930s–40s, leftist films turned attention to pressing social problems such as flood and famine in the countryside, or unemployment and housing shortage in the city, thereby strengthening the functions of social criticism and political intervention in Chinese films. Memorable examples include ***Song of the Fishermen*** (*dir.* **Cai Chusheng**, 1934), ***Crossroads*** (*dir.* **Shen Xiling**, 1937), ***Myriad of Lights*** (*dir.* **Shen Fu**, 1948) and ***Crows and Sparrows*** (*dir.* **Zheng Junli**, 1949). Since the 1950s, mainland productions have been concerned – indeed, obsessed – with all kinds of social problems, and the moralist tone of most social problem films did not subside until the late 1980s, when market factors pressured the industry to produce films on lighter themes. However, social problems continue to be explored in mainland films of the 1990s, for example, violence in ***Bloody Morning*** (*dir.* **Li Shaohong**, 1990), disability in ***Mama*** (*dir.* **Zhang Yuan**, 1991), and poverty in *Country Teachers* (*dir.* **He Qun**, 1993).

Similar treatments of social problems are found in Taiwan and, to a more limited extent, in Hong Kong as well. In Taiwan, many New Wave films of the 1980s contain social criticism of some kind, for instance *The Son's Big Doll* (*dir.* **Hou Hsiao-hsien**, 1983), ***Terrorizer*** (*dir.* Edward **Yang**, 1986) and ***Banana Paradise*** (*dir.* **Wang Tung**, 1989). In Hong Kong, Ann **Hui**'s *The Story of Woo Viet* (1981) and ***Boat People*** (1982) are genuine films of social problems. Indeed, even a **comedy** like ***Eat Drink Man Woman*** (*dir.* Ang **Lee**, 1994), a **gangster film** like *A Better Tomorrow* (*dir.* John **Woo**, 1986), or an **art film** like *Chungking Express* (*dir.* **Wong Kar-Wai**, 1994) will inevitably reflect certain social tension in the real world.

Further Reading
J. Ma (1993), on Zheng Zhengqiu's films on social problems.

(YZ)

socialist construction

Socialist construction is a major theme in mainland films in the 1950s–70s. Although the official press still insists on the term 'socialism', mainland

Plate 39   *Li Shuangshuang* (1962)

films of the 1980s–90s are characterized by a multiplicity that goes far beyond the coverage of a term like 'socialism'.

Apart from glorifying the **Communist revolution** on the screen, mainland films of the 1950s–70s were devoted to a positive portrayal of the government's achievements in socialist construction in urban and rural areas. Helplessly caught in the propaganda machinery, feature film productions closely followed the Communist policies on industrial and agricultural fronts. *Sisters, Stand Up* (*dir.* Chen Xihe, 1951) praises the government's initiative to eradicate **prostitution** and to integrate former prostitutes into the work force. *City Without Night* (*dir.* **Tang Xiaodan**, 1957) depicts the transformation of Shanghai capitalists during the campaign for the nationalization of private industries. *Huang Baomei* (*dir.* **Xie Jin**) and *Girls from Shanghai* (*dir.* Cheng Yi, both 1958) demonstrate how enthusiastic the new generation of workers and technicians were in their work at factories or construction sites; *Young People in Our Village* (*dir.* Su Li, 1959, 1963) and *Li Shuangshuang* (*dir.* Lu Ren, 1962) show how rural people whole-heartedly participated in collective farming in the People's Communes and worked for the well-being of the entire community rather than of one's own family. Films of ethnic minorities in this period, such as *Five Golden Flowers* (1959), *Daji and Her Fathers* (1961, both *dir.* Wang Jiayi) and *Red Flowers by Tianshan Mountains* (*dir.* **Cui Wei**, Chen Huaiai, 1964) also illustrate the devotion minority people displayed to the glorious cause of socialist construction in remote regions. All in all, films of socialist construction aimed to give audiences feelings of accomplishment, pride and solidarity.

See also: ethnic minorities, film of; propaganda and film

(YZ)

socialist realism

A term used to describe mainland film productions of the 1950s–70s, characterized by dramatic acting, typical or stock characterization, prolonged dialogue, and formulaic plot concerning class struggle, **Communist revolution** or **socialist construction**.

See also: Chinese cinema (in Historical essays)

(YZ)

soft film

See under: Chinese cinema (in Historical essays)

Song of China

aka *Filial Piety* (Tianlun)

dir. **Fei Mu**, **Luo Mingyou**
sc. Zhong Shigen
with **Zheng Junli**, **Chen Yanyan**, Lin Chuchu, Zhang Yi, Li Zhuozhuo
Shanghai: Lianhua Film, 1935

This film constitutes one of Lianhua's attempts to participate in the New Life Movement which, among other things, sought to re-establish traditional moral tenets. The film was one of the few Chinese productions to be distributed in the USA during the 1930s.

A wandering son returns home just before his father dies. The old man asks his son to extend his love for the **family** to the whole of society. Several decades later, the son has himself become an old man who is disappointed with his children, particularly his son and daughter-in-law who indulge themselves in the pleasures of city life. He moves his family to the countryside and devotes himself to the building of an orphanage. But after his son and daughter-in-law leave him, his daughter also runs away.

Many years later, the old man's grandson comes to live with him. His daughter, having been abandoned by her lover, also returns home. On his death bed, the old man admonishes his children in terms similar to those used by his father to admonish him years earlier: 'Go beyond personal love and extend love to all mankind.' The film ends with orphans proudly marching to their bright future.

(ZX)

Song of the Exile

(Ke tu qiu hen)

dir. Ann **Hui**
sc. **Wu Nien-chen**
With Maggie **Cheung**, Lu Xiaofen, Waise Lee
Hong Kong: Gaoshi Film/Taipei: CMPC, 1990

This autobiographical film revisits Japanese–Chinese relations after World War II and analyses the immigrant experience of **exile** and diaspora. It opens with a flashback showing Hueyin during her London college days in summer 1973. She applies, unsuccessfully, for a job at the BBC before being pressured into returning to Hong Kong for her sister's wedding. Hueyin's estrangement from her mother Aiko began in early childhood. A flashback shows Hueyin with her mother and grandparents in Macao while her father works in Hong Kong. Grandfather's artistic traditionalism impresses Hueyin, but her mother Aiko remains very withdrawn. Aiko does not get along with the family and plans to return to Japan permanently. For her part, Hueyin remembers moving to the 'strange' Hong Kong environment in 1963. After she argues with her father over Aiko's irresponsible behaviour, he tells her that Aiko is actually Japanese and he explains something of the frustrations she has experienced. Hueyin then leaves for boarding school.

In 1973 Hueyin offers to accompany her mother on a visit to Japan. They are met by Aiko's brother, and Hueyin slowly begins to understand the cultural estrangement her mother had lived through as a foreigner in Hong Kong. Aiko visits some former schoolmates and fights with her embittered younger brother. Another flashback depicts Aiko meeting Hueyin's father, who helped her even though she was Japanese. She tells Hueyin that while her father never visited Japan she is proud that her daughter has now done so. The two are finally reconciled. Hueyin secures a job at a Hong Kong television station and later visits Canton after grandfather has a stroke. She is told not to 'lose hope for China'.

(KH)

Song of the Fishermen

(Yu guang qu)

dir./sc. **Cai Chusheng**
with **Wang Renmei**, Yuan Congmei, Han Lan'gen, Tang Tianxiu
Shanghai: Lianhua Film, 1934

In a village near Shanghai a poor fisherman's wife struggles with her twins – a son Hou and a daughter Mao. After her husband's death, she has become the wet-nurse of He Ziying, son of the owner of many fishing boats. Ziying becomes friend and playmate to the twins.

When the twins grow up they become fishermen like their father, while Ziying travels abroad to study new techniques that will modernize his father's (later his own) fishing company. As the poor fishermen cannot compete against He's industrialized form of organization, the twins emigrate to Shanghai with their mother and make their living singing songs on the street. One day Ziying meets Mao and gives her some money, but after being discovered in possession of such an unusually large sum Mao and Hou are arrested on suspicion of theft. When released they learn that their mother, shocked and desperate after their arrest, accidentally caused a fire which killed her and their uncle. They also learn that Ziying's father was completely ruined by his mistress and committed suicide. The three childhood friends meet again and decide to restart their fishing business together.

Song of the Fishermen won the first international prize for a Chinese film at the 1935 Moscow FF.

(PV)

Song of Youth
(Qingchun zhi ge)

dir. **Cui Wei**, Chen Huaiai
sc. Yang Mo
with Xie Fang, Yu Yang, Yu Shizhi, Qin Wen, **Qin Yi**
Beijing: Beijing Film, 1959

Adapted from a novel of the same title, this film depicts a young woman's transformation from housewife to loyal Communist. This process is presented as 'natural' – possessed of inherent logic rather than merely 'incidental'. Hence, the film is really about **Communist revolution** that won over the hearts and minds of Chinese youth.

To escape an arranged marriage, Lin Daojing runs away from home. Having failed to find her relative in Beijing and becoming homeless, she decides to commit suicide. She is saved by a Beijing University student named Yu Yongze, who subsequently helps her find a school-teaching job. However, Lin is soon expelled from the school

Plate 40   *Song of Youth* (1959)

after making an anti-Japanese speech. Lin marries Yu, but remains unhappy that she is financially dependent on him. Their marriage begins to deteriorate.

An underground Communist, Lu Jiachuan, who is also a student movement leader, draws Lin into social activities that Yu resents. One day, while trying to evade the Nationalist police, Lu seeks refuge in Yu's house, but is turned away. Lu's subsequent arrest and execution results in Lin's split from Yu. After a kidnap and an escape, Lin finds a job in a rural school and attempts to mobilize peasant resistance against the government. She is later arrested after being betrayed by an informer. During Lin's period of imprisonment her cell mate, Lin Hong, strengthens her faith in Communism. Upon release, Lin joins the CCP and devotes herself to the revolutionary cause.

(ZX)

Sorrows and Joys of a Middle-Aged Man

(Ai le zhongnian)

dir./sc. **Sang Hu**
with **Shi Hui**, Han Fei, Li Huanqing, Zhu Jiachen
Shanghai: Wenhua Film, 1949

This film about generational conflict and traditional virtue leaves aside political issues to focus on an ordinary man's life. Chen Shaochang is a school principal who is unwilling to remarry after his wife's death. He loves his three children and his job and is happy with his modest life.

Ten years later, his oldest son Jianzhong marries a banker's daughter. Now possessed of higher social standing, Jianzhong is so ashamed of his father's mediocre job that he pressures him into retirement, but when his daughter also marries Chen begins to feel lonely and depressed. Jianzhong tries to cheer him up by purchasing an expensive tomb site in the suburb for him! When his youngest son then prepares for marriage, Chen discovers that he is not too old to have an active life. He finds out that one of his former students at his old school, herself now a teacher, is actually in love with him. Chen needs her understanding and companionship. He marries her over his children's objections and decides to transform the tomb site into a house and school. In the end, Chen fathers another child and enthusiastically teaches a new class of children. This humanistic triumph for a 'productive' Confucian father foreshadows Ang **Lee**'s surprise ending in ***Eat Drink Man Woman*** (1994).

(PV)

Sorrows of the Forbidden City

(Qing gong mishi)

dir. **Zhu Shilin**
sc. Yao Ke
with Shu Shi, **Zhou Xuan**, Tang Ruoqing
Hong Kong: Yonghua Film, 1948

This historical drama is based on the rise to power of Empress Dowager Cixi. The film depicts the 'Hundred Days Reform' of the late Qing period by focusing on the exploits of a few individuals closely associated with the court.

The film begins with a fanfare announcing Emperor Guangxu's wedding. Due to the interference of Empress Dowager Cixi, Emperor Guangxu is not able to take Zhenfei, the woman he truly loves, as his first wife. Instead, with Cixi's endorsement, Longyu is to become Empress. Guangxu's tutor Weng Tonghe influences Guangxu with his new ideas, but is expelled from the palace after Guangxu vetoes a proposal to appropriate navy funds for Cixi's birthday celebrations. However, Zhenfei supports Guangxu by setting up a private navy fund.

After China's defeat in the first Sino-Japanese War (1894–5), Emperor Guangxu is determined to reform the political system. He brings a group of reform-minded intellectuals into the government, shuts down numerous superfluous government agencies, and fires many incompetent bureaucrats. Meanwhile, Cixi watches Guangxu's every move. She forces Guangxu's abdication, thus making it easier for her allies to arrest all his followers. Guangxu becomes desperate and asks the general of the New Army, Yuan Shikai, to assassinate Ronglu, one of Cixi's supporters, and put Cixi under house arrest. Instead Yuan reports Guangxu's scheme to Ronglu. Now Cixi has Guangxu put under house arrest before she takes control of the government.

Two years later, Beijing falls under attack by the Allied troops dispatched to China after the Boxer uprising. Before Cixi flees Beijing, she orders Zhenfei to commit suicide.

See also: historical film

(ZX)

Soul of the Painter, The

(Hua hun)

dir. **Huang Shuqin**
sc. Liu Heng, Min Anqi, Huang Shuqin
with **Gong Li**, Er Dongsheng, Da Shichang
Shanghai: Shanghai Film/Taipei: Golden
Tripod, 1994

This film about a woman who worked in a brothel
before becoming a renowned artist with a passion
for painting is based on a true story. With **Zhang
Yimou** acting as technical director and Gong Li
as the female lead, the film is as concerned to
achieve certain visual effects as it is to account for
the details of its biographical material. The female
nude, whether situated in the brothel or a work of
art, provides an important visual motif.

After the death of courtesan Miss Hong, her
maid Zhang Yuliang is coerced into **prostitution**
by the owner of a brothel. She is sent as a gift to
serve Mr. Pan, who has recently returned from
studying in Japan to become the local governor.
In Pan's household, Yuliang is treated fairly and
learns how to read and write. Mr. Pan, with one
wife already in his rural home, marries Yuliang
and moves to Shanghai. In the city, Yuliang learns
painting from Pan's friend. After years of practice,
Yuliang is finally accepted into art school while
Pan is away on business. The nude female body
becomes her subject of obsession. For a woman to
be an art student in the 1920s is already the cause
of gossip; a woman drawing female nudes is a positive scandal. Because she is denied a female model,
Yuliang has to hide herself in the public showers;
after being beaten up by angry bathers she turns
to her own body image in the mirror.

Yuliang is a traditional wife who regrets her
inability to bear a child for Mr. Pan (a consequence of the anti-pregnancy drink she took while
in the brothel). She writes a letter to Pan's first
wife inviting her to join in the production of a male
heir. Unavoidable conflicts ensue. Through a
series of dissolves Yuliang is shown painting a nude
figure; these are followed by images of the couple's
lovemaking. Feeling confined by China's conservative traditions and her own family situation,
Yuliang seizes the opportunity to leave for Paris.
She spends seven years in France earning her
artistic reputation. Her painting 'Woman After
Shower' wins an award. She returns to China to
meet her husband and the first wife's son, and she
becomes a professor at Nanking Art School. But

Chinese audiences of the 1930s do not appreciate
Western art, much less nudes: when Yuliang
prepares for her exhibition even Mr. Pan objects;
the local newspaper attacks her work and her
personal reputation. At this point, Pan's first wife
rejoins them from the countryside in order to
consult a doctor about her blindness and also visit
her son. In the 1940s, social and familial pressures
once again force Yuliang to flee to Paris. She
witnesses the death of a close friend and begins to
lose hope. A Chinese friend, Mr. Wang, expresses
his concern. Yuliang recovers to devote the rest of
her life to painting. In the 1950s, Yuliang receives
a letter from China telling her that her husband
has died in a house fire accidentally caused by the
blind wife. With no home or family left in China,
Yuliang stays in Paris. She dies in 1977.

Further Reading

J. Dai and M. Yang (1995), an informative interview; S. Huang (1995), a brief account of her own
work.

(SC)

sound film

See under: Chinese cinema (in
Historical essays)

Sparkling Fox

(Huo hu)

dir. **Wu Ziniu**
sc. Wang Chunbo, Wu Ziniu
with Gong Hanlin, Tu Men
Changchun: Changchun Film/Hong Kong:
Senxin Entertainment, 1993

A highly avant-garde film from a **Fifth
Generation** director, *Sparkling Fox* uses two
hunters' pursuit of a legendary sparkling fox in
snow mountains as an allegorical quest for the
meaning of life. An urban cinema projectionist
completes his last picture show before the theatre
is closed for remodelling as a restaurant. He goes
to the hospital for a medical check-up and is reas-
sured of his perfect health. He then travels deep
into the forests and starts fox-hunting. He meets a
bearded man, who has spent six years hunting for
the same elusive fox. The two rivals confront each
other on several occasions. During one stormy
night, the bearded man rescues the urban projectionist. After the storm, the two realize that it is

easier to survive natural storms than one's inner turmoils. As they part on the edge of the forest, another young man heads toward the mountains.

Alternating between scenes of snow-covered forests and long sequences of **documentary**-style interviews where the two hunters and their wives directly face the camera and speak in monologues, the film achieves a surrealist quality that prompts the viewers to examine their own existential problems.

See also: avant-garde, experimental or exploratory film

(YZ)

Sparkling Red Star

(Shanshan de hongxing)

dir. **Li Jun**, Li Ang
sc. collective
with Zhu Xinyun, Gao Baocheng, Liu Jiang, Li Xuehong
Beijing: August First Film, 1974

This is one of the few feature films produced during the **Cultural Revolution**. It takes as its subject matter one young boy's initiation into the **Communist revolution**.

As the Red Army is forced to leave its Jiangxi Soviet base areas, Pan Xingyi, a Red Army officer, leaves his teenage son, Dongzi, a red star and tells him that he will return. The landlord from the village returns with the Nationalist army and takes revenge on all those who took part in the land reform programme under the CCP's regional government. Dongzi witnesses his mother being burned to death and determines to become a revolutionary. He joins the guerrilla forces and performs several tasks with extraordinary skill and maturity. Finally, he kills the landlord who earlier put his mother to death. After the Sino-Japanese war breaks out, Dongzi's father returns to his home village to recruit some new soldiers for the Red Army. Dongzi shows him the red star he has kept all these years and follows him to the front to fight the Japanese.

(ZX)

sports

Sports was not a major theme in the 1920s–40s. A few documentaries of sports events were produced in the 1930s, and one notable feature film, *Queen of Sports* (*dir.* **Sun Yu**, 1934),

emphasizes the issue of morality while displaying the modern woman's athletic body and the usual temptations of **urban life** (e.g., money and fame). In the 1950s–60s, mainland filmmakers used sports to promote **nationalism**, as in *Girl Basketball Player No. 5* (*dir.* **Xie Jin**, 1957), as well as the sense of collective achievement, as in *Two Boys' Soccer Teams* (*dir.* **Liu Qiong**, 1956), *Ice-Skating Sisters* (*dir.* Wu Zhaodi, 1959) and *Girl Divers* (*dir.* Liu Guoquan, 1964). In the 1980s, however, more attention was given to individual athletes' feelings, although national pride and a sense of collectivity remain constant in mainland productions. *Drive to Win* (*dir.* **Zhang Nuanxin**, 1981) shows the determination of a woman volleyball player to win the world championship. *A Probationary Member* (*dir.* **Wu Ziniu**, Chen Lu, 1983) illustrates the important role sports plays in the development of an otherwise timid schoolboy. Unlike their mainland counterparts, Hong Kong and Taiwan filmmakers have seldom tried to cover a wide range of sports in their film productions.

See also: documentary

(YZ)

Spring Comes to the Withered Tree

(Kumu fengchun)

dir. **Zheng Junli**
sc. Wang Lian, Zheng Junli
with You Jia, Xu Zhihua, **Shangguang Yunzhu**, Liu Hongshen, Xu Ming, Hu Siqing
Shanghai: Haiyan Film, 1961

This film demonstrates how **socialist construction** brings fundamental changes to the lives of peasants dwelling in poverty-stricken, disease-ridden areas. Ku Meizi is an orphan who grows up with Fang and her son Dong. During their escape from an epidemic that hits their home village, Ku Meizi becomes separated from her friends. Ten years later she is married but soon loses her husband through illness. Dong is now a tractor driver and he meets Ku Meizi again by accident. He and his mother learn that Ku Meizi also has contracted the deadly disease. Mother fears for their safety and wants to leave the area, but Dong wants to stay – he is in love with Ku Meizi and believes that a cure can be found.

Two doctors, Liu Xiang and his sister Liu Hui, arrive from Shanghai to start work on a cure, assisted by the village chief, Luo Xunde. After meeting with Mao Zedong, Luo reports to all villagers that the Chairman encourages everyone to collaborate in the search for a cure. Even Liu Xiang, who initially cared only about his reputation, realizes that the cure can only be found through cooperation with other people and a sincere concern for his patients' well-being. The miracle occurs: Ku Meizi is cured. She marries Dong and gives birth to healthy twins. The final scene shows Dong teaching Ku Meizi how to drive the tractor as they work happily together with other peasants in the field.

Further Reading

E. Yau (1990), a study of representations of women in mainland films of the 1950s–60s.

(PV)

Spring in a Small Town
(Xiao cheng zhi chun)

dir. **Fei Mu**
sc. Li Tianji
with Wei Wei, Shi Yu, Li Wei, Zhang Hongmei, Cui Chaoming
Shanghai: Wenhua Film, 1948

This exceptional film devotes full attention to the psychology of a passionate love triangle. The story takes place in a small town in Southern China where a small family lives in a house surrounded by a decaying wall. Zhou Yuwen has been married for eight years to Dai Liyan, a fragile and ill man whom she does not love. Her only companions are an old servant and her sister-in-law Dai Xiu, although the latter's youth and enthusiasm actually disturb Yuwen and make her feel even more lonely.

One day Zhang Zhichen arrives to break the melancholic stagnation of the house. A young doctor and an old friend of Liyan, Zhichen used to be Yuwen's lover. The inevitable happens – a passionate love reignites between the two. Feeling guilty and yet unable to repress her passion, Yuwen experiences contradictory desires – to love, to escape and maybe even to murder. Liyan realizes what is going on and decides to kill himself. He fails. However, his actions convince both Yuwen and Zhichen that they should give up their love for each other and remain loyal to Liyan instead. The film ends with Zhichen's departure from the house.

A different type of Chinese woman emerges in this film – a character who personifies,

simultaneously, the Confucian ideal of sacrificial and submissive wife and a 'feminist' image of the independent woman. The film also presents an original and modern film style. The abstract *mise-en-scène*, together with camera positioning, approximates the complex psychological world inhabited by the protagonists.

Further Reading

X. Ying (1993), a study of Oriental film aesthetics; C. Li (1985), an analysis of the film's innovative techniques in relation to Chinese aesthetic traditions.

(PV)

Spring River Flows East
(Yi jiang chunshui xiang dong liu)

dir./sc. **Cai Chusheng**, **Zheng Junli**
with **Bai Yang**, Shu Xiuwen, **Wu Yin**, **Shangguan Yunzhu**, Tao Jin
Shanghai: Kunlun Film, 1947

One of the most influential post-war productions, this film focuses on the moral corruption of a young man and contrasts his upward social mobility with the suffering and sacrifices of his wife and his mother. It is extremely critical of social conditions under the KMT regime and set a box-office record in Shanghai.

Zhang Zhongliang joins the patriotic volunteer unit at the outbreak of the Sino-Japanese war. When the Chinese armed forces retreat from Shanghai, he leaves his wife, Sufen, his new born son and his mother behind and follows the government troops first to Nanjing and then on to Wuhan. During the battle of Wuhan, Zhang is captured by the Japanese, but manages to escape to Chongqing. Meanwhile, Sufen and Zhang's mother join Zhang's father in the countryside after the fall of Shanghai. However, the Japanese forces kill Zhang's father for his alleged anti-Japanese activities. Sufen and her mother-in-law return again to Shanghai. While Zhang's mother takes in washing to help make ends meet, Sufen works at a refugee camp: both anxiously wait for news of Zhang.

In Chongqing, Zhang becomes a refugee after the government refuses to honour his service credits. An old female acquaintance, Wang Lizhen, helps him find a job in a company, but Zhang is dismayed that the people around him care little for national affairs. He gradually becomes romantically involved with Wang and ends up functioning smoothly in the war-time capital's business district.

Zhang returns to Shanghai after the Japanese surrender. But instead of looking for his family, he uses his credibility as a resistance hero to help clear Wang's brother-in-law from charges of treason. In the process, he takes over this man's wife, He Wenyan, who is Wang's cousin. As Zhang enjoys his new status, his family continues to live in hardship, all the while hopeful that everything will be fine once he returns. Sufen, who finds a maid's position at He's residence, is shocked to see her husband entwined with Wang during a party there. After being insulted by Wang, Sufen leaves a note for her son and then commits suicide by drowning in the river that carries her unending sorrows. 'Don't follow your dad's example,' reads her note.

(ZX)

Spring Silkworms

(Chuncan)

dir. **Cheng Bugao**
sc. **Cai Chusheng**, **Xia Yan**
with Xiao Ying, **Gong Jianong**, Zheng Xiaoqiu, Gao Qianping, Ai Xia
Shanghai: Mingxing Film, 1933

An adaptation of Mao Dun's story, *Spring Silkworms* depicts poor silkworm farmers unwittingly caught up in competition with foreign industries during the early 1930s. In a village in Zhejiang province, Tongbao's family would do anything to make their silkworms healthier and more marketable. While taking care of their silkworms they fight against nature and their own superstitions. Yet, against Tongbao's wishes, his youngest son likes to play with Hehua, a woman believed to bring bad luck. In revenge for Tongbao's hostility towards her, Hehua throws a handful of his silkworms into the river.

Tongbao's family get into debt and try out many different methods in their attempt to produce high quality cocoons. When he travels to a nearby town to sell his produce, Tongbao finds all the shops closed because of a local battle between warlords. This forces him to travel further afield and, due to the fierce competition, to sell his cocoons at lower prices. Tongbao gets depressed because his family's hard work is not paying off.

The film, praised as one of the first successful leftist films, was shot in a **documentary** style (it records the growth of silkworms in real time, for example).While commenting on the consequences of superstition and the lack of solidarity among farmers, *Spring Silkworms* also dramatizes the impact political and economic change exerts on the lives of the poor.

See also: leftist film (under Chinese cinema in Historical essays)

(PV)

spy film

A type of film that focuses on espionage activities and usually carries political implications for the case involved.

See also: detective film

(YZ)

Stage Sisters

(Wutai jiemei)

dir. **Xie Jin**
sc. Lin Gu, Xu Jin, Xie Jin
with Xie Fang, Li Wei, Cao Yindi, **Shangguan Yunzhu**
Shanghai: Tianma Film, 1965

This film contrasts the lives of two actresses, one who seeks happiness and fulfilment through family life, and the other through political activism. Not surprisingly, the former is portrayed as a failure.

A peasant girl, Zhu Chunhua, is sold as a child bride. She runs away and joins a touring performance troupe. The music instructor's daughter, Yuehong, likes Zhu and the two become sworn sisters. When the troupe stops in Shaoxing, a local dandy tries to make a pass at Yuehong. After being rejected, he makes the police ban the show and arrest Yuehong. Zhu fights them off in an attempt to protect Yuehong, but she is tied to a post and subjected to public humiliation.

The troupe is dismantled, and Zhu and Yuehong move on to Shanghai, where their excellent acting skills prove highly successful. Their new manager, Tang, asks Zhu to perform a more suggestive act, but the request is turned down. After Yuehong marries Tang for financial security, the two sisters begin to drift apart.

Zhu stages a play, *New Year's Sacrifice* (based like the famous film of that title on Lu Xun's work),

Plate 41   *Stage Sisters* (1964)

which the KMT authorities instruct Tang to ban. When this fails Tang orders Ah Gan to throw limestone into Zhu's face: Zhu is severely injured as a result of the attack. Under public pressure, the KMT authorities reluctantly try the case in court. Tang persuades Yuehong to accept all responsibility, but Zhu points out in the court room that the act was actually politically motivated.

After 1949, Zhu goes on a performance tour and runs into Yuehong in a village. Yuehong has been abandoned by Tang. The two stage sisters are reconciled, and the film ends with them sitting side by side on a motor boat charging forward.

Further Reading

G. Marchetti (1989), a critical study of revolutionary aesthetics.

(ZX)

Stand Up, Don't Bend Over

(Zhan zhi le, bie paxia)

dir. **Huang Jianxin**

sc. Huang Xin

with Feng Gong, Da Shichang, Niu Zhenhua

Xi'an: Xi'an Film, 1992

The encounters between three urban neighbours provide a microcosm of contemporary life in China. Like Huang's early films this is a satiric **comedy**, although its absurdities spring from the peculiar state of mind, language, and social position of individual characters rather than from the depiction of unexpected events. As well as being an individual, each character represents a social type, and they collectively embody the faces of everyday life in contemporary China.

The viewer is invited to join a neighbour gazing though a peephole on a young couple moving house. The couple, a writer and his artist wife, are welcomed by their new neighbours in different ways: an old doorkeeper warns them of violent events in the past; Cadre Liu comforts them in language popular during the **Cultural Revolution**; when the wife opens the door in the morning she finds a pile of stinking watermelon shells. Writer Gao comes to realize why the neighbours describe the rascal Zhang and his wife as two wolves. Complicated neighbourhood conflicts begin to unfold between the three households.

The film ridicules intellectuals for their strong words but cowardly inaction. Gao becomes such a respected writer that Liu invites him to tutor his daughter for her college entrance examinations. When Zhang starts a family business raising exotic fish in his apartment, electrical shortages and other problems disrupt his neighbours' lives. Brainwashed by political ideology, Liu calls the police while Zhang takes revenge through violence. Gao mediates between the two, trying to support one neighbour without offending the other. Tragicomic moments occur when the writer, who has been expressing himself freely and loudly behind his closed door, stops the moment the door is opened.

The three neighbours find common ground once China's economic reforms stir their dreams of becoming rich. Zhang's fish business returns large profits, and neighbours begin to make money by furnishing him with supplies. Among them is Liu, who secretly phones a relative to make a deal with Zhang. Money does not bring happiness, however. Zhang pays the writer Gao to exchange apartments, and the powerless intellectual bows before the newly empowered entrepreneur.

(SC)

Star, Moon, Sun

aka *Sun, Moon, Star* (Xingxing, yueliang, taiyang)

dir. Yi Wen
sc. Qin Yifu
with You Min, **Ge Lan**, Ye Feng, Zhang Yang, Ouyang Shafei
Hong Kong: MP & GI, 1961

This two-part **melodrama** tells an unfulfilled love story between a man and three women. Xu Jianbai loves Lan, an orphan girl working for her uncle in the village. When Xu's rich father learns of his trysts, Xu is beaten and sent to a city school. Xu's cousin Qiuming is Xu's schoolmate. Soon the two fall in love, and Xu's father is happy with this situation. Xu becomes sick when he hears the rumours that Lan is married. Qiuming takes good care of him and later accompanies him back home for his mother's funeral. To his surprise, Xu discovers that Lan is not married. Qiuming notices their love and decides to withdraw from the triangle, but Lan herself wants Xu to marry Qiuming. The two women from different backgrounds become friends.

Troubled by his mixed feelings, Xu attends a college in Beijing and participates in the anti-Japanese student movement. He is acquainted with Yan'an, a lovely girl from Southeast Asia, and the two fall in love. Yan'an leads the students retreating to the south, and they all join the army. Many of them die in a battle, and several survivors get married on the front. By this time Yan'an has learned of the other two women in Xu's life and refuses to marry him. The two are injured in another battle and are rushed to a hospital. Lan, now a nurse in the medical team, cares for Xu but leaves him when she notices Yan'an's photo in his pocket.

The three women meet on the front and become good friends. Yan'an is injured and loses a leg. Lan is sick and is transferred to the hinterland. After the war, Qiuming and Yan'an visit Lan before she dies. Xu pays a visit to Lan's grave. He meets Yan'an in Hong Kong, but she does not want to burden him now that she is crippled. After Yan'an leaves for Southeast Asia, Xu looks for Qiuming and finds her in a nunnery. They meet in the courtyard, but Qiuming pretends not to recognize him, leaving him alone to figure out his unfulfilled love with three bright women.

The film won prizes of Best Film, Best Screenplay and Best Actress (You Min) at the first Taipei GHA in 1962.

(YZ)

Steeled Fighters

(Gangtie zhanshi)

dir./sc. **Cheng Yin**
with Zhang Ping, Sun Yu, Hu Peng
Changchun: Northeast Film, 1950

This film glorifies the heroism of three Communist prisoners-of-war and condemns the cruelty of the Nationalists.

During the civil war, Zhang and his platoon are assigned the task of hindering the advance of the pursuing Nationalist army. After their mission is accomplished, however, Zhang and two of his soldiers, Wang and Liu, are captured by enemy troops looking for information about the location of some food and equipment buried by the CCP before the Nationalists arrived. Zhang and his comrades refuse to cooperate: Wang dies of his wounds after his captors fail to provide him with adequate medical care, and Liu is shot to death when he tries to grab a gun. Zhang remains tight-lipped. A prison guard moved by his bravery helps Zhang escape to a village. The pursuing Nationalist soldiers arrive in the village to look for him. Not wanting to see any harm befall the locals, Zhang turns himself in. Now his captors bring his mother to him in an attempt to persuade him to talk, but, to their great disappointment, she only encourages him to stand firm. The town is soon taken by Communist forces and Zhang is released. His commander awards him a banner that reads 'Steeled Soldier'.

The film won the Peace Award at the 1951 Karlovy Vary FF and the First Prize from the Ministry of Culture in 1957.

(ZX)

Storm on the Border

(Sai shang fengyun)

dir. **Ying Yunwei**
sc. **Yang Hansheng**
with **Li Lili**, Shu Xiuwen, Zhou Boxun, **Wu Yin**
Chongqing: China Motion Picture, 1940

The purpose of this propaganda film is to promulgate unity between the Han Chinese and ethnic minorities in the fight against a common enemy, namely Japanese aggression.

A Mongolian youth, Diluwa, falls in love with a girl named Jinhuar. However, a young Chinese man, Ding Shixiong, is also trying to win Jinhuar's affection, thus making Diluwa jealous. A Japanese spy tries to turn this triangular love affair into an ethnic conflict between the Chinese and the Mongolians. Jinhuar's brother sees through the scheme and tries to calm down the two feuding parties, but the Japanese spy has him kidnapped. Diluwa's sister witnesses the kidnapping and reports this to her brother, who then realizes his mistake and makes peace with Ding Shixiong. They set out together to rescue Jinhuar's brother. The spy accuses them of rebellion and successfully convinces the leader of Diluwa's tribe that he should fortify his castle. Diluwa's sister, who works inside the castle, reveals the true identity of the Japanese spy to the commander of the guards, who then changes sides by helping the allied force of Diluwa and Ding Shixiong take the castle. The Japanese spy is killed, but so is Jinhuar. As she watches Ding Shixiong and Diluwa fighting side by side, a smile appears on her face.

Plate 42   *Storm on the Border* (1940)

The film sets the narrative pattern for many films of ethnic minorities in the 1950s–60s that stress ethnic harmony and national security.

See also: ethnic minorities, film of; propaganda and film

(ZX)

Story of Liubao Village

(Liubao de gushi)

dir. **Wang Ping**
sc. Shi Yan, Huang Zongjiang
with Liao Youliang, Tao Yuling
Beijing: August First Film, 1957

In this film that glorifies self-sacrifice for the **Communist revolution**, a squadron of the Communist soldiers is stationed in Liubao Village. A sergeant, Li Jin, falls in love with his landlord's daughter, Ermeizi, a turn of events not permitted by military regulation. His commander persuades him to back out of the affair and transfers him to a different location. Although Li promises to stop seeing Ermeizi, he just can't get her out of his mind.

After the squadron leaves the village, the puppet Japanese forces return. One of the Japanese officers takes an interest in Ermeizi, and when his proposal is rejected he takes her by force. Upon hearing this news, Li's commander and comrades immediately go on a rescue mission. The kidnappers are killed and Ermeizi is rescued. Li, however, keeps his promise and suppresses his feelings for her.

Five years later, Li is promoted to lieutenant while Ermeizi has also joined the Communist militia force. He and Ermeizi are finally reunited when Li returns to Liubao village on a new mission.

(ZX)

Story of Qiuju, The

(Qiuju da guansi)

dir. **Zhang Yimou**
sc. Liu Heng
with **Gong Li**, Liu Peiqi, Lei Luosheng, Yang Liuchun
Hong Kong: Sil-Metropole/Beijing: BFA Youth Film, 1992

With *The Story of Qiuju* Zhang Yimou attempts to move in a new stylistic direction. The film's use of concealed cameras, location shooting, and non-professional actors gives it a strong realistic quality.

The narrative traces a simple cause-and-effect plot line. Qiuju's husband offends the village head by ridiculing the man's propensity to produce only daughters, not a son. The village head responds to this insult by viciously kicking Qiuju's husband in the groin. The pregnant Qiuju insists that action be taken over the assault, but while the local authorities order the offender to pay all medical bills, no actual apology is forthcoming. Qiuju decides to take the case to the courts.

She makes a series of trips in her quest for justice, ascending the court system from district town to provincial city. The trips are linked stylistically. The image of red peppers loaded on to a wagon indicates the financial base of the venture: transportation scenes develop from wagon to bicycle, tractor to long-distance bus. The pregnant Qiuju and her sister-in-law emerge from, or disappear into, crowds of real people in the streets. Folk music is heard whenever Qiuju appears on the same old country road. Moreover, to ensure authenticity, actors dress and act like local people and speak in regional dialect.

Qiuju's unflagging search for someone to hear her case elicits sympathy from court officials, lawyers, and hotel staff. The relationship between Qiuju and the village head changes dramatically on the night Qiuju goes into labour. The village head and others carry Qiuju to the hospital where, after a difficult delivery period, she gives birth to a son. Later, as Qiuju waits for the village head to attend her son's first month celebrations, she learns that the Public Security Bureau is finally going to act on the assault charge by imprisoning the offender for fifteen days. In an ambiguous final image, the camera follows Qiuju as she runs after the police car receding away into the distance.

The film is significant for its utilization of a **documentary** film aesthetic, its exploration of the heroine's self-consciousness, and its moral interpretation of day-to-day social realities in contemporary China.

(SC)

Strange Circle

(Guaiquan)

dir. Sun Sha
sc. Fu Yannan
with Huang Meiying, Ge Yunping, Zhang Baishuang, Shen Min, Li Li
Changchun: Changchun Film, 1986

What seems at first glance an unconventional film about sisterhood and female **sexuality** turns out to be a reaffirmation of mainstream values. All estranged women find their men in the end, except for one who genuinely chooses to remain single.

Four young women, Zhenni, Meizhen, Ah Man and Ah Chun, are determined to remain single. They live together as a surrogate family. A driver, Xiaoying, also insists on joining the circle of single women. However, their 'unity' gradually begins to collapse as each becomes attracted to a man. Only the oldest, Zhenni, remains firm in her commitment to staying single. One day the others wake up to find Zhenni gone: a note left behind beseeches them to start new lives by leaving the 'strange circle'. Ah man immediately announces that she and Xiao Cheng, the young man who always waits outside for her, are in love. Xiaoying marries Ah Long without her parents' consent. Meizhen goes to look for her artist friend. Only Ah Chun, who has been hurt before and now hates all men, is left alone in the house. When a college graduate, Wang Shicai, proposes to her, she rejects him. Unexpectedly, Zhenni returns and tells Ah Chun that her disappearance was a scheme designed to break their circle. She convinces Ah chun that she should go to see Wang. Now Zhenni turns out to be the only remaining member of this strange circle.

(ZX)

Strawman

(Daocao ren)

dir. **Wang Tung**
sc. Wang Xiaodi, Song Hong
with Yang Guimei, Zhuo Zhengli, Chang Bozhou, **Ko Chun-hsiung**
Taipei: CMPC, 1987

Strawman opens with the image of a peasant mother placing cow pies on her two sons' eyes so that they will both be unfit for military service in the imperial Japanese army. Thus begins this satirical **comedy** about the legacies of Japanese colonialism in Taiwan. Life on the home front is not easy, and the Chen brothers suffer from food shortages, poverty and American bombing during the Pacific War. One day a bomb lands but does not explode. The brothers carry it all the way to town and present it to the Japanese captain, hoping to be rewarded for their loyalty. They are

scolded and told to drop the bomb in the ocean instead. They comply, and the bomb explodes at the last moment. However, their disappointment turns to unexpected luck as hundreds of dead fish float toward the shore – instead of a cash reward the brothers return with a bounty of seafood for their village. The film ends with a happy seafood feast and the children saying, 'We hope the Americans drop more bombs so that we can have fish every day.'

Such implausible scenes of wartime absurdity and incongruity give this film the touch of a parable or fable which hints at darker realities. After making it Wang Tung and his collaborator, the scriptwriter/filmmaker Wang Xiaodi, worked together on **Banana Paradise** (1989). The two films demonstrate their comic gift for producing historical satires that forcefully illustrate different stages of political suppression in Taiwanese history.

(YY)

Street Angel

(Malu tianshi)

dir./sc. **Yuan Muzhi**
with **Zhao Dan**, **Zhou Xuan**, Wei Heling, Zhao Huishen
Shanghai: Mingxing Film, 1937

Street Angel dramatizes the struggle of good-hearted urban youth to escape from a corrupt environment in the poorest district of Shanghai. The film opens with a comic marriage procession in which Chen Xiaoping plays trumpet for the band. Chen is in love with his neighbour Hong, who fled from Manchuria with her sister Yun after the Japanese occupation. While Yun has been forced into prostitution, Hong travels around with her tutor singing songs.

One day the tutor decides to sell Hong to a small-time gangster. Chen and his friends want to free her and decide to consult the lawyer Zhang. They soon discover, however, that without money the law will not help the poor. Running away provides the only solution, and Hong does this with the help of Chen. They live together in another district of the city. Yun comes for a visit and dreams of starting a new life with Chen's friend, Wang, but the evil tutor asks a gangster to track them down. Although Hong manages to escape Yun is stabbed by the two men. Friends

Plate 43   *Street Angel* (1937)

gathered around Yun's bedside can do nothing but watch her die.

This story of solidarity, friendship, and love amongst the dregs of urban society has been interpreted in different ways. It is certainly a critique of Shanghai's semi-colonialist society; it might have been inspired by Frank Borzage's *Street Angel* (1928); it has even been described as a Chinese forerunner of Italian neo-realism. A canonized leftist film, it combines Hollywood and Soviet film techniques with traditional Chinese narrative arts.

See also: leftist film (under Chinese cinema in Historical essays)

Further Reading
M. Feng (1989), a discussion of foreign influences; L. Lee (1999), an insightful analysis of urban perception; N. Ma (1989), a critical study of film techniques; T. Sato (1985), a comparative study.

(PV)

Struggle in an Ancient City
(Yehuo chunfeng dou gucheng)

dir. Yan Jizhou
sc. Li Yingru, Li Tian, Yan Jizhou

with Wang Xiaotang, **Wang Xin'gang**, Chen Lizhong, Wang Runshen
Beijing: August First Film, 1963

This film concerns a group of devoted underground Communists and their heroic struggle against Japanese occupation forces and puppet Chinese troops.

During the Sino-Japanese war a Communist officer, Yang Xiaodong, is sent to Beijing on a mission to persuade the city's Chinese puppet security force to defect to the resistance side. Disguising himself as a merchant, Yang makes contact with two sisters, Jinhuan and Yinhuan, both of whom are underground agents. After some discussion, the three agree that one of the security force commanders, Guan Jingtao, carries the greatest potential to switch allegiance. The resistance had captured Guan during an earlier ambush, but then decided to release him. Because of that event, Guan has been viewed with suspicion by his superiors ever since. At the same time, the police arrest a member of the resistance who then betrays his comrades. With information provided by him, the police arrest Jinhuan. Now Guan's superiors want to use Jinhuan to test

Guan's loyalty, but when the two are brought together, Jinhuan sees through the scheme and protects Guan. Meanwhile, Yang has also been captured by the Japanese. In order to make him talk, the police have his mother arrested. However, not wanting her son to give in to the enemy just for her sake, she commits suicide. While Jinhuan is killed by the Japanese, Yinhuan falls in love with Yang and helps organize a daring rescue of Yang from jail. They both visit Guan and manage to persuade him to switch sides.

(ZX)

Summer at Grandpa's, A

(Dongdong de jiaqi)

dir. **Hou Hsiao-hsien**
sc. **Chu Tien-wen**
with Chen Bocheng, Yang Liyin, Gu Jun
Taipei: Wanbaolu Film, 1984

A Summer at Grandpa's reveals Hou Hsiao-hsien's talent for making children's films. It begins when Dongdong is attending his primary school leaving ceremony. At the very moment when he should be celebrating the start of his summer vacation, his mother is hospitalized. His father sends him and his little sister to spend the summer with his grandparents in the country. To Dongdong and his sister, who have spent most of their life in Taipei, the countryside is an unknown place. Dongdong's grandfather, a respected local physician, will not allow Dongdong to spend most of his time playing; he requires that every day Dongdong practice calligraphy and recite classical poems. Yet Dongdong becomes fascinated by the countryside. He quickly makes friends with village boys, explores the wilderness, discovers natural wonders and plays tricks on his sister. Driven away as a pest by the boys, the sister finds comfort with a local madwoman who later saves her life. One day Dongdong witnesses the murder of a truck driver by some local hoodlums who also happen to be friends of his uncle. When his uncle is framed by the murderers, Dongdong has to reveal the truth so as to save him. The film ends when the summer vacation ebbs away and Dongdong's father comes to take them back to Taipei.

A Summer at Grandpa's is a prototypical Hou Hsiao-hsien movie. It has a centrifugal narrative structure composed of vignettes. It replays Hou's favourite themes of initiation and rites of passage:

Dongdong and his sister begin to experience the cruelties of life after witnessing illness, madness, violence and death. Moreover, it exemplifies Hou's talent for drawing the most natural and unaffected performances from child actors.

See also: children's film

Further Reading
G. Cheshire (1993), an excellent analysis of Hou's films; H. Chiao (1993b), an interview with critical comments.

(YY)

Summer Snow

(Nüren sishi)

dir. Ann **Hui**
sc. Chan Man Keung
with Josephine **Siao**, Roy Chiao, Law Kar-ying
Hong Kong: Golden Harvest, 1994

This comic-serious film about Alzheimer's disease concerns the Sun family: May, Bing, and their son Allen. May does not get along with Bing's father, who is brusque and rude at the table. One day the mother-in-law suffers a fatal attack: May and Allen try to get help while the father-in-law, an ex-pilot, watches a video game. At the subsequent funeral he calls his daughter, Lan, 'old woman'. Not long afterwards he is diagnosed with Alzheimer's. Bing cannot persuade his brother's family to help them out.

May and Bing experience a deterioration in their relationship. Bing, who is normally an easy-going test-drive examiner, fails a driver. May sends the father-in-law to a centre for senior citizens where a friend of her mother-in-law, Mrs Han, also lives. One day Allen loses his grandfather at the centre. A taxi hunt by May ends at the police station with the grandfather making an unexpected appearance. He wants to leave the centre so much that he actually parachutes off the Suns' roof with an umbrella (he is not seriously hurt). An old companion tells Allen that decades earlier the grandfather had saved his life during a dogfight.

As Mrs Han dies of cancer, May realizes how much she loves her husband and begins to re-evaluate their relationship. After she takes the grandfather home in summer it suddenly starts to snow – much to his wonder. Bing finally passes the driver whom he had earlier failed. The grandfather recovers after days in a coma: he picks flowers in the countryside, recognizes his daughter Lan, and after telling May that 'life . . . is all about fun', quietly dies. The film ends on a positive vision of life: Allen and his girlfriend declare their mutual love and May sees the grandfather's 'imaginary' pigeons on the roof.

This film won Josephine Siao the Best Actress award at Berlin FF.

(KH)

Sun Daolin

b. 1921, Beijing
Actor, director

A famous actor of the 1940s–60s, Sun Daolin came from a well-to-do family. His father studied engineering in Belgium in the 1910s and Sun himself majored in philosophy from 1938 at the American-run Yenching University. He made his first film appearance in *The Reunion* (*dir.* Ding Li, 1948). Sun's successful portrayal of a timid but honest schoolteacher in **Crows and Sparrows** (*dir.* **Zheng Junli**, 1949) earned acclaim from both critics and audiences: his performance earned an achievement award from the Ministry of Culture in 1957.

In the post-1949 period, Sun played a variety of characters, including a resolute Communist officer in **Reconnaissance Across the Yangtze** (*dir.* **Tang Xiaodan**, 1954), a weak-minded brother in *Family* (*dir.* Chen Xihe, Ye Ming, 1956), a confused intellectual in **Early Spring in February** (*dir.* **Xie Tieli**, 1963), and a patriotic chess master in *The Go Master* (*dir.* Duan Jishun, Junya Sato, 1982). Sun began to write screenplays and direct films himself after 1984. His recent titles include *Thunderstorm* (1984) and *The Provisional President* (1986).

Further Reading

ZDX (1982–6: 6: 134–47), a short biography.

(ZX)

Sun Shiyi

b. 1904
d. 3 October 1966
Screen writer

A noted leftist screen and songwriter of the 1930s, Sun Shiyi had an eventful early life. He was an active participant in political movements while still a student at the Industrial Institute in Jiangxi province. The school officials withheld his diploma, and Sun was threatened with arrest by the police. He fled to Beijing and studied English at Huiwen University. In 1924, he went to Shanghai to take classes at the National University of Politics. He became fascinated with Marxism and translated numerous Marxist writings into Chinese, whereupon he was expelled from the university in 1926.

Sun found employment at the Great Wall Film Company. At the same time, he also worked for the Motion Picture Department of the Commercial Press and China Film Company. His responsibilities included the editing of studio publications, writing film scripts and occasional acting jobs. After China Film Company was closed, Sun briefly became involved with theatre.

Sun resumed his film activities in 1934. His script of **New Woman** (*dir.* **Cai Chusheng**), was made into a film by Lianhua Film Company that year. He also wrote the theme songs for **Big Road** (*dir.* **Sun Yu**, 1934), *Goddess of Liberty* (*dir.* **Situ Huimin**, 1935) and other titles. In 1936, Sun took over the directorship of the Department of Motion Pictures and Radio at Jiangsu College of Education, and he became one of the early advocates of **film education** in China. During the war, he made a **documentary**, *The Resonance of Peace*, and wrote the theme song for *White Clouds of Home* (*dir.* Situ Huimin, 1940).

Sun went to Hong Kong in 1949 and served as chief editor of *Wenhui Daily*, but the newspaper was closed by the British authorities in 1951. After returning to China in 1957, Sun helped to found the China Film Archives. He died of a heart attack in 1966.

See also: theatre and film

Further Reading

ZDX (1982–6: 1: 65–70), a short biography.

(ZX)

Sun Yu

(Sun Chengyu)

b. 21 March 1900, Chongqing, Sichuan province
d. 11 July 1990
Director

One of the most prominent directors in China during the 1930s–40s, Sun Yu made numerous films considered classics by today's critics. A graduate of Qinghua University, Sun went on to study drama at the University of Wisconsin with the financial support of the Boxer Funds. He later studied film writing and directing at Columbia University as well as cinematography, film developing and editing at New York University. He returned to China in 1926 and directed his first film, *A Romantic Swordsman* (1929), for Minxin Film Company.

As one of the four pillar directors at Lianhua Film Company in the 1930s, Sun made a great contribution by introducing new approaches to filmmaking. Partly through his efforts, Chinese films attained an unprecedented level of artistic success. Sun's first two Lianhua titles, *Memories of the Old Capital* and **Wild Flower** (both 1930), established his reputation as a socially conscious artist. He became so associated with other leftist filmmakers that the messages in his films seem indistinguishable from the political positions advocated by underground Communists at the time. For instance, *Wild Rose* (1932) contains unmistakable anti-Japanese themes, *Revenge by the Volcano* (1932) calls for open revolt against the oppressors, **Daybreak** (1932) presents revolution as the only hope for the working classes, and both **Little Toys** (1933) and **Big Road** (1934) direct attention to the impending national crisis.

After the outbreak of the Sino-Japanese war, Sun moved to Chongqing, where he directed *The Sky Rider* (1940), a **war film** about the Chinese air force, and *A Bloody Lesson* (1941), the story of a traitor who changes his mind after witnessing Japanese atrocities. Sun visited the USA in the post-war period, and upon returning to China, began work on a film **biography** called *The Life of Wu Xun* (1950). In 1951, after Mao Zedong personally wrote an article denouncing the film, Sun was devastated by widespread criticism. During the next four decades, Sun directed or co-directed only three more titles, none of which could match the artistic quality of his pre-1949 work.

Further Reading

C. Berry (1988c), a psychoanalytic study of *Big Road*; C. Li (1991), a survey of Sun's early film career; Y. Sun (1987), a memoir; ZDX (1982–6: 2: 81–7), a short biography; Y. Zhang (1994a), with analysis of *Wild Flower*.

(ZX)

Sun Zhou

b. 1954, Shandong province
Director

A close associate of the **Fifth Generation**, Sun Zhou started out as a cameraman at the Shandong TV station and made dozens of TV dramas, including *Wu Song* (1981), *Garlands at the Foot of the Mountain* (1983) and *Snowstorm* (1984). In 1984 he attended a special directing class at the Beijing Film Academy. He was later transferred to Pearl River Film Studio to direct *Put Some Sugar in the Coffee* (1987). His next feature, **Bloodshed at Dusk** (1989), a detective and **gangster film**, clearly demonstrates how influenced he has been by this major Hong Kong genre. The **True Hearted** (1992), a touching story of a retired opera singer and his 'abandoned' grandson who finally communicate with each other, won Sun Zhou critical acclaim, including a Special Jury award at the 1992 Hawaii FF. The film bears the influence of an earlier Pearl River production, **Swan Song** (*dir.* **Zhang Zeming**, 1985).

See also: detective film

(YZ)

Sunshine and Showers

(Taiyang yu)

dir. **Zhang Zeming**
sc. Liu Xihong, Zhang Zeming
with Yan Xiaopin, Sun Chun, Yi Xinxin, Zhang Ling
Guangzhou: Pearl River Film, 1987

A refreshing look at **urban life** in China, this film traces the emotional life of Liu Yaxi, a librarian in Shenzhen, a special economic zone bordering Hong Kong. Her boyfriend Liu Yadong runs an advertising agency and has little time to spend with her even during weekends. Yaxi understands Yadong but still feels lonely. A friend introduces her to a lively teenage girl, Kong Lingkai, and the two become good friends. Meanwhile He Nan, Yadong's former taxi driver girlfriend, tells Yaxi that she still loves Yadong and will not back out. Yaxi feels puzzled and talks to Yadong.

Lingkai decides not to attend college and joins a fashion model workshop. Yaxi takes a business trip and is disappointed when Yadong does not come to send her off. For months she keeps a distance from him, and is delighted when Lingkai drops by and spends a night with her. At the fashion show, Yaxi meets Yadong, and the two are reconciled again. Yaxi does not know what to say when a close friend decides to marry her Hong Kong boss. Yadong's advertising agency is bankrupt, and he has to move to another place. When Yaxi sees him off, she discovers the driver is He Nan. She is angry at Yadong and feels lonely once he leaves with his staff. The title symbolically captures Yaxi's moods and the changing urban landscapes.

The film's depiction of the intimate relationship between Yaxi and Lingkai has led some critics to pursue a lesbian reading. In any case, the film addresses urban disillusionment in a period of profound changes.

(IJS)

Super Citizens

(Chaoji shimin)

dir. **Wan Jen**
sc. Wan Jen, **Wu Nien-chen**
with Li Zhiqi, Su Mingming, Chen Bozheng, Lin Xiuling
Taipei: Wanbaolu Film, 1985

Super Citizens opens with a young man from the countryside looking for his sister who works in Taipei. It is a story of urban adventure in which the man encounters all sorts of dark urban realities that are completely unlike his past rural experiences. His ethical moorings begin to loosen when exposed to the attractions of city life. He becomes fascinated by a beautiful prostitute, although when he actually buys her time he is too embarrassed to look at her nude body. His innocent ways lead him to believe stories made up by a teenage drug addict. He becomes the good friend of a thief. Then he witnesses a whole family committing suicide. However, none of these encounters shock him so much as when he sees his friend being beaten up by a car owner after trying to steal a car stereo.

The film combines comedy and suspense in a way that generates sympathy for its working class heroes. Its main plot line is modelled after the kind of 'captivity narrative' depicted in *The Searchers* (*dir.* John Ford, 1959), and it is significant that its location, Taipei, physically resembles the American wilderness – both being places which can seem dangerous and unknown, and which can be deployed in the representation of an alien, mysterious and corrupt moral other. But unlike John Wayne, the protagonist of *Super Citizens* never finds his woman, let alone rescue her: by the end of the film the young man has decided to stay on in the city and continue his search.

(YY)

Swan Song

(Juexiang)

dir./sc. **Zhang Zeming**
with Kong Xianzhu, Mo Shaoying, Liang Yujin, Feng Diqing, Liu Qianyi
Guangzhou: Pearl River Film, 1985

The film is about the life of a traditional musician whose contributions to Cantonese music have never been fully recognized. He is misunderstood by his son, undervalued by society, abused by political power and taken advantage of by those who fail to make proper acknowledgement of their debts to him.

Ou Laoshu had his glorious days when he was young. But his biggest unfulfilled wish is to publish a collection of Cantonese music he has written over the years. Ou's son, Guanzi, has been living with his father since his parents divorced. Under his father's influence, Guanzi has become quite talented in music himself. However, during the **Cultural Revolution**, Ou is politically persecuted and Guanzi is led to believe that his father is guilty of the many charges levelled against him. He leaves home and breaks his relationship with his father. After many years, Guanzi comes home to visit his father, who now makes a living by selling paper boxes. Ou cooks his best dish to entertain his son, and the two are reconciled. When Ou learns that Guanzi is planning to flee to Hong Kong, he is worried and tries to stop him. But Guanzi does not listen to his father and ends up losing his money to a smuggler. His girl friend tries to talk him into continuing his music study, but Guanzi remains uninterested. Ou dies in poverty. Some of his music scores are lost, others are published under other people's names. Guanzi's mother, who is remarried and has become a famous Cantonese opera actress by now, comes to look for him. Guanzi's step sister has a huge success by performing a piano concerto based on Ou's music score, but Ou's name is not acknowledged. Guanzi finally begins to understand his father and the contribution he made to Cantonese music.

The film received a Special Award at the 1986 International Youth FF in Italy.

Further Reading

M. Lang (1993), a historical study of the film and traditional music.

(ZX)

swordplay film

Sometimes termed 'swordsman film', this is a type of film that is set in ancient China and features knight-errants (*youxia* or *jianxia*) roaming the country righting wrongs committed by evil local tyrants or corrupt imperial court officials.

See also: martial arts film

(YZ)

Swordsman, II

(Dongfang bu bai)

dir. **Ching Siu Tung**
sc. **Tsui Hark**, Hanson Chan, Tang Pik Yin
with Jet **Li**, **Lin Ching Hsia**, Rosamund Kwan, Fannie Yuen, Michelle Li
Hong Kong: Golden Princess, 1992

Swordsman, II is the centre-piece of Ching Siu Tung and Tsui Hark's dazzling *Swordsman* trilogy. The first instalment, *Swordsman* (1990), co-directed in part by the great King **Hu**, took Louis Cha's novel *The Smiling, Proud Warrior* and turned it into a high-powered piece of film entertainment. The narrative – a Ming-era account of the scramble to gain possession of a centuries-old sacred scroll called the Sunflower Scriptures – is impossible to summarize, but what matters most is the film's ambitious combination of humour, special effects, and over-the-top stunts.

This basic recipe was retained for the superior sequel, although a number of top stars (Samuel Hui, Jacky Cheung, Cecilia Yip) did not survive the transition to round two. *Swordsman, II*'s masterstroke is its gender inversion. The **Cultural Revolution**-era novel may have contained, in its evocation of a power-obsessed leader who castrates himself in order to obtain sacred martial arts skills, sly political references to Chairman Mao, but the film turns the castrated character into a woman, Invincible Asia. Out of control

sexually after his/her gender transformation, Invincible Asia falls in love with Ling, the swordsman of the title, although things do not go smoothly for either of them, because they have to battle a demonic adversary as well as each other.

Invincible Asia returns in *Swordsman, III: The East Is Red* (1993). Now Spanish and Japanese invaders are attempting to plunder China's resources, and Asia encounters Snow, her former concubine, who is still leading Asia's Sun-Moon sect from a masochistic sense of devotion.

These three titles have helped popularize the perverse pleasures of Hong Kong action cinema. Herein lie great soundtracks, high-wire action, wild sartorial statements, beautiful stars and kinky sex.

See also: action film; martial arts film

Further Reading

R. Chu (1994), on entertainment and gender; H. Hampton (1996), on the star image of **Lin Ching Hsia**.

(JS)

Swordsman in Double-Flag Town, The

(Shuangqizhen daoke)

dir. **He Ping**
sc. Yang Zhengguang, He Ping
with Gao Wei, Zhao Mana, Chang Jiang, Sun Haiying, Wang Gang
Xi'an: Xi'an Film, 1990

This highly stylish **kungfu film** is set in the northwestern deserts. Haige, a boy swordsman, follows his father's dying words and arrives in Double-Flag Town to look for his child bride. Upon his arrival, he sees how 'One-Strike Swordsman' kills two men who have come for revenge. The crippled inn-keeper lets Haige stay but is not willing to marry his daughter Haomei to the boy, in spite of his previous agreement with the boy's father. Haige peeps at Haomei when she is taking a bath. He is caught and beaten by the innkeeper, but Haomei feels sympathetic for him. The inn-keeper thinks very little of Haige when he sits on his bed and practises a special kind of kungfu.

One day, a swordsman gets drunk in the inn and attempts to rape Haomei. Haige challenges him and miraculously kills this powerful man. The whole town is shocked. They plead with him to stay and take his responsibility. Inside their house, the innkeeper marries Haomei to Haige. Haige seeks aid from 'Flying Sand', whom he met a while back. Three days later, 'One-Strike Swordsman' comes to revenge the death of his brother. In an elaborate sequence that resembles the fight scenes in **Westerns**, he kills several townspeople, including the innkeeper. When he sees his contestant is a boy, he feels puzzled. Nevertheless, they both draw out their swords. When the dust settles, Haige's face is covered with blood. 'One-Strike Swordsman' smiles and turns back. He walks a few steps and falls down dead. After watching the fight on the town's wall, 'Flying Sand' rides into the street to claim the victory. Haige ignores this cheat and leaves the mysterious desert town with his young wife.

(JJS)

T

Taipei Story

(Qingmei zhuma)

dir. Edward **Yang**
sc. Edward Yang, **Chu Tien-wen**
with **Hou Hsiao-hsien**, Cai Qing, **Wu Nien-chen**
Taipei: Edward Yang Film Workshop, 1985

Taipei Story is a striking prelude to the main achievements of New Taiwan Cinema. Using the acting talents of the blossoming director Hou and the brilliant writer Wu, director Yang offers a portrait of Taipei that situates its colonial past against its increasingly globalized future. Hou plays the protagonist, Long, who comes from a successful merchant family which capitalized on the sudden departure of American military councils after the Vietnam war. Long's privileged, traditional and patriarchal background is challenged by his girl-friend Qin, who has embraced American-style modern bourgeois values and mistaken them for women's liberation. Long's fortunes are also under siege by a new class of young, predatory entre-preneurs who disregard old community ties and abandon themselves to a global consumer culture instead. This group is represented by Qin's younger sister Ling, who frequents underground dance clubs as against the comfortable pubs favoured by Qin and the Fukien-Japanese style of karaoke houses patronized by Long.

Yang's representation of the mood and make-up of distinct musical environments is richly evocative of competing cultural practices in Taipei. The narcissism of the karaoke bar, for example, where sodden men sing to themselves, is set off against a number of alternative locations for musical diversion – alternatives marked by divisions of nation, class and gender. It is also a testament to Yang's directorial vision that he does not turn Long's struggle – namely, the questioning of his ethics, his masculinity, and his community – into a sentimental lament for a lost Taipei, even though the character has come to develop a much colder, alienated city persona.[6]

See also: New Taiwan Cinema (under Taiwan cinema in Historical essays)

(YY)

Tang Xiaodan

b. 22 February 1910
Director

A veteran director whose career spanned over half a century, Tang Xiaodan was born into a merchant family. He spent most of his childhood with his parents in Southeast Asia. His interest in film was kindled by a toy bought by his father, namely a hand-cranked film projector and three hundred feet of *The Great Train Robbery*. Enrolled at an agricultural college in Xiamen (Amoy), Tang became more interested in literature and theatre. He was finally expelled from the college in 1928 for his involvement in student protests against the Japanese massacre at Ji'nan. Tang went to Shanghai and became acquainted with **Shen Xiling**, a leftist filmmaker, who helped him get a job as stage designer at Tianyi Film Company in 1931. During the filming of *The Platinum Dragon* (1933), the original director fell ill and the producer asked Tang to take over.

Tang's success with *The Platinum Dragon* brought him recognition. In 1934, Tianyi decided to open a Hong Kong branch of the studio for the produc-tion of Cantonese-dialect films, and Tang was subsequently transferred. However, unhappy with Tianyi's lack of concern for the quality of produc-tion, Tang moved on to Yihua Film Company. His film *The Foolish Father-in-Law* (1934) raked in huge profits, while two other hit titles, *The Turn-Over* (1934) and *Twelve Beauties* (1936), both produced for Grandview Film Company (Daguan), were highly critical of social conditions. In 1938, Tang made three anti-Japanese films. When Hong Kong fell in 1942, Tang refused to collaborate with the Japanese and fled to Chongqing.

Tang's best work of the post-war period includes **Dream in Paradise** (1947), *Rejuvenation* (1948) and *The Lost Love* (1949). Tang made a total of fourteen titles after 1949, mostly war films depicting the Communist victory over the Nationalist troops. Amongst these, **From Victory to Victory** (*co-dir.* **Cheng Yin**, 1952), **Reconnaissance Across the Yangtze** (1954) and *Red Sun* (1963) are well-crafted works that were extremely popular with audiences. Although Tang suffered political persecution during the **Cultural Revolution**, he was cleared of all charges earlier than most other veteran filmmakers. In the post-Cultural Revolution period, Tang directed a few historical films, including *The Nanchang Uprising* (1981) and *Liao Zhongkai* (1983) – the latter won him a Best Director prize at the 1985 China GRA.

See also: historical film; theatre and film; war film

Further Reading

T. Chen (1984), a profile; ZDX (1982–6: 2: 100–9), a short biography.

(ZX, YZ)

Te Wei

b. 22 August 1915, Shanghai
Director

One of the best **animation** filmmakers in China, Te Wei regularly contributed political cartoons to such major Shanghai publications of the 1930s as *Shanghai Cartoons* (Shanghai manhua), *Independent Cartoons* (Duli manhua) and *Evening Daily* (Da wanbao). During the Sino-Japanese war, he devoted himself to drawing cartoons promoting **nationalism**. He joined the CCP in 1949 and was appointed Head of the Animation Division of the newly founded Northeast Film Studio. In the following year, he was transferred to Shanghai Film Studio's Animation Department, and when the department was expanded into the Shanghai Animation Film Studio in 1957, served as its first general manager.

As a director of animated films, Te has produced some remarkable work. While his *Good*

Friends (1954) was runner-up for the Ministry of Culture's Achievement Award in 1957, *Where Is Mama?* (1961) won several titles: the Silver Sail at the 1961 Locarno FF, Best Animation award at the 1962 HFA, and an honourable mention at the 1964 Cannes FF. Similarly, his other titles, such as *The Cowherd's Flute* (1963) and *The Magic Tune* (1988) have received high acclaim both inside and outside China.

Further Reading

ZDX (1982–6: 6: 314–25), a short biography.

(ZX)

Temptation of a Monk, The

(You seng)

dir. Clara **Law**
sc. Eddie Fong, Lilian Lee
with Joan **Chen**, Wu Xingguo, Zhang Fengyi
Hong Kong: Tedpoly Films, 1993

Tang Dynasty Generals Shi and Huo Da become friends. Shi meets Princess 'Scarlet'. Huo claims that the Crown Prince, Shi's master, schemes to kill his brother Shi-min, but Shi-min (Huo's master) actually plots to kill his two brothers. Shi arrives too late to protect the Prince's family after a savage battle.

Before killing herself, Shi's mother makes Shi swear to 'wander' while Shi-min lives. Scarlet asks to accompany him. He and some loyalists become monastery acolytes – Shi, now known as Jing Yi, takes vows – but they disagree on battle plans. Scarlet turns up amongst their number dressed in common clothing. While his followers enjoy themselves, Jing takes Scarlet to the bath for love-making, before being shown a wanted poster with his name on it.

A party come to arrest Jing surprises the men outside the monastery. Scarlet is struck down and all except Jing and a loyalist are killed. Jing departs alone and wanders as far as an isolated temple, where he begs an aged abbot to admit him. A mysterious noblewoman, actually the psychologically unhinged Scarlet in disguise, requests a funeral service for her husband. The woman is ill and so is taken inside to be cured by Jing: he becomes very aroused and later yields to her advances. She tries to kill him during their love-making, but the abbot manages to kill her instead. Huo brings a decree that Jing be promoted Generalissimo at the Palace. Huo's men set fire to the temple after Jing declines the offer – Huo approaches Jing with a sword but is felled by an axe blow to the neck. The film ends when Jing, wandering towards the hills, sees a white horse and rides away on it. This is a beautifully sensuous, if sometimes too deliberate, meditation on discovering life's true simplicity.

Further Reading

T. S. Kam *et al.* (1994–5), a brief discussion.

(KH)

Temptress Moon
(Fengyue)

dir. **Chen Kaige**
sc. Shu Kei
with Leslie **Cheung**, **Gong Li**, Kevin Lin, He Saifei
Hong Kong: Tomson, 1995

Immediately following his award-winning *Farewell My Concubine* (1993), this film of urban seduction and corruption has turned out to be a disappointment for many eager critics and fans of Chen Kaige. In spite of his star-sparkling cast and his good intention of presenting a psychological struggle that would capture the agony of an era, the film fails to engage the viewer for the most part and, instead, delivers a spectacle of splendid sets, elegant camera work and sensuous performance.

Set in the 1920s, which bear a close resemblance to the 1990s in the director's mind, the story follows Zhongliang, a young man from the countryside who arrives in Suzhou, a traditional city, to serve in the household of his opium-addict cousin, Ruyi. Zhongliang leaves to study in Beijing and returns years later as a gigolo employed by Biggie, member of a Shanghai triad. Zhongliang is sent to seduce Ruyi, who is in charge of her clan. The scheme fails because Zhongliang falls in love with Ruyi and has to return to Shanghai. The drama of seduction takes an ironic turn near the end of the film when Biggie brings Ruyi to Shanghai to observe her gigolo lover at work in seducing other women.

If nothing else, Chen's film intensifies a **nostalgia** for Shanghai culture of the 1920s–30s that has been articulated in such titles as *The Actress* (*dir.* Stanley **Kwan**, 1992) and *Shanghai Triad* (*dir.* **Zhang Yimou**, 1995).

(YZ)

Teng Wenji
b. 8 November 1944, Beijing
Director

A prolific mainland director of the 1980s, Teng graduated from the Directing Department of BFA in 1968 and worked for Xi'an Film Studio in 1973. Officially a member of the 'Fourth Generation', Teng's films actually share a number of features common to the work of the **Fifth Generation** directors. Firstly, Teng places great emphasis on the film medium's specific audio-visual qualities: certainly, his directing début, *Reverberations of Life* (*co-dir.* **Wu Tianming**, 1979), helped renovate Chinese cinema in the post-**Cultural Revolution** period. Secondly, the thematic thrust of Teng's films is usually inspired by contemporary intellectual discourse: for example, both *A Village in the Metropolis* (1982) and *On the Beach* (1984) deal with the tensions between tradition and modernity that were at the centre of intellectual debate during the mid-1980s. Finally, like his Fifth Generation colleagues, Teng enjoys high international visibility even though some of his films have failed at the domestic box office: *Ballad of the Yellow River* (1989) won him a Best Director award at the 1990 Montreal FF.

(ZX)

Terrorizer
(Kongbu fenzi)

dir. Edward **Yang**
sc. Xiao Ye, Edward Yang
with Li Liqun, Cora Miao, Wang An
Taipei: CMPC, 1986

A landmark of New Taiwan Cinema, *Terrorizer* is a sophisticated treatment of **urban life** in modern society. The film starts with a crime scene in Taipei. A Eurasian prostitute escapes the police by jumping from a balcony and is sent to hospital by a young photographer. The film then follows Zhou Yufen, a washed-out writer whose relationship with her husband Li Lizhong takes a drastic turn when she receives a prank phone call from the prostitute. Ironically, the call taps Zhou's imagination and she fabricates an award-winning story. The photographer rents the apartment raided by the police and transforms it into a darkroom. The prostitute enters and is surprised to see a giant picture of herself on the wall. The photographer talks to her in monologue. When he wakes up next day, she has disappeared again. Meanwhile, Li is rejected by Zhou and denied a job promotion; he visits his detective friend and they get drunk. Several endings are played out. Li wakes up, goes out to the street, and shoots his boss. The detective is woken up and finds his handgun missing. Li kills Zhou's lover and enters a hotel room with the prostitute. As she pulls out a hidden knife, the detective rushes to the hotel. The gun shots are repeated. This time the detective wakes up to find Li dead in the bathroom. Zhou also wakes up. In bed with her lover, she feels nauseated, and the film ends with her puzzled look.

Terrorizer explores issues of **modernity** by questioning technologies (e.g., camera, telephone, and TV), which do not reduce but add to the sense of urban alienation and unpredictability. It won awards of Best Film at Taipei GHA in 1986, a silver prize at Locarno FF and Best Director at Pesaro FF, both in 1987.

See also: New Taiwan Cinema (under Taiwan cinema in Historical essays)

Further Reading
F. Jameson (1994), a treatise on modernism; Y. Zhang (1994b), a study of rural–urban configurations.

(YZ)

That Day on the Beach
(Haitan shang de yitian)

dir. Edward **Yang**
sc. Edward Yang, **Wu Nien-chen**
with Sylvia **Chang**, Hu Yinmeng, Ma Xuewei, Xu Ming, Li Lei
Taipei: CMPC, 1983

The first feature-length film by Edward Yang, *That Day on the Beach* can also be considered the first 'woman's film' from Taiwan. It depicts the various stages of a woman's fight against patriarchy on the road to finding her own autonomy. The story itself may sound relatively straightforward, but the narrative is quite complicated, especially when compared to most Taiwanese films of the period.

Lin Jiali pays a visit to an internationally known pianist who used to be her brother's lover. The main part of the film then unfolds as Jiali proceeds to recount the story of her life to the pianist. After graduating from college she had eloped with her boyfriend, although, cut off from family support, the couple struggled to build their new life together. They rode the national economic boom of the 1980s and became members of the middle class. Jiali's brother died of overwork and dissatisfaction with his marriage to a woman chosen by their father. As Jiali and her husband became wealthier they began to experience marriage difficulties. Jiali's husband continued to work too much even though suffering from stress and general bad health. She struggled with boredom and the suspicion that her husband was having extramarital affairs. Finally, when their marriage came to a crisis point, the husband went missing. He was last seen at a beach, but his body was never found. The day of her husband's disappearance, however, was also the day that Jiali decided to start her new life, to become a new woman. Yang's film successfully employs a fragmented pattern of storytelling to dramatize the story of one woman's pursuit of independence.

(YY)

theatre and film

Chinese film has been heavily influenced by theatre. Such influence is especially visible in the genre of **filmed stage performances**, in which classic pieces of Peking or other types of operas are restaged in front of the camera and are delivered to audiences nationwide. The influence of the performing arts are found in Chinese filmmakers' emphasis on theatrical acting, dramatic action and exaggerated gestures and facial expressions, as well as characterization of easily distinguished good and bad guys. The modern spoken drama, which was introduced to China via Japan at the turn of the twentieth century, has also left its influence on Chinese film. Due to the popularity of film **adaptations of drama and literature**, Chinese filmmakers pay a great deal of attention to dramatic tension, plot complications, and climactic moments in film narrative. Dialogue is often conceived as an art in itself. Unfortunately, this conception has resulted in a general preference for lengthy dialogue at the expense of other aspects (especially the visual) of film aesthetics in Chinese films. The preference for the theatrical, dramatic, and literary qualities of film has created an imbalance between film as narrative and film as visual art. Since the early 1980s, however, the New Wave directors in Hong Kong (e.g., **Tsui Hark** and **Wong Kar-Wai**), Taiwan (e.g., **Hou**

Hsiao-hsien and Edward **Yang**) and the mainland (**Chen Kaige**, **Tian Zhuangzhuang** and **Zhang Yimou**) have attempted to redress this imbalance. Consequently, a new visual aesthetic of film has gradually come into being in contemporary Chinese cinema.

Further Reading
G. Semsel *et al.* (1990: 1–20), Chinese debates on the theatricality of film.

(YZ)

Third Sister Liu
(Liu sanjie)

dir. Su Li
sc. Qiao Yu
with Huang Wanqiu, Xia Zongxue, Liu Shilong
Changchun: Changchun Film, 1960

Inspired by a Zhuang minority folktale, this cheerful **musical** presents the story of a courageous woman in southwestern China who, during the Tang dynasty, sings folk 'mountain songs' and rebels against oppressive landlords. The film opens with a natural scene of the Li River, one of China's most beautiful resorts. Third Sister Liu has survived an attempted murder by a landlord and is drifting on the river. She is invited by an old fisherman to stay in his riverside village, and Ah Niu, the fisherman's son, falls in love with her.

Soon after her arrival, Liu creates trouble for the local landlord, Mo Huairen. She first breaks his prohibition against collecting tea-leaves; then, knowing that Mo plans to forbid the peasants to sing, challenges him to a musical competition that will determine their right to sing. Her witty, improvised songs defeat the efforts of Mo's literati friends, who have to rely on song books. Mo is publicly humiliated and decides to take his revenge. He kidnaps Liu and locks her up in his mansion. With Ah Niu's help she manages to escape into the night mist of the river, leaving Mo and his servants chasing after her in vain. Next day, under a giant tree, Third Sister Liu expresses her love for Ah Niu by throwing him an embroidered ball.

A clear allegory of the **Communist revolution**, this film of ethnic minorities, like *Serfs* (*dir.* **Li Jun**, 1963), presents minority peoples as participants in class struggle and, therefore, as ideologically identifiable with the Han majority. At a time of strict film censorship, this musical also manages to exoticize **romance** by setting the story in a minority area. A ballet version was directed by **Wu Yonggang** and Chen Zhenghong in 1978.

See also: censorship and film; ethnic minorities, film of

Further Reading
P. Clark (1987b), a survey of films of ethnic minorities; W. Huang (1988), the actress Huang Wanqiu's memoir; W. Loh (1984), a study of folklore sources; Y. Zhang (1997a), a critical study of nationhood and ethnicity.

(PV)

This Life of Mine
(Wo zhe yibeizi)

dir. **Shi Hui**
sc. Yang Liuqing
with Shi Hui, Shen Yang, Cheng Zhi, Wei Heling, Li Wei, Cui Chaoming
Shanghai: Wenhua Film, 1950

By focusing on the tragic life of a policeman, this film is extremely critical of social conditions under the KMT regime. Its happy ending pays obvious tribute to the PRC.

The narrative is told through the first person. 'I' became a policeman in the late Qing period. After the 1911 Revolution, I was assigned to guard a Mr Qin who turned out to be a corrupt official. Although he was removed from his post, I became disillusioned with the prospects for a better society. During the May Fourth Movement, I was acquainted with a student movement leader, Shen Yuan, who brought me new hope and the belief that things might change for the better. But Mr Qin was soon rehabilitated and appointed to an even higher position: when he asked me to arrest Shen Yuan, I gave up on him. My wife died of an illness shortly before the Nanjing government was established. While my daughter was married off, my son also became a policeman. The Japanese came and took my son's sweetheart: he was so angered that he went and joined the CCP resistance force. After the Sino-Japanese war, I was jailed by the Nationalists because my son was with the Communists. During my imprisonment I ran into Shen Yuan once again. He taught me that the solution to the problems faced by poor folk lies

Plate 44   *This Life of Mine* (1950)

in the reformation of the whole of society. Beijing was liberated and my son came home. 'I' was finally able to enjoy my retirement.

(ZX)

Three Modern Women

(San ge modeng nüxing)

dir. **Bu Wancang**
sc. **Tian Han**
with **Ruan Lingyu**, **Jin Yan**, **Chen Yanyan**
Shanghai: Lianhua Film, 1933

This film contrasts the lives of three women and explores the true meaning of being modern. While each of the three protagonists embodies certain traits of modern womanhood, Zhou is presented as an exemplary modern woman who lives a simple life style, is close to the working class, does not indulge in personal affairs, and devotes herself to national causes.

A college student from Manchuria, Zhang Yu, refuses to marry the girl his parents have arranged for him and runs away from home. The would-be bride, Zhou Shuzhen, feels humiliated, but makes up her mind that she will earn respect from people. Three years later, she finishes high school with honours. Meanwhile, Zhang has become a movie star in Shanghai.

The Japanese invasion of Manchuria drives Zhou and her parents to Shanghai. Zhou finds a job as a switch-board operator and learns that Zhang is also living in the city. The Japanese attack on Shanghai in 1932 awakens Zhang's sense of patriotism. He joins the Red Cross so as to be able to take care of wounded soldiers. But when he asks his girl friend, Yu Yu, to become involved also, she declines and tells him that she will soon marry a Hong Kong businessman. Zhang tries to get over Yu by devoting himself to resistance causes. During one rescue mission, he himself is wounded and taken to a hospital where Zhou works as a volunteer. When Zhang is in need of blood for a transfusion, Zhou offers her own. After Zhang recovers, he tries to approach Zhou, but her aloofness frustrates him.

Yu returns from Hong Kong. Her husband has just died of an illness and she wants to resume her relationship with Zhang. Meanwhile, one of

Zhang's fans, Chen Ruoying, who lives in a different city, hears of Zhang's injuries and comes to visit him in Shanghai. Zhang tells Chen that he is in love with someone else, but as a consolation, offers her an opportunity to star in a film with him. However, Chen commits suicide during shooting.

As his relationship with Zhou progresses, Zhang shows her the glamorous side of Shanghai, whereas Zhou takes him to see the city's dark side. During a strike at Zhou's company, Zhou represents the striking workers. She is injured during a fight with the police and fired from her position. But she has earned Zhang's admiration.

Further Reading

Y. Zhang (1994a), a critique of gender politics in the 1930s.

(ZX)

Three Summers

(Gege de qingren)

dir. Lawrence Ah Mon
sc. Sylvia **Chang**, Bill Yip, Lawrence Ah Mon, Cheng Tat Ming
with Tony Chiu-Wai Leung, Ng Sin-lin, Cherie Chan, Veronica Yip
Hong Kong: Paka Hill Film, 1993

This gentle initiation story opens with students making wishes on Tai O island off the Hong Kong coast. Half Pint recalls spending three summers there together with her brother Wai and other love-sick teenagers. Flora, Lam, and Sean are inseparable. Young Half Pint loves Lam, but he leaves for school without being made aware of her feelings. Next summer, criminals threaten Half Pint and Wai, who deny having seen their boss's wife. A 'demon' (actually the morbid Sean) plagues the village. After Wai competes in the dragon-boat race, he goes to meet the boss's wife and they make love. She has left her husband and will not tell Wai her destination. The students play a spin-the-bottle virtues game: Lang is very nice about Flora, but Sean is offended and insults Lang. Flora rejects Sean, who 'prays' madly to her, defaces the school with obscene drawings, makes monkey noises in a tree, and kills Anna's dog. Remembering Flora had a miscarriage, Half Pint calls the summer a 'confusing detective movie'. In the third summer, Half Pint buries the necklace Flora gave her under a tree. She will stay with her aunt in Hong Kong and look for a job. The film ends with Wai

fishing in his boat and nicely conveys a sense of **nostalgia** for the lost innocence of childhood.

(KH, YZ)

thriller

A type of film that creates excitement and suspense, such as the **action film** or **gangster film**. The term may also be used for the **mystery film**, **detective film** or **spy film**.

(YZ)

Ti Lung

(Di Long)

b. 1946, Guangdong province
Actor, director

Ti Lung was educated at Eton School in Hong Kong. After working as a tailor, he auditioned for the lead role in **Chang Che**'s *Dead End* in 1968. Shaw Brothers put him under contract and featured him in films often directed by Chang Che and co-starring David **Chiang**, such as *The Return of the One-Armed Swordsman* (1968), *Vengeance* (1970), *The New One-Armed Swordsman*, *Duel of Fists* (both 1971) and ***Blood Brothers*** (1972), which gained him popularity with Hong Kong audiences. Like Chiang, he also starred in an English-speaking role in the Hammer co-production *Shatter* (1973). In the mid-1970s he briefly joined Chang Che's Taiwan-based film company and appeared in films such as *Five Shaolin Masters* (1975) and *Eight Man Army* (1976). He also directed a series of urban films with social leanings such as *Young Lovers on Flying Wheels* (1974) and *The Young Rebel* (1975).

An experienced martial artist, Ti Lung also appeared in Shaw Brothers adaptations of Gu Long novels. But, like Sammo **Hung**, he links both the first and second Hong Kong New Waves. John **Woo** cast him as the noble Triad Ho in *A **Better Tomorrow*** (1986) and *A Better Tomorrow, II* (1987) for his Shaw Brothers associations. However, Ti Lung is a very versatile actor whose range encompasses **comedy** as well as modern or historical drama, as *Run, Don't Walk* (1989), *First Shot* (1993) and his 1995 television role as Judge Dee reveal. In *First Shot*, the Governor of Hong Kong applauds Lung's character for embodying true Chinese values.

(TW)

Tian Fang

b. 3 January 1911, Baoding, Hebei province
d. 27 August 1974
Actor and producer

A noted actor turned film administrator, Tian Fang attended Furen University in Beijing and began working for Tianyi Film Company in 1931. Initially employed to teach other actors how to speak standard Mandarin, he was soon offered his own part in *Willow Catkin* (*dir.* **Tang Xiaodan**, 1933). Tian subsequently starred in a number of other Tianyi productions, including *Struggle* (*dir.* Qiu Qixiang, 1933), *The Land of Fortune* (*dir.* **Shao Zuiweng**, 1933) and *Sea Burial* (*dir.* Wang Bin, 1935). In 1935, Tian played the lead male protagonist in Xinhua Film Company's first major production, *A Knight-Errant Named Hongyang* (*dir.* **Yang Xiaozhong**, 1935).

During the Sino-Japanese war, Tian went to Yan'an and joined the CCP. He took on several stage roles as well as some administrative responsibilities. After the Japanese surrender, Tian led a team sent to take charge of Manchurian Motion Pictures. After 1949, Tian helped organize Beijing Film Studio and became its first general manager. He also served as Associate Director of the Film Bureau and Vice-President of All China Filmmakers' Association. Despite his numerous administrative responsibilities Tian still managed to star in another half-dozen films, including ***Revolutionary Family*** (*dir.* **Shui Hua**, 1961) and ***Heroic Sons and Daughters*** (*dir.* Wu Zhaodi, 1964). Tian suffered political persecution during the **Cultural Revolution** and died in 1974.

Further Reading
ZDX (1982–6: 1: 37–46), a short biography.

(ZX)

Tian Han

b. 12 March 1898, Hunan province
d. 10 December 1968
Screen writer, playwright

One of the most prominent writers of modern China, Tian Han greatly influenced Chinese cinema by contributing a large number of screenplays, especially during the 1930s. He became interested in film while still a student in Japan. By 1926 he had begun to write and produce films, although none of his earliest work is particularly

significant. Tian was always a politically engaged, high-profile leftist intellectual. He joined the CCP in 1932 and became an active participant in the League of Chinese Leftist Writers.

Tian wrote numerous screenplays advocating Communist ideology. Centred on issues of **nationalism**, class struggle and social justice, his work constituted the heart of 1930s leftist cinema. Tian wrote the lyrics for 'The Marching of the Volunteers', initially the theme song of *Children of Troubled Times* (*dir.* Xu Xingzhi, 1935), but later adopted as the PRC national anthem. During the Sino-Japanese war, Tian wrote three more scripts, only one of which was actually turned into a completed film. In the post-war years, two of Tian's scripts were filmed: *A Tale of Two Girls* (*dir.* **Ying Yunwei**, Wu Tian, 1947) and ***Female Fighters*** (*dir.* **Chen Liting**, 1949).

After 1949, Tian was a member of the National Political Consultative Committee and the First National Congress. He was also in charge of the bureau for the arts under the Ministry of Culture and served as chairman of the Association of Chinese Dramatists. During the 1950s–60s, Tian primarily focused his creative energies on the writing of historical dramas, demonstrating once and for all that he was an accomplished dramatist as well as a distinguished screenwriter. Tian was persecuted during the **Cultural Revolution** and died in jail in 1968.

Further Reading
H. Tian (1981), a memoir; ZDX (1982–6: 2: 55–67), a short biography.

(ZX)

Tian Hua

(Liu Tianhua)

b. 3 August 1928
Actress, producer

A famous actress of the 1950s–60s, Tian came from a poor peasant family. She was recruited by an Eighth Route Army theatre troupe in 1940 and changed her name to Tian Hua. ·

Tian had been active on stage before making her first film appearance in *The **White-Haired Girl*** (*dir.* Wang Bin, **Shui Hua**, 1950). Her portrayal of the peasant girl in this film won her an Individual Achievement award from the Ministry of Culture in 1957. After performing in many other productions, Tian studied acting at

Central Academy of Drama between 1955 and 1957. Upon graduation, she starred in *The Full Moon* (*dir.* Guo Wei) and *Daughter of the Party* (*dir.* **Lin Nong**, both 1958). She officially joined August First Film Studio in 1959 and has worked there ever since. Amongst the August First titles, **Secret Document** (*dir.* Hao Guang, 1965) contains her most mature performance of the pre-**Cultural Revolution** period. Tian has appeared in over a dozen films since the late 1970s, among them the critically acclaimed *The Trial* (*dir.* Cong Lianwen, Lu Xiaoya, 1980) and *Xu Mao and His Daughters* (*dir.* **Li Jun**, 1981). Tian is currently the general manager of August First Film Studio.

Further Reading

ZDX (1982–6: 5: 84–96), a short biography.

(ZX)

Tian Zhuangzhuang

b. 1952, Beijing
Director

A leading figure in the **Fifth Generation**, Tian Zhuangzhuang was born into a film family. His father **Tian Fang** was a well-known actor from the 1930s and veteran Communist who served as first director of Beijing Film Studio in the 1950s. His mother **Yu Lan**, a popular star of the 1950s–60s, became head of Beijing Children's Film Studio in the 1980s. Tian Zhuangzhuang was lucky enough to sit in on censorship screenings when he was young. He was sent to the country-side in Jilin province in 1968 and later joined the army. He managed to return to Beijing and find work as an assistant cinematographer at Agricultural Film Studio, where he participated in **documentary** and educational projects. He studied in the Directing Department of BFA in 1978–82 and co-directed a student video-film, *Our Corner* (1980) with Xie Xiaojing and Cui Xiaoqiu. After graduation he was assigned to Beijing Film Studio but did not get the chance to direct a film there until 1987. In the meantime, he produced a five-part TV series, *The Summer Experience* (1983), and made various films for other studios. Among these, *Red Elephant* (1982), co-directed with **Zhang Jianya** and Xie Xiaojing, is a **children's film** made for Children's Film Studio in Beijing, and *September* (1984) is a **melodrama** shot for Kunming Film Studio.

Tian attracted critical attention with **On the Hunting Ground** (1985), a documentary-style feature about the enigmatic hunting codes of Inner Mongolian society. This highly experimental film sold only four prints, inflicting huge losses on Inner Mongolia Film Studio. Tian's equally experimental **Horse Thief** (1986), commissioned by Xi'an Studio's ambitious director **Wu Tianming**, did not fare much better at the box office; in fact, it provoked criticism from old-timers who accused Tian of neglecting or despising the contemporary audience. From a historical perspective, Tian's angry rebuttal – namely, that his films are meant for sophisticated audiences of the twentieth-first century – proved highly ironic, partly because many of his subsequent features are definite crowd-pleasers, and partly because by the 1990s he himself had come to regret his controversial statement. He shot a conventional film based on Lao She's novel, **Drum Singers** (1987), for Beijing Film Studio, and for Youth Film Studio he made **Rock 'n' Roll Kids** (1988), an entertainment film aimed at the urban youth market. Supported by Hong Kong financiers, he directed **Li Lianying: The Imperial Eunuch** (1991), which bears a stronger resemblance to Hong Kong director **Li Han-hsiang**'s historical films than to Tian's earlier work. In addition, Tian has reportedly made *Illegal Lives* (1990), a film that has not yet been released in China, and composed the music for his *Horse Thief* and **Chen Kaige**'s **King of the Children** (1987) and **Life on a String** (1991). For most of his own features, Tian has relied on Hou Yong (*b.* 1960), a classmate from the Cinematography Department of BFA, as cinematographer.

The variety of such creative activity fully demonstrates the range of Tian's eclectic taste. As he once told a reporter, he likes Italian neo-realism, Antonioni, **Hou Hsiao-hsien**, Ozu and many other celebrated filmmakers. In the late 1980s, he turned from an exclusive interest in the formal beauty of film (shared by other directors of his generation, like Chen Kaige and **Zhang Yimou**) to the pursuit of sincere, psychologically sophisticated portrayals of common people. The change in style, already manifest in **Family Portrait** (*dir.* **Li Shaohong**, 1992), a film he produced for Taiwan's Era International, is more directly reflected in his own controversial epic, *The* **Blue Kite** (1993), co-produced with Hong Kong. Because of its sensitive subject matter (the **Cultural Revolution**) and the fact that it was exhibited overseas without first gaining government approval, the film was banned in the mainland: Tian himself was prohibited from making any more films until 1996. On the other hand, *The Blue Kite* was a major international hit. In 1993 it won the Grand Prize at Tokyo FF, the Hawaii East-West Center Award, and an award from the Society of Film Critics in New York. The film was widely distributed in Europe and North America.

See also: avant-garde, experimental or exploratory film; censorship and film; historical film

Further Reading

K. Eder and D. Rossell (1993: 104–8), with an interview; D. Gladney (1995), on Tian and films of ethnic minorities; P. Lopate (1994), a critical interview; T. Rayns (1989: 39–43), an analysis of Tian's early works; G. Semsel (1987: 128–33), an interview; R. Sklar (1994), an interview; Z. Tian (1989), the director's own reflections.

(YZ, ZX)

Time to Live, a Time to Die, A

(Tongnian wangshi)

dir. **Hou Hsiao-hsien**
sc. **Chu Tien-wen**, Hou Hsiao-hsien
with You Anshun, Xin Shufen, Tien Feng, Mei Fang
Taipei: CMPC, 1985

An autobiographical film from Hou Hsiao-hsien, *A Time to Live, a Time to Die* is perhaps the single best film produced in Taiwan up until 1985. As the Chinese title, 'Childhood Stories', indicates, the film documents the life of Ah Hao (a shortened name for the young Hou Hsiao-hsien himself) from childhood to teenage years. Separation, illness, violence, sex and death mark the key points of Ah Hao's youthful experiences. The film tries to present these experiences as part of a natural, coincidental course of events rather than as a chain of causality. In order to achieve this, Hou uses temporal ellipses to organize the narrative rather than strict linear progressions. He also uses long shots in many scenes involving violence in order to reduce their dramatic potential. These stylistic devices work to support the theme of the representation of memory, as recollections here seem fragmentary and incomplete.

Despite telling such a personal story, however, the film resonates with the life experiences of many other Taiwanese people. It is full of moments that suggest life is like a circle in which death and

growth occur simultaneously. Ah Hao's father dies suddenly on a dark stormy night when the protagonist has just turned thirteen and does not yet know how to grieve. His mother tells him she has cancer on the night he experiences his first ejaculation. Profundities jostle cheek-by-jowl with absurdities, subverting the border between the mundane and the sublime. In its mixing of history and personal memory, Hou's film aspires to the status of epic, thus initiating the shift in emphasis towards the historical concerns of his Taiwan trilogy.

Further Reading

G. Cheshire (1993), an excellent analysis of Hou's films; H. Chiao (1993b), an interview with critical comments.

(YY)

Ting Shan-hsi

(Ding Shanxi)

b. 1936
Director, screen writer

Ting Shan-hsi graduated from the Screenplay and Directing Department of National Taiwan College of Arts and entered Shaw Brothers in 1963. After writing several film scripts he returned to Taiwan in 1968 to start his directing career. He has made more than sixty films. His *Martyrs* (1974) won Best Screenplay and *Bloodstained Yellow Flowers* (1980) Best Director awards at Asian Film Festivals; *Battle for the Republic of China* (1982) won Best Film award at Taipei GHA. His other noted works include *Qiu Jin* (1972) and *Eight Hundred Heroic Soldiers* (1975).

Further Reading

R. Huang (1994: 388), a brief entry.

(YZ)

To Live (Huozhe)

dir. **Zhang Yimou**
sc. Yu Hua, Lu Wei
with Ge You, **Gong Li**
Hong Kong: Era/Shanghai: Shanghai Film, 1994

An epic film comparable to **Farewell My Concubine** (*dir.* **Chen Kaige**, 1993) and *The Blue Kite* (*dir.* **Tian Zhuangzhuang**, 1993), *To Live* uses one family's continuous struggle for survival as the microcosm of a modern China wrenched by a series of socio-political upheavals. A shadow-puppet play ties the segments of this family **melodrama** together. As the film opens, Fugui is addicted to gambling, and his predicament foreshadows the family's downfall. In the gambling house, with the puppet show in the background and Qinqiang tunes (local opera popular in the Shaanxi region) on the sound track, Fugui finally runs through the family fortune, losing the ancestral mansion and all their possessions. Fugui's pregnant wife eventually leaves him, taking their daughter with her.

Ironically, this shattering loss proves to be the family's salvation. Fugui witnesses the new owner of his mansion being executed because he is a landlord, while his new identity as puppet player and local opera singer earns him working-class membership status. Upon returning to his family from the battlefields of the civil war, Fugui enables them to survive an absurd society that promises a bright future but instead inflicts one disaster after another.

The tragic deaths of Fugui's two children underscore the chaos and irrationality of life in China. During the Great Leap Forward anything made of steel, even cooking pots and farm implements, is melted down in a futile effort to boost China's steel production. The couple's son, Youqing, an elementary school pupil assigned to participate in this collective work effort, is killed when a car driven by a local official hits the wall behind which the exhausted boy is sleeping. During the **Cultural Revolution**, when doctors are persecuted, the couple's daughter Fengxia dies while giving birth to the family's grandchild. The young Red Guards staffing the hospital cannot handle the complications of Fengxia's labour, while the doctor, ostracized and made to wear a placard on his chest, passes out after ravenously gorging seven bread rolls out of sheer starvation. The film intercuts scenes of birth and death, food and hunger, but still manages to end on a positive note: 'Life will get better when you have grown up,' Fugui tells his grandson, Little Bun, as they walk back from the graves of Fugui's daughter and son, who never knew such a life.

To Live received the Grand Jury prize and Best Actor (Ge You) award at the 1994 Cannes FF.

(SC)

Tonight Nobody Goes Home
(Jintian bu huijia)

dir. Sylvia **Chang**
sc. Kang Lee
with Lung Sihung, Gua Ah-Leh, Winston Chao
Taipei: Unique Films, 1996

This CMPC-invested family **melodrama** aimed to attract the Taiwan audience back to domestic productions, which had decreased to a dismal level by the mid-1990s. The screen writer Kang Lee (Li Gang) followed his brother Ang **Lee**'s formula for urban **comedy**, and the veteran filmmaker Sylvia Chang directed attention to a dysfunctional **family** in modern-day Taipei.

The father openly indulges in an extra-marital affair with a young woman. The mother feels indignant and goes out to seek comfort in a gigolo bar run by her son. The son has failed in several business ventures and is always planning ahead for some grand projects. He cares very little when his mother hooks up with a 'cowboy' in his bar. The daughter has been living with her boyfriend for some time and is questioning the wisdom of formally getting married.

Once the disintegration of the family reaches the point of seemingly no return, the film reverses the course of action and surprises the audience – as Ang Lee's films do – by leading the family members back home one by one, except for the son who has fled overseas to avoid paying his debts. The homecoming begins with the daughter, followed by the father. The mother is next to return when the father falls sick and is hospitalized. As if to prove that women are after all more 'virtuous' than men, the film lets the daughter withdraw her personal savings and clear her brother's debts, thus leaving the possibility that he, too, will eventually return home. Even more surprising is the daughter's decision to get married and stay with her parents, in spite of the messy family life the film is eager to dramatize in the first place.

(YZ)

Touch of Zen, A
(Xia nü)

dir./sc. King **Hu**
with Shih Chun, **Hsu Feng**, Bai Ying, Roy Chiao
Taiwan: Union Film, 1970

A Touch of Zen is the greatest achievement of Taiwan cinema, approaching the unusual realm of **art film** status in a highly commercialized industry. The Chinese title, 'The Magnanimous Girl', is based on the similarly titled story from Pu Songling's famous collection *Strange Stories from a Chinese Studio*. King Hu has extended the story about the initial relationship between poor scholar Ku and a mysterious girl who moves near him into an epic drama set in Northern China during the Ming dynasty.

Like *Dragon Gate Inn* (1967) and *The Valiant Ones* (1975), *A Touch of Zen* deals with conflicts between honour and treachery in a turbulent political era. But King Hu paints an epic artistic canvas in which different characters move across time and space within personal, political, and spiritual relationships. Although the film covers similar territory to *Dragon Gate Inn*, involving a persecuted family's flight from the Eastern clan, King Hu uses three different levels of narrative, beginning with the world of nature and moving into a transcendental realm.

The film opens with shots of a spider's web trapping various insects – a beautiful metaphor for the dangerous game affecting everyone. Scholar Ku becomes intrigued by strange sounds from an abandoned fort near where he lives with his mother. He discovers a mysterious girl and her mother living there, fugitives from the Eastern clan. Aided by loyal patriots and Buddhist monk Hui, she escapes. But all characters face a final battle between the forces of good and evil in a world where the spiritual and material forces must always exist in uneasy cohesion. A visually beautiful film impossible to summarize.

(TW)

Transmigration

aka *Samsara* (Lunhui)

dir. **Huang Jianxin**
sc. Wang Shuo
with Lei Han, Tan Xiaoyan
Xi'an: Xi'an Film, 1988

This film's ending encapsulates its meditation on the nature of human identity. The camera pans from a photo of a naked baby boy on the wall to a crippled man, Shiba, gazing intently at his self-image in the mirror. With a violent smashing sound, the mirror becomes shards of glass on the floor. The man adjusts a lamp to project his shadow on the blank wall. His silhouette appears larger than life: two fists rising up from a lean masculine body. He then steps out onto a balcony overlooking the street. After a series of shots/reverse shots of him and the moon, he jumps over the rail and falls into the darkness. Chinese subtitles then explain that Shiba's wife gives birth to a boy named Shi Xiaoba (i.e., Little Shiba) six months later. The baby in the photo, the male image on the wall, the death of the man, and the birth of his son thus complete a cycle – a process of finding oneself during a moment of loss.

Shiba has been soul-searching so as to rebel against the past, yet he is unable to find new meaning in life. A generation of lost urban youth in contemporary China is defined by alienation and disaffection. In Beijing, a man wanders the subway following an unknown young woman for adventure. We find out his name is Shiba from the voice message on his answer-machine, and we meet him again at a dinner party. Numerous guests who do not know each other come to his house. Shiba's involvement with illegal business brings him money but also threats. To his male friends Shiba is a successful entrepreneur; to the girl he stalks he is a hoodlum.

The question of who Shiba really is continues to be posed through his relationship with a beautiful dance student. From Yujing's perspective, Shiba is hardly an ideal male figure, despite his wit and personality. The son of high-ranking Communist cadres, Shiba once served in the navy. But the death of his parents and the failures of the socialist system transform him into an anti-hero who believes in nothing but himself. Thus he makes a fetish out of individual difference: the use of language, fashion, one's behaviour. Shiba finally wins Yujing's interest. 'He is a real man,' she says.

Shiba paints the walls of his house red to suggest his love for Yujing, but the colour comes to signify a bloody blackmail. Some gang members power-drill screws into Shiba's leg when he refuses to give them money. Now a cripple, Shiba refuses to see Yujing any more and paints his house black. Yujing finds him and they marry, but happiness remains elusive. Shiba's efforts to maintain essential human dignity always end in alienation. Yujing exchanges her promising career for a meaningless marriage. Finally, Yujing explodes: 'Stop cheating me and yourself. You have never loved anyone but yourself.' Shiba slaps her face and shuffles away to the living room where he ends his life: a dark picture of post-socialist nihilism.

Further Reading

P. Pickowicz (1994), a study of post-socialism; Y. Wang (1991), a discussion of representation of self.

(SC)

Trouble Shooters, The

(Wan zhu)

dir. Mi Jiashan
sc. Wang Shuo, Mi Jiashan
with Zhang Guoli, Liang Tian, Li Geng, Ge You, Ma Xiaoqing, **Pan Hong**
Chengdu: Emei Film, 1988

This film is a satire of the post-Mao social reality. A profound cynicism is what distinguishes this film from many contemporary Chinese titles.

Three unemployed young men, Yu, Yang, and Ma, set up a company called 3T Co. Ltd. and provide services tailored to their customers' needs. A doctor calls them for help because he has an emergency case and cannot go to meet his blind date. The company sends Yang to comfort the girl. But the girl immediately falls for Yang, who has to call Yu and Ma to his rescue. A mediocre writer wants to feel good about himself and asks 3T people to organize an award ceremony for him. But none of the well-known writers who are invited to the ceremony shows up. So Yu passes the celebrity name tags to whoever is present for the fashion show, which is part of the award giving ceremony. In the end, the writer receives a large pickle jug as the award for his literary achievement.

An ethics professor confides his interest in women to the three young men, but the next day, he ridicules them during a public speech. One day, Yu is assigned to accompany an old lady whose children have left her in hospital. In despair the old lady commits suicide, and Yu is blamed for his negligence. Meanwhile, the writer files a law suit against the 3T Co. on the ground that the company has made illegal profits through his award ceremony. In response, the neighbourhood party branch suspends the operations of the 3T Co. and orders the three men to pay the family members of the old lady. In a desperate attempt to find money, Yu offers himself up to a film crew as a stunt man, but is turned down because his asking price is too high. Just as the three men are

at a loss as to what to do next, they see a long line of people waiting outside the front entrance to their company.

Further Reading

P. Pickowicz (1995), a brief discussion of the film.

(ZX)

True Hearted, The

aka *Heartstrings* (Xin xiang)

dir. **Sun Zhou**
sc. Miao Yue, Sun Zhou
with Wang Yumei, Zhu Xu, Fei Yang
Guangzhou: Pearl River Film, 1992

A close associate of the **Fifth Generation** directors, Sun Zhou focuses on everyday life and ordinary people in contemporary China. The film unfolds the relationship between Grandpa and his long separated grandson. Shown from the boy's point of view, the film considers questions of love and communication between different generations, genders, and traditions in a modern society.

Peking opera frames the story – the film starts and ends with opera performances – and provides a backdrop for the characters. In preparation for divorce, Jingjing's mother decides to send him to her father, a well-known opera singer in the south. His parents see Jingjing off at the train station as the camera shifts from one to the other, indicating their split relationship.

At first, Jingjing's life with Grandpa, whom he has never met before, is rife with conflict and misunderstanding. As he observes the love-relationship between Grandpa and an elderly woman, Liangu, Jingjing gradually changes. Liangu has been a fan of Grandpa and takes care of him after Grandma dies. Grandpa and Liangu are in love but continue to live separately. One day they learn that Liangu's husband, who fled to Taiwan forty years before and rebuilt a family there, plans to visit his mainland hometown. Gossip flares and Grandpa seeks strength in singing opera. Liangu's husband dies before his expected arrival, however, and Liangu succumbs to illness. The scenes of love and caring unto death make a deep impression on Jingjing, who learns to care for Grandpa and befriends a neighbour's girl.

When he recovers from Liangu's death, Grandpa tries to sell his opera fiddle to collect money for a ritual funeral for Liangu and her husband. Jingjing takes the street as a stage, articulating his emotions through opera-singing. Grandpa's instrument and Jingjing's voice reverberate with the beauty of human love, their heartstrings in harmony. The film ends with Grandpa biding farewell to Jingjing as the latter leaves for the north again.

(SC)

True Story of Ah Q, The

(A Q zhengzhuan)

dir. Cen Fan
sc. **Chen Baichen**
with Yan Shunkai, Li Wei, Jin Yikang, Wang Suya
Shanghai: Shanghai Film, 1981

Adapted from Lu Xun's short story of the same title, this film portrays a man whose many shortcomings are meant to reflect the Chinese 'national character'. His self deceptions, his down-to-earth understanding of revolutionary changes, and his duplicitous actions are all stressed by the filmmakers.

A man named Ah Q is the habitual object of ridicule by his villagers. Although he does not even have a family name, when a local gentry's son passes the civil service examination, he claims his name as his own as a result of his family's inherited genes. Members of the gentry family are so offended by this outlandish claim that they slap him in the face until he apologizes. Ah Q wants to marry one of the maids working for the gentry family, but he can't afford a wedding. In an effort to make money, he goes to a gambling house, but is robbed of all his winnings. Fortunately, he is then hired by the gentry family and has the opportunity to meet the maid whom he intends to marry. His clumsy proposition scares her, however, and she accuses him of harassment. Ah Q is fired. He next travels to a nearby city in search of work: later, when he returns to the village with a small fortune, he is envied by some and suspected of being a thief by others.

The news of the 1911 Revolution makes the well-to-do families nervous. Ah Q, on the other hand, openly exhibits his enthusiasm, which makes some people take him to be a revolutionary. Before long, though, the local gentry have all joined the revolution and Ah Q is left the odd one out. Through a bizarre turn of events, Ah Q is accused of robbery and sentenced to death. Without even knowing what all this means, he signs a confession and is taken off to be executed.

The film won Best Actor award (Yan Shunkai) at the 1983 HFA.

(ZX)

Tsai Ming-liang

(Cai Mingliang)

b. 1958, Malaysia
Director

Tsai Ming-liang grew up in an ethnic Chinese family in Malaysia and graduated from the Drama and Cinema Department of Taiwan's Chinese Culture University in 1982. Over the last decade he has established himself as a leading figure of the 'second-wave' of Taiwan's New Cinema. His feature début, **Rebel of the Neon God** (1992), attracted critical attention for its depiction of a group of alienated Taipei youth hemmed in by life in the modern metropolis. Hsiao-kang, a rebellious son kicked out of the family by his father, reappears in Tsai's **Vive l'amour** (1994), another study of a depressed teenager and a lovesick young woman who can find no meaning in their aimless urban existence. The influence of Hong Kong **art film** director **Wong Kar-Wai** on Tsai's work is most apparent here. The film won a Golden Lion award at the 1994 Venice FF. In the third of Tsai's Taipei trilogy, *The River* (1997), Hsiao-kang returns to confront his father – a hopeful scenario barely glimpsed in Tsai's two previous films. All Tsai's urban characters have no meaningful life to cling to and commit various 'irrational' acts ranging from vandalism, theft, and gang activity, to crossdressing, masturbation and attempted suicide.

In addition to films, Tsai has directed several TV dramas in Taiwan, such as *All Corners of the World* (1989) and *Youngsters* (1991), both of which describe the miserable, even tragic situations within which urban youth have to struggle as they grow up. Tsai also made a videotape in the mid-1990s, *My New Friends*, Taiwan's first AIDS **documentary**, which is full of psychological and sociological insights.

See also: Taiwan cinema (in Historical essays); urban life

Further Reading

C. Berry (1995b), a critical study; M. Cai (1994), the script of *Vive l'amour* with reviews and an interview;

J. Hwang (1995), a short interview; C. Stephens (1996a), a perceptive analysis of Tsai's work.

(YZ)

Tseng Chuang-hsiang

(Zeng Zhuangxiang)

b. 1947
Director

An early figure in New Taiwan Cinema, Tseng Chuang-hsiang grew up in Hong Kong, attended the Foreign Languages Department of Taiwan University and received his MA in Film Studies from the University of Texas, Austin. He wrote film reviews for Hong Kong newspapers and came to Taiwan to shoot **documentary** films in 1982. He directed the second episode, *Xiao Qi's Hat*, of the three-part **Sandwich Man** (1983) and received critical acclaim. His other works include *The Flute Sound in the Mist* (1984) and *The* **Woman of Wrath** (1984).

See also: New Taiwan Cinema (under Taiwan cinema in Historical essays)

(YZ)

Tsui Hark

(Xu Ke)

b. 15 February 1951, Vietnam
Director, producer, actor

After growing up in Vietnam, Tsui Hark moved to Hong Kong in 1966 and started taking film classes at the University of Texas, Austin in 1969. He worked at a Chinese cable television station in New York City in the mid-1970s before returning to Hong Kong and making an important television mini-series, *The Gold Dagger Romance*, in 1978. With the release of his early feature films, *The Butterfly Murders* (1979), *Dangerous Encounter – First Kind* and *We're Going To Eat You* (both 1980), Tsui Hark earned his reputation as the *wunderkind* of the Hong Kong New Wave. His early work is ground-breaking, in terms both of subject matter and style – not to mention box-office records. With his partner, Nansun Shi, Tsui formed the Film Workshop production company in 1984 which, under a tight regime of managerial control, quickly established itself as one of the major players on the Hong Kong movie scene.

Tsui Hark's work rate is astonishing. While critics perceive his output to be erratic in terms of quality, there is no doubting the quantity. His filmography oscillates between period titles (**Peking Opera Blues**, 1986; *Green Snake*, 1993) and contemporary dramas (*Twin Dragons*, 1991; *The Master*, 1992). He has worked in **comedy** (*Aces Go Places*, *III*, 1984), martial arts (**Once Upon a Time in China**, 1991), fantasy (*Zu: Warriors From the Magic Mountain*,1982), and action genres (*A Better Tomorrow, III*, 1989). Tsui has also produced some of the most internationally popular of all modern Hong Kong titles, including *A* **Better Tomorrow** (*dir.* John **Woo**, 1986), *A* **Chinese Ghost Story** (**Ching Siu Tung**, 1987) and *The Wicked City* (*dir.* Mak Tai Kit, 1992). Despite all their faults, such films epitomize an inventive, dynamic and crowd-pleasing cinema of attractions.

Tsui Hark won Best Director award at Taipei GHA in 1981. He followed in the footsteps of some of his Hong Kong colleagues (e.g., John **Woo**, Ringo **Lam**, Ronny Yu) by making the move to Hollywood. His Jean-Claude Van Damme action title, *Double Team* (1997), hedges its bets but should still secure him further commissions. Apart from his status as a genuine cult director, Tsui Hark can also claim the distinction of being one of the few filmmakers to be immortalized in song by a decent pop group (cf. 'Tsui Hark' on Sparks' 1995 CD *Gratuitous Sax and Senseless Violins*).

See also: action film; fantasy film; martial arts film

Further Reading
P. Aufderheide (1988), C. Reid (1995a), two career overviews; C. Li (1993b), on Western interest in Tsui; T. Kam (1996), on Tsui and the censors.

(JS)

Tunnel Warfare

(Didao zhan)

dir. Ren Xudong
sc. Ren Xudong, Pan Yunshan, Wang Junlan, Xu Guoteng
with Wang Binghuo, Zhu Longguang, Zhang Yongshou, Liu Xiujie, Wang Lizong
Beijing: August First Film, 1965

An education **war film** showcasing guerrilla warfare tactics used against the Japanese, *Tunnel Warfare* aspires to demonstrate how peasants can learn from Chairman Mao's teachings to become invincible in all forms of warfare. The story takes place in 1942. An entire village in Central China unites to transform its defensive tunnels into offensive weapons. Originally used merely as hiding places, the tunnels are re-routed to strategic locations in the village, enabling the inhabitants to shoot their enemies without being seen. The tunnels are connected to those in other villages and eventually extend beneath the enemy's own battalion. After initial setbacks, the villagers work with local guerrilla units to trap the Japanese soldiers in an open field. The film ends with the guerilla leader's execution of the Japanese captain and the villagers' celebration of their complete victory under Mao's guidance. *Tunnel Warfare* best illustrates the close links that exist between **propaganda and film** in mainland China.

See also: education film

(PV, YZ)

Twenty-Four Hours in Shanghai

(Shanghai ershisi xiaoshi)

dir. **Shen Xiling**
sc. **Xia Yan**
with Gu Lanjun, Chen Qiuning, **Zhao Dan**
Shanghai: Mingxing Film, 1933

This representative leftist film supposedly 'records' a 'typical' day in Shanghai by contrasting the lives of the working class with those of the capitalists. While the former live in poor conditions but maintain their moral dignity, the latter are decadent, hypocritical and ruthless.

It is four o'clock in the afternoon and a child labourer has been injured in Mr Zhou's factory. In need of money for a doctor, the child's brother Chen goes to Mr Zhou's residence to look for his wife, who works there as a maid, in the hope that she may have some. Chen is astonished to see Mrs Zhou paying more than thirty yuan to a doctor for treatment for her dog. Chen's unemployed friend, Zhao, angry with such social injustice and economic disparity, breaks into Mr Zhou's home. Meanwhile, after having dinner, going to the theatre, and visiting a gambling house with his mistress, Mr Zhou brings her to a dance hall where they run into Mrs Zhou and her lover. Everybody pretends to be terribly civilized. The police investigation of the burglary leads to Chen's arrest as a suspect because of his visit to Zhou's residence the night before the incident. Chen's wife is also

fired as a result of her husband's alleged crime. As Zhao generously distributes his loot among family and friends, Mr Zhou is conducting an illegitimate business deal: he sells imported goods with a label that reads 'Made in China'.

The injured boy finally dies dues to a lack of proper medical care and Zhao learns of Chen's wrongful imprisonment. Tormented by his conscience, Zhao turns himself in so as to clear Chen of all charges. Chen is released, but saddened that his brother is gone. It is four o'clock again. Another day in Shanghai begins.

See also: leftist film (under Chinese cinema in Historical essays)

(ZX)

Twin Sisters

(Zimei hua)

dir./sc. **Zheng Zhengqiu**
with **Hu Die**, Zheng Xiaoqiu, Tan Zhiyuan, Xuan Jinglin
Shanghai: Mingxing Film, 1933

Like many leftist films of the same period, *Twin Sisters* exhibits a concern for social justice by contrasting the lives of two siblings. In depicting people with wealth and power as decadent, corrupt, cruel and evil, and poor folk as honest, caring, and hardworking, the film takes a clear anti-establishment stand.

Mr Zhao is an illegal arms dealer who seldom stays with his wife and their twin daughters, Dabao and Erbao. After Zhao's release from jail, he is eager to leave the village again. Mrs Zhao, fearing she will not be able to support both children, begs him to take one of them with him, and so Zhao takes Erbao. Years later Erbao has become the seventh wife of a warlord, whereas Dabao is married to a carpenter and still lives in the village with her mother. The collapse of the rural economy forces them to flee the countryside and move to the city. Erbao also happens to be living in the city and is looking for a nanny for her newborn son. Dabao comes for the job, even though her own baby is also in need of care. The twin sisters – one a mistress, the other a servant – do not even recognize each other.

One day Dabao's husband falls off a roof while working. To pay his hospital bills, Dabao begs Erbao to give her a loan; instead, she gets a slap in the face from Erbao. In desperation, Dabao steals a gold ornament from Erbao's baby, but she is seen by Erbao's sister-in-law. Dabao panics and tries to escape, but she accidentally stumbles over a huge vase which then falls on Erbao's sister-in-law's head and kills her. Dabao is arrested for murder and put in jail.

Her mother comes to visit her in prison and accidentally runs into Mr Zhao, her former husband, who is in charge of Dabao's case. Zhao is now the garrison commander because he had given Erbao to the warlord. Mrs Zhao threatens that if he does not release Dabao, she will reveal his past. Since the victim is the warlord's sister, Zhao has received orders from him to punish Dabao severely: therefore, Zhao does not want to jeopardize his future by giving Dabao a light sentence. In the end, it is Erbao who brings her twin sister and mother to see the warlord, leaving Mr Zhao alone in his office.

See also: leftist film (under Chinese cinema in Historical essays)

(ZX)

U

Under the Bridge
(Da qiao xiamian)

dir. Bai Chen
sc. Bai Chen, Ling Qiwei, Zhu Tian
with Gong Xue, Wang Pin, Ji Mengshi
Shanghai: Shanghai Film, 1983

This is a film about the lives of ordinary people. Its main concern is to criticize traditional 'feudalistic' views, particularly the notion of chaste womanhood. The film also implicitly alludes to the impact the **Cultural Revolution** has made on people's lives.

Qin Nan, a youth just returned to Shanghai, makes her living as a tailor. She is having difficulty finding an appropriate place to set up shop. Her neighbour, Gao Zhihua, who has also just returned from the countryside, offers her a place next to his bicycle repair shop. Because of their similar backgrounds, the two soon develop a liking for each other. Gao's mother, in particular, hopes the relationship will lead to marriage. But when Qin brings her young son from the countryside, she becomes the subject of gossip and speculation. The boy is seen as an indication of Qin's morally dubious past. In the light of her illegitimate son, Gao's mother finds her hard to accept, but Gao has fallen in love with Qin and decided to disregard her past. His sincerity moves Qin – she then reveals to him that when she lived in the countryside she had a relationship with a man and became pregnant. The man later went to Canada and was never heard from again. Gao assures her that they will leave the past behind and start anew.

In 1983–4 the film won awards of Best Actress (Gong Xue) at both China GRA and HFA, as well as Best Film from the Ministry of Culture.

(ZX)

Uproar in Heaven
(Da'nao tiangong)

dir. **Wan Laiming**
sc. Li Keruo, Wan Laiming
Shanghai: Shanghai Animation, 1961 (first part), 1964 (second part)

Based on a well-known episode from the classic novel *Journey to the West*, *Uproar in Heaven* is a two-hour, 11,000 foot-long cartoon full of beautiful drawings and supernatural feats. The ever-playful monkey king Sun Wukong makes a trip to the Dragon Palace and takes possession of the pillar holding the sky vault. By magic, he shrinks the pillar to the size of a needle and stores it in his ear. With this powerful weapon, he disturbs the peace in Heaven by beating up the Jade Emperor's gatekeepers. He is temporarily recruited to a petty celestial job but, feeling bored, proceeds to steal the peaches of longevity, swallow the elixir of immortality and ruin the banquet prepared for the Queen Mother of the West. What is more, no deities or generals in Heaven can prove his equal in battle. Travelling between Heaven and Earth, he is an enduring – and, indeed, endearing – symbol of intelligence, courage, and free will in Chinese culture.

For Wan Laiming, *Uproar in Heaven* was a dream come true, because he had been forced to abandon his initial plans for the film in the early 1940s. The film won a number of international prizes, including one at the 1978 London FF. It has broken export records for Chinese **animation**. By 1984, it had been distributed to forty-four countries and regions. In June 1983, nearly 100,000 people saw the film after it premièred in twelve Paris theatres. The film has also been screened on French and British television.

Plate 45   *Uproar in Heaven* (1961, 1964)

Further Reading

H. Chen (1989: 2: 114–6), an official account;
M.C. Quiquemelle (1991: 184–6), a succinct
summary.

(YZ)

urban life

In spite of the high concentration of film studios
in large cities like Shanghai and Hong Kong,
urban life rarely enjoys a completely favourable
depiction in Chinese films. Unlike **rural life**,
which may be given an idyllic portrayal and thus
conveys a sense of peace and tranquillity, urban
life is usually rendered as chaotic and disruptive.
In the course of the century, a number of urban
configurations have emerged to dominate the
Chinese screen: the city is negatively imaged as
a site of corruption, degradation, deprivation,
destruction, alienation, confusion, and only occasionally imagined as a place of personal fulfilment,
collective achievement or cultural **nostalgia**.

The theme of corruption was articulated
as early as the 1920s–30s, when the city was
presented as an evil entity that allured and
corrupted young people from rural areas.
Combining visual and sound effects, *Cityscape*
(*dir.* **Yuan Muzhi**, 1935) presents a kaleidoscopic
view of what the city does to its rural newcomers.
Innocent country folks are shown to be corrupted
by powerful urban forces, especially money and
sex. The theme of degradation surfaced not only
in the tragic tales of country women sold into
houses of **prostitution**, as in *Daybreak* (*dir.* **Sun
Yu**, 1932), but also in films like *A New Year's
Coin* (*dir.* **Zhang Shichuan**, 1937), where
performing singers and dancers are forced to
become hired partners at cheap dance halls. The
theme of deprivation is prominent in films
like *Little Toys* (*dir.* Sun Yu, 1933), where a rural
family is forced to migrate to the city, as well as
in numerous other films that address the problem
of housing shortage in Shanghai, such as *Dream
in Paradise* (*dir.* **Tang Xiaodan**, 1947),
Myriad of Lights (*dir.* **Shen Fu**, 1948) and
Crows and Sparrows (*dir.* **Zheng Junli**, 1949).
The theme of destruction demonstrates by far the
most sinister aspect of urban life. While *New
Woman* (*dir.* **Cai Chusheng**, 1934) dramatizes

the death of an aspiring woman writer, ***Plunder of Peach and Plum*** (*dir.* **Ying Yunwei**, 1934) narrates the tragic story of an educated couple whose dream of a happy family life is completely destroyed by evil urban forces.

Contrary to most films of the 1920s–40s, ***Sorrows and Joys of a Middle-Aged Man*** (*dir.* **Sang Hu**, 1949) is an exceptional story that reveals the potential of the city as a place of personal fulfilment. The happy ending of a retired schoolteacher who marries a young woman and becomes a father again is echoed forty-five years later in ***Eat Drink Man Woman*** (*dir.* Ang **Lee**, 1994), where an old widower marries a young woman and anticipates the birth of his child. However, this kind of fairy-tale ending rarely occurs without first bringing confusions and complications to urban adventurers. In many Taiwan melodramas that focus on issues of **love and marriage**, especially those based on **Chiung Yao**'s novels, young couples experience their personal fulfilment only after a series of trials and tribulations. Similarly, in many urban romances produced in mainland China in the 1980s, such as *Back-Lit Pictures* (*dir.* Ding Yinnan, 1982) and ***Under the Bridge*** (*dir.* Bai Chen, 1983), filmmakers pay more attention to social problems than to individuals' feelings. In films like ***Good Morning, Beijing*** (*dir.* **Zhang Nuanxin**, 1990), one sees an attempt to capture a sense of pride in collective achievements that was prevalent in many films of the 1950s–60s, such as ***It's My Day Off*** (*dir.* Lu Ren, 1959).

Since the mid-1980s, several mainland directors joined their Taiwan and Hong Kong counterparts in exploring new urban films. The feelings of alienation and existential crisis become major concerns in films such as ***Transmigration*** (*dir.* **Huang Jianxin**, 1988), ***Black Snow*** (*dir.* **Xie Fei**, 1989), ***Yesterday's Wine*** (*dir.* **Xia** **Gang**, 1995), ***Terrorizer*** (*dir.* Edward **Yang**, 1986), ***Daughter of the Nile*** (*dir.* **Hou Hsiao-hsien**, 1987), ***Vive l'amour*** (*dir.* **Tsai Ming-liang**, 1994), ***Song of the Exile*** (*dir.* Ann **Hui**, 1990), ***Days of Being Wild*** (1991) and *Fallen Angels* (1995, both *dir.* **Wong Kar-Wai**). Apart from these more or less serious urban explorations, urban films that treat alienation and existential crisis may be done in the **comedy** genre. For instance, behind hilarious shows of human follies in both *The* ***Trouble Shooters*** (*dir.* Mi Jiashan, 1988) and *A* ***Confucius Confusion*** (*dir.* Edward Yang, 1995) lies a deep concern with the meaning of life in a time of profound socio-economic change. In ***Rouge*** (1987) and *The* ***Actress*** (1992, both *dir.* Stanley **Kwan**), urban culture of the bygone days becomes an imaginary site for the director to project a strong feeling of nostalgia. On the other hand, gangster films, especially those Hong Kong productions, use the city as a metaphor for a chaotic world beyond human control. Both the police and criminals fight a losing battle in their futile efforts to reclaim the urban territory in films such as ***Long Arm of the Law*** (*dir.* Johnny **Mak**, 1984) and *A* ***Better Tomorrow*** (*dir.* John **Woo**, 1986).

See also: gangster film; melodrama; romance; social problems, film of

Further Reading
C. Berry (1988a), a discussion of mainland urban cinema of the 1980s; F. Luo (1995), on cinema and the decadent city; P. Pickowicz (1991), a survey of 1930s films; P. Pickowicz (1994), on Huang Jianxin; P. Pickowicz (1995), on urban film and politics; X. Tang (1994), a study of images of Beijing; Y. Zhang (1994b), on the urban–rural dichotomy.

(YZ)

V

Visitor on Ice Mountain

(Bingshan shang de laike)

dir. Zhao Xinshui
sc. Bai Xin
with Liang Yin, Gu Yuying, Abudulimiti
Changchun: Changchun Film, 1963

This film includes several key elements: sabotage by undercover enemies, ethnic conflict, exotic **romance** and beautiful regional songs.

In the early 1950s, several dozen Communist soldiers are stationed in a Uighur village near the border. A villager named Nawu Ruzi is getting married. The bride, 'Gulandanmu', is really a secret agent working for Relipu, the leader of a band of armed separatists in the region. A Communist soldier, Amier, who dated the real Gulandanmu when they were both teenagers, feels sad at the thought of her wedding to someone else. The impostor Gulandanmu learns of Amier's past romantic episode and tries to befriend him. Amier's frequent visits to the military camp cause Gulandanmu's commander to put her under surveillance. A group of bandits are foiled in their attempt to cross the border by the Communist's border patrol. Just as the true identity of the impostor Gulandanmu is being discovered, her controller has her killed. Finally, the Communist commander learns of the enemy's plan and sets a trap. The bandits are wiped out, and the real Gulandanmu reunited with Amier.

See also: ethnic minorities, film of

(ZX)

Vive l'amour

(Aiqing wansui)

dir. **Tsai Ming-liang**
sc. Tsai Ming-liang, Yang Biying, Cai Yijun
with Yang Guimei, Chen Zhaorong,
Li Kangsheng
Taipei: CMPC, 1994

This urban film opens with someone taking away a key left in a house door. Kang is a loner wandering along Taipei on his scooter. He enters the empty house, takes a bath, and tries to cut open his wrist with a knife. Meanwhile, Meimei, a real estate agent, runs into Rong and takes him 'home' with her. Meimei strips off Rong's clothes and kisses his body. Amid their moaning sounds, Kang quietly leaves the house. After love-making, Rong notices a big 'For Sale' sign on the window.

Meimei posts advertisements along the streets and makes phonecalls in another empty house. Kang rides his scooter and distributes advertisements for funeral urns. Meimei discovers she has lost a key and returns to the real estate office to get another one. Kang sees her enter and leave the house. Rong returns from a business trip abroad and enters the house. While he is taking a shower, Kang arrives with a watermelon. The two strangers meet and question each other. When Kang leaves, Rong feels puzzled.

Meimei talks on her cellular phone while eating a bowl of oyster noodles. She drives along a street packed with cars, enters the house and uses the bathroom. The two men secretly run downstairs. In a fast food store, they exchange names and start smoking. Rong puts two pornographic magazines inside Kang's briefcase, and the two visit the funeral parlour.

Meimei swats mosquitos in the house, but there are just too many of them. She returns home and takes a bath, feeling extremely depressed. Meanwhile, Rong and Kang eat from a hotpot in the apartment. Kang washes Rong's dirty clothes and puts on a black skirt and high-heeled shoes. Later, in the night market, Rong meets Meimei. The two return to the house and make love. Under the trembling bed, Kang unzips his trousers and places his hand inside. Early in the morning, Meimei leaves, and Kang climbs on to the bed and kisses Rong's handsome face while the latter is asleep. Outside, Meimei sits on a park bench and starts weeping.

An avant-garde film on urban alienation and disillusionment, the film won the Golden Lion at Venice FF as well as Best Film and Best Director awards at Taipei GHA in 1994.

See also: avant-garde, experimental or explorarory film; urban life

Further Reading

C. Berry (1995b), a discussion of Tsai's films; M. Cai *et al.* (1994), the film script and select reviews; C. Stephens (1996a), an excellent profile of Tsai Ming-liang.

(YZ)

W

Wan Jen

(Wan Ren)

b. 1950
Director

An important figure in New Taiwan Cinema, Wan Jen graduated from the Foreign Languages Department at Tung Wu University and received an MA in Film from Columbia College in California. He made two 16 mm films before entering the industry in 1983. *The Taste of the Apple*, last episode in the three-part **Sandwich Man** (1983), established his reputation. In other noted films such as **Rapeseed Woman** (1983), **Super Citizens** (1985), *The Coast of Departure* (1987) and *Super Citizen Ko* (1995), Wan Jen pays particular attention to the Taiwanese experience.

See also: New Taiwan Cinema (under Taiwan cinema in Historical essays)

(YZ)

Wan Laiming

b. 18 January 1899
Director

The founding father of **animation** film in China, Wan Laiming was self-taught in the fine arts. In 1919, he found employment as an editor in the graphics department of the Commercial Press. At the same time, he also worked as an art editor for a popular pictorial named *The Young Companion* (Liangyou huabao). Wan contributed numerous illustrations, cartoons and cover designs to both publishing groups. To help other aspiring young artists, he also published two textbooks, *The Beauty of the Human Body* (Renti biaoqing mei) and *The Pattern of the Human Body* (Renti tuhua mei).

When American animated films were first brought to China in the early 1920s, Wan became fascinated by the new medium. He and his three brothers began to make their own movies. In 1925, they produced the first-ever Chinese animated film, a commercial for a typewriter manufacturer, and a year later released *Turmoil in a Workshop* (1926). The Wan brothers consolidated these successes by producing their first sound animation, *Dancing Camel*, in 1935.

After the outbreak of the Sino-Japanese war in 1937, the Wan brothers made a number of animated propaganda films, even though they were not paid for several months because of the dire financial position of their employer, the Nationalist Central Film Studio. The Wan brothers moved back to Shanghai in 1939, the year Disney's *Snow White* was exported to China. They were deeply impressed by the level of craftsmanship in this film and decided to produce a Chinese film that matched it for quality. The result – **Princess Iron Fan** (1941) – was to remain for twenty years the lengthiest Chinese animated title. The film demonstrates the Wan brothers' artistic maturity as well as their ability to combine traditional Chinese aesthetics with Western techniques.

The Pacific War interrupted Wan Laiming's film career. To survive under extremely difficult wartime conditions, he worked as a sculptor and an interior decorator. For a while, Wan believed his career as an animation filmmaker was over. But in 1954, he joined a Hong Kong tourist group visiting mainland China and was so impressed with what he saw that he decided to stay on. Following an invitation from the Shanghai Animation Film Studio, Wan was finally able to resume making cartoons. After two shorts, Wan embarked on production of the two-part **Uproar in Heaven** (1961–4), Wan's highest achievement in animation filmmaking, and a film that has won numerous international awards. Unfortunately, though, the film also turned out to be Wan Laiming's swan song.

See also: propaganda and film

Further Reading

L. Wan (1986), a memoir; M.C. Quiquemelle (1991), on the Wan brothers and animation; ZDX (1982–6: 2: 12–7), a short biography.

(ZX)

Wang Danfeng

(Wang Yufeng)

b. 23 August 1925, Shanghai
Actress

One of the most popular mainland actresses of the 1940s–60s, Wang Danfeng has starred in more than sixty films. She was discovered by **Zhu Shilin**, who changed her name and spotlighted her in his *New Fisherman's Song* (1942), a sensational box-office success. On the basis of her engaging performance, Wang established herself as a rising star. She appeared in no less than two dozen titles during the 1940s.

Wang stayed in Hong Kong between 1948 and 1951, but finally decided to return to China. Before the **Cultural Revolution**, she acted in ten films of varying quality for the Shanghai Film Studio. Although she managed to appear in three films during the post-Cultural Revolution period, her attempts at a comeback were largely unsuccessful.

As an actress, Wang has played a wide range of characters. Her portrayal of an innocent young maid in *Family* (*dir.* Chen Xihe, Ye Ming, 1956), a patriotic courtesan in *The Peach Blossom Fan* (*dir.* Sun Jing, 1963) and a devoted wife in *Jade Butterfly* (*dir.* Zhang Fengxiang, Yang Gaisen, 1980) established her reputation as a 'tragic actress'. But she is equally good at **comedy**, as demonstrated by her performances in *Woman Barber* (*dir.* Ding Ran, 1962) and *The Son, the Grandson and the Seeds* (*dir.* Liang Tingduo, 1978).

Further Reading

D. Wang *et al.* (1954), a recollection; ZDX (1982–6: 6: 20–30), a short biography.

(ZX)

Wang Ping

(Wang Guangzhen)

b. 2 September 1916, Nanjing
d. 1 December 1990
Actress, director

A veteran woman director from mainland China, Wang Ping was interested first in theatre before she entered the world of film. While teaching in 1935 at a primary school in Nanjing, she took the lead role in a Chinese adaptation of Ibsen's *A Doll's House*. As this was a time when the acting profession was not particularly respectable socially, officials from the Education Bureau of Nanjing Municipal Government disapproved of any teacher involvement in show business. When they discovered that Wang was performing in this play, they fired her and banned all schools in Nanjing from hiring her. Meanwhile, Wang's father also viewed her involvement in theatre as a disgrace to the family and refused to accept her back into his home. Only a number of leftist intellectuals supported Wang, and she joined their cause.

In 1936, Wang was hired by Northwest Film Company in Taiyuan as an actress. She married Song Zhide, a leading leftist intellectual, not long after. During the Sino-Japanese war, Wang was mostly involved in theatrical performances. In the post-war period, while still continuing her career as a stage actress, she played supporting roles in a number of leftist films. Meanwhile, she also worked for the Communist party as an underground contact in Shanghai. Her services to the party were rewarded after 1949 with a director position in the film division of the army's political department. In 1952, she made an instructional film for the army. Wang's first feature was *Darkness Before Dawn* (1956). By the time she directed **Story of Liubao Village** (1957), Wang had clearly demonstrated her artistic maturity and individual style. After a few successful films, *Locust Tree Village* (1962) brought her Best Director award at the 1962 HFA.

Wang also directed two spectacular musicals glorifying the **Communist revolution**: *The East Is Red* (1965) and *Song of the Chinese Revolution* (*co-dir.* Huang Baoshan, 1985), the latter a special award winner at the 1986 China GRA.

See also: musical, the; theatre and film

Further Reading

ZDX (1982–6: 5: 36–49), a short biography.

(ZX)

Wang Renmei

(Wang Shuxi)

b. December 1914, Changsha, Hunan province
d. 12 April 1987
Actress

A famous actress of the 1930s, Wang Renmei was a member of Li Jinhui's China Song and Dance Troupe. She became a singer and gained publicity during performance tours. In 1931, Li's troupe, which by then had changed its name to Bright Moon Song and Dance, joined Lianhua Film Company, and the entire membership came to comprise Lianhua's core of stock players.

Among Wang's first films were *Twin Stars* (*dir.* **Shi Dongshan**, 1931) and *Wild Rose* (*dir.* **Sun Yu**, 1932). The realistic quality of Wang's performances brought a sense of spontaneity to a national cinema long dominated by exaggeration and mannerism. She refined her precise and natural style in ***Dawn Over the Metropolis*** (*dir.* **Cai Chusheng**, 1933). After taking the lead role in ***Song of the Fishermen*** (*dir.* Cai Chusheng, 1934), Wang achieved recognition as one of the most accomplished actresses of her time.

In 1935, Wang joined Diantong Film Company, then largely run by underground Communists. After a minor role in *Children of Troubled Times* (*dir.* Xu Xingzhi, 1935), she left Diantong for Xinhua and starred in *The Pioneers* (*dir.* **Wu Yonggang**, 1936). Wang then married **Jin Yan**, the most popular male star of the era. The fact that Wang's private life was not perceived to be particularly glamorous may actually have contributed to her star appeal. During the years of the Sino-Japanese war, she travelled between Hong Kong, Guilin, Kunming and Chongqing, participating in stage performances and acting only once, in *The Sky Rider* (*dir.* Sun Yu, 1940).

After the war, Wang starred in a few more films, but her celebrity status gradually faded. After 1949, she appeared in *Two Families* (*dir.* Qu Baiyin, Xu Bingduo, 1951) but never again played any major roles.

Further Reading

R. Wang (1985), a memoir; ZDX (1982–6: 2: 39–45), a short biography.

(ZX)

Wang Tung

(Wang Tong)

b. 1942, Taihe, Anhui province
Director, art designer

An important figure in New Taiwan Cinema, Wang Tung moved to Taiwan in 1949 and studied fine arts at National Taiwan College of Arts in 1962–4. He entered CMPC in 1966 and worked as artistic designer on many feature productions. In 1971 he pursued research work in stage design at the East-West Centre in Hawaii and returned in 1973 to join **Pai Ching-jui**'s production team. His directorial début, *If I Were for Real* (1981), was based on a controversial screenplay about an army sex scandal that the mainland government had prohibited from being adapted for the screen; it won him Best Film award at Taipei GHA. He directed a Taiwan version of *Unrequited Love* (1982), which tells the story of the persecution of an artist by the Communists during the **Cultural Revolution**. The original mainland production of this film was completed in 1981 but never publicly released, and its screen writer, Bai Hua, was fiercely attacked by conservatives.

With *A Flower in the Rainy Night* (1983), a film based on Hwang Chun-ming's famous nativist story, Wang Tung turned his attention to the Taiwan experience. Many of his later features, such as ***Strawman*** (1987) and ***Banana Paradise*** (1989), are set during crucial moments of Taiwanese history (respectively, the Japanese occupation and the Nationalist take-over) and they emphasize the lack of political consciousness found among ordinary people. Both films contain a mixture of **comedy** and **melodrama** and reveal Wang's unique vision of history, which differs from the overtly intellectual contemplations of **Hou Hsiao-hsien** and Edward **Yang**. *Strawman* won Best Director and Best Film award at Taipei GHA. With *The **Hills of No Return*** (1992), a moving tale of two miners and a woman toiling in the days of Japanese exploitation, Wang completed his 'Taiwan trilogy'; the film was granted Best Film award at the first Shanghai FF.

See also: New Taiwan Cinema (under Taiwan cinema in Historical essays)

Further Reading

R. Chen (1993b: 172–3), a brief entry; T. Wang (1991), on his *Banana Paradise*.

(YZ)

Wang Xiaoshuai

Independent filmmaker

A noted figure in the **Sixth Generation**, Wang Xiaoshuai studied in the Directing Department of the BFA between 1985 and 1989. After graduation he was assigned to Fujian Film Studio and did miscellaneous jobs for a number of years. He then decided to start out as an independent filmmaker and borrowed the money to make his first feature. *The **Days*** (1993) depicts the daily routine of an artist couple whose relationship slowly deteriorates. Wang reportedly lived on only one meal a day (instant noodles or bread and preserved cabbage) for weeks while working on the project. *The Days* was critically acclaimed in Europe and is held in the collection of the Museum of Modern Art in New York. With grants from Rotterdam and elsewhere, Wang was able to proceed with his other projects. In 1997 he released two new features: *A Vietnam Girl*, a film produced by **Tian Zhuangzhuang** that tells of two country boys' urban adventures, and *The Big Game*.

See also: independent film

Further Reading

X. Han (1995), an informative piece on the post-Fifth Generation.

(YZ)

Wang Xin'gang

b. January 1932, Dalian
Actor

A famous actor of the 1960s–80s, Wang Xin'gang was already an accomplished stage actor by the time of his first guest appearance, in *Quiet Forest* (*dir.* Zhu Wenshun, 1956). He joined August First Film Studio in 1958.

Wang's memorable performances in *The Everlasting Radio Signals* (*dir.* **Wang Ping**, 1958), ***Red Detachment of Women*** (*dir.* **Xie Jin**, 1961) and ***Struggle in an Ancient City*** (*dir.* Yan Jizhou, 1963) established his reputation, but some critics were quick to point out traces in his work of a residual 'stage habit'. After the **Cultural Revolution**, Wang's starring role in ***Regret for the Past*** (*dir.* **Shui Hua**, 1981) showed a marked improvement in the quality of his acting. (Wang himself considered this film a career landmark). He won Best Actor award at the 1982 HFA for his superb performance in *Intimate Friends* (*dir.* **Xie Tieli**, Chen Huaiai, Ba Hong, 1981), and was appointed deputy director of August First Film Studio not long after. However, much to his fans' disappointment, Wang has now more or less retired from filmmaking.

Further Reading

ZDX (1982–6: 5: 8–18), a short biography.

(ZX)

Wang Yin

b. 25 June 1900, Shanghai
d. 13 April 1988
Actor, director, screen writer

A veteran filmmaker whose career spans the late 1920s to the mid-1970s, from Shanghai to Hong Kong and Taiwan, Wang Yin is actually more acclaimed as an actor than as a director. After a successful career in Shanghai during the 1930s–40s, he moved to Hong Kong to establish Liangyou Film Company in 1947 and Tiannan Films in 1959. In addition to writing screenplays, he acted in and directed numerous films of different genres, including martial arts and a **melodrama**, *Whose Belongings?* (1966). He twice won Best Actor award at Taipei GHA, in 1962 and 1971 respectively. He retired from the film world in 1977 and received a special achievement award at Taipei GHA in 1981.

See also: martial arts film

(YZ)

Wang Yu

b. 1944
Actor, director

Though overshadowed by Bruce **Lee** in the 1970s, Wang Yu's role as one of the leading figures in pre-1985 Hong Hong cinema deserves re-evaluation. Shaw Brothers offered him a contract in 1963. His first starring role was in *Tiger Boy* (*dir.* **Chang Che**, 1964). Although uneven and commercially unsuccessful, the film led to star and director reuniting for *One-Armed Swordsman* (1967), which made both famous in Hong Kong. The film classified Wang in the role of a brooding, masochistic hero, suffering both dishonour and dismemberment before he finally returns to settle scores and regain his lost honour. Chang then directed Wang in what may be his greatest role as the heroic, death-embracing Silver Roc, in *Golden Swallow* (1968), an ostensible sequel to *Come Drink With Me* (1966). After starring in *The Return of the One-Armed Swordsman* (1968) and *The Chinese Boxer* (1969), Wang broke his Shaw Brothers contract and went independent as both actor and director, establishing his screen persona in films such as *One-Armed Boxer* (1971) and *Beach of the War Gods* (1973). After attempting an international breakthrough in *The Man from Hong Kong* (1974), his career declined. However, Wang returned to the screen with a distinguished character role as Jet **Li**'s martial arts antagonist in ***Once Upon a Time in China*** (1991) and as producer and co-star of *Island of Fire* (*dir.* Chu Yen-ping, 1992) featuring Jackie **Chan**, Sammo **Hung** and Andy **Lau**.

(TW)

war film

Although documentaries of battles were shot as early as the 1910s, as in *The Shanghai Battle* (1912), the war film did not emerge as a genre until the late 1930s, when the Sino-Japanese war broke out on a national scale and the KMT government retreated to Wuhan and then Chongqing. ***Protect Our Land*** (*dir.* **Shi Dongshan**) and *Eight Hundred Heroic Soldiers* (*dir.* **Ying Yunwei**, both 1938) are two early examples from the Nationalist-controlled studios. In the 1940s, the Nationalist studios continued to make war films, such as *The Sky Rider* (*dir.* **Sun Yu**, 1940), the first Chinese film about air battles. After a period of hiatus, the reorganized government studios in Taiwan resumed production of war films as part of their overall propaganda operation. Notable titles include *Martyrs* (1974) and *Eight Hundred Heroic Soldiers* (1975, both *dir.* **Ting Shan-hsi**). In the meantime, pro-Nationalist studios in Hong Kong also invested in war films, releasing titles such as ***Star, Moon, Sun*** (*dir.* Yi Wen, 1961).

War films constitute one of the most significant parts of the Communist propaganda machinery in the mainland. Starting from ***Daughters of China*** (*dir.* **Ling Zifeng**, Zhai Qiang, 1949), a film about eight women soldiers who sacrificed their lives in defending the country from the Japanese invaders, the production of this popular genre has continued to the 1990s, with only a brief interruption during the early years of the **Cultural Revolution**. War films may restage major battles, such as ***From Victory to Victory*** (*dir.* **Cheng Yin**, 1952) and *The **Battle of Taierzhuang*** (*dir.* Yang Guangyuan, Zai Junjie, 1987). It may present famous war heroes, such as

Plate 46   *The Battle of Taierzhuang* (1987)

Dong Cunrui (*dir.* Guo Wei, 1955) and *Heroic Sons and Daughters* (*dir.* Wu Zhaodi, 1964). It may also demonstrate military strategies or individuals' wisdom, such as *Capture Mount Hua by Stratagem* (*dir.* Guo Wei, 1953), *Reconnaissance Across the Yangtze* (*dir.* Tang Xiaodan, 1954) and *Guerillas on the Plain* (*dir.* Zhao Ming, 1955). The obvious purpose of all these war films is to reinforce **nationalism** and to educate the masses with lessons from the **Communist revolution**.

Almost all imaginable types of warfare are projected on the mainland screen, from old-fashioned sea battles like *Naval Battle of 1894* (*dir.* **Lin Nong**, 1962) to modern air fights like *Silver Flowers in the Blue Sky* (*dir.* **Sang Hu**, 1960), from epic land battles like *The Decisive Engagements, I-III* (*dir.* **Li Jun** *et al.*, 1991–2) to guerilla wars like *Tunnel Warfare* (*dir.* Ren Xudong, 1965). The typical heroism in mainland (and most of Taiwan) productions, however, was challenged in the mid-1980s by the **Fifth Generation** directors. *One and Eight* (*dir.* **Zhang Junzhao**, 1984) sought to reveal the war's psychological impact on individuals, and **Wu Ziniu** continued such startling revelations in his *Secret Decree* (1984), *Evening Bell* (1988) and *The Big Mill* (1990). In fact, this new, mostly humanitarian representation of wars was so emotionally powerful and so ideologically subversive that two titles from the the Fifth Generation were banned: *The Dove Tree* (*dir.* Wu Ziniu, 1985) and *In Their Prime* (*dir.* **Zhou Xiaowen**, Guo Fangfang, 1986). The ban was effective in that no more subversive war films have appeared in the mainland since then. At the same time the government-subsidized war films are no longer as popular as they were in the 1950s–70s, mainly due to the emergence of other entertaining genres like **comedy** and gangster films.

See also: documentary; gangster film; propaganda and film

Further Reading
R. Huang (1994), a Taiwan perspective; ZDYYZ (1984), an official mainland account; Z. Zhou and D. Zhang (1995), on war films set in the Sino-Japanese war.

(YZ)

Wedding Banquet, The
(Xiyan)

dir. Ang **Lee**
sc. Ang Lee, Neil Peng, James Schamus
with Lung Sihung, Gua Ah-Leh, Winston Chao, Mitchell Lichtenstein, May Chin
Taipei: CMPC/Good Machine, 1992

Plate 47   *The Wedding Banquet* (1992)

The film is Ang Lee's second instalment of a contemporary cinematic comedy of manners which led to international prestige rivalling that of *Sense and Sensibility* (1995).

Taiwanese-American citizen Kao Wai-Tung receives frequent cassette tapes from his mother urging him to marry. But Wai-Tung is gay and lives with his Caucasian lover Simon. Simon suggests a marriage of convenience which will satisfy Wai-Tung's parents as well as facilitate a green card for Shanghai artist Wei-Wei. When Wai-Tung's parents arrive, Simon poses as his landlord.

Wai-Tung's father, a retired Nationalist army officer, insists on a formal ceremony and a traditional wedding banquet. His former army chauffeur, Chen, suggests they use his plush Manhattan restaurant. Wai-Tung, Wei-Wei, and Simon reluctantly agree to this and undergo the excessive strain of food, alcohol, and raucous behaviour associated with Chinese wedding banquets. Wei-Wei seduces Wai-Tung later that evening. When Simon learns of her pregnancy he explodes in anger before everyone. Mr Kao suffers a mild stroke. Wai-Tung confesses his sexual orientation to his mother at the hospital. She makes him promise not to tell his father. Several weeks later, Mr Kao reveals his knowledge of the actual situation to Simon. He makes him promise not to tell his wife and son. When Wei-Wei decides against an abortion, Simon accepts the position of 'one of the fathers'. After presenting the Kaos with a wedding photo album, the newly reconstituted family watch them leave for Taiwan.

Further Reading

C. Berry (1993c), a discussion of the film and melodrama; W. Dariotis and E. Fung (1997), a critical study of Ang Lee's films.

(TW)

Wedding Maidens, The

(Chujia nü)

dir. Wang Jin
sc. He Mengfan
with Jin Dai, Wu Aiji, Shen Rong, Wei Jie, Zhang Liwei
Guangzhou: Pearl River Film/Hong Kong: Sil-Metropole, 1990

Five Girls and a Rope

(Wu ge nüzi yu yi gen shengzi)

dir. Yeh Hong-wei
sc. Ye Weilin
with Ai Jing, Yang Jiemei, Lu Yuanqi, Zhang Shi
Taipei: Tomson Film, 1991

The two films are based on the same story by mainland writer Ye Weilin. Although the narrative is the same, specific details differ in these two films. In a remote mountain village, five innocent girls are attracted to a legend about 'touring the garden'. According to the legend, a girl may hang herself before marriage and preserve her purity. Her soul would turn into a white bird and soar to the heavenly garden, where there is only beauty and peace. The five girls then go to work on a hillside. Nineteen-year-old Mingtao takes off the outer layer of her clothes, and three others follow suit. They try to force sixteen-year-old Jinmei to do the same, but their undressing 'show' is seen by an idiot. To punish the idiot's 'indecent' act, they pull down his pants. Terrified at what they see, they quickly run away.

Back at the village, the five girls have to confront the ugly reality. Mingtao's step-mother has found a sick husband for Mingtao. Aiyue is shocked to learn that her grandmother is not allowed to eat at the dinner table even on her eightieth birthday. Hexiang knows her own fate when she sees how her brother abuses his wife. Guijuan witnesses the horrifying process whereby the family of her sister's husband only cares for the newborn and lets her sister die unattended after childbirth. And Jinmei is reluctant to follow her father's plan to marry at a young age. On a spring day, the five girls gather in an old temple outside the village. They use a long piece of white cloth to make five nooses and hang it on the beam. All dressed in red, they hang themselves, and the idiot is the only witness of this tragic group suicide.

The two directors take two different approaches to the story. While both aim to expose the miserable fate of Chinese women, Wang Jin chose the southern landscape and made his film's natural setting resemble a traditional painting. From this predominantly aesthetic view, even superstition has its own charm. Yeh Hong-wei, on the other hand, is fascinated with the northern type of barren landscape. As a result, his *mis-en-scène* and style resemble those of the **Fifth Generation** directors.

See also: painting and film

(JJS)

Westerns

Chinese 'Westerns' (*xibu pian*) is a term **Wu Tianming** coined in 1985–6 to designate a new direction Xi'an Film Studio began to take under his leadership. This elastic term covers all films set in Western China – an enormous territory stretching from Xi'an in the mid-west to as far north as Xinjiang autonomous region and as far south as Yunnan province. However, films like *King of the Children* (*dir.* **Chen Kaige**, 1987) are rarely associated with the new term, and as most of the so-called Chinese 'Westerns' are set in the deserts and mountains of the northwest they are visually linked to the conception of 'yellow culture' (*huangtu wenhua*) with its primitive landscapes and grotesque characters. Among the most remarkable features in this category are *Ballad of the Yellow River* (*dir.* **Teng Wenji**, 1989), *The Swordsman in Double-Flag Town* (*dir.* **He Ping**, 1990) and *The Wooden Man's Bride* (*dir.* **Huang Jianxin**, 1993). In terms of storyline and *mise-en-scène*, these films are obviously indebted to *Red Sorghum* (*dir.* **Zhang Yimou**, 1987), a film set in Shandong province but produced by Xi'an Studio, where the other three films were also made.

(YZ)

White-Haired Girl, The

(Baimao nü)

dir./sc. Wang Bin, **Shui Hua**
with **Tian Hua**, **Chen Qiang**, Li Baiwan, Hu Peng
Changchun: Northeast Film, 1950

The central theme of this film is class exploitation and conflict. The saviours of the poor peasants are the Communist army.

A peasant girl, Xi'er, and her neighbour, Dachun, are in love with each other. Xi'er's father, Yang Bailao, and Dachun's mother plan to see them married after the fall harvest. A local landlord, Huang Shiren, takes an interest in Xi'er and uses the debts Yang owes him as a leverage. Unable to pay his debts to Huang, Yang is pressured into signing a document contracting her as Huang's maid. Ashamed to face his daughter, Yang commits suicide. Huang takes back more of the land that Dachun is renting from him and drives Dachun out of the village.

Xi'er is raped by Huang and becomes pregnant. With the help of another maid, she runs away from Huang's residence and hides in the mountains. After years of living in the cave, her hair turns completely white. In order to survive, she frequently steals sacrifices from the temple, acts which are interpreted by the worshippers as visits from the deity. After the outbreak of the Sino-Japanese war, Dachun, now a Communist army officer, returns to his home village to mobilize the peasants. In an attempt to find the truth behind the local legend, he follows Xi'er to her cave. Truth is revealed, lovers are reunited, and the evil landlord is executed.

The film won a special award at the 1951 Karlovy Vary FF as well as Best Film award from the Ministry of Culture in 1957.

(ZX)

Widow Village

(Guafu cun)

dir. Wang Jin
sc. Chen Lizhou, Wang Yan
with Hao Jialing, Liang Yujin, Yu Li, Tao Zeru, Xie Yuan
Guangzhou: Pearl River Film/Hong Kong: Sil-Metropole, 1988

This film attempts to reflect critically on traditional Chinese culture by examining marriage practices in a small fishing village.

As a severe sea storm took the lives of most able-bodied men and left behind a throng of widows, a local community is known as Widow Village. The marriage practices and family lives of this village are ruled by a strange custom. The rules stipulate that husbands and wives have to live separately, and that the wives are only allowed to visit their husbands three times a year. Furthermore, husbands and wives are not supposed to have sex within the first three years of marriage, and a wife must start producing children for her husband within three years. Those who violate such rules become social outcasts and are usually forced into committing suicide.

Three orphaned sisters in the village, Tingjie, Dumei and Alai, live together and take good care of each other. Tingjie has been married for ten years and has not yet produced a child. She happens to have her periods on visiting days, much to the disappointment of her husband. Duomei has been married just over two years and so cannot yet sleep with her husband. She does not even know what her husband looks like, as she can only watch him from behind a curtain during visiting hours. When Tingjie falls ill, Duomei goes to the market to sell their ox so that she can buy medicine for Tingjie. The buyer turns out to be Duomei's husband, Side, but Duomei fails to recognize him. After the transaction, Duomei falls in love with him and begins to reject her own husband: one night, when Side attempts to take her to bed, she even hits him with a tile without realizing that Side is the man who bought her ox. Alai and her husband have been married for just one year. They decide to disregard tradition by sleeping together. That very night, the Nationalist troops pass by on their way to Taiwan and conscript all the men in the village, leaving the women husbandless once more.

Widow Village won the Best Film award at the 1989 HFA.

See also: love and marriage

(ZX)

Wild Flower

(Ye cao xian hua)

dir./sc. **Sun Yu**
with **Ruan Lingyu**, **Jin Yan**, Liu Jiqun
Shanghai: Lianhua Film, 1930

The film condemns the practice of arranged marriage and shows the tragic consequences of parental interference in young people's romantic affairs.

When the film begins, a young mother and her baby girl are dying from starvation. A carpenter and his wife happen to pass by. Too late to save the mother, they adopt the girl and name her Lilian. Sixteen years later, they settle in Shanghai. Lilian sells flowers to help support the family. One day Lilian has an accident on the street. A young man named Huang Yun saves her life. Huang is a runaway musician who refuses to accept the marriage his parents have arranged for him. The carpenter offers Huang room and board. Huang in turn discovers Lilian's talents in singing and teaches her music. With the help of an old servant, Huang raises enough funds to stage his opera, which stars himself and Lilian. The show is well received, and Huang and Lilian become celebrities overnight.

Without consulting their parents, the two are engaged. When Huang's father learns of this he is upset and tries to interfere. On the eve of Huang and Lilian's wedding, Huang's father and other relatives come to Lilian's home, accusing her of being a gold digger. They say to Lilian that she will ruin Huang's future if she marries him. Deeply hurt by this, Lilian decides to break her engagement with Huang. Not knowing the true cause behind her sudden change of heart, Huang is greatly saddened and blames her in public. The theatre manager wants to continue the opera show because of its popularity and replaces Huang's role with someone else. When Lilian sees Huang's substitute, she realizes her loss and faints on the stage. Meanwhile, Huang has learned of the truth. He leaves his family again and goes to Lilian.

Further Reading

Y. Zhang (1994a), a critical study of women's images in 1930s Shanghai.

(ZX)

Wild Torrents

(Kuang liu)

dir. **Cheng Bugao**
sc. **Xia Yan**
with **Hu Die**, **Gong Jianong**, Xia Peizhen, Wang Xianzai
Shanghai: Mingxing Film, 1933

As a representative leftist film, this film focuses on the social tensions and economic disparities between peasants and landlord. The film uses much footage shot during the actual flooding of Southern China in 1932: many of the images of flood refugees are also **documentary** in nature.

After a village along the Yangtze River is threatened by flood, the villagers build a levee to hold the rising water. A school teacher, Liu Tiesheng, is their leader. As the sandbags are in short supply, they decide to ask the village head, Fu Boren, for help, but Fu is busy preparing a wedding for his daughter Xiujuan. Despite the fact that Xiujuan is already in love with Liu, Fu wants to marry her off to Li Heqing, the son of the county magistrate. Fu refuses to help the villagers and flees to Hankou with his family. Once there he raises funds for the flood, but uses the money to build a house for himself instead.

As the flood situation continues to worsen, hundreds of thousands of people lose their homes and have to fight for survival. Yet Fu and his family then embark on a sightseeing tour of the flooded area. Xiujuan's fiancée Li is jealous of Liu because Xiujuan is still attached to Liu. So Li hires a country doctor to murder him. Meanwhile, Xiujuan becomes suspicious of Liu's relationship with a girl he rescues from the river. As more rain falls, the villagers rush to Fu's house to fetch his building materials so that they can strengthen the levee. Finally, the levee breaks. Liu manages to bring Xiujuan to safety before reaching out to the others still struggling in the water.

See also: leftist film (under Chinese cinema in Historical essays)

(ZX)

Winner, The

(Yingjia)

dir. Huo Jianqi
sc. Si Wu
with Shao Bing, Ning Jing, Geng Le
Beijing: Beijing Film/Hangzhou: China-Hong Kong Industries, 1996

This **sports** film is unusual because of its focus on a handicapped athlete who demonstrates not only a competitive spirit but also a strong sense of pride. Set in Beijing in the summer of 1994, the film opens with a breathtaking scene in which a young man runs after a taxi. The driver has just hit a pedestrian and tries to get away, but he is caught by the man and is forced to apologize to the woman, who turns out only to have a minor scratch. After letting the driver go, the man introduces himself as Chang Ping and discovers the woman's name is Lu Xiaoyang.

Lu is a bank teller and feels unhappy because her boyfriend, a rich entrepreneur, is too busy making money to care for her feelings. Her acquaintance with Chang brings new light to her life, but she does not know that Chang is a handicapped athlete who trains hard in preparation for a major competition. Lu's mother also disapproves of Lu's dating with Chang. When Lu's boyfriend finds out that Chang is handicapped, he is shocked and wishes Chang the best. In the competition, Chang's team wins the gold medal for the relay. Lu is moved to tears. She goes to the locker room and wants to help Chang put on his artificial leg. Chang, however, refuses Lu, saying that he can lose a race but will not accept help. The film ends with a long shot of Lu kneeling by Chang's side in the dark locker room.

The director graduated from the Art Department of BFA in 1982 and served as art designer in *On the Hunting Ground* (*dir.* **Tian Zhuangzhuang**, 1985) and *After Separation* (*dir.* **Xia Gang**, 1992).

(YZ)

Woman Demon Human

(Ren gui qing)

dir. **Huang Shuqin**
sc. Huang Shuqin, Li Ziyu, Song Guoxun
with Xu Shouli, Pei Yanling, Li Baotian
Shanghai: Shanghai Film, 1987

Drawing on the real-life story of an opera actress, Pei Yanling, the film portrays her passionate engagement with the opera role of a male ghost, Zhong Kui, and her desire for a female identity. Considered the most feminist **woman's film** produced in China, *Woman Demon Human* embodies a poetics of female self-representation that narrates personal experience from a woman's perspective.

The character's early identity crisis stems from a mother–daughter conflict. Qiuyun grows up in an opera family and spends her childhood around the stage, watching as her father and mother perform 'Zhong Kui Marries His Sister Off'. Off stage, though, her parents experience marital problems. One evening Qiuyun runs into a barnyard where she sees her mother making love with an unidentified man. Her mother runs away a few days later in the middle of an opera performance. Abandoned in this way, Qiuyun is taunted by her peers and spends her childhood under a cloud of confusion.

To become someone who is not identified with her mother thus forms the core of Qiuyun's life-long struggle for selfhood, but it also brings trouble to the relationships she forms with each male figure in her life. She expresses interest in an opera career, yet agrees with her father that she will only play male roles so as to avoid the pitfalls female roles might engender. Her talent and arduous training in kungfu, singing, and acting win her the reputation of a prodigy. She is selected for the provincial troupe to train under Zhang, himself a well-known young actor. Mesmerized by Qiuyun's acting talents and frustrated by his unhappy marriage, Zhang expresses his love for her. However, their forbidden relationship forces Zhang's resignation and a swirl of humiliating gossip about Qiuyun.

On-stage Qiuyun continues to masquerade in male roles. Off-stage, she carries out the female role of wife and mother. While she raises two children and resumes her training after the **Cultural Revolution**, her husband (unseen throughout the film) devotes himself to gambling and sends home a stream of unpaid bills. The theatrical role of Zhong Kui and the opera itself provide Qiuyun with an alternate world. Torn between the demands of different roles, she achieves international fame by 'marrying' herself to the stage and identifying with her male persona Zhong Kui. The film ends with her visit to her hometown, where she and her father talk about driving all demons from the human world.

Further Reading

J. Dai (1995), a feminist critique of woman's film in the mainland; J. Dai and M. Yang (1995), an informative interview; S. Huang (1995), a brief account of her own work.

(SC, YZ)

Woman from the Lake of Scented Soul, The

aka *Woman Sesame-Oil Maker*
(Xiang hun nü)

dir./sc. **Xie Fei**
with **Siqin Gaowa**, Wu Yujuan, Lei Luosheng, Chen Baoguo
Tianjin: Tianjin Film/Changchun: Changchun Film, 1992

The film is set in contemporary China. A Japanese businesswoman likes the sesame oil made by Xiang and wants to invest in her sesame-oil shop near the Lake of Scented Soul. This investment changes Xiang's financial and social status in the village. Her idiotic son loves Huanhuan, whose father has just lost five thousand yuan in his small fishing business. With a dowry of ten thousand yuan, Huanhuan is married to the idiot, who publicly humiliates her on their wedding day. Xiang tries to comfort Huanhuan by relating her own unhappy marriage to a lame good-for-nothing.

Xiang's husband does not work. He enjoys drinking wine and watching theatre shows. Once drunk, he goes home in the middle of the night and beats up Xiang. Huanhuan sees all this and soon notices that Xiang has a lover, a married truck driver who delivers goods for her. One night, when her lover wants to end their relationship and Xiang is angry, the husband unexpectedly comes home early. The driver jumps out of the window and bumps into Huanhuan, but Huanhuan does not reveals the secret.

While Xiang is sick, Huanhuan takes good care of her. The two unhappy women seem to communicate in silence. Suddenly, Xiang sees the scars of tooth bites on Huanhuan's shoulders and realizes how much her idiotic son has done to this miserable young woman. The next morning, Xiang suggests that Huanhuan file a divorce, but Huanhuan does not feel relieved, for she knows no other man will marry her because of her relations with the idiot.

A moving tale of women's suffering, the film won the Golden Bear at the 1993 Berlin FF.

Further Reading

J. Lent (1996/7), an interview with the director.

(JJS)

Woman of Wrath, The

(Sha fu)

dir. **Tseng Chuang-hsiang**
sc. **Wu Nien-chen**
with Xia Wenxi, Bai Ying
Taipei: Tomson Film, 1984

The suffering woman is the most conspicuous image in films of the New Taiwan Cinema. But no other film depicts a woman's victimization like *The Woman of Wrath*. A sexually abused woman avenges herself by killing her husband, a butcher by trade. She is convicted and sentenced to death. The film caused a lot of attention when it was released because it was adapted from a controversial novel entitled 'Shafu' (literally, 'killing the husband'). The novel was written by Li Ang, one of the leading woman writers in Taiwan in the 1980s. Li is known for her poignant depictions of sexuality and critiques of patriarchy. In the novel, she argues that men equate women with sex and food: women provide sex in exchange for food. But they are ultimately punished for their rebellion against sexual oppression.

The film unfolds with a little girl witnessing her mother having sex with a Japanese soldier in exchange for food. As the mother is eating her food while the soldier is on top of her, the villagers catch and condemn her. This food-sex cycle befalls the little girl herself as she grows up. Her uncle sells her to a butcher to avoid a life of hunger. Perhaps because sex is such an unusual subject in Taiwanese literature and cinema, the film was a box-office flop in 1984. Yet the most common complaint is that its restrained style and non-expressive acting make it virtually unwatchable. It seems few people want to pay attention to the brutalities a butcher husband can inflict upon his illiterate peasant wife.

See also: New Taiwan Cinema (under Taiwan cinema in Historical essays)

(YY)

woman's film

'Woman's film' (*nüxing dianying*) is a relatively new phenomenon which started to attract critical attention in mainland China in the mid-1980s. As a general term, it refers to all films made by women directors and is thus to be distinguished from **representations of women** by male directors. In a critical sense, 'woman's film' designates a special type of film which explores what it means to be female and which usually contains elements resistant to the dominant ideology.

Historically, Chinese women were not cast in film until *Zhuangzi Tests His Wife* (dir. **Li Beihai**, 1913), in which the screen writer **Li Minwei**'s wife, Yan Shanshan, played a supporting role. In 1925, Xie Caizhen reportedly became the first Chinese woman director by scripting, directing and acting in her own film. The actress Ai Xia followed suit but soon ended her career in a tragic suicide in the early 1930s. During the chaotic years of war from the mid-1930s to the late 1940s, there were practically no opportunities for women to direct major films. It was only after 1949 that women were assigned important roles in filmmaking in the mainland. An impressive line-up of women directors has been established since that date. According to one source, fifty-nine women directors were working by the late 1980s and 182 feature films bear their signatures. In Shanghai Film Studio alone, there were six women among twenty-five active directors, and in one particular year a third of the studio's feature productions were directed by women. More than that, since 1979 women directors have regularly won domestic and international prizes.

Woman's film evolved through several stages in the mainland. In the 1950s–60s, **Wang Ping** was the only women director at work. She took pride in producing films which glorify **Communist revolution** and **socialist construction** but which offer no clues as to their director's gender. She produced a number of representative films of the period, including *The Everlasting Radio Signals* (1958), which portrays an underground Communist martyr; *Locust Tree Village* (1962), which depicts social change in rural areas from the land reform to the people's commune; *Sentinels under the Neon Lights* (1964), which is set in the newly liberated Shanghai; and the epic musical *The East Is Red* (1965), which represents revolutionary history as a grand spectacle. Wang Ping became a model for the new generation of women directors who received professional training in the 1950s–60s but, due to the **Cultural Revolution**, did not start directing until the 1980s. Many followed in her footsteps by directing mainstream socialist-realist films which praise the way individuals make sacrifices in the interests of revolution or social welfare.

Wang Haowei (*b.* 1940), who entered the Directing Department of BFA in 1958, can be taken as a representative figure from the second phase of social film by women directors. Moving away from the earlier conception of the socialist country as a giant **family**, her award-winning *What a Family!* (1979) and the acclaimed *Sunset Street* (1983) focus on a smaller community and the humane – rather than politicized – aspects of its everyday life. With *The Invisible Web* (1981) and *Ormosia From the North* (1984), she confronts moral issues of **love and marriage** which have provided a central focus for many women directors since the 1980s. In these films, love – in its pure, spiritual form untarnished by sex – is conceptualized as an expression of individual freedom and is contrasted with various social evils (e.g., feudalist mentality and ultra-leftist ideology).

The centrality of love and compassion is also a recurring theme in the work of Shi Shujun (*b.* 1939), a 1964 graduate from the Directing Department of the Central Drama Academy in Beijing. Her interest in female adolescents is reflected in *Girl Students' Dormitory* (1984), *The Missing Middle-School Girl* (1985) and *Death of a College Girl* (1992), films that address social issues without privileging female experience. Shi Xiaohua, who entered the Directing Class of the Shanghai Film School in 1960, insists that women directors should not confine themselves to the production of only women's films; she herself has directed **children's** film, comedy, and even action film and is proud of her non-gendered perspective. Clearly, social commitment and political consciousness still govern the beliefs of this group of women who uphold film's educational function.

Nevertheless, since the mid-1980s several women directors have consciously set out to make women's films, and the results have been remarkable. **Zhang Nuanxin**'s *Sacrificed Youth* (1985) and **Hu Mei**'s *Army Nurse* (1985) probe the psychology of their women protagonists as they gradually perceive the painful loss of their gender identity in a repressive society. Enhanced by subjective voice-over techniques, these two films explore 'women's consciousness' (*nüxing yishi*) or subjectivity and establish a female lyrical narrative style characterized by a lingering **nostalgia** and idealization of youth. Concern for youth also finds its way into **Huang Shuqin**'s early films, including *Forever Young* (Qingchun wansui, 1983). It was not until *Woman Demon Human* (1987), however, a film about an actress playing a man's role on stage and struggling with her irreconcilable gender identity, that Huang was credited with producing a genuine woman's film in China. She tried to sustain a pro-feminist perspective in *The Soul of the Painter* (1994), the story of a

prostitute and concubine who becomes a famous painter, but the film was not so successful. The same holds true for Zhang Nuanxin's *Good Morning, Beijing* (1990) and Hu Mei's *Far from the War* (1987), both of which lack their respective directors' earlier dedication to female subjectivity.

It is obvious that no striking generation gap exists when it comes to the production of women's films in the mainland, as both Huang Shuqin and Zhang Nuanxin belong to the **Fourth Generation**. Among the **Fifth Generation**, **Peng Xiaolian**'s confrontational manner differs from Hu Mei's lyrical style. By tracing the formation of sisterhood among three country women working in the hostile city, Peng's *Women's Story* (1987) is more critical of patriarchal values and more subversive than Hu's *Army Nurse*. In contrast to Peng's and Hu's pursuit of female experience, their classmate **Li Shaohong** cares little about female gender identity in her *Bloody Morning* (1990) and *Family Portrait* (1992), two psychological studies of urban and rural problems in contemporary China.

Among the Fourth Generation, there is a third group who occupy the middle ground by approaching social issues through the exploration

Plate 48   *Woman Demon Human* (1988)

of distinct female experiences. Wang Junzheng (*b.* 1945), who graduated from the Directing Department of the BFA in 1968, directed *The First Woman in the Forest* (1987) and *Women, Taxi, Women* (1991), both of which feature strong female protagonists who nevertheless do not desire a 'room of their own'. The veteran director Dong Kena (*b.* 1930), who had started work in the 1960s, began to make women's films in the mid-1980s. In such titles as *Who Is the Third Party?* (1988), *Women of Huangtupo Village* (1990) and *The World of Women* (1992), she tries to view the world from a woman's perspective by exploring issues of motherhood, **femininity**, **sexuality**, and the conflicts between career and family. Staged as **melodrama** and versed in ethico-moral concerns, her films often begin with an anti-patriachal stance (e.g. attacking male chauvinism) but invariably end with a conventional scene wherein the audience is compelled to feel sympathy for both male and female protagonists. Again, love or true feeling is cherished as the only thing that endures, survives, and occasionally triumphs. Indeed, this seems to be the overriding theme that has united the work of most women directors in the mainland since the 1980s, as evidenced by Wang Haowei's *Divorce* (1993) and Zhang Nuanxin's *A Yunnan Story* (1994).

Among other prominent women directors in the mainland are Bao Zhifang (*The Golden Fingernail*, 1988), Guang Chunlan, Ji Wenyan, Ling Zi (*Savage Land*, 1981), **Liu Miaomiao**, Lu Xiaoya (*b.* 1941, *Girl in Red*, 1984), **Ning Ying**, Qin Zhiyu (*A Single Woman*, 1991), and Wu Zhennian (a TV series *Women*, 1988–90).

In Taiwan, filmmaking is dominated by men, and only one woman director, **Huang Yu-shan**, has attracted attention for her documentaries and features. (The famous Taiwan actress Sylvia **Chang** later directed films in Hong Kong.) The situation is a little different in Hong Kong. Although their works are not discussed as 'women's films', women directors have been in the vanguard of the Hong Kong New Waves. In the early 1970s, Tang Shuxuan's *The Arch* 1970), a 16 mm black and white experimental film, proposed a critique of patriarchal society and foreshadowed the technological changes that would take place a decade later; her *China Behind* (1974), another prophetic work, explores the identity crisis experienced by Hong Kong's mainland émigrés during the Cultural Revolution. In 1979, Ann **Hui**'s *The Secret*, a product of her collaboration with Sylvia Chang (actress), Joyce Chan (screen

writer) and Violet Lam (composer), contributed to the rise of the first New Wave in Hong Kong. Under commercial pressure Ann Hui made numerous action films, but her reputation rests on her art films, such as **Song of the Exile** (1990), which examines the mother–daughter relationship and the identity question in Hong Kong, mainland China and Japan. In the late 1980s, Mabel Cheung (Zhang Wanting) and Clara **Law** were among the outstanding figures of the Second Wave. Many of their works, like Cheung's An **Autumn's Tale** (1987) and Law's *The* **Reincarnation of Golden Lotus** (1989), offer unique female perspectives on issues of desire, betrayal, exile and sexual politics. From Tang Shuxuan to Clara Law, one may delineate a worthy tradition of woman's film in Hong Kong.

See also: art film; avant-garde, experimental or exploratory film; documentary; Hong Kong cinema (in Historical essays); socialist realism

Further Reading

C. Berry (1988b), interviews with an introduction on mainland directors; J. Dai (1995), a feminist, historical survey of mainland productions; S. Donald (1995), a study of orientalism and silence; K. Hu (1988), a critical survey of mainland filmmaking in the 1980s; S. Teo (1994–5), a discussion of Hong Kong filmmaking; E. Yau (1990), a dissertation on filmic discourse on women in China.

(YZ)

Women Flowers

(Nüren hua)

dir./sc. Wang Jin
with Pu Chaoying, Yuan Li, Liu Wei, Zhu Hongbo, Zhou Yan
Guangzhou: Pearl River Film, 1994

After his **Widow Village** (1988) and *The* **Wedding Maidens** (1990), this film is the third in Wang Jin's trilogy on women who are bound by age-old traditions. According to a local custom in the Pearl River delta, young girls always wear long braids, while married women wear their hair up in a bun. Women who do not want to get married become 'self-combed women' by undergoing the rituals and wearing a special type of hair bun. Formed as a society of their own, 'self-combed women' also adopt young girls and train them in music and song; when these 'sister flowers'

Plate 49   *Women Flowers* (1994)

grow up, they are sold to rich officials and merchants as concubines.

Living in a large, secluded compound, Shang Meiju is the head of a self-combed women's society. She conducts the initiation ritual for a silk factory worker, Ah Di. Because her marriage was arranged years ago by her parents, Ah Di is kidnapped by her husband Ah Fu. Shang brings a group of self-combed women, all wearing black, to Ah Fu's village, demanding Ah Di's release. When they pull out scissors to threaten group suicide, the village head negotiates a fake marriage between Ah Di and Ah Fu. On the wedding night, Ah Di is taken away from Ah Fu by Ah Yin, a strong-muscled woman.

Eighteen-year-old Yanzhi, Shang's adopted 'sister flower', has grown up to be a beautiful songstress. Shang sends her to perform at a famous teahouse in Guangzhou, and sets her prize at twenty thousand silver dollars. Back at their compound, Yanzhi is shocked to find Shang and Ah Yin in bed together, and the rumours about Shang's lesbian lifestyle seem confirmed. Ah Qin, another self-combed woman, falls in love with the brother of her diseased 'husband'. She soon finds herself pregnant and commits suicide in despair. Meanwhile, in spite of their fake marriage, Ah Di and Ah Fu are genuinely in love. Their dating is

discovered, and Shang decides to punish Ah Di by drowning her in the river, as tradition dictates. On the day of the punishment, Ah Di is rescued by Ah Fu, who accuses Shang of extreme cruelty.

A rich merchant comes to purchase Yanzhi. Shang recognizes that he is none other than her missing lover years ago. Yanzhi realizes that 'sister flowers' like her are commodity items and that Shang uses self-combed women for her own revenge against men in general. In protest, Yanzhi pulls out a pair of scissors and stabs herself to death. Shang goes insane as her society of self-combed women falls apart.

(IJS)

Women's Story

(Nüren de gushi)

dir. **Peng Xiaolian**
sc. Xiao Mao
with Zhang Wenrong, Zhang Min, Song Ruhui
Shanghai: Shanghai Film, 1987

When life in a poor village becomes too hard to endure, three peasant women make their way to the city to sell yarn. Each goes for a different purpose. Laizi's mother hopes to earn enough money to buy her son candy and help her two brothers-in-law find wives. Xiaofeng is from a family with four daughters but no son and wants to show the villagers that a woman can be useful. Forced to marry a deaf mute in exchange for a bride for her brother, Jinxiang is fleeing her husband. With these three women, the director tries to explore and express the workings of feminine psychology.

The country women stick out in the city like a sore thumb and they have to endure many insults. Laizi's mother sells her yarn in a residential district, but her first customer is a swindler who pays for her produce with counterfeit money. The three friends spend a frustrating night in a public bathhouse being ridiculed by city women. They then travel to a distant mountain conurbation. At last they begin to make money and enjoy a taste of city life. Laizi's mother saves every penny for her family. Jinxiang admires the attractions of **urban life**. Xiaofeng enters into a relationship with a construction worker from her home town: her premarital sexual engagement suggests that even a peasant girl can choose a man and live according to her desires. As each woman perceives the differences between city and village, and between money and poverty, their self-consciousness and self-confidence increases.

The journey to the city brings not only money but also new ideas. The women return well dressed and self-reliant. Yet rural poverty and ignorance still remain. As they enter the village, the deaf mute prepares to kidnap Jinxiang and drag her back to his house. Xiaofeng and Laizi's mother stand firm next to Jinxiang as they prepare for the confrontation with the approaching male figures.

(SC)

Wong, Anthony

(Huang Qiusheng)

b. 1961, Hong Kong
Actor, director

One of the most bizarre and talented actors in Hong Kong, Anthony Wong is its only movie star with formal stage training. Abandoned by his British father while a boy, he suffered prejudice for his Eurasian background while at boarding school. After studying for three years at a local TV station's training programme for actors, he decided to learn his craft properly at Hong Kong's prestigious Academy for the Performing Arts, where he played classical roles in *Cyrano de Bergerac*,

Oedipus Rex, and *Othello*. He returned to television acting and entered films.

Wong played a number of diverse roles before finding his screen persona as Hong Kong's favourite psychopath in Category 3 films. During 1992 he delivered strong performances in John **Woo**'s *Hard Boiled* and Ringo **Lam**'s *Full Contact*. In 1993, he won Best Actor award at HKFA for his leading role in **Bunman: the Untold Story** (dir. Herman Yau), which is based on a real crime about a restaurant worker who kills his boss and family and uses their bodies to make pork buns. He refined his psychopathic persona that same year appearing in *The Heroic Trio*, *The Executioners* (both dir. Johnny To), *Daughter of Darkness*, *Taxi Hunter* (dir. Herman Yau), and *Underground Banker* (dir. Bosco Lam). The last film satirized Category 3 with Wong teaming up with Dr. Lamb to avenge his wife's treatment by brutal Triads. One hilarious scene showed a berserk Wong chasing his enemy while incessantly muttering, 'Human Pork Buns' – a reference to *Bunman*.

Wong has also turned to directing. He merged Fassbinder and Polanski in *The New Tenant* (1995) and attempted to seduce three lesbians in *Top Banana Club* (1996). However, he can also perform light **comedy**, as his 'wannabee' role in *Cop Image* (1994) revealed. It parodied American and Hong Kong gangster films with a closing dedication to Danny **Lee**.

See also: Category 3 film; gangster film

Further Reading

F. Dannen and B. Long (1997: 138–41), a profile with a selected filmography.

(TW)

Wong, Che Kirk

(Huang Zhiqiang)

b. 1949, Hong Kong
Director

Che Kirk Wong studied fashion design at Jacob Kramer College in Leeds, England in 1974. After graduation, he attended Croydon College of Art to study stage design and film production. He subsequently worked for Anglia Television and at Covent Garden. He became a TV producer after returning to Hong Kong in 1978. His first film as director was *The Club* (1981), and he has recently appeared in a starring role in *Crystal Fortune Run* (1994).

Wong brings a stylish ambiguity to the **action film**, which he has cultivated without being imitative of the powerful examples of John **Woo** and Ringo **Lam**. His action sequences are direct and generally umromanticized but nevertheless poetic. His *Gunmen* (1988) and *Organized Crime and Triad Bureau* (1993) both employ the evocative talents of composer Danny Chung, and the latter stars **gangster film** icon Danny **Lee**. Wong does not shrink from exposing the less attractive side of the police or the more humane side of the criminal. This facet of his work has caused him to be characterized as a subtler and more enigmatic director than John Woo or **Tsui Hark**. Wong's direction of the fact-based *Crime Story* (1993) lent a new intensity and depth to Jackie **Chan**'s usual screen image.

Further Reading

S. Hammond and M. Wilkins (1996: 198), a brief discussion.

(KH)

Wong Jing

(Wang Jing)

b. 1956, Hong Kong
Director, actor, producer, screen writer

One of the most prolific directors in the 1990s, Wong Jing is regarded as a representative of fast-pace commercial filmmaking in Hong Kong. He often directed two films at the same time, in addition to writing screenplays and supervising productions.

Wong is the son of Wang Tianlin (*b.* 1928), a veteran director of Cantonese movies. Wong graduated from the Chinese Department at the Chinese University of Hong Kong and served as script writer for TV dramas. After his directorial début with *Challenge of the Gamesters* (1981), Wong did not go full speed until *God of Gamblers* (1989) and its numerous sequels. Since then, he has tried various genres or **mixed genres**, such as **comedy**, gangster, martial arts as well as Category 3 films. Among his other notable titles are *City Hunter* (1993), starring Jackie **Chan**, *Naked Killer* (1992, with Wong as producer), featuring lesbian killers, and *The Last Hero in China* (1993), starring Jet **Li** in a parody of *Once Upon a Time in China* (*dir.* **Tsui Hark**, 1991).

See also: Cantonese cinema (under Hong Kong cinema in Historical essays); Category 3 film; gangster film; genre films; martial arts film

Further Reading

F. Dannen and B. Long (1997: 48–9, 141–3), a profile with a selected filmography.

(YZ)

Wong, Joey

(Wang Zuxian)

b. 1967, Taipei
Actress

Famous for being habitually cast in the role of romantic ghost, Joey Wong made her film début while still in high school. She played an enigmatic female ghost for the first time in *This Year It Will Be Cold by the River Bank* (1982). From then on she became a regular performer in Hong Kong films, attracting most attention for *A **Chinese Ghost Story*** (*dir.* **Ching Siu Tung**, 1987) and its sequels. She is popular in Japan, where she was invited to star in a series of TV dramas.

(YZ)

Wong Kar-Wai

(Wang Jiawei)

b. 1958
Director, screen writer

Wong Kar-Wai is one of the most talented of Hong Kong's post-1988 'second wave' of young directors. With a mere five feature films under his belt, and with domestic critics still divided in their estimation of his work, Wong has already established a secure worldwide reputation as one of the most daring avant-garde filmmakers active in the various Chinese communities throughout the world. His films are celebrated for their flamboyant narrative transitions and spatial mismatches, their charming character observations, and for the productive collaborations the director has forged with cinematographer Christopher Doyle (Du Kefeng, who prefers hand-held cameras and stop-motion techniques that achieve unique visual effects), production designer William Chang, and musicians Frankie Chan and Roel A. Garcia – not to mention a veritable throng of charismatic actors and superstars.

Wong Kar-Wai started screenplay writing in 1982 and turned to directing with *As Tears Go By* (1988). Although firmly located in the Hong Kong gangster film genre, Wong's first film feels completely fresh and original. The influence for a number of subsequent titles, the most accomplished of which is *Moment of Romance* (*dir.* Benny Chan, 1990), Wong's sensitive dissection of fragmented and broken lives was taken further in his extraordinary second title, **Days of Being Wild** (1991). This big budget **melodrama** was beset by production difficulties but still managed to attract excellent notices for its sharp insights on the nature of love and memory. (The film also evidences Wong's own creative transformation of influences such as Nicholas Ray and Orson Welles). A study of alienation and deracination in contemporary **urban life**, *Days of Being Wild* features three protagonists who walk aimlessly around the city talking to themselves more than other people. This deep sense of existential crisis is further examined in **Chungking Express** (1994), which provides a more hopeful though equally ambivalent ending, and which brought Wong to the attention of international critics of **art film**. Shot back-to-back with *Chungking Express*, the epic *Ashes of Time* (1994) pushes the **martial arts film** in completely new directions, combining specifically Asian philosophical wisdoms with a modernist deconstruction of narrative.

Wong Kar-Wai's *Fallen Angels* (1995) is a film noir-ish account of night-time Hong Kong. While not as groundbreaking as its predecessors, the film is still different and innovative enough to confirm the director's presence on the international scene. At the 1997 Cannes FF, Wong Kar-Wai won Best Director award for his *Happy Together*, a story of two frustrated Chinese gay men struggling in the beautiful but alienating landscape of Argentina. Wong Kar-Wai occupies a special place in contemporary film history in that he moves effortlessly between the cult and mainstream marketplaces. Though still young, he has exerted a sizeable impact on Taiwanese (e.g., **Tsai Ming-liang**) and Asian American filmmakers.

See also: avant-garde, experimental or exploratory film

Further Reading

A. Abbas (1997: 48–62), a chapter on Wong; L. Gross (1996), a discussion of *Fallen Angels*; F. Luo (1995: 37–59), on Wong and *fin-de-siècle* decadence; C. Stephens (1996b), on Wong's vision of memory; C. Tsui (1995), a critical study of Wong's films.

(YZ, JS)

Wong, Raymond
(Huang Baiming)

b. 1948
Actor, screen writer, producer

Raymond Wong worked at a radio station and a theatre troupe before joining TVB as an actor in 1970. He wrote several TV scripts and screenplays in the 1970s. In 1980 he co-founded, with Carl **Mak** and Dean Shek (Shi Tian, *b.* 1950), Cinema City (Xin yicheng), which soon became a leading force in the Hong Kong film industry. His screenplays are mostly comedies, including the immensely popular *Aces Go Places* (*dir.* Eric Tsang, 1982) and its sequels. **Papa, Can You Hear Me Sing?** (*dir.* Yu Kanping, 1983), a film he co-wrote with **Wu Nien-chen**, Taiwan's leading screen writer, was highly acclaimed.

See also: comedy

(YZ)

Woo, John
(Wu Yusen)

b. Canton, 1946
Director

After his family fled the Communist mainland when he was three years old, John Woo spent a poverty-ridden childhood in Hong Kong. Schooled, in part, through funds donated to a Christian Methodist church, he soon developed a passion for movies. Woo experimented with short films during the late 1960s before finding script-supervising work at Cathay Studios. His fortunes really began to change when he was employed at Shaw Brothers as assistant to veteran director **Chang Che**.

Woo made his feature film début in 1974 with *The Young Dragons*. Now working for Golden Harvest, he oversaw the production of a dozen titles in as many years, including martial arts (*Hand of Death*, 1976, starring Jackie **Chan**), Cantonese opera (*Princess Chang Ping*, 1975), and comedy (*From Rags to Riches*, 1980). In 1986, aided by producer **Tsui Hark** and actor **Chow Yun-Fat**, Woo's career went ballistic. *A **Better Tomorrow*** looks like a **gangster film**, sounds like a **melodrama**, and is shot through with martial chivalry; it became an enormous hit at the Hong Kong box office. From there, the director never looked back, producing a string of blistering gunplay flicks, notably *A Better Tomorrow, II* (1987), *The **Killer*** (1989), and *Hard Boiled* (1992), the first two winning top prizes at HKFA and Taipei GHA. Curiously, though, Woo's most intense and deeply personal film, the Vietnam drama *A Bullet in the Head* (1989), is the only one of his major productions since 1986 not to feature his alter ego, Chow Yun-Fat.

John Woo moved to North America in 1992. He made the respectable *Hard Target* (1993) for Universal, and the more financially successful *Broken Arrow* (1996) for Twentieth Century Fox. Woo also shot an insipid remake of his 1991 Cinema City title *Once a Thief* for Fox Television in 1996. While the director's experiences in Hollywood have not been completely happy ones, the thrill of his post-*Better Tomorrow* slaughterfests will bring a smile to the face of any true action fan.

Further Reading

A. Ciecko (1997), on Woo and transnational action; B. Logan (1996), with a career overview; M. McDonagh (1993a, b), a profile with an interview; J. Sandell (1996), on male intimacy; J. Stringer (1997b), on masculinity; T. Williams (1997a, b), on Woo's crisis cinema and his Hollywood ventures.

(JS)

Wooden Man's Bride, The

aka *The Porter* (Yan shen, *aka* Wukui)

dir. **Huang Jianxin**
sc. Yang Zhengguang
with Wang Lan, Wang Fuli, Wang Yumei, Chang Shih
Xi'an: Xi'an Film/Taipei: Longxiang Film, 1993

In sharp contrast to his early urban films, Huang Jianxin here follows **Zhang Yimou**'s model of sexual repression and transgression, which means that *The Wooden Man's Bride* is a Chinese 'western' set in the northwestern desert, concerning an isolated community and a legend about adultery and punishment. The film opens with a caravan taking a new bride to her groom's family. Sword-wielding horsemen sweep down and kidnap the bride. She is released unharmed when her porter, Wukui, follows her to the bandits' camp and impresses their chief with his loyalty. As Wukui carries the bride back to the Liu family, they learn that the groom has died in a freak accident.

The wealthy Liu family is very influential in the village. Madame Liu, a widow and the owner of a tofu mill, not only rules the business but also defends the traditional morals associated with female virtue. She subjects the bride to a chastity test. Kneeling naked on a white sheet strewn with ashes, the bride sneezes when tickled with chicken feathers. The ashes remain undisturbed, demonstrating that her virginity remains intact. Madame Liu insists that the bride be married with a wooden statue of the dead groom. The wedding procession inside the courtyard is transformed into a funeral rite via a single crane shot. As white lanterns and paper money fill the screen, the bride, hands tied behind her, is confined inside a white sedan and married off to the dead.

Young Mistress cannot endure the wooden man. After a number of unsuccessful attempts to escape she finds solace with Wukui. When their affair is discovered, Madame Liu banishes Wukui from the village and punishes Young Mistress by having her Achilles tendons severed. Wukui returns a year later with a band of followers and asks Madame Liu to hang herself. At the very moment Madame Liu's foot kicks the chair, Wukui carries the crippled Young Mistress away. The film ends with a shot of a memorial archway the villagers erected to honour Madame Liu's chastity.

(SC)

Wu Di

Independent filmmaker

A member of the **Sixth Generation**, Wu Di attended a special cinematography class at BFA. He directed a little known **independent film**, *Yellow Goldfish* (1995), with the assistance of the screen writer and actor Ma Xiaoyong, who studied in BFA's Directing Department between 1985 and 1989.

Further Reading

X. Han (1995), an informative piece on the Sixth Generation.

(YZ)

Wu Nien-chen

(Wu Nianzhen)

b. 1952, Taipei, Taiwan
Screen writer, director

One of the most important screen writers of New Taiwan Cinema, Wu Nien-chen was born into a miner's family and worked his way through high school. He started publishing stories in the early 1970s and won several literary prizes. In 1980 he entered CMPC and began his prolific screen career. His screenplays number more than sixty and several have won top prizes at Taipei GHA. His major works include *That Day on the Beach* (*dir.* Edward **Yang**, 1983), *Osmanthus Alley* (*dir.* **Chen Kun-hou**, 1987), and those directed by **Hou Hsiao-hsien**: *Sandwich Man* (1983), *Dust in the Wind* (1986), *A City of Sadness* (1989), and *The* **Puppet Master** (1993), some of them co-written with **Chu Tien-wen**.

Wu turned to directing with *A Borrowed Life* (1993), an autobiographical depiction of his father's difficult transition from the period of Japanese occupation to that of modern Taiwan. The film won a top prize at Turin FF. His second feature, *Buddha Bless America* (1996), is a light **comedy** dramatizing the devastating effect US military training rituals inflict on a Taiwanese village in the 1960s.

See also: New Taiwan Cinema (under Taiwan cinema in Historical essays)

Further Reading
S. Teng (1996c), an informative piece.

(YZ)

Wu Tianming

b. 1939, near Xi'an, Shaanxi province
Director, producer

An important figure in mainland film production of the 1980s, Wu earned his international reputation not only by directing his own award-winning films but, more significantly, by making Xi'an Film Studio a home base for both trend-setting art films (*yishu pian*) and commercial films (*shangye pian*). He entered Xi'an Studio as an actor in the early 1960s and performed in several dramas and films. He attended a special directing class at BFA in 1976 and returned to Xi'an to serve as deputy director. Elected studio head at the end of 1983, he started to recruit promising young directors from around the country. During 1985–8 he successfully engaged on two fronts by producing crowd-pleasing entertainment films (so as to give the studio a stable financial base) while subsidizing the experimental or 'exploratory' films (*tansuo pian*) that would earn the studio's international reputation. In the first category, the

two-part *Legend of the Dowager Empress's Tomb* (*dir.* Li Yundong, 1986), *Desperation* (*dir.* **Zhou Xiaowen**, Shi Chenfeng, 1987) and *The* **Price of Frenzy** (*dir.* Zhou Xiaowen, 1988) took the market by storm. In the second category, **Horse Thief** (*dir.* **Tian Zhuangzhuang**, 1986), *King of the Children* (*dir.* **Chen Kaige**) and *Red Sorghum* (*dir.* **Zhang Yimou**, both 1987) captured critical attention in China and abroad. In addition, Wu formulated a new genre for Xi'an, Chinese **Westerns**, thereby securing his studio a legitimately 'central' place in the mainland.

Wu is himself an accomplished director. *Reverberations of Life* (*co-dir.* with **Teng Wenji**, 1979) is a passionate indictment of the 'Gang of Four' who ruined the entire country during the **Cultural Revolution**. His solo feature, *The* **River Without Buoys** (1983), continues his reflection on the devastating political events of the past. With *Life* (1984) he turned his attention to such contemporary issues as the rural–urban divide. *Old Well* (1987), featuring Zhang Yimou as both cinematographer and male lead, won the grand prize at Tokyo FF. An outspoken studio head, Wu has been under constant political pressure. He left for the USA in 1989 and decided to stay on in Los Angeles. He returned to China to shoot *The* **King of Masks** (1996), an award-winning co-production between Youth Film Studio and Shaw Brothers of Hong Kong that concerns a wandering local artist and his troublesome quest for a 'male' heir.

See also: art film; avant-garde, experimental or exploratory film

Further Reading
H. Liang and J. Shapiro (1986: 165–77), an early profile; X. Luo (1989), a biographic sketch; T. Rayns (1989: 19–26), a historical treatment.

(YZ)

Wu Wenguang

b. 1956, Yunnan province
Independent filmmaker, video journalist

After spending four years in the countryside, Wu Wenguang studied Chinese literature at Yunnan University during 1978–84. He worked as a journalist for a Kunming TV station producing documentaries. His independent films include *Chinese People: Artists* (1989), *Chinese People: Kungfu*

(1989), *Bumming in Beijing – The Last Dreamers* (1990), and *1966: My Times with the Red Guards* (1992–3). These documentaries were shot entirely on video and have helped redefine *cinéma vérité* in the Chinese context. Wu's in-depth analyses and fresh perspectives have provided a model for the 'New Chinese Documentary Movement' and attracted critical attention at home and abroad. Wu ignored the official ban on his work to complete *At Home in the World* (1995), a sequel to *Bumming in Beijing*, which concerns some of his earlier subjects – namely, a group of marginalized artists surviving in Beijing outside the official system – who are now in **exile** in various parts of the world and struggle to find the meaning of life. Wu has been invited to screen his work in the West.

See also: documentary; independent film

Further Reading

K. Eder and D. Rossell (1993: 109); B. Reynaud (1996), a brief discussion of his two documentaries.

(YZ)

Wu Yigong

b. 1 December 1938, Hangzhou, Zhejiang province
Director

A noted mainland director of the 1980s, Wu Yigong graduated from the Directing Department of BFA in 1960 and was assigned to Haiyan Film Studio in Shanghai. He worked as assistant director on a number of productions. *Night Rain on the River* (*co-dir.* **Wu Yonggang**, 1980), which won Best Film at 1981 China GRA, placed Wu Yigong's name in the public spotlight. His solo feature, *My Memory of Old Beijing* (1982), which won Best Director award at 1983 China GRA as well as the Golden Eagle at the Second FF held in Manila, further consolidated Wu's reputation as one of the most talented directors of the 1980s. Like many directors of his generation who also hold administrative positions (e.g., **Wu Tianming**, **Xie Fei**), Wu does not direct films on a year-by-year basis. His *The Descendants of Confucius* (1992) was awarded Best Director and Best Film prizes by MBFT in 1993.

Wu has served as manager of Shanghai Film Studio, general manager of the United Film Company of Shanghai, and director of the Bureau of Motion Pictures under Shanghai Municipal government.

Further Reading

K. Eder and D. Rossell (1993: 110–12), with an interview.

(ZX)

Wu Yin

(Yang Ying)

b. 2 August 1909, Tianjin
d. 10 April 1991
Actress

A noted actress of the 1930s–40s, Wu Yin accompanied a friend to Lianhua Film Company in 1934: while her friend's application was rejected by the studio, Wu was invited to appear in *New Woman* (*dir.* **Cai Chusheng**, 1934). She accepted the invitation and changed her name to Wu Yin.

In fact, Wu was no stranger to the film world. She had frequented cinemas in her childhood and attended Mingxing Film Company's film school when she was sixteen. After her début, Wu worked with several minor studios before signing up with Mingxing in 1936. She appeared in many films now considered classics, such as *A New Year's Coin*, *A Woman of Devotion* (both *dir.* **Zhang Shichuan**) and *Crossroads* (*dir.* **Shen Xiling**, all 1937). Although Wu mostly played supporting roles in these films, her performances were superb.

During the Sino-Japanese war, Wu took minor roles in four films, two of which were written by the Communist screenwriter **Yang Hansheng**. After the war, she returned to Shanghai and participated in the work of Kunlun Film Company. During the next twenty years she was involved in the production of over twenty films. Her performances in *Spring River Flows East* (*dir.* Cai Chusheng, **Zheng Junli**, 1947), *Myriad of Lights* (*dir.* **Shen Fu**, 1948) and *Crows and Sparrows* (*dir.* Zheng Junli, 1949) earned praise from critics and audiences. Since Wu tended to play elderly ladies in her films, she was sometimes labelled the 'Number One Old Lady of the Orient'.

Further Reading

Y. Wu (1993), a memoir; ZDX (1982–6: 2: 147–55), a short biography.

(ZX)

Wu Yonggang

b. 1 November 1907, Jiangsu province
d. 18 December 1982
Director

A famous director of the 1930s, Wu Yonggang began working with film at the age of nineteen. His father did not think highly of the medium and encouraged him to study fine arts at the Commercial Press. However, Wu found employment at Lily (Baihe) Film Company and was soon discovered by **Shi Dongshan**, who promoted him to stage designer.

Wu's directing début, **Goddess** (1934), a Lianhua Film Company production, was well received by both critics and audiences. He next directed *Little Angel* (1935), which was based on a prize-winning screenplay. Although his name is often associated with leftist films, Wu was a socially conscious artist in broader terms. In *The Desert Island* (1936), for example, Wu searched for a common humanism that could unite people, and he lamented the divisions brought about by class consciousness. Yet when it came to foreign encroachments against China, Wu was a staunch nationalist. In the patriotic *The Pioneers* (1936), Wu advocated unity among the Chinese and armed resistance against foreign invaders.

Wu's films became more diverse during the period 1937–41. There were entertaining action flicks, costume dramas and romantic tearjerkers. Eventually, Wu went to Chongqing, where he worked for Nationalist Central Film Studio and began to film *The Path to National Reconstruction*. However, the project ran into problems. First, the original female lead, **Hu Die**, had to be replaced because of Hu's entangled relationship with Dai Li, head of the Nationalist secret police. Then the crew became caught up in a Japanese bombing raid during location shooting and lost most of its footage and equipment. The project was finally aborted. After the war, Wu directed several noteworthy films, including *Loyal Family* (1946) and *Decision of a Lifetime* (1947). He also founded Daye Film Company and produced *Waiting for Spring* (1947).

During the 1950s Wu directed three films: *The Far Away Village* (1950) deals with land reform, *Hasen and Jiamila* (1952) tackles issues of ethnicity, and *Qiu Meets the Goddess of Flowers* (1956) is a fairy tale. In 1957 Wu wrote an essay criticizing the party's excessive control over the film industry. He

was labelled a Rightist and deprived of any opportunity to direct more films. (He was not able to to make another film until 1962.) Wu made two popular, politically 'safe' opera movies. In the post-**Cultural Revolution** period, he directed the highly acclaimed **Night Rain on the River** (*co-dir.* **Wu Yigong**, 1980), which won Best Film award at the 1981 China GRA. Wu Yonggang then retired from filmmaking.

See also: action film; costume drama; filmed stage performances

Further Reading
W. Rothman (1993), an analysis of *Goddess*; Y. Wu (1986), a memoir; ZDX (1982–6: 2: 156–63), a short biography.

(ZX)

Wu Ziniu

b. 3 November 1953, Leshan, Sichuan province
Director, screen writer

One of the most productive members of the **Fifth Generation**, Wu Ziniu has made a number of controversial films since graduating from the Directing Department of BFA in 1982. Like many of his classmates, he spent several years in the countryside during the **Cultural Revolution**, during which time he took up creative writing. He published literary works while studying at BFA. After graduation, he was assigned to Xiaoxiang Film Studio, where he co-directed, with Chen Lu, *A Probation Member* (1983), a **children's film** that makes extensive use of direct-sound recording and won a special prize at China GRA. Wu's next feature, *Secret Decree* (1984), co-directed with Li Jingmin, resembles **One and Eight** (*dir.* **Zhang Junzhao**, 1984) in its graphic rendition of bloody wars, and reportedly broke box-office records. Wu has been obsessed by war films ever since, but a major setback occurred when the government banned *The Dove Tree* (1985) for the sensitivity of its subject matter (the Sino-Vietnam border war). It was the first ban on a Fifth Generation work.

The Last Day of Winter (1986) was the fourth film Wu directed for Xiaoxiang Studio before starting work at other studios. **Evening Bell** (1988), produced by August First Film Studio, presents a disturbingly candid account of hatred, hunger and humiliation amongst soldiers in action. The film had to pass through four stages of film censorship, resulting in numerous changes that took months to complete. When it was finally released it won several awards, among them a Silver Bear at Berlin FF and Best Director at China GRA. Wu's *Joyous Heroes* (1988) and its sequel, *Between the Living and the Dead* (1988), produced by Fujian Film Studio, again emphasize the irrationalities of rape, decapitation and other acts of human violence. By the end of the film, most of the characters, including an unborn baby, are murdered or ruthlessly gunned down. These two films again proved popular and won Wu another Best Director award at China GRA.

Wu returned to Xiaoxiang to shoot *The **Big Mill*** (1990), a film about love and revenge in the 1920s civil war. Financed by Hong Kong's Sil-Metropole, the film was entered at the Berlin FF but abruptly withdrawn by the Chinese government. Wu's *Mountains of the Sun* (1991) was followed by *Nanjing 1937* (Nanjing 1937, 1994), a **historical film** about war crimes committed by the Japanese in Nanjing during World War II. With Hong Kong backing he made an avant-garde film, ***Sparkling Fox*** (1993), posing, in the process, existential questions for audiences by isolating two self-exiled men amidst snow-covered mountains and letting them find the true meaning of life. The film won several festival awards around the world. In spite of his unpleasant encounters with the processes of censorship, Wu has never lost his combative spirit and seems determined to pursue his iconoclastic vision. In addition to films, he has produced dozens of TV dramas.

See also: avant-garde, experimental or exploratory film; censorship and film; war film

Further Reading

W. Liu (1988), an informative interview; T. Rayns (1989: 44–7), a brief discussion; Z. Wu *et al.* (1995), on *Nanjing 1937*.

(YZ)

X

Xia Gang

b. 1953, Beijing

Director, producer

A late runner amongst the **Fifth Generation**, Xia Gang started attracting critical attention in the late 1980s. After graduating from the Direction Department at BFA in 1982, he started to work at Beijing Film Studio. Unlike many of his classmates who acquired fame by making war films (**Wu Ziniu** and **Zhang Junzhao**) or films of **rural life** (**Chen Kaige**, **Li Shaohong**, **Peng Xiaolian** and **Zhang Yimou**), Xia Gang has stayed within the realms of contemporary **urban life**. *Half Flame, Half Brine* (1989), adapted from Wang Shuo's novel, is a study of the urban underground world emphasizing disillusionment and the renewed quest for identity. The theme of disillusionment is further explored in *Unexpected Passion* (1991), which focuses on an improbable love relationship between a terminally ill woman and her aggressive suitor. Xia's two early films are marked by certain superficialities of characterization and inconsistencies of narrative structure, but with **After Separation** (1992) he both develops a more nuanced treatment of human emotions and continues to display his trade mark of satirical humour. *No One Cheers* (1993), co-written by Wang Shuo, continues Xia Gang's studies on deteriorating relationships between urban couples. **Yesterday's Wine** (1995), a psychological film about the maturation of an urban girl tormented by the memory of her loveless childhood and her sexual relationships with a father and his son, marks Xia's change in style. In terms of urban sensibility and humour, Xia is more akin to **Huang Jianxin** than his Fifth Generation classmates, but he pays more attention to issues of **love and marriage** than Huang does.

See also: war film

Further Reading

K. Eder and D. Rossell (1993: 113–7), with an interview.

(YZ)

Xia Meng

b. 1932, Shanghai

Actress, producer

Xia Meng entered Hong Kong's Changcheng Film Company in 1950 and starred in about forty films, most notably *New Widow* (1956) and *Between Tears and Smiles* (1964), both directed by **Zhu Shilin**. She formed Blue Bird Film Company (Qingniao) in the 1980s, which has produced films like **Homecoming** (*dir.* **Yim Ho**, 1984).

(YZ)

Xia Yan

(Shen Duanxian, Shen Naixi)

b. 30 October 1900, Zhejiang province

d. 6 February 1995

Screenwriter, critic

By any standard the most influential figure in Chinese filmmaking for over a half century, Xia Yan won a scholarship to study at Meiji Technical School in Japan in 1921. He became inspired by Marxism and befriended numerous Chinese revolutionaries in exile. In 1927, Xia was expelled by the Japanese authorities because of his involvement in political activity. He returned to Shanghai, joined the CCP, and took over the organization of the League of Leftist Writers.

In 1932, Mingxing Film Company invited Xia and his friends, **Ah Ying** and Zheng Boqi, to work for the studio. Xia accepted the invitation and formed a secret underground CCP team there. Under Xia's leadership, the leftist film movement gained momentum. In addition to writing screenplays and criticism, Xia made a great contribution by introducing the Soviet film to Chinese audiences.

Xia's first screenplay, **Wild Torrents** (*dir.* **Cheng Bugao**, 1933), used the great flood of 1931 as a background for the staging of class struggle between peasants and landlords. Xia then adapted Mao Dun's story **Spring Silkworms** (*dir.* Cheng Bugao, 1933) into a screenplay. While these two films deal with rural bankruptcy, Xia also portrayed the difficulties of **urban life** in *The Market of Beauty* (*dir.* **Zhang Shichuan**), *Children of Our Time* (*dir.* **Li Pingqian**), *Twenty-Four Hours in Shanghai* (*dir.* **Shen Xiling**, all 1933) and *Goddess of Liberty* (*dir.* **Situ Huimin**, 1935).

After 1949, Xia served as the cultural chief in Shanghai. He was then appointed Deputy Minister of Culture in 1954. Xia continued his interest in film, and in 1962 shared with **Shui Hua** a Best Screenplay award for *Revolutionary Family* (*dir.* Shui Hua, 1961). Like many veteran filmmakers of the pre-1949 period, Xia suffered political persecution during the **Cultural Revolution**. In 1965, he was removed from his official position and spent the next eight years in prison. In the post-Cultural Revolution period, Xia devoted himself mostly to writing memoirs and editing his earlier writings for publication.

Further Reading

Y. Xia (1985), a memoir; ZDX (1982–6: 1: 261–77), a short biography.

(ZX)

Xi'an Incident

(Xi'an shibian)

dir. **Cheng Yin**
sc. Zheng Zhong, Cheng Yin
with Jin Ange, Gu Yue, Sun Feihu, Xin Jing, Wang Tiecheng
Xi'an: Xi'an Film, 1981

This historical film is based on an actual event that shocked the country in 1936. Despite its pro-Communist bias, the film is nevertheless 'objective' in its representation of various historical figures, particularly the Nationalists.

In 1935, Japan steps up its aggression against China. Generals Zhang Xueliang and Yang Hucheng, who were ordered by Chiang Kai-shek to fight the Communists in Northwestern China, suffer heavy losses and reach a truce with the CCP. As tensions between the KMT central authorities and the forces belonging to the two generals flare up in Xi'an, where Zhang and Yang's headquarters are located, Chiang flies to the city to present Zhang and Yang with two alternatives: either continue to fight the Communists or relocate somewhere else. Zhang and Yang try to persuade Chiang to turn his attention from fighting the Communists to fighting the Japanese, but Chiang refuses to listen.

Student demonstrators march towards Chiang's residence. Chiang's guards receive the order to fire on anyone who comes within shooting distance. Zhang halts the students and promises them that he will satisfy their demands to fight the Japanese. Later that evening, Zhang and Yang arrest Chiang and force him into changing his position.

The news of Chiang's kidnapping shocks the nation. The KMT government in Nanjing is divided as to how to respond to the situation. While the CCP sends a delegation, headed by Zhou Enlai, to Xi'an, Chiang's wife also flies to Xi'an. After a series of negotiations, a peaceful settlement to the Xi'an Incident is reached. Chiang agrees to stop his military campaign against the Communists and turn his attention to fighting the Japanese, and Zhang prepares to escort Chiang back to Nanjing. Zhou tries to stop Zhang from going with Chiang, but by the time Zhou arrives at the airport, the plane is already airborne.

The film won awards of Best Director at the 1982 China GRA as well as Best Film from the Ministry of Culture in 1981.

(ZX)

Xian Xinghai

b. 13 June 1905, Guangdong
d. 30 October 1945
Composer

A well-known musician who composed musical scores for films during the 1930s, Xian Xinghai was born in Macao and became interested in music during his high school years. In 1915 he passed a competitive examination and enrolled in the Music Department at Beijing Academy of Arts. In 1928 he was admitted into the Shanghai

Conservatory. After being expelled from the school for his involvement in student protests, Xian went to Paris in 1930 to study musical composition at the Paris Conservatory. He returned to China and worked for Baidai Record Company in Shanghai. Meanwhile, he also served as a music consultant for Xinhua Film Company. Between 1935 and 1937, Xian composed scores for more than a dozen films. His music for *Singing at Midnight* (*dir.* **Ma-Xu Weibang**, 1937) finally brought him public recognition.

In 1938, Xian went to Yan'an and taught at Lu Xun College of Arts. On his way to Yan'an, he composed the theme song for *Storm Over Taihang Mountains* (*dir.* He Mengfu, 1940). Xian joined the CCP in 1939 and was sent to the former Soviet Union. Xian died of cancer in Moscow before getting the chance to finish the score for a **documentary** called *Yan'an and the Eighth-Route Army*.

Further Reading

ZDX (1982–6: 2: 205–11), a short biography.

(ZX)

Xie Fei

b. 14 August 1942, Yan'an province
Director

A famous mainland director of the 1980s–90s, Xie Fei graduated from the Directing Department of BFA in 1965 and has been teaching there ever since. He has also served as department chair and vice-president of BFA. However, Xie's real achievement lies in the number of highly acclaimed films he has directed.

After co-directing two films with his BFA colleagues Zheng Dongtian and Wang Xinyu, Xie independently directed *Our Field* (1983), a moving drama about educated youth that earned much critical acclaim. *A Girl from Hunan* (*co-dir.* Wu Lan, 1986), though, earned international recognition: in 1988, this cinematic study of female **sexuality** and bizarre marriage practices in rural China won the Golden Panda award at a French film festival and a 'Don Quixote' award at a Spanish festival. Although the film was a failure at the domestic box office, it was one of the few Chinese films to achieve overseas distribution in the mid-1980s. Xie visited the USA in 1988 and conducted a year's worth of research at the University of Southern California.

Xie's next film, *Black Snow* (1989), takes a refreshing look at contemporary **urban life**. It

fared much better than his previous films both in and outside China, winning awards of Best Film at HFA and a Silver Bear at the 1990 Berlin FF. Riding high on this success, he then directed *The Woman from the Lake of Scented Soul* (1992), a **melodrama** set in contemporary rural China, which won the Golden Bear at the 1993 Berlin FF. With the release of his highly acclaimed *A Mongolian Tale* (1995), Xie further established his reputation as one of the most important film directors in China.

See also: love and marriage

Further Reading

J. Lent (1996/7), D. Sterritt (1997), two interviews; L. Padgaonkar (1996), an account of *A Mongolian Tale*.

(ZX, YZ)

Xie Jin

b. 21 November 1923
Director

One of the most popular and influential mainland directors of the 1950s–90s, Xie Jin studied theatre in 1941 and participated in stage performances in the mid-1940s. He majored in directing at National Nanjing School of Theatre in 1946 and joined Datong Film Company in 1948. After studying at a political training school in 1950, Xie served as assistant director and director in Changjiang Film Studio and Shanghai Film Studio. Since then, he has directed more than two dozens films, at least eight of which have won top awards in and out of China.

Xie drew critical attention with *Girl Basketball Player No. 5* (1957), China's first colour **sports** film, which won a silver prize at the 1957 World Youth Festival. After *Huang Baomei* (1958), a docudrama enthusiastically endorsing model workers in **socialist construction**, Xie's *Red Detachment of Women* (1961) took away several major awards at the 1962 HFA, including Best Film, Best Director and Best Actress. Although *Stage Sisters* (1965), a powerful **melodrama** about two Shanghai actresses, was completed before the **Cultural Revolution**, the film came to receive international recognition more than a decade later, winning an award at the 1980 London FF and a Golden Eagle at the 1981 Manila FF.

Xie did not suffer much during the Cultural Revolution, and he was allowed to direct **Chun Miao** (1975) and other titles favoured by ultra-leftist leaders like Jiang Qing. Since the late 1970s, he has directed a dozen films, all of which have secured some kind of award. While *The Cradle* (1979) received a Best Film award from the Ministry of Culture in 1979, *The **Legend of Tianyun Mountain*** (1980) took Best Film at the 1980 China GRA and HFA, as well as at the 1982 HKFA. His *The **Herdsman*** (1982), ***Garlands at the Foot of the Mountain*** (1984) and **Hibiscus Town** (1986) continued to command domestic as well as international attention. Considering this record number of awards, Xie's achievement in Chinese film history is truly unprecedented.

In the 1980s, Xie's films became the subject of numerous Western academic studies. His success at producing both highly popular and critically acclaimed films earned him a high level of prestige: he was invited to be a judge at the 1983 Manila FF, had a solo retrospective show in five major cities in the USA in 1985, and was granted membership of the Academy of Motion Picture Arts and Science in 1987. Even such famous **Fifth Generation** directors as **Chen Kaige**, **Tian Zhuangzhuang** and **Zhang Yimou** cannot yet boast such recognition, even though their films actually enjoy wider commercial distribution in international markets than Xie's.

Xie's importance as director lies in his representation of a particular approach to filmmaking, one the critics have dubbed the 'Xie Jin model'. The key elements of this model include an emphasis on Confucian values, the choice of popular subject matter, and the use of conventional melodramatic narratives. This approach became so dominant in mainland filmmaking of the 1980s that a number of younger directors attempted to force change by challenging the Xie Jin model. They rejected the conservatism of Xie's films, particularly his defence of the current political system, but met with little success domestically. The Xie Jin model is still the golden formula that guarantees ticket sales. In this sense, Xie continues to influence the way films are made in China.

In the 1990s, Xie founded his own film company (Xie Jin-Hengtong) and produced such titles as *An Old Man and His Dog* (1993). In 1997, he released an epic **historical film**, *The Opium War*, which was endorsed by top CCP leaders and

hit the market at the exact time Hong Kong was being handed over to mainland China.

See also: theatre and film

Further Reading

N. Browne (1994), a theoretical discussion of political melodrama; H. Da (1989), an interview; N. Ma (1994), a critical study of family melodrama; T. Tung (1987), a comment on Xie's work; P. Tyler (1996), a report on *The Opium War*; ZDX (1982–6: 6: 481–95), a short biography.

(ZX, YZ)

Xie Tian

(Xie Hongkun, Xie Jun)

b. 18 June 1914, Tianjin
Actor, director

A veteran actor and director, Xie Tian became a freelance writer and advertising agent before participating in theatre activities in the early 1930s. His first film role came along by chance, when, during the shooting of *Night Tryst* (*dir.* **Li Pingqian**, 1936), one of the actors became sick and Xie was cast as his substitute. Xie went on to star in a number of films of the late 1930s. He played supporting roles in **Street Angel** (*dir.* **Yuan Muzhi**), *A **New Year's Coin*** (*dir.* **Zhang Shichuan**) and *Four Daughters* (*dir.* Wu Cun), and lead roles in *Dream World* (*dir.* **Cheng Bugao**, all 1937) and other titles.

After the Sino-Japanese war, Xie worked for Nationalist Central Film Studio and played the male leads in *The Holy City* (1946), *Pursuit* (1947, both *dir.* **Shen Fu**) and *Haunted House No. 13* (*dir.* Xu Changlin, 1948). Xie's most memorable screen images after 1949 include a traitor in *New Heroes and Heroines* (*dir.* **Shi Dongshan**, Lü Ban, 1951), a mafia boss in *Gate No. 6* (*dir.* Lü Ban, 1952) and a shop manager in *The **Lin Family Shop*** (*dir.* **Shui Hua**, 1959).

Between 1955 and 1957, Xie studied film directing at BFA, although he did not earn fame as a director until the early 1980s. *Sweet Business* (1979) won him Best Director award at the 1980 HFA. *A Lowly County Magistrate* (1979), a filmed stage performance, earned him another Best Director prize at the 1981 HFA. Furthermore, *The Teahouse* (1982), an adaptation of Lao She's famous play, won special awards in 1983 at China GRA and from the Ministry of Culture.

See also: adaptations of drama and literature; filmed stage performances; theatre and film

Further Reading

ZDX (1982–6: 4: 501–12), a short biography.

(ZX)

Xie Tieli

b. 27 December 1925
Director

A noted mainland director of the 1960s–80s, Xie Tieli's career has developed slowly. His first film, *A Nameless Island* (1959), was a flop, but *Hurricane* (1960) showed his potential. After a spectacular success with ***Early Spring in February*** (1963), Xie became widely recognized as one of the best directors in China.

Although *Early Spring in February* was considered a masterpiece by many critics, the CCP authorities launched a nationwide campaign criticizing its 'erroneous' ideological orientation. They charged that the film indulged in petty bourgeois sentimentality and ignored working-class struggle.Devastated by the accusations and eager to prove his political loyalty, Xie made *Never Forget Class Struggle* (1964), a title reminiscent of pure propaganda.

Xie evidently won back the party's trust. During the **Cultural Revolution**, he was one of the few directors allowed to work on films. He was even given a key role in the adaptation to the screen of a number of 'revolutionary model operas' (*geming yangban xi*). His direction of *Haixia* (1975) caused some rifts among the inner circle of the party's cultural élites.

Xie continued to direct films in the post-Cultural Revolution period. His ***Intimate Friends*** (*co-dir*. Chen Huaiai, Ba Hong, 1981) was warmly received. After directing a few other titles, Xie served as chief director on the six-part

costume drama *Dream of the Red Chamber* (1988–9).

See also: propaganda and film

Further Reading

D. Ma and G. Dai (1994: 179–84), a chapter on Xie Tieli; ZDX (1982–6: 4: 491–500), a short biography.

(ZX)

Xu Xinfu

b. 1897
d. 8 May 1965, Hong Kong
Director, producer

A veteran director whose career spanned over forty years from early cinema to Taiwan cinema, Xu Xinfu graduated from a public school in Shanghai's international settlements in 1920 and co-founded the Society for Chinese Shadowplay Studies. After participating in the production of China's first long feature, ***Yan Ruisheng*** (*dir.* Ren Pengnian, 1921), he joined Great China Film Company and co-directed with Lu Jie (1894–1967) *Victory* (1925). In the 1930s–40s, he worked for Mingxing, Xinhua and Cathay, directing such films as *The Uprising* (1933), *A Bible for Girls* (*dir*. **Zhang Shichuan**, **Cheng Bugao**, **Shen Xiling**, **Zheng Zhengqiu**, 1934), *Gunshots in a Rainy Evening* (1941) and *Shadows in an Ancient House* (1948). He founded the private Wanxiang Film Company in 1948 and produced Taiwan's first Mandarin film, *Wind and Cloud on Ali Mountain* (*dir*. **Chang Che**, 1949). He directed *Never to Part* (1951), *Women Soldiers* (1952) and other titles before taking up administrative positions in Taiwan.

See also: Taiwan cinema (in Historical essays)

(YZ)

Y

Yam, Simon
(Ren Dahua)

b. 1955
Actor

Simon Yam is the son of a senior Hong Kong police officer and one of the most talented contemporary film actors. His star persona represents an Eastern mixture of Cary Grant's charisma and Charles Bronson's brooding menace. Although capable of 'walk-on' performances in roles he regards as uninteresting – as in *Queen's High* (1991) and *Gun and Rose* (1992) – Simon Yam can deliver a diverse number of distinctive characterizations in contemporary Hong Kong cinema.

While an early role as a goofy 'Wayne's World' adolescent in *Lucky Stars* (1983) appears surprisingly uncharacteristic, it demonstrates the type of versatility he can bring to a particular part. His first distinctive performance is as the Eurasian hitman, Luke, in John **Woo**'s *A Bullet in the Head* (1989). Woo clearly models Yam's role according to his reworking of Alain Delon's romantically doomed killer in Jean-Pierre Melville's *Le Samourai* (1966). Yam is normally at his best in sympathetic roles, as *Killer's Romance* (1990) and *Naked Killer* (1992) reveal, but he can also flourish in more menacing roles. As gay psychopathic killer Judge in Ringo **Lam**'s *Full Contact* (1992), Yam delivers an accomplished performance mixing excessive camp with brooding menace in one of Hong Kong cinema's darkest works. However, Yam can redeem the exploitative features of Category 3 productions with nuanced acting ability as both *Doctor Lamb* (1992) and *Run and Kill* (1993) reveal. The revelation of his real character in *Tiger Cage* (1988) is masterly. Although dream-teaming of Yam with Hong Kong's favourite psycho, Anthony **Wong**, failed in *Awakening* (1994), *Twist*

(1995) contains his best performance since *A Bullet in the Head*.

See also: Category 3 film

(TW)

Yan Chuntang

b. unknown, Shanghai
d. 1949
Producer

An influential producer of the 1930s, Yan Chuntang was one of the prominent mafia figures in Shanghai. In 1932, one of his protégés, Zha Ruilong, who had starred in numerous martial arts films as a kungfu master, decided to set up a film studio of his own and asked Yan to loan him the needed capital. Instead, Yan established Yihua Film Company and became its general manager.

Yihua's first two releases, *The Survival of the Nation* (*dir.* **Tian Han**) and *Bloodbath* (*dir.* Hu Tu, both 1933), were both scripted by Tian Han, a high-profile leftist writer. Amazingly, they did well at the box office. This convinced Yan that filmmaking could be a lucrative business. He expanded Yihua and relied on Tian to run the studio, which took a leftist turn and made two more leftist films in 1933. These films alarmed the right-wing elements within the KMT, who, nevertheless were unable to intervene through official channels. On 12 November 1933, a group of such extremists went to Yihua and trashed the studio. They warned studio personnel not to film any scripts by Tian Han and other known leftists. Under this pressure, Yan shifted to the right, but not before releasing a few more leftist films. *The Golden Age* (*dir.* **Bu Wancang**, 1934), *Triumph* (*dir.* Bu Wancang), *Life of Sadness* (*dir.* Hu Rui) and *Escape* (*dir.* Yao Feng, all 1935) were made after the November incident.

As a businessman Yan was not particularly interested in politics. Yihua became the centre of soft film production, a trend that started with *Fairies of the Mortal World* (*dir.* **Dan Duyu**, 1935), a Chinese imitation of Hollywood musicals, and culminated with *Girl in Disguise* (*dir.* Fang Peilin, 1936). During the Japanese occupation of Shanghai, Yihua was incorporated into United China Film Company with Yan himself serving as an assistant manager. After the war, he tried, but largely failed, to re-establish Yihua Film Studio.

See also: martial arts film; musical, the

Further Reading

ZDX (1982–6: 2: 110–15), a short biography.

(ZX)

Yan Ruisheng

(Yan Ruisheng)

dir. Ren Pengnian
sc. **Yang Xiaozhong**
with Chen Shouzhi, Wang Caiyun, Shao Peng
Shanghai: Shanghai Film, 1921

This film is based on a sensational Shanghai murder case of the 1920s. The case involved a young man named Yan Ruisheng who kills a prostitute for money. The victim, Wang Lianying, was not an ordinary hooker, but a concubine of great renown: in the pleasure quarters of Shanghai she carried the title 'Queen of the Flowers'. A a result of this, the case attracted an unusually large amount of publicity. Members of the Shanghai Society of Film Studies tried to cash in on the scandal by making this film about Yan's life. They even asked Yan's good friend, Chen Shouzhi, to play Yan. Chen not only looked like Yan, he had many of the same mannerisms as well. To achieve a heightened sense of authenticity, a retired prostitute was found to play the actual victim, Wang Lianying.

As a college student, Yan Ruisheng is more interested in pleasure than study. After squandering his money in brothels, gambling houses and restaurants, he and his friends plot to rob Wang Lianying, a well-known prostitute in Shanghai and an acquaintance of Yan's. One day Yan arrives at Wang's brothel and invites her to go out with him. Wang's friend, Xiaolin Daiyu, happens to be visiting Wang, so Yan extends the invitation to her as well. Xiaolin declines. Yan drives Wang to a remote part of the suburb where Wu and Fang are waiting. Wang realizes what is happening and begs them to take only her jewellery, not her life. Not wanting to leave any witnesses behind, Yan kills Wang and leaves her corpse in a rice field. The brothel manager becomes concerned after Wang fails to return that night. After she learns from Xiaolin that Wang has gone out with Yan, the manager goes to the police station to report the incident. The manager actually does run into Yan, but the latter disappears into the crowd. After hiding himself in several places, Yan is finally arrested in Xuzhou, some several hundred miles from Shanghai. His two accomplices are also arrested and brought back to Shanghai. The three murderers are tried and sentenced to death.

(ZX)

Yang, Edward

(Yang Dechang)

b. 1947, Shanghai
Director

One of the most distinguished figures of New Taiwan Cinema, Edward Yang moved to Taiwan in 1949 with his family (originally from Meixian, Guangdong province). He received an engineering degree from Taiwan's Chiao-tung University in 1969 and an MA in computer science from the University of Florida in 1974. He spent one year in the film programme at the University of Southern California and then worked as a computer engineer before returning to Taiwan in 1981. He directed *Floating Leaf* (1981), an episode in the TV series *Eleven Women* (1982), and *Desires*, a section of the four-part film *In Our Time* (1982). The latter, produced by CMPC, is recognized as the starting point of the New Cinema movement in Taiwan.

Yang's solo feature, *That Day on the Beach* (1983), investigates the problems of an urban bourgeois marriage from a distinctively female point of view. With its extensive use of flashbacks and voice-over, the film demonstrates Yang's mature individual style and his fascination with experimental film. *Taipei Story* (1984) continues his cinematic study of **urban life** as experienced by people of different social classes. *Terrorizer* (1986) proceeds further into the realms of the irrational and the mysterious and generates an acute sense of metropolitan alienation and deracination.

The film earned a Best Director award at the 1987 Pesaro FF. Following the example of the successful **historical film** *A City of Sadness* (*dir*. **Hou Hsiao-hsien**, 1989), Yang turned his attention to Taiwan's ambivalent past in *A* **Brighter Summer Day** (1991), a touching story of a group of rebellious teenagers caught between conflicting cultural forces in the late 1950s. In 1991 the film was awarded a special prize at Tokyo FF and Best Director at Nantes.

With *A* **Confucius Confusion** (1995), Yang returns to urban life, now plagued as it were by 'post-modern' sentiment. He examines the existential problems suffered by middle-class youth in the 'age of independence' (the meaning of its Chinese title). Unlike *Terrorizer*, Yang incorporates both comic and ironic elements into the film and he succeeds in juxtaposing serious contemplation with hilarious fights and misunderstandings. Yang's next feature was **Mah-jong** (1996), another urban comedy exploring juvenile delinquency in Taipei.

In addition to films, Yang has directed stage dramas and produced MTV videos.

See also: avant-garde, experimental or exploratory film; New Taiwan Cinema (under Taiwan cinema in Historical essays)

Further Reading
C. Berry (1991a: 199–200); R. Chen (1993b: 171), both brief entries; J. Huang (1995), a book-length study.

(YZ)

Yang Hansheng
(Ouyang Benyi, Ouyang Jixiu)

b. 7 November 1902, Sichuan province
d. 7 June 1993
Screenwriter, playwright

One of the most famous leftist screenwriters of the 1930s, Yang Hansheng committed himself to politics before beginning to work with film. He joined the CCP while studying sociology at Shanghai University, and served as a branch secretary for his university and Zhabei district of Shanghai. Yang was also one of the founder members of the League of Leftist Writers.

After Yang wrote his first screenplay, *Oppression* (*dir*. **Hong Shen**, 1933), he was offered a position by Yihua Film Company as a screenwriter. He contributed such titles as *The Wrath of the China*

Sea (*dir*. Yao Feng, 1933), *Life of Sadness* (*dir*. Hu Rui) and *Escape* (*dir*. Yao Feng, both 1935). In February 1935, he was arrested by the Nationalist authorities. While in jail he wrote more screenplays: *Hearts United* (*dir*. **Ying Yunwei**, 1936), *To the Light* (*dir*. **Cheng Bugao**, 1937) and **Storm on the Border** (*dir*. Ying Yunwei, 1940). Yang was released from jail as a result of the Second United Front between the CCP and the KMT. He contributed four more screenplays to the Nationalist Central Film Studio during the Sino-Japanese war period, including *Eight Hundred Heroic Soldiers* (*dir*. Ying Yunwei, 1938), *Young China* (*dir*. Su Yi, 1940) and *Japanese Spy* (*dir*. Yuan Meiyun, 1943).

After the war, Yang returned to Shanghai and helped found Kunlun Film Company. He co-wrote **Myriad of Lights** (*dir*. **Shen Fu**, 1948), which was highly critical of social conditions under the KMT regime. He also adapted a popular comic series into a screenplay, *An* **Orphan on the Streets** (*dir*. Zhao Ming, 1949). After 1949, Yang took up a number of prestigious positions in the party and the government, but also pretty much ceased his creative writing activities. Besides *Southern Wind Blowing North* (*dir*. Shen Fu, 1963), which he co-authored with the director, Yang wrote one more screenplay in 1979. It was never filmed.

Further Reading
ZDX (1982–6: 2: 115–30), a short biography.

(ZX)

Yang Xiaozhong
(Yang Baotai, Mi Tisheng)

b. 11 December 1899, Changzhou, Jiangsu province
d. January 1969
Director, screen writer

An important figure whose career spans over half a century, Yang Xiaozhong worked at the Commercial Press, which set up its Motion Picture Department in 1918. Yang became fascinated with film and directed **Yan Ruisheng** (1921), a dramatization of a sensational real-life murder case involving a Shanghai prostitute. Yang wrote some more screenplays, such as *Good Brothers* (*dir*. Ren Pengnian, 1922), and wrote and directed *The Tragedy of a Drunkard* (1924). He was among the first Chinese filmmakers to utilize location shooting, props, and special effects. By 1926, the Motion Picture Department of the Commercial

Press had split from the press and become an independent film studio, with Yang in charge of its directing and script departments. Within a year the company had released three films directed by Yang, *Mother's Heart*, *The Journey Home* and *The Vagabond Ma* (all 1926).

Yang joined the Great Wall Film Company in 1927 and directed *Hatred* (1927), an account of the tensions which exist between peasants and the local gentry. Yang made another two costume dramas and three martial arts movies before the end of the decade. During the 1930s, Yang worked for several studios and made some twenty films. While some continued to be 'entertainment' crowd-pleasers, others were more concerned with social issues.

Yang was in Shanghai during the Sino-Japanese war. His most important films from this period are *Autumn* (1942) and *The Wedding March* (1943). Among his post-war films, *Mother's Daughter* (1948) stands out as particularly well made. After 1949, Yang made several opera movies and three children's films, including *Lanlan and Dongdong* (1958) and *The Secret of a Precious Gourd* (1963). He died during the **Cultural Revolution**, a victim of political persecution.

See also: children's film; costume drama; filmed stage performances; martial arts film

Further Reading
ZDX (1982–6: 1: 154–60), a short biography.

(ZX)

Yellow Earth
(Huang tudi)

dir. **Chen Kaige**
sc. Zhang Ziliang
with Xue Bai, Wang Xuexi
Nanning: Guangxi Film, 1984

Yellow Earth departs radically from earlier Chinese film traditions and marks a defining moment in the emergence of the **Fifth Generation**. The striking visual composition of such cultural images as the Loess Plateau and the Yellow River encapsulates Chen Kaige's philosophical statement on the interdependencies of heaven–earth–human. The main narrative concerns the attempt by the Communists to forge links with peasants in the northern Shaanxi region, while a secondary discourse questions whether the Communists can really save the poor.

Gu Qing, an army officer, is sent to a village to collect 'xintianyou', a set of local folk tunes. While living with a poor peasant family – father, daughter Cuiqiao, and son Hanhan – Gu Qing educates them with new ideas; in turn, he receives instruction in ancient values concerning life and the universe. Gu Qing succeeds in teaching the silent Hanhan a song with a line that runs: 'Only Communists can save the poor', and he prompts Cuiqiao to question her forthcoming arranged marriage. When Gu Qing leaves the village he promises to return and take Cuiqiao to join the army in Yan'an, but after her marriage Cuiqiao drowns herself in the Yellow River on her way to join the revolutionaries (her singing of the revolutionary song Gu Qing had taught her brother ending abruptly on the soundtrack). In a series of dissolves and slow-motion images, Gu Qing returns but seems unable to reach Hanhan who is struggling to make his way through a crowd of poor peasants frantically praying to the Dragon King for rain.

Yellow Earth emphasizes visual imagery over narrative plot, philosophical meditation over political ideology. The use of high horizons and wide-angle shots of the landscape captures the interdependence of nature and human in a manner reminiscent of traditional Chinese landscape painting.

See also: painting and film

Further Readings
G. Barmé and J. Minford (1988: 251–69), a section on the film; M. Farquhar (1992), an exploration of gender structure; C. Berry and M. Farquhar (1994), a comparative study of film and painting; H. Chiao (1990a), the Chinese script and reviews; H. C. Li (1989), a study of colour and character; B. McDougall (1991), the English script and background information; E. Yau (1987–8), a theoretical treatise.

(SC)

Yeoh, Michelle
(Michelle Khan, Yang Ziqiong)

b. 1962, Malaysia
Actress

As a 'Bond girl' in *Tomorrow Never Dies* (1997), Michelle Yeoh appears destined to equal Jackie **Chan**'s success at Western screen stardom. After earning a BA at London's Royal Academy of Dance, she returned to her country of birth and was crowned Miss Malaysia of 1983. She achieved her Hong Kong screen breakthrough in *Yes, Madam!* (*dir.* Correy Yuen, 1985). This action-**comedy-thriller** featured her alongside Cynthia Rothrock and was a major success. After making *Easy Money* (*dir.* Stephen Shin) and *Magnificent Warriors* (*dir.* David Chung, both 1987), she took the traditional route of retirement after marrying Dickson Poon of D&B Films. But, unlike Cheng Pei Pei and Angela **Mao** Ying, she returned to stardom after her divorce with a new surname (changed from Kahn to Yeoh) and new acting talents far exceeding those of her action movie replacement Cynthia Khan.

In *Supercop* (*dir.* Stanley Tong, 1992) Yeoh complemented Jackie Chan in both acting and action. She appeared as the 'Invisible Woman' in *The Heroic Trio* (*dir.* Johnny To, 1993) alongside two other Hong Kong cinematic divas, Anita **Mui** and Maggie **Cheung**, and its dark sequel *The Executioners* (*dir.* Johnny To, 1993), holding her own against her major cinematic rivals. Yeoh clearly overcame her earlier 'Girls 'n' Guns' stereotype. She repeated her mainland Chinese police inspector role from *Supercop* in *Project S* (*dir.* Stanley Tong, 1993) and matched Jet **Li**'s performance as *The Tai-chi Master* (*dir.* Yuen Woo-ping, 1993). However, *Wing Chun* (*dir.* Yuen Woo-ping, 1993) also revealed Yeoh's subtle acting talents as a martial artist wearing male attire following the advice of her master (played by Cheng Pei Pei) to protect her from male assault earlier in life. Despite this Wing Chun also yearns for the life of a normal woman, yearnings Yeoh conveys by subtle facial expression.

Before leaving for the USA, Yeoh starred in two films made by two of Hong Kong's talented female directors. Ann **Hui** directed Yeoh in *Stunt Woman* (1996), and Mabel Cheung featured Yeoh as one of *The Soong Sisters* (1997) set in the Qing dynasty. Yeoh is currently managed by Terence **Chang**.

See also: action film; martial arts film

(TW, YZ)

Yesterday's Wine
(Yu wangshi ganbei)

dir. **Xia Gang**
sc. Meng Zhu

with Liu Yan, Pu Cunxin, Shao Bing
Hainan: Nanyang Film/Beijing: Beijing Film, 1995

This sentimental urban **romance** represents a sincere attempt at depicting female psychology and female **sexuality** by a latecomer in the **Fifth Generation**. Narrated throughout by female voice-over, the film traces the painful process of the sexual maturation of a teenage girl, Mengmeng. She grows up in a loveless family where her alcoholic father reigns like a tyrant. In the hot summer days, Mengmeng prepares for her college entrance examinations in a courtyard where she lives with her divorced mother. Her best classmate, Tingting, is afraid that her parents will get a divorce. When Tingting later learns that they have been legally divorced without informing her, she commits suicide.

Mengmeng's neighbour is a kind, middle-aged doctor. He takes good care of Mengmeng while her mother is busy dating a former lover. Mengmeng has never experienced fatherly love and tries to distance herself from the neighbour, but she cannot control herself one rainy evening and eagerly gives herself to the man. The man caresses her beautiful body and promises to protect the 'virgin soil'. He shows a photo of his son, who was taken away from him years ago and now lives in the USA. The love affair has to stop when Mengmeng and her mother move to a new apartment.

One summer vacation during her college years, Mengmeng meets a Chinese American on a beach. They fall in love, and she names him Lao Ba. Soon Lao Ba sends visa documents and asks Mengmeng to join him in California. Mengmeng flies there and enjoys their brief life together in the 'paradise'. When Lao Ba visits his grandfather in Baltimore to prepare for their wedding, Mengmeng discovers in his albums the same photograph her neighbour showed her years ago. Lao Ba is that long lost son, and Mengmeng is seeking in this young man the love she lost in his father. Unable to continue her relationship with Lao Ba, Mengmeng returns home. A letter arrives from Baltimore with the tragic news that Lao Ba has died in a car accident.

The film ends with Mengmeng's hallucinations: she meets the neighbour again, who gladly tells her that his son is coming for a visit. She sits on a sofa at home, and Lao Ba cheerfully walks through the door. Standing up to greet him, Mengmeng knocks down a fish bowl, and the fish flips on the floor.

(YZ)

Yim Ho
(Yan Hao)

b. 1952
Director

Like his contemporaries in the Hong Kong New Wave, Yim Ho enjoyed a successful career in TV before turning to film, but his first few films were not well received. It was not until **Homecoming** (1984) that he found a suitable expression for his humanist concerns. Partially shot in the mainland, this film features mainland actress **Siqin Gaowa** in a study of the contrasts between Hong Kong and China. Yim's interest in mainland subjects inspired him to combine two well-known stories of the same title in China and Taiwan into *The King of Chess* (1992), but he did not manage to complete the film (it was picked up years later by **Tsui Hark**). Yim explores the love–hate relationship between mother and son in *The **Day the Sun Turned Cold*** (1994), which won Best Film award at Tokyo FF. Among Yim's other notable films are **Red Dust** (1990), a mixture of soap opera, folk tale and historical panorama, and *The Sun Has Ears* (1995), a film produced by **Zhang Yu**, an award-winning mainland actress who returned to East Asia after a decade spent studying in the USA. *The Sun Has Ears* won Best Director award for Yim Ho and the Fipresci Prize at the 1996 Berlin FF.

See also: Hong Kong cinema (in Historical essays)

Further Reading
C. Li (1994), E. Yau (1994a), include critical studies of *Homecoming*.

(YZ)

Ying Yunwei
(Ying Yuchen, Ying Yangzhen)

b. 7 September 1904, Shanghai
d. 16 January 1967
Director

A noted director of the 1930s–40s, Ying Yunwei became interested in theatre in 1921 while still working for a shipping company. He joined Shanghai Theatre Society and acted in a number of plays. In 1934, Diantong Film Company offered him a position as a film director. His directing début, the leftist **Plunder of Peach and Plum** (1934), won critical acclaim. After directing *Heroes*

of the Circumstances (1935), Ying joined Mingxing Film Company and directed *Hearts United* (1936). During the Sino-Japanese war, he worked for Nationalist Central Film Studio and directed *Eight Hundred Heroic Soldiers* (1938) and **Storm on the Border** (1940), both scripted by the leftist writer **Yang Hansheng**. Ying's accomplishments in the post-war period included many films scripted by leftists. He continued to be productive after 1949, directing feature films as well as **filmed stage performances**.

See also: leftist film (under Chinese cinema in Historical essays); theatre and film

(ZX)

youth culture

This entry covers films that appeal particularly to young adults rather than children; the latter are treated in **children's film**. In the 1920s–40s, there was no special effort to produce films that represent youth life as a distinctive type of culture. Film romances with emphases on **love and marriage** often addressed concerns of the youth as part of **family** or social problems. In this sense, **Zheng Zhengqiu**'s family dramas of the 1920s are not about youth culture alone. Although many later films, such as **Wild Flower** (*dir.* **Sun Yu**, 1930) and **New Woman** (*dir.* **Cai Chusheng**, 1934), focused almost exclusively on young people, they did not develop a discernible type of youth culture. Instead, they used different kinds of characters (e.g., traditional, modern, self-sacrificing or decadent) to chart out different roads the urban youths could take at a time of national crisis. In the 1940s, young people's lives were generally inserted into an overall picture of the economic and political landscapes in post-war China. In mainland productions of the 1950s–70s, young people are seen everywhere enthusiastically participating in **socialist construction**; or elsewhere they are portrayed as heroes and heroines completely devoted to the **Communist revolution** in the past.

Youth culture found expression in Hong Kong and Taiwan in the 1950s–70s. The musicals that dominated the Hong Kong screen in this period appealed to young audiences in particular, and so did Taiwan romances based on **Chiung Yao**'s novels. However, youth culture as a sub-culture or counter-culture did not appear until the late 1980s in Hong Kong and Taiwan. Violent youth gangs are featured in *As Tears Go By* (*dir.*

Wong Kar-Wai), *Gangs* (*dir.* Lawrence Ah Mon, both 1988), ***Daughter of the Nile*** (*dir.* **Hou Hsiao-hsien**, 1987), *A **Brighter Summer Day*** (*dir.* Edward **Yang**, 1991) and ***Rebel of the Neon God*** (*dir.* **Tsai Ming-liang**, 1992). These unglamorous treatments of **urban life** form a sharp contrast to a group of mainland films that present youth culture as a fascinating counter-culture. In ***Rock 'n' Roll Kids*** (*dir.* **Tian Zhuangzhuang**, 1988), ***Black Snow*** (*dir.* **Xie Fei**, 1989), ***Beijing Bastards*** (*dir.* **Zhang Yuan**, 1993), ***In the Heat of the Sun*** (*dir.* **Jiang Wen**, 1994) and ***Dirt*** (*dir.* Guan Hu, 1994), violence is often more psychological than physical, and rebellions more symbolic than real. However, a deep sense of urban disillusionment in these mainland films links them to their Hong Kong and Taiwan counterparts.

See also: musical, the; romance; social problems, film of

(YZ)

Yu Lan

(Yu Peiwen)

b. 3 June 1921, Liaoning province
Actress

One of the most talented actresses of the 1950s–60s, Yu Lan drew critical attention with her performance in *Red Flag Over Cuigang Mountain* (*dir.* **Zhang Junxiang**, 1951). She exhibited an extraordinary maturity as an actress and was recruited by Beijing Film Studio in 1953. She studied in the Acting Department of the Central Academy of Drama in Beijing during 1954–6 and starred in *The **Lin Family Shop*** (*dir.* **Shui Hua**, 1959). Her performance in ***Revolutionary Family*** (*dir.* Shui Hua, 1961) won her Best Actress award at the 1961 Moscow FF. Since that time, Yu has retired from film acting, making just one more appearance, in ***Red Crag*** (*dir.* Shui Hua, 1964).

In the post-**Cultural Revolution** period, Yu served in various administrative functions, such as general manager of Beijing Children's Film Studio, vice-president of the All China Filmmakers' Association, and member of the National Congress. She is the mother of the internationally known **Fifth Generation** director **Tian Zhuangzhuang**.

Further Reading

ZDX (1982–6: 4: 9–16), a short biography.

(ZX)

Yu Ling

(Ren Xigui, Yu Cheng, You Jing)

b. 14 February 1907, Jiangsu province
Screenwriter, critic

One of the most accomplished screenwriters and film critics of the 1930s–40s, Yu Ling joined the Communist Youth League while still in high school and was involved in organizing the Beijing branch of the League of Leftist Writers while a law student at Beijing University. During a University drama performances, Yu got into trouble with the Nationalist police and promptly set out to join the CCP.

In 1933, Yu was transferred to Shanghai, where he took charge of the Leftist League's organizational work. He began to write film criticism, which constituted a significant component of the leftist film movement's activities. After Shanghai fell to the Japanese in 1937, Yu stayed on to lead the cultural resistance and wrote numerous plays promoting **nationalism**. Two of these, *Women's Dormitory* (*dir.* Cheng Kengran, 1939) and *Fallen Flower* (*dir.* **Zhang Shichuan**, Zheng Xiaoqiu, 1941) were adapted into films. In the post-war period, Yu wrote *Mr Nobody* (*dir.* **Ying Yunwei**, 1947) then turned his attention solely to the writing of stage plays.

After 1949, Yu was put in charge of the takeover of Nationalist cultural establishments in Shanghai. He served as the first general manager of Shanghai Film Studio, which at that time also incorporated numerous independent studios. Despite his busy schedule as a high ranking administrator in the PRC government, Yu managed to write another screenplay, *Nie Er* (*dir.* **Zheng Junli**, 1959). He survived the **Cultural Revolution** and has been serving as the vice-president of the All China Filmmakers' Association ever since.

Further Reading

ZDX (1982–6: 2: 1–11), a short biography.

(ZX)

Yuan Muzhi

(Yuan Jialai)

b. 3 March 1909, Ningbo, Zhejiang province
d. 30 January 1978
Actor, screen writer, director

A talented filmmaker of the 1930s–40s, Yuan Muzhi became involved in theatre while still at high school. During his college years, he played the lead role in a Chinese stage adaptation of Chekov's *Uncle Vanya*. In 1930 Yuan was drawn into the leftist theatre movement. However, his parents' disapproval of his involvement in theatre, together with their active interference in his work, served to estrange Yuan from his family.

Yuan joined Diantong Film Company, a centre of the leftist film movement, in 1934. He wrote and starred in **Plunder of Peach and Plum** (*dir.* **Ying Yunwei**, 1934), which deals with the widespread problem of unemployment and is highly critical of social conditions in the 1930s. Yuan also starred in another Diantong production, *Children of Troubled Times* (*dir.* Xu Xingzhi, 1935). In 1935, he wrote and directed **Cityscape** (1935), a musical focusing on the dark side of **urban life**. Yuan joined Mingxing Film Company after Diantong was shut down because of its leftist orientation. He starred in *Hearts United* (*dir.* Ying

Yunwei, 1936) and then scripted and directed **Street Angel** (1937), one of the best known films of the 1930s.

During the Sino-Japanese war, Yuan appeared in *Eight Hundred Heroic Soldiers* (*dir.* Ying Yunwei, 1938) before leaving for Yan'an. In 1940 Yuan joined the CCP and was sent to the Soviet Union. In the post-war period, Yuan played a major role in the CCP take-over of Manchurian Motion Pictures. Northeast Film Studio was established under his leadership in 1946. After 1949, Yuan left his post as Northeast Studio's manager and was appointed chief director of the Film Bureau under the Ministry of Culture.

See also: leftist film (under Chinese cinema in Historical essays); musical, the; theatre and film

Further Reading

ZDX (1982–6: 1: 278–88), a short biography.

(ZX)

Z

Zhang Ga, a Boy Soldier

(Xiao bing Zhang Ga)

dir. **Cui Wei**, Ouyang Hongying
sc. Xu Guangyao
with An Jisi, Yu Shaokang, Zhang Ping, Ge
Cunzhuang
Beijing: Beijing Film, 1963

In this children's **war film**, the wisdom of
the Chinese people triumphs over the Japanese
invaders.

The orphaned boy Zhang Ga is brought up by
his grandmother. A wounded Communist officer,
Zhong Liang, lives with them while his wounds
are healing. When the Japanese military discover
this, they come to the village and have Zhong
arrested and the grandmother executed.

To avenge the Japanese, Zhang Ga himself
joins the Communist troops and becomes one
of their special agents. Despite his excellent
performance during an operation, he violates military rules by hiding a pistol captured from the
enemy. He is later arrested while on an informa-
tion-collecting mission, but refuses to yield any
information even when tortured by the Japanese.
While in prison he manages to set fire to one of
the enemy's block houses and then help his
comrades surrounding the compound to win a
victory. After the battle is over, Zhang Ga decides
voluntarily to hand over the pistol he has stashed
away. His superiors authorize his use of the hand
gun as a reward for his honesty and bravery, and
the villagers cheer.

See also: children's film

(ZX)

Zhang Jianya

b. May 1951, Shanghai
Director

An emerging figure from the **Fifth Generation**,
Zhang Jianya worked as a carpenter before
entering Shanghai Film Studio as an actor in 1975.
He studied in the Directing Department of BFA
in 1978–82 and upon graduation joined his classmates **Tian Zhuangzhuang** and Xie Xiaojing
in directing *Red Elephant* (1982). He did various
odd jobs at Shanghai Studio before directing his
solo features: *Trapped on a Frozen River* (1986), *The
Tribulations of a Young Master* (under the general
direction of **Wu Yigong**, 1987), *Kidnapping Karajan*
(1988), *San Mao Joins the Army* (1992), *Mr Wang:
Flames of Desire* (1993), *Superwoman* (1994) and
Narrow Escape (1994). Most of his films are comedies, marked at times by black humour and
'post-modern' sentiment. It is Zhang's ambition to
create a type of film **comedy** unique to the city
of Shanghai, something comparable to Woody
Allen's New York films. Besides making several
TV dramas, Zhang started work in 1996 on
China's first computer animation/CGI feature
film, *Uproar in Heaven*, with a budget of US$150
million.

Further Reading

C. Wu (1996), an interview.

(YZ)

Zhang Junxiang

(Yuan Jun)

b. 27 December 1910, Zhejiang province
Screenwriter, director

A noted director of the 1940s, Zhang Junxiang is
one of the few Chinese filmmakers to have been

educated overseas. A graduate of the prestigious Department of Foreign Languages and Literatures at Qinghua University, Zhang studied drama and received his MFA from Yale's College of Theater in 1939. After returning to China he wrote and directed numerous stage plays.

His film career began in 1947, when Nationalist Central Film Studio offered him a position as director and screen writer. Zhang wrote several screenplays that were subsequently turned into films, including **Diary of a Homecoming** (1947) and *The Lucky Son-in-law* (1948), which he directed under his pseudo-name Yuan Jun. He moved to Hong Kong and directed *The Cremation* (1948) for Yonghua Film Company before returning to China. Like many other well-known filmmakers, Zhang served in numerous administrative positions in the PRC government: as president of Shanghai Film School, president of the Shanghai Filmmakers' Association, and as a member of the National Congress. Between 1951 and 1982, Zhang directed four feature films, including *Red Flag Over Cuigang Mountain* (1951). He also wrote three screenplays during the 1950s, the most popular of which was **Letter with Feather** (*dir.* **Shi Hui**, 1954). Zhang was once married to the actress **Bai Yang**.

Further Reading

ZDX (1982–6: 7: 319–34), a short biography; J. Zhang (1985), a memoir.

(ZX)

Zhang Junzhao

b. 1952, Henan province
Director

An important early figure of the **Fifth Generation**, Zhang Junzhao joined the army and became actively involved in directing and performing plays, which led to his assignment as head of publicity at a theatre. He studied in the Directing Department of BFA in 1978–82. He was assigned to Guangxi Film Studio, where he directed the first landmark Fifth Generation film, **One and Eight** (1984), with **Zhang Yimou** as cameraman. Zhang Junzhao subsequently made two undistinguished films, *Come On, China* (1985) and *The Loner* (1986), before turning to *Arc Light* (1988), a study of a mental patient in hospital which aims to pose existential questions and capture a certain mood of oriental mysticism.

(YZ)

Zhang Nuanxin

b. 27 October 1940, Liaoning province
d. 28 May 1995, Beijing
Director.

One of the most famous women film directors in China, Zhang Nuanxin first attracted critical attention in the early 1980s when she published 'The Modernization of Film Language' (Lun dianying yuyan de xiandaihua), co-authored with her husband Li Tuo, a noted literary critic. The essay criticized the conventional Chinese approach to filmmaking, which views film as no more than an illustration for literary works. Zhang urged her colleagues to pay greater attention to the visual qualities of the cinema. The essay sparked a debate among mainland filmmakers and critics and contributed greatly to the rise of a new Chinese cinema.

Graduating from the Directing Department of BFA as early as 1962, Zhang had to wait until 1981 to direct her first feature, **Drive to Win**. This **sports** film was awarded Best Film prize by the Ministry of Culture in 1981 and earned Zhang Best Director award at the 1982 China GRA. In many ways, *Drive to Win* is a demonstration of the artistic principles advocated by Zhang in her essay, and it helped to bring about changes in Chinese filmmaking. Zhang's next film, **Sacrificed Youth** (1985) was an even bigger success. Zhang went to France to study film in 1985. After returning to China, she directed **Good Morning, Beijing!** (1990). In contrast to the avant-garde style of her earlier films, this new film of **urban life** centres around the lives of a group of ordinary Beijing citizens. It received a Best Film award from MBFT in 1991 and seemed to signal a significant change in Zhang's career. Unfortunately, shortly after the release of *A Yunnan Story* (1994), an ethnographic film about a Japanese girl growing up in an ethnic minority region in China, Zhang died of breast cancer.

See also: avant-garde, experimental or exploratory film

Further Reading

G. Semsel *et al.* (1990: 10–20), a translation of Zhang and Li's essay; X. Tang (1994), a critical study of *Good Morning, Beijing!*; E. Yau (1994b), an analysis of *Sacrificed Youth*; Z. Zhang (1988), a discussion of Zhang Nuanxin's early works.

(ZX, YZ)

Zhang Ruifang

b. 15 June 1918, Baoding, Hebei province
Actress

A famous actress of the 1950s–60s, Zhang Ruifang was initially a student of fine arts, but soon became involved in theatre. Having established her reputation as a major star of the stage, she made the transition to film by taking a supporting role in *The Light of East Asia* (*dir.* He Feiguang, 1940) and the female lead in *A Bloody Lesson* (*dir.* **Sun Yu**, 1941). While she gave excellent performances in such titles as ***Along the Sungari River*** (*dir.* **Jin Shan**, 1947), *Family* (*dir.* Chen Xihe, Ye Ming, 1956) and *Nie Er* (*dir.* **Zheng Junli**, 1959), it was her portrayal of a peasant woman in ***Li Shuang-shuang*** (*dir.* Lu Ren, 1962) that earned her Best Actress award at the 1963 HFA. In the post-**Cultural revolution** period, she starred in three more films but had retired from filmmaking by 1982.

See also: theatre and film

Further Reading

ZDX (1982–6: 7: 335–49), a short biography.

(ZX)

Zhang Shankun

b. 1905, Zhejiang province
d. 7 January 1957, Japan
Producer

An influential but controversial producer of the 1930s–40s, Zhang Shankun came from a wealthy family. While still a college student at Nanyang University in Shanghai, he exhibited a smart business sense by managing movie shows on campus and thus making money for himself. After college, Zhang worked as an advertising agent for a tobacco company. Meanwhile, he joined Shanghai's underworld and became a protégé of Huang Jinrong, one of the city's most notorious mafia bosses. With Huang's support, Zhang took control of two popular and lucrative entertainment centres in the city, The Big World and The Gong Theatre. He experimented with screening movies during the intervals of theatrical performances and thus started his adventures in film.

Zhang formed Xinhua Film Company in 1934. His first two releases, *A Knight-Errant Named Hongyang* (*dir.* **Yang Xiaozhong**, 1935) and *The New Peach Blossom Fan* (*dir.* **Ouyang Yuqian**, 1935), were both box-office hits. Within two years Zhang had churned out a number of socially conscious and technically well-crafted titles: *A Sorrowful Song* (*dir.* **Shi Dongshan**), *The Pioneers* (*dir.* **Wu Yonggang**, both 1936), ***Singing at Midnight*** (*dir.* **Ma-Xu Weibang**, 1937) and *Marching Youth* (*dir.* Shi Dongshan, 1937) can be considered representative of Xinhua's output during this period.

After November 1937, Shanghai became an 'Isolated Island' in Japanese-occupied China, and many established studios left the city. Just as the nation's domestic film production ground to a halt, however, Zhang seized the opportunity and made eighteen films in one year, most of which catered to the tastes of 'low-brow' urbanites. But he also released ***Mulan Joins the Army*** (*dir.* **Bu Wancang**, 1939), a film charged with patriotic sentiment. A shrewd businessman, Zhang registered his film studio under an American business interest so to avoid harassment by the Japanese.

After the outbreak of the Pacific War, Zhang served as the general manager of the Japanese-controlled China United Film Production Corporation (Zhonglian), an umbrella company incorporating twelve film studios in Shanghai. Under Zhang's management CUFPC produced 130 titles between 1942 and 1945, some of which are clearly propaganda pieces for the Japanese. Ironically, Zhang was jailed for twenty days by the Japanese on suspicion of having connections with the Chinese resistance. However, this could not save Zhang from a charge of treason in the post-war period. Zhang fled to Hong Kong before the time of his trial and then toured Europe and the USA, acquainting himself with Western film industries as he went. Returning to Hong Kong, Zhang took charge of Yonghua Film Company and produced several big budget movies, including *The Spirit of the Nation* (*dir.* Bu Wancang, 1948) and ***Sorrows of the Forbidden City*** (*dir.* **Zhu Shilin**, 1948). After these titles did not rake in the expected monetary returns, Zhang tried to make a comeback. He died of a heart attack in 1957 while shooting on location in Japan.

See also: propaganda and film

Further Reading

ZDX (1982–6: 2: 302–7), a short biography.

(ZX)

Zhang Shichuan

b. 1 January 1889, Ningbo, Zhejiang province
d. 8 July 1953
Director, producer

One of the founding fathers of Chinese cinema, Zhang used to work as a compradore for an advertising agency. In 1913, two Americans formed Asia Film Company and asked Zhang to be their advisor. Zhang took over all work responsibilities for the company instead. Though having little experience in filmmaking, he enlisted **Zheng Zhengqiu**, a famous dramatist of the time, and together they made the first Chinese short feature, *The **Difficult Couple*** (1913). After finishing the film, Zhang formed Huanxian Film Company (Fantasy) in 1916 and directed *Wronged Ghosts in Opium Den* (1916). In 1922, Zhang co-founded Mingxing Film Company with his friends **Zhou Jianyun** and Zheng Zhengqiu.

A shrewd businessman primarily concerned with profit, Zhang differed from Zheng, who viewed cinema as a vehicle for social reform. If their didactic films such as ***Orphan Rescues Grandfather*** (1923) could become box-office hits, Zhang didn't have a problem with repeating the formula. But when his **martial arts film** *The **Burning of Red Lotus Temple*** (1928) sold well, Zhang rushed to make sequel after sequel.

In the early 1930s, increasing Japanese aggression against China produced a sense of national crisis. Under Zhang's management, Mingxing hired a group of leftist writers to work for its script department. As a result, a large number of leftist films were produced by the studio.

The Mingxing studio site was destroyed by a Japanese bombardment during the 1932 battle of Shanghai. While Zhang managed to rescue some equipment and film stock, he was never again able to revive Mingxing's former glory. After the outbreak of the Pacific War, the Japanese took over Shanghai and incorporated all of the city's major film studios into the China United Film Production Corporation. Zhang served as a branch manager as well as director of the production department, duties which led to charges of treason after Japan surrendered in 1945. Although not officially indicted, Zhang never recovered from the resulting public humiliation. He died in 1953, aged sixty four.

See also: leftist film (under Chinese cinema in Historical essays)

Further Reading

X. He (1982), on Zhang and Mingxing; ZDX (1982–6: 1: 222–30), a short biography.

(ZX)

Zhang Yimou

b. 1950, Xi'an, Shaanxi province
Director, cinematographer, actor

One of the best-known directors from the **Fifth Generation**, Zhang Yimou was already twenty-eight by the time he sat the entrance examination to BFA in 1978. He was initially rejected on the grounds of his age but entered the Cinematography Department after a direct appeal to the Ministry of Culture. Before that, he had spent three years in the countryside and seven years in a factory. He developed his interest in drawing and photography at an early age and is reported to have sold his blood in order to buy his first camera. At BFA, Zhang kept a low profile and did not attract as much attention as his classmates **Chen Kaige** and **Tian Zhuangzhuang**,

Plate 50   Zhang Yimou

two friends with strong connections to the Beijing film world. Upon graduation, Zhang was assigned to Guangxi Film Studio, where he worked as cinematographer on a number of important features: **One and Eight** (*dir*. **Zhang Junzhao**, 1984), **Yellow Earth** (1984) and *The* **Big Parade** (1985, both *dir*. Chen Kaige). He moved to his home town, Xi'an, on **Wu Tianming**'s invitation and served as both cinematographer and male lead on Wu's **Old Well** (1987). The film won Wu Best Film and Zhang Best Actor awards at Tokyo FF.

After this success, Zhang was allowed to direct his first feature, **Red Sorghum** (1987), an exuberant, earthy film about legendary figures of bygone days. With its unconventional narrative and its ravishing images, the film won China its first Golden Bear at the 1988 Berlin FF; it was also the first Fifth Generation film to appeal to the mass domestic audience. Except for a trivial entertainment film, *Code Name Puma* (1988), Zhang's subsequent works have regularly been exhibited in the West, and his name is intimately associated with film awards around the world. *Ju* **Dou** (1989), a story of forbidden love between a battered wife and her 'nephew', won him a first Oscar nomination for Best Foreign Film. Although Zhang was prevented from attending the American Academy awards ceremony by the Chinese government – which temporarily banned the film – he had better luck with his next feature, **Raise the Red Lantern** (1991), a study of **sexuality** and power relations within a household of four wives. He was allowed to visit the USA, where the film was named most successful foreign language title of 1992 by *Variety*. The film was a popular hit in Europe, too, and won a Silver Lion at Venice FF.

Shifting his attention from a 'timeless' rural China to the contemporary situation, Zhang directed *The* **Story of Qiuju** (1992), a highly theatrical docudrama about a stubborn country woman who goes all the way to the provincial courts to redress a wrong committed against her husband. This theme fell perfectly in line with the needs of legal education in the mainland so the government loved it; they released Zhang's two previous films and paraded him as a kind of 'national' hero who had 'conquered' the West. The film added a Golden Lion from Venice FF to Zhang's long list of international prizes. Zhang's **To Live** (1994) presents a less glamorous picture of Chinese history by following a family through political turmoil and personal tragedy over the course of half a century. His **Shanghai Triad** (1995), however, reverts to the spectacular display of exotica, this time as a **gangster film** set in the metropolitan Shanghai of the 1920s–30s.

Zhang's casting of **Gong Li** as lead actress in all his films up to 1995 brought her international fame. Ever since *Ju Dou*, the director has received the backing of investors from Japan, Taiwan and other places. He turned to the **comedy** of contemporary **urban life** with *Keep Cool* (1997), which stars **Jiang Wen** as the male lead and a young fashion model, Qu Ying, as his new heroine. In 1996, with his international reputation for the production of art films, Zhang was invited to direct a film version of Puccini's *Turnandot*, a famous Italian opera about a beautiful but cruel Eastern princess who slays the men who love her.

See also: art film

Further Reading

M. Chen (1995), a book-length study; S. Cheng (1994), a useful background piece; *Cinemaya* (1995), a tribute to the director; S. Klawans (1995), a profile; H. Kong (1996/7), an analysis of Zhang's symbolism; S. Lu (1997b), on cultural critique and transnational cinema; T. Rayns (1989: 47–51), a brief discussion; G. Semsel (1987: 134–40), an interview; D. Sutton (1994), on history and ritual; M. Yang (1993), an informative interview with critical comments; M. Yue (1996), a critique of Zhang's films.

(YZ)

Zhang Yu

b. 1957, Shanghai
Actress, producer

A well-known mainland actress in the early 1980s, Zhang Yu entered Shanghai Film Studio in 1973. Her roles in *Romance on Lu Mountain* (*dir*. Huang Zumo) and **Night Rain on the River** (*dir*. **Wu Yonggang**, **Wu Yigong**, both 1980) won her Best Actress award at the 1980 China GRA and HFA. Her other notable films include **Narrow Street** (*dir*. Yang Yanjin), *Intimate Friends* (*dir*. **Xie Tieli**, Chen Huai'ai, Ba Hong, both 1981) and *Thunderstorm* (*dir*. **Sun Daolin**, 1984).

Zhang went to the USA in 1985 and studied media production at California State University, Northridge. She returned to star in a TV drama *Legend of Li Shishi* (1991) in Taiwan and in a Shanghai **comedy**, *Mr Wang: Flames of Desire*

(1993), directed by her husband **Zhang Jianya**. She also invested over one million US dollars and produced *The Sun Has Ears* (*dir.* **Yim Ho**, 1995), which won Best Director award and a Fipresci prize at the 1996 Berlin FF.

(YZ)

Zhang Yuan

b. 1963, Nanjing
Independent filmmaker

Zhang Yuan studied in the Cinematography Department of BFA during 1985–9. Upon graduation, he rejected an official posting to August First Film Studio for the life of an independent. He was involved in the preparation of *The Tree of the Sun*, a film about handicapped children which was later abandoned by both Beijing Children's Film Studio and August First Studio. With merely US$1,300, Zhang worked on the film by himself, renaming it *Mama* (1991). He rented the equipment necessary for shooting and the studio space necessary for post-production.

Zhang has made TV commercials and music videos for MTV in Hong Kong and the USA. His second independent film, *Beijing Bastards* (1993), cuts frequently between its improvised sequences and semi-documentary footage of China's leading rock star, Cui Jian, who also acted as co-producer. Zhang began shooting *Chicken Feathers on the Ground* in October 1993, but by April 1994 he had been banned from any future work in the mainland by the government. Nevertheless, he defiantly proceeded to make a **documentary**, *The Square* (1995). A year later, he had completed *Sons* (1996), a docudrama about a dysfunctional family which was acclaimed at Rotterdam FF. His *East Palace, West Palace* (1997), reputedly China's first 'gay film', was screened at the Cannes FF, but he has himself been barred from leaving the country by the Chinese authorities. Due to his independent spirit, Zhang has been regarded as a leading representative of China's 'underground' filmmakers.

See also: independent film

Further Reading

K. Eder and D. Rossell (1993: 124–6), with an interview; T. Rayns (1996), an informative interview.

(YZ)

Zhang Zeming

b. 1951, Fuzhou, Fujian province
Director, screen writer

An associate of the **Fifth Generation**, Zhang Zeming grew up in Guangzhou under a strong film influence. His father, a playwright and screen writer, and his mother, a director of documentaries, were both attached to Pearl River Film Studio. He was sent to a farm in Hainan Island in 1968 and returned a decade later to his parents' place of work. He twice failed the entrance examinations to BFA and started writing screenplays in 1983. He wrote and directed his first feature, *Swan Song* (1985), a film about a local Cantonese musician. Based on a story by Kong Jiesheng, a noted Guangzhou writer, this acclaimed film takes a look at a distinctive regional culture in an unglamorized fashion that probably influenced a later Pearl River production, *The True Hearted* (*dir.* **Sun Zhou**, 1992). Zhang's attention to literary quality is evident in his two-part TV drama, *Auntie Dan* (1986). *Sunshine and Showers* (1987) focuses on the younger generation and captures certain moods of contemporary **urban life** that have also been addressed by other urban films made since the late 1980s, such as those by **Huang Jianxin** and **Xia Gang**.

See also: documentary

Further Reading

W. Chong and A. Keyser (1990), the director on *Swan Song*; M. Lang (1993), a historical study of traditional musicians; T. Rayns (1989: 51–5), a brief discussion.

(YZ)

Zhao Dan

(Zhao Fengxiang)

b. 27 June 1915, Yangzhou, Jiangsu province
d. 10 October 1980, Shanghai
Actor, director

One of the most talented Chinese film actors of all time, Zhao Dan developed an early interest in film by frequenting the movie house managed by his father. The large number of films he watched constituted his film education. In 1933 he began to appear in supporting roles. His popularity soared with two 1937 titles, *Crossroads* (*dir.* **Shen Xiling**) and *Street Angel* (*dir.* **Yuan**

Muzhi). Zhao took the male lead in both titles and demonstrated his wide range. During the Sino-Japanese war, Zhao starred in *Children of China* (*dir.* Shen Xiling, 1939).

Zhao went to Xinjiang in 1939 as an active participant in the leftist theatre movement, hoping to promote progressive theatre. The local authorities, irritated by the activities of Zhao and his associates, had them jailed for five years. Upon his release in 1945, Zhao returned to Shanghai to resume his career as a film actor. *Crows and Sparrows* (*dir.* **Zheng Junli**, 1949) includes his finest screen work. After 1949 Zhao starred in a dozen films, including the controversial *The Life of Wu Xun* (*dir.* **Sun Yu**, 1950) as well as the highly acclaimed *Lin Zexu* (Zheng Junli, Cen Fan, 1959).

In contrast to his achievements and popularity as a movie star, Zhao's attempts at directing were never particularly significant. His earlier association with Jiang Qing, an actress of the 1930s who later became Mao Zedong's wife, caused Zhao a great deal of trouble during the period of the **Cultural Revolution**. Although he survived political persecution and remained an outspoken artist throughout the late 1970s, his failing health prevented him from making any more films.

Further Reading

D. Zhao (1980), a memoir; ZDX (1982–6: 1: 237–54), a short biography.

(ZX)

Zheng Junli

(Zheng Zhong, Qian Li)

b. 6 December 1911, Shanghai
d. 23 April 1969
Director, actor

A noted figure of the 1930s–60s, Zheng Junli was a stage actor before joining Lianhua Film Company in 1932. After the release of *Revenge by the Volcano* (*dir.* **Sun Yu**, 1932), he starred in another dozen or so productions for the studio.

When film production in Shanghai ground to a halt after the outbreak of the Sino-Japanese war, Zheng resorted to stage work as a way of contributing to the resistance. With his background in theatre, Zheng quickly established himself as a star. In 1938 he left Shanghai and went to the interior to work for the KMT government. He participated in the making of a **documentary**, *Long Live*

the Nation (1942), but devoted most of his energies to the translating of drama textbooks. In addition, he also wrote *The Birth of Character* (Jiaose de dansheng), a monograph published in 1948 and adapted as a textbook by many drama and film schools throughout the country.

After the war, Zheng made the transition from acting to directing. His most noteworthy achievements are *Spring River Flows East* (*co-dir.* **Cai Chusheng**, 1947) and *Crows and Sparrows* (1949). Like many artists of his generation, Zheng had to adapt to the new political environment of the post-1949 period. His *Husband and Wife* (1951) was widely criticized for its bourgeois sentiment, a reaction that greatly annoyed and discouraged him. He then switched to the production of documentaries and did not shoot another feature until *The Rebels* in 1955. This biographical film was based on the life of an historical figure, Song Jingshi, who led a peasant uprising against the Manchu rulers. To avoid getting himself into more political trouble, Zheng carefully studied the party line on this man's life and times. Although only a moderate success artistically, the film prepared Zheng for *Lin Zexu* (*co-dir.* Cen Fan, 1959), an **historical film** set during the time of the Opium Wars. Despite its propagandist nature, *Lin Zexu* is technically well crafted and can stand as representative of the best pre-**Cultural Revolution** filmmaking from the PRC. Zheng's other films since *Lin Zexu* have met with varying degrees of success. While *Nie Er* (1959) won a top prize in the category of **biography** film at Karlovy Vary FF, *Spring Comes to the Withered Tree* (1961) was critically acclaimed domestically. However, his last film, *Li Shanzi* (1964), was for political reasons never released.

See also: propaganda and film; theatre and film

Further Reading

ZDX (1982–6: 2: 286–97), a short biography; J. Zheng (1948, 1979), his monograph and a memoir.

(ZX)

Zheng Zhengqiu

(Zheng Fangze, Zheng Bo Chang, Zheng Yao Feng)

b. 25 January 1889, Shanghai
d. 16 July 1935, Shanghai
Screen writer, director, playwright

One of the founding fathers of Chinese cinema, Zheng Zhengqiu was an influential figure in theatre and wrote theatrical reviews for major newspapers. In 1913, his friend **Zhang Shichun** joined Asia Film Company and asked him to be his partner. Together they made China's first short feature, *The **Difficult Couple*** (*dir.* Zhang Shichuan, 1913), a film highly critical of the practice of arranged marriage. However, Asia Film Company dissolved soon after the film was completed, and the two did not work together again until 1922, when Zhang organized Mingxing Film Company. Besides writing and directing, Zheng also served as assistant manager of the studio and was in charge of training company employees.

Zheng always believed that film should be socially conscious and morally uplifting. Between 1923 and 1930 he wrote and directed a total of fifty-three titles, the best known of which are ***Cheng the Fruit Seller*** (1922), ***Orphan Rescues Grandfather*** (1923, both *dir.* Zhang Shichuan), *Little Darling* (1926), *My Fair Lady* (1927), *The White Cloud Pagoda* (1928), *Flower of Freedom* (1932) and ***Twin Sisters*** (1933). One consistent theme in all these films is the plight of the poor and powerless. Zheng once commented on his films, 'To seek justice on behalf of the weak has always been my philosophy. In my films I have always tried to find a position from which I can speak for the poor'. Indeed, many of his films denounce the moral corruption of those in power. For instance, his most important title of the 1930s, *Twin Sisters*, contrasts the lives of two sisters: while the one married to a wealthy warlord is mean and cruel, the one who works as a maid to support her husband and child is kind and loving. This critical thrust in Zheng's films mirrored the ideological orientation of the 1930s leftists.

Zheng suffered from chronic illness, a condition only exacerbated by his manic work rate. When he died in 1935, a deep sense of loss was felt by both the leftist filmmakers and the KMT officials. In death as in life, Zheng Zhenqiu transcended political differences.

See also: theatre and film

Further Reading

C. Tang (1992a, b), two studies of Zheng Zhengqiu; ZDX (1982–6: 1: 202–9), a short biography; Z. Zhang (1999), on *Cheng the Fruit Seller*.

(ZX)

Zhou Jianyun

b. 1883
d. 1967
Producer

An influential producer of the 1920s–30s, Zhou Jianyun co-founded Mingxing Film Company with **Zhang Shichuan** and **Zheng Zhengqiu** in 1922. He served in numerous positions at the studio. In 1928, he played a major role in organizing Liuhe Film Company (United Six), which merged six Shanghai film studios into one huge corporation with the aim of squeezing smaller rivals out of the market. He later served as Mingxing Film Company's manager, finance director and film distributor. In the early 1930s, Zhou was instrumental in bringing into the industry a group of leftist intellectuals, and so indirectly contributed to the rise of leftist films. As a widely recognized industry business leader, Zhou led a Chinese film delegation to Moscow in 1935 to attend a film festival. He moved to Hong Kong after the Sino-Japanese war and retired from the film world after 1949.

See also: leftist film (under Chinese cinema in Historical essays)

Further Reading

ZDX (1982–6: 1: 176–82), a short biography.

(ZX, YZ)

Zhou Xiaowen

b. 1954, Beijing
Director, cinematographer

A close associate of the **Fifth Generation**, Zhou Xiaowen did not earn international recognition until 1994, when his Hong Kong-financed ***Ermo*** (1994) was distributed overseas. Like several other directors of his generation, Zhou joined the army in 1969 (at the age of fifteen). He managed to get hold of a book on cinematography by Wu Yinxian and was surprised to learn, when he entered BFA three years later, that Wu's was the only textbook used to train newsreel cameramen like himself. After training he was assigned to Xi'an Film Studio, where he struggled for years to move into directing. His wish came true in 1984 after **Wu Tianming** had been elected head of the studio. Zhou first served as assistant director on ***In the Wild Mountain*** (*dir.* Yan Xueshu, 1985) and then co-directed ***In Their***

Prime (1986) with Guo Fangfang. Like *The Dove Tree* (*dir.* **Wu Ziniu**, 1985), this film about the Sino-Vietnam border war was banned in China.

Greatly upset, Zhou then accepted Wu's proposal to make two gangster films: ***Desperation*** (1987) and *The **Price of Frenzy*** (1988). The immense commercial success of these two films led to a number of imitations produced by other studios, for example Pearl River's ***Bloodshed at Dusk*** (*dir.* **Sun Zhou**, 1989), but it did not convince Zhou that he should abandon his quest for **art film**. He directed and shot *The **Black Mountain Road*** (1990), an experimental film about an uninhibited woman and her relations with two forest workers. The film was shelved without apparent reason for a number of years, but it finally cleared film censorship in the mid-1990s with just minor cuts. Meanwhile, Zhou made three more low-budget features at Xi'an, among them *No Regrets* (1991) which bears a strongly autobiographical imprint. Zhou made *The Lie Detector* (1993) while suffering from depression; admittedly his worst film to date, it was shot in twenty days while the director drank heavily on set. He also directed a **gangster film** *Presumed Guilty* (1993), a co-production with Youth Film Studio and Dragon Air Entertainment Company in Hong Kong.

The production history of the acclaimed *Ermo* features as many ups and downs as Zhou's own career. Zhou decided to go it alone when he failed to secure support from any mainland studio. Fortunately, Hong Kong backing came just in time for post-production work, and the film went on to win four major prizes at Locarno FF. Zhou and his producers continued their successful partnership on the director's next feature, *The **Emperor's Shadow*** (1996), an epic historical drama about the First Emperor of China, a tyrant responsible for the building of the Great Wall.

See also: avant-garde, experimental or exploratory film; censorship and film; documentary; historical drama

Further Reading

T. Rayns (1995d), an excellent biography.

(YZ)

Zhou Xuan

(Su Pu)

b. 1 August 1918, Changzhou, Jiangsu province
d. 22 September 1957
Actress, singer

One of the most popular movie stars and singers of the 1930s–40s, Zhou experienced a series of tragic events in her personal life. Her biological parents abandoned her after she was born, and her foster parents almost sold her into **prostitution** while still a teenager. She was recruited by Li Minghui's Bright Moon Song and Dance Troupe and gained a basic musical education. When the troupe's leading lady failed to turn up for a show, the stage manager substituted Zhou in her place. Zhou's superb performances immediately attracted critical notices. Zhou won a singing competition sponsored by several Shanghai radio stations in 1934 and was affectionately dubbed the 'Golden Voice'.

Zhou's first movie role was as a minor character in *A Lady's Favour* (*dir.* Wen Yimin, 1935). Her engaging performance impressed audiences, and over the next few years she played one female lead after another in films produced by Yihua and Xinhua. The fact that Zhou was also a singer only increased her appeal, and many of the songs she sang on screen became popular tunes of the 1930s, for example, from ***Street Angel*** (*dir.* **Yuan Muzhi**).

Zhou's relationship with her first husband, Yan Hua, deteriorated rapidly after their marriage. A contract dispute caused her a great deal of stress and resulted in a miscarriage. Yet her estranged husband continued to pester her. Out of desperation, Zhou attempted suicide. During the Sino-Japanese war, Zhou participated in stage performances and toured the Philippines to promote the resistance. She acted in about twenty films from this period, most of them costume dramas produced by Guohua and United China film companies.

Zhou moved to Hong Kong after the war and starred in ***Night Inn*** (*dir.* **Huang Zuolin**, 1947), *A Tale of Two Girls* (*dir.* **Ying Yunwei**, Wu Tian, 1947) and ***Sorrows of the Forbidden City*** (*dir.* **Zhu Shilin**, 1948). For several years she suffered from a mental illness. After making a partial recovery, she returned to Shanghai in 1950, but unfortunately died before she could complete another film.

See also: costume drama

Further Reading

ZDX (1982–6: 2: 184–92), a short biography.

(ZX, YZ)

Zhu Shilin

b. 27 July 1899
d. 5 January 1967
Director, screen writer

Zhu Shilin was a production manager for Lianhua in 1930 and co-wrote the screenplay for *Memories of the Old Capital* (*dir.* **Sun Yu**, 1930) with **Luo Mingyou**. He started directing in 1934 and contributed a segment to the omnibus film ***Lianhua Symphony*** (1937). He directed many historical films in occupied Shanghai. After moving to Hong Kong in 1946, he directed several excellent features, including ***Sorrows of the Forbidden City*** (1948), *New Widow* (1956) and *Between Tears and Smiles* (1964), the last an adaptation of a famous novella by Ba Jin. Zhu was regarded as the prime exponent of a new school of film realism in Hong Kong in the 1950s–60s.

See also: adaptations of drama and literature; historical film

(YZ)

Zhuangzi Tests His Wife

(Zhuangzi shiqi)

dir./sc. Li Minwei
with **Li Beihai**, Li Minwei, Yan Shanshan
Shanghai: Huamei Film, 1913

One of the first Chinese feature films ever made, this Hong Kong production was also the first to star an actress.

The two-reel film is an adaptation of a Chinese legend based on the Taoist sage, Zhuangzi, and his relationship with his wife. The film begins with Zhuangzi's suspicions about his wife's infidelity. He decides to test her by pretending that he is dead, all the while disguising himself as a prince so as then to seduce his unsuspecting 'widow'. While the director, Li Minwei, took the roles of both Zhuangzi and his wife, Li's own wife, Yan Sansan, played a maid – the first woman ever to star in a Chinese film.

See also: legends and myths

(ZX)

Bibliography
Yingjin Zhang and Jean J. Su

Items of essential reading are preceded by asterisks. Chinese titles are limited to book-length studies, general surveys or major sources.

Abbas, Ackbar (1996) 'Cultural Studies in a Postculture', in C. Nelson and D. P. Gaonkar (eds) *Disciplinarity and Dissent in Cultural Studies*, New York: Routledge, 289–312.

* — (1997) *Hong Kong: Culture and the Politics of Disappearance*, Minneapolis: University of Minnesota Press.

An, Jingfu (1994) 'The Pain of a Half Taoist: Taoist Principles, Chinese Landscape Painting, and *King of the Children*', in L. Ehrlich and D. Desser (eds) *Cinematic Landscapes*, 117–25.

Armes, Roy (1987) *Third World Film Making and the West*, Berkeley: University of California Press.

Asiaweek (1994) 'From Concubine to Crone, and Then Joan Chen Wants to Play Burma's Heroine', *Asiaweek* (Feb. 16): 29.

Atkinson, Michael (1996) 'Songs of Crushed Love: The Cinema of Stanley Kwan', *Film Comment* 32, 3: 42–9.

Aufderheide, Pat (1987) 'Oriental Insurgents', *Film Comment* 23, 6: 73–6.

— (1988) 'Dynamic Duo', *Film Comment* 24, 3: 43–5.

Bai, Yan (1955) *Yige nü yanyuan de zishu* (Pak Yin: autobiography of a film actress), Hong Kong: Wenzong chubanshe.

Baker, Rick and Toby Russell (1994) *The Essential Guide to Hong Kong Movies*, London: Eastern Heroes Publications.

Bao, Wenqing (1983) 'Two Films About the Empress Dowager', *China Reconstructs* (Dec.): 42–7.

— (1991) 'Three Award-Winning Women Film Directors', *China Today* 3: 24–8.

Bao, Yuheng (1985) 'The Mirror of Chinese Society', *Chinese Literature* 4: 190–201.

Barmé, Geremie (1983) 'Shi Hui: A Profile', *Chinese Literature* 8: 96–104.

Barmé, Geremie and John Minford (1988) *Seeds of Fire: Chinese Voices of Conscience*, New York: Hill and Wang.

* Bergeron, Régis (1977) *Le Cinéma chinois, 1905–1949*, Lausanne: Alfred Eibel.

* — (1982) 'Le Cinéma chinois et les luttes politiques en Chine de 1949 à 1981', in *Ombres électriques*, 75–82.

* — (1984) *Le Cinéma chinois, 1949–1983*, 3 vols., Paris: L'Harmattan.

— (1996/7) 'The Making of a Passion: 40 Years of Living with the World of Chinese Films', *Asian Cinema* 8, 2: 116–25.

Berry, Chris (1982) 'Stereotypes and Ambiguities: An Examination of the Feature Films of the Chinese Cultural Revolution', *Journal of Asian Culture* 6: 37–72.

— (1988a) 'Chinese Urban Cinema: Hyper-realism Versus Absurdism', *East-West Film Journal* 3, 1: 76–87.

* — (1988b) 'Chinese "Women's Cinema"', *Camera Obscura* 18: 5–41.

— (1988c) 'The Sublimative Text: Sex and Revolution in *Big Road*', *East-West Film Journal* 2, 2: 66–86.

— (1989a) 'Now You See It, Now You Don't', *Cinemaya* 4: 46–55.

— (1989b) 'Poisonous Weeds or National Treasures: Chinese Left Films in the 1930s', *Jump Cut* 34: 87–94.

* — (ed.) (1991a) *Perspectives on Chinese Cinema*, London: BFI Publishing.

— (1991b) 'Sexual Difference and the Viewing Subject in *Li Shuangshuang* and *The In-laws*', in C. Berry (ed.) *Perspectives*, 30–9.

— (1992) 'Race: Chinese Film and the Politics of Nationalism', *Cinema Journal* 31, 2: 45–58.

— (1993a) 'At What Price Success?' *Cinemaya* 20: 20–2.

— (1993b) 'Interview with Peng Xiaolian', *Modern Chinese Literature* 7, 2: 103–8.

— (1993c) 'Taiwanese Melodrama Returns with a Twist in *The Wedding Banquet*', *Cinemaya* 21: 52–4.

— (1994a) 'A Nation T(w/o)o: Chinese Cinema(s) and Nationhood(s)', in W. Dissanayake (ed.) *Colonialism*, 42–64.

— (1994b) 'Neither One Thing Nor Another: Toward a Study of the Viewing Subject and Chinese Cinema in the 1980s', in N. Browne *et al.* (eds), *New Chinese Cinemas*, 109–10.

— (1995a) 'Hidden Truths', *Cinemaya* 28–29: 52–5.

— (1995b) 'Tsai Ming-liang: Look at All the Lonely People', *Cinemaya* 30: 18–20.

— (1996a) 'Outrageous Fortune: China's Film Industry Takes a Roller-Coaster Ride', *Cinemaya* 33: 17–19.

— (1996b) 'Sexual DisOrientations: Homosexual Rights, East Asian Films, and Postmodern Postnationalism', in X. Tang and S. Snyder (eds) *In Pursuit of Contemporary East Asian Culture*, Boulder: Westview Press, 157–82.

— (1996c) 'Zhang Yuan: Thriving in the Face of Adversity', *Cinemaya* 32: 40–4.

Berry, Chris and Mary Ann Farquhar (1994) 'Post-Socialist Strategies: An Analysis of *Yellow Earth* and *Black Cannon Incident*', in L. Ehrlich and D. Desser (eds) *Cinematic Landscapes*, 81–116.

Block, Alex Ben (1974) *The Legend of Bruce Lee*, New York: Dell.

Browne, Nick (1994) 'Society and Subjectivity: On the Political Economy of Chinese Melodrama', in N. Browne *et al.* (eds), *New Chinese Cinemas*, 40–56.

— (1996) 'Hou Hsiao-hsien's *Puppetmaster*: The Poetics of Landscape', *Asian Cinema* 8, 1: 28–37.

* Browne, Nick, Paul G. Pickowicz, Vivian Sobchack and Esther Yau (eds) (1994) *New Chinese Cinemas: Forms, Identities, Politics*, New York: Cambridge University Press.

Cai, Hongsheng (1995) 'Xianggang dianying bashinian' (Eighty years of Hong Kong cinema), *Dangdai dianying* 2: 105–12.

Cai, Mingliang *et al.* (1994) *Aiqing wansui: Cai Mingliang de dianying* (*Vive l'amour*: Tsai Mingliang's film), Taipei: Wanxiang.

Callahan, W.A. (1993) 'Gender, Ideology, Nation: *Ju Dou* in the Cultural Politics of China', *East-West Film Journal* 7, 1: 52–80.

Cambon, Marie (1995) 'The Dream Palaces of Shanghai: American Films in China's Largest Metropolis Prior to 1949', *Asian Cinema* 7, 2: 34–45.

Chan, Evans (1990) 'A China of No Returns: Notes on *China, My Sorrow*', *Cinemaya* 9: 20–3.

Chang, Michael G. (1999) 'The Good, the Bad, and the Beautiful: Movie Actresses and Public Discourse in Shanghai, 1920s–1930s', in Y. Zhang (ed.) *Romance, Sexuality, Identity*.

Chen, Baoguang (1993) 'Young Actress Gong Li', *Chinese Literature* 2: 180–3.

* Chen, Bo (ed.) (1993) *Zhongguo zuoyi dianying yundong* (The leftist film movement in China), Beijing: Zhongguo dianying chubanshe.

Chen, Dieyi (1984) *Xianggang yingtan mishi* (A secret history of the Hong Kong film circles), Hong Kong: Benma chubanshe.

* Chen, Feibao (1988) *Taiwan dianying shihua* (A history of Taiwan cinema), Beijing: Zhongguo dianying chubanshe.

— (1994) 'Chutan Taiwan dianying daoyan jiegou ji qi dianying meixue tezheng' (Generations of Taiwan directors and their aesthetic styles), *Dianying yishu* 1: 36–9, 2: 24–30.

* Chen, Huangmei (ed.) (1989) *Dangdai Zhongguo dianying* (Contemporary Chinese cinema), 2 vols, Beijing: Zhongguo shehui kexue chubanshe.

Chen, Kaige (1989–90) 'Encounter: Chen Kaige Talks to Aruna Vasudev', *Cinemaya* 6: 18–23.

— (1990) 'Breaking the Circle: The Cinema and Cultural Change in China', *Cineaste* 17, 3: 28–31.

— (1991) *Shaonian Kaige* (The young Kaige), Taipei: Yuanliu.

* Chen, Kaige and Tony Rayns (1989) *King of the Children and the New Chinese Cinema*, London: Faber and Faber.

Chen, Mo (1995) *Zhang Yimou dianying lun* (On Zhang Yimou's films), Beijing: Zhongguo dianying chubanshe.

Chen, Pauline (1994) 'History Lessons', *Film Comment* 30, 2: 85–7.

* Chen, Ru-shou Robert (1993a) 'Dispersion, Ambivalence and Hybridity: A Cultural-Historical Investigation of Film Experience in Taiwan in the 1980s', Ph.D. dissertation, University of Southern California.

— (1993b) *Taiwan xindianying de lishi wenhua jingyan* (Historical and cultural experiences in new Taiwan cinema), Taipei: Wanxiang.

— (1995) *Dianying diguo: ling yizhong zhushi* (Screen empire: a different gaze), Taipei: Wanxiang.

Chen, Tongyi (1984) 'Veteran Director Tang Xiaodan', *China Screen* 4: 20–1.

Chen, Wei (ed.) (1992) *Ke Ling dianying wencun* (Ke Ling's film essays), Beijing: Zhongguo dianying chubanshe.

Chen, Xihe (1990) 'Shadowplay: Chinese Film Aesthetics and Their Philosophical and Cultural Fundamentals', in G. Semsel *et al.* (eds), *Chinese Film Theory*, 192–204.

Chen, Zhaoyu (1985) 'Film Actress Bai Yang', *Chinese Literature* 4: 202–6.

Cheng, Bugao (1983) *Yingtan yijiu* (Reminiscences of the film circles), Beijing: Zhongguo dianying chubanshe.

Cheng, Jessie (1995) 'Shaky Foundation', *Free China Review* (Feb.): 28–33.

* Cheng, Jihua, Li Shaobai and Xing Zuwen (eds) (1963) *Zhongguo dianying fazhan shi* (History of the development of Chinese cinema), 2 vols., Beijing: Zhongguo dianying chubanshe.

Cheng, Scarlet (1993) 'The Great Wall of Cinema', *The World & I* (May): 116–21.

— (1994) 'The Story of Zhang Yimou', *The World & I* (May): 122–5.

Cheshire, Godfrey (1993) 'Time Span: The Cinema of Hou Hsiao-hsien', *Film Comment* 29, 6: 56–63.

— (1994) 'Chinese Checkers', *Film Comment* 30, 4: 65.

Chiao, (Peggy) Hsiung-Ping (1981) 'Bruce Lee: His Influence on the Evolution of the Kung Fu Genre', *Journal of Popular Film and Television* 9, 1: 30–42.

* — (ed.) (1987) *Xianggang dianying fengmao* (Aspects of Hong Kong cinema), Taipei: Shibao chuban gongsi.

* — (ed.) (1988) *Taiwan xindianying* (New Taiwan cinema), Taipei: Shibao chuban gongsi.

— (ed.) (1990a) *Huang tudi* (Yellow earth), Taipei: Wanxiang.

— (ed.) (1990b) *Laojing* (Old well), Taipei: Wanxiang.

— (1991a) 'The Distinct Taiwanese and Hong Kong Cinemas', in C. Berry (ed.) *Perspectives*, 155–65.

— (1991b) *Tai Gang dianying zhongde zuozhe yu leixing* (Auteurs and genres in Taiwan and Hong Kong), Taipei: Yuanliu.

— (1993a) *Gaibian lishi de wunian: Guolian dianying yanjiu* (Five years that changed history: Studies on Guolian studio), Taipei: Wanxiang.

— (1993b) 'History's Subtle Shadows: Hou Hsiao-hsien's *The Puppet Master*', *Cinemaya* 21: 4–11.

— (1993c) 'Reel Contact Across the Taiwan Straits: A History of Separation and Reunion', in K. Eder and D. Rossell (eds) *New Chinese Cinema*, pp. 48–57.

— (1994) 'Stan Lai: Illusions, Lies and Realities', *Cinemaya* 24: 48–54.

— (1996a) '*Mahjong*: Urban Travails [*sic*] – An Interview with Edward Yang', *Cinemaya* 33: 24–7.

— (1996b) 'Second Wave from Taiwan: Three Interviews', *Cinemaya* 34: 4–13.

China Screen collective (1997) 'Zhongguo dianying houji ? ren' (Who are the new generation of Chinese filmmakers?), *Zhongguo yinmu* 1: 34–9.

Chong, W. L. and A. S. Keyser (1990) 'Director Zhang Zeming on His Film *Swansong*', *China Information* 4, 4: 37–43.

Chow, Rey (1993) 'A Souvenir of Love', *Modern Chinese Literature* 7, 2: 59–78.

* — (1995) *Primitive Passions: Visuality, Sexuality, Ethnography, and Contemporary Chinese Cinema*, New York: Columbia University Press.

Chu, Rolanda (1994) '*Swordsman II* and *The East is Red*: The "Hong Kong film", Entertainment, and Gender', *Bright Lights Film Journal* 13: 30–35, 46.

Chute, David (ed.) (1988) 'Made in Hong Kong', *Film Comment* 24, 3: 33–56.

— (1994) 'Beyond the Law', *Film Comment* 30, 1: 60–2.

Ciecko, Anne T. (1997) 'Transnational Action: John Woo, Hong Kong, Hollywood', in S. Lu (ed.) *Transnational Chinese Cinemas*.

Cinemaya (1995) 'A Tribute to Zhang Yimou', a special forum, *Cinemaya* 30: n.p.

Clark, Paul (1984) 'The Film Industry in the 1970s', in B. McDougall (ed.) (1984) *Popular Chinese Literature and Performing Arts in the People's Republic of China, 1949–1979*, Berkeley: University of California Press, 177–96.

* —— (1987a) *Chinese Cinema: Culture and Politics Since 1949*, New York: Cambridge University Press.

—— (1987b) 'Ethnic Minorities in Chinese Films: Cinema and the Exotic', *East-West Film Journal* 1, 2: 15–31.

—— (1989) 'Reinventing China: The Fifth-Generation Filmmakers', *Modern Chinese Literature* 5: 121–36.

—— (1994–95) 'Chronicles of Chinese Life', *Cinemaya* 25–26: 4–6.

CMPC (ed.) (1994) *Yinshi nannü: dianying juben yu paishe shimo* (*East Drink Man Woman*: the film script and the production process), Taipei: Wanxiang.

Coward, Rosalind and John Ellis (1981) 'Hong Kong – China 1981', *Screen* 22, 4: 91–100.

Cui, Shuqin (1997) 'Gendered Perspective: The Construction and Representation of Subjectivity and Sexuality in *Ju Dou*', in S. Lu (ed.) *Transnational Chinese Cinemas*.

Da, Huo'er (1989) 'An Interview with Xie Jin', *Jump Cut* 34: 107–9.

* Dai, Jinhua (1995) 'Invisible Women: Contemporary Chinese Cinema and Women's Film', *Positions* 3, 1: 255–80.

Dai Jinhua and Mayfair Yang (1995) 'A Conversation with Huang Shuqin', *Positions* 3, 3: 790–805.

Dai, Qing (1993) 'Raised Eyebrows for *Raise the Red Lantern*', *Public Culture* 5: 333–6.

* Dannen, Fredric and Barry Long (1997) *Hong Kong Babylon: An Insider's Guide to the Hollywood of the East*, London: Faber and Faber.

Dariotis, Wei Ming and Eileen Fung (1997) 'Breaking the Soy Sauce Jar: Diasporas and Displacement in the Films of Ang Lee', in S. Lu (ed.) *Transnational Chinese Cinemas*.

Delmar, R. and M. Nash (1976) 'Breaking with Old Ideas: Recent Chinese Films', *Screen* 17, 4: 67–84.

Dissanayake, Wimal (ed.) (1988) *Cinema and Cultural Identity: Reflections on Films from Japan, India, and China*, Lanham, MD: University Press of America.

—— (ed.) (1993) *Melodrama and Asian Cinema*, New York: Cambridge University Press.

—— (ed.) (1994) *Colonialism and Nationalism in Asian Cinema*, Bloomington: Indiana University Press.

Dolcini, M. (ed.) (1978) *Cinema e spettacolo in Cina oggi*, quaderno informativo n. 75 a cura dell'ufficio documentazione della Mostra.

Donald, Stephanie (1995) 'Women Reading Chinese Films: Between Orientalism and Silence', *Screen* 36, 4: 325–40.

Du, Yunzhi (1978) *Zhongguo de dianying* (Film in China), Taipei: Huangguan chubanshe.

* —— (1988) *Zhonghua minguo dianying shi* (A history of cinema in the Republic of China), 2 vols, Taipei: Xingzhengyuan wenhua jianshe weiyuanhui.

* Eberhard, Wolfram (1972) *The Chinese Silver Screen: Hong Kong and Taiwan Motion Pictures*, Taipei: Orient Cultural Service.

Edelstein, David (1988) 'Eastern Haunts', *Film Comment* 24, 3: 48, 50–2.

* Eder, Klaus and Deac Rossell (eds) (1993) *New Chinese Cinema*, London: National Film Theatre.

* Ehrlich, Linda and David Desser (eds) (1994) *Cinematic Landscapes: Observations on the Visual Arts and Cinema of China and Japan*, Austin: University of Texas Press.

Ehrlich, Linda and Ning Ma (1990) 'College Course File: East Asian Cinema', *Journal of Film and Video* 42, 2: 53–70.

Ellis, John (1982) 'Electric Shadows in Italy', *Screen* 23, 2: 79–83.

Eng, David L. (1993/4) 'Love at Last Site: Waiting for Oedipus in Stanley Kwan's *Rouge*', *Camera Obscura* 32: 74–101.

Ertong dianying lilun yanjiu ziliao (Research materials on children's film) (1988), 2 vols, Beijing: Zhongguo heping chubanshe.

Farquhar, Mary Ann (1992) 'The "Hidden" Gender in *Yellow Earth*', *Screen* 33, 2: 154–64.

—— (1995) '*Sanmao*: Classic Cartoons and Chinese Popular Culture', in John A. Lent (ed.) *Asian Popular Culture*, Boulder: Westview Press, 109–25.

Feng, Min (1989) '*Malu tianshi* yu xin xianshi zhuyi' (*Street Angel* and neorealism), *Dandai dianying* 5: 95–100.

* Feng Min, Shao Zhou and Jin Fenglan (1992) *Zhongguo dianying yishu shigang* (An outline history of Chinese film art), Tianjin: Nankai daxue chubanshe.

Filed, Andrew (1999) 'Selling Souls in Sin City: Shanghai Singing and Dancing Girls in Print, Film and Politics, 1920–1949', in Y. Zhang (ed.) *Romance, Sexuality, Identity*.

Fong, Allen (1990) 'A Feel for the Real', *Cinemaya* 8: 22–5.

Fong, Suzie Young-Sau (1995) 'The Voice of Feminine Madness in Zhang Yimou's *Raise the Red Lantern*', *Asian Cinema* 7, 1: 12–23.

* Fonoroff, Paul (1988) 'A Brief History of Hong Kong Cinema', *Renditions* 29–30: 293–308.

— (1990/91) 'King of the Island: Chow Yun-Fat', *Cinemaya* 10: 58–9.

* — (1997) *Silver Light: A Pictorial History of Hong Kong Cinema, 1920–1970*, Hong Kong: Joint Publishing.

Fore, Steve (1993) 'Tales of Recombinant Femininity: *The Reincarnation of Golden Lotus*, the *Chin P'ing Mei*, and the Politics of Melodrama in Hong Kong', *Journal of Film and Video* 45, 4: 57–70.

— (1994) 'Golden Harvest Films and the Hong Kong Movie Industry in the Realm of Globalization', *The Velvet Light Trap* 34: 40–58.

— (1997) 'Jackie Chan and the Cultural Dynamics of Global Entertainment', in S. Lu (ed.) *Transnational Chinese Cinemas*.

Gallagher, Mark (1997) 'Masculinity in Translation: Jackie Chan's Trans-cultural Star Text', *The Velvet Light Trap* 39: 23–41.

Gladney, Dru C. (1995) 'Tian Zhuangzhuang, the Fifth Generation, and Minorities Film in China', *Public Culture* 8: 161–75.

Glaessner, Verina (1974) *Kung Fu: The Cinema of Vengeance*, London: Lorrimer.

Gong, Jianong (Robert Kung) (1967) *Gong Jianong congying huiyi lu* (Gong Jianong's memoirs of his silver screen life), 3 vols., Taipei: Wenxing shudian.

* Gongsun, Lu (1977) *Zhongguo dianying shihua* (A history of Chinese cinema), Hong Kong: Nantian.

Gross, Larry (1996) 'Nonchalant Grace', *Sight and Sound* (Sep.): 6–10.

Guan, Wenqing (Moon Kwan) (1976) *Zhongguo yintan waishi* (Unofficial history of the Chinese screen), Hong Kong: Guangjiaojing chubanshe.

Hammer, Tad Bentley (1991) *International Film Prizes: An Encyclopedia*, New York: Garland.

* Hammond, Stefan and Mike Wilkins (1996) *Sex and Zen and a Bullet in the Head: The Essential Guide to Hong Kong's Mind-Bending Films*, New York: Fireside/Simon & Schuster.

Hampton, Howard (1996) 'Venus, Armed: Brigitte Lin's Shanghai Gesture', *Film Comment* 32, 5: 42–8.

Han, Xiaolei (1995) 'Dui diwudai de wenhua tuwei: houwudai de geren dianying xianxiang' (A cultural breakaway from the Fifth Generation: the phenomenon of individualist film in the post-Fifth Generation), *Dianying yishu* 2: 58–63.

Hao, Dazheng (1994) 'Chinese Visual Representation: Painting and Cinema', in L. Ehrlich and D. Desser (eds) *Cinematic Landscapes*, 45–62.

Harris, Kristine (1995) '*The New Woman*: Image, Subject, and Dissent in 1930s Shanghai Film Culture', *Republican China* 20, 2: 55–79.

— (1999) 'Adaptation and Innovation: Costume Drama Spectacle and *Romance of the Western Chamber*', in Y. Zhang (ed.) *Romance, Sexuality, Identity*.

He, Keren *et al.* (1986) *Ruan Lingyu zhisi* (The death of Ruan Lingyu), Changsha: Yulu shushe.

He, Xiujun (1982) 'Zhang Shichuan et la compagnie cinématographique Mingxing', in *Ombres électriques*, 67–74.

Hitchcock, Peter (1992) 'The Aesthetics of Alienation, or China's "Fifth Generation"', *Cultural Studies* 6, 1: 116–41.

HKIFF (1978) *Cantonese Cinema Retrospective, 1950–1959*, a publication for the 2nd Hong Kong International Film Festival (HKIFF), Hong Kong: Urban Council.

— (1979) *Hong Kong Cinema Survey, 1946–1968*, a publication for the 3rd HKIFF, Hong Kong: Urban Council.

— (1980) *A Survey of the Hong Kong Martial Arts Film*, a publication for the 4th HKIFF, Hong Kong: Urban Council.

— (1981) *A Study of the Hong Kong Swordplay Film, 1945–1980*, a publication for the 5th HKIFF (rev. edition, 1996), Hong Kong: Urban Council.

— (1982a) *Cantonese Cinema Retrospective, 1960–69*, a publication for the 6th HKIFF (rev. edition, 1996), Hong Kong: Urban Council.

— (1982b) *Hong Kong Contemporary Cinema*, a publication for the 6th HKIFF, Hong Kong: Urban Council.

— (1983) *A Comparative Study of Post-War Mandarin and Cantonese Cinema: The Films of Zhu Shilin, Qin Jian and Other Directors*, a publication for the 7th HKIFF, Hong Kong: Urban Council.

— (1984) *A Study of Hong Kong Cinema in the Seventies*, a publication for the 8th HKIFF, Hong Kong: Urban Council.

— (1985) *The Traditions of Hong Kong Comedy*, a publication for the 9th HKIFF, Hong Kong: Urban Council.

— (1986a) *Cantonese Melodrama, 1950–1969*, a publication for the 10th HKIFF (rev. edition, 1997), Hong Kong: Urban Council.

— (1986b) *Ten Years of Hong Kong Cinema, 1976–1985*, a publication for the 10th HKIFF, Hong Kong: Urban Council.

— (1987) *Cantonese Opera Film Retrospective*, a publication for the 11th HKIFF (rev. edition, 1996), Hong Kong: Urban Council.

— (1988) *Changes in Hong Kong Society through Cinema*, a publication for the 12th HKIFF, Hong Kong: Urban Council.

— (1989) *Phantoms of the Hong Kong Cinema*, a publication for the 13th HKIFF, Hong Kong: Urban Council.

— (1990) *The China Factor in Hong Kong Cinema*, a publication for the 14th HKIFF (rev. edition, 1997), Hong Kong: Urban Council.

— (1991) *Hong Kong Cinema in the Eighties*, a publication for the 15th HKIFF, Hong Kong: Urban Council.

— (1992) *Overseas Chinese Figures in Cinema*, a publication for the 16th HKIFF, Hong Kong: Urban Council.

— (1993) *Mandarin Films and Popular Songs: 40's-60's*, a publication for the 17th HKIFF, Hong Kong: Urban Council.

— (1994) *Cinema of Two Cities: Hong Kong–Shanghai*, a publication for the 18th HKIFF, Hong Kong: Urban Council.

— (1995) *Early Images of Hong Kong & China*, a publication for the 19th HKIFF, Hong Kong: Urban Council.

— (1996a) *The Restless Breed: Cantonese Stars of the Sixties*, a publication for the 20th HKIFF, Hong Kong: Urban Council.

— (1996b) *The 20th Anniversary of the Hong Kong International Film Festival, 1977–1996*, Hong Kong: Urban Council.

Hoare, Stephanie (1993) 'Innovation through Adaptation: The Use of Literature in New Taiwan Film and Its Consequences', *Modern Chinese Literature* 7, 2: 33–58.

Hong, Hong and Yue Hui (eds) (1992) *Wo anlian de Taohuayuan* (My secret love of Peach Blossom Land), Taipei: Yuanliu.

* Hong Kong Arts Centre and Hong Kong Chinese Film Association (eds) (1984) *Early Chinese Cinema: The Era of Exploration*, a programme for the Hong Kong Arts Festival 1984.

Hong, Shi (1995) 'Diyici langchao: mopian qi Zhongguo shangye dianying xianxiang shuping' (The first wave: a discussion of commercial films in the silent era of Chinese cinema), *Dangdai dianying* 2: 5–12.

Hsiung, Deh-ta (1960) 'The Chinese Cinema To-day', *China Quarterly* 4: 82–7.

Hu, Die (1988) *Hu Die huiyi lu* (Hu Die's memoirs), Beijing: Wenhua yishu chubanshe.

Hu, Jinquan (King Hu) and Zhong Ling (1979) *Shanke ji* (Mountain visitors), Taipei: Yuanjing.

Hu, Ke (1988) 'Menglong de xiandai nüxing yishi' (The ambiguous modern female consciousness), in *Xinshiqi dianying shinian* (A decade of film in the new era), Chongqing: Chongqing chubanshe.

Hu, Xu (1986) *Xin Zhongguo dianying de yaolan* (The cradle of film in new China), Changchun: Jili wenshi chubanshe.

Huang, Jianxin (1991) 'Dis-Located! Huang Jianxin Talks to Chris Berry', *Cinemaya* 11: 20–3.

Huang, Jianye (1995) *Yang Dechang dianying yanjiu – Taiwan xin dianying de zhixing sibian jia* (Films by Edward Yang: a critical thinker in new Taiwan cinema), Taipei: Yuanliu.

Huang, Mingchuan (1990) *Duli zhipian zai Taiwan* (Independent filmmaking in Taiwan), Taipei: Qianwei chubanshe.

— (ed.) (1994) *Baodao dameng* (Bodo), Taipei: Qianwei chubanshe.

Huang, Ren (1994) *Dianying yu zhengzhi xuanchuan* (Film and political propaganda), Taipei: Wanxiang.

Huang, Shuqin (1995) 'Nü daoyan zibai' (Woman director's own comments), *Dangdai dianying* 5: 69–71.

Huang, Wanqiu (1988) *Wo yu Liu Sanjie* (Third Sister Liu and Me), Nanning: Guangxi renmin chubanshe.

Hui, Ann (1990) 'State of Flux: Ann Hui Talks to Rashmi Doraiswamy', *Cinemaya* 7: 22–4.

Hulsbus, Monica (1997) 'On the Oppositional Politics of Chinese Everyday Practices', *Cineaction* 42: 10–14.

Hwang, Jim (1995) 'Turning Talent Into Awards', *Free China Review* (Feb.): 18–19.

Jaehne, Karen (1984) '*Boat People*: An Interview with Ann Hui', *Cineaste* 13, 2: 16–19.

Jaivin, Linda (1995) 'Defying a Ban, Chinese Cameras Roll', *The Wall Street Journal* 18 Jan.: A12.

Jameson, Fredric (1994) 'Remapping Taipei', in N. Browne *et al.* (eds), *New Chinese Cinemas*, 117–50.

Jarvie, I.C. (1979) 'The Social and Cultural Significance of the Demise of the Cantonese Movie', *Journal of Asian Affairs* 4, 2: 40–51.

Jia, Leilei (1995) 'Luanshi chu haoxia, shenhua zao yingxiong: Zhongguo wuxia dianying, 1931–1949' (Knights-errant born in chaotic times, heroes created by legends: Chinese martial arts film), *Dangdai diangying* 2: 27–30.

Jing, Ray (1992) 'Taiwan Film Archive', *Cinemaya* 15: 10–12.

Kam, Tan See (1993) 'The Hong Kong Cantonese Vernacular as Cultural Resistance', *Cinemaya* 20: 12–15.

— (1996) 'Ban(g)! ban(g)! Dangerous Encounter – 1st Kind: Writing with Censorship', *Asian Cinema* 8, 1: 83–108.

Kam, Tan See, Justin Clemens and Eleanor Hogan (1994–5) 'Clara Law: Seeking an Audience Outside Hong Kong', *Cinemaya* 25–6: 50–4.

Kaplan, E. Ann (1989) 'Problematizing Cross-Cultural Analysis: The Case of Women in the Recent Chinese Cinema', *Wide Angle* 11, 2: 40–50.

* — (1991) 'Melodrama/Subjectivity/Ideology: The Relevance of Western Melodrama Theories to Recent Chinese Cinema', *East-West Film Journal* 5, 1: 6–27.

— (1997) 'Reading Formations and Chen Kaige's *Farewell My Concubine*', in S. Lu (ed.) *Transnational Chinese Cinemas*.

Kennedy, Harlan (1983) '*Boat People*', *Film Comment* 19, 5: 41–43, 47.

Keng, Chua Siew (1992) 'An Interview with Hou Hsiao-hsien', *Cinemaya* 15: 9.

Kipnis, Andrew (1996/7) 'Anti-Maoist Gender: *Hibiscus Town*'s Naturalization of a Dengist Sex/Gender/Kinship System', *Asian Cinema* 8, 2: 66–75.

Klawans, Stuart (1995) 'Zhang Yimou: Local Hero', *Film Comment* 31, 5: 11–18.

Ko, S.N. (1995) 'Rhythms: Hongkong Independent Shorts', *Cinemaya* 28–29: 14–21.

Kong, Haili (1996/7) 'Symbolism Through Zhang Yimou's Subversive Lens in His Early Films', *Asian Cinema* 8, 2: 98–115.

Kou, Liguang and Li Yuzhi (1991) *Zhongguo dangdai youxiu yingpian xinshang* (Appreciation of excellent contemporary Chinese films), Taiyuan: Shanxi jiaoyu chubanshe.

Kowallis, Jon (1997) 'The Diaspora in Postmodern Taiwan and Hong Kong Films: Framing Stan Lai's *The Peach Blossom Land* with Allen Fong's *Ah Ying*', in S. Lu (ed.) *Transnational Chinese Cinemas*.

Kraicer, Shelly (1997) 'Allegory and Ambiguity in Zhang Yimou's *Shanghai Triad*', *Cineaction* 42: 15–17.

Lang, Miriam (1993) '*Swan Songs*: Traditional Musicians in Contemporary China – Observations from a Film', *East Asian History* 5: 149–82.

Larson, Wendy (1997) 'The Concubine and the Figure of History: Chen Kaige's *Farewell My Concubine*', in S. Lu (ed.) *Transnational Chinese Cinemas*.

Lau, Jenny Kwok Wah (1991a) 'A Cultural Interpretation of the Popular Cinema of China and Hong Kong', in C. Berry (ed.) *Perspectives*, 166–74.

— (1991b) '*Judou*: A Hermeneutical Reading of Cross-Cultural Cinema', *Film Quarterly* 45, 2: 2–10.

— (1994) '*Judou*: An Experiment in Color and Portraiture in Chinese Cinema', in L. Ehrlich and D. Desser (eds) *Cinematic Landscapes*, 127–45.

— (1995) '*Farewell My Concubine*: History, Melodrama, and Ideology in Contemporary Pan-Chinese Cinema', *Film Quarterly* 49, 1: 16–27.

Law, Wai Ming (1993) 'Stanley Kwan: Carrying the Past Lightly', *Cinemaya* 19: 10–13.

Lee, David (1994) 'Ang Lee: Thoughts After the Oscars', *Sinorama* (May): 6–24.

Lee, Joan (1996) 'Zhang Yimou's *Raise the Red Lantern*: Contextual Analysis of Film Through a Confucian/Feminist Matrix', *Asian Cinema* 8, 1: 120–7.

* Lee, Leo Ou-fan (1991) 'The Tradition of Modern Chinese Cinema: Some Preliminary Explorations and Hypotheses', in C. Berry (ed.) *Perspectives*, 6–20.
— (1994) 'Two Films from Hong Kong: Parody and Allegory', in N. Browne *et al.* (eds), *New Chinese Cinemas*, 202–16.
— (1999) 'The Urban Milieu of Shanghai Cinema, 1930–1940: Some Explorations of Film Audience, Film Culture, and Narrative Conventions', in Y. Zhang (ed.) *Romance, Sexuality, Identity*.

Lee, Tain-Dow (1995) 'Rereading the Cultural Significance of Taiwan's Cinema of the 1990s', *Asian Cinema* 7, 1: 3–11.

* Lent, John A. (1990) *The Asian Film Industry*, Austin: University of Texas Press, 1990.
— (1996/7) 'Teach for a While, Direct for a While: An Interview with Xie Fei', *Asian Cinema* 8, 2: 91–7.

* Leyda, Jay (1972) *Dianying: An Account of Films and the Film Audience in China*, Cambridge, Mass.: MIT Press.

Li, Cheuk-to (1985) 'Le printemps d'une petite ville, un film qui renouvelle la tradition chinoise', in Quiquemelle and Passek (eds) *Le Cinéma chinois*, 73–6.
— (1989) 'Political Censorship: The Fatal Blow', *Cinemaya* 4: 42–5.
— (1991) 'Eight Films of Sun Yu', *Cinemaya* 11: 54–63.
— (1993a) *Guanni ji: Xianggang dianying pian* (Watching counter currents: Hong Kong cinema), Hong Kong: Ci wenhua.
— (1993b) 'Tsui Hark and Western Interest in Hong Kong Cinema', *Cinemaya* 21: 50–1.

* — (1994) 'The Return of the Father: Hong Kong New Wave and Its Chinese Context in the 1980s', in N. Browne *et al.* (eds), *New Chinese Cinemas*, 160–79.

Li, Erwei (1996) 'Breaking Up Is Hard to Do: Zhang Yimou Speaks About His New Film', *Cinemaya* 34: 27–9.

Li, Hanxiang (1984) *Sanshinian xishuo congtou* (Detailed account of my thirty-year career), 3 vols, Hong Kong: Tiandi tushu.

Li, H.C. (1989) 'Color, Character, and Culture: On *Yellow Earth*, *Black Cannon Incident*, and *Red Sorghum*', *Modern Chinese Literature* 5: 91–119.

* — (1993) 'Chinese Electric Shadows: A Selected Bibliography of Materials in English', *Modern Chinese Literature* 7, 2: 117–53.

* — (1994) 'More Chinese Electric Shadows: A Supplementary List', *Modern Chinese Literature* 8: 237–50.

Li, Lihua (1969) *Li Lihua de zuori, jinri, mingri* (Li Lihua's film career), ed. Liang Ruizhou, Taipei: Huabao she.

Li, Minwei (1993) 'Wo yu Zhongguo dianying', *Dangdai dianying* 6: 83–6.

Li, Shaobai (1991) *Dianying lishi ji lilun* (Film history and film theory), Beijing: Wenhua yishu chubanshe.

* Li, Suyuan and Hu Jubin (1996) *Zhongguo wusheng dianying shi* (A history of Chinese silent films), Beijing: Zhongguo dianying chubanshe.

Li, Wei (1994) 'Ning Ying Declares No More Fantasy', *China Screen* 3: 12–13.

Li, Yizhuang (1994) 'Xianggang dianying yu Xianggang shehui bianqian' (Hong Kong cinema and Hong Kong social changes), *Dianying yishu* 2: 15–23.

Li Youxin (ed.) (1986a) *Dianying, dianyingren, dianying kanwu* (film, film people, film publications), Taipei: Zili wanbao she.
— (ed.) (1986b) *Gang Tai liu da daoyan* (Six major directors in Hong Kong and Taiwan), Taipei: Zili wanbao she.

Liang, Heng and Judith Shapiro (1986) *After the Nightmare*, New York: Knopf.

Liao, Ping-hui (1993) 'Rewriting Taiwanese National History: The February 29 Incident as Spectacle', *Public Culture* 5: 281–96.

Liao, Xianhao (1994) 'Nanfang yilei: Yi houzhimin shijiao kan *Beiqing chengshi* yu *Niupeng* zhongde yuyan, chenmo yu lishi' (The south as other: a postcolonial study of language, silence and history in *A City of Sadness* and *China, My Sorrow*), *Zhongwai wenxue* 22, 8: 59–73.

Liu, Chenghan (1992) *Dianying fubixing ji* (Studies in Chinese cinema), 2 vols., Taipei: Yuanliu.

Liu, Lihsing (1992) 'The Chinese Cinema in the 1980s: Toward a Systematic Study of Its Socialist Realism', Ph.D. dissertation, Brigham Young University.

Lin, Niantong (1985) 'A Study of the Theories of Chinese Cinema in their Relationship to Classical Aesthetics', *Modern Chinese Literature* 1, 2: 185–200.

— (1991) *Zhongguo dianying meixue* (Chinese film aesthetics), Taipei: Yunchen.

Liu, Siping and Xing Zuwen (eds) (1981) *Lu Xun yu dianying* (Lu Xun and film), Beijing: Zhongguo dianying chubanshe.

Liu, Weihong (1988) 'Yu Wu Ziniu tan Wu Ziniu' (A conversation with Wu Ziniu about Wu Ziniu), *Dangdai dianying* 4: 264–84.

Liu, Xiaoqing (1992) *Wo zhe banian* (The past eight years of my career), Taipei: Huangguan.

Lo, Kwai-Cheung (1993) '*Once Upon A Time*: Technology Comes to Presence in China', *Modern Chinese Literature* 7, 2: 79–96.

Logan, Bey (1996) *Hong Kong Action Cinema*, New York: Overlook Press.

Loh, Wai-fong (1984) 'From Romantic Love to Class Struggle: Reflections on the Film *Liu Sanjie*', in B. McDougall (ed.) *Popular Chinese Literature and Performing Arts in the People's Republic of China, 1949–1979*, Berkeley: University of California Press, 165–76.

Lopate, Phillip (1994) 'Odd Man Out: Interview with Tian Zhuangzhuang', *Film Comment* 30, 4: 60–4.

* Lösel, Jörg (1980) *Die politische Funktion des Spielfilms in der Volksrepublik China zwischen 1949 und 1965*, Munich: Minerva Publikation.

* Lu, Sheldon Hsiao-peng (ed.) (1997a) *Transnational Chinese Cinemas: Identity, Nationhood, Gender*, Honolulu: University of Hawaii Press.

— (1997b) 'National Cinema, Cultural Critique, Transnational Capital: The Films of Zhang Yimou', in S. Lu (ed.) *Transnational Chinese Cinemas*.

* Lu, Si (1962) *Yingping yijiu* (Film criticism in recollection), Beijing: Zhongguo dianying chubanshe.

Lü, Sushang (1961) *Taiwan dianying xiju shi* (History of Taiwan cinema and drama), Taipei: Dongfang chubanshe.

Luo, Feng (1995) *Shijimo chengshi* (The decadent city), Hong Kong: Oxford University Press.

Luo, Xueying (1989) 'Wu Tianming's Rise to Fame', *Chinese Literature* 3: 188–95.

— (1990) 'The Ambitions of Zhang Yimou', *Chinese Literature* 4: 168–76.

— (1994a) 'Born for Art – Jiang Wen', *China Screen* 1: 26–7.

— (1994b) 'Return to Commonality – About Director He Qun', *China Screen* 3: 24–5.

Luo, Yijun (ed.) (1988) *Zhongguo xinwenyi daxi, 1949–1966* (Anthology of modern Chinese literature and arts), *Film sections*, 2 vols, Beijing: Zhongguo wenlian chubanshe.

* Luo, Yijun, Li Jinsheng and Xu Hong (eds) (1992) *Zhongguo dianying lilun wenxuan, 1920–1989* (Chinese film theory: an anthology), 2 vols, Beijing: Wenhua yishu chubanshe.

Ma, Debo and Dai Guangxi (1994) *Daoyan chuangzuo lun: lun Beiying wuda daoyan* (On five major directors of Beijing Film Studio), Beijing: Zhongguo dianying chubanshe.

Ma, Junrang (1993) 'Minzu zhuyi suo suzao de xiandai Zhongguo dianying' (modern Chinese film as fashioned by nationalism), *Ershiyi shiji* 15: 112–19.

* Ma, Ning (1987a) 'Notes on the New Filmmakers', in G. Semsel (ed.) *Chinese Film*, 63–93.

— (1987b) '*Satisfied or Not*: Desire and Discourse in the Chinese Comedy of the 1960s', *East-West Film Journal* 2, 1: 32–49.

— (1989) 'The Textual and Critical Difference of Being Radical: Reconstructing Chinese Leftist Films of the 1930s', *Wide Angle* 11, 2: 22–31.

— (1993) 'Symbolic Representation and Symbolic Violence: Chinese Family Melodrama of the Early 1980s', in W. Dissanayake (ed.) *Melodrama*, 29–58.

— (1994) 'Spatiality and Subjectivity in Xie Jin's Film Melodrama of the New Period', in N. Browne *et al.* (eds), *New Chinese Cinemas*, 15–39.

McDonagh, Maitland (1993a) 'Action Painter: John Woo', *Film Comment* 29, 5: 46–9.

— (1993b) 'Things I Felt Were Being Lost: Interview with John Woo', *Film Comment* 29, 5: 50–2.

McDougall, Bonnie S. (1991) *The Yellow Earth: A Film by Chen Kaige, with a Complete Translation of the Filmscript*, Hong Kong: Chinese University Press.

Mackerras, Colin (1981) *The Performing Arts in Contemporary China*, London: Routledge & Kegan Paul.

Marchetti, Gina (1989) 'The Blossoming of a Revolutionary Aesthetic: *Two Stage Sisters*', *Jump Cut* 34: 95–106.

Meishu dianying chuangzuo yanjiu (Studies in animated films) (1984), Beijing: Zhongguo dianying chubanshe.

Mills, Ian (1983) 'Why Did Chiang Ching Close down Chinese Film Production? Or, the Garden of Eden Re-Opened', *Australian Journal of Screen Theory* 15–16: 7–34.

Mintz, Marilyn (1978) *The Martial Arts Film*, New York: A.S. Barnes.

Ni, Zhen (1994) 'Classical Chinese Painting and Cinematographic Signification', in L. Ehrlich and D. Desser (eds) *Cinematic Landscapes*, 63–80.

Ombre elettriche: Saggi e ricerche sul cinema cinese (1982), Milan: Regione Piemonte/Electa.

Ombres électriques: Panorama du cinéma chinois 1925–1982 (1982), Paris: Centre de Documentation sur le Cinéma Chinois.

Ouyang, Yuqian (1984) *Dianying banlu chujia ji* (Entering the film world in my mid-career), Beijing: Zhongguo dianying chubanshe.

Padgaonkar, Latika (1996) 'Xie Fei: Twixt Teaching and Shooting . . . Time for a Good Story', *Cinemaya* 32: 34–8.

Petitprez, Veronique (1993) 'Being a Woman in the Films of the Fifth Generation', *Cinemaya* 21: 32–6.

Pickowicz, Paul (1989) 'Popular Cinema and Political Thought in Post-Mao China: Reflections on Official Pronouncements, Film, and the Film Audience', in P. Link, R. Madsen and P. Pickowicz (eds) *Unofficial China: Popular Culture and Thought in the People's Republic*, Boulder: Westview Press, 37–53.

* — (1991) 'The Theme of Spiritual Pollution in Chinese Films of the 1930s', *Modern China* 17, 1: 38–75.

* — (1993a) 'Melodramatic Representation and the "May Fourth" Tradition of Chinese Cinema', in E. Widmer and D. Wang (eds) *From May Fourth to June Fourth: Fiction and Film in Twentieth-Century China*, Cambridge, Mass.: Harvard University Press, 295–326.

— (1993b) 'Sinifying and Popularizing Foreign Culture: From Maxim Gorky's *The Lower Depths* to Huang Zuolin's *Ye dian*', *Modern Chinese Literature* 7, 2: 7–31.

— (1994) 'Huang Jianxin and the Notion of Postsocialism', In N. Browne *et al.* (eds), *New Chinese Cinemas*, 57–87.

* — (1995) 'Velvet Prisons and the Political Economy of Chinese Filmmaking', in Deborah Davis, Richard Kraus, Barry Naughton, and Elizabeth Perry (eds) *Urban Spaces in Contemporary China: The Potential for Autonomy and Community in Post-Mao China*, New York: Cambridge University Press, 193–220.

Qiu, Liang and Yu Muyun (eds) (1995) *Zuoye xingguang* (Starlight of the bygone days), 2 vols, Hong Kong: Sanlian.

Quiquemelle, Kwok and M.C. Quiquemelle (1982) 'Le Cinéma chinois et le réalisme', in *Ombres électriques*, 87–96.

— (1987) 'Chinese Cinema and Realism', in J. Downing (ed.) *Film and Politics in the Third World*, New York: Praeger, 181–9.

Quiquemelle, Marie-Claire (1991) 'The Wan Brothers and Sixty Years of Animated Film in China', in C. Berry (ed.) *Perspectives*, 175–86.

* Quiquemelle, Marie-Claire and Jean-Loup Passek (eds) (1985) *Le Cinéma chinois*, Paris: Centre Georges Pompidou.

Rashkin, Elissa (1993) 'Rape as Castration as Spectacle: *The Price of Frenzy*'s Politics of Confusion', in Tonglin Lu (ed.) *Gender and Sexuality in Twentieth-Century Chinese Literature and Society*, Albany: State University of New York Press, 107–19.

Rayns, Tony (1976) 'Director: King Hu', *Sight and Sound* 45: 8–13.

— (1987) 'The Position of Women in New Chinese Cinema', *East-West Film Journal* 1, 2: 32–44.

* — (1989) 'Chinese Vocabulary: An Introduction', in Chen Kaige and T. Rayns, *King of the Children*, 1–58.

— (1990) 'Review of *Rouge* and Notes on Stanley Kwan', *Monthly Film Bulletin* (Feb.): 31–3.

— (1992) 'Hard Boiled', *Sight and Sound* (Aug.): 20–3.

— (1993) 'Dream On', *Sight and Sound* (July): 16–9.

— (1995a) 'Poet of Time', *Sight and Sound* (Sept.): 12–16.

— (1995b) 'Review of *The Days*', *Sight and Sound* (Mar.): 36–7.

— (1995c) 'Review of *Ermo*', *Sight and Sound* (July): 47–8.

— (1995d) 'The Ups and Downs of Zhou Xiaowen', *Sight and Sound* (July): 22–4.

— (1996) 'Provoking Desire', *Sight and Sound* (July): 26–9.

* Rayns, Tony and Scott Meek (eds) (1980) *Electric Shadows: 45 Years of Chinese Cinema*, London: British Film Institute.

Reid, Craig D. (1994) 'An Evening with Jackie Chan', *Bright Lights Film Journal* 13: 18–25.

— (1995a) 'Fant-asia Filmmaker: Producer Tsui Hark', *Imagi-Movies* 2, 4: 21–3, 27–30.

— (1995b) 'Interview with Tsui Hark', *Film Quarterly* 48, 3: 34–41.

Reynaud, Berenice (1994–5) 'Li Shaohong', *Cinemaya* 25–26: 8–9.

— (1996) 'Hong Kong', *Cinemaya* 33: 53–4.

Richie, Donald (1996) '*The Day the Sun Turned Cold*': Some Aspects of Yim Ho's Film', *Cinemaya* 31: 16–18.

Rodriguez, Hector (1997) 'Hong Kong Popular Culture as an Interpretive Arena: The Huang Feihong Film Series', *Screen* 38, 1: 1–24.

Rothman, William (1993) '*The Goddess*: Reflections on Melodrama East and West', in W. Dissanayake (ed.) *Melodrama*, 59–72.

Ryan, Barbara (1995) 'Blood, Brothers, and Hong Kong Gangster Movies: Pop Culture Commentary on "One China"', in John A. Lent (ed.) *Asian Popular Culture*, Boulder: Westview Press, 61–77.

Sandell, Jillian (1994) 'A Better Tomorrow?: American Masochism and Hong Kong Action Films', *Bright Lights Film Journal* 13: 40–5, 50.

— (1996) 'Reinventing Masculinity: The Spectacle of Male Intimacy in the Films of John Woo', *Film Quarterly* 49, 4: 23–34.

Sato, Tadao (1985) 'Le Cinéma japonais et le cinéma chinois face à la tradition', in Quiquemelle and Passek (eds) *Le Cinéma chinois*, 77–83.

— (1992) 'A Passage to Taiwan', *Cinemaya* 15: 4–8.

Scott, A.C. (1965) *Literature and the Arts in Twentieth Century China*, London: Allen.

* Semsel, George S. (ed.) (1987) *Chinese Film: The State of the Art in the People's Republic*, New York: Praeger.

Semsel, G., Chen Xihe, and Xia Hong (eds) (1993) *Film in Contemporary China*, New York: Praeger.

Semsel, G., Xia Hong, and Hou Jianping (eds) (1990) *Chinese Film Theory: A Guide to the New Era*, New York: Praeger.

Severson, Matt (1996) 'Silent Behind the Great Wall', *Film Comment* 32, 3: 47–8.

Shanghai dianying sishinian (Forty years of Shanghai cinema) (1991), Shanghai: Xuelin chubanshe.

Shao, Mujun (1988) 'Chinese Films Amidst the Tide of Reform', in W. Dissanayake (ed.) *Cinema and Cultural Identity*, 199–208.

— (1989) 'Notes on *Red Sorghum*', *Chinese Literature* 1: 172–80.

Shen, Shiao-ying (1995) 'Where Has All the Capital Gone: The State of Taiwan's Film Investment', *Cinemaya* 30: 4–12.

Sheng, Virginia (1995) 'The Father Figure of Taiwan Film', *Free China Review* (Feb.): 20–3.

Shi, Yin (1991) 'The Tenth Anniversary of China Children's Studio', *China Screen* 3: 10.

Shu, Kei (1993) 'Letter to Chen Kaige', *Cinemaya* 20: 18–20.

Si shui liu nian – cong juben dao yingpian (*Homecoming*: from the script to the film) (1986), Beijing: Zhongguo dianying chubanshe.

Singer, Michael (1988) 'Chow Must Go On', *Film Comment* 24, 3: 46–7.

Sklar, Robert (1994) 'People and Politics: Simple and Direct: An Interview with Tian Zhuangzhuang', *Cineaste* 20, 4: 36–8.

Stephens, Chuck (1996a) 'Intersection: Tsai Ming-liang's Yearning Bike Boys and Heartsick Heroines', *Film Comment* 32, 5: 20–3.

— (1996b) 'Time Pieces: Wong Kar-Wai and the Persistence of Memory', *Film Comment* 32, 1: 12–18.

Stephenson, Shelley (1999) '"Her Traces Are Found Everywhere": Shanghai, Li Xianglan, and the "Greater East Asia Film Sphere"', in Y. Zhang (ed.) *Romance, Sexuality, Identity*.

Sterritt, David (1997) 'Exploring Women's Lot in Changing Culture: Interview with Chinese Director Xie Fei', *Christian Science Monitor* 1 Apr.: 14.

Stockbridge, Sally (1994) 'Sexual Violence and Hong Kong Films: Regulation and Cultural Difference', *Media Information Australia* 74: 86–92.

Stringer, Julian (1995) 'Review of *Peking Opera Blues*', *Film Quarterly* 48, 3: 34–42.

— (1996/7) 'Problems with the Treatment of Hong Kong Cinema as Camp', *Asian Cinema* 8, 2: 44–65.

— (1997a) '*Centre Stage*: Reconstructing the Bio-Pic', *Cineaction* 42: 28–39.

— (1997b) '"Your Tender Smiles Give Me Strength": Paradigms of Masculinity in John Woo's *A Better Tomorrow* and *The Killer*', *Screen* 38, 1: 25–41.

— (1998a) 'Category 3: Sex and Violence in Postmodern Hong Kong,' in Christopher Sharrett (ed.) *Mythologies of Violence in Postmodern Media*, Detroit: Wayne State University Press.

— (1998b) 'Cultural Identity and Diaspora in Contemporary Hong Kong Cinema,' in Darrell Hamamoto and Sandra Liu (eds) *Asian American Screen Cultures*, Philadelphia: Temple University Press.

Su, Shuyang (1996) 'Qianwan bie qiwu lishi – xiaotan lishi ticai yingpian' (Don't ever take advantage of history – thoughts on historical films), *Zhongguo yinmu* 7–8: 44–5.

Sun, Yu (1987) *Yinhai fanzhou – huiyi wode yisheng* (Sailing across the sea of the silver screen – my life in recollection), Shanghai: Shanghai wenyi chubanshe.

Sutton, Donald S. (1994) 'Ritual, History, and the Films of Zhang Yimou', *East-West Film Journal* 8, 2: 31–46.

Tan, Chunfa (1992a), *Kai yidai xianhe – Zhongguo dianying zhifu Zheng Zhengqiu* (Opening a new road – Zheng Zhengqiu, the father of Chinese cinema), Beijing: Guoji wenhua chuban gongsi.

— (1992b) 'Zheng Zhengqiu yu Zhongguo san da dianying zhongxin tixi' (Zheng Zhengqiu and three major Chinese film systems), *Dangdai dianying* 6: 86–95.

— (1995) 'Changqi bei wudu bei lengluo de yiye – zaoqi de Zhongguo dianying' (A period long misunderstood and long neglected – early Chinese cinema), *Dangdai dianying* 2: 13–20.

Tan, Patrick (1997) 'East/West Politics', *Cineaction* 42: 47–9.

Tang, Xiaobing (1994) 'Configuring the Modern Space: Cinematic Representation of Beijing and Its Politics', *East-West Film Journal* 8, 2: 47–69.

Tay, William (1994) 'The Ideology of Initiation: The Films of Hou Hsiao-hsien', in N. Browne *et al.* (eds), *New Chinese Cinemas*, 151–9.

Teng, Sue-Feng (1996a) 'The Hottest Lens in the East – Cinematographer Christopher Doyle', *Sinorama* (Jan.): 94–101.

— (1996b) 'King of the Pop Flick – Film Director Chu Yen-ping', *Sinorama* (Feb.): 102–9.

— (1996c) 'Wu Nien-chen, Master Storyteller', *Sinorama* (May): 36–43.

— (1996d) 'From Bruce Lee to Jackie Chan – The Kungfu Film Carries On', *Sinorama* (June): 28–35.

Teo, Stephen (1991) 'A New Kind of Alienation: Edward Yang's *A Brighter Summer Day*', *Cinemaya* 13: 41–4.

— (1992) '*A Brighter Summer Day*: The Four-Hour Version Reviewed and Reassessed', *Cinemaya* 14: 44–7.

— (1994) 'The Hong Kong New Wave: Before and After', *Cinemaya* 23: 28–32.

— (1994–5) 'The Silken Screen', *Cinemaya* 25–26: 47–9.

Tessier, Max (1992) 'Hsu Feng: Steel in Velvet', *Cinemaya* 15: 13–15.

— (1993) '*Farewell to My Concubine*: Art Over Politics', *Cinemaya* 20: 16–18.

Tian, Han (1981) *Yingshi zhuihuai lu* (Recollections of film activities), Beijing: Zhongguo dianying chubanshe.

Tian, Zhuangzhuang (1989) 'Reflections', *Cinemaya* 5: 14–18.

Toroptsev, Sergei (1992) 'The Space of the Subjective: Pre-Fifth Generation Chinese Cinema', *Cinemaya* 16: 14–17.

Tsui, Curtis K. (1995) 'Subjective Culture and History: The Ethnographic Cinema of Wong Kar-wai', *Asian Cinema* 7, 2: 93–124.

Tung, Timothy (1987) 'The Work of Xie Jin: A Personal Letter to the Editor', in J. Downing (ed.) *Film and Politics in the Third World*, New York: Praeger, 199–207.

Tuohy, Sue (1999) 'Metropolitan Sounds: Music in Chinese Films of the 1930s', in Y. Zhang (ed.) *Romance, Sexuality, Identity*.

Tyler, Patrick E. (1996) 'In China, Letting a Hundred Films Wither', *New York Times* 1 Dec.: H2, 26.

Wan, Laiming (1986) *Wo yu Sun Wukong* (Monkey King and me), Taiyuan: Beiyue wenyi chubanshe.

Wang, Ban (1997) *The Sublime Figure of History: Aesthetics and Politics in Twentieth-Century China*, Stanford University Press.

Wang, Danfeng *et al.* (1954) *Wode congying shenghuo* (My film careers), Hong Kong: Changcheng huabao she.

Wang, Fei-yun (1995) 'Flowers Blooming in Barren Soil', *Free China Review* (Feb.): 4–17.

Wang, Renmei (1985) *Wode chengming yu buxing – Wang Renmei huiyi lu* (My fame and misfortunes: a memoir), Shanghai: Shanghai wenyi chubanshe.

Wang, Tugen (1990) 'Wuchang jieji wenhua dageming: shi, xushi, yishixingtai, huayu' (History, narration, ideology, discourse from the Cultural Revolution), *Dangdai Dianying* 3: 34–45.

Wang, Tung (1991) 'Banana Paradise', *Cinemaya* 12: 52–3.

Wang, Wei (1995) *Xunqiu jiaxiang xian de yinmu: dangdai Taiwan dianying guancha* (In search of a projected screen: perspectives on contemporary Taiwan cinema), Taipei: Wanxiang.

Wang, Yuejin (1988) 'The Old Well: A Womb or Tomb? The Double Perspective in Wu Tianming's *Old Well*', *Framework* 35: 73–82.

— (1989a) 'The Cinematic Other and the Cultural Self? De-centering the Cultural Identity on Cinema', *Wide Angle* 11, 2: 32–9.

— (1989b) 'Mixing Memory and Desire: *Red Sorghum*, a Chinese Version of Masculinity and Femininity', *Public Culture* 2, 1: 31–53.

— (1991) 'The Rhetoric of Mirror, Shadow, and Moon: *Samsara* and the Problem of Representation of Self in China', *East-West Film Journal* 5, 2: 69–92.

Weakland, John H. (1971) 'Chinese Film Images of Invasion and Resistance', *China Quarterly* 47: 439–70.

Wei, Yanmei (1997) 'Music and Femininity in Zhang Yimou's Family Melodrama', *Cineaction* 42: 18–27.

Weisser, Thomas (1997) *Asian Cult Cinema*, New York: Boulevard Books.

White, Jerry (1997) 'The Films of Ning Ying: China Unfolding in Miniature', *Cineaction* 42: 2–9.

Williams, Tony (1997a) 'From Hong Kong to Hollywood: John Woo and His Discontents', *Cineaction* 42: 40–6.

— (1997b) 'Space, Place, and Spectacle: The Crisis Cinema of John Woo', *Cinema Journal* 36, 2: 67–84.

Wilson, Patricia (1987) 'The Founding of the Northeast Film Studio', in G. Semsel (ed.) *Chinese Film*, 15–33.

Woo, Catherine Yi-Yu Cho (1991) 'The Chinese Montage: From Poetry and Painting to the Silver Screen', in C. Berry (ed.) *Perspectives*, 21–9.

Wu, Chengji (1996) 'Wo xiang gen jiejin guanzhong yidian' (I want to get closer to the audiences: an interview with Zhang Jianya), *Dianying yishu* 2: 37–42.

Wu, Hao (1993) *Xianggang dianying minsuxue* (Ethnography of Hong Kong film), Hong Kong: Ci wenhua.

Wu, Xianggui (1992) 'The Chinese Film Industry since 1977', Ph.D. dissertation: University of Oregon.

Wu, Yin (1993) *Huishou yi dangnian* (Recollections of the past), Beijing: Zhongguo dianying chubanshe.

Wu, Yonggang (1986) *Wode tansuo he zhuiqiu* (My explorations and quests), Beijing: Zhongguo dianying chubanshe.

Wu, Ziniu, *et al.* (1995) *Nanjing 1937: Wu Ziniu de dianying* (*Nanjing 1937*: Wu Ziniu's film), Taipei: Wanxiang.

Xia, Hong (1987) 'Film Theory in the People's Republic of China: The New Era', in G. Semsel (ed.) *Chinese Film*, 35–62.

Xia, Yan (1985) *Lanxun jiumeng lu* (Pursuing old dreams with reluctance), Beijing: Sanlian shudian.

Xiao, Li (1992) 'Huang Shuqin: A Woman Film Director', *Chinese Literature* 2: 178–81.

Xiao, Xiangzi (1964) *Yinghou Lin Dai chuanqi* (Legends of the movie queen Lin Dai), Hong Kong: Wanxiang shudian.

Xiao, Zhiwei (1997) 'Anti-Imperialism and Film Censorship During the Nanjing Decade, 1927–1937', in S. Lu (ed.) *Transnational Chinese Cinemas*.

— (1999) 'Constructing a New National Culture: Film Censorship and the Issues of Cantonese Dialect, Superstition and Sex in the Nanjing Decade', in Y. Zhang (ed.) *Romance, Sexuality, Identity*.

Xie, Fei (1990) '"Disidai" de zhengming' (A testimony to the 'fourth generation'), *Dianying yishu* 3: 17–29.

Yang, Mayfair (1993) 'Of Gender, State Censorship, and Overseas Capital: An Interview with Chinese Director Zhang Yimou', *Public Culture* 5: 297–313.

Yang, Mingyu (1995) 'China: Once Upon A Time / Hong Kong: 1997: A Critical Study of Contemporary Martial Arts Films', Ph.D. dissertation: University of Maryland.

Yau, Esther C.M. (1987–8) '*Yellow Earth*: Western Analysis and a Non-Western Text', *Film Quarterly* 41, 2: 22–33.

— (1989) 'Cultural and Economic Dislocations: Filmic Phantasies of Chinese Women in the 80s', *Wide Angle* 11, 2: 6–21.

* — (1990) 'Filmic Discourse on Women in Chinese Cinema (1949–65): Art, Ideology and Social Relations', Ph.D. dissertation, University of California, Los Angeles.

* — (1993) 'International Fantasy and the "New Chinese Cinema"', *Quarterly Review of Film and Video* 14, 3: 95–107.

— (1994a) 'Border Crossing: Mainland China's Presence in Hong Kong Cinema', in N. Browne *et al.* (eds), *New Chinese Cinemas*, 180–201.

— (1994b) 'Is China the End of Hermeneutics?; or, Political and Cultural Usage of Non-Han Women in Mainland Chinese Films', in D. Carson, L. Dittmar and J. R. Welsch (eds) *Multiple Voices in Feminist Film Criticism*, Minneapolis: University of Minnesota Press, 280–92.

Ye, Longyan (1995) *Guangfu chuqi Taiwan dianying shi* (A history of Taiwan cinema in the early postwar period), Taipei: Guojia dianying ziliaoguan.

Ying, Xiong (1993) '*Xiao cheng zhi chun* yu "dongfang dianying"' (*Spring in a Small Town* and 'Oriental cinema'), *Dianying yishu* 1: 11–18, 2: 46–51.

Yip, June (1997) 'Constructing a Nation: Taiwanese History and the Films of Hou Hsiao-hsien', in S. Lu (ed.) *Transnational Chinese Cinemas*.

Yong yanjing kan de Zhongguo dianying shi (A history of Chinese cinema seen through the eyes) (1979), Taipei: Longjiang.

Yu, Lan (1985) 'Ertong dianying sanshiwu nian xunli' (An overview of 35 years of children's film), in *Zhonghua renmin gonghe guo dianying shiye sanshiwu nian, 1949–1984* (Thirty-five years of film industry in the People's Republic of China), Beijing: Zhongguo dianying chubanshe, 224–35.

* Yu, Muyun (1996) *Xianggang dianying shihua* (A historical account of Hong Kong cinema), vol. 1, Hong Kong: Ci wenhua, 1996.

Yue, Ming-Bao (1996) 'Visual Agency and Ideological Fantasy in Three Films by Zhang Yimou', in Wimal Dissanayake (ed.) *Narratives of Agency: Self-Making in China, India, and Japan*, Minneapolis: University of Minnesota Press, 56–73.

Yun, Duo (1994) 'Liu Miaomiao – A Fervent Director', *China Screen* 3: 22–3.

* ZDX (ed.) (1982–6) *Zhongguo dianyingjia liezhuan* (Biographies of Chinese film people), 7 vols, Beijing: Zhongguo dianying chubanshe.

— (ed.) (1985) *Zhonghua renmin gongheguo dianying shiye sanshiwu nian, 1949–1984* (Thirty-five years of film development in the People's Republic of China), Beijing: Zhongguo dianying chubanshe.

— (ed.) (1995) *Lishi yu xianzhuang* (History and current situation), Beijing: Zhongguo dianying chubanshe.

ZDYYZ (ed.) (1984) *Lishi, zhanzheng, dianying mei* (History, wars, and the beauty of films), Beijing: Jiefangjun wenyi chubanshe.

— (ed.) (1995) *Zhongguo dianying tuzhi* (Illustrated annals of Chinese film), Guangxi: Zhuhai chubanshe.

* — (ed.) (1996) *Zhongguo wusheng dianying* (Chinese silent film), Beijing: Zhongguo dianying chubanshe.

* — (ed.) (1996–7) *Zhongguo yingpian dadian: gushi pian, xiqu pian* (Encyclopedia of Chinese films: feature films and filmed stage performances), 4 vols, Beijing: Zhongguo dianying chubanshe.

Zha, Jianying (1995) *China Pop: How Soap Operas, Tabloids, and Bestsellers Are Transforming a Culture*, New York: New Press.

Zhang, Aihua (1987) 'Lun Fei Mu de yishu tese' (On the artistic features of Fei Mu's films), in *Dianying yanjiu* (Studies in cinema), Beijing: Zhongguo dianying chubanshe, 215–45.

Zhang, Che (Chang Che) (1989), *Huigu Xianggang dianying sanshinian* (Thirty years of Hong Kong cinema in recollection), Hong Kong: Sanlian shudian.

Zhang, Chengshan (1989) *Zhongguo dianying wenhua toushi* (Cultural perspectives on Chinese film), Shanghai: Xuelin chubanshe.

Zhang, Dan (1993) 'The Great Mind Matures Slowly – An Introduction to Li Shaohong', *China Screen* 2: 14–15.

Zhang, Junxiang (1985) *Yingshi suoyi* (Miscellaneous thoughts on film), Beijing: Zhongguo dianying chubanshe.

* Zhang, Junxiang and Cheng Jihua (eds) (1995) *Zhongguo dianying da cidian* (China cinema encyclopedia), Shanghai: Shanghai cishu chubanshe.

Zhang, Litao (1987) *Zhonggong dianying shi gailun* (A general survey of the film history of Communist China), Hong Kong: Tomokazu.

* Zhang, Xudong (1997) *Chinese Modernism in the Era of Reforms: Cultural Fever, Avant-garde Fiction, and the New Chinese Cinema*, Durham, NC: Duke University Press.

Zhang, Yingjin (1990) 'Ideology of the Body in *Red Sorghum*: National Allegory, National Roots, and Third Cinema', *East-West Film Journal* 4, 2: 38–53.

— (1994a) 'Engendering Chinese Filmic Discourse of the 1930s: Configurations of Modern Women in Shanghai in Three Silent Films', *Positions* 2, 3: 603–28.

— (1994b) 'The Idyllic Country and the Modern City: Cinematic Configurations of Family in *Osmanthus Alley* and *The Terrorizer*', *Tamkang Review* 25, 1: 81–99.

— (1994c) 'Rethinking Cross-Cultural Analysis: The Questions of Authority, Power, and Difference in Western Studies of Chinese Films', *Bulletin of Concerned Asian Scholars* 26, 4: 44–53.

— (1996) *The City in Modern Chinese Literature and Film: Configurations of Space, Time, and Gender*, Stanford University Press.

* — (1997a) 'From "Minority Film" to "Minority Discourse": Questions of Nationhood and Ethnicity in Chinese Film Studies', *Cinema Journal* 36, 3: 73–90.

* — (1997b), 'Review Essay: Screening China – Recent Studies of Chinese Cinema in English,' *Bulletin of Concerned Asian Scholars* 29, 2.

* — (ed.) (1999a) *Romance, Sexuality, Identity: Cinema and Urban Culture in Shanghai, 1910s–1940s*, Stanford University Press. Scheduled for publication 1999.

— (1999b) 'Prostitution and Urban Imagination: An Aspect of Chinese Film in the 1930s', in Y. Zhang (ed.) *Romance, Sexuality, Identity*.

Zhang, Zhen (1999) 'Teahouse, Shadowplay, *Bricolage*: *Laborer's Love* and the Question of Early Chinese Cinema', in Y. Zhang (ed.) *Romance, Sexuality, Identity*.

Zhang, Zhenqin (1988), 'Cong "zijue" xiang "ziyou" de qiusuo – lun Zhang Nuanxin he tade dianying chuanzuo' (From 'self-awareness' to 'freedom' – on Zhang Nuanxin's films), in *Xin shiqi dianying shinian* (Ten years of film in the new era), Sichuan: Chongqing chubanshe, 254–78.

Zhao, Dan (1980) *Diyu zhi men* (The gate of hell), Shanghai: Shanghai wenyi chubanshe.

Zhao, Wentao (1994) 'Huang Jun and his Triology', *China Screen* 4: 30–1.

Zheng, Junli (1936) 'Xiandai Zhongguo dianying shilüe' (A concise history of Chinese film), Shanghai: Liangyou; reprinted in nine instalments, in *Dianying chuangzuo* (Feb.–Oct. 1989).

— (1948) *Jiaose de dansheng* (The birth of character), Shanghai: Shenghuo shudian.

— (1979) *Huawai yin* (Off-screen sound), Beijing: Zhongguo dianying chubanshe.

Zheng, Yi (1997) 'Narrative Images of the Historical Passion: Those *Other* Women – On the Alterity in the New Wave of Chinese Cinema', in S. Lu (ed.) *Transnational Chinese Cinemas*.

Zheng, Yimei (1982) *Yingtan jiuwen – Dan Duyu he Yin Mingzhu* (Old stories about the film circles – Dan Duyu and Yin Mingzhu), Shanghai: Shanghai wenyi chubanshe.

Zhong, Dafeng (1993) 'A Historical Survey of Yingxi Theory', in G. Semsel, Chen Xihe and Xia Hong (eds), *Film in Contemporary China*, 65–73.

Zhong, Dafeng, Zhen Zhang and Yingjin Zhang (1997) 'From *Wenmingxi* (Civilized Play) to *Yingxi* (Shadowplay): The Foundation of Shanghai Film Industry in the 1920s', *Asian Cinema* 9, 1 (Fall 1997): 46–64.

Zhong, Dafeng and Shu Xiaoming (1995) *Zhongguo dianying shi* (A history of Chinese cinema), Beijing: Zhongguo guangbo dianshi chubanshe.

* Zhou, Xiaoming (1985) *Zhongguo xiandai dianying wenxue shi* (A history of film literature in modern China), 2 vols., Beijing: Gaodeng jiaoyu chubanshe.

Zhou, Zhengbao and Zhang Dong (1995) 'Zhanzheng pian yu Zhongguo kangzhan ticai gushi pian' (War films and Chinese feature films on the war of resistance against Japan), *Wenyi yanjiu* 5: 13–20.

Zhu, Chunting (1995) *Gongfu huangdi: Li Xiaolong zhuan* (King of kungfu: a biography of Bruce Lee), Guangzhou: Guangdong renmin chubanshe.

Select Internet web sites on Chinese cinema
Jean J. Su

Web sites with substantial information are preceded by asterisks.

* http://razzle.Stanford.EDU/hk
    This site, 'Hong Kong Cinema', offers a comprehensive home page that includes box-office reports, news of the week, annual awards, relevant articles, editorial features and related links. Its movie database and people database are searchable by titles and names.

http://ms418qzh.ms.u-tokyo.ac.jp/~utcsa/links/China/china06.html
    This site provides several links related to Asian movies.

http://www.asahi.co.jp/asia/asia-movie/movie-listE.html
    This site contains a selected list of Asian movies with brief synopses.

* http://www.geocities.com/Tokyo/Towers/2038
    This site, 'Hong Kong Top Ten Box Office Home Page', contains 'Fluff of the Week', featuring updated news items drawn from leading Hong Kong newspapers. It also furnishes information regarding top ten box-office hits (including foreign titles), such as how many screens were signed on and how many weeks these films were shown, as well as these films' weekly gross and cumulative incomes. It provides colour pictures, extensive texts and some related links.

* http://www.movieworld.com.hk
    This site, 'Movie World H. K.', claims to provide all Hong Kong movies between 1960 and 1997. The best feature about this database is that its contents are searchable by titles, performers, directors, screen writers, crew, and all persons involved. The user can use English, pinyin, Cantonese or the quick method to search. The site has a search guide and invites users' participation.

* http://www.nanhai.com/video.html
    This site for Nan Hai Co., Inc., USA contains a partial listing of the company's large collection of Chinese film and TV programmes. It carries brief synopses of films arranged in genre categories.

http://www.siff.com/main.html
    This site for the Shanghai International Film Festival contains the festival's history, activities, awards and other news.

* http://filmcritics.org.hk
    This site for Hong Kong Film Critics Society features events, current reviews, archival reviews since 1995, and some short essays.

Glossary of Chinese characters

Zhiwei Xiao

The Glossary is intended for the use of the specialist. It includes most of the proper names (film titles, people and studios) listed in the Indexes. Pinyin forms are listed in the left-hand column. Alternative forms (e.g., Wade-Giles, Cantonese or English) are in the right-hand column. If you do not know the Pinyin version of the name you wish to consult, you will readily find it via the entry headings (for people's names and film titles) or the Indexes which also include Studios, and which list all proper name versions used in this encyclopedia.

Pinyin	**Characters**	**Other**
A Dai	阿呆	Ah Dai
A Fei zhengzhuan	阿飛正傳	Days of Being Wild
A Gan zhengzhuan	阿甘正傳	Forrest Gump
A jihua	A 計劃	Project A
A Jin de gushi	阿金的故事	Stunt Woman
A Q zhengzhuan	阿Q正傳	The True Story of Ah Q
A, Yaolan	啊，搖籃	The Cradle
A Ying	阿英	Ah Ying, *aka* Qian Defu, Qian Xingcun
Afandi	阿凡堤	Effendi
Ai chang ru jia	愛廠如家	Love the Factory as One's Home
Ai le zhongnian	哀樂中年	Sorrows and Joys of a Middle-Aged Man
Ai Xia	艾霞	
Ai yu zhi zheng	愛欲之爭	Conflict between Love and Lust
Ai zai biexiang de jijie	愛在別鄉的季節	Farewell, China
Aiguo san	愛國傘	Umbrella of Patriotism
Aiqing wansui	愛情萬歲	Vive l'amour
Aiqing yu huangjin	愛情與黃金	Love and Gold
Alishan fengyun	阿里山風雲	Wind and Cloud on Ali Mountain
Anlian Taohua yuan	暗戀桃花源	Peach Blossom Spring
Ashima	阿詩瑪	Ashma
Ba dao louzi	八道樓子	Eight Man Army
Ba Hong	巴鴻	
Babai zhuangshi	八百壯士	Eight Hundred Heroic Soldiers
Bage de gushi	拔哥的故事	The Life of Wei, I–II
Bai Chen	白沉	
Bai Jingrui	白景瑞	Pai Ching-jui
Bai Qiuen daifu	白求恩大夫	Doctor Bethune

Pinyin	**Characters**	**Other**
Bai Xuexian	白雪仙	Pak Suet-sin
Bai Yan	白燕	Pak Yin
Bai Yang	白楊	Yang Chengfang
Baihe yingpian gongsi	百合影片公司	Lily Film Company
Baihua gongzhu	百花公主	Princess of a Hundred Flowers
Baijin long	白金龍	The Platinum Dragon
Baimao nü	白毛女	The White-Haired Girl
Baiyun guxiang	白雲故鄉	White Clouds of Home
Baiyun ta	白雲塔	The White Cloud Pagoda
Ban wo chuang tianya	伴我闖天涯	Wild Search
Banbian ren	半邊人	Ah Ying
Bangjia Kalayang	綁架卡拉楊	Kidnapping Karajan
Banjin baliang	半斤八兩	The Private Eyes
Bansheng yuan	半生緣	An Interrupted Love
Baochou	報仇	Vengeance
Baodao da meng	寶島大夢	Bodo
Baofeng yan	暴風眼	Crystal Fortune Run
Baofeng zhouyu	暴風驟雨	Hurricane
Baofengyu zhong de xiongying	暴風雨中的雄鷹	Eagle in the Storm
Baohulu de mimi	寶葫蘆的秘密	The Secret of a Precious Gourd
Baolian deng	寶蓮燈	The Magic Lamp
Baowei women de tudi	保衛我們的土地	Protect Our Land
Baqianli lu yun he yue	八千里路雲和月	Eight Thousand Li of Cloud and Moon
Bashan yeyu	巴山夜雨	Night Rain on the River
Bawang bieji	霸王別姬	Farewell My Concubine
Baxian fandian zhi renrou chashao bao	八仙飯店之人肉叉燒包	Bunman: The Untold Story
Bayi dianying zhipianchang	八一電影制片廠	August First Film Studio
Bei aiqing yiwang de jiaoluo	被愛情遺忘的角落	The Corner Forsaken by Love
Bei guoqi de ren	背國旗的人	The Man Who Carries the National Flag
Beican shijie	悲慘世界	Les Misérables
Beiguo hongdou	北國紅豆	Ormosia from the North
Beiguo Jiangnan	北國江南	Southern Wind Blowing North
Beijing nizao	北京，你早	Good Morning, Beijing
Beijing ren zai Niuyue	北京人在紐約	A Native of Beijing in New York
Beijing zazhong	北京雜種	Beijing Bastards
Beikaobei, lianduilian	背靠背，臉對臉	Back to Back, Face to Face
Beilie paibang	悲烈排幫	The Prostitute and the Raftsmen
Beiqing chengshi	悲情城市	A City of Sadness
Benming nian	本命年	Black Snow
Biancheng	邊城	Border Town
Bianlian	變臉	The King of Masks
Bianzhai fenghuo	邊寨烽火	Bonfires in the Border Village
Bianzou bianchang	邊走邊唱	Life on a String
Biao	表	The Watch

Pinyin	Characters	Other
Biaojie, nihao ye	表姐，你好嘢	Her Fatal Ways
Bikong yinhua	碧空銀花	Silver Flowers in the Blue Sky
Bing lin cheng xia	兵臨城下	The Besieged City
Binghe siwang xian	冰河死亡綫	Trapped on a Frozen River
Bingshan shang de laike	冰山上的來客	Visitor on Ice Mountain
Bingshang jiemei	冰上姐妹	Ice-Skating Sisters
Bixue huanghua	碧血黃花	Bloodstained Yellow Flowers
Boai	博愛	Universal Love
Bohai yingpian gongsi	渤海影片公司	Bohai Film Studio
Bohao	跛豪	To Be Number One
Bu Wancang	卜萬蒼	
Bukan huishou	不堪回首	You Can't Look Back
Buliao qing	不了情	Lingering Passion
Buru gui	不如歸	The Journey Home
Buye cheng	不夜城	City without Night
Cai Chusheng	蔡楚生	
Cai Mingliang	蔡明亮	Tsai Ming-liang
Cai Yangming	蔡揚名	
Cai Yuanyuan	蔡元元	
Caotai KTV	草臺KTV	Hay Stall KTV
Cehuang qi	測謊器	The Lie Detector
Cen Fan	岑範	
Chaguan	茶館	The Teahouse
Changcheng huapian gongsi	長城畫片公司	Great Wall Film Company, Shanghai
Changchun dianying zhipianchang	長春電影制片廠	Changchun Film Studio
Changhen ge	長恨歌	A Sorrowful Song
Changjiang dianying zhipianchang	長江電影製片廠	Changjiang Film Studio
Changkong wanli	長空萬里	The Sky Rider
Chaoba nülang	超霸女郎	Superwoman
Chaoji jihua	超級計劃	Project S
Chaoji jingcha	超級警察	Supercop, *aka* Police Story, III
Chaoji shimin	超級市民	Super Citizens
Chen Baichen	陳白塵	Chen Zhenghong
Chen Baozhu	陳寶珠	Connie Chan
Chen Chong	陳冲	Joan Chen
Chen Huaiai	陳懷皚	
Chen Jiashang	陳嘉上	Gordon Chan
Chen Kaige	陳凱歌	
Chen Kengran	陳鏗然	
Chen Kexin	陳可辛	Peter Chan
Chen Kunhou	陳坤厚	Chen Kun-hou
Chen Liting	陳鯉庭	
Chen Peisi	陳佩斯	
Chen Pi	陳皮	Chan Pei

Pinyin	**Characters**	**Other**
Chen Qiang	陳強	Chen Qingsan
Chen Shouyin	陳壽蔭	
Chen Xihe	陳西禾	
Chen Yanyan	陳燕燕	
Chen Yaoxin	陳耀忻	
Chen Yi shizhang	陳毅市長	Mayor Chen Yi
Chen Yunshang	陳雲裳	Nancy Chan
Chen Yuxun	陳玉勛	
Cheng Bugao	程步高	
Cheng Jihua	程季華	
Cheng Long	成龍	Jackie Chan
Cheng Xiaodong	程小東	Ching Siu Tung
Cheng Yin	成蔭	Cheng Yunbao
Chenglong kuaixu	乘龍快婿	The Lucky Son-in-Law
Chengnan jiushi	城南舊事	My Memory of Old Beijing
Chengshi lieren	城市獵人	City Hunter
Chengshi zhi ye	城市之夜	City Night
Chiluo gaoyang	赤裸羔羊	Naked Killer
Chongpo liming qian de heian	冲破黎明前的黑暗	Darkness Before Dawn
Chongqing senlin	重慶森林	Chunking Express
Chu Yuan	楚原	
Chuandao Fangzi	川島芳子	Kawashima Yoshiko
Chuangwai	窗外	Outside the Window
Chuangye	創業	The Pioneers
Chuanjia nü	船家女	Boatman's Daughter
Chuilian tingzheng	垂簾聽政	Reign Behind a Curtain
Chujia nü	出嫁女	The Wedding Maidens
Chulu	出路	The Way Out
Chun	春	Spring
Chun dao renjian	春到人間	Spring on Earth
Chun jiang yihen	春江遺恨	The Sorrow of Spring River
Chun man renjian	春滿人間	The World of Love
Chuncan	春蠶	Spring Silkworms
Chunguang zhaxie	春光乍洩	Happy Together
Chunmiao	春苗	Chunmiao
Chuntao	春桃	A Woman for Two
Chunxiang nao xue	春香鬧學	Chunxiang Disturbs the School
Cike	刺客	The Assassin
Cima	刺馬	Blood Brothers
Cimu qu	慈母曲	Mother's Song
Cong Lianwen	叢連文	
Congming de xiao yazi	聰明的小鴨子	Little Duckling
Cui Wei	崔嵬	Cui Jingwen
Cui Xiaoqin	崔小琴	
Cuicui	翠翠	Cuicui
Cuigang hongqi	翠崗紅旗	Red Flag over Cuigang Mountain
Cuowei	錯位	Dislocation, *aka* The Stand-In

Pinyin	Characters	Other
Da bianzi de youhuo	大辮子的誘惑	Enchanted by Her Long Braid
Da cuo che	搭錯車	Papa, Can You Hear Me Sing?
Da di chong guang	大地重光	The Return of Spring
Da feng ge	大風歌	The Song of a Hero
Da fo de tongkong	大佛的瞳孔	Eyes of the Buddha
Da ge da	大哥大	Big Brother
Da hong denglong gaogao gua	大紅燈籠高高挂	Raise the Red Lantern
Da juezhan	大決戰	The Decisive Engagements, I–III
Da junfa	大軍閥	The Warlord
Da Li, Xiao Li he Lao Li	大李小李和老李	Big Li, Young Li and Old Li
Da lu	大路	Big Road, *aka* The Highway
Da mofang	大磨坊	The Big Mill
Da nao tiangong	大鬧天宮	Uproar in Heaven
Da nei mitan linglingfa	大內密探靈靈發	Forbidden City Cop
Da pibao	大皮包	A Big Briefcase
Da qiao xiamian	大橋下面	Under the Bridge
Da saba	大撒把	After Separation
Da taijian Li Lianying	大太監李蓮英	Li Lianying: the Imperial Eunuch
Da tuanyuan	大團圓	The Reunion
Da yuebing	大閱兵	The Big Parade
Da Zhonghua Baihe yingpian gongsi	大中華百合影片公司	Great China – Lily Film Company
Da Zhonghua yingye gongsi	大中華影業公司	Great China Film Company
Da zui xia	大醉俠	Come Drink with Me
Daguan yingpian gongsi	大觀影片公司	Grandview Film Company
Dai Sijie	戴泗杰	
Daihao meizhoubao	代號美洲豹	Code Name Puma
Daijian de xiaohai	帶劍的小孩	Child with a Sword
Daji he ta de fuqin	達吉和她的父親	Daji and Her Fathers
Dan Duyu	但杜宇	
Dan yi	丹姨	Auntie Dan
Dang de nüer	黨的女兒	Daughter of the Party
Dangdai ren	當代人	Contemporary People
Danni'er de gushi	丹尼爾的故事	The Story of Daniel
Dao ma dan	刀馬旦	Peking Opera Blues
Dao ma zei	盜馬賊	Horse Thief
Dao ming lai	道名來	Show Your ID
Dao xibei qu	到西北去	To the Northwest
Daocao ren	稻草人	Strawman
Dashu cun	大樹村	Big Tree Village
Datong dianying qiye gongsi	大同電影企業公司	
Dayang yingye gongsi	大洋影業公司	Ocean Film Company
Daye yingpian gongsi	大業影片公司	
Dayimieqin	大義滅親	Secret Told at Last
Debao dianying gongsi	德寶電影公司	D&B Films
Deng Yimin	鄧一民	
Dengdai liming	等待黎明	Hong Kong 1941

Pinyin	**Characters**	**Other**
Di ba tiantang	第八天堂	Eighth Heaven
Di Long	狄龍	Ti Lung
Di nü hua	帝女花	Princess Chang Ping
Di xue huanghun	滴血黃昏	Bloodshed at Dusk
Di yi leixing weixian	第一類型危險	Dangerous Encounter – First Kind
Diantong yingpian gongsi	電通影片公司	Diantong Film Company
Dianying gongzuo shi	電影工作室	Film Workshop
Dianying maoye gongsi	電影懋業公司	Dianmao, *aka* MP & GI
Diao Chan	貂蟬	Diau Charn of the Three Kingdoms
Diao Chan	貂蟬	Sable Cicada
Didao zhan	地道戰	Tunnel Warfare
Didi di rizi	蒂蒂的日子	The Diary of Didi
Die bian	蝶變	The Butterfly Murders
Diexue heigu	喋血黑谷	Secret Decree
Diexue shuang xiong	喋血雙雄	The Killer
Ding Junshan	定軍山	Conquering Jun Mountain, *aka* Dingjun Mountain
Ding Shanxi	丁善璽	Ting Shan-hsi
Ding Yinnan	丁蔭楠	
Dishi panguan	的士判官	Taxi Hunter
Dixia qing	地下情	Love Unto Waste
Diyu wu men	地獄無門	We're Going to Eat You
Dong chun de rizi	冬春的日子	The Days
Dong Cunrui	董存瑞	
Dong furen	董夫人	The Arch
Dong Kena	董克娜	
Dong xie xi du	東邪西毒	Ashes of Time
Dongbei dianying zhipianchang	東北電影制片廠	Northeast Film Studio
Dongbei er nüzi	東北二女子	Two Orphan Girls from the Northeast
Dongdong de jiaqi	冬冬的假期	A Summer at Grandpa's
Dongfang bu bai	東方不敗	Swordsman, II
Dongfang hong	東方紅	The East is Red
Dongfang huazhu	洞房花燭	The Difficult Couple
Dongfang san xia	東方三俠	The Heroic Trio
Dongfang tuying	東方禿鷹	Eastern Condors
Dongfang ye tan	東方夜譚	Oriental Nights
Donggong xigong	東宮西宮	East Palace, West Palace
Dongling dadao	東陵大盜	Legend of the Dowager Empress's Tomb
Dongmei	冬梅	The Life of Dongmei
Dongya zhi guang	東亞之光	The Light of East Asia
Du bi dao	獨臂刀	One-Armed Swordsman
Du jiang zhencha ji	渡江偵察記	Reconnaissance Across the Yangtze
Du Kefeng	杜可風	Christopher Doyle
Du Qifeng	杜琪風	Johnny To
Du shen	賭神	God of Gamblers
Du shen xuji	賭神續集	God of Gamblers' Return

Pinyin	**Characters**	**Other**
Du sheng	賭聖	All for the Winner
Du shiniang	杜十娘	Lady Du
Du xia	賭俠	God of Gamblers, II
Du xia zhi Shanghai tan du sheng	賭俠之上海灘賭聖	God of Gamblers III: Back to Shanghai
Duan di yu yin	斷笛余音	The Melody from a Broken Flute
Duan jian	斷箭	Broken Arrow
Duhui de zaochen	都會的早晨	Dawn Over Metropolis
Duli shidai	獨立時代	A Confucius Confusion
Duoluo tianshi	墮落天使	Fallen Angels
Duosang	多桑	A Borrowed Life
Dushen nüren	獨身女人	A Single Woman
Dushi fengguang	都市風光	Cityscape
Dushi li de cunzhuang	都市里的村莊	A Village in the Metropolis
Emei dianying zhipianchang	峨眉電影制片廠	Emei Film Studio
Emeng chu xing	惡夢初醒	Awakening from Nightmare
Er Dongsheng	爾東升	Derek Yee
Erba jiaren	二八佳人	My Fair Lady
Ermo	二嫫	
Erzi	兒子	Sons
Erzi de da wan'ou	兒子的大玩偶	Sandwich Man
Erzi de da wan'ou	兒子的大玩偶	The Son's Big Doll
Erzi kai dian	二子開店	Erzi Runs an Inn
Erzi, sunzi he zhongzi	兒子，孫子和種子	Son, the Grandson and the Seeds
Fandui xijun zhan	反對細菌戰	Opposing Biological Warfare
Fang Lingzheng	方令正	Eddie Fong
Fang Peilin	方沛霖	
Fang Shiyu	方世玉	Fong Sai Yuk
Fang Yuping	方育平	Allen Fong
Fangfang	方方	
Fantianfudi	翻天覆地	The Turn-Over
Fating neiwai	法庭內外	The Trial
Fei Mu	費穆	
Fei xia A Da	飛俠阿達	The Red Lotus Society
Feichang da zongtong	非常大總統	The Provisional President
Feihu xiongxin	飛虎雄心	Final Option
Feilong mengjiang	飛龍猛將	Dragons Forever
Feizhou heshang	非洲和尚	Crazy Safari
Fendou	奮斗	Struggles
Feng Baobao	馮寶寶	Bobo Fung
Feng da shaoye	馮大少爺	Young Master Feng
Feng jie	瘋劫	The Secret
Fengbao	風暴	Storm
Feng'er tita cai	風兒踢踏踩	Cheerful Wind
Fenggui lai de ren	風櫃來的人	The Boys from Fengkuei

Pinyin	**Characters**	**Other**
Fenghuang qin	鳳凰琴	Country Teachers
Fenghuang yingye gongsi	鳳凰影業公司	Phoenix Films
Fengkuang de daijia	瘋狂的代價	The Price of Frenzy
Fengliu jianke	風流劍客	A Romantic Swordsman
Fengnian	豐年	The Year of Harvest
Fengxue Taihangshan	風雪太行山	Storm over Taihang Mountains
Fengyue	風月	Temptress Moon
Fengyun ernü	風雲兒女	Children of Troubled Times
Fengyun zai qi	風雲再起	Swordsman, III: The East is Red
Fengzheng	風箏	The Kite
Fenhongse de meng	粉紅色的夢	Pink Dream
Fenhongse de zhadan	粉紅色的炸彈	Pink Bomb
Fu Shunnan	符舜南	
Fugui bi ren	富貴逼人	It's a Mad, Mad World
Fuhuo de meigui	復活的玫瑰	Revived Rose
Fujian dianying zhipianchang	福建電影制片廠	Fujian Film Studio
Fuping	浮萍	Floating Leaf
Furen de shenghuo	富人的生活	The Life of the Wealthy
Furong zhen	芙蓉鎮	Hibiscus Town
Fushi	腐蝕	Erosion
Fuzi qing	父子情	Father and Son
Gangren tiema	鋼人鐵馬	Steel Man and Iron Horse
Gangtie shi zheyang liancheng de	鋼鐵是這樣煉成的	This is How Steel is Made
Gangtie zhanshi	鋼鐵戰士	Steeled Fighters
Gao Yuan	高遠	
Gaoshan xia de huahuan	高山下的花環	Garlands at the Foot of the Mountain
Gaoyang yisheng	羔羊醫生	Doctor Lam
Ge chang chunse	歌場春色	A Singer's Story
Ge Lan	葛蘭	Grace Chang, *aka* Zhang Yuying
Ge lü qing chao	歌侶情潮	Singing Lovers
Ge Xin	葛鑫	
Ge You	葛優	
Gege de qingren	哥哥的情人	Three Summers
Gei kafei jia dian tang	給咖啡加點糖	Put Some Sugar in the Coffee
Geming jiating	革命家庭	Revolutionary Family
Genü Hongmudan	歌女紅牡丹	Sing-Song Girl Red Peony
Gewu shengping	歌舞升平	Last Song in Paris
Gezi shu	鴿子樹	Dove Tree
Gong fu guonan	共赴國難	Facing the National Crisis
Gong Jianong	龔稼農	Robert Kung
Gong Li	鞏俐	
Gongpu	公僕	The Law with Two Phases
Gu Changwei	顧長衛	
Gu Dezhao	谷德昭	Vincent Kok
Gu feng	股瘋	Shanghai Fever

Pinyin	**Characters**	**Other**
Gu Kenfu	顧肯夫	
Gu Rong	古榕	
Guafu cun	寡婦村	Widow Village
Guai quan	怪圈	Strange Circle
Guaming de fuqi	挂名的夫妻	Marriage in Name
Guan Dexing	關德興	Kwan Tak-hing
Guan Haifeng	管海峰	
Guan Hanqing	關漢卿	
Guan Hu	管虎	
Guan Jinpeng	關錦鵬	Stanley Kwan
Guan lianzhang	關連長	Commander Guan
Guan Wenqing	關文清	Moon Kwan
Guangchang	廣場	The Square
Guangxi dianying zhipianchang	廣西電影制片廠	
Guangyin de gushi	光陰的故事	In Our Time
Gucheng lienü	孤城烈女	The Heroine in the Besieged City
Gudao tiantang	孤島天堂	Orphan Island Paradise
Gudu chunmeng	故都春夢	Memories of the Old Capital
Gudu zhe	孤獨者	The Loner
Guer jiu zu ji	孤兒救祖記	Orphan Rescues Grandfather
Gugong xin yuan	故宮新怨	Sad Song from an Old Palace
Guhuozai	古惑仔	Young and Dangerous
Gui da gui	鬼打鬼	Encounters of the Spooky Kind, *aka* Close Encounters of the Spooky Kind
Gui ma shuang xing	鬼馬雙星	Games Gamblers Play
Gui mi xinqiao	鬼迷心竅	Awakening
Guihua xiang	桂花巷	Osmanthus Alley
Guixinsijian	歸心似箭	The Call of the Front
Gujin dazhan Qinyong qing	古今大戰秦俑情	The Terracotta Warrior
Gujing chong bo ji	古井重波記	The Revival of an Old Well
Gulingjie shaonian sharen shijian	牯嶺街少年殺人事件	A Brighter Summer Day
Gungun hongchen	滾滾紅塵	Red Dust
Guo feng	國風	The Spirit of the Nation
Guo hun	國魂	Spirit of the Nation
Guo Wei	郭維	
Guochan lingling qi	國產凌凌漆	From Beijing with Love
Guonian	過年	Spring Festival
Guoqing shi dian zhong	國慶十點鐘	Ten o'Clock on the National Day
Guosetianxiang	國色天香	The Musician
Guotai jigou youxian gongsi	國泰機構有限公司	Cathay Films
Gushu yiren	鼓書藝人	Drum Singers, *aka* Travelling Players
Guwu guairen	古屋怪人	The Ghost in an Old House
Guwu moying	古屋魔影	Shadows in an Ancient House
Guwu xingshi ji	古屋行尸記	Walking Corpse in an Old House
Guyuan chunmeng	故園春夢	Between Tears and Smiles

Pinyin	Characters	Other
Hai hun	海魂	The Spirit of the Sea
Hai ou	海鷗	Sea Gull
Hai shi	海誓	Sea Oath
Haigang	海港	On the Docks
Haitan	海灘	On the Beach
Haitan shang de yi tian	海灘上的一天	That Day on the Beach
Haixia	海霞	Haixia
Haiyan dianying zhipianchang	海燕電影制片廠	Haiyan Film Studio
Haizang	海葬	Sea Burial
Haizi wang	孩子王	King of the Children
Han ye	寒夜	Cold Night
Hao Guang	郝光	
Hao nan hao nü	好男好女	Good Men, Good Women
Hao pengyou	好朋友	Good Friends
Hao xiongdi	好兄弟	Good Brothers
Hao zhangfu	好丈夫	Good Husband
Hasen yu Jiamila	哈森與加米拉	Hasen and Jamila
He Feiguang	何非光	
He Jianjun	何建軍	He Yi
He Mengfu	何孟斧	
He Ping	何平	
He Qun	何群	
He Yi	何一	He Jianjun
Hei bai dao	黑白道	One-Armed Boxer
Hei ji yuan hun	黑籍冤魂	Wronged Ghosts in Opium Den
Hei junma	黑駿馬	A Mongolian Tale
Hei mingdan	黑名單	Black List
Hei pao shijian	黑炮事件	Black Cannon Incident
Heishan lu	黑山路	Black Mountain Road
Heixia	黑俠	Black Mask
Heiye dao tianming	黑夜到天明	From Night to Dawn
Heiye guhun	黑夜孤魂	A Lonely Soul of the Dark Night
Heliu	河流	The River
Heping fandian	和平飯店	Peace Hotel
Heping zhi yingsheng	和平之應聲	The Resonance of Peace
Hong fan qu	紅番區	Rumble in the Bronx
Hong gaoliang	紅高粱	Red Sorghum
Hong Jinbao	洪金寶	Sammo Hung
Hong meigui, bai meigui	紅玫瑰，白玫瑰	Red Rose, White Rose
Hong Shen	洪深	Hong Da
Hong tiane	紅天鵝	Red Swan
Hong xiang	紅象	Red Elephant
Hong yi shaonü	紅衣少女	Girl in Red
Hong yingtao	紅櫻桃	Red Cherry
Hongdeng ji	紅燈記	Legend of the Red Lantern
Hongdeng ting, lüdeng xing	紅燈停，綠燈行	Signal Left, Turn Right
Hongfen	紅粉	Blush

Pinyin	Characters	Other
Hongfen kulou	紅粉骷髏	The Vampire
Honghu chiweidui	洪湖赤衛隊	Red Guards of Lake Hong
Honglou meng	紅樓夢	Dream of the Red Chamber
Hongqi pu	紅旗譜	Legend of the Banner
Hongri	紅日	Red Sun
Hongse niangzijun	紅色娘子軍	Red Detachment of Women
Hongyang haoxia zhuan	紅羊豪俠傳	A Knight-Errant Named Hongyang
Hou Xiaoxian	候孝賢	Hou Hsiao-hsien
Hou Yao	候曜	
Hou Yong	侯咏	
Houbu duiyuan	候補隊員	A Probationary Member
Hu Die	胡蝶	Butterfly Wu
Hu Jinquan	胡金銓	King Hu
Hu Mei	胡玫	
Hu Peng	胡鵬	Wu Pang
Hu Rui	胡睿	
Hu Tu	胡涂	
Hu Xuehua	胡雪華	
Hu Xueyang	胡雪揚	
Hu Yue de gushi	胡越的故事	The Story of Woo Viet
Hua hun	畫魂	The Soul of the Painter
Hua jian lei	花濺泪	Fallen Flower
Hua luo shui jia	花落誰家	Whose Belongings?
Huabei dianying gongsi	華北電影公司	North China Film Company
Huabian	嘩變	Mutiny
Huacheng yingye gongsi	華成影業公司	Huacheng Film Company
Huaguang dianying gongsi	華光電影公司	Huaguang Film Company
Huahaoyueyuan	花好月圓	The Full Moon
Huaishu zhuang	槐樹莊	Locust Tree Village
Huamei yingpian gongsi	華美影片公司	Wah Mei Films
Huang Baiming	黃百鳴	Raymond Wong
Huang Baomei	黃寶妹	Huang Baomei
Huang Baoshan	黃寶善	
Huang Feihong	黃飛鴻	Wong Fei-hung
Huang Feihong	黃飛鴻	Once Upon a Time in China
Huang Feihong zhuan	黃飛鴻傳	The True Story of Wong Fei-hung
Huang Jiamo	黃嘉謨	
Huang Jianxin	黃建新	
Huang Jianye	黃建業	
Huang Jianzhong	黃建中	
Huang jinyu	黃金魚	Yellow Goldfish
Huang Jun	黃軍	
Huang Manli	黃曼梨	Wong Man-lei
Huang Mingchuan	黃明川	
Huang Qiusheng	黃秋生	Anthony Wong
Huang Shaofen	黃紹芬	Huang Ke
Huang Shuqin	黃蜀芹	

Pinyin	Characters	Other
Huang tudi	黃土地	Yellow Earth
Huang Yushan	黃玉珊	Huang Yu-shan
Huang Zhiqiang	黃志強	Che Kirk Wong
Huang Zumo	黃祖模	
Huang Zuolin	黃佐臨	Zuolin
Huanghe yao	黃河謠	Ballad of the Yellow River
Huangjia shijie	皇家師姐	Yes, Madam!
Huangjin shidai	黃金時代	The Golden Age
Huangjin zhi lu	黃金之路	Golden Road
Huangpu jun hun	黃埔軍魂	Spirit of the Huangpu Military Academy
Huangtupo de nürenmen	黃土坡的女人們	Women of Huangtupo Village
Huanle yingxiong	歡樂英雄	Joyous Heroes
Huanxian dianying gongsi	幻仙電影公司	Fantasy Film Company
Huanxiang riji	還鄉日記	Diary of a Homecoming
Huashen guniang	化身姑娘	Girl in Disguise
Huaxin yingye gongsi	華新影業公司	Huaxin Film Company
Huaying	華影	United China Film Company
Hudie meng	蝴蝶夢	Rebecca
Hudumen	虎渡門	Stage Door
Huguang	弧光	Arc Light
Hunhou wenti	婚后的問題	Post-Marital Problems
Huo de xili	火的洗禮	A Bloody Lesson
Huo hu	火狐	Sparkling Fox
Huo Jianqi	霍建起	
Huo shao dao	火燒島	Island of Fire
Huo shao Honglian si	火燒紅蓮寺	The Burning of Red Lotus Temple
Huo shao Honglian si	火燒紅蓮寺	Burning Paradise
Huo shao Yuanmingyuan	火燒圓明園	The Burning of the Imperial Palace
Huo tong	火童	Fire Boy
Huoshan qing xue	火山情血	Revenge by the Volcano
Huozang	火葬	The Cremation
Huozhe	活着	To Live
Hutu waijiao	糊涂外交	The Foolish Father-in-law
Ji dao zhuizong	極道追踪	Zodiac Killers
Ji tong ya jiang	雞同鴨講	Chicken and Duck Talk
Jia	家	Family
Jia feng xu huang	假鳳虛凰	Phony Phoenixes
Jia he sheng chun	嘉禾生春	Spring Comes to the Rice Field
Jia jin gong li de nanren	嫁進宮里的男人	The Man Married to the Imperial Court
Jia you xishi	家有喜事	All's Well, Ends Well
Jia zai Taibei	家在臺北	Home, Sweet Home
Jiachou	家丑	Family Scandal
Jiahe dianying gongsi	嘉禾電影公司	Golden Harvest Film Company
Jiandan renwu	簡單任務	First Strike, *aka* Police Story, IV

Pinyin	Characters	Other
Jiang Dawei	姜大衛	David Chiang
Jiang Wen	姜文	
Jiangnan dianying zhipianchang	江南電影制片廠	Jiangnan Film Studio
Jiangshi xiansheng	僵尸先生	Mr Vampire
Jianguo zhi lu	建國之路	The Path to National Reconstruction
Jianmei yundong	健美運動	Body Builders
Jianyu fengyun	監獄風雲	Prison on Fire
Jiao wo ruhe bu xiang ta	教我如何不想她	Because of Her
Jiao Xiongping	焦雄屏	Peggy Hsiung-Ping Chiao
Jiaru wo shi zhende	假如我是真的	If I Were for Real
Jiawu fengyun	甲午風雲	Naval Battle of 1894
Jidi	吉地	The Land of Fortune
Jidong qixia	急凍奇俠	Iceman Cometh, *aka* Time Warriors
Jidu maoxian	極度冒險	Maximum Risk
Jiehun	結婚	Marriage
Jiehun jinxing qu	結婚進行曲	The Wedding March
Jiejie meimei zhanqilai	姐姐妹妹站起來	Sisters, Stand Up
Jietouxiangwei	街頭巷尾	Head of Street, End of Lane
Jijing de shanlin	寂靜的山林	Quiet Forest
Jimao xin	鷄毛信	Letter with Feather
Jimo de shiqi sui	寂寞的十七歲	Lonely Seventeen
Jin lianhua	金蓮花	Golden Lotus
Jin Shan	金山	Zhao Mo
Jin Yan	金焰	Jin Delin
Jin yanzi	金燕子	Golden Swallow
Jin Yuji	金玉姬	Story of Jin Yuji
Jin zhuang xiangjiao julebu	金裝香蕉俱樂部	Top Banana Club
Jinding yingye gongsi	金鼎影業公司	Golden Tripod Film Company
Jinfen nishang	金粉霓裳	All That Glitters
Jing	井	The Well
Jingcha gushi	警察故事	Police Story
Jingwumen	精武門	Fist of Fury, *aka* The Chinese Connection
Jinnian de hupan hui hen leng	今年的湖畔會很冷	This Year it Will be Cold by the River Bank
Jinping shuang yan	金瓶雙艷	Golden Vase Beauties
Jinqian bao	金錢豹	The Leopard
Jinse zhijia	金色指甲	The Golden Fingernail
Jintian bu huijia	今天不回家	Tonight Nobody Goes Home
Jintian wo xiuxi	今天我休息	It's My Day Off
Jinwu shi'er chai	金屋十二釵	Twelve Beauties
Jinxing yingye gongsi	金星影業公司	Golden Star Film Company
Jinxiuheshan	錦繡河山	Beautiful Country
Jinye you baofengxue	今夜有暴風雪	Snowstorm
Jinzhiyuye	金枝玉葉	He's a Woman, She's a Man
Jiu yue	九月	September

Pinyin	Characters	Other
Jiushi liuliude ta	就是溜溜的她	A Cute Girl
Ju Dou	菊豆	
Juejing feng sheng	絕境逢生	Narrow Escape
Juelie	決裂	Breaking with Old Ideas
Juexiang	絕響	Swan Song
Jun zhong fangcao	軍中芳草	Women Soldiers
Kaige	凱歌	Triumph
Kanhai de rizi	看海的日子	A Flower in the Rainy Night
Ke Junxiong	柯俊雄	Ko Chun-hsiung
Ke Ling	柯靈	
Ke nü	蚵女	Oyster Girl
Ke tu qiu hen	客途秋恨	Song of the Exile
Ke Yizheng	柯一正	Ko Yi-cheng
Kelian tianxia fumu xin	可憐天下父母心	All These Pitiable Parents
Kong fuzi	孔夫子	Confucius
Kongbu fenzi	恐怖分子	Terrorizer
Konggu lan	空谷蘭	Orchid in the Deep Valley
Kongshan lingyu	空山靈雨	Raining in the Mountain
Ku lian	苦戀	Unrequited Love
Kuaican che	快餐車	Wheels on Meals
Kuang	狂	Ripples Across Stagnant Water
Kuang liu	狂流	Wild Torrents
Kuanghuan zhi ye	狂歡之夜	The Night of Debauchery
Kucai hua	苦菜花	Sowthistle
Kumu fengchun	枯木逢春	Spring Comes to the Withered Tree
Ku'nao ren de xiao	苦惱人的笑	Bitter Laughter
Kunlun yingye gongsi	昆侖影業公司	Kunlun Film Company
Lai ke	來客	The Boy from Vietnam
Lai Shengchuan	賴聲川	Stan Lai
Lan fengzheng	藍風箏	The Blue Kite
Lang tao sha	浪淘沙	The Desert Island
Langshan diexue ji	狼山喋血記	Wolf Hunting
Lanlan he Dongdong	蘭蘭和冬冬	Lanlan and Dongdong
Lanling wang	蘭陵王	Warrior Lanling
Lao jing	老井	Old Well
Lao Mo de di'erge chuntian	老莫的第二個春天	Lao Mo's Second Spring
Laobing xinzhuan	老兵新傳	New Story of an Old Soldier
Laodong hua kai	勞動花開	Work is Beautiful
Laogong aiqing	勞工愛情	Labourer's Love
Laohu tianji	老虎田鷄	Tiger and Frogs
Laoren yu gou	老人與狗	An Old Man and His Dog
Lei hen	淚痕	Traces of Tears
Leiyu	雷雨	Thunderstorm (TV series)
Leng yue shihun	冷月詩魂	Lonely Soul
Li An	李安	Ang Lee

Pinyin	Characters	Other
Li Ang	李昂	
Li Beihai	黎北海	Lai Pak-hoi
Li Bihua	李碧華	Lilian Lee
Li Chenfeng	李晨風	Lee Sun-fung
Li Guoli	李國立	
Li Haishan	黎海山	Lai Hoi-san
Li Hanxiang	李翰祥	Li Han-hsiang
Li Jia	李嘉	
Li Jun	李俊	
Li Lianjie	李連杰	Jet Li
Li Lichi	李力持	Lee Lik-chi
Li Lihua	李麗華	
Li Lili	黎莉莉	Qian Zhenzhen
Li Minwei	黎民偉	Lai Man-wai
Li Pingqian	李萍倩	Li Chunshou
Li Shaohong	李少紅	
Li Shishi chuanqi	李師師傳奇	Legend of Li Shishi
Li Shizhen	李時珍	Li Shizhen
Li Shuangshuang	李雙雙	Li Shuangshuang
Li Tianlu	李天祿	Li Tien-lu
Li Tie	李鐵	Lee Tit
Li Wenhua	李文化	
Li Xiaolong	李小龍	Bruce Lee
Li Xin	李欣	
Li Xing	李行	Lee Hsing
Li Xiuxian	李修賢	Danny Lee, *aka* Lee Sau-yin
Li Yalin	李亞林	
Li Youning	李佑寧	
Li Zhun	李準	
Li Ziyu	李子羽	
Li Zuyong	李祖永	Lee Tsu Yung
Lian'ai yu yiwu	戀愛與義務	Love and Responsibility
Liang ge xiao zuqiu dui	兩個小足球隊	Two Boys' Soccer Teams
Liang ge youqi jiang	兩個油漆匠	Two Sign-Painters
Liang gong huangtaihou	兩宮皇太后	Two Empress Dowagers
Liang jia chun	兩家春	Two Families
Liang Jiahui	梁家輝	Tony Kar-Fei Leung
Liang Puzhi	梁普智	Leong Po-chih
Liang Shanbo yu Zhu Yingtai	梁山伯與祝英臺	Liang Shanbo and Zhu Yingtai
Liang Shanbo yu Zhu Yingtai	梁山伯與祝英臺	Love Eterne
Liang Shanbo zaihui Zhu Yingtai	梁山伯再會祝英臺	Liang Shanbo's Second Meeting with Zhu Yingtai
Liang Shaopo	梁少坡	Leung Siu-po
Liang Tingduo	梁廷鐸	
Liang Zhu henshi	梁祝恨史	Tragic Story of Liang Shanbo and Zhu Yingtai
Liangjiafunü	良家婦女	Good Woman

Pinyin	Characters	Other
Liangxin	良心	Conscience
Lianhua jiaoxiangqu	聯華交響曲	Lianhua Symphony
Lianhua yingye gongsi	聯華影業公司	United Photoplay Service
Lianhua yingyishe	聯華影藝社	Lianhua Film Society
Lianlian fengchen	戀戀風塵	Dust in the Wind
Liao Zhongkai	廖仲愷	Liao Zhongkai
Liaoyuan	燎原	Fire on the Plain
Liaoyuan de xiangcun	遼遠的鄉村	The Far Away Village
Lidichengfo	立地成佛	A Change of Heart
Liechang zhasa	獵場扎撒	On the Hunting Ground
Liehuo jingang	烈火金剛	Steel Meets Fire
Liehuo zhong yongsheng	烈火中永生	Red Crag
Liening zai shiyue	列寧在十月	Lenin in October
Liening zai 1918	列寧在一九一八	Lenin in 1918
Lihun	離婚	Divorce
Lihun le, jiu bie zai lai zhao wo	離婚了就別再來找我	No Visit after Divorce
Lin Chuchu	林楚楚	Lam Cho-cho
Lin Dai	林黛	Linda Lin
Lin Fengjiao	林鳳嬌	Lin Feng-chiao
Lin jia puzi	林家鋪子	The Lin Family Shop
Lin Lingdong	林嶺東	Ringo Lam
Lin Niantong	林年同	
Lin Nong	林農	
Lin Qinglong	林慶隆	Bosco Lam
Lin Qingxia	林青霞	Lin Ching Hsia, *aka* Brigitte Lin
Lin Zexu	林則徐	Lin Zexu
Ling yu rou	靈與肉	Soul and Flesh
Ling Zi	凌子	
Ling Zifeng	凌子風	
Linju	鄰居	Neighbours
Liren xing	麗人行	Female Fighters, *aka* Three Women
Liu Dehua	劉德華	Andy Lau
Liu Guanwei	劉觀偉	Lau Kwoon-wai
Liu Guochang	劉國昌	Lawrence Ah Mon
Liu Guoquan	劉國權	
Liu hao men	六號門	Gate No. 6
Liu Heng	劉桓	
Liu Jiachang	劉家昌	
Liu Jialiang	劉家良	Lau Kar-leung, *aka* Liu Chia Liang
Liu Miaomiao	劉苗苗	
Liu Na'ou	劉吶鷗	
Liu Qiong	劉瓊	
Liu Sanjie	劉三姐	Third Sister Liu
Liu Weiqiang	劉偉強	Andrew Lau
Liu Xiaoqing	劉曉慶	
Liu Zhenwei	劉鎮偉	Jeff Lau

Pinyin	Characters	Other
Liubao de gushi	柳堡的故事	Story of Liubao Village
Liuhe yingxi yingye gongsi	六合影戲營業公司	United Six Film Company
Liulang Beijing	流浪北京	Bumming in Beijing – The Last Dreamers
Liulang shaonian lu	流浪少年路	Wandering Youth
Liushou nüshi	留守女士	Lady Left Behind
Liuxu	柳絮	Willow Catkin
Long hu dou	龍虎斗	The Chinese Boxer
Long hu fengyun	龍虎風雲	City on Fire
Long min	籠民	Cageman
Long nian jingguan	龍年警官	Dragon Year Cops
Long teng sihai	龍騰四海	Gun and Rose
Long teng Zhongguo	龍騰中國	Presumed Guilty
Longma yingpian gongsi	龍馬影片公司	Longma Film Company
Longmen kezhan	龍門客棧	Dragon Gate Inn
Longxiang yingye gongsi	龍祥影業公司	Longxiang Film Company
Longxiong hudi	龍兄虎弟	Armour of God
Longzhenghudou	龍爭虎斗	Enter the Dragon
Lou Ye	婁燁	
Lü Ban	呂班	
Lu Jie	陸潔	
Lu Ren	魯韌	
Lü Sushang	呂訴上	
Lu Wei	蘆葦	
Lu Xiaoya	陸小雅	
Lu Xuechang	路學長	
Lu Yu	盧鈺	
Lu Yuntao	陸運濤	Loke Wan Tho
Luanshi fengguang	亂世風光	The Chaotic World
Lubing hua	魯冰花	Cold Ice-Flower
Lunhui	輪回	Transmigration, *aka* Samsara
Luo Jingyu	羅靜予	
Luo Mingyou	羅明佑	
Luo Qirui	羅啟銳	Alex Law
Luo Wei	羅維	Lo Wei
Luo Zhuoyao	羅卓瑤	Clara Law
Luotuo xian wu	駱駝仙舞	Dancing Camel
Luotuo Xiangzi	駱駝祥子	Camel Xiangzi, *aka* Rickshaw Boy
Ma langdang	馬郎當	Vagabond Ma
Ma-Xu Weibang	馬徐維邦	Xu Weibang
Mai Dangjie	麥當杰	Michael Mak
Mai Dangxiong	麥當雄	Johnny Mak
Mai hua guniang	賣花姑娘	Flower Girl
Mai Jia	麥嘉	Carl Mak
Maifu	埋伏	Surveillance
Maishenqi	賣身契	The Contract

Pinyin	Characters	Other
Majiang	麻將	Mah-jong
Malu tianshi	馬路天使	Street Angel
Mama	媽媽	Mama, *aka* The Tree of the Sun
Manbo guniang	曼波姑娘	Mambo Girl
Mang gunü	盲孤女	Blind Orphan Girl
Manyi bu manyi	滿意不滿意	Satisfied or Not
Manzhou yinghua xiehui	滿洲映畫協會	Manchurian Motion Pictures
Mao Ying	茅瑛	Angela Mao
Mao Zedong de gushi	毛澤東的故事	The Story of Mao Zedong
Mati sheng cui	馬蹄聲脆	Women on the Long March
Mei Yanfang	梅艷芳	Anita Mui
Meigui duo ci	玫瑰多刺	Thorny Rose
Meigui piaoling	玫瑰飄零	Fallen Rose
Meiguo xin	美國心	Just Like the Weather
Meili bao dao	美麗寶島	Beautiful Island
Meiren en	美人恩	A Lady's Favour
Meiren xue	美人血	Beauty's Blood
Meiyou hangbiao de heliu	沒有航標的河流	The River without Buoys
Meng li qiankun	夢裏乾坤	Dream World
Meng long guo jiang	猛龍過江	Return of the Dragon
Menglongsha	勐隴沙	Menglongsha Village
Mi Jiashan	米家山	
Miaojie huanghou	廟街皇后	Queen of Temple Street
Mimi tuzhi	秘密圖紙	Secret Document
Minjing gushi	民警故事	On the Beat
Mingxing yingpian gongsi	明星影片公司	Star Film Company
Minxin dianying gongsi	民新電影公司	China Sun Film Company
Minzu shengcun	民族生存	The Survival of the Nation
Minzu wansui	民族萬歲	Long Live the Nation
Mitu de gaoyang	迷途的羔羊	Lost Children
Mo Kangshi	莫康時	Mok Hong-see
Mo Yan	莫言	
Modai huanghou	末代皇后	The Last Empress
Modeng baobiao	摩登保鏢	Security Unlimited
Moshushi de qiyu	摩術師的奇遇	The Adventure of a Magician
Mu di	牧笛	The Cowherd's Flute
Mu ma ren	牧馬人	The Herdsman
Mu zhi xin	母之心	Mother's Heart
Mudan niao	牡丹鳥	Peony Birds
Mulan congjun	木蘭從軍	Mulan Joins the Army
Muqin	母親	Mother
Muqin sanshi sui	母親三十歲	Story of Mother
Muxing zhi guang	母性之光	Motherly Love
Nanchang qiyi	南昌起義	The Nanchang Uprising
Nan'er dang ziqiang	男兒當自強	Once Upon a Time in China, II
Nanfu nanqi	難夫難妻	The Difficult Couple

Pinyin	Characters	Other
Nanguo zaijian, nanguo	南國再見，南國	Goodbye, South, Goodbye
Nanguo zhi chun	南國之春	Southern Spring
Nanhai changcheng	南海長城	The Great Wall of the South China Sea
Nanhai chao	南海潮	Waves of the Southern Sea
Nanhai meiren	南海美人	The Beauty from the Southern Sea
Nanjing 1937	南京一九三七	Nanjing 1937
Nanwei le meimei	難為了妹妹	The Sister
Nanyang fengguang	南洋風光	Scenes from the South Seas
Nanyang yingpian gongsi	南洋影片公司	South Seas Film Company
Nanyue yingpian gongsi	南越影片公司	Nam Yuet Film Company
Nanzhengbeizhan	南征北戰	From Victory to Victory
Neimenggu (see next entry)		
Neimenggu dianying zhipianchang	內蒙古電影制片廠	Inner Mongolian Film Studio
Nezha nao hai	哪吒鬧海	Nezha Conquers the Dragon King
Ni Zhen	倪震	
Niandai yingshi shiye gongsi	年代影視事業公司	Era International Films
Nie Er	聶耳	Hie Tianshi, Nie Shouxin; Nie Er (film)
Nie yuan	孽緣	Evil Fates
Niezi	孽子	The Outcasts
Niguang	逆光	Back-Lit Pictures
Nihongdeng xia de shaobing	霓虹燈下的哨兵	Sentinels under the Neon Lights
Niluohe de nüer	尼羅河的女兒	Daughter of the Nile
Ning Ying	寧瀛	
Niulang zhinü	牛郎織女	Cowherd and Fairy Maiden
Niupeng	牛棚	China, My Sorrow
Nongnu	農奴	Serfs
Nongye jiaoyu dianying gongsi	農業教育電影公司	Agricultural Education Motion Picture Company
Nü cike	女刺客	The Valiant Ones
Nü daxuesheng sushe	女大學生宿舍	Girl Students' Dormitory
Nü daxuesheng zhi si	女大學生之死	Death of a College Girl
Nü fuma	女駙馬	The Daughter-in-Law
Nü jixieren	女機械人	Robotrix
Nü lan wu hao	女籃五號	Girl Basketball Player No. 5
Nü lifashi	女理髮師	Woman Barber
Nü tiaoshui duiyuan	女跳水隊員	Girl Divers
Nü xia Li Feifei	女俠李飛飛	A Female Knight-Errant
Nüer jing	女兒經	A Bible for Girls
Nüer lou	女兒樓	Army Nurse
Nuli de nüer	奴隸的女兒	A Slave's Daughter
Nüren	女人	Women
Nüren de gushi	女人的故事	Women's Story
Nüren hua	女人花	Women Flowers
Nüren men	女人們	Women
Nüren sishi	女人四十	Summer Snow

Pinyin	Characters	Other
Nüren, TAXI, nüren	女人，TAXI，女人	Women, Taxi, Women
Nüren xin	女人心	Women
Nüxing de nahan	女性的吶喊	The Protest of Women
Nüxing shijie	女性世界	The World of Women
Nüzi gongyu	女子公寓	Women's Dormitory
O, xiangxue	哦！香雪	Oh! Sweet Snow
Ouyang Hongying	歐陽紅櫻	
Ouyang Shafei	歐陽莎菲	
Ouyang Yuqian	歐陽予倩	Ouyang Liyuan
Pan Hong	潘虹	
Pan Jinlian zhi qianshi jinsheng	潘金蓮之前世今生	The Reincarnation of Golden Lotus
Pan si dong	盤絲洞	The Spider Cave
Pan Wenjie	潘文杰	Poon Man Kit
Pao da shuang deng	炮打雙燈	Red Firecracker, Green Firecracker
Peng Xiaolian	彭小蓮	
Pingguo de ziwei	蘋果的滋味	The Taste of the Apple
Pingyuan youjidui	平原游擊隊	Guerrillas on the Plain
Pulaiweitiche gongsi	普來維梯徹公司	Private Teaching Company
Putong zhanshi	普通戰士	An Ordinary Soldier
Qi fu	弃婦	Abandoned Woman
Qi pin zhima guan	七品芝麻官	A Lowly County Magistrate
Qi wang	棋王	King of Chess
Qi xiaofu	七小福	Painted Faces
Qi zheng piaopiao	旗正飄飄	The Flag is Flying
Qi zhong qi	奇中奇	Wonder of Wonders
Qian jiao bai mei	千嬌百媚	Smiling Beauty
Qian nü youhun	倩女幽魂	A Chinese Ghost Story
Qian wang	潛網	The Invisible Web
Qian Zhuangfei	錢壯飛	
Qian zuo guai	錢作怪	From Rags to Riches
Qiancheng wanli	前程萬里	The Boundless Future
Qiang shen	槍神	Hard Boiled
Qianwan buyao wangji jieji douzheng	千萬不要忘記階級斗爭	Never Forget Class Struggle
Qiao	橋	Bridge
Qiao zhe yi jiazi	瞧這一家子	What a Family
Qidai *see* Zhi wang	期待	
Qielifei	茄哩啡	The Extras
Qin Fan	秦範	
Qin song	秦頌	The Emperor's Shadow
Qin Yi	秦怡	Qin Dehe
Qing chang yi shen	情長誼深	Loyal Partners
Qing chao	情潮	Love Tide
Qing gong mishi	清宮秘史	Sorrows of the Forbidden City

Pinyin	Characters	Other
Qing she	青蛇	Green Snake
Qing yan	情焰	Flames of Passion
Qingbai	清白	The Innocent
Qingcheng zhi lian	傾城之戀	Love in the Fallen City
Qingchun	青春	Youth
Qingchun ji	青春祭	Sacrificed Youth
Qingchun wansui	青春萬歲	Forever Young
Qingchun wuhui	青春無悔	No Regrets
Qingchun zhi ge	青春之歌	Song of Youth
Qingmeizhuma	青梅竹馬	Taipei Story
Qingnian dianying zhipianchang	青年電影制片廠	Youth Film Studio
Qingnian jinxing qu	青年進行曲	Marching Youth
Qingnian Zhongguo	青年中國	Young China
Qingniao dianying zhipian youxian gongsi	青鳥電影制片有限公司	Bluebird Film Company
Qingshaonian Nezha	青少年哪咤	Rebel of the Neon God
Qingshishan	青石山	Green Rock Mountain
Qingxu meng	清虛夢	An Empty Dream
Qingyu baojian	情欲寶鑒	Amorous Lesson
Qiong lou hen	瓊樓恨	The Haunted House
Qiong Yao	瓊瑤	Chiung Yao
Qishi'er jia fangke	七十二家房客	House of Seventy-two Tenants
Qiu	秋	Autumn
Qiu Fusheng	丘復生	
Qiu Gangjian	丘剛健	Qiu-Dai Anping
Qiu Jin	秋瑾	Qiu Jin
Qiu jue	秋決	Execution in Autumn
Qiu Litao	邱禮濤	Herman Yau
Qiu weng yu xian ji	秋翁遇仙記	Qiu Meets the Goddess of Flowers
Qiu yue	秋月	Autumn Moon
Qiu-Dai Anping	邱戴安平	Qiu Gangjian
Qiuju da guansi	秋菊打官司	The Story of Qiuju
Qiutian de tonghua	秋天的童話	An Autumn's Tale
Qixingdong tu	七星洞圖	Map of the Seven-Star Cave
Qiyi de hunpei	奇异的婚配	The Strange Marriage
Qizhuang shanhe	氣壯山河	To Die a Heroic Death
Qu Baiyin	瞿白音	
Quangao feidie zishou	勸告匪諜自首	Advice to the Communist Spy
Quanji shou	拳擊手	The Boxer
Queli renjia	闕里人家	The Descendants of Confucius
Redai yu	熱帶魚	Tropical Fish
Ren Dahua	任達華	Simon Yam
Ren dao zhongnian	人到中年	At the Middle Age
Ren Fengtai	任豐泰	
Ren gui qing	人，鬼，情	Woman Demon Human

Pinyin	**Characters**	**Other**
Ren Jianhui	任劍輝	Yam Kim-fai
Ren Jinping	任矜苹	
Ren Pengnian	任彭年	
Ren Xudong	任旭東	
Ren zai Niuyue	人在紐約	Full Moon in New York
Ren zhi chu	人之初	Lost Innocence
Rendao	人道	Humanity
Renhai guhong	人海孤鴻	The Orphan
Renjian xianzi	人間仙子	Fairies of the Mortal World
Renmin de juzhang	人民的巨掌	Inescapable
Rensheng	人生	Life
Renxin	人心	The Human Heart
Renzhe wudi	仁者無敵	The Magnificent Butcher
Rexue zhonghun	熱血忠魂	The Loyal Warriors
Rexue zhonghun	熱血忠魂	The Patriotic Family
Riben jiandie	日本間諜	Japanese Spy
Richu	日出	Sunrise
Riguang xiagu	日光峽谷	Sun Valley
Roubo	肉搏	Bloodbath
Ruan Lingyu	阮玲玉	Ruan Agen, *aka* Ruan Yuying
Ruan Lingyu	阮玲玉	The Actress, *aka* Centre Stage
Ruci fanhua	如此繁華	Extravaganza
Ruozhe, ni de mingzi shi nüren	弱者，你的名字是女人	Weakness, Thy Name is Woman
Ruyi	如意	As You Wish
Sai shang fengyun	塞上風雲	Storm on the Border
San ge heshang	三個和尚	Three Monks
San ge modeng nüxing	三個摩登女性	Three Modern Women
San ge nüren de gushi *see* Ren zai niuyue	三個女人的故事	
San Mao congjun ji	三毛從軍記	San Mao Joins the Army
San Mao liulang ji	三毛流浪記	An Orphan on the Streets, *aka* The Winter of Three Hairs
San Mao zuo shengyi	三毛做生意	San Mao Runs a Business
San nian yihou	三年以後	Three Years Later
San ren shijie	三人世界	Heart to Hearts
San xiao	三笑	Tang Bohu Picks Qiuxiang
San zimei	三姊妹	Three Sisters
Sang Hu	桑弧	Li Peilin
Sha fu	殺夫	Woman of Wrath
Sha Ou	沙鷗	Drive to Win
Shan jian lingxiang mabang lai	山間鈴響馬幫來	The Caravan
Shan shen	山神	God of the Mountain
Shan zhong chuanqi	山中傳奇	Legend of the Mountain
Shang shi	傷逝	Regret for the Past
Shang yi dang	上一當	Conned-Once Restaurant

Pinyin	Characters	Other
Shangganling	上甘嶺	Shanggan Ridges
Shangguan Yunzhu	上官雲珠	Wei Junluo
Shanghai dianying zhipianchang	上海電影制片廠	Shanghai Film Studio
Shanghai ershisi xiaoshi	上海二十四小時	Twenty-four Hours in Shanghai
Shanghai guniang	上海姑娘	Girls from Shanghai
Shanghai huoxian hou	上海火綫后	Behind the Shanghai Front
Shanghai jiaofu	上海教父	Shanghai 1920
Shanghai jiaqi	上海假期	My American Grandson
Shanghai meishu dianying zhipianchang	上海美術電影制片廠	Shanghai Animation Film Studio
Shanghai yi furen	上海一婦人	A Shanghai Woman
Shanghai yingxi gongsi	上海影戲公司	Shanghai Film Company
Shanghai zhanyi	上海戰役	The Shanghai Battle
Shanghai zhi ye	上海之夜	Shanghai Blues
Shangrao jizhongying	上饒集中營	Shangrao Concentration Camp
Shanhe lei	山河泪	My Mountains, My Rivers
Shanlin zhong touyige nüren	山林中頭一個女人	The First Woman in the Forest
Shanshan de hongxing	閃閃的紅星	Sparkling Red Star
Shanshui qing	山水情	The Magic Tune
Shao Renmei	邵仁枚	Runme Shaw
Shao shi fuzi	邵氏父子	Shaw and Sons
Shao shi xiongdi	邵氏兄弟	Shaw Brothers
Shao Yifu	邵逸夫	Run Run Shaw
Shao Zuiweng	邵醉翁	Shao Renjie
Shaolin men	少林門	Hand of Death
Shaolin si	少林寺	Shaolin Temple
Shaolin wu zu	少林五祖	Five Shaolin Masters
Shaonainai de shanzi	少奶奶的扇子	The Mistress's Fan
Shaonian fan	少年犯	Juvenile Delinquents
Shaoye de monan	少爺的磨難	The Tribulations of a Young Master
Shashou hao	殺手壕	Young Master
Shazai dongfang	傻崽洞房	The Fool's Wedding Night
Shazi nao fang	傻子鬧房	An Idiot Disturbs the House
She xing diao shou	蛇形刁手	Snake in the Eagle's Shadow
Shehui zhi hua	社會之花	A Woman of Devotion
Shen bian	神鞭	Magic Braid
Shen Fu	沈浮	Shen Aijun, aka Shen Baiming
Shen Xiling	沈西苓	Shen Xuecheng, aka Ye Shen
Shen-Tu shi	申屠氏	Story of Lady Shen-Tu
Sheng zhi aige	生之哀歌	Life of Sadness
Shengcheng ji	聖城記	The Holy City
Shenggang qibing	省港旗兵	Long Arm of the Law
Shenghuo de chanyin	生活的顫音	Reverberations of Life
Shengli jinxingqu	勝利進行曲	The Victory March
Shengming xian	生命綫	Life Line
Shengsi guan	生死關	Justice, My Foot

Pinyin	**Characters**	**Other**
Shengsi hen	生死恨	Remorse at Death
Shengsi jue	生死決	Duel to the Death
Shengsi tongxin	生死同心	Hearts United
Shenmi de dafo	神秘的大佛	A Mysterious Giant Buddha
Shenmi de lüban	神秘的旅伴	The Mysterious Traveller
Shennü	神女	Goddess
Shenzhen yingye gongsi	深圳影業公司	Shenzhen Film Company
Shenzhou yingpian gongsi	神州影片公司	Shenzhou Film Company
Shi bu fangcao	十步芳草	Mother's Daughter
Shi Chenfeng	史晨風	
Shi Dongshan	史東山	Shi Kuangshao
Shi Hui	石揮	Shi Yutao
Shi Tian	石天	Dean Shek
Shi zu hen	失足恨	Regrets
Shidai de ernü	時代的兒女	Children of Our Time
Shijia yingye gongsi	事佳影業公司	Skai Film Company
Shiqu de aiqing	失去的愛情	The Lost Love
Shiqu jiyi de ren	失去記憶的人	The Man Who Lost His Memory
Shisan hao xiongzhai	十三號凶宅	Haunted House No. 13
Shishi zao yingxiong	時勢造英雄	Heroes Circumstance
Shiyi ge nüren	十一個女人	Eleven Women
Shiyue fengyun	十月風雲	The October Storm
Shizi jietou	十字街頭	Crossroads
Shizishan xia	獅子山下	Below Lion Rock
Shizong de nü zhongxuesheng	失踪的女中學生	The Missing Middle-School Girl
Shou de yun kai jian mingyue	守得雲開見明月	Waiting for the Moon
Shu jian en chou lu	書劍恩仇錄	The Romance of Book and Sword
Shu Qi	舒琪	Shu Kei
Shuang zhuo	雙鐲	Twin Bracelets
Shuangqizhen daoke	雙旗鎮刀客	The Swordsman in Double Flag Town
Shui Hua	水華	Zhang Yufan
Shui shi di san zhe	誰是第三者	Who is the Third Party?
Shui zhi guo	誰之過	Whose Fault is This?
Si qianjin	四千金	Four Daughters
Si qianjin	四千金	Our Sister Hedy
Si shui liu nian	似水流年	Homecoming
Sihai wei jia	四海為家	At Home in the World
Siqin Gaowa	斯琴高娃	
Sishi buhuo	四十不惑	Family Portrait
Situ Huimin	司徒慧敏	Situ Zhu
Siwang youxi	死亡游戲	Game of Death
Song Chuyu	宋楚瑜	James Soong
Song Cunshou	宋存壽	
Song jia san jiemei	宋家三姐妹	The Soong Sisters
Song Jingshi	宋景詩	The Rebels
Song Shijie	宋士杰	Rebel Song
Songhua jiang shang	松花江上	Along the Sungari River

Pinyin	Characters	Other
Su Li	蘇里	
Su Xiaoxiao	蘇小小	Miss Su
Sun Daolin	孫道臨	
Sun Jing	孫敬	
Sun Sha	孫沙	
Sun Shiyi	孫師毅	
Sun Yu	孫瑜	Sun Chengyu
Sun Zhou	孫周	
Ta lia he ta lia	她倆和他倆	Twins Come in Pairs
Taiji Zhang Sanfeng	太極張三豐	The Tai-chi Master
Taiping tianguo	太平天國	Buddha Bless America
Taipingyang shang de fengyun	太平洋上的風雲	Storms over the Pacific
Taishan yingye gongsi	泰山影業公司	Taishan Film Company
Taitai wansui	太太萬歲	Long Live the Mistress!
Taiwan gongye	臺灣工業	Taiwan Industry
Taiwan nongye	臺灣農業	Taiwan Agriculture
Taiwan sheng dianying zhipianchang	臺灣省電影制片廠	Taiwan Motion Picture Studio
Taiwan yinghua yanjiu hui	臺灣映畫研究會	Taiwan Motion Picture Study Society
Taiwan yinghua zhizuo suo	臺灣映畫制作所	Taiwan Motion Picture Production Office
Taiyang shan	太陽山	Mountains of the Sun
Taiyang you er	太陽有耳	The Sun Has Ears
Taiyang yu	太陽雨	Sunshine and Showers
Tamen zheng nianqing	他們正年輕	In Their Prime
Tan qing shuo ai	談情說愛	Falling in Love
Tan Xinpei	譚鑫培	
Tang Bohu dian Qiuxing	唐伯虎點秋香	The Flirting Scholar
Tang Jili	唐季禮	Stanley Tong
Tang Shuxuan	唐書璇	
Tang Xiaodan	湯曉丹	
Tangchen yingye gongsi	湯臣影業公司	Tomson Film Company
Tangshan daxiong	唐山大兄	The Big Boss
Tao Dechen	陶德辰	Jim Tao
Tao Qin	陶秦	
Taofan	逃犯	Prison on Fire, II
Taohua jiang	桃花江	Peach Flower River
Taohua shan	桃花扇	The Peach Blossom Fan
Taoli jie	桃李劫	Plunder of Peach and Plum, *aka* Fate of Graduates
Taowang	逃亡	Escape
Taoxue weilong	逃學威龍	Fight Back to School
Te jing tu long	特警屠龍	Tiger Cage
Te Wei	特偉	
Teng Wenji	滕文驥	
Ti xiao yinyuan	啼笑因緣	Fate in Tears and Laughter

Pinyin	**Characters**	**Other**
Tian Fang	田方	
Tian guan ci fu	天官賜福	The Lucky Bureaucrat
Tian Han	田漢	
Tian Hua	田華	Liu Tianhua
Tian liang hao ge qiu	天涼好個秋	Cool Autumn
Tian mimi	甜蜜蜜	Comrades: Almost a Love Story
Tian ruo you qing	天若有情	A Moment of Romance
Tian Zhuangzhuang	田壯壯	
Tian zi di yi hao	天字第一號	Code Name Heaven No. 1
Tiancai yu baichi	天才與白痴	The Last Message
Tianguo nizi	天國逆子	The Day the Sun Turned Cold
Tianlun	天倫	Song of China, *aka* Filial Piety
Tianluo diwang	天羅地網	Gunmen
Tianma dianying zhipianchang	天馬電影制片廠	Tianma Film Studio
Tianmi de shiye	甜蜜的事業	Sweet Business
Tianming	天明	Daybreak
Tianshan de honghua	天山的紅花	Red Flowers by Tianshan Mountains
Tianshan dianying zhipianchang	天山電影制片廠	Tianshan Film Studio
Tiantang chunmeng	天堂春夢	Dream in Paradise
Tianxian pei	天仙配	The Heavenly Match
Tianya genü	天涯歌女	The Singer in Exile
Tianyi yingpian gongsi	天一影片公司	Tianyi Film Company
Tianyunshan chuanqi	天雲山傳奇	The Legend of Tianyun Mountain
Tiao hui	跳灰	Jumping Ash
Tiao wa	跳蛙	Leap Frog
Tie ji dou wugong	鐵鷄斗蜈蚣	The Last Hero in China
Tie niao	鐵鳥	Iron Bird
Tieban honglei lu	鐵板紅泪錄	Oppression
Tiedao youji dui	鐵道游擊隊	Railroad Guerrillas
Tieshan gongzhu	鐵扇公主	Princess Iron Fan
Tiyu huanghou	體育皇后	Queen of Sports
Tongdang	童黨	Gangs
Tongju zhi ai	同居之愛	The Love Story
Tongnian de pengyou	童年的朋友	Childhood Friends
Tongnian wangshi	童年往事	A Time to Live, a Time to Die
Tongnian zai Ruijin	童年在瑞金	Childhood in Ruijin
Tongtian dadao	通天大盜	Easy Money
Tou shaoya	偷燒鴨	Stealing the Roast Duck
Touben nuhai	投奔怒海	Boat People
Toufa luanle	頭發亂了	Dirt
Tu Guangqi	屠光啟	
Tuanjie qilai dao mingtian	團結起來到明天	Unity for Tomorrow
Tuishou	推手	Pushing Hands
Wan chun qing shi	晚春情事	Passion in Late Spring
Wan Guchan	萬古蟾	

Pinyin	Characters	Other
Wan Laiming	萬籟鳴	
Wan Ren	萬仁	Wan Jen
Wan zhang mo	萬丈魔	The Intrigue
Wan zhong	晚鐘	Evening Bell
Wan zhu	頑主	The Trouble Shooters
Wang Bin	王濱	
Wang Binglin	王秉林	
Wang Cilong	王次龍	
Wang Danfeng	王丹鳳	Wang Yufeng
Wang Haowei	王好為	
Wang Jiawei	王家衛	Wong Kar-Wai
Wang Jiayi	王家乙	
Wang Jin	王進	
Wang Jing	王晶	Wong Jing
Wang Laowu	王老五	The Life of Mr Wang
Wang Ping	王蘋	Wang Guangzhen
Wang Qimin	王啟民	
Wang Renmei	王人美	Wang Shuxi
Wang Rui	王瑞	
Wang Shuo	王朔	
Wang Tianlin	王天林	
Wang Tong	王童	Wang Tung
Wang Weiyi	王為一	
Wang xiansheng zhi yuhuo fen shen	王先生之欲火焚身	Mr Wang: Flames of Desire
Wang Xiaoshuai	王曉帥	
Wang Xin'gang	王心剛	
Wang Yan	王炎	
Wang Yi	王毅	
Wang Yin	王引	
Wang Yu	王羽	
Wang Zuxian	王祖賢	Joey Wong
Wangjiao kamen	旺角卡門	As Tears Go by
Wangshi ru yan	往事如烟	Shadow of Dreams
Wangu liufang	萬古流芳	Famed Forever
Wangyang zhong de yitiao chuan	汪洋中的一條船	A Boat in the Ocean
Wanhe yingshi gongsi	萬和影視公司	Vanke Film and TV Company
Wanjia denghuo	萬家燈火	Myriad of Lights
Wanjun	婉君	Wanjun
Wanshi liufang	萬世流芳	The Opium War
Wanxiang huichun	萬象回春	Rejuvenation
Wawa	娃娃	Babies
Wei cheng	圍城	Fortress Beseiged
Wei lou chun xiao	危樓春曉	In the Face of Demolition
Weida de qidian	偉大的起點	The Point of Departure
Weile heping	為了和平	For Peace

Pinyin	Characters	Other
Wen Yimin	文逸民	
Wenhua yingye gongsi	文華影業公司	Wenhua Film Company
Wo ai Mali	我愛瑪麗	I Love Mary
Wo ai taikong ren	我愛太空人	The Other Half and the Other Half
Wo de yeye	我的爺爺	My Grandpa
Wo he wo de tongxue men	我和我的同學們	Me and My Classmates
Wo ta lang er lai	我踏浪而來	I Came with the Waves
Wo ye you baba	我也有爸爸	I Have My Daddy, Too
Wo zhe yibeizi	我這一輩子	This Life of Mine
Wo zheyang guole yisheng	我這樣過了一生	Kuei-mei, a Woman
Women cunli de nianqing ren	我們村里的年輕人	Young People in Our Village
Women de tiankong	我們的天空	Our Sky
Women de tianye	我們的田野	In Our Field
Women dou shi zheyang zhangda de	我們都是這樣長大的	Reunion
Women fufu zhijian	我們夫婦之間	Husband and Wife
Women shi shijie	我們是世界	We Are the World
Wu Chufan	吳楚帆	Cho-fan Ng
Wu Cun	吳村	
Wu daban *see* Wuniu	舞大班	
Wu Di	鄔迪	
Wu duo jinhua	五朵金花	Five Golden Flowers
Wu fu xing	五福星	Lucky Stars
Wu ge nüzi yu yi gen shengzi	五個女子與一根繩子	Five Girls and a Rope
Wu Hui	吳回	Ng Wui
Wu Lan	烏蘭	
Wu li de di sheng	霧里的笛聲	Flute Sound in the Mist
Wu Ma	午馬	
Wu Nianzhen	吳念真	Wu Nien-chen
Wu Renzhi	吳韌之	
Wu shu	烏鼠	Run and Kill
Wu Song	武松	Wu Song
Wu Tian	吳天	
Wu Tianming	吳天明	
Wu tu wu min	吾土吾民	Our Land, Our People
Wu Wenchao	吳文超	
Wu Wenguang	吳文光	
Wu Xun zhuan	武訓傳	The Life of Wu Xun
Wu Yigong	吳貽弓	
Wu Yin	吳茵	Yang Ying
Wu Yonggang	吳永剛	
Wu Yusen	吳宇森	John Woo
Wu zhai	霧宅	Haunted House
Wu Zhaodi	武兆堤	
Wu Ziniu	吳子牛	
Wudang	武當	The Undaunted Wudang
Wuhan zhanyi	武漢戰役	The Wuhan Battle

Pinyin	Characters	Other
Wukui	五魁	The Porter, *aka* The Wooden Man's Bride
Wulin zhi	武林志	Pride's Deadly Fury
Wuming dao	無名島	A Nameless Island
Wuming shi	無名氏	Mr Nobody
Wuniu	舞牛	Dancing Bull
Wuqiang de qiangshou	無槍的槍手	Gunslinger Without a Gun
Wuqing de qingren	無情的情人	Ruthless Lovers
Wuren hecai	無人喝彩	No One Cheers
Wushan yunyu	巫山雲雨	Rainclouds Over Wushan
Wushi niandai yingye gongsi	五十年代影業公司	Fiftieth Film Company
Wutai chunse	舞臺春色	Stage Glamour
Wutai jiemei	舞臺姐妹	Stage Sisters
Wuya yu maque	烏鴉與麻雀	Crows and Sparrows
Wuyan de shanqiu	無言的山丘	The Hills of No Return
Xi bu lai de ren	西部來的人	The Man from Island West
Xi Chu bawang	西楚霸王	Great Conqueror's Concubine
Xi meng rensheng	戲夢人生	The Puppet Master
Xi Shi	西施	The Story of Xi Shi, I–II
Xi taihou	西太后	The Empress Dowager, II–III
Xi xiang ji	西廂記	Romance of the Western Chamber, *aka* Way Down West
Xi xing qiuche	西行囚車	Westbound Convict Train
Xi ying men	喜迎門	The In-Laws
Xia Chifeng	夏赤鳳	
Xia dao gao fei	俠盜高飛	Full Contact
Xia Gang	夏剛	
Xia Meng	夏夢	
Xia nü	俠女	A Touch of Zen
Xia Yan	夏衍	Shen Duanxian, Shen Naixi
Xia Yu	夏雨	
Xialu yinghao *see* Long teng Zhongguo	狹路英豪	
Xi'an dianying zhipianchang	西安電影制片廠	Xi'an Film Studio
Xi'an shibian	西安事變	Xi'an Incident
Xian Xinghai	冼星海	
Xiandai haoxia zhuan	現代豪俠傳	The Executioners
Xiang Huasheng	向華勝	Jimmy Heung
Xiang hun nü	香魂女	The Woman from the Lake of Scented Soul, *aka* Woman Sesame-Oil Maker
Xiang nü Xiaoxiao	湘女瀟瀟	A Girl from Hunan
Xiangchou	鄉愁	Homesick
Xianggang qi an zhi xixue guili wang	香港奇案之吸血貴利王	Underground Banker
Xiangjiao tiantang	香蕉天堂	Banana Paradise
Xiangxue hai	香雪海	A Nun's Love
Xiangyin	鄉音	A Country Wife

Pinyin	Characters	Other
Xiannü san hua	仙女散花	Fairy Maidens Spread Flowers
Xiao baba de tiankong	小爸爸的天空	Daddy's Sky
Xiao bing Zhang Ga	小兵張嘎	Zhang Ga, a Boy Soldier
Xiao cheng gushi	小城故事	Story of a Small Town
Xiao cheng zhi chun	小城之春	Spring in a Small Town
Xiao dingdang	小叮當	Little Dingdang
Xiao Fangfang	蕭芳芳	Josephine Siao
Xiao hua	小花	Little Flower
Xiao jie	小街	Narrow Street
Xiao kedou zhao mama	小蝌蚪找媽媽	Where is Mama
Xiao Lang	蕭朗	
Xiao lingzi	小玲子	Story of Lingzi
Xiao longtou	小龍頭	Little Dinosaurs
Xiao Qi de na ding maozi	小琪的那頂帽子	Xiao Qi's Hat
Xiao qingren	小情人	Little Darling
Xiao tianshi	小天使	Little Angel
Xiao wanyi	小玩藝	Little Toys
Xiao Ye	小野	
Xiao zuqiu dui	小足球隊	The Boy Soccer Team
Xiao'ao jianghu	笑傲江湖	Swordsman
Xiaobi de gushi	小畢的故事	Growing Up
Xiaoquan guaizhao	笑拳怪招	Fearless Hyena
Xiaoshi de nüren	消失的女人	The Woman Who Disappeared
Xiaoxiang dianying zhipianchang	瀟湘電影制片廠	Xiaoxiang Film Studio
Xiayi shaonian	俠義少年	A Chivalrous Boy
Xibei dianying gongsi	西北電影公司	Northwest Film Company
Xibie de hai'an	惜別的海岸	The Coast of Departure
Xie Fei	謝飛	
Xie Jin	謝晉	
Xie Tian	謝添	Xie Hongkun, *aka* Xie Jun
Xie Tieli	謝鐵驪	
Xin buliao qing	新不了情	C'est la vie, mon chéri
Xin Dubidao	新獨臂刀	The New One-Armed Swordsman
Xin ernü yingxiong zhuan	新兒女英雄傳	New Heroes and Heroines
Xin fangke	新房客	The New Tenant
Xin gua	新寡	New Widow
Xin gui yuan	新閨怨	The Sorrows of Women
Xin Jingwumen	新精武門	New Fist of Fury
Xin juzhang daolai zhiqian	新局長到來之前	Before the New Director Arrives
Xin nüxing	新女性	New Woman
Xin ren de jiating	新人的家庭	The New Family
Xin Shushan jianxia	新蜀山劍俠	Zu-Warriors of the Magic Mountain
Xin taohua shan	新桃花扇	The New Peach Blossom Fan
Xin xiang	心香	The True Hearted, *aka* Heartstrings
Xin Yuguang qu	新漁光曲	New Fisherman's Song
Xingfu kuangxiang qu	幸福狂想曲	Rhapsody of Happiness

Pinyin	Characters	Other
Xinghua sanyue tian	杏花三月天	Apricot Blossom, *aka* The Story of Xinghua
Xingxing, yueliang, taiyang	星星，月亮，太陽	Star, Moon, Sun
Xinhai shuang shi	辛亥雙十	Battle for the Republic of China
Xinhua yingye gongsi	新華影業公司	Hsin Hwa Film Company
Xinjiu shidai	新舊時代	Transition
Xinlian yingye gongsi	新聯影業公司	Sun Luen Films
Xinniang yu wo	新娘與我	My Bride and I
Xinyicheng yingye gongsi	新藝城影業公司	Cinema City
Xiwang zai renjian	希望在人間	Hope in the World
Xiyan	喜宴	The Wedding Banquet
Xiyang zhi ge	夕陽之歌	A Better Tomorrow, III
Xiyou ji di yibai lingyi hui zhi yueguang baohe	西游記第一百零一回之月光寶盒	Chinese Odyssey, I: Pandora's Box
Xizhao jie	夕照街	Sunset Street
Xu Anhua	許鞍華	Ann Hui
Xu Changlin	徐昌霖	
Xu Feng	徐鳳	Hsu Feng
Xu Guanjie	許冠杰	Sam Hui
Xu Guanwen	許冠文	Michael Hui
Xu Ke	徐克	Tsui Hark
Xu Mao he ta de nüer men	許茂和他的女兒們	Xu Mao and His Daughters
Xu Shunnan	徐舜南	
Xu Tao	徐韜	
Xu Xinfu	徐欣夫	
Xu Xingzhi	許幸之	
Xu Zhuodai	徐卓呆	
Xuanlian	懸戀	Red Beads
Xuanya lema	懸崖勒馬	Turning Back
Xue fu men	血符門	Angry River
Xue jian yinghua	血濺櫻花	Blood on the Cherry
Xue Juexian	薛覺先	Sit Kok-sin
Xuefu yingye gongsi	學甫影業公司	Scholar Film Company
Xuehen	血痕	Bloodstain
Xuehua pianpian	雪花片片	Snowflake
Xuerou changcheng	血肉長城	The Will to Resist
Xuese qingchen	血色清晨	Bloody Morning
Xuezhan Taierzhuang	血戰臺兒莊	The Battle of Taierzhuang
Ya qi	啞妻	The Silent Wife
Yan chao	鹽潮	The Uprising
Yan Chuntang	嚴春堂	
Yan Gong	嚴恭	
Yan Hao	嚴浩	Yim Ho
Yan Jizhou	嚴寄洲	
Yan Jun	嚴俊	
Yan Ruisheng	閻瑞生	Yan Ruisheng

Pinyin	Characters	Other
Yan Shanshan	嚴珊珊	Yim San-san
Yan shen	驗身	The Wooden Man's Bride
Yan shi	艷屍	An Exotic Corpse
Yan Xueshu	顏學恕	
Yan'an yu balu jun	延安與八路軍	Yan'an and the Eighth-Route Army
Yang Dechang	楊德昌	Edward Yang
Yang Gaisen	楊溉森	
Yang guifei	楊貴妃	Beautiful Concubine Yang
Yang Hansheng	陽翰笙	Ouyang Benyi, *aka* Ouyang Jixiu
Yang Jiming	楊霽明	
Yang men nü jiang	楊門女將	Women Warriors of the Yang Family
Yang Xiaozhong	楊小仲	Mi Tisheng, *aka* Yang Baotai
Yang ya renjia	養鴨人家	Beautiful Duckling
Yang Yanjin	楊延晉	
Yang Yazhou	楊亞洲	
Yang Yin	陽陰	Yang Yin: Gender in Chinese Cinema
Yang Ziqiong	楊紫瓊	Michelle Yeoh, *aka* Michelle Khan
Yangcheng anshao	羊城暗哨	Secret Guards in Canton
Yangguang canlan de rizi	陽光燦爛的日子	In the Heat of the Sun
Yanghua hen	楊花恨	Flirting with Disaster
Yangzi jiang fengyun	揚子江風雲	Storms over the Yangtze River
Yanmo de qingchun	淹沒的青春	Drowned Youth
Yanshan yin xia	燕山隱俠	Invisible Swordsman
Yanyang tian	艷陽天	Bright Sky
Yanzhi	胭脂	Rouge
Yanzhi kou	胭脂扣	Rouge
Yanzhi lei	胭脂淚	Rouge Tears
Yanzi dao	燕子盜	The Swallow
Yao	藥	Medicine
Yao a yao, yao dao waipo qiao	搖啊搖，搖到外婆橋	Shanghai Triad
Yao Feng	姚鳳	
Yao Li	姚力	
Yaogun qingnian	搖滾青年	Rock 'n' Roll Kids
Yaoshan qing	瑤山情	Romance in Yao Mountains
Yaoshou dushi	妖獸都市	The Wicked City
Yaoyuan de ai	遙遠的愛	The Love of Far Away
Yapian zhanzheng	鴉片戰爭	The Opium War
Yasui qian	壓歲錢	A New Year's Coin
Yaxiya yingxi gongsi	亞細亞影戲公司	Asia Film Company
Ye ben	夜奔	To the Light
Ye cao xian hua	野草閑花	Wild Flower
Ye Daying	葉大鷹	Ye Ying
Ye dian	夜店	Night Inn
Ye haizi	野孩子	Wild Children
Ye Hongwei	葉鴻偉	
Ye hui	夜會	Night Tryst
Ye meigui	野玫瑰	Wild Rose

Pinyin	Characters	Other
Ye meigui zhi lian	野玫瑰之戀	Wild, Wild Rose
Ye Mingwei	葉鳴偉	
Ye shan	野山	In the Wild Mountain
Yeban gesheng	夜半歌聲	The Phantom Lover
Yeban gesheng	夜半歌聲	Singing at Midnight
Yehuo chunfeng dou gucheng	野火春風斗古城	Struggle in an Ancient City
Yezhu lin	野豬林	Boar Forest
Yi bu yingpian wei wancheng yinqi de taolun	一部影片未完成引起的討論	Discussions Caused by a Film Being Stopped
Yi chang fengbo	一場風波	An Accident
Yi dan qun ying	義膽群英	A Bullet in the Head
Yi di jimao	一地雞毛	Chicken Feathers on the Ground
Yi ge he ba ge	一個和八個	One and Eight
Yi ge sizhe dui shengzhe de fangwen	一個死者對生者的訪問	Questions for the Living
Yi jian chou	一見仇	Hatred
Yi jiang chunshui xiang dong liu	一江春水向東流	Spring River Flows East
Yi Jiangnan	憶江南	Tale of Two Girls
Yi pan meiyou xiawan de qi	一盤沒有下完的棋	The Go Master
Yi Wen	易文	Evan Yang
Yiban shi huoyan, yiban shi haishui	一半是火焰，一半是海水	Half Flame, Half Brine
Yihua yingye gongsi	藝華影業公司	Yihua Film Company, Shanghai
Yin Li	尹力	
Yin Xiucen	殷秀岑	
Yindu jigou youxian gongsi	銀都機構有限公司	Sil-Metropole Organization
Ying fei renjian	鶯飛人間	The Singer
Ying Yunwei	應雲衛	Ying Yangzhen, *aka* Ying Yuchen
Yingchun qu	迎春曲	Waiting for Spring
Yingchunge zhi fengbo	迎春閣之風波	The Fate of Lee Khan
Yingge yanwu	鶯歌燕舞	Mad about Music
Yingguo bengkui zhi ri	英國崩潰之日	The Day of England's Collapse
Yingjia	贏家	The Winner
Yinglie qianqiu	英烈千秋	Martyrs
Yingsheng A Ge	應聲阿哥	Brother Echo
Yingxiong bense	英雄本色	A Better Tomorrow
Yingxiong ernü	英雄兒女	Heroic Sons and Daughters
Yinhan shuang xing	銀漢雙星	Twin Stars
Yinrong jie	音容劫	Misfortune
Yinshe mousha an	銀蛇謀殺案	The Silver Snake Murder Case
Yinshi nannü	飲食男女	Eat Drink Man Woman
Yinyang jie	陰陽界	Between the Living and the Dead
Yiren Wu Feng	義人吳鳳	Wu Feng the Righteous Man
Yishujia Qi Baishi	藝術家齊白石	The Artist Qi Baishi
Yizhi banshi chuang jianghu	一知半識闖江湖	Half a Load of Kung Fu
Yong bu fenli	永不分離	Never to Part

Pinyin	Characters	Other
Yong bu xiaoshi de dianbo	永不消失的電波	The Everlasting Radio Signals
Yong Chun	咏春	Wing Chun
Yonghua yingye gongsi	永華影業公司	Yung Hwa Film Company, Shanghai
Yongsheng yingye gongsi	永勝影業公司	Win's Films
You hua haohao shuo	有話好好説	Keep Cool
You ren pianpian aishang wo	有人偏偏愛上我	Someone Happened to Fall in Love with Me
You seng	誘僧	The Temptation of a Monk
You yuan	郵緣	Stamp Collector
You yuan jing meng	游園驚夢	Startling Tour in the Garden
Youchai	邮差	The Postman
Yougu lian'ge	幽谷戀歌	Love Song in the Valley
Youma caizi	油麻菜籽	Rapeseed Woman
Yu bang xiangzheng	鷸蚌相爭	Snipe-Clam Grapple
Yu guang qu	漁光曲	Song of the Fisherman
Yu guo tian qing	雨過天晴	Reconciliation
Yu Hua	余華	
Yu Kanping	虞勘平	
Yu Lan	于籃	Yu Peiwen
Yu Ling	于伶	Ren Xigui, *aka* You Jing, Yu Cheng
Yu meiren	虞美人	Yu the Beauty
Yu ni tongzhu	與你同住	Living with You
Yu wangshi ganbei	與往事干杯	Yesterday's Wine
Yuan	源	The Pioneers
Yuan Congmei	袁叢美	
Yuan Heping	袁和平	Yuen Woo-ping
Yuan Jun	袁俊	Zhang Junxiang
Yuan Kui	元奎	Yuen Correy, *aka* Yuen Fei
Yuan Meiyun	袁美雲	
Yuan Muzhi	袁牧之	Yuan Jialai
Yuan xiang ren	原鄉人	China, My Native Land
Yuanli zhanzheng de niandai	遠離戰爭的年代	Far from the War
Yuanyang yishi	遠洋逸事	Stories of the Voyage
Yuanye	原野	Savage Land
Yuanzi dianying gongsi	原子電影公司	Atom Films, Taipei
Yue Feng	岳楓	
Yuenan guniang	越南姑娘	A Vietnam Girl
Yujie bingqing	玉潔冰清	Innocence
Yunnan gushi	雲南故事	A Yunnan Story
Yupu tuan	玉蒲團	Sex and Zen
Yuqing sao	玉卿嫂	Jade Love
Yuse hudie	玉色蝴蝶	Jade Butterfly
Yuye qiangsheng	雨夜槍聲	Gunshots in a Rainy Evening
Zai na hepan qing cao qing	在那河畔青草青	Green, Green Grass of Home
Zaijian Zhongguo	再見中國	China Behind
Zao'an Taibei	早安，臺北	Good Morning, Taipei

Pinyin	Characters	Other
Zaochun eryue	早春二月	Early Spring in February
Zaoyu jiqing	遭遇激情	Unexpected Passion
Zazui zi	雜嘴子	An Innocent Babbler
Zeiwang	賊王	Twist
Zeng Weizhi	曾未之	
Zeng Zhiwei	曾志偉	Eric Tsang
Zeng Zhuangxiang	曾壯祥	Tseng Chuang-hsiang
Zhan gong	戰功	Victory
Zhan zhi le, bie paxia	站直了，別趴下	Stand Up, Don't Bend Over
Zhang Aijia	張艾嘉	Sylvia Chang
Zhang Ailing	張愛玲	Eileen Zhang
Zhang Che	張徹	Chang Che
Zhang Fengxiang	張鳳翔	
Zhang Guorong	張國榮	Leslie Cheung
Zhang Huaxun	張華勛	
Zhang Huoyou	張活游	Cheung Wood-yau
Zhang Jianting	張堅廷	Alfred Cheung
Zhang Jianya	張建亞	
Zhang Junxiang	張駿祥	Yuan Jun
Zhang Junzhao	張軍釗	
Zhang Ke	張客	
Zhang Manyu	張曼玉	Maggie Cheung
Zhang Ming	章明	
Zhang Nuanxin	張暖忻	
Zhang Qi	張其	
Zhang Ruifang	張瑞芳	
Zhang Shankun	張善琨	
Zhang Shichuan	張石川	
Zhang Wanting	張婉婷	Mabel Cheung
Zhang Xian	張弦	
Zhang Xianliang	張賢亮	
Zhang Xinsheng	張欣生	Zhang Xinsheng
Zhang Xinyan	張鑫炎	
Zhang Yi	張毅	Chang Yi
Zhang Yimou	張藝謀	
Zhang Ying	張瑛	Cheung Ying
Zhang Yu	張瑜	
Zhang Yuan	張元	
Zhang Yunhe	張雲鶴	
Zhang Zeming	張澤鳴	
Zhang Zien	張子恩	
Zhang Zhiliang	張之亮	Jacob Cheung
Zhang Zuoji	張作驥	
Zhanshen tan	戰神灘	Beach of the War Gods
Zhao Dan	趙丹	Zhao Fengxiang
Zhao Huanzhang	趙煥章	
Zhao le	找樂	For Fun

Pinyin	Characters	Other
Zhao Ming	趙明	
Zhao Shushen	趙樹燊	Chiu Shu-sen
Zhao Wenzhuo	趙文卓	Wing Chow
Zhao Xinshui	趙心水	
Zhen nü	貞女	Two Virtuous Women
Zheng Boqi	鄭伯奇	
Zheng Dongtian	鄭洞天	
Zheng Junli	鄭君里	Qian Li, *aka* Zheng Zhong
Zheng Xiaoqiu	鄭小秋	
Zheng Zhegu	鄭鷓鴣	
Zheng Zhengqiu	鄭正秋	Zheng Bo Chang, *aka* Zheng Fangze, Zheng Yao Feng
Zhengzha	掙扎	Struggle
Zhi guo yuan	擲果緣	Cheng the Fruit Seller
Zhi qu Huashan	智取華山	Capture Mount Hua by Stratagem
Zhi qu Weihushan	智取威虎山	Taking Tiger Mountain by Stratagem
Zhi wang, *aka* Qidai	至望	Desires
Zhifen shichang	脂粉市場	The Market of Beauty
Zhiren daoluan ji	紙人搗亂記	Turmoil in a Workshop
Zhiyin	知音	Intimate Friends
Zhong Acheng	鐘阿城	Ah Cheng
Zhong an shilu ou ji	重案實錄偶記	Organized Crime and Triad Bureau
Zhong an zu	重案組	The Crime Story
Zhong Qing	鐘情	
Zhongdian	中電	Central Film Studio
Zhong sheng	鐘聲	Alarm Bell
Zhong You	鐘游	
Zhong zai	忠仔	Ah Chung
Zhongguo de zuihou yi ge taijian	中國的最后一個太監	Lai Shi, China's Last Eunuch
Zhongguo dianying gongsi	中國電影公司	China Film Corporation
Zhongguo dianying hezuo zhipian gongsi	中國電影合作制片公司	China Film Co-production Corporation, Beijing
Zhongguo dianying zhipianchang (Zhongzhi)	中國電影制片廠 (中制)	China Motion Picture Studio
Zhongguo dui, jiayou	中國隊，加油	Come On, China
Zhongguo geming zhi ge	中國革命之歌	Song of the Chinese Revolution
Zhongguo hai de nuchao	中國海的怒潮	The Wrath of the China Sea
Zhonghua dianying gongsi	中華電影公司	China Film Company, Shanghai; Chung Wah Films, Hong Kong
Zhonghua dianying lianhe gongsi	中華電影聯合公司	United China Film Company, Shanghai
Zhonghua ernü	中華兒女	Children of China
Zhonghua lianhe zhipian gongsi	中華聯合制片公司	China United Film Production Corporation
Zhonghua nüer	中華女兒	Daughters of China
Zhonghua zhanshi	中華戰士	Magnificent Warriors

Pinyin	**Characters**	**Other**
Zhonglian dianying gongsi	中聯電影公司	Union Film Enterprises
Zhongnanhai baobiao	中南海保鏢	The Bodyguard from Beijing
Zhongshen dashi	終身大事	Decision of a Life Time
Zhongyang dianying gongsi	中央電影公司	Central Film Studio
Zhongyang dianying shiye youxian gongsi	中央電影事業有限公司	Central Motion Picture Company
Zhongyi zhi jia	忠義之家	Loyal Family
Zongying *see* Zhonghua dianying gongsi	中影	China Film Company, Shanghai
Zhou Jianyun	周劍雲	
Zhou Runfa	周潤發	Chow Yun-Fat
Zhou Xiaowen	周曉文	
Zhou Xingchi	周星馳	Stephen Chow, *aka* Stephen Chiau
Zhou Xuan	周璇	Su Pu
Zhou Yu	周予	
Zhoumo qingren	周末情人	Weekend Lovers
Zhu Bajie chi xigua	豬八戒吃西瓜	Zhu Bajie Eats the Watermelon
Zhu Shilin	朱石麟	
Zhu Tianwen	朱天文	Chu Tien-wen
Zhu Wenshun	朱文順	
Zhu Yanping	朱延平	Chu Yen-ping
Zhuang dao zheng	撞到正	The Spooky Bunch
Zhuangzhi ling yun	壯志凌雲	The Pioneers
Zhuangzi shi qi	莊子試妻	Zhuangzi Tests His Wife
Zhufu	祝福	New Year's Sacrifice
Zhui	追	Pursuit
Zhujiang dianying zhipianchang	珠江電影制片廠	Pearl River Film Studio
Zhujiang lei	珠江泪	Tears over the Pearl River
Zimei hua	姊妹花	Twin Sisters
Ziye	子夜	Midnight
Ziyou ren	自由人	Killer's Romance
Ziyou shen	自由神	Goddess of Liberty
Ziyou zhi hua	自由之花	Flower of Freedom
Zongheng sihai	縱橫四海	Once a Thief
Zou Wenhuai	鄒文懷	Raymond Chow
Zui ai	最愛	Passion
Zui xiangnian de jijie	最想念的季節	The Season of Fond Memory
Zuihou de dongri	最后的冬日	The Last Day of Winter
Zuihou de fengkuang	最后的瘋狂	Desperation
Zuihou guantou	最后關頭	The Last Minute Call
Zuijia paidang	最佳拍擋	Aces Go Places
Zuiquan	醉拳	Drunken Master
Zuixian yihen	醉仙遺恨	The Tragedy of a Drunkard
Zun Long	尊龍	John Lone

Index of titles

Note: This index contains all film and television titles – including foreign productions – mentioned in the entries. The **bold** type indicates those that carry individual entries. Titles of publications and stage plays are not included.

Index of names

Note: In addition to people who are treated in individual entries (and whose names are printed below in **bold** type), this index includes most directors and a select number of screen writers, producers, actors and actresses.

Index of studios

Note: This index does not include all studios mentioned in the entries.